Lecture Notes in Computer Science 5382

Frank S. de Boer Marcello M. Bonsangue
Susanne Graf Willem-Paul de Roever (Eds.)

Formal Methods for Components and Objects

6th International Symposium, FMCO 2007
Amsterdam, The Netherlands, October 24-26, 2007
Revised Papers

Springer

Volume Editors

Frank S. de Boer
Centre for Mathematics and Computer Science, CWI
Kruislaan 413, 1098 SJ Amsterdam, The Netherlands
E-mail: F.S.de.Boer@cwi.nl

Marcello M. Bonsangue
Leiden University, Leiden Institute of Advanced Computer Science
P.O. Box 9512, 2300 RA Leiden, The Netherlands
E-mail: marcello@liacs.nl

Susanne Graf
VERIMAG
2 Avenue de Vignate, Centre Equitation, 38610 Grenoble-Gières, France
E-mail: Susanne.Graf@imag.fr

Willem-Paul de Roever
Christian-Albrechts University Kiel
Institute of Computer Science and Applied Mathematics
Hermann-Rodewald-Straße 3, 24118 Kiel, Germany
E-mail: wpr@informatik.uni-kiel.de

Library of Congress Control Number: 2008940690

CR Subject Classification (1998): D.2, D.3, F.3, D.4

LNCS Sublibrary: SL 2 – Programming and Software Engineering

ISSN 0302-9743
ISBN-10 3-540-92187-7 Springer Berlin Heidelberg New York
ISBN-13 978-3-540-92187-5 Springer Berlin Heidelberg New York

Springer is a part of Springer Science+Business Media

springer.com

Printed in Germany

Typesetting: Camera-ready by author, data conversion by Scientific Publishing Services, Chennai, India
Printed on acid-free paper SPIN: 12582655 06/3180 5 4 3 2 1 0

Preface

Large and complex software systems provide the necessary infrastructure in all industries today. In order to construct such large systems in a systematic manner, the focus in development methodologies has switched in the last two decades from functional issues to structural issues: both data and functions are encapsulated into software units which are integrated into large systems by means of various techniques supporting reusability and modifiability. This encapsulation principle is essential to both the object-oriented and the more recent component-based software engineering paradigms.

Formal methods have been applied successfully to the verification of medium-sized programs in protocol and hardware design. However, their application to the development of large systems requires more emphasis on specification, modeling and validation techniques supporting the concepts of reusability and modifiability, and their implementation in new extensions of existing programming languages like Java.

The 6th Symposium on Formal Methods for Components and Objects was held in Amsterdam, The Netherlands, during October 24–26, 2007. It was realized as a concertation meeting of European projects focussing on formal methods for components and objects. This volume contains the contributions submitted after the symposium by the speakers of each of the following European IST projects involved in the organization of the program jointly with the bilateral NWO/DFG project MobiJ:

- The IST-FP6 project Mobius aiming at developing the technology for establishing trust and security for the next generation of global computers, using the proof-carrying code paradigm. The contact persons are Martin Hofmann (Ludwig Maximilians University Munich, Germany) and Gilles Barthe (IMDEA Software, Spain).
- The IST-FP6 project SelfMan on self-management for large-scale distributed systems based on structured overlay networks and components. The contact person is Peter Van Roy (Université Catholique de Louvain, Belgium).
- The IST-FP6 project GridComp and the FP6 CoreGRID Network of Excellence on grid programming with components. The contact person is Denis Caromel (INRIA Sophia-Antipolis, France).
- The Real-time component cluster of the Network of Excellence on Embedded System Design ARTIST. This cluster focuses on design processes and architectures for real-time embedded systems. The contact person is Albert Benveniste (INRIA / IRISA, France)
- The IST-FP6 project CREDO on modelling and analysis of evolutionary structures for distributed services. The contact person is Frank de Boer (CWI, The Netherlands).

The proceedings of the previous editions of FMCO have been published as volumes 2852, 3188, 3657, 4111, and 4709 of Springer's *Lecture Notes in Computer Science*. We believe that these proceedings provide a unique combination of ideas on software engineering and formal methods which reflect the expanding body of knowledge on modern software systems.

Finally, we thank all authors for the high quality of their contributions, and the reviewers for their help in improving the papers for this volume.

September 2008

Frank de Boer
Marcello Bonsangue
Susanne Graf
Willem-Paul de Roever

Organization

The FMCO symposia are organized in the context of the project Mobi-J, a project founded by a bilateral research program of The Dutch Organization for Scientific Research (NWO) and the Central Public Funding Organization for Academic Research in Germany (DFG). The partners of the Mobi-J projects are: the Centrum voor Wiskunde en Informatica, the Leiden Institute of Advanced Computer Science, and the Christian-Albrechts-Universität Kiel.

This project aims at the development of a programming environment which supports component-based design and verification of Java programs annotated with assertions. The overall approach is based on an extension of the Java language with a notion of component that provides for the encapsulation of its internal processing of data and composition in a network by means of mobile asynchronous channels.

Sponsoring Institutions

The Dutch Organization for Scientific Research (NWO)
The Dutch Institute for Programming research and Algorithmics (IPA)
The Centrum voor Wiskunde en Informatica (CWI), The Netherlands
The Leiden Institute of Advanced Computer Science (LIACS), The Netherlands

Table of Contents

The MOBIUS Project

The MOBIUS Proof Carrying Code Infrastructure (An Overview) 1
Gilles Barthe, Pierre Crégut, Benjamin Grégoire, Thomas Jensen, and David Pichardie

Certification Using the Mobius Base Logic 25
Lennart Beringer, Martin Hofmann, and Mariela Pavlova

Safety Guarantees from Explicit Resource Management 52
David Aspinall, Patrick Maier, and Ian Stark

Universe Types for Topology and Encapsulation 72
Dave Cunningham, Werner Dietl, Sophia Drossopoulou, Adrian Francalanza, Peter Müller, and Alexander J. Summers

COSTA: Design and Implementation of a Cost and Termination Analyzer for Java Bytecode 113
Elvira Albert, Puri Arenas, Samir Genaim, German Puebla, and Damiano Zanardini

The GridCOMP Project

Active Objects and Distributed Components: Theory and Implementation 133
Denis Caromel, Ludovic Henrio, and Eric Madelaine

The SELFMAN Project

Self Management for Large-Scale Distributed Systems: An Overview of the SELFMAN Project 153
Peter Van Roy, Seif Haridi, Alexander Reinefeld, Jean-Bernard Stefani, Roland Yap, and Thierry Coupaye

The ARTIST Project

Causal Semantics for the Algebra of Connectors (Extended Abstract) ... 179
Simon Bliudze and Joseph Sifakis

Multiple Viewpoint Contract-Based Specification and Design 200
Albert Benveniste, Benoît Caillaud, Alberto Ferrari, Leonardo Mangeruca, Roberto Passerone, and Christos Sofronis

The CREDO Project

Coordination: Reo, Nets, and Logic 226
Dave Clarke

An Object-Oriented Component Model for Heterogeneous Nets 257
Einar Broch Johnsen, Olaf Owe, Joakim Bjørk, and Marcel Kyas

Coordinating Object Oriented Components Using Data-Flow Networks 280
Mohammad Mahdi Jaghoori

Author Index 313

The MOBIUS Proof Carrying Code Infrastructure
(An Overview)

Gilles Barthe[1], Pierre Crégut[3], Benjamin Grégoire[2], Thomas Jensen[4], and David Pichardie[4]

[1] IMDEA Software, Madrid, Spain
[2] INRIA Sophia-Antipolis Méditerranée, France
[3] France Télécom, France
[4] INRIA Rennes Bretagne, Fance

Abstract. The goal of the MOBIUS project is to develop a Proof Carrying Code architecture to secure global computers that consist of Java-enabled mobile devices. In this overview, we present the consumer side of the MOBIUS Proof Carrying Code infrastructure, for which we have developed formally certified, executable checkers. We consider wholesale Proof Carrying Code scenarios, in which a trusted authority verifies the certificate before cryptographically signing the application. We also discuss retail Proof Carrying Code, where the verification is performed on the consumer device.

1 Introduction

MOBIUS [BBC+06] is a European integrated project developing basic technologies to ensure reliability and security in global computers formed of a host of Java-enabled devices, such as phones, PDAs, PCs, which provide a common runtime environment for a vast number of mobile applications. Its aim is to give users independent guarantees of the safety and security of mobile applications, using the concept of security through verifiable evidence emphasized by the Proof Carrying Code (PCC) paradigm [Nec97]. The fundamental view behind PCC is that mobile code components come equipped with a certificate that can be checked efficiently and independently by the code consumer to ensure that that downloaded components issued by the producer respects its policy.

PCC complements standard security infrastructures such as PKI, which only guarantee the origin and the integrity of code, and makes an appropriate basis for security of global computers; however, there remain significant challenges to generalize its use in security architectures for global computing, in particular:

- *Need for comprehensive policies*: PCC has mostly been used to enforce safety properties of applications, including type safety, and memory management safety. One goal of the MOBIUS project is to show the adequacy of PCC for enforcing basic security policies such as non-interference and resource control, and for the verification of functional properties of applications.
- *Need for enhanced PCC tools*: programming logics and type systems are the two basic enabling technologies for PCC. However, developing programming logics and type systems in the context of a full-blown, object-oriented, programming

F.S. de Boer et al. (Eds.): FMCO 2007, LNCS 5382, pp. 1–24, 2008.

language such as Java raises a number of challenging issues about efficiency, scalability, and trustworthiness of the PCC infrastructure itself. One goal of the MOBIUS project is to develop efficient and scalable mechanisms to generate and to check certificates, and to prove formally that the security-critical part of the PCC infrastructure is correct.

The purpose of this article is to present intermediate achievements of the project with respect to its goal of achieving efficient and trustworthy PCCs tools. We consider two scenarios, *wholesale* and *retail* Proof Carrying Code, and detail for each scenario how to achieve reliable certificate checking.

2 Proof Carrying Code

The purpose of this section is to recall existing approaches to Proof Carrying Code, and to present the main characteristics of the MOBIUS approach.

2.1 Type-Based Proof Carrying Code

The most successful instance and widely deployed application of PCC technology to date, namely the use of stackmaps in lightweight bytecode verification, uses type systems as its enabling technology.

A primer on bytecode verification. Bytecode verification [Ler03] is a central element of the Java security architecture. Its purpose is to check that applets are correctly formed and correctly typed, and that they do not attempt to perform malicious operations during their execution. To this end, the bytecode verifier (BCV) performs a structural analysis and a static analysis of bytecode programs.

The structural analysis checks the absence of basic errors such as calling a method that does not exist, jumping outside the scope of the program, or not respecting modifiers such as `final`. While simple to enforce, these checks are important and failing to enforce them may open the door to attacks [Gow04].

The second analysis is a static analysis of the program and is meant to ensure that programs execute in adherence with a set of safety properties, and in particular that values are used with their correct type (to avoid forged pointers). This second pass of bytecode verification is implemented as a data-flow analysis using Kildall's algorithm [Kil73]. The analysis aims at computing solutions of data-flow equations over a lattice derived from the subtyping relation between JVM types, and from a typed virtual machine which operates on the same principles as the standard JVM except for two crucial differences: the typed virtual machine manipulates *types* instead of *values*, and executes one method at a time. In a nutshell, the algorithm manipulates so-called *stackmaps* that store, for each program point, an abstract state (stack type) that is the least upper bound of the abstract states that have been previously reached at this program point. The stackmap is initialized to the initial state of the method being verified for the first program point, and to a default state for the other program points. One step of execution proceeds by iterating the execution function of the virtual machine over the stackmap. A non-default state is chosen and the result of the execution of the typed virtual machine on this state is propagated to its possible successors (by taking pointwise the least upper bound of the computed and stored abstract states types). Termination of the analysis is guaranteed since the set of states does not have infinite ascending chains, and the state stored in the history structure is increasing.

Lightweight bytecode verification. In the context of devices with limited resources, applications are verified off-device and, in case of a successful verification, signed and loaded on-device. Such a solution is not optimal in the sense that it leaves a crucial component of the security architecture outside of the perimeter of the device.

In order to remedy this deficiency, there are several proposals for circumscribing the trusted computing base to the device using on-device bytecode verification. The KVM overcomes this deficiency by relying on on lightweight bytecode verification (LBCV) [Ros03], a variant of bytecode verification whose objective is to minimize computations by requiring that the program comes equipped with the solution to the dataflow equations. Thus, the role of the lightweight verifier is confined to checking that the solution is correct, which can be performed in one pass. More technically, a certificate in lightweight bytecode verification is a function that attaches a stackmap to each junction point in the program, where a junction point is a program point with more than one predecessor, i.e., a program point where the results of execution potentially need to be merged. Instead of performing the merging, a lightweight bytecode verifier will merely verify that for each program point the stackmap computed by dataflow analysis, using the stackmaps of its predecessors, is compatible with the stackmap provided by the certificate, and continues its computation with the latter. In this way, a lightweight bytecode verifier essentially checks that the candidate fixpoint is indeed a fixpoint, and that it relates suitably to the program. Such a procedure minimizes computations since one just needs to check that the stackmap is indeed a fixpoint. This, as already mentioned, can be done in a single pass over the program, while simultaneously computing a stackmap for program points that are not junction points. Lightweight bytecode verification is sound and complete with respect to bytecode verification, in the sense that if a program P equipped with a certificate c is accepted by a LBCV, then P is accepted by a BCV, and conversely, if P is accepted by a BCV, then there exists a certificate c (that can be extracted directly from the fixpoint computed by the BCV) such that P equipped with the certificate c is accepted by a LBCV.

Although lightweight bytecode verification is currently limited to verifying basic typing and initialisation properties of downloaded code, there is technological potential for verifying a much richer set of program properties that are useful to further secure a code. Abstraction-carrying code (ACC) [APH05] is a generalization of bytecode verification approach to PCC which is based throughout on the use of *abstract interpretation* [CC77] as enabling technology. The use of abstract interpretation allows ACC to generate certificates which encode complex properties, including traditional safety issues but also resource-related properties like, e.g., resource consumption. Intuitively, the abstract interpreter implements a logic dedicated to a particular verification, making it possible to develop efficient and dedicated checkers that manipulate condensed certificates.

Figure 1 shows the overall PCC architecture and protocol for certificates based on type systems or abstract interpretation.

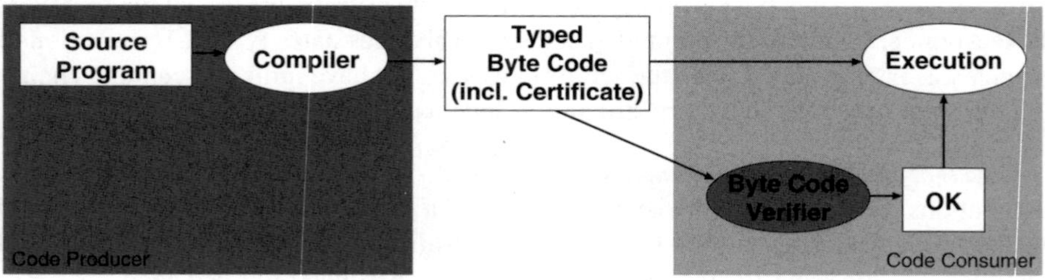

Fig. 1. PCC architecture and protocol for type-based certificates. Compilers add type information to byte code, which therefore includes a certificate. The code consumer type checks the code before executing it. Only the type checker (byte code verifier) is part of the trusted computing base.

2.2 Logic-Based Proof Carrying Code

The original PCC infrastructure proposed by Necula and Lee, which is described in Figure 2, is built upon several elements:

A formal logic for specifying and verifying policies. The specification language is used to express requirements on the incoming component, and the logic is used to verify that the component meets the expected requirements. Requirements are typically expressed as pre-conditions, post-conditions or invariants.

A verification condition generator (VCGen). The VCGen produces, for each component and safety policy, a set of proof obligations whose provability will be sufficient to ensure that the component respects the safety policy.

A proof checker. Certificates provide a formal representation of proofs, and are used to convey to the code consumer efficiently verifiable evidence that the code it receives satisfies its specification. The proof checker verifies that the certificate does indeed establish the proof obligations generated by the VCGen.

Although it builds upon ideas from program verification, which in its full generality requires interactive proofs, PCC is transparent for end-users, and does not require the code consumers to build proofs; rather, it requires code consumers to check proofs, which is fully automatic. Second, logic-based PCC is general and can be used for different policies; in particular, the VCGen and the proof checker are independent of the policy. Besides, the only restriction on the security policy is that it should be expressible in the formal logic, which is often very expressive.

Certifying compilation and proof-transforming compilation. One fundamental issue to be addressed by any practical deployment of logic-based PCC is the generation of certificates. If logic-based certificates are to be used to verify basic safety properties of code, and it is expected that large classes of programs carry a certificate, then it is important that certificates are generated automatically. Certifying compilers [NL98] extend traditional compilers with a mechanism to generate automatically certificates for sufficiently simple safety properties, exploiting the information available about a program during its compilation to produce a certificate that can be checked by the proof

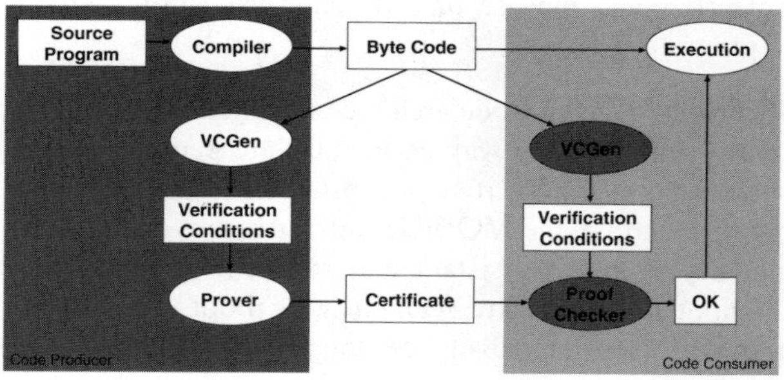

Fig. 2. PCC architecture and protocol. Code producers generate verification conditions by applying the VCGen to the compiled bytecode program. The conditions are then proved by the prover, resulting in a PCC certificate. Like producers, consumers apply the VCGen to bytecode. The certificate must contain sufficient information to allow the proof checker to discharge these conditions. Only after successful checking, the code is executed.

checker. The certifying compiler does not form part of the Trusted computing Base (TCB); nevertheless, it is an essential ingredient of PCC, since for specific properties it reduces the burden of verification on the code producer side.

MOBIUS also develops proof-transforming compilers as a means to generate certificates interactively for more complex properties that cannot be established automatically. The primary objective of proof-transforming compilation is to provide a means to generate a certificate of the bytecode program using interactive program verification environments for source code programs [BGP08, MN07].

2.3 Foundational Proof Carrying Code

The verification infrastructure on the consumer side is the central element in the PCC security architecture, and it is therefore of utmost importance to achieve the highest guarantees that its design and implementation are correct. However, providing a correct implementation of a verification infrastructure for a realistic language is a significant challenge. Thus, subtle errors may arise both at the conceptual level (e.g. by formulating unsound proof rules), or at an implementation level (e.g. by omitting some checks). In order to prevent such flaws that could be exploited by malicious code, Appel [App01] suggests to pursue a foundational approach in which the adherence of the program against the policy is formally justified using a model of the code semantics formalized in a proof assistant. This foundational approach offers several advantages:

1. *small TCB*: Foundational Proof Carrying Code (FPCC) considerably reduces the TCB, since the verification condition generator is formally proved sound w.r.t. the operational semantics. In addition, FPCC provides the highest level of guarantee for the correctness of the certificate checking infrastructure;
2. *uniform support for verification methods*: since all justifications are ultimately given in terms of the operational semantics, FPCC naturally supports a vast range of security policies (more precisely policies that can be expressed in terms of the

program semantics) and the use of different verification methods, such as type systems and program logics.

The MOBIUS Proof Carrying Code architecture is heavily inspired from FPCC, but departs significantly from it in the way certificates are generated and checked. FPCC is deductive by nature, i.e. typing rules are proved as lemmas and combined using the rules of logic. In contrast, the MOBIUS infrastructure exploits the computational power of the underlying proof assistant and relies on a tight integration between deduction and computation to ensure scalability of proof checking. In particular, the MOBIUS architecture uses intensively computational reflection, whose goal is to replace deduction by computation, and which provides an effective means to carry computation-intensive proofs for facts that cannot be established by purely deductive means. In Section 2.3, we illustrate the *reflective proof carrying code* used in MOBIUS by considering a verification condition generator and an information flow checker that have been implemented in a reflective style, and that have been verified formally. Since we provide proof objects of their semantical correctness, the verifiers are removed from the TCB (as is the case for FPCC), which now only contains the Coq type checker and the semantics of the JVM. At last, the table below summarizes the TCB of the different PCC approaches presented in this section.

PCC approach	TCB components
Type-based PCC	Byte code lightweight verifier
Logic-based PCC	VCGen + Proof checker
Foundational PCC	Coq type checker + semantics of JVM

3 Informal Development

The purpose of this section is to provide a brief introduction to the proof assistant Coq [Coq04], and an overview of the approach pursued within MOBIUS.

Coq is a general purpose proof assistant based on the Calculus of Inductive Constructions, a dependent type theory that supports higher-order logic. Coq features a specification language that is sufficiently expressive to model programming language semantics, program analysis and verification. Section 4 describes Bicolano, which provides a formalisation of the Java Virtual Machine as a state transition relation `exec:program→ state→ state→` **`Prop`**. Following the approach of FPCC, we use this semantics to prove the correctness of certificate checkers.

One essential feature of Coq is its support for writing executable specifications, which can be extracted to a functional programming language, or run inside the system itself. In the latter case, Coq warrants the use of computations to prove properties of programs, and allows to combine deduction and computation, in particular to rely on computation in place where deductive reasoning is too cumbersome.

For example, the Coq system can be used in the following manner to prove the correctness and execute (in the system itself) type-based certificate checkers, as reported in Section 5.2:

- program a computable function `check:program→bool` that is a verification procedure for a safety property on program;
- formalise rigorously the safety predicate `Safe:program→`**`Prop`** with respect to the semantics of the language given by Bicolano;
- prove that `check` is indeed a correct verification procedure. That is, build a term `check_correct` of type `∀ p, check p = true →Safe p.`

Then, to prove `Safe p` for a particular program `p`, if we know that `check p` *reduces* to `true`, we can simply use `check_correct p (refl_equal true)` where `(refl_equal true)` is a proof of `true = true`. Indeed, the conversion rule of Coq allows to change the type of a term by an equivalent one, and thus the term `(refl_equal true)` is also a proof that `check p = true` because `check p` reduces to `true`, so `true=true` is convertible with `check p = true`.

The above technique, called reflection, is also of interest to reason about program correctness, as illustrated in Section 5.3. Consider for example that we have a verification condition generator that computes a sufficient condition for safety:

```
Parameter vcg : program → form
Parameter interp : form → Prop
Parameter vcg_correct : ∀ p, interp (vcg p) → Safe p.
```

where `form` is an inductive definition of formulae, and `interp` is an interpretation of the formulae in the logic of Coq. Then, we can prove program safety for `p` with the term `vcg_correct p c`, where `c` is a proof of `interp (vcg p)`. One can improve the overall efficiency of the approach by combining `vcg` with an executable simplifier for formulae:

```
Parameter smp: form → form
Parameter smp_correct : ∀ f, interp (smp f) → interp f.
```

In this case, the proof of safety of `p` will be of the form `po_correct p c`, where `c` is a proof of `interp (smp (vcg p))` and `po_correct` is the correctness lemma obtained by composition of `smp_correct` and `vcg_correct`.[1]

Proofs by reflection are efficient and yield smaller certificates (of course, the proof term `check_correct` may be large, but the proof is only done and type-checked once, and is shared by all the instantiations). However, proofs by reflection are not appropriate for PCC scenarios where the consumer infrastructure is subject to resource constraints, as considered in Section 6. Rather than using a complete proof assistant as a checker and a logic as the language for proof certificates, it is possible to design a lightweight form of PCC where the certificate checker is a functional program extracted from Coq. Intuitively, the extraction mechanism in Coq produces Caml programs from Coq terms by eliding those parts of the terms that do not have computational content. Such parts are only necessary to ensure the well typing of the Coq term (and by the same the

[1] Our approach introduces an inductive representation of formulae (known as a deep embedding in the literature) in the above example. In fact, it is often possible to use a shallow embedding and model proof obligation generation as a **`Prop`**-valued function, but our presentation is based on a deep embedding for efficiency reasons (in particular, the use of a simplifier is more natural for a deep embedding).

correctness of the corresponding programs) but are not necessary to reduce the term to normal form (to evaluate programs).

In particular, we can use the extraction mechanism to obtain a *certified* Caml implementation of the procedure `check` above. The correction of the Coq extraction mechanism ensures that the extracted Caml checker satisfy the same soundness property as its Coq ancestor. While this approach is effective for several program verification techniques (as for examples static analysis based or type system based), it is not completely adapted for verifying programs using proof obligations since the checker does not return a boolean but a formula which should be proved. To be able to apply the extraction scenario to proof obligations the simplifier of formula should be sufficiently powerful to reduce valid formulas to the trivial one *true* (i.e. the simplifier should be a certified automatic prover).

4 Bicolano

The soundness of all the MOBIUS Proof Carrying Code infrastructure requires a formal specification of the JVM. This specification is formalised in the Coq proof assistant [Coq04] and is called Bicolano.

Bicolano is situated at the bottom of the trusted base of the MOBIUS PCC infrastructure. It is a formal description of the Java Virtual Machine (JVM), giving a rigorous mathematical description of Java bytecode program executions. It closely follows the official description of the JVM [LY99] as provided by Sun. Since the correctness of Bicolano is not formally provable, the close connection with the official specification is essential to gain trust in the specification.

This requirement results in two important design decisions for Bicolano. First, we formalize a small step semantics to relate consecutive JVM states during program execution, as it is done in the official description. Second, we try to keep our description of the JVM at the same level of detail as in the official specification. Nevertheless some simplifications have been made with respect the official documentation, some of which are motivated by the fact that we concentrate on the Connected Limited Device Configuration (CLDC), which is the primary Java configuration for mobile devices [Sun03].

Figure 3 presents the global architecture of the development. At the core of Bicolano is the axiomatic base that describes the notion of program, and specifies the semantic domains and machine arithmetic that we use. We use the Coq module system to model these different components. The operational semantics is defined on top of this axiomatic base. We define a small step and a big step semantics, and we prove equivalence between these. Finally, to show that the axiomatisations that we use are consistent, we give concrete instantiations of the different modules that allow to represent particular bytecode programs. The instantiations can also be used to obtain executable verifiers.

4.1 Axiomatic Base

The starting point of Bicolano is an axiomatisation of program syntax, semantic domains and machine arithmetic. For simplicity, we adopt a post-linking view of programs: in

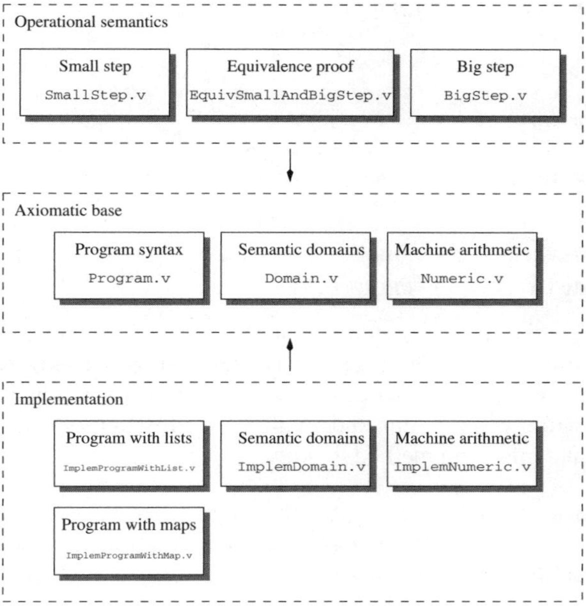

Fig. 3. Bicolano architecture

particular, we only handle complete programs and hence is not able to deal with dynamic linking. This choice simplifies the specification considerably, because a large part of the description in the official Sun specification is related to linking. Furthermore, we omit some of the numerical domains: 64 bits values (`double` and `long`) and `float` numbers are not considered.

Program syntax. The syntax of a JVM program is modelled abstractly, using signatures of the Coq module system to achieve a cleaner separation of concerns in the formalisation of the semantics. The whole set of axioms is put in a module type named `PROGRAM`. This axiomatisation is based on various abstract data types:

```
Parameter Program Class Interface Method Field
          Var MethodSignature FieldSignature PC : Set.
```

Note that some notions, such as methods and fields, are modelled in two forms: the standard form and the signature form. Such a distinction is necessary because bytecode instructions do not contain direct pointers to methods or fields.

Each abstract type has a list of accessors to manipulate them. We group the accessors of a given type in the same sub-module type. Here we give an example of `Program` accessors:

```
(** Contents of a Java program *)
Module Type PROG_TYPE.
  (** accessor to a class from its qualified name *)
  Parameter class : Program → ClassName → option Class.
```

```
    Parameter name_class_invariant1 : ∀ p cn cl,
      class p cn = Some cl → cn = CLASS.name cl.

    (** accessor to an interface from its qualified name *)
    Parameter interface : Program →
                          InterfaceName → option Interface.
    Parameter name_interface_invariant1 : ∀ p cn cl,
      interface p cn = Some cl → cn = INTERFACE.name cl.

  End PROG_TYPE.
  Declare Module PROG : PROG_TYPE.
```

Notice that the `Program` structure contains several internal invariants like `name_class_invariant1`. These are properties that we require to hold for any instantiation of the module, and that can be assumed in the operational semantics.

The axiomatisation of programs ends with a list of definitions using the previous notions such as subtyping and method lookup.

Semantic domains. Semantic domains are axiomatised in a module type named `SEMANTIC_DOMAIN`. Each sub-domain is specified in a sub-module type. For example, the set of local variables is specified as follows.

```
Module Type LOCALVAR.
  Parameter t : Set.
  Parameter get : t → Var → option value.
  Parameter update : t → Var → value → t.
  Parameter get_update_new : ∀ l x v,
    get (update l x v) x = Some v.
  Parameter get_update_old : ∀ l x y v,
    x<>y → get (update l x v) y = get l y.
End LOCALVAR.
Declare Module LocalVar : LOCALVAR.
```

The most complex axiomatisation of this file concerns the heap, for which we provide an axiomatic treatment based on the work of Poetzsch-Heffter and Müller [PHM98].

```
Module Type HEAP.
  Parameter t : Set.

  Inductive AddressingMode : Set :=
    | StaticField : FieldSignature → AddressingMode
    | DynamicField : Location →
                     FieldSignature → AddressingMode
    | ArrayElement : Location → Int.t → AddressingMode.

  Inductive LocationType : Set :=
    | LocationObject : ClassName → LocationType
    | LocationArray : Int.t → type → LocationType.

  Parameter get : t → AddressingMode → option value.
  Parameter update : t → AddressingMode → value → t.
```

```
Parameter typeof : t → Location → option LocationType.
Parameter new : t → Program →
                   LocationType → option (Location * t).
...
```

The abstract type of heaps (called `t` inside the module type `HEAP`) has two accessors `get` and `typeof` and two modifiers `update` and `new`. These functions are based on the notions of `AddressingMode` and `LocationType`. `AddressingMode` gives the kind of entry in the heap: a field signature for static fields, a location together with a field signature for field values of objects, and a location together with an integer for the element of an array. The definition `get` gives access to the value attached to an indicated address. The definition `typeof` gives the type associated with a location (if there is any). This type is either a class name for objects or a length and a type of elements for arrays. The definition `update` allows to modify a value at a given address. Finally, the definition `new` allows to allocate a new object or a new array.

4.2 Operational Semantics

Bicolano proposes two different operational semantics for sequential JVM bytecode: a small step and a big step, for which equivalence is proved formally.

Small step semantics. The small step semantics follows exactly the reference semantics given in the official specification. It consists of an elementary relation named `step` between states of the virtual machine. A standard state is of the form `(St h (Fr m pc s l) sf)` where `h` is a heap; `(Fr m pc s l)` is the current frame composed of the current method `m`, the current program point `pc`, the local variables `l` and the operand stack `s`; and finally `sf` is the call stack. An exceptional state is of the form `(StE h (FrE m pc loc l) sf)` where all elements are similar to those found in a standard state, except the location of the exception object `loc`, which replaces the operand stack. Exceptional states occur when an exception is thrown, but control has not yet reached the corresponding exception handler.

The `step` relation is given by an inductive relation. We give here a fragment describing the semantics of the `getfield` instruction.

```
Inductive step (p:Program) : State.t → State.t → Prop :=
...
| getfield_step_ok : ∀ h m pc pc' s l sf loc f v cn,

  instructionAt m pc = Some (Getfield f) →
  next m pc = Some pc' →
  Heap.typeof h loc = Some (Heap.LocationObject cn) →
  defined_field p cn f →
  Heap.get h (Heap.DynamicField loc f) = Some v →

  step p (St h (Fr m pc (Ref loc::s) l) sf)
         (St h (Fr m pc' (v::s) l) sf)
...
```

This case reads as follows: if the current instruction (given by `instructionAt m pc`) is `Getfield f` then a normal execution step is possible under several conditions: the next program counter is valid (`next m pc = some pc'`), the current operand stack is non empty and starts with a reference of class name `cn` such that the field signature `f` is defined in the class named `cn`. Under these conditions, the value `v` of the field `f` in the object pointed by the location `loc` is pushed on top of the operand stack. We omit here the second case where the top of the operand stack is `null` and an exceptional state is created.

The definition of this relation closely follows the definition given in the official specification. Together with the axiomatisation presented above, it forms the trusted base of Bicolano.

Big step semantics. Since JVM states contain a frame stack to handle method invocations, it is often convenient to use an equivalent semantics where method invocations are performed in one big step transition for showing the correctness of static analyses and program logics. Therefore we introduce a new semantics relation:

```
IntraStep (p:Program) : Method →
    IntraNormalState → IntraNormalState + ReturnState → Prop
```

This relation denotes transitions of a method between two internal states, i.e. JVM states that only contain one frame (instead of a frame stack), or between an internal state and a return state, i.e. a pair of a heap and a final result (a JVM value or an exception object in case of termination by an uncaught exception). While small-step semantics uses a call stack to store the calling context and retrieve it during a return instruction, the big step semantics directly calls the full evaluation of the called method from an initial state to a return value and uses it to continue the current computation.

We have formally proved the correctness of the big step semantics with respect to the reference small step semantics, by showing that the notion "evaluation of method m in program p from states s terminates with the final value ret" coincides in both semantics.

Semantics of programs with safety annotations. We rely on preliminary exception analyses to reduce the control flow graph of applications. Curbing the explosion in the control flow graph is essential for maintaining a minimum of precision in an information flow analysis or reducing the size of verification conditions. This is especially a problem in a language like Java because a large number of bytecode instructions are *defensive*, *i.e* they perform dynamic verifications (such as testing nullity of pointers that must be dereferenced or testing if index are between the bounds of arrays they try to access) on the current state before executing the instruction. When these verifications fail at execution time, a JVM exception is thrown and the control flow is redirected towards an adequate handler of the current method, if it has one, or the current method is stopped and the exception is recursively handled by the next method in the call stack. If the call stack is empty the program halts with an uncaught exception. Exceptions substantially complicate the control flow graph. Moreover, in most Java applications, JVM exceptions are not intentionally manipulated by the programmer and only the normal branch of these instructions are executed in practice. Part of these unreachable branches can be detected by static analysis. Bicolano uses a notion of *safety annotations* that allows to execute a static exception checker before any other verification tool and hence let such verification tools benefit from these control flow simplifications at a semantic level.

Safety annotations are exploited in an instrumented semantics, where extra properties taken from annotation information are assumed in the premise of the transition rules. Annotations take the form of flags safe attached to program points where the pre-analyser predict that no exception may be thrown here. Exceptions hence only happen at program points which are not annotated as safe. We also equip each method with an over-approximation of the set of exceptions that can be raised from it without being caught (building such an over-approximation is feasible since we consider complete programs). Assuming the annotations are correct, it is straightforward to prove that each judgment of the big step semantics implies the corresponding judgment of the instrumented big step semantics.

This pre-verification technique fits well in a PCC approach, as explained in Figure 4. Annotations are first generated by an exception analyser and then transmitted with the program. Using lightweight verification techniques, they are then checked on the consumer side by fixpoint verification. With this scheme, any verification tool can then safely reason on the annotated semantics of the program.

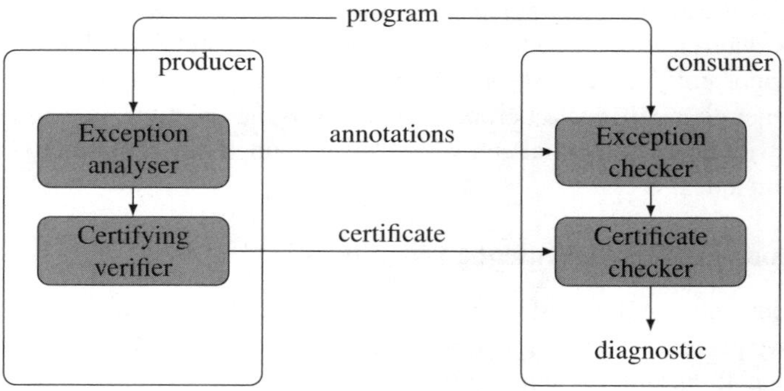

Fig. 4. Hybrid certificate with safety annotations

4.3 Implementations of Module Interfaces

Bicolano also provides implementations of the different modules used in the formalization of the JVM. These implementations serve two purposes: they guarantee that the axiomatizations are consistent, and they can also be used to get executable verifiers (in which case efficiency is important). We currently propose two different implementations of these modules; one is based on lists and is more readable whereas the second is based on maps and is more efficient.

5 Reflective Proof Carrying Code for Wholesale Checking

The purpose of this section is to present the first MOBIUS scenario, and to elaborate on the presentation of Section 3.

5.1 Scenario and Requirements

In wholesale Proof Carrying Code, mobile code transits through a trusted intermediary, e.g. a mobile phone operator. As explained in Figure 5, PCC is used by code producers (that are external to the phone operators and untrusted by them) with proofs which establish that the application is secure. The operator then digitally signs the code before distributing it to the code consumers (the customers, who rely on the operator).

This scenario for "wholesale" verification by a code distributor effectively combines the best of both PCC and trust, and brings important benefits to all participating actors. For the end user in particular, the scenario does not add PCC infrastructure complexity to the device, but still allows effective enforcement of advanced security policies.

From the point of view of phone operators, the proposed scenario enables achieving the required level of confidence in applications developed by third parties, since they can reproduce the program verification process performed by producers, but completely automatically and thus with low cost. Furthermore, Foundational Proof Carrying Code is an appropriate approach, since it brings the highest guarantees and there are no stringent restrictions on resource (memory, CPU, bandwidth) consumption.

From the software producer perspective, the scenario removes the bottleneck of the manual approval/rejection of code by the operator. This results in a significant increase in market opportunity. Of course, this comes at a cost: producers have to verify their code and generate a certificate before shipping it to the operator, in return for access to a market with a large potential and which has remained rather closed to independent software companies.

5.2 Information Flow Lightweight Type Checker

As a first instance of the reflective Proof Carrying Code approach developed in MOBIUS, we present a lightweight type checker [BPR07] that enforces confidentiality of JVM applications with the same modularity principles as Java bytecode verification: provided class files are suitably extended with appropriate security annotations, a program can be checked method by method without fixpoint iterations.

More concretely, we suppose that the levels of confidentiality of data is abstracted into a lattice of security levels (a level k_1 is lower than a level k_2, written $k_1 \sqsubseteq k_2$, if k_1 is less confidential as k_2), and that programs are equipped with security annotations (whose type is named `secure_annots` in the rest of the section), indicating the confidentiality level of each method local variables, method returns (if any) and class fields. Each method is also equipped with a security environment se that tracks the potential indirect flows (when the execution of a given instruction indirectly depends on a branching instruction involving confidential information) and assigns a security level to each program point. In order to abstract the operand stacks, the type system computes for each program point a stack of security levels. This information is reconstructed thanks to *stackmaps*, in the same spirit that those that are used in bytecode verification.

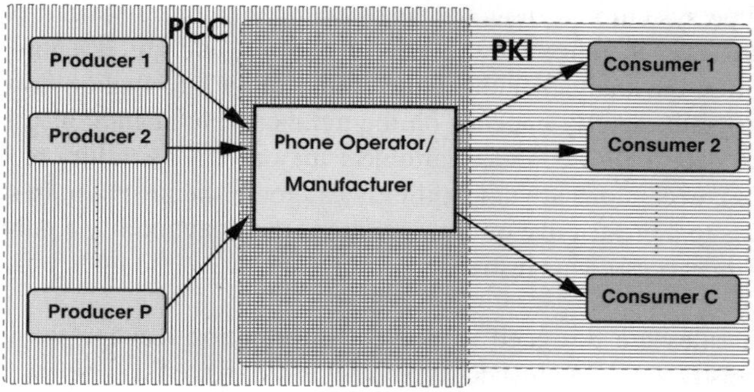

Fig. 5. The MOBIUS scenario

The semantic property enforced by the type checker is a non-interference property, which ensures that there is no flow of information from secret to public data [SM03]. It depends on a security level k_{obs} that determines the observational capabilities of the attacker. Essentially, the attacker can observe fields, local variables, and return values whose level is below k_{obs}. This is modeled with a notion of equivalence $\sim_{in}$ (for program inputs) and $\sim_{out}$ (for program outputs) between Bicolano memory states. These relations depends on the security annotations of a program. A program is non-interferent if for each method m, two terminating runs of m with $\sim_{in}$-equivalent inputs, i.e. inputs that cannot be distinguished by an attacker, yield $\sim_{out}$-equivalent results, i.e. results that cannot be distinguished by the attacker. Formally, the security condition is expressed relative to the Bicolano big step semantics, which is captured by judgments of the form $h_{in}, a \Downarrow_m r, h_{out}$, meaning that executing the method m with initial heap h_{in} and parameters a yields the final heap h_{out} and the result r. The semantic notion of non-interference is then expressed in Coq with a predicate `non_interferent:program→ secure_annots→` **`Prop`** that models the following property on a program p

$$\forall m, h_{in}, a, r, h_{out}, h'_{in}, a', r', h'_{out} \quad \left.\begin{array}{c} h_{in}, a \Downarrow_m r, h_{out} \\ h'_{in}, a' \Downarrow_m r', h'_{out} \\ (h_{in}, a) \sim_{in} (h'_{in}, a') \end{array}\right\} \Rightarrow (h_{out}, r) \sim_{out} (h'_{out}, r')$$

The type checker operates on annotated programs, and is parametrized by *control dependence region* (CDR) that approximate the scope of branching instructions, i.e. the set of instructions that execute under the scope of a given branching instruction. CDRs are required to detect indirect flows and to enforce global constraints that prevent assignments of public information to occur under guards that depend on confidential data. Formally, a point j is in a control dependence region of a branching points i if j is reachable from i (in the current method), and there may be an execution path from i to a return point which do not contain j. Although CDRs can be computed using post-dominators, we follow a lightweight verification approach and require the CDR to be transmitted with the program and develop a CDR checker.

Both the type system and the CDR analyzer operate on annotated programs. The annotations are used to minimize the size of regions, and are essential to guarantee some precision in the analysis: indeed, the ability of an information flow type system to accept a program directly depends on the number of branching instructions in this program. Each access to a confidential object may reveal its nullity to an attacker if `NullPointer` exceptions are not explicitly caught in the program. In such cases the type system has to be restrictive on the operations that may modify a public part of the memory after this access. This restriction is not necessary if the nullity case is provably unreachable.

The typing rules are designed to prevent information leakage through imposing appropriate constraints. In a nutshell, typing rules are of the form below (we omit here the special case of return instructions):

$$\frac{P[i] = ins \quad constraints}{se, i \vdash st \Rightarrow st'}$$

where st, st' are stacks of security levels before and after the execution of the instruction ins found at point i in program P, and se is the security environments of the current method. For the special case of the `getfield` instruction the rule looks like this one

$$\frac{\begin{array}{c} P[i] = \texttt{getfield}\, f \qquad \neg \mathit{Safe}(i) \Rightarrow \forall j \in \mathit{region}(i),\ k \leq se(j) \\ st' = \begin{cases} (\mathsf{ft}(f) \sqcup se(i)) :: st & \text{if } \mathit{Safe}(i) \\ \mathrm{lift}_k((\mathsf{ft}(f) \sqcup se(i)) :: st) & \text{otherwise} \end{cases} \end{array}}{se, i \vdash k :: st \Rightarrow st'}$$

The instruction `getfield` f at program point i is typable if the current type stack is of the form $k :: st$ with k the security level of the object which is read. The constraint $\forall j \in \mathit{region}(i),\ k \leq se(j)$ imposes that all points j in the control dependence region of i have a security environment $se(j)$ whose confidentiality is equal or greater than level k because reaching one of the program points $\mathit{region}(i)$ may depend on the nullity of the read object. $\mathit{Safe}(i)$ represents here the safety annotation that predicts the absence of `NullPointer` exception if the predicate holds and is inconclusive otherwise. The previous constraint is only imposed if $\mathit{Safe}(i)$ does not hold, otherwise the current point i is not a branching point. The next stack type depends also on $\mathit{Safe}(i)$. If the predicate holds, we pop the top of the stack and push a security level at least greater than the level $\mathsf{ft}(f)$ of field f and the level k of the location (to prevent explicit flows) and at least greater than $se(i)$ for implicit flows. If the predicate does not hold, we use the same stack type but *lift* it. Here lift_k is the point-wise extension to stack types of $\lambda l.\ k \sqcup l$. It is necessary to perform this lifting operation to avoid implicit flows through operand stack leakage.

Finally, the checker we formalize in Coq is of type

```
iflow_check : program →secure_annots →iflow_annots →bool
```

As indicated above, annotations are composed of safety annotations, control dependence regions and security environments and stackmaps of security levels. The checker successively checks these different annotations and finally ensures that the program is typable according to the information flow typing rules and the security annotations that express its security policy. The soundness theorem establishes the soundness of the checker with respect to the non-interference policy.

```
iflow_check_correct :
∀ p policy annot,
  iflow_check p policy annot = true → non_interferent p policy
```

This checker is fully executable, and can be run inside Coq to obtain a foundational proof of the confidentiality of a program, as described in Section 3. Alternatively, it can be extracted into a stand-alone Caml type checker and executed on-device as described in Section 6.

5.3 Verification Condition Generator

As another instance of reflective Proof Carrying Code, we present a verification condition generator (VCgen) that can be used to ensure functional and non-functional properties of programs. The VCgen operates on annotated programs, and returns a set of proof obligations whose validity ensures that the program meets its specification. More precisely, program annotations are contained in a method specification table, that assigns to every method a pre- and a post-condition, and a local specification table, that attaches to some program points an assertion (in general a loop invariant) that should be valid each time the program execution reaches them; the annotations are logical formulae that may refer to the current and initial states (heap and operand stack), and in the case of the postcondition to the termination mode and the result.

The semantic property ensured by the VCgen is expressed using the Coq predicate `correct:program→ funct_annots→ Prop` modeling the following property on an annotated program p:

$$\forall m, h_{in}, a, r, h_{out}, [h_{in}, a \Downarrow_m r, h_{out} \wedge pre\ m\ (h_{in}, a) \Rightarrow post\ m\ ((h_{in}, a), (r, h_{out}))]$$

The validity of the proof obligations ensures that, upon termination of the execution of a method m, the post-condition $post\ m$ of m will hold, provided the method was called in a initial state satisfying the pre-condition $pre\ m$. There are two kinds of proof obligations: to ensure the coherence of the annotations at a global level, e.g. that the specification respects *behavioral subtyping* [LW94], and to ensure the coherence of the annotations for each method. The latter are computed using a weakest precondition calculus, and ensure that the the annotation is valid each time the program execution reaches an annotated program point i (a local annotation is attached to i, or i is an exit point). In order to be effective, the weakest precondition calculus assumes that the methods are sufficiently annotated. Under such a condition, the weakest precondition $\mathsf{wp_i}$ at program point k is defined using the general scheme:

$$\mathsf{wp_i}(k)(s_0, s) = \bigwedge_{l \in succ(k)} C_{(k,l)}(s) \Rightarrow P_{(k,l)}(\mathsf{wp_l}(k), s_0, s)$$

where s_0 is the initial state (initial heap and arguments) $C_{(k,l)}(s)$ is the condition that needs to be satisfied by s in order for the execution to go from k to l in one step, and $P_{(k,l)}(\mathsf{wp_l}(l), s_0, s)$ is a predicate transformer updating s in correspondence with the instruction at k and applying it to the weakest precondition of the successor j ($\mathsf{wp_l}(j)$).

Computing $P_{(k,l)}(\mathsf{wp_l}(k), s_0, s)$. The function $\mathsf{wp_l}(k)$ simply searches the local annotation table; if k is annotated the precondition is the annotation else it is $\mathsf{wp_i}(k)$, so the two functions are defined using a mutual recursion. For the `getfield` instruction the rule is:

$$\frac{P[k] = \texttt{getfield}\, f \qquad \phi = \begin{cases} \mathsf{wp_l}(l, s_0, (h', v' :: [], \rho)) \text{ if } \texttt{Handler}(k, \texttt{NullPointer}) = l \\ m.\texttt{post}(s0, h', v') \qquad \text{otherwise} \end{cases}}{\begin{array}{l} \mathsf{wp_i}(k)(s_0, (h, v :: os, \rho)) = \\ \quad v \neq \texttt{null} \Rightarrow \mathsf{wp_l}(k+1)(s_0, (h(v.f) :: os, \rho)) \\ \quad \wedge v = \texttt{null} \Rightarrow \forall h'\ v',\ New(h, \texttt{NullPointer}) = (h', v') \Rightarrow \phi \end{array}}$$

In the rule above, $(h, v :: os, \rho)$ represents the current state, h stands for the heap, $v :: os$ is the operand stack and ρ is the mapping from local variables to their values. For a `getfield` instruction, the stack should be not empty. If the top value v is not null, the instruction executes normally pushing the field value of f in the top of the stack. If the top value is null, a runtime exception v' is created, leading to a new heap h' ($New(h, \texttt{NullPointer}) = (h', v')$). In that case, two cases can appear. The exception may be caught ($\texttt{Handler}(k, \texttt{NullPointer}) = l$), and the execution continues to the program counter l, in which case the postcondition of k is the precondition of l. Otherwise, the exception is uncaught and the method terminates abruptly, in which case the postcondition of k is the exceptional postcondition of the method $m.\texttt{post}$ applied to the initial state, the final heap h' and the raised exception v'. Since the exception handler is statically known, the precondition of the `getfield` is a conjunction of two postconditions.

Computing $C_{(k,l)}(s)$. The function $C_{(k,l)}$ uses safety information to eliminate impossible branches: if the program point k is annotated as safe and $Safe(k)$ is incompatible with the condition $C_{(k,l)}$ the new condition is simply `False`, and then the simplifier can remove the trivially true proposition $\texttt{False} \Rightarrow P_{(k,l)}(\mathsf{wp_l}(k), s_0, s)$ from the conjunction corresponding to $\mathsf{wp_i}(k)(s_0, s)$.

Here the VCgen uses information provided by static analyses. It is also possible [GS07] to transfer the part of the assertions contained in the specification to the analysis, so that the analysis can produce more accurate results which can be used by the VCgen to simplify the proof obligations, leading to a kind of cross fertilization between the static analyses and the VCgen.

Correctness. Finally, the VCgen we implement in Coq is of type

```
vcgen:program→ funct_annots→ Prop
```

(strictly speaking, it takes as additional argument a proof that the program is well-annotated). Its correctness lemma is:

```
vcgen_correct : ∀ p annot, vcgen p annot → correct p annot
```

The verification condition generator is executable, and can be run inside Coq, as described in Section 3.

6 Certified Static Analysis as Lightweight Proof Carrying Code

The purpose of this section is to present the first MOBIUS scenario, and to elaborate on the presentation of Section 3.

6.1 Scenario and Requirements

Rather than using a complete proof assistant as a checker and a logic as the language for proof certificates, it is possible to rely on a lightweight form of PCC, inspired from ACC, where the code consumer checks the certificate itself.

Compared to the "wholesale" scenario, this scenario does not require a PKI infrastructure and a trusted third party, as the checking phase can be done directly on the end-user device. This form of retail PCC is beneficial to the trusted intermediary, for which the cost of digital signatures can be prohibitive—it is not unusual to have hundreds of versions of a single application, because of the fragmentation of execution platforms, networks and internationalization—and to the code consumers, who may be offered an opportunity to customize policies they want to be enforced.

These embedded verifiers are part of the *trusted computing base*, and should therefore be validated with respect to Bicolano–implementing a verifier is simpler than implementing an analyser but it is still error prone. The formal framework for this validation is certified abstract interpretation [BJP06b], which proposes an unified framework to specify both an analysis to infer program invariant and a checker to verify them. The correctness of the checker is proved formally in Coq. This results in a proof-carrying code architecture—outlined in Figure 6—where both correctness proofs and actual program certificates arise from abstract interpretation. In this architecture, a verified fixpoint checker is combined with an untrusted fixpoint engine that the code producer uses to produce the stackmaps. Stackmaps are further reduced by a (still untrusted) fixpoint compression technique, yielding the final stackmap for the program. On the code consumer side, the verification proceeds in two stages. The first stage is off-device and only takes place when the consumer must update his on-device verifier. The consumer first receives a proposed fixpoint checker together with a proof of its semantic correctness. He combines this proof with a formalisation of the language semantics and the targeted security policy (here given by Bicolano) and then checks the proof off-device with the type checker of the Coq kernel. Once the proof has been checked, the code consumer extracts the fixpoint verifier using Coq's program extraction mechanism and installs it on the device. This extracted verifier can then be used to verify (on-device) the stackmaps accompanying a piece of downloaded software.

6.2 Embedding the Verifiers: Design Choices

There are several technical choices to make for porting a checker to a mobile handset:

- at least three underlying OS could be used: Windows Mobile, Symbian or Linux;
- the extraction from Coq could target Scheme, Objective Caml, Haskell or F# (for Windows mobile phones).

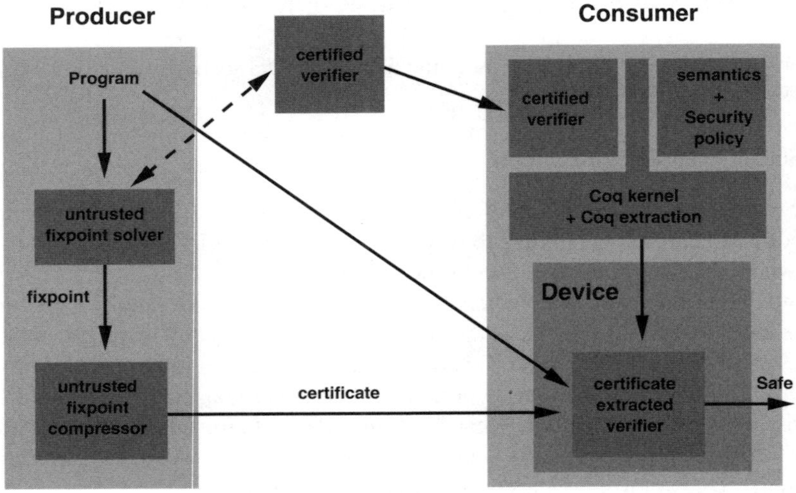

Fig. 6. A PCC architecture based on certified abstract interpretation

Because Bicolano makes a heavy use of functors, it seems natural to use Objective Caml as target language because Objective Caml also natively support this feature. To ease the porting process of the Objective Caml back-end, we have selected two Linux-based devices: a Nokia 770 tablet, an open Linux-based "web-appliance" with a very easy to use development environment and a Motorola A780 phone that runs a closed version of Linux (Montavista). Both are based on an ARM application processor. The resource constaints of the mobile handset (the operating system only leaves 1.5Mb of RAM to share among all the applications) are very typical of medium-end smartphones.

One main technical difficulty is adapting the Objective Caml compiler due to the lack of hardware floating-point support on the limited processors of those devices. We have chosen to disable completely the support for floating point as the code extracted from Coq does not need it.

6.3 Embedding the Verifiers: Case Study

In order to illustrate the feasibility of verifying the results of an analysis on-device, we have considered the interval analysis from [BJPT07]. The analysis operates on a restricted instruction set, which is sufficiently expressive to program a simple search algorithm, which is shown below with its annotations, consisting of linear relations between variables. The annotations provide pre- and post-conditions as well as invariants between local variables and parameters. With these invariants it is possible to prove *e.g.*, that all accesses to buffers (arrays) happens within their bounds and do not overflow to the surrounding memory.

```
  //      PRE: True
static int bsearch(int key, int[] vec) {
  // (I'_1) |vec_0| = |vec| ∧ 0 ≤ |vec_0|
```

```
  int low = 0, high = vec.length - 1;
 // (I'_2) |vec_0| = |vec| ∧ 0 ≤ low ≤ high + 1 ≤ |vec_0|
  while (0 < high-low) {
 // (I'_3) |vec_0| = |vec| ∧ 0 ≤ low < high < |vec_0|
     int mid = (low + high) / 2;
 // (I'_4) |vec| − |vec_0| = 0 ∧ low ≥ 0 ∧ mid − low ≥ 0∧
 //       2 · high − 2 · mid − 1 ≥ 0 ∧ |vec_0| − high − 1 ≥ 0
     if (key == vec[mid]) return mid;
     else if (key < vec[mid]) high = mid - 1;
     else low = mid + 1;
 // (I'_5) |vec_0| = |vec| ∧ −1 + low ≤ high ∧ 0 ≤ low ∧ 5 + 2 · high ≤ 2 · |vec|
  }
 // (I'_6) 0 ≤ |vec_0|
  return -1;
} //    POST: −1 ≤ res < |vec_0|
```

The invariants given here are already compressed using an automatic pruning technique. As an example the original invariant (I_5) was:

$// \ (I_5)\ \mathtt{key}_0 = \mathtt{key} \wedge |\mathtt{vec}_0| = |\mathtt{vec}| \wedge -2+3\cdot\mathtt{low} \leq 2\cdot\mathtt{high}+\mathtt{mid} \wedge -1+2\cdot\mathtt{low} \leq \mathtt{high} + 2\cdot\mathtt{mid} \wedge -1+\mathtt{low} \leq \mathtt{mid} \leq 1+\mathtt{high} \wedge \mathtt{high} \leq \mathtt{low}+\mathtt{mid} \wedge 1+\mathtt{high} \leq 2\cdot\mathtt{low}+\mathtt{mid} \wedge 1+\mathtt{low}+\mathtt{mid} \leq |\mathtt{vec}_0|+\mathtt{high} \wedge 2 \leq |\mathtt{vec}_0| \wedge 2+\mathtt{high}+\mathtt{mid} \leq |\mathtt{vec}_0|+\mathtt{low}$

As invariant reconstruction can be expensive, the optimal amount of information to supply to the checker is (I'_2) and (I'_5) so that checking is limited to verifying the inclusion of polyhedrons. Notice that (I'_2) would have been sufficient if the checker could compute a convex hull of two polyhedron. As this is a rather expensive operation, the MOBIUS project has developed a technique for producing extremely compact and easily verifiable certificates of polyhedra inclusion, which often can replace a convex hull computation—see [BJPT07] for details.

6.4 Case Study: Benchmarks

Time measurements in figure 7 are given for the interval analysis [BJP06b] on the Motorola handset. The certified function `Coq.BytecodeChecker.cheker` is iterated 100 times to avoid problems with the resolution of the timer. Parsing time is negligible. Those figures show that the phone is roughly ten times slower than the machine used in [BJP06b]. Time measurements in figure 8 are given for ten iteration of the polyhedral checker of [BJPT07].

6.5 Research Agenda

We intend to improve these preliminary experiments along three directions:

program	Bubble Sort	Convolution Product	Floyd Wharshall	HeapSort	Polynom Product	QuickSort
Time	3.92	2.94	8.49	49.48	5.77	56.91

Fig. 7. Benchmarks of the interval-based array bound checker

program	BSearch	FFT	HeapSort	Jacobi	LU	QuickSort	Random	SparseCompRow
Time	0.30	5.65	0.97	0.23	3.02	34.86	1.70	0.14
Checks made	4	29	12	5	30	12	24	2
% Checked	100	78	100	50	44	100	82	33

Fig. 8. Benchmarks of the polyhedral array bound checker

- *property coverage:* many of the properties that are relevant for security can be checked by static analysis. We intend to study the feasibility of embedding verifiers for a resource analysis that counts the number of calls to a given method, and also for a points-to analysis. The latter is used by several other analysis (eg to resolve virtual method dispatch statically) and which can be used directly to compute an approximation of the arguments of all the calls to dangerous methods (see [CA05] or [LL05]);
- *language coverage:* the language recognised by the checker must be extended to accommodate a more complete fragment of the CLDC/MIDP specification. It involves extending the instruction set to a large subset of CLDC bytecodes and refining the semantics of Bicolano to account for at least the intricate details of method dispatch, object initialisation and exception handling. Furthermore, t he MIDP libraries with their links to the native platform must be taken into account. Such an extension opens several software engineering challenges in terms of modularity and maintainability.
- *constraints:* the code of the checker must fit on constrained devices such as mobile phones. Benchmarks have shown that the CPU load is reasonable on very small examples but that we must improve the size of the representation of the bytecode handled by the checker before we extend our analysis to the complete bytecode instruction set. A modified version of the Bicolano representation of the JVM bytecode is under development. Other ideas such as mapping Coq integer types to native Objective Caml integers during the extraction of the checker (as used in [Chl0x]) should also be considered.

7 Conclusion

This article presents two PCC scenarios explored in MOBIUS, and their associated infrastructures for checking certificates. Both approaches rely on proof assistants to ensure the trustworthiness of certificate checkers: we advocate the use of reflective PCC for wholesale scenarios, and the use of certified certificate checkers for retail scenarios. In parallel to developing certified certificate checkers, the MOBIUS project has been actively investigating certificate generation: relevant material is available from the project web page:

`http://mobius.inria.fr`

Acknowledgments. This work is supported by the Integrated Project MOBIUS, within the Global Computing II initiative.

References

[APH05] Albert, E., Puebla, G., Hermenegildo, M.V.: Abstraction-carrying code. In: Baader, F., Voronkov, A. (eds.) LPAR 2004. LNCS, vol. 3452, pp. 380–397. Springer, Heidelberg (2005)

[App01] Appel, A.W.: Foundational proof-carrying code. In: Halpern, J. (ed.) Logic in Computer Science, p. 247. IEEE Press, Los Alamitos (2001)

[BBC+06] Barthe, G., Beringer, L., Crégut, P., Grégoire, B., Hofmann, M., Müller, P., Poll, E., Puebla, G., Stark, I., Vétillard, E.: MOBIUS: Mobility, ubiquity, security. In: Montanari, U., Sannella, D., Bruni, R. (eds.) TGC 2006. LNCS, vol. 4661, pp. 10–29. Springer, Heidelberg (2007)

[BGP08] Barthe, G., Grégoire, B., Pavlova, M.: Preservation of proof obligations from java to the java virtual machine. In: Armando, A., Baumgartner, P., Dowek, G. (eds.) IJCAR 2008. LNCS, vol. 5195, pp. 83–99. Springer, Heidelberg (2008) (to appear, 2008)

[BJP06a] Besson, F., Jensen, T., Pichardie, D.: A PCC architecture based on certified abstract interpretation. In: Emerging Applications of Abstract Interpretation. Elsevier, Amsterdam (2006)

[BJP06b] Besson, F., Jensen, T., Pichardie, D.: Proof-Carrying Code from Certified Abstract Interpretation and Fixpoint Compression. Theoretical Computer Science 364(3), 273–291 (2006); Extended version of [BessonP06]

[BJPT07] Besson, F., Jensen, T., Pichardie, D., Turpin, T.: Result certification for relational program analysis. Research Report 6333, IRISA (September 2007)

[BPR07] Barthe, G., Pichardie, D., Rezk, T.: A certified lightweight non-interference java bytecode verifier. In: De Nicola, R. (ed.) ESOP 2007. LNCS, vol. 4421, pp. 125–140. Springer, Heidelberg (2007)

[CA05] Crégut, P., Alvarado, C.: Improving the security of downloadable Java applications with static analysis. In: Bytecode Semantics, Verification, Analysis and Transformation. Electronic Notes in Theoretical Computer Science, vol. 141. Elsevier, Amsterdam (2005)

[CC77] Cousot, P., Cousot, R.: Abstract interpretation: a unified lattice model for static analysis of programs by construction or approximation of fixpoints. In: Principles of Programming Languages, pp. 238–252 (1977)

[Chl0x] Chlipala, A.: Modular development of certified program verifiers with a proof assistant. Journal of Functional Programming (to appear)

[Coq04] Coq development team. The Coq proof assistant reference manual V8.0. Technical Report 255, INRIA, France (March 2004), `http://coq.inria.fr/doc/main.html`

[Gow04] Gowdiak, A.: Java 2 Micro Edition (J2ME) security vulnerabilities. In: Hack In The Box Conference, Kuala Lumpur, Malaysia (2004)

[GS07] Grégoire, B., Sacchini, J.: Combining a verification condition generator for a bytecode language with static analyses. In: Barthe, G., Fournet, C. (eds.) TGC 2007 and FODO 2008. LNCS, vol. 4912, pp. 23–40. Springer, Heidelberg (2008)

[Kil73] Kildall, G.A.: A unified approach to global program optimization. In: Principles of Programming Languages, pp. 194–206. ACM Press, New York (1973)

[Ler03] Leroy, X.: Java bytecode verification: algorithms and formalizations. Journal of Automated Reasoning 30(3-4), 235–269 (2003)

[LL05] Livshits, V., Lam, M.: Finding security vulnerabilities in java applications with static analysis. In: USENIX Security Symposium (2005)

[LW94] Liskov, B., Wing, J.M.: A behavioral notion of subtyping. ACM Transactions on Programming Languages and Systems 16(6) (1994)

[LY99] Lindholm, T., Yellin, F.: The Java™ Virtual Machine Specification, 2nd edn. Sun Microsystems, Inc. (1999), `http://java.sun.com/docs/books/vmspec/`

[MN07] Müller, P., Nordio, M.: Proof-transforming compilation of programs with abrupt termination. In: SAVCBS 2007: Proceedings of the 2007 conference on Specification and verification of component-based systems, pp. 39–46. ACM, New York (2007)

[Nec97] Necula, G.C.: Proof-carrying code. In: Principles of Programming Languages, pp. 106–119. ACM Press, New York (1997)

[NL98] Necula, G.C., Lee, P.: The design and implementation of a certifying compiler. In: Programming Languages Design and Implementation, vol. 33, pp. 333–344. ACM Press, New York (1998)

[PHM98] Poetzsch-Heffter, A., Müller, P.: Logical foundations for typed object-oriented languages. In: Gries, D., De Roever, W. (eds.) Programming Concepts and Methods (PROCOMET), pp. 404–423 (1998)

[Ros03] Rose, E.: Lightweight bytecode verification. Journal of Automated Reasoning 31(3-4), 303–334 (2003)

[SM03] Sabelfeld, A., Myers, A.: Language-based information-flow security. IEEE Journal on Selected Areas in Communication 21, 5–19 (2003)

[Sun03] Sun Microsystems Inc., 4150 Network Circle, Santa Clara, California 95054. Connected Limited Device Configuration.Specification Version 1.1. Java™ 2 Platform, Micro Edition (J2ME™) (March 2003)

Certification Using the Mobius Base Logic

Lennart Beringer[1], Martin Hofmann[1], and Mariela Pavlova[2]

[1] Institut für Informatik, Universität München
Oettingenstrasse 67, 80538 München, Germany
{beringer,mhofmann}@tcs.ifi.lmu.de
[2] Trusted Labs, Sophia-Antipolis, France
Mariela.Pavlova@trusted-labs.fr

Abstract. This paper describes a core component of Mobius' Trusted Code Base, the Mobius base logic. This program logic facilitates the transmission of certificates that are generated using logic- and type-based techniques and is formally justified w.r.t. the Bicolano operational model of the JVM. The paper motivates major design decisions, presents core proof rules, describes an extension for verifying intensional code properties, and considers applications concerning security policies for resource consumption and resource access.

1 Introduction: Role of the Logic in Mobius

The goal of the Mobius project consists of the development of proof-carrying code (PCC) technology for the certification of resource-related and information-security-related program properties [16]. According to the PCC paradigm, code consumers are invited to specify conditions ("policies") which they require transmitted code to satisfy before they are willing to execute such code. Providers of programs then complement their code with formal evidence demonstrating that the program adheres to such policies. Finally, the recipient validates that the obtained evidence ("certificate") indeed applies to the transmitted program and is appropriate for the policy in question before executing the code.

One of the cornerstones of a PCC architecture is the trusted computing base (TCB), i.e. the collection of notions and tools in whose correctness the recipient implicitly trusts. Typically, the TCB consists of a formal model of program execution, plus parsing and transformation programs that translate policies and certificates into statements over these program executions. The Mobius architecture applies a variant of the *foundational* PCC approach [2] where large extents of the TCB are represented in a theorem prover, for the following reasons.

- Formalising a (e.g. operational) semantics of transmitted programs in a theorem prover provides a precise definition of the model of program execution, making explicit the underlying assumptions regarding arithmetic and logic.
- The meaning of policies may be made precise by giving formal interpretations in terms of the operational model.

F.S. de Boer et al. (Eds.): FMCO 2007, LNCS 5382, pp. 25–51, 2008.

– Theorem provers offer various means to define formal notions of certificates, ranging from proof scripts formulated in the user interface language (including tactics) of the theorem prover to terms in the prover's internal representation language for proofs (e.g. lambda-terms).

In particular, the third item allows one to employ a variety of certificate notions in a uniform framework, and to explore their suitability for different certificate generation techniques or families of policies. In contrast to earlier PCC systems which targeted mostly type- and memory-safety [2,27], policies and specifications in Mobius are more expressive, ranging from (upper) bounds on resource consumption, via access regulations for external resources and security specifications limiting the flow of information to lightweight functional specifications [16]. Thus, the Mobius TCB is required to support program analysis frameworks such as type systems and abstract interpretation, but also logical reasoning techniques.

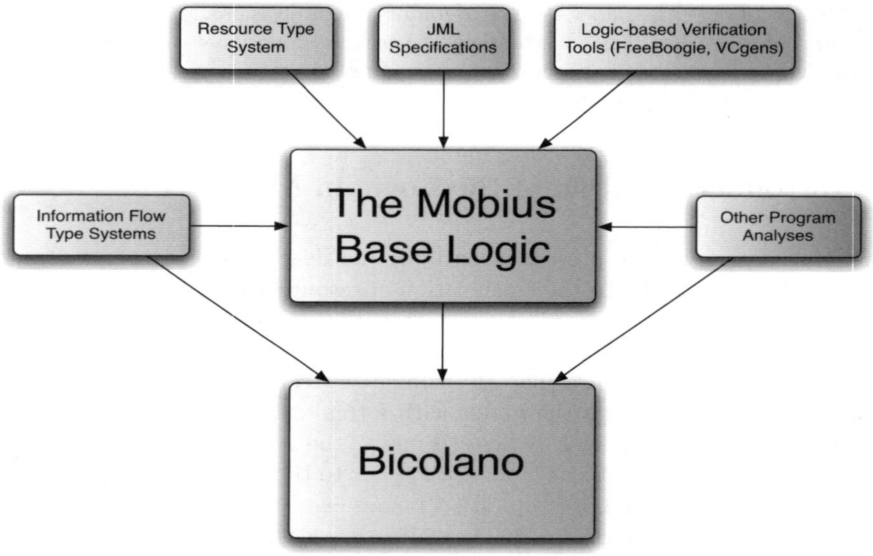

Fig. 1. Core components of the MOBIUS TCB

Figure 1 depicts the components of the Mobius TCB and their relations. The base of the TCB is formed by a formalised operational model of the Java Virtual Machine, Bicolano [30], which will be briefly described in the next section. Its purpose is to define the meaning of JVML programs unambiguously and to serve as the foundation on which the PCC framework is built. In order to abstract from inessential details, a program logic is defined on top of Bicolano. This provides support for commonly used verification patterns such as the verification of loops. Motivated by verification idioms used in higher-level formalisms such as type systems, the JML specification language, and verification condition generators, the logic complements partial-correctness style specifications by two further assertion forms: *local annotations* are attached to individual program points and are guaranteed to hold whenever the annotated program point is visited during a program execution. *Strong invariants* assert that a particular property will continue to hold for all future states during the execution of a method, including states inside inner method invocations. The precise interpretation of these assertion forms, and a selection of proof rules will be described in Section 3.

We also present an extension of the program logic that supports reasoning about the effects of computations. The extended logic arises uniformly from a corresponding generic extension of the operational semantics. Using different instantiations of this framework one may obtain domain-specific logics for reasoning about access to external resources, trace properties, or the consumption of resources. Polices for such domains are difficult if not impossible to express purely in terms of relations between initial and final states. The extension is horizontal in the sense of Czarnik and Schubert [20] as it is conservative over the non-extended ("base") architecture.

The glue between the components is provided by the theorem prover Coq, i.e. many of the soundness proofs have been formalised. The encoding of the program logics follow the approach advocated by Kleymann and Nipkow [25,29] by employing a shallow embedding of formulae. Assertions may thus be arbitrary Coq-definable predicates over states. Although the logic admits the encoding of a variety of program analyses and specification constructs, it should be noted that the architecture does not mandate that all analyses be justified with respect to this logic. Indeed, some type systems for information flow, for example, are most naturally expressed directly in terms of the operational semantics, as already the definition of information flow security is a statement over two program executions. In neither case do we need to construct proofs for concrete programs by hand which would be a daunting task in all but the simplest examples. Such proofs are always obtained from a successful run of a type system or program analysis by an automatic translation into the Mobius infrastructure. Examples of this method are given in Sections 4 and 5.2.

Outline. We give a high-level summary of the operational model Bicolano [30], restricted to a subset of instructions relevant for the present paper, in Section 2. In Section 3 we present the program logic. Section 4 contains an example of a type-based verification and shows how a bytecode-level type system guaranteeing a constant upper bound on the number of heap allocations may be encoded in the logic. The extended program logic is outlined in Section 5, together with an application concerning a type system for numeric correspondence assertions [34]. We first discuss some related work.

1.1 Related Work

The basic design decisions for the base logic were presented in [8], and the reader is referred to loc.cit. for a more in-depth motivation of the chosen format of assertions and rules. In that paper, we also presented a type-system for constant heap space consumption for a functional intermediate language, such that typing derivations could be translated into program logic derivations over an appropriately restricted judgement form. In contrast, the type system given in the present paper works directly on bytecode and hence eliminates the language translation from the formalised TCB.

The first proposal for a program logic for bytecode we are aware of is the one by Quigley [31]. In order to justify a rule for while loops, Quigley introduces various auxiliary notions for relating initial states to intermediate states of an execution sequence, and for relating states that behave similarly but apply to different classes. Bannwart and Müller [4] present a logic where assertions apply at intermediate states and are interpreted as preconditions of the assertions decorating the successor instructions. However, the occurrence of these local specifications in positive and negative positions in this interpretation precludes the possibility of introducing a rule of consequence. Indeed, our proposed rule format arose originally from an attempt to extend Bannwart and Müller's logic with a rule of consequence and machinery for allowing assertions to mention initial states. Strong invariants were introduced by the Key project [6] for reasoning about transactional safety of Java Card applications using dynamic logics [7].

Regarding formal encodings of type systems into program logics, Hähnle et al. [23], and Beringer and Hofmann [9] consider the task of representing information flow type systems in program logics, while the MRG project focused on a formalising a complex type system for input-dependent heap space usage [10].

Certified abstract interpretation [11] complements the type-based certificate generation route considered in the present paper. Similar to the relationship between Necula-Lee-style PCC [27] and foundational PCC by Appel et al. [2], certified abstract interpretation may be seen as a foundational counterpart to Albert et al.'s Abstraction-carrying code [1]. Bypassing the program logic, the approach chosen in [11] justifies the program analysis directly with respect to the operational semantics. A generic framework for certifying program analyses based on abstract interpretation is presented by Chang et al. [14]. The possibility to view abstract interpretation frameworks as inference engines for invariants and other assertions in program logics in general was already advocated in one of the classic papers by Cousot & Cousot in [18].

Nipkow et al.'s VeryPCC project [33] explores an alternative foundational approach by formally proving the soundness of verification condition generators. In particular, [32] presents generic soundness and completeness proofs for VCGens, together with an instantiation of the framework to a safety policy preventing arithmetic overflows. Generic PCC architectures have recently been developed by Necula et al. [15] and the FLINT group [22].

2 Bicolano

Syntax and States. We consider an arbitrary but fixed bytecode program P that assigns to each method identifier M a method implementation mapping instruction labels l to instructions. We use the notation $M(l)$ to denote the instruction at program point l in M, and $init_M$, $suc_M(l)$, and par_M to denote the initial label of M, the successor label of l in M, and the list of formal parameters of M, respectively. While the Bicolano formalisation supports the full sequential fragment of the JVML, this paper treats the simplified language given by the *basic* instructions

$$basic(M,l) \equiv M(l) \in \left\{ \begin{array}{l} \mathsf{load}\ x, \mathsf{store}\ x, \mathsf{dup}, \mathsf{pop}, \mathsf{push}\ z, \\ \mathsf{unop}\ \mathsf{u}, \mathsf{binop}\ o, \mathsf{new}\ c, \mathsf{athrow}, \\ \mathsf{getfield}\ c\ f, \mathsf{putfield}\ c\ f, \mathsf{getstatic}\ c\ f, \mathsf{putstatic}\ c\ f \end{array} \right\}$$

and additionally conditional and unconditional jumps $\mathsf{ifz}\ l$ and $\mathsf{goto}\ l$, static and virtual method invocations $\mathsf{invokestatic}\ M$ and $\mathsf{invokevirtual}\ M$, and $\mathsf{vreturn}$.

Values and states. The domain $\mathcal{V}$ of values is ranged over by $v, w, \ldots$ and comprises constants (integers z and Null), and addresses $a, \ldots \in \mathcal{A}$. States are built from operand stacks, stores, and heaps

$$O \in \mathcal{O} = \mathcal{V}\ list \qquad S \in \mathcal{S} = \mathcal{X} \rightharpoonup_{fin} \mathcal{V} \qquad h \in \mathcal{H} = \mathcal{A} \rightharpoonup_{fin} \mathcal{C} \times (\mathcal{F} \rightharpoonup_{fin} \mathcal{V})$$

where $\mathcal{X}$, $\mathcal{C}$ and $\mathcal{F}$ are the domains of variables, class names, and field names, respectively. In addition to local states comprising operand stacks, stores, and heaps,

$$s, r \in \Sigma = \mathcal{O} \times \mathcal{S} \times \mathcal{H},$$

we consider initial states Σ_0 and terminal states $\mathcal{T}$

$$s_0 \in \Sigma_0 = \mathcal{S} \times \mathcal{H} \qquad t \in \mathcal{T} ::= NormState(h, v) + ExcnState(h, a)$$

These capture states which occur at the beginning and the end of a frame's execution. Terminal states t are tagged according to whether the return value represents a pointer to an unhandled exception object (constructor $ExcnState(.,.)$) or an ordinary return value (constructor $NormState(.,.)$). For $s_0 = (S, h)$ we write $state(s_0) = ([\,], S, h)$ for the local state that extends s_0 with an empty operand stack. For $par_M = [x_1, \ldots, x_n]$ and $O = [v_1, \ldots, v_n]$ we write $par_M \mapsto O$ for $[x_i \mapsto v_i]_{i=1,\ldots,n}$. We write $heap(s)$ to access the heap component of a state s, and similarly for initial and terminal states. Finally, $lv(.)$ denotes the local variable component of a state and $getClass(h, a)$ extracts the dynamic class of the object at location a in heap h.

Operational judgements. Bicolano defines a variety of small-step and big-step judgements, with compatibility proofs where appropriate. For the purpose of the present paper, the following simplified setup suffices[1] (cf. Figure 2):

[1] The formalisation separates the small-step judgements for method invocations from the execution of basic instructions and jumps, and then defines a single recursive judgement combining the two. See [30] for the formal details.

Non-exceptional steps. The judgement $\vdash_M l, s \Rightarrow_{\mathsf{norm}} l', r$ describes the (non-exceptional) execution of a single instruction, where l' is the label of the next instruction (given by $suc_M(l)$ or jump targets). The rules are largely standard, so we only give a rule for the invocation of static methods, InvsNorm.

Exceptional steps. The judgement $\vdash_M l, s \Rightarrow_{\mathsf{excn}} h, a$ describes exceptional small steps where the execution of the instruction at program point M, l in state s results in the creation of a fresh exception object, located at address a in the heap h. In the case of method invocations, a single exceptional step is also observed by the callee if the invoked method raised an exception that could not be locally handled (cf. rule InvsExcn).

Small step judgements. Non-exceptional and handled exceptional small steps are combined to the small step judgement $\vdash_M l, s \Rightarrow l', r$ using the two rules NormStep and ExcnStep. The reflexive transitive closure of this relation is denoted by $\vdash_M l, s \Rightarrow^* l', r$.

Big-step judgements. The judgement form $\vdash_M l, s \Downarrow t$ captures the execution of method M from the instruction at label l onwards, until the end of the method. This relation is defined by the three rules Comp, VRet and Uncaught.

Deep step judgements. The judgement $\vdash_M l, s \Uparrow r$ is defined similarly to the big-step judgement, by the rules D-Refl, D-Trans D-Invs, and D-Uncaught. This judgement associates states across invocation boundaries, i.e. r may occur in a subframe of the method M. This is achieved by rule D-Invs which associates a call state of a (static) method with states reachable from the initial state of the callee. A similar rule for virtual methods is omitted from this presentation.

Small and big-step judgements are mutually recursive due to the occurrence of a big-step judgement in hypotheses of the rules for method invocations on the one hand and rule Comp on the other.

3 Base Logic

This section outlines the non-resource-extended program logic.

3.1 Phrase-Oriented Assertions and Judgements

The structure of assertions and judgements of the logic are governed by the requirement to enable the interpretation of type systems as well as the representation of core idioms of JML. High-level type systems typically associate types (in contexts) to program phrases. Compiling a well-formed program phrase into bytecode yields a code segment that is the postfix of a JVM method, i.e. all program points without control flow successors contain return instructions. Consequently, judgements in the logic associate assertions to a program label which represents the execution of the current method invocation from the current point (i.e. a state applicable at the program point) onwards. In case of method termination, a partial-correctness assertion (post-condition) applies that relates this

$$\textsc{InvsNorm}\ \frac{M(l) = \mathsf{invokestatic}\ M' \qquad \vdash_{M'} \mathit{init}_{M'}, ([\,], \mathit{par}_{M'} \mapsto O, h) \Downarrow \mathit{NormState}(k, v)}{\vdash_M l, (O@O', S, h) \Rightarrow_{\mathsf{norm}} \mathit{suc}_M(l), (v :: O', S, k)}$$

$$\textsc{InvsExcn}\ \frac{M(l) = \mathsf{invokestatic}\ M' \qquad \vdash_{M'} \mathit{init}_{M'}, ([\,], \mathit{par}_{M'} \mapsto O, h) \Downarrow \mathit{ExcnState}(k, a)}{\vdash_M l, (O@O', S, h) \Rightarrow_{\mathsf{excn}} k, a}$$

$$\textsc{NormStep}\ \frac{\vdash_M l, s \Rightarrow_{\mathsf{norm}} l', r}{\vdash_M l, s \Rightarrow l', r} \qquad \textsc{ExcnStep}\ \frac{\vdash_M l, (O, S, h) \Rightarrow_{\mathsf{excn}} k, a \qquad \mathit{getClass}(k, a) = e \quad \mathit{Handler}(M, l, e) = l'}{\vdash_M l, (O, S, h) \Rightarrow l', ([a], S, k)}$$

$$\textsc{Comp}\ \frac{\vdash_M l, s \Rightarrow l', s' \qquad \vdash_M l', s' \Downarrow t}{\vdash_M l, s \Downarrow t} \qquad \textsc{VRet}\ \frac{M(l) = \mathsf{vreturn}}{\vdash_M l, (v :: O, S, h) \Downarrow \mathit{NormState}(h, v)}$$

$$\textsc{Uncaught}\ \frac{\vdash_M l, s \Rightarrow_{\mathsf{excn}} h, a \quad \mathit{getClass}(h, a) = e \quad \mathit{Handler}(M, l, e) = \emptyset}{\vdash_M l, s \Downarrow \mathit{ExcnState}(h, a)}$$

$$\textsc{D-Refl}\ \frac{}{\vdash_M l, s \Uparrow s} \qquad \textsc{D-Trans}\ \frac{\vdash_M l, s \Rightarrow l', s' \qquad \vdash_M l', s' \Uparrow s''}{\vdash_M l, s \Uparrow s''}$$

$$\textsc{D-Invs}\ \frac{M(l) = \mathsf{invokestatic}\ M' \qquad \vdash_{M'} \mathit{init}_{M'}, ([\,], \mathit{par}_{M'} \mapsto O, h) \Uparrow s}{\vdash_M l, (O@O', S, h) \Uparrow s}$$

$$\textsc{D-Uncaught}\ \frac{\vdash_M l, s \Rightarrow_{\mathsf{excn}} h, a \quad \mathit{getClass}(h, a) = e \quad \mathit{Handler}(M, l, e) = \emptyset}{\vdash_M l, s \Uparrow ([a], \emptyset, h)}$$

Fig. 2. Bicolano: selected judgements and operational rules

current state to the return state. As the guarantee given by type soundness results often extends to infinite computations (e.g. type safety, i.e. absence of type errors), judgements furthermore include assertions that apply to non-terminating computations. These *strong invariants* relate the state valid at the subject label to each future state in the current method invocation. This interpretation includes states in subframes, i.e. in method invocations that are triggered in the phrase represented by the subject label.

Infinite computations are also covered by the interpretation of local annotations in JML, i.e. assertions occurring at arbitrary program points which are to be satisfied whenever the program point is visited. The logic distinguishes these explicitly given annotation from strong invariants as the former ones are not necessarily present at all program points. A further specification idiom of JML that has a direct impact on the form of assertions is `\old` which refers to the initial state of a method invocation and may appear in post-conditions, local annotations, and strong invariants.

Formulae that are shared between postconditions, local annotations, and strong invariant, and additionally only concern the relationship between the subject state and the initial state of the method may be captured in pre-conditions.

Thus, the judgement of the logic are of the form $\mathcal{G} \vdash \{A\}\, M, l\, \{B\}\, (I)$ where M, l denotes a program point (composed of a method identifier and an instruction label), and the assertions forms are as follows, where $\mathcal{B}$ denotes the set of booleans.

Assertions. $A \in \mathit{Assn} = \Sigma_0 \times \Sigma \to \mathcal{B}$ occur as preconditions A and local annotations Q, and relate the current state to the initial state of the current frame.

Postconditions. $B \in \mathit{Post} = \Sigma_0 \times \Sigma \times \mathcal{T} \to \mathcal{B}$ relate the current state to the initial and final state of a (terminating) execution of the current frame.

Invariants. $I \in \mathit{Inv} = \Sigma_0 \times \Sigma \times \Sigma \to \mathcal{B}$ relate the initial state of the current method, the current state, and any future state of the current frame or a subframe of it.

The component $\mathcal{G}$ of a judgement represents a proof context and is represented as an association of specification triples $(A, B, I) \in \mathit{Assn} \times \mathit{Post} \times \mathit{Inv}$ to program points.

The behaviour of methods is described using three assertion forms.

Method preconditions. $R \in \mathit{MethPre} = \Sigma_0 \to \mathcal{B}$ are interpreted hypothetically, i.e. their satisfaction implies that of the method postconditions and invariants but is not directly enforced to hold at all invocation points.

Method postconditions. $T \in \mathit{MethSpec} = \Sigma_0 \times \mathcal{T} \to \mathcal{B}$ constrain the behaviour of terminating method executions and thus relate only initial and final states.

Method invariants. $\Phi \in \mathit{MethInv} = \Sigma_0 \times \Sigma \to \mathcal{B}$ constrain the behaviour of terminating and non-terminating method executions by relating the initial state of a method frame to any state that occurs during its execution.

A program specification is given by a method specification table $\mathcal{M}$ that associates to each method a method specification $\mathcal{S} = (R, T, \Phi)$, a proof context $\mathcal{G}$, and a table $\mathcal{Q}$ of local annotations $Q \in \mathit{Assn}$. From now on, let $\mathcal{M}$ denote some arbitrary but fixed specification table satisfying $\mathit{dom}\ \mathcal{M} = \mathit{dom}\ P$.

3.2 Assertion Transformers

In order to notationally simplify the presentation of the proof rules, we define operators that relate assertions occurring in judgements of adjacent instructions. The following operators apply to the non-exceptional single-step execution of basic instructions.

$$\begin{aligned}
\mathsf{Pre}(M, l, l', A)(s_0, r) &= \exists\, s.\ \vdash_M l, s \Rightarrow_{\mathsf{norm}} l', r \wedge A(s_0, s) \\
\mathsf{Post}(M, l, l', B)(s_0, r, t) &= \forall\, s.\ \vdash_M l, s \Rightarrow_{\mathsf{norm}} l', r \to B(s_0, s, t) \\
\mathsf{Inv}(M, l, l', I)(s_0, r, t) &= \forall\, s.\ \vdash_M l, s \Rightarrow_{\mathsf{norm}} l', r \to I(s_0, s, t)
\end{aligned}$$

These operators resemble WP-operators, but are separately defined for pre-conditions, post-conditions, and invariants.

Exceptional behaviour of basic instructions is captured by the operators

$$\begin{aligned}
\mathsf{Pre}^{\mathsf{excn}}(M,l,e,A)(s_0,r) &= \exists\ s\ h\ a.\ \vdash_M l,s \Rightarrow_{\mathsf{excn}} h,a \wedge \mathit{getClass}(h,a)=e \wedge \\
&\qquad r = ([a], lv(s), h) \wedge A(s_0,s) \\
\mathsf{Post}^{\mathsf{excn}}(M,l,e,B)(s_0,r,t) &= \forall\ s\ h\ a.\ \vdash_M l,s \Rightarrow_{\mathsf{excn}} h,a \rightarrow \mathit{getClass}(h,a)=e \rightarrow \\
&\qquad r = ([a], lv(s), h) \rightarrow B(s_0,s,t) \\
\mathsf{Inv}^{\mathsf{excn}}(M,l,e,I)(s_0,r,t) &= \forall\ s\ h\ a.\ \vdash_M l,s \Rightarrow_{\mathsf{excn}} h,a \rightarrow \mathit{getClass}(h,a)=e \rightarrow \\
&\qquad r = ([a], lv(s), h) \rightarrow I(s_0,s,t)
\end{aligned}$$

In the case of method invocations, we replace the reference to the operational judgement by a reference to the method specifications, and include the construction and destruction of a frame. For example, the operators for non-exceptional execution of static methods are

$$\begin{aligned}
&\mathsf{Pre}_{\mathsf{sinv}}(R,T,A,[x_1,\ldots,x_n])(s_0,s) = \\
&\quad \exists\ O\ S\ h\ k\ v\ v_i.\ (R([x_i \mapsto v_i]_{i=1}^n, h) \rightarrow T(([x_i \mapsto v_i]_{i=1}^n, h),(k,v))) \wedge \\
&\qquad s = (v :: O, S, k) \wedge A(s_0, ([v_1,\ldots,v_n]@O, S, h)) \\
&\mathsf{Post}_{\mathsf{sinv}}(R,T,B,[x_1,\ldots,x_n])(s_0,r,t) = \\
&\quad \forall\ O\ S\ k\ k\ v\ v_i.\ (R([x_i \mapsto v_i]_{i=1}^n, h) \rightarrow T(([x_i \mapsto v_i]_{i=1}^n, h),(k,v))) \rightarrow \\
&\qquad r = (v :: O, S, k) \rightarrow B(s_0, ([v_1,\ldots,v_n]@O, S, h), t) \\
&\mathsf{Inv}_{\mathsf{sinv}}(R,T,I,[x_1,\ldots,x_n])(s_0,s,r) = \\
&\quad \forall\ O\ S\ k\ k\ v\ v_i.\ (R([x_i \mapsto v_i]_{i=1}^n, h) \rightarrow T(([x_i \mapsto v_i]_{i=1}^n, h),(k,v))) \rightarrow \\
&\qquad s = (v :: O, S, k) \rightarrow I(s_0, ([v_1,\ldots,v_n]@O, S, h), r)
\end{aligned}$$

The exceptional operators for static methods cover exceptions that are raised during the execution of the invoked method but not handled locally. Due to space limitations we omit the operators for exceptional (null-pointer exceptions w.r.t. the invoking object) and non-exceptional behaviour of virtual methods.

3.3 Selected Proof Rules

An addition to influencing the types of assertions, type systems also motivate the use of a certain form of judgements and proof rules. Indeed, one of the advantages of type systems is their compositionality i.e. the fact that statements regarding a program phrase are composed from the statements referring to the constituent phrases, as in the following typical proof rule for a language of expressions

$$\frac{\vdash e_1 : \mathbf{int} \qquad \vdash e_2 : \mathbf{int}}{\vdash e_1 + e_2 : \mathbf{int}}.$$

Transferring this scheme to bytecode leads to a rule format where hypothetical judgements refer to the control flow successors of the phrase in the judgement's conclusion. In addition to supporting syntax-directed reasoning, this orientation renders the explicit construction of a control flow graph unnecessary, as no control flow predecessor information is required to perform a proof.

Figure 3 presents selected proof rules. These are motivated as follows.

$$\textsc{Instr}\ \frac{\begin{array}{l} \quad basic(M,l) \qquad SC_1 \qquad SC_2 \qquad l'' = suc_M(l) \\ \quad \mathcal{G} \vdash \{\mathsf{Pre}(M,l,l'',A)\}\, M,l'\, \{\mathsf{Post}(M,l,l'',B)\}\, (\mathsf{Inv}(M,l,l'',I)) \\ \forall\, l'\ e.\ Handler(M,l,e) = l' \rightarrow \\ \quad \mathcal{G} \vdash \{\mathsf{Pre}^{\mathsf{excn}}(M,l,e,A)\}\, M,l'\, \{\mathsf{Post}^{\mathsf{excn}}(M,l,e,B)\}\, (\mathsf{Inv}^{\mathsf{excn}}(M,l,e,I)) \\ \quad \forall\, s_0\ s\ h\ a.\ (\forall\, e.\ getClass(h,a) = e \rightarrow Handler(M,l,e) = \emptyset) \rightarrow \\ \quad \vdash_M l, s \Rightarrow_{\mathsf{excn}} h, a \rightarrow A(s_0,s) \rightarrow B(s_0,s,(h,a)) \end{array}}{\mathcal{G} \vdash \{A\}\, M,l\, \{B\}\, (I)}$$

$$\textsc{Goto}\ \frac{\begin{array}{c} M(l) = \mathsf{Goto}\ l' \qquad SC_1 \qquad SC_2 \\ \mathcal{G} \vdash \{\mathsf{Pre}(M,l,l',A)\}\, M,l'\, \{\mathsf{Post}(M,l,l',B)\}\, (\mathsf{Inv}(M,l,l',I)) \end{array}}{\mathcal{G} \vdash \{A\}\, M,l\, \{B\}\, (I)}$$

$$\textsc{If0}\ \frac{\begin{array}{c} M(l) = \mathsf{ifz}\ l' \qquad SC_1 \qquad SC_2 \qquad l'' = suc_M(l) \\ \mathcal{G} \vdash \{\mathsf{Pre}(M,l,l',A)\}\, M,l'\, \{\mathsf{Post}(M,l,l',B)\}\, (\mathsf{Inv}(M,l,l',I)) \\ \mathcal{G} \vdash \{\mathsf{Pre}(M,l,l'',A)\}\, M, suc_M(l)\, \{\mathsf{Post}(M,l,l'',B)\}\, (\mathsf{Inv}(M,l,l'',I)) \end{array}}{\mathcal{G} \vdash \{A\}\, M,l\, \{B\}\, (I)}$$

$$\textsc{InvS}\ \frac{\begin{array}{l} \quad M(l) = \mathsf{invokestatic}\ M' \quad \mathcal{M}(M') = (R,T,\Phi) \quad SC_1 \quad SC_2 \\ \forall\, s_0\ O\ S\ h\ O'\ r\ v_i.\ (R(par_{M'} \mapsto O, h) \rightarrow \Phi((par_{M'} \mapsto O, h), r)) \rightarrow \\ \qquad A(s_0,(O@O',S,h)) \rightarrow I(s_0,(O@O',S,h),r) \\ \quad A_1 = \mathsf{Pre}_{\mathsf{sinv}}(R,T,A,par_{M'}) \qquad B_1 = \mathsf{Post}_{\mathsf{sinv}}(R,T,B,par_{M'}) \\ \quad \mathcal{G} \vdash \{A_1\}\, M, suc_M(l)\, \{B_1\}\, (\mathsf{Inv}_{\mathsf{sinv}}(R,T,I,par_{M'})) \\ \forall\, l'\ e.\ Handler(M,l,e) = l' \rightarrow \\ \quad \mathcal{G} \vdash \{\mathsf{Pre}^{\mathsf{excn}}_{\mathsf{sinv}}(R,T,A,e,par_{M'})\}\, M,l'\, \{\mathsf{Post}^{\mathsf{excn}}_{\mathsf{sinv}}(R,T,B,e,par_{M'})\} \\ \qquad (\mathsf{Inv}^{\mathsf{excn}}_{\mathsf{sinv}}(R,T,I,e,par_{M'})) \\ \forall\, s_0\ O\ S\ h\ O'\ k\ a.\ (R(par_{M'} \mapsto O, h) \rightarrow \Phi((par_{M'} \mapsto O, h),(k,a))) \rightarrow \\ \qquad (\forall\, e.\ getClass(k,a) = e \rightarrow Handler(M,l,e) = \emptyset) \rightarrow \\ \qquad A(s_0,(O@O',S,h)) \rightarrow B(s_0,(O@O',S,h),(k,a)) \end{array}}{\mathcal{G} \vdash \{A\}\, M,l\, \{B\}\, (I)}$$

$$\textsc{Ret}\ \frac{\begin{array}{c} M(l) = \mathsf{vreturn} \qquad SC_1 \qquad SC_2 \\ \forall\, s_0\ v\ O\ S\ h.\ A(s_0,(v :: O,S,h)) \rightarrow B(s_0,(v :: O,S,h),(h,v)) \end{array}}{\mathcal{G} \vdash \{A\}\, M,l\, \{B\}\, (I)}$$

$$\textsc{Conseq}\ \frac{\begin{array}{ll} \mathcal{G} \vdash \{A'\}\, \ell\, \{B'\}\, (I') & \forall\, s_0\ s.\ A(s_0,s) \rightarrow A'(s_0,s) \\ \forall\, s_0\ s\ t.\ B'(s_0,s,t) \rightarrow B(s_0,s,t) & \forall\, s_0\ s\ r.\ I'(s_0,s,r) \rightarrow I(s_0,s,r) \end{array}}{\mathcal{G} \vdash \{A\}\, \ell\, \{B\}\, (I)}$$

$$\textsc{Ax}\ \frac{\begin{array}{c} \mathcal{G}(\ell) = (A,B,I) \qquad \forall\, s_0\ s.\ A(s_0,s) \rightarrow I(s_0,s,s) \\ \forall\, Q.\ \mathcal{Q}(\ell) = Q \rightarrow (\forall\, s_0\ s.\ A(s_0,s) \rightarrow Q(s_0,s)) \end{array}}{\mathcal{G} \vdash \{A\}\, \ell\, \{B\}\, (I)}$$

Fig. 3. Program logic: selected syntax-directed rules

Rule INSTR describes the behaviour of basic instructions. The hypothetical judgement for the successor instruction involves assertions that are related to the assertions in the conclusion by the transformers for normal termination. A further hypothesis captures exceptions that are handled locally, i.e. those exceptions e to which the exception handler of the current method associates a handling instruction (predicate $\mathit{Handler}(M, l, e) = l'$). Exceptions that are not handled locally result in abrupt termination of the method. Consequently, these exceptions are modelled in a side condition that involves the method postcondition rather than a further judgemental hypothesis.

Finally, the side conditions SC_1 and SC_2 ensure that the invariant I and the local annotation Q (if existing) are satisfied in any state reaching label l.

$$SC_1 = \forall s_0\ s.\ A(s_0, s) \rightarrow I(s_0, s, s)$$
$$SC_2 = \forall Q.\ \mathcal{Q}(M, l) = Q \rightarrow (\forall s_0\ s.\ A(s_0, s) \rightarrow Q(s_0, s))$$

In particular, SC_2 requires us to prove any annotation that is associated with label l. Satisfaction of I in later states, and satisfaction of local annotations Q' of later program points are guaranteed by the judgement for $\mathit{suc}_M(l)$.

The rules for conditional and unconditional jumps include a hypotheses for the control flow successors, and the same side conditions for local annotations and invariants as rule INSTR. No further hypotheses or side conditions regarding exceptional behaviour are required as these instructions do not raise exceptions. These rules also account for the verification of loops which on the level of bytecode are rendered as jumps. Loop invariants can be inserted as postconditions B at their program point. Rule AX allows one to use such invariants whereas according to Definition 1 they must be established once in order for a verification to be valid.

In rule INVS, the invariant of the callee, namely Φ (more precisely: the satisfaction of Φ whenever the initial state of the callee satisfies the precondition R), and the local precondition A may be exploited to establish the invariant I. This ensures that I will be satisfied by all states that arise during the execution of M', as these states will always conform to Φ. The callee's post-condition T is used to construct the assertions that occur in the judgement for the successor instruction l'. Both conditions reflect the transfer of the method arguments and return values between the caller and the callee. This protocol is repeated in the hypothesis and the side condition for the exceptional cases which otherwise follow the pattern mentioned in the description of the rule INSTR.

A similar rule for virtual methods is omitted. The rule for method returns, RET, ties the precondition A to the post-condition B w.r.t. the terminal state that is constructed using the topmost value of the operand stack.

Finally, the *logical rules* CONSEQ and AX arise from the standard rules by adding suitable side conditions for strong invariants and local assertions.

3.4 Behavioural Subtyping and Verified Programs

We say that method specification (R, T, Φ) *implies* (R', T', Φ') if

- for all s_0 and t, $R(s_0) \rightarrow T(s_0, t)$ implies $R'(s_0) \rightarrow T'(s_0, t)$, and
- for all s_0 and s, $R(s_0) \rightarrow \Phi(s_0, s)$ implies $R'(s_0) \rightarrow \Phi'(s_0, s)$

Furthermore, we say that $\mathcal{M}$ satisfies *behavioural subtyping* for P if whenever P contains an instruction invokevirtual M' with $\mathcal{M}(M') = (\mathcal{S}', \mathcal{G}', \mathcal{Q}')$, and M overrides M', then there are $\mathcal{S}$, $\mathcal{G}$ and $\mathcal{Q}$ with $\mathcal{M}(M) = (\mathcal{S}, \mathcal{G}, \mathcal{Q})$ such that $\mathcal{S}$ implies $\mathcal{S}'$. Finally, we call a derivation $\mathcal{G} \vdash \{A\}\, M, l\, \{B\}\, (I)$ *progressive* if it contains at least one application of a non-logical rule.

Definition 1. *P is* verified *with respect to $\mathcal{M}$, notation $\mathcal{M} \vdash P$, if*

- *$\mathcal{M}$ satisfies behavioural subtyping for P, and*
- *for all M, $\mathcal{M}(M) = (\mathcal{S}, \mathcal{G}, \mathcal{Q})$, and $\mathcal{S} = (R, T, \Phi)$*
  - *a progressive derivation $\mathcal{G} \vdash \{A\}\, M, l\, \{B\}\, (I)$ exists for any l, A, B, and I with $\mathcal{G}(M, l) = (A, B, I)$, and*
  - *a progressive derivation $\mathcal{G} \vdash \{A\}\, M, init_M\, \{B\}\, (I)$ exists for*

$$
\begin{aligned}
A(s_0, s) &\equiv s = state(s_0) \wedge R(s_0) \\
B(s_0, s, t) &\equiv s = state(s_0) \rightarrow T(s_0, t) \\
I(s_0, s, r) &\equiv s = state(s_0) \rightarrow \Phi(s_0, r).
\end{aligned}
$$

As the reader may have noticed, behavioural subtyping only affects method specifications but not the proof contexts $\mathcal{G}$ or annotation tables $\mathcal{Q}$. Technically, the reason for this is that no constraints on these components are required in order to prove the logic sound. Pragmatically, we argue that proof contexts and local annotations tables of overriding methods indeed should not be related to contexts and annotation tables of their overridden counterparts, as both kinds of tables expose the internal structure of method implementations. In particular, entries in proof contexts and annotation tables are formulated w.r.t. specific program points, which would be difficult to interprete outside the method boundary or indeed across different (overriding) implementations of a method.

The distinction between progressive and non-progressive derivations prevents attempts to justify a proof context or method specification table simply by applying the axiom rule to all entries. In program logics for high-level languages, the corresponding effect is silently achieved by the unfolding of the method body in the rule for method invocations [29]. As our judgemental form does not permit such an unfolding, the auxiliary notion of progressive derivations is introduced. In our formalisation, the separation between progressive and other derivations is achieved by the introduction of a second judgement form, as described in [8].

3.5 Interpretation and soundness

Definition 2. *The triple $(\mathcal{Q}, B, I)$ is* valid *at (M, l) for (s_0, s) if*

- *for all r, if $\vdash_M l, s \Downarrow t$ then $B(s_0, s, t)$*
- *for all l' and r, if $\vdash_M l, s \Rightarrow^* l', r$ and $\mathcal{Q}(l') = Q$, then $Q(s_0, r)$, and*
- *for all r, if $\vdash_M l, s \Uparrow r$ then $I(s_0, s, r)$.*

Note that the second clause applies to annotations Q associated with arbitrary labels l' in method M that will be visited during the execution of M from (l, s) onwards. Although these annotations are interpreted without recourse to the state s, the proof of $Q(s_0, r)$ may exploit the precondition $A(s_0, s)$.

The soundness result is then as follows.

Theorem 1. *For* $\mathcal{M} \vdash P$ *let* $\mathcal{M}(M) = (\mathcal{S}, \mathcal{G}, \mathcal{Q})$, $\mathcal{G} \vdash \{A\}\, M, l\, \{B\}\, (I)$ *be a progressive derivation, and* $A(s_0, s)$*. Then* $(\mathcal{Q}, B, I)$ *is valid at* (M, l) *for* (s_0, s)*.*

In particular, this theorem implies that for $\mathcal{M} \vdash P$ all method specifications in $\mathcal{M}$ are honoured by their method implementations. The proof of this result may be performed in two ways. Following the approach of Kleymann and Nipkow [25,29,3], one would first prove that the derivability of a judgement entails its validity, under the hypothesis that contextual judgements have already been validated. For this task, the standard technique involves the introduction of relativised notions of validity that restrict the interpretation of judgements to operational judgements of bounded height. Then, the hypothesis on contextual judgements is eliminated using structural properties of the relativised validity. An alternative to this approach has been developed by Benjamin Gregoire in the course of the formalisation of the present logic. It consists of (i) defining a family of syntax-directed judgements (one judgement form for each instruction form, inlining the rule of consequence), (ii) proving that property $\mathcal{M} \vdash P$ implies that the last step in a derivation of $\mathcal{G} \vdash \{A\}\, M, l\, \{B\}\, (I)$ can be replaced by an application of the syntax-directed judgement corresponding to the instruction at M, l (in particular, an application of the axiom rule is replaced by the derivation for the corresponding code blocks from $\mathcal{G}$), and (iii) proving the main claim of Theorem 1 by treating the three parts of Definition 2 separately, each one by induction over the respective operational judgement.

4 Type-Based Verification

In this section we present a type system that ensures a constant bound on the heap consumption of bytecode programs. The type system is formally justified by a soundness proof with respect to the MOBIUS base logic, and may serve as the target formalism for type-transforming compilers.

The requirement imposed on programs is similar to that of the analysis presented by Cachera et al. in [13] in that recursive program structures are denied the facility to allocate memory. However, our analysis is presented as a type system while the analysis presented in [13] is phrased as an abstract interpretation. In addition, Cachera et al.'s approach involves the formalisation of the calculation of the program representation (control flow graph) and of the inference algorithm (fixed point iteration) in the theorem prover. In contrast, our presentation separates the algorithmic issues (type inference and checking) from semantic issues (the property expressed or guaranteed) as is typical for a type-based formulation. Depending on the verification infrastructure available at the code consumer side, the PCC certificate may either consist of (a digest of) the typing derivation or an expansion of the interpretation of the typing judgements into the MOBIUS logic. The latter approach was employed in our earlier work [10] and consists of understanding typing judgements as derived proof rules in the program logic and using syntax-directed proof tactics to apply the rules in an automatic fashion. In contrast to [10], however, the interpretation given in the present section extends to non-terminating computations, albeit for a far simpler type system.

The present section extends the work presented in [8] as the type system is now phrased for bytecode rather than an intermediate functional language and includes the treatment of exceptions and virtual methods.

Bytecode-level type system. The type system consists of judgements of the form $\vdash_{\Sigma,\Lambda} \ell : n$, expressing that the segment of bytecode whose initial instruction is located at ℓ is guaranteed not to allocate more than n memory cells. Here, ℓ denotes a program point M, l while signatures Σ and Λ assign types (natural numbers n) to identifiers of methods and bytecode instructions (in particular, when those are part of a loop), respectively.

$$\text{C-NEW}\,\frac{n \geq 1 \qquad M(l) = \mathsf{New}\ C \qquad \vdash_{\Sigma,\Lambda} M, \mathit{suc}_M(l) : n-1}{\vdash_{\Sigma,\Lambda} M, l : n}$$

$$\text{C-INSTR}\,\frac{\begin{array}{c} n \geq 1 \qquad \mathit{basic}(M,l) \qquad \neg M(l) = \mathsf{New}\ C \qquad \vdash_{\Sigma,\Lambda} M, \mathit{suc}_M(l) : n \\ \forall l'\ e.\ \mathit{Handler}(M,l,e) = l' \ \rightarrow \vdash_{\Sigma,\Lambda} M, l' : n-1 \end{array}}{\vdash_{\Sigma,\Lambda} M, l : n}$$

$$\text{C-IF}\,\frac{n \geq 0 \qquad M(l) = \mathsf{ifz}\ l' \qquad \vdash_{\Sigma,\Lambda} M, l' : n \qquad \vdash_{\Sigma,\Lambda} M, \mathit{suc}_M(l) : n}{\vdash_{\Sigma,\Lambda} M, l : n}$$

$$\text{C-INVOKE}\,\frac{\begin{array}{c} M(l) \in \{\mathsf{invokestatic}\ M', \mathsf{invokevirtual}\ M'\} \qquad \Sigma(M') = k \\ n \geq 1 \qquad k \geq 0 \qquad \vdash_{\Sigma,\Lambda} M, \mathit{suc}_M(l) : n \\ \forall l'\ e.\ \mathit{Handler}(M,l,e) = l' \ \rightarrow \vdash_{\Sigma,\Lambda} M, l' : n-1 \end{array}}{\vdash_{\Sigma,\Lambda} M, l : n+k}$$

$$\text{C-RET}\,\frac{M(l) = \mathsf{vreturn}}{\vdash_{\Sigma,\Lambda} M, l : 0} \qquad \text{C-SUB}\,\frac{\vdash_{\Sigma,\Lambda} \ell : n \qquad n \leq k}{\vdash_{\Sigma,\Lambda} \ell : k} \qquad \text{C-ASSUM}\,\frac{\Lambda(\ell) = n}{\vdash_{\Sigma,\Lambda} \ell : n}$$

Fig. 4. Type system for constant heap space

The rules are presented in Figure 4. The first rule, C-NEW, asserts that the memory consumption of a code fragment whose first instruction is new C is the increment of the remaining code. Rule C-INSTR applies to all basic instructions (in the case of goto l' we take $\mathit{suc}_M(l)$ to be l'), except for new C – the predicate $\mathit{basic}(m, l)$ is defined as in Section 3.3. The memory effect of these instructions is zero, as is the case for return instructions, conditionals, and (static) method invocations in the case of normal termination. For exceptional termination, the allocation of a fresh exception object is accounted for by decrementing the type for the code continuation by one unit. The rule C-Assum allows for using the annotation attached to the instruction if it matches the type of the instruction.

A typing derivation $\vdash_{\Sigma,\Lambda} \ell : k$ is called *progressive* if it does not solely contain applications of rules C-Sub and C-Assum. Furthermore, we call P *well-typed* for Σ, notation $\vdash_{\Sigma} P$, if for all M and n with $\Sigma(M) = n$ there is a local specification table Λ such that a progressive derivation $\vdash_{\Sigma,\Lambda} M, init_M : n$ exists, and for all ℓ with $\Lambda(\ell) = k$ we have a progressive derivation $\vdash_{\Sigma,\Lambda} \ell : k$.

Type checking and inference. The tasks of checking and automatically finding (inference) of typing derivations are not our main concern here. Nevertheless, we discuss briefly how this can be achieved.

For this simple type system checking a given typing derivation amounts to verifying the inequations that arise as side conditions. Furthermore, given Σ, Λ a corresponding typing derivation can be reconstructed by applying the typing rules in a syntax-directed fashion. In order to construct Σ, Λ as well (type inference) one writes down a "skeleton derivation" with indeterminates instead of actual numeric values and then solves the arising system of linear inequalities. Alternatively, one can proceed by counting allocation statements along paths and loops in the control-flow graph.

Our main interest here is, however, the use of existing type derivations however obtained in order to mechanically construct proofs in the program logic. This will be described now.

Interpretation of the type system. The interpretation for the above type system is now obtained by defining for each number n a triple $[\![n]\!] = (A, B, I)$ consisting of a precondition A, a postcondition B, and an invariant I, as follows.

$$[\![n]\!] \equiv \begin{pmatrix} \lambda\,(s_0, s).\ \mathit{True}, \\ \lambda\,(s_0, s, t).\ |\mathit{heap}(t)| \leq |\mathit{heap}(s)| + n, \\ \lambda\,(s_0, s, r).\ |\mathit{heap}(r)| \leq |\mathit{heap}(s)| + n \end{pmatrix}$$

Here, $|h|$ denotes the size of heap h and $\mathit{heap}(s)$ extracts the heap component of a state. We specialise the main judgement form of the bytecode logic to

$$\mathcal{G} \vdash \ell\,\{n\} \equiv \mathit{let}\ (A, B, I) = [\![n]\!]\ \mathit{in}\ \mathcal{G} \vdash \{A\}\,\ell\,\{B\}\,(I).$$

By the soundness of the MOBIUS logic, the derivability of a judgement $\mathcal{G} \vdash \ell\,\{n\}$ guarantees that executing the code located at ℓ will not allocate more that n items, in terminating (postcondition B) and non-terminating (invariant I) cases, provided that $\mathcal{M} \vdash P$ holds. For $(A, B, I) = [\![n]\!]$ we also define the method specification

$$\mathit{Spec}\ n \equiv (\lambda\, s_0.\ \mathit{True}, \lambda\,(s_0, t).\ B(s_0, \mathit{state}(s_0), t), \lambda\,(s_0, s).\ I(s_0, \mathit{state}(s_0), s)),$$

and for a given Λ we define $\mathcal{G}_\Lambda$ pointwise by $\mathcal{G}_\Lambda(\ell) = [\![\Lambda(\ell)]\!]$.

Finally, we say that $\mathcal{M}$ satisfies Σ, notation $\mathcal{M} \models \Sigma$, if for all methods M, $\mathcal{M}(M) = (\mathit{Spec}\ n, \mathcal{G}_\Lambda, \emptyset)$ holds precisely if $\Sigma(M) = n$, where Λ is the context associated with M in $\vdash_\Sigma P$. Thus, method specification table $\mathcal{M}$ contains for each method the precondition, postcondition and invariant from Σ, the (complete) context determined from Λ, and the empty local annotation table $\mathcal{Q}$.

We can now prove the soundness of the typing rules with respect to this interpretation. By induction on the typing rules, we first show that the interpretation of a typing judgement is derivable in the logic.

Proposition 1. *For $\mathcal{M} \models \Sigma$ let M be provided in $\mathcal{M}$ with some annotation table Λ such that $\vdash_{\Sigma,\Lambda} M, l : n$ is progressive. Then $\mathcal{G}_\Lambda \vdash M, l \; \{n\}$.*

From this, one may obtain the following, showing that well-typed programs satisfy the verified-program property:

Theorem 2. *Let $\mathcal{M} \models \Sigma$ and $\vdash_\Sigma P$, and let $\mathcal{M}$ satisfy behavioural subtyping for P. Then $\mathcal{M} \vdash P$.*

Discussion. In order to improve the precision of the analysis, a possibility is to combine the type system with a null-pointer analysis. For this, we would specialise the proof rules for instructions which might throw a null-pointer exception. At program points for which the analysis guarantees absence of such exceptions, we may then use a specialised typing rule. For example, a suitable rule for the field access operation is the following.

$$\text{C-GETFLD1}\,\frac{\mathit{getField}(m,l) \quad \mathit{refNotNull}(m,l) \quad \vdash_{\Sigma,\Lambda} m, \mathit{suc}_m(l) : n}{\vdash_{\Sigma,\Lambda} m, l : n}$$

Program points for which the analysis is unable to discharge the side condition $\mathit{refNotNull}(m,l)$ would be dealt with using the standard rule. Similarly, instructions that are guaranteed not to throw runtime exceptions (like load x, store x, dup) may be typed using the optimised rule

$$\text{C-NORTE}\,\frac{\vdash_{\Sigma,\Lambda} m, \mathit{suc}_m(l) : n \quad \mathit{noExceptionInstr}(m,l)}{\vdash_{\Sigma,\Lambda} m, l : n}$$

We expect that justifying these specialised rules using the program logic would not pose major problems, while the formal integration with other program analyses (such as the null-pointer analysis) is a topic for future research.

5 Resource-Extended Program Logic

In this section we give a brief overview of an extension of the MOBIUS base logic as described in Section 3 for dealing with resources in a generic way. The extension addresses the following shortcoming of the basic logic:

Resource consumption. Specific resources that we would like to reason about include instruction counters, heap allocation, and frame stack height. A well-known technique for modelling these resources is *code instrumentation*, i.e. the introduction of (real or ghost) variables and instructions manipulating these. However, code instrumentation appears inappropriate for a PCC environment, as it does not provide an end-to-end guarantee that can be understood without reference to the program at hand. In particular, the overall satisfaction of a resource property using code instrumentation requires an analysis of the annotated program, i.e. a proof that the instrumentation variables are introduced and manipulated correctly. Furthermore, the interaction between additional variables of different domains, and between auxiliary variables and proper program variables is difficult to reason about.

Execution traces. Here, the goal is to reason about properties concerning a full terminating or non-terminating execution of a program, for example by imposing that an execution satisfies a formula expressed in temporal logics or a policy given in terms of a security automaton. Such specifications may concern the entire execution history, i.e. be defined over a sequence of (intermediate) Bicolano states, and are thus not expressible in the MOBIUS base logic.

Ghost variables are heavily used in JML, both for resource-accounting purposes as well as functional specifications, but are not directly expressible in the base logic.

In this section we extend the base logic by a generic resource-accounting mechanism that may be instantiated to the above tasks. In addition to the work reported here, we have also performed an analysis of the usage made of ghost variables in JML, and have developed interpretations of ghost variables in native and resource-extended program logics [24]. In particular, loc.cit. contains a formalised proof demonstrating how resource counting using ghost variables in native logics may be effectively eliminated, by translating each proof derivation into a derivation in the resource-extended logic.

5.1 Semantic Modelling of Generic Resources

In order to avoid the pitfalls of code instrumentation discussed above, a semantic modelling of resource consumption was chosen. The logic is defined over an extended operational semantics, the judgements of which are formulated over the same components as the standard Bicolano operational semantics, plus a further resource-accounting component [20]. The additional component is of the a priori unspecified type ACT, and occurs as a further component in initial, final, and intermediate states. In addition, we introduce transfer functions that update the content of this component according to the other state components, including the program counter. The operational semantics of the extended framework is then obtained by embedding each non-extended judgement form in a judgement form over extended states and invoking the appropriate transfer functions on the resource component. While these definitions of the operational semantics are carried out once and for all, the implementation of the transfer functions themselves is programmable. Thus, realisations of the framework for particular resources may be obtained by instantiating the ACT to some specific type and implementing the transfer functions as appropriate. The program logic remains conceptually untouched, i.e. it is structurally defined as the logic from Section 3, but the definitions of assertion transformers and rules, and the soundness proof, are adapted to extended states and modified operational judgements.

In comparison to admitting the definition of ad-hoc extensions to the program logic, we argue that the chosen approach is better suited to the PCC applications, as the consumer has a single point of reference where to specify his policy, namely the implementation of the transfer functions.

5.2 Application: Block-Booking

As an application of the resource-extended program logic, we consider a scenario where an application repeatedly sends some data across a network provided that each such operation is sanctioned by an interaction with the user. In order to avoid authorisation requests for individual send operations, a high-level language might contain a primitive **auth**(n) that asks the user to authorise n messages in one interaction. A reasonable resource policy for the code consumer then is to require that no send operation be carried out without authorisation, and that at each point of the execution, the acquired authorisations suffice for servicing the remaining **send** operations. (For simplicity, we assume that refusal by the user to sanction an authorisation request simply blocks or leads to immediate non-termination without any observable effect.)

We note that as in the case of the logic loop constructs from the high-level language are mapped to conditional and unconditional jumps that must be typed using the corresponding rules.

We now outline a bytecode-level type and effect system for this task, for a sublanguage of scalar (integer) values and unary static methods. Effects τ are rely-guarantee pairs (m, n) of natural numbers: a code fragment with this effect satisfies the above policy whenever executed in a state with at least m unused authorisations, with at least n unused authorisations being left over upon termination. The number of authorisations that are additionally acquired, and possibly used, during the execution are unconstrained. Types $C, D, \ldots$ are sets of integers constraining the values stored in variables or operand stack positions. Judgements take the form $\Delta, \eta, \Xi \vdash_{\Sigma,\Lambda} \ell : C, \tau$, with the following components:

- the abstract store Δ maps local variables to types
- the abstract operand stack η is represented as a list of types
- Ξ is an equivalence relation relation ranging over identifiers ρ from $dom\ \Delta \cup dom\ \eta$ where $dom\ \eta$ is taken to be the set $\{0, \ldots, |\eta| - 1\}$. The role of Ξ is to capture equalities between values on the operand stack and the store.
- instruction labels $\ell = (M, l)$ indicate the current program point, as before
- the type C describes the return type
- the effect τ captures the pre-post-behaviour of the subject phrase with respect to authorisation and send events
- the proof context Λ associates sets of tuples $(\Delta, \eta, \Xi, C, \tau)$ to labels l (implicitly understood with respect to method M).
- the method signature table Σ maps method names to type signatures of the

form $\forall i{\in}I.\ C_i \xrightarrow{(m_i,n_i)} D_i$. Limiting our attention to static methods with a single parameter, such a poly-variant signature indicates that for each i in some (unspecified) index set I, the method is of type $C_i \xrightarrow{(m_i,n_i)} D_i$, i.e. takes arguments satisfying constraint C_i to return values satisfying D_i with (latent) effect (m_i, n_i).

In addition to ignoring virtual methods (and consequently avoiding the need for a condition enforcing behavioural subtyping of method specifications), we also ignore exceptions. Finally, while our example program contains simple objects we do not give proof rules for object construction or field access. We argue that this impoverished fragment of the JVML suffices for demonstrating the concept of certificate generation for effects, and leave an extension to larger language fragments as future work.

For an arbitrary relation R, we let $Eq(R)$ denote its reflexive, transitive and symmetric closure. We also define the operations $\varXi - \rho$, $\varXi + \rho$ and $\varXi[\rho := \rho']$ on equivalence relation $\varXi$ and identifiers ρ and ρ', as follows.

$$\begin{aligned} \varXi - \rho &\equiv \varXi \setminus \{(\rho_1, \rho_2) \mid \rho = \rho_1 \vee \rho = \rho_2\} \\ \varXi + \rho &\equiv \varXi \cup \{(\rho, \rho)\} \\ \varXi[\rho := \rho'] &\equiv Eq((\varXi - \rho) \cup \{(\rho, \rho')\}) \end{aligned}$$

The interpretation of position ρ in a pair (O, S) is given by $[\![x]\!]_{(O,S)} = S(x)$ and $[\![n]\!]_{(O,S)} = O(n)$. The interpretation of a triple $\Delta, \eta, \varXi$ in a pair (O, S) is given by the formula

$$[\![\Delta, \eta, \varXi]\!]_{(O,S)} = \begin{cases} dom\ \Delta \subseteq dom\ S \wedge |\eta| = |O| \wedge \\ \forall x \in dom\ \Delta.\ S(x) \in \Delta(x) \wedge \\ \forall i < |\eta|.\ O(i) \in \eta(i) \wedge \\ \forall (\rho, \rho') \in \varXi.\ [\![\rho]\!]_{(O,S)} = [\![\rho']\!]_{(O,S)} \end{cases}$$

With the help of these operations, the type system is now defined by the rules given in Figure 5. Due to the formulation at the bytecode level, the authorisation primitive does not have a parameter but obtains its argument from the operand stack.

The rule for conditionals, E-IF, exploits the outcome of the branch condition by updating the types of all variables associated with the top operand stack position in $\varXi$. This limited form of copy propagation will be made use of in the verification of an example program below.

In the rule of consequence, E-SUB, subtyping on types is denoted by $C <: D$ and given by subset inclusion, and is extended to abstract stores (notation $\Delta <: \Delta'$) and abstract operand stacks (notation $\eta <: \eta'$) in a pointwise fashion. Sub-effecting is given by the reflexive closure of the rule

$$\frac{k \geq m + d \quad l \leq n + d}{(m, n) <: (k, l)}.$$

$$\text{E-SEND}\frac{M(l) = \textbf{send} \qquad \Delta, \eta, \Xi \vdash_{\Sigma,\Lambda} M, suc_M(l) : D, (m-1, n)}{\Delta, \eta, \Xi \vdash_{\Sigma,\Lambda} M, l : D, (m, n)}$$

$$\text{E-AUTH}\frac{M(l) = \textbf{auth} \qquad \forall i \in C.\, i \geq k \quad \Delta, \eta, \Xi - |\eta| \vdash_{\Sigma,\Lambda} M, suc_M(l) : D, (m+k, n)}{\Delta, C :: \eta, \Xi \vdash_{\Sigma,\Lambda} M, l : D, (m, n)}$$

$$\text{E-GOTO}\frac{M(l) = \mathsf{goto}\ l' \qquad \Delta, \eta, \Xi \vdash_{\Sigma,\Lambda} M, l' : D, (m, n)}{\Delta, \eta, \Xi \vdash_{\Sigma,\Lambda} M, l : D, (m, n)}$$

$$\text{E-IF}\frac{\begin{array}{c} M(l) = \mathsf{ifz}\ l' \qquad \Xi' = \Xi - |\eta| \\ \Delta_1 = \Delta[x \mapsto \Delta(x) \cap (\mathbf{Z} \setminus \{0\})]_{(|\eta|,x)\in\Xi} \\ \eta_1 = \eta[i \mapsto \eta(i) \cap (\mathbf{Z} \setminus \{0\})]_{(|\eta|,i)\in\Xi \ \wedge\ 0 \leq i < |\eta|} \\ \Delta_2 = \Delta[x \mapsto \Delta(x) \cap \{0\}]_{(|\eta|,x)\in\Xi} \\ \eta_2 = \eta[i \mapsto \eta(i) \cap \{0\}]_{(|\eta|,i)\in\Xi \ \wedge\ 0 \leq i < |\eta|} \\ \Delta_1, \eta_1, \Xi' \vdash_{\Sigma,\Lambda} M, suc_M(l) : (m, n) \qquad \Delta_2, \eta_2, \Xi' \vdash_{\Sigma,\Lambda} M, l' : D, (m, n) \end{array}}{\Delta, C :: \eta, \Xi \vdash_{\Sigma,\Lambda} M, l : D, (m, n)}$$

$$\text{E-STORE}\frac{\begin{array}{c} M(l) = \mathsf{store}\ x \qquad \Xi' = (\Xi[x := |\eta|]) - |\eta| \\ \Delta[x \mapsto C], \eta, \Xi' \vdash_{\Sigma,\Lambda} M, suc_M(l) : D, (m, n) \end{array}}{\Delta, C :: \eta, \Xi \vdash_{\Sigma,\Lambda} M, l : D, (m, n)}$$

$$\text{E-LOAD}\frac{\begin{array}{c} M(l) = \mathsf{load}\ x \qquad \Xi' = \Xi[|\eta| := x] \\ \Delta, \Delta(x) :: \eta, \Xi' \vdash_{\Sigma,\Lambda} M, suc_M(l) : D, (m, n) \end{array}}{\Delta, \eta, \Xi \vdash_{\Sigma,\Lambda} M, l : D, (m, n)}$$

$$\text{E-PUSH}\frac{M(l) = \mathsf{push}\ c \quad \Delta, \{c\} :: \eta, \Xi + |\eta| \vdash_{\Sigma,\Lambda} M, suc_M(l) : D, (m, n)}{\Delta, \eta, \Xi \vdash_{\Sigma,\Lambda} M, l : D, (m, n)}$$

$$\text{E-BINOP}\frac{\begin{array}{c} M(l) = \mathsf{binop} \oplus \qquad C = \{z | z = x \ \oplus\ y, x \in C_1, y \in C_2\} \\ \Delta, C :: \eta, ((\Xi - |\eta|) - (|\eta| + 1)) + |\eta| \vdash_{\Sigma,\Lambda} M, suc_M(l) : D, (m, n) \end{array}}{\Delta, C_1 :: C_2 :: \eta, \Xi \vdash_{\Sigma,\Lambda} M, l : D, (m, n)}$$

$$\text{E-INVS}\frac{\begin{array}{c} M(l) = \mathsf{invokestatic}\ M' \qquad \Sigma(M') = \forall i {\in} I.\ C_i \xrightarrow{\tau_i} D_i \qquad k \in I \\ \Xi' = (\Xi - |\eta|) + |\eta| \qquad \Delta, D_k :: \eta, \Xi' \vdash_{\Sigma,\Lambda} M, suc_M(l) : D, (n_k, n) \end{array}}{\Delta, C_k :: \eta, \Xi \vdash_{\Sigma,\Lambda} M, l : D, (m_k, n)}$$

$$\text{E-VRET}\frac{M(l) = \mathsf{vreturn}}{\Delta, D, \Xi \vdash_{\Sigma,\Lambda} M, l : D, (0, 0)} \qquad \text{E-AX}\frac{(\Delta, \eta, \Xi, D, \tau) \in \Lambda(l)}{\Delta, \eta, \Xi \vdash_{\Sigma,\Lambda} M, l : D, \tau}$$

$$\text{E-SUB}\frac{\begin{array}{c} \Delta', \eta', \Xi' \vdash_{\Sigma,\Lambda} \ell : C, \tau' \\ \Delta <: \Delta' \qquad \eta <: \eta' \\ C <: D \quad \tau' <: \tau \quad \Xi' \subseteq \Xi \end{array}}{\Delta, \eta, \Xi \vdash_{\Sigma,\Lambda} \ell : D, \tau} \qquad \text{E-UNIV}\frac{\forall\, O\ S.\ [\![\Delta, \eta, \Xi]\!]_{(O,S)} = \mathit{False}}{\Delta, \eta, \Xi \vdash_{\Sigma,\Lambda} M, l : D, (m, n)}$$

Fig. 5. Type and effect system for block-booking

The final rule, E-UNIV, allows us to associate an arbitrary effect and result type to a code segment under the condition that the constraints Δ, η, Ξ on the initial state are unsatisfiable. The main use of this rule is in cases where branch conditions render one branch dead code.

In order to prove the soundness of the type system in the extended program logic, we instantiate the parameter ACT to the type of finite words over the set $\{\mathbf{send}\} \cup \{\mathbf{auth}(z) \mid z \geq 0\}$ and implement the transfer functions such that each execution of the primitives **send** and **auth** results in appending the appropriate action to the trace - in case of authorisation events, the number z is obtained by inspecting the topmost value of the operand stack.

We interpret a judgement $\Delta, \eta, \Xi \vdash_{\Sigma,\Lambda} M, l : D, (m, n)$ as the logic statement

$$[\![\Lambda]\!]_M \vdash \{\lambda\, s_0.\ \mathit{True}\}\, M, l\, \{[\![(\Delta, \eta, \Xi, m, n, D)]\!]\}\ ([\![(\Delta, \eta, \Xi, m)]\!]),$$

with the following components. The postcondition $[\![(\Delta, \eta, \Xi, m, n, D)]\!]$ is

$$\begin{aligned}&\lambda\,(s_0, (O, S, h, X), (h, v, Y)).\ [\![\Delta, \eta, \Xi]\!]_{(O,S)} \to \\ &\qquad\qquad (\exists Z.\, v \in D \wedge Y = XZ \wedge |Z|_{\mathsf{auth}} + m \geq |Z|_{\mathsf{send}} + n).\end{aligned}$$

For any terminating execution starting in an initial store and operand stack conforming to the abstractions Δ and η, and respecting the equivalence relation Ξ, this property guarantees that the return value satisfies D. Furthermore, the sub-traces for authorisation and send events (obtained by projecting from the trace Z of all events encountered during the execution of the phrase) satisfy the inequality interpreting the effect.

A similar explanation holds for the definition of the invariant $[\![(\Delta, \eta, \Xi, m)]\!]$,

$$\begin{aligned}&\lambda\,(s_0, (O, S, h, X), (O', S', h', X')).\ [\![\Delta, \eta, \Xi]\!]_{(O,S)} \to \\ &\qquad\qquad (\exists Z.\ X' = XZ \wedge |Z|_{\mathsf{auth}} + m \geq |Z|_{\mathsf{send}}).\end{aligned}$$

The local proof context $[\![\Lambda]\!]_M$ is given by

$$[(M, l) \mapsto (\mathit{True}, [\![(\Delta, \eta, \Xi, m, n, D)]\!], [\![(\Delta, \eta, \Xi, m)]\!])]_{\Lambda(l)=(\Delta,\eta,\Xi,D,(m,n))},$$

i.e. by translating the entries of Λ pointwise. Finally, each specification entry $\Sigma(M) = \forall i{\in}I.\ C_i \xrightarrow{(m_i,n_i)} D_i$ results in an entry $\mathcal{M}(M) = (R, T, \Phi)$ in the bytecode logic specification table, where

$$\begin{aligned}R(s_0) &= \mathit{True} \\ T((S, h, X), (h, v, Y)) &= \forall i \in I.\, S(\mathrm{arg}) \in C_i \to \\ &\qquad (\exists\, Z.\, v \in D_i \wedge Y = XZ \wedge \\ &\qquad\qquad |Z|_{\mathsf{auth}} + m_i \geq |Z|_{\mathsf{send}} + n_i) \\ \Phi((S, h, X), (O, S', h', X')) &= \forall i \in I.\, S(\mathrm{arg}) \in C_i \to \\ &\qquad (\exists\, Z.\ X' = XZ \wedge |Z|_{\mathsf{auth}} + m_i \geq |Z|_{\mathsf{send}})\end{aligned}$$

where arg is the formal parameter. Based on this interpretation, certificate generation may now be obtained by deriving the typing rules from the program logic and introducing appropriate notions of progressive derivations and well-typed programs (in the absence of virtual methods: without a behavioural subtyping condition), in a similar way as in Section 4. The formalisation of this is left as future research.

5.3 Example

We assume two builtin integer-valued functions `size_string` yielding the number of SMS messages required to send a given string, and `size_book` which gives the size of an address book. Figure 6 presents Java-style pseudocode for sending a given string to all addresses of a given address book after requiring the necessary permissions. The program first computes the total number of SMS messages

```
public interface Parameters {
  int p=...; //some constant >= 0
}
class BlockBooking {
  static void send () {...};
  static void auth (int p) {...};
  void block_send(Java.lang.String s, addrbook b) {
       int n = size_string(s);
       int m = size_book(b);
       int nb_sms = n * m;
       int j = 0;
       int sent = 0;
       while (nb_sms - sent > 0) {
         if j > 0 {
           //current authorisations suffice
           send();
           sent = sent + 1;
           j = j - 1
         } else {
           //acquire p new authorisations
           auth (Parameters.p);
           j = Parameters.p;
         }
       }
       return 0;
  }
}
```

Fig. 6. Program for sending a message using authorisation chunks of size p

and then sends the messages where authorisations are acquired in blocks of size p, for arbitrary fixed $p \geq 0$. The primitives for sending and authorising messages are modelled as additional (static) methods.

```
0  aload_1 //variable s
1  invokestatic sizestring
4  istore_3 //variable n
5  aload_2 // variable b
6  invokestatic sizebook
9  istore 4 //variable m
11 iload_3
12 iload 4
14 imul
15 istore 5 //variable nbms
17 iconst_0
18 istore 6 //variable j
20 iconst_0
21 istore 7 //variable sent

23 iload 5
25 iload 7
27 isub
28 ifle 64

31 iload 6
33 ifle 54

36 invokestatic send
39 iload 7
41 iconst_1
42 iadd
43 istore 7
45 iload 6
47 iconst_1
48 isub
49 istore 6
51 goto 23

54 iconst_3 // parameter p
55 invokestatic auth
58 iconst_3
59 istore 6
61 goto 23

64 iconst_0
65 ireturn
```

Fig. 7. Bytecode for method `BlockBooking.block_send`

Figure 7 shows the bytecode for method `block_send`, which comprises six basic blocks. In order to verify that this method does not send more messages than authorised, we derive the typing

$$[s \mapsto C, b \mapsto D], [\,], \emptyset \vdash_{\Sigma,\Lambda} \texttt{block\_send}, 0 : \{0\}, (0, 0)$$

where C and D are arbitrary and

$$\begin{aligned}
\Sigma &\equiv [\texttt{sizestring} \mapsto \{(C, 0, 0, \mathbf{Z})\}, \texttt{sizebook} \mapsto \{(D, 0, 0, \mathbf{Z})\}] \\
\Lambda &\equiv [23 \mapsto \{\mathit{spec}_d \mid 0 \leq d\}] \\
\mathit{spec}_d &\equiv (\Delta_d, [\,], \Xi_d, \{0\}, (d, 0)) \\
\Delta_d &\equiv [n \mapsto \mathbf{Z}, m \mapsto \mathbf{Z}, \mathit{nbsms} \mapsto \mathbf{Z}, j \mapsto \{d\}, \mathit{sent} \mapsto \mathbf{Z}^{\geq 0}] \\
\Xi_d &\equiv \{(n, n), (m, m), (\mathit{nbsms}, \mathit{nbsms}), (j, j), (\mathit{sent}, \mathit{sent})\}.
\end{aligned}$$

The proof context Λ contains a single entry, namely a polyvariant loop invariant for instruction 23. The invariant contains one entry for each $0 \leq d$, where the index specifies precisely the content of variable j and links this value to the pre-effect. The equivalence relation relevant at this program point contains merely the reflexive entries for all (integer) variables. The verification of the above judgement applies the rules syntax-directedly for instructions $0, \ldots, 21$, and then applies the axiom rule for label 23, guarded by an application of rule E-Sub.

The overall verification complements the verification of the above judgement with a justification of the context Λ, by providing a progressive derivation for the loop invariant. Again, this verification proceeds syntax-directedly through the loop, terminating in (subtyping-protected) applications of the rule E-Ax. At the point where method `send` is invoked (instruction label 36) a case-split is performed on the condition $d = 0$. If this condition holds, a vacuous statement is obtained as the invocation occurs in the branch $j > 0$, and our invariant ensures that j contains the value d. The vacuity is detected as the entry for j in Δ is $\emptyset$ at that point: the load instruction at label 36 inserts $(0, j)$ into Ξ, hence the type associated with j in the fall-through-hypothesis of the branch at label 33 (in particular: at label 36) is $\{d\} \cap (\mathbf{Z} \setminus \{0\}) = \emptyset$ where the term $\{d\}$ was propagated unmodified to instruction 36 from instruction 23. Consequently, the case $d = 0$ may be immediately discharged by an invocation of rule E-Univ. The case $d > 0$ admits the application of the proof rule E-Send, and the remainder of the branch is again proven in a syntax-directed fashion.

Type checking and inference. Again, we briefly discuss these issues for this system. The type system is generic in that types may be arbitrary sets of integers. In order to support effective typechecking and inference one must of course restrict these sets themselves and also the sets of types that arise in annotations and method specifications. A popular and for our intended application sufficient way consists of restricting types to convex polyhedra specified by a system of linear inequalities and to confine sets of types to those arising by intersecting a fixed convex polyhedron with a hyperplane specified by one or more additional parameters. Notice that the types in our running example are all of this form.

When we make this restriction (formally by applying the subtyping rule immediately after each rule to bring the types back into the polyhedral format) then type checking amounts to checking inclusion of convex polyhedra which can be efficiently performed by linear programming. Furthermore, Farkas' Lemma also furnishes short, efficiently computable, and efficiently checkable certificates [21,28]. Indeed, since any convex polyhedron is the intersection of hyperplanes, deciding containment of convex polyhedra reduces to deciding whether a convex polyhedron $H = \{\boldsymbol{x} \mid A\boldsymbol{x} \leq \boldsymbol{b}\}$ is contained in a hyperplane of the form $P = \{\boldsymbol{x} \mid \boldsymbol{c}^T\boldsymbol{x} \leq d\}$. This, however, is the case iff $\max\{\boldsymbol{c}^T\boldsymbol{x} \mid \boldsymbol{x} \in H\} \leq d$; a linear programming problem. Now, the latter inequality can be certified by providing a vector $\boldsymbol{r} \geq 0$ (componentwise) such that $\boldsymbol{r}^T A = \boldsymbol{c}^T$ and $\boldsymbol{r}^T\boldsymbol{b} \leq d$. For then, whenever $\boldsymbol{x} \in H$, i.e., $A\boldsymbol{x} \leq \boldsymbol{b}$ then $\boldsymbol{c}^T\boldsymbol{x} = \boldsymbol{r}^T A\boldsymbol{x} \leq \boldsymbol{r}^T\boldsymbol{b} \leq d$. Farkas' lemmas asserts that such a vector $\boldsymbol{r}$ exists whenever $\max\{\boldsymbol{c}^T\boldsymbol{x} \mid \boldsymbol{x} \in H\} \leq d$. Given its existence we can efficiently compute it by minimising $\boldsymbol{y}^T\boldsymbol{b}$ subject to $\boldsymbol{y}^T A = \boldsymbol{c}^T$ and $\boldsymbol{y} \geq 0$.

Regarding automatic type inference as opposed to type checking one has to find unknown convex polyhedra specified by fixpoint equations. Besson et al. [12] report that this can be done by iteration using widening heuristics from [19]. The range and efficiency remains, however, unexplored in loc. cit. In our particular application we expect constraints to be sufficiently simple so that these heuristics or those proposed in [26] will be successful. Inference of the equivalence relations Ξ can be achieved by employing standard copy-propagation techniques known from compiler constructions.

6 Discussion

We have described the use of the Mobius base logic as a unified backend for both program analyses and type systems. The Mobius base logic has been formally proved sound with respect to the Bicolano formalisation of the JVM. Compared to direct soundness proofs of type systems and analyses with respect to Bicolano the use of the Mobius base logic as an intermediary offers two distinctive advantages. First, the soundness proof of the Mobius base logic already does much of the work that is common to soundness proofs, in particular inducting on steps in the operational semantics and stack height. The Mobius logic is more transparent and allows for proof by invariant and recursion. Secondly, the standardised format of assertions in the Mobius base logic makes it easier to compare results of different type systems and analyses and also to assess whether the asserted property coincides with the intuitively desired property.

The resource extension to both Bicolano and the Mobius base logic allows for direct specification and certification of resource-related intensional properties without having to go through indirect observations such as values of ordinary program variables that are externally known to reflect some resource behaviour. This is particularly important in the PCC scenario where providers and users of specifications and certificates do not coincide and might have different objectives.

Similarly, the strong invariants enhance the expressive power of the Mobius base logic compared to standard Hoare logics in that resource behaviour of non-terminating programs is appropriately accounted for. In this way, the usual strong guarantees of type systems and program analyses may be adequately reflected in the logic.

We have demonstrated this use of the Mobius base logic on one of the Mobius case studies: a block-booking scheme whose deployment could avoid the inflation of permission requests that lead to social vulnerabilities.

Acknowledgements. This work was funded in part by the Information Society Technologies programme of the European Commission, Future and Emerging Technologies under the IST-2005-015905 MOBIUS project. This paper reflects only the author's views and the Community is not liable for any use that may be made of the information contained therein. We are grateful to all members of the MOBIUS Working Group on work package 3, in particular Benjamin Gregoire, David Pichardie, Aleksy Schubert and Randy Pollack, for the numerous discussions on program logics, JML, and types, and on formalising these in theorem provers. The constructive feedback from the reviewers helped us to improve content and presentation of the paper.

References

1. Albert, E., Puebla, G., Hermenegildo, M.V.: Abstraction-carrying code. In: Baader, F., Voronkov, A. (eds.) LPAR 2004. LNCS, vol. 3452, pp. 380–397. Springer, Heidelberg (2005)
2. Appel, A.W.: Foundational proof-carrying code. In: Halpern, J. (ed.) Logic in Computer Science, p. 247. IEEE Press, Los Alamitos (invited talk, 2001)
3. Aspinall, D., Beringer, L., Hofmann, M., Loidl, H.-W., Momigliano, A.: A program logic for resource verification. In: Slind, K., Bunker, A., Gopalakrishnan, G.C. (eds.) TPHOLs 2004. LNCS, vol. 3223, pp. 34–49. Springer, Heidelberg (2004)
4. Bannwart, F.Y., Müller, P.: A program logic for bytecode. In: Spoto, F. (ed.) Bytecode Semantics, Verification, Analysis and Transformation. Electronic Notes in Theoretical Computer Science, vol. 141, pp. 255–273. Elsevier, Amsterdam (2005)
5. Barthe, G., Fournet, C. (eds.): TGC 2007 and FODO 2008. LNCS, vol. 4912. Springer, Heidelberg (2008)
6. Beckert, B., Hähnle, R., Schmitt, P.H. (eds.): Verification of Object-Oriented Software. LNCS, vol. 4334. Springer, Heidelberg (2007)
7. Beckert, B., Mostowski, W.: A program logic for handling JAVA cARD's transaction mechanism. In: Pezzé, M. (ed.) FASE 2003. LNCS, vol. 2621, pp. 246–260. Springer, Heidelberg (2003)
8. Beringer, L., Hofmann, M.O.: A bytecode logic for JML and types. In: Kobayashi, N. (ed.) APLAS 2006. LNCS, vol. 4279, pp. 389–405. Springer, Heidelberg (2006)
9. Beringer, L., Hofmann, M.: Secure information flow and program logics. In: IEEE Computer Security Foundations Workshop. IEEE Press, Los Alamitos (2007)
10. Beringer, L., Hofmann, M., Momigliano, A., Shkaravska, O.: Automatic certification of heap consumption. In: Baader, F., Voronkov, A. (eds.) LPAR 2004. LNCS, vol. 3452, pp. 347–362. Springer, Heidelberg (2005)
11. Besson, F., Jensen, T., Pichardie, D.: Proof-Carrying Code from Certified Abstract Interpretation and Fixpoint Compression.Theoretical Computer Science (2006)
12. Besson, F., Jensen, T., Pichardie, D., Turpin, T.: Result certification for relational program analysis. Inria Research Report 6333 (2007)
13. Cachera, D., Jensen, T.P., Pichardie, D., Schneider, G.: Certified memory usage analysis. In: Fitzgerald, J.S., Hayes, I.J., Tarlecki, A. (eds.) FM 2005. LNCS, vol. 3582, pp. 91–106. Springer, Heidelberg (2005)
14. Chang, B., Chlipala, A., Necula, G.: A framework for certified program analysis and its applications to mobile-code safety. In: Emerson, E.A., Namjoshi, K.S. (eds.) VMCAI 2006. LNCS, vol. 3855, pp. 174–189. Springer, Heidelberg (2005)
15. Chang, B., Chlipala, A., Necula, G., Schneck, R.: The open verifier framework for foundational verifiers. In: Morrisett, J., Fähndrich, M. (eds.) Proceedings of TLDI 2005: 2005 ACM SIGPLAN International Workshop on Types in Languages Design and Implementation, pp. 1–12. ACM Press, New York (2005)
16. MOBIUS Consortium. Deliverable 1.1: Resource and information flow security requirements (2006), `http://mobius.inria.fr`
17. MOBIUS Consortium. Deliverable 3.1: Bytecode specification language and program logic (2006), `http://mobius.inria.fr`
18. Cousot, P., Cousot, R.: Automatic synthesis of optimal invariant assertions: mathematical foundations. In: ACM Symposium on Artificial Intelligence & Programming Languages, Rochester, NY; ACM SIGPLAN Not 12(8), 1–12 (1977)

19. Cousot, P., Halbwachs, N.: Automatic discovery of linear restraints among variables of a program. In: Conference Record of the Fifth ACM Symposium on Principles of Programming Languages, pp. 84–97 (1978)
20. Czarnik, P., Schubert, A.: Extending operational semantics of the java bytecode. In: Barthe, Fournet [5], pp. 57–72
21. Detlefs, D., Nelson, G., Saxe, J.B.: Simplify: a theorem prover for program checking. Journal of the ACM 52(3), 365–473 (2005)
22. Feng, X., Ni, Z., Shao, Z., Guo, Y.: An open framework for foundational proof-carrying code. In: Proc. 2007 ACM SIGPLAN International Workshop on Types in Language Design and Implementation (TLDI 2007), pp. 67–78. ACM Press, New York (2007)
23. Hähnle, R., Pan, J., Rümmer, P., Walter, D.: Integration of a security type system into a program logic. In: Montanari, U., Sannella, D., Bruni, R. (eds.) TGC 2006. LNCS, vol. 4661, pp. 116–131. Springer, Heidelberg (2007)
24. Hofmann, M., Pavlova, M.: Elimination of ghost variables in program logics. In: Barthe, Fournet [5], pp. 1–20
25. Kleymann, T.: Hoare Logic and VDM: Machine-Checked Soundness and Completeness Proofs. PhD thesis, LFCS, University of Edinburgh (1998)
26. Müller-Olm, M., Seidl, H.: Precise interprocedural analysis through linear algebra. In: Proc. ACM POPL 2004, pp. 330–341 (2004)
27. Necula, G.C.: Proof-carrying code. In: Principles of Programming Languages, pp. 106–119. ACM Press, New York (1997)
28. Nelson, G.: Techniques for program verification. Technical Report CSL-81-10, Xerox PARC Computer Science Laboratory (June 1981)
29. Nipkow, T.: Hoare logics for recursive procedures and unbounded nondeterminism. In: Bradfield, J. (ed.) CSL 2002 and EACSL 2002. LNCS, vol. 2471, pp. 103–119. Springer, Heidelberg (2002)
30. Pichardie, D.: Bicolano – Byte Code Language in Coq. Summary appears in [7] (2006), `http://mobius.inia.fr/bicolano`
31. Quigley, C.L.: A Programming Logic for Java Bytecode Programs. In: Basin, D.A., Wolff, B. (eds.) TPHOLs 2003. LNCS, vol. 2758, pp. 41–54. Springer, Heidelberg (2003)
32. Wildmoser, M.: Verified Proof Carrying Code. PhD thesis, Institut für Informatik, Technische Universität München (2005)
33. Wildmoser, M., Nipkow, T., Klein, G., Nanz, S.: Prototyping proof carrying code. In: Levy, J.-J., Mayr, E.W., Mitchell, J.C. (eds.) Theoretical Computer Science, pp. 333–347. Kluwer Academic Publishing, Dordrecht (2004)
34. Woo, T.Y., Lam, S.S.: A semantic model for authentication protocols. In: RSP: IEEE Computer Society Symposium on Research in Security and Privacy (1993)

Safety Guarantees from Explicit Resource Management

David Aspinall, Patrick Maier, and Ian Stark

Laboratory for Foundations of Computer Science
School of Informatics, The University of Edinburgh, Scotland
{David.Aspinall,Patrick.Maier,Ian.Stark}@ed.ac.uk

Abstract. We present a language and a program analysis that certifies the safe use of flexible resource management idioms, in particular advance reservation or "block booking" of costly resources. This builds on previous work with *resource managers* that carry out runtime safety checks, by showing how to assist these with compile-time checks. We give a small ANF-style language with explicit resource managers, and introduce a type and effect system that captures their runtime behaviour. In this setting, we identify a notion of *dynamic safety* for running code, and show that dynamically safe code may be executed without runtime checks. We show a similar *static safety* property for type-safe code, and prove that static safety implies dynamic safety. The consequence is that typechecked code can be executed without runtime instrumentation, and is guaranteed to make only appropriate use of resources.

1 Introduction

Safe management of resources is a crucial aspect of software correctness. Bad resource management impacts reliability and security. The more expensive a resource or the more complex its usage pattern, the more important is good management. For example, a media player could crash badly, leaving the hardware in a messy state, if its memory management was governed by the overly optimistic assumption that every request for memory will succeed. Malware on a mobile phone can defraud an unaware user by maliciously sending text messages to premium rate numbers, if there is no effective management of network access [12]. On current mobile platforms such as Java MIDP 2.0, management of network access is commonly left to the user, but users can easily be deceived by social engineering attacks.

Unfortunately, current programming languages do not provide special mechanisms for resource management. Therefore, programmers can only hope that their applications are resource safe, or use necessarily imprecise analyses to try to show this. For example, there are type systems that over-approximate (hopefully tightly) the memory requirements of an application [6], and static analyses that over-approximate the number of text messages being sent by an application [7].

These approaches may fail if a dynamic set of resources must be managed, as with *bulk messaging* where the user wants to send a text message to a number of recipients selected from an address book. Because of the cost of sending text messages, the user must authorise each recipient (i. e., their phone number) explicitly. This could happen individually, just before each message is being sent, or collectively, before sending the

F.S. de Boer et al. (Eds.): FMCO 2007, LNCS 5382, pp. 52–71, 2008.

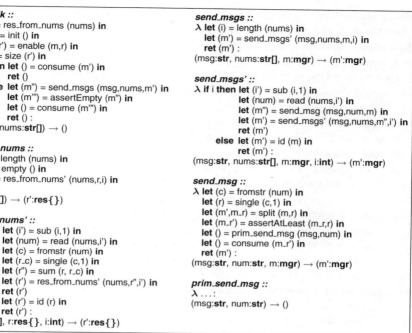

```
send_bulk ::
λ let (r) = res_from_nums (nums) in
   let (m) = init () in
   let (m',r') = enable (m,r) in
   let (n) = size (r') in
   if n then let () = consume (m') in
             ret ()
        else let (m'') = send_msgs (msg,nums,m') in
             let (m''') = assertEmpty (m'') in
             let () = consume (m''') in
             ret () :
(msg:str, nums:str[]) → ()

res_from_nums ::
λ let (i) = length (nums) in
   let (r) = empty () in
   let (r') = res_from_nums' (nums,r,i) in
   ret (r') :
(nums:str[]) → (r':res{})

res_from_nums' ::
λ if i then let (i') = sub (i,1) in
             let (num) = read (nums,i') in
             let (c) = fromstr (num) in
             let (r_c) = single (c,1) in
             let (r'') = sum (r, r_c) in
             let (r') = res_from_nums' (nums,r'',i') in
             ret (r')
        else let (r') = id (r) in
             ret (r') :
(nums:str[], r:res{}, i:int) → (r':res{})

send_msgs ::
λ let (i) = length (nums) in
   let (m') = send_msgs' (msg,nums,m,i) in
   ret (m') :
(msg:str, nums:str[], m:mgr) → (m':mgr)

send_msgs' ::
λ if i then let (i') = sub (i,1) in
             let (num) = read (nums,i') in
             let (m'') = send_msg (msg,num,m) in
             let (m') = send_msgs' (msg,nums,m'',i') in
             ret (m')
        else let (m') = id (m) in
             ret (m') :
(msg:str, nums:str[], m:mgr, i:int) → (m':mgr)

send_msg ::
λ let (c) = fromstr (num) in
   let (r) = single (c,1) in
   let (m',m_r) = split (m,r) in
   let (m_r') = assertAtLeast (m_r,r) in
   let () = prim_send_msg (msg,num) in
   let () = consume (m_r') in
   ret (m') :
(msg:str, num:str, m:mgr) → (m':mgr)

prim_send_msg ::
λ . . . :
(msg:str, num:str) → ()
```

Fig. 1. Bulk messaging application

first message. Collective authorisation, or *block booking* of resources, is preferable but requires detailed resource management, keeping track of the (multi-)set of authorised resources – in this case the permitted phone numbers.

In this paper, we present a language-based mechanism that provides programmers with a safe way to control complex resource usage patterns using a notion of *resource manager*. Figure 1 shows the code of a bulk messaging application using resource managers in our intermediate-level functional programming language. The language and functions used will be explained in full detail in Section 2; for now, we just give an outline of operation. The function send_bulk calls send_msgs to send the message msg to the phone numbers stored in the array nums. Along with these two arguments send_msgs takes a resource manager m' which encapsulates the resources that have been authorised (during the call to enable) to send the messages. For each phone number in nums, send_msgs calls the wrapper function send_msg, passing along a resource manager. Prior to calling the primitive send function prim_send_msg, the wrapper checks (using assertAtLeast) whether its input manager m contains the resource required to send a message to num; if the resource is not present, the program will abort with a runtime error, otherwise send_msg removes the resource from the manager (using split), and returns the modified manager as m'.

The bulk messaging application is (dynamically) resource safe by construction, as the resource managers will trap attempts to abuse resources. The resource manager abstraction works in tandem with a static analysis, so that programs which can be proved resource safe statically can be treated more efficiently at runtime by removing the dynamic accounting code. In Section 3.2, we prove resource safety statically for the bulk messaging application.

Our contribution is two-fold. In Section 2, we develop a functional programming language for coding complex resource idioms, such as block booking resources in the bulk messaging application. The language is essentially a first-order functional language in administrative normal form (ANF) [10] with a novel type system serving two purposes. First, the type system names input and output parameters of functions and avoids shadowing of previously bound names, thus admitting to view functions as relations (expressed by logical formulae) between their input and output parameters. Second, the language includes a special, linear type for resource managers, where linearity serves as a means of introducing stateful objects into an otherwise pure functional language. Resource managers track what resources a program is allowed to use, and the operational semantics causes the program to go wrong (i. e., abort with a runtime error) as soon as it attempts to abuse resources. This induces a notion of *dynamic resource safety*, which holds if a program never attempts to abuse resources. In this case, accounting is not necessary. As our first result, we show that erasing resource managers does not alter the semantics of dynamically resource safe programs.

Decisions about which resources programs may use are typically guided by *resource policies*. From the point of view of a program, a policy is simply an oracle determining what resources to grant; and we abstract this as a non-deterministic operation on resource managers. This covers many concrete policy mechanisms, both static (e. g., Java-style policy files) or dynamic (e. g., user interaction); see [3] for more on the interaction of resource managers and policies.

In Section 3 we present our second contribution, an effect type system for deriving relational approximations of functions. These approximations are expressed as pairs of constraints in a first-order logic, specifying a pre- and postcondition (or rather, state transforming action) of a given function, similar to Hoare type theory [11]; note that the use of logical formulae as effects is the rationale behind choosing a programming language where functions have named input and output parameters. Typability of functions in the effect type system induces a notion of *static resource safety*. As our second result, we prove a soundness theorem stating that static implies dynamic resource safety. As a corollary, we show that resource managers can always be erased from statically resource safe programs. Proofs have been omitted due to lack of space.

2 A Programming Language for Resource Management

We introduce a simple programming language with built-in constructs for handling resource managers. The language is essentially a simply-typed first-order functional language in ANF [10], with the additional features that functions take and return tuples of values, function types name input and output arguments, scoping avoids shadowing, and the type of resource managers enforces a linearity restriction on its values. The first three of these features are related to giving the language a relational appeal: for the purpose of specifying and reasoning logically, functions ought to be viewed as relations

$\langle\text{fundecl}\rangle ::=$	$\langle\text{prodtype}\rangle \longrightarrow \langle\text{prodtype}\rangle$	*(built-in function)*
$\mid$	$\boldsymbol{\lambda}\langle\text{exp}\rangle \,\mathbf{:}\, \langle\text{prodtype}\rangle \longrightarrow \langle\text{prodtype}\rangle$	*(λ-abstraction)*
$\langle\text{exp}\rangle ::=$	$\mathbf{if}\ \langle\text{val}\rangle\ \mathbf{then}\ \langle\text{exp}\rangle\ \mathbf{else}\ \langle\text{exp}\rangle$	*(conditional)*
$\mid$	$\mathbf{let}\ \mathbf{(}\langle\text{var}\rangle\mathbf{,}\ldots\mathbf{,}\langle\text{var}\rangle\mathbf{)} = \langle\text{fun}\rangle\ \mathbf{(}\langle\text{val}\rangle\mathbf{,}\ldots\mathbf{,}\langle\text{val}\rangle\mathbf{)}\ \mathbf{in}\ \langle\text{exp}\rangle$	*(function call)*
$\mid$	$\mathbf{ret}\ \mathbf{(}\langle\text{var}\rangle\mathbf{,}\ldots\mathbf{,}\langle\text{var}\rangle\mathbf{)}$	*(return)*
$\langle\text{val}\rangle ::=$	$\langle\text{const}\rangle \mid \langle\text{var}\rangle$	
$\langle\text{prodtype}\rangle ::=$	$\mathbf{(}\langle\text{var}\rangle\mathbf{:}\langle\text{type}\rangle\mathbf{,}\ldots\mathbf{,}\langle\text{var}\rangle\mathbf{:}\langle\text{type}\rangle\mathbf{)}$	
$\langle\text{type}\rangle ::=$	$\langle\text{datatype}\rangle \mid \mathbf{mgr}$	
$\langle\text{datatype}\rangle ::=$	$\mathbf{unit} \mid \mathbf{int} \mid \mathbf{str} \mid \mathbf{res} \mid \mathbf{res\{\}} \mid \langle\text{datatype}\rangle\mathbf{[]}$	

Fig. 2. BNF grammar

between input and output parameters. The fourth feature is a means of introducing state into a functional language.

The choice for such a language has been inspired by Grail [2], another first-order functional language in ANF. Moreover, Appel [1] argues that ANF, the intermediate language used by many compilers for functional languages, and SSA, the intermediate representation used by most compilers for imperative languages, are essentially the same thing. Therefore, our language should capture the essence of first-order programming languages, whether functional or imperative.

2.1 Syntax and Static Semantics

Grammar. Figure 2 shows the grammar of the programming language. The nonterminals $\langle\text{fun}\rangle$, $\langle\text{var}\rangle$ and $\langle\text{const}\rangle$ represent *functions*, *variables* and *constants*, respectively. A *program* Π is a partial function from $\langle\text{fun}\rangle$ to $\langle\text{fundecl}\rangle$, i. e., Π maps functions to function declarations, which are either type declarations for built-in functions or λ-abstractions (with type annotations serving as variable binders). We use the notation $\Pi(f) = [\boldsymbol{\lambda}\ldots]\sigma \longrightarrow \sigma'$ if we are only interested in the type of f, regardless whether f is built-in or a λ-abstraction. By $dom(\Pi)$, we denote the domain of Π. We denote the restriction of Π to the built-in functions by Π_0, i. e., $\Pi(f)$ is a λ-abstraction if and only if $f \in dom(\Pi) \setminus dom(\Pi_0)$. We assume that Π_0 declares exactly the functions that are shown in Figure 4.

The grammar of *expressions* $e \in \langle\text{exp}\rangle$ and *values* $v \in \langle\text{val}\rangle$ is quite standard for a first-order functional language in ANF. Throughout, functions operate on tuples of values, which is reflected by the syntax for function call and return. The sets of free and bound (by the let-construct) variables of an expression e, denoted by *free*(e) and $bound(e)$ respectively, are defined in the usual way.

Datatypes $\tau \in \langle\text{datatype}\rangle$ comprise the unit type, integers, strings, resources, multisets of resources, and arrays. A *type* $\tau \in \langle\text{type}\rangle$ is either a datatype or the special type of resource managers, denoted $\mathbf{mgr}$. See Section 2.2 for the interpretations of types. A tuple $(x_1{:}\tau_1,\ldots,x_n{:}\tau_n) \in \langle\text{prodtype}\rangle$ is a *product type* if the variables $x_1,\ldots,x_n$ are pairwise distinct. Product types appear to associate types to variables, but they really associate variables *and* types to positions in tuples. A pair of product types of the form $(x_1{:}\tau_1,\ldots,x_m{:}\tau_m) \longrightarrow (x'_1{:}\tau'_1,\ldots,x'_n{:}\tau'_n)$ forms a *function type* if the variable sets $\{x_1,\ldots,x_m\}$ and $\{x'_1,\ldots,x'_n\}$ are disjoint. We call the product types to the left and right of the arrow *argument type* and *return type*, respectively. As an example consider the type of the function send_msg from Figure 1. It states that send_msg takes two strings and a resource manager and returns a resource manager, while at the same time binding the names of the formal input parameters msg, num and m and announcing that the formal output parameter will be m'.

Static typing. A *type environment* Γ is a functional association list of type declarations of the form $x{:}\tau$, where x is a variable and τ a type. Being functional implies that whenever Γ contains two type declarations $x{:}\tau$ and $x{:}\tau'$ we must have $\tau = \tau'$. Therefore, Γ can be seen as a partial function mapping variables to types. By $dom(\Gamma)$, we denote the domain of this partial function, and for $x \in dom(\Gamma)$, we may write $\Gamma(x)$ for the unique type which Γ associates to x. We write type environments as comma-separated lists, the empty list being denoted by $\emptyset$. The restriction $\Gamma|_X$ of Γ to a set of variables X, is defined in the usual way and induces a partial order $\succeq$ type environments, where $\Gamma' \succeq \Gamma$ iff $\Gamma'|_{dom(\Gamma)} = \Gamma$.

We call a type environment $\Gamma = x_1{:}\tau_1,\ldots,x_n{:}\tau_n$ *linear* if the variables $x_1,\ldots,x_n$ are pairwise distinct. Note that such a linear type environment Γ may be viewed as a product type $\sigma = (x_1{:}\tau_1,\ldots,x_n{:}\tau_n)$, and vice versa. Occasionally, we will write $\Pi(f) = [\boldsymbol{\lambda}\ldots]\Gamma \longrightarrow \Delta$ to emphasise that argument and return types of the function f are to be viewed as linear type environments.

Figure 3 shows the typing rules for the programming language. The judgement $C;\Gamma \vdash v : \tau$ expresses that the value v has type τ in type environment Γ and context C, where a *context* is a set of variables (generally the set of variables occurring in some super-expression of v). Note that (T-const) restricts program constants to the unit value, integers and strings, which are the interpretations of the types **unit**, **int** and **str**, respectively (see Section 2.2). All other types are abstract in the sense that their values can only be accessed through built-in functions.

The judgement $C;\Gamma \vdash_\Pi e : \sigma$ means that the expression e has product type σ in type environment Γ, context C and program Π. If the program is understood we may write $C;\Gamma \vdash e : \sigma$. There are three things worth noting about expression typing. First, although the type system is linear, weakening and contraction are available to all types but **mgr**, rendering **mgr** the sole linear type of the language. Second, the side condition of (T-let) ensures that let-bound variables do not shadow any variables in the context (which is generally a superset of the set of variables occurring in the let-expression). Third, the rule (T-ret) matches the variables in the return expression to the variables in the product type, thus enforcing that an expression uniformly uses the same variables to return its results (even though these return variables may be let-bound in different branches of the expression). Note that (T-ret) is the only rule to exploit type information about variables. Finally, the judgement $\Gamma \vdash e : \sigma$ (or $\Gamma \vdash_\Pi e : \sigma$ if we want to stress the program Π) means that e has product type σ in a linear type environment Γ.

The judgement $\Pi \vdash f$ states that f is a well-typed λ-abstraction in program Π. Note that the syntax of λ-abstractions does not appear to bind variables, yet it does bind the variables hidden in the argument type. Note also that the restriction on function

Typing of values $C; \Gamma \vdash v : \tau$

$$\text{(T-var)}\ \frac{}{C; x{:}\tau \vdash x : \tau}\ \text{if } x \in C \qquad \text{(T-const)}\ \frac{}{C; \emptyset \vdash d : \tau}\ \text{if } \begin{cases} d \in \tau\ \wedge \\ \tau \in \{\mathbf{unit}, \mathbf{int}, \mathbf{str}\} \end{cases}$$

Typing of expressions $C; \Gamma \vdash e : \sigma$

$$\text{(T-weak)}\ \frac{C; \Gamma \vdash e : \sigma}{C; \Gamma, x{:}\tau \vdash e : \sigma}\ \text{if } \begin{cases} x \in C\ \wedge \\ \tau \neq \mathbf{mgr} \end{cases} \qquad \text{(T-contr)}\ \frac{C; \Gamma, x{:}\tau, x{:}\tau \vdash e : \sigma}{C; \Gamma, x{:}\tau \vdash e : \sigma}\ \text{if } \tau \neq \mathbf{mgr}$$

$$\text{(T-if)}\ \frac{C; \Gamma \vdash v : \mathbf{int} \qquad C; \Gamma' \vdash e_1 : \sigma \qquad C; \Gamma' \vdash e_2 : \sigma}{C; \Gamma, \Gamma' \vdash \mathbf{if}\ v\ \mathbf{then}\ e_1\ \mathbf{else}\ e_2 : \sigma} \qquad \text{(T-xch)}\ \frac{C; \Gamma, \Gamma' \vdash e : \sigma}{C; \Gamma', \Gamma \vdash e : \sigma}$$

$$\text{(T-ret)}\ \frac{C; \Gamma_1 \vdash x_1 : \tau_1 \quad \ldots \quad C; \Gamma_n \vdash x_n : \tau_n}{C; \Gamma_1, \ldots, \Gamma_n \vdash \mathbf{ret}\ (x_1, \ldots, x_n) : (x_1{:}\tau_1, \ldots, x_n{:}\tau_n)}$$

$$\text{(T-let)}\ \frac{\begin{array}{c} \Pi(f) = [\boldsymbol{\lambda} \ldots](z_1{:}\tau_1, \ldots, z_m{:}\tau_m) \to (z'_1{:}\tau'_1, \ldots, z'_n{:}\tau'_n) \\ C; \Gamma_1 \vdash v_1 : \tau_1 \quad \ldots \quad C; \Gamma_n \vdash v_m : \tau_m \\ C \cup \{x'_1, \ldots, x'_n\}; \Gamma', x'_1{:}\tau'_1, \ldots, x'_n{:}\tau'_n \vdash e' : \sigma'' \end{array}}{C; \Gamma_1, \ldots, \Gamma_m, \Gamma' \vdash \mathbf{let}\ (x'_1, \ldots, x'_n) = f\ (v_1, \ldots, v_m)\ \mathbf{in}\ e' : \sigma''}\ \text{if } (*)$$

$$\text{where } (*) \begin{cases} x'_1, \ldots, x'_n \text{ pairwise distinct } \wedge \\ x'_1, \ldots, x'_n \notin C \cup dom(\Gamma') \end{cases}$$

Typing of expressions $\Gamma \vdash e : \sigma$

$$\text{(T-lin)}\ \frac{dom(\Gamma); \Gamma \vdash e : \sigma}{\Gamma \vdash e : \sigma}\ \text{if } \Gamma \text{ linear}$$

Well-typedness of λ-abstractions $\Pi \vdash f$

$$\text{(T-lam)}\ \frac{\begin{array}{c} \Pi(f) = \boldsymbol{\lambda} e : (x_1{:}\tau_1, \ldots, x_m{:}\tau_m) \to \sigma' \\ x_1{:}\tau_1, \ldots, x_m{:}\tau_m \vdash e : \sigma' \end{array}}{\Pi \vdash f}$$

Fig. 3. Typing rules (for a fixed program Π)

types means that the return variables of the body of a λ-abstraction must be disjoint from its argument variables. Finally, we call a program Π *well-typed* if $\Pi \vdash f$ for all $f \in dom(\Pi) \setminus dom(\Pi_0)$.

Lemma 1. *Let e be an expression (referring to an implicit program Π), Γ a type environment and σ a product type.*

1. *If $\Gamma \vdash e : \sigma$ then $free(e) \subseteq dom(\Gamma)$ and $bound(e) \cap dom(\Gamma) = \emptyset$.*
2. *If $\Gamma \vdash e : \sigma$ and $X \supseteq free(e)$ then $\Gamma|_X \vdash e : \sigma$.*

2.2 Interpretation of Types and Effects of Built-in Functions

Constraints. To provide a formal semantics for the built-in functions, we introduce a many-sorted first-order language $\mathcal{L}$ with equality. Sorts of $\mathcal{L}$ are the datatypes of the programming language (note that this excludes the type $\mathbf{mgr}$). Formulae of $\mathcal{L}$ are formed from atomic formulae using the usual Boolean connectives $\neg$, $\wedge$, $\vee$, $\Rightarrow$ and $\Leftrightarrow$ (in decreasing order of precedence), and the quantifiers $\forall x{:}\tau$ and $\exists x{:}\tau$, where $x \in \langle\text{var}\rangle$ is a variable and $\tau \in \langle\text{datatype}\rangle$ a sort. Atomic formulae are the Boolean constants $\top$ and $\bot$, or are constructed from terms using the binary equality predicate $\approx$ (which is available for all sorts), the binary inequality predicate $\leq$ on sort **int** or the binary inclusion predicate $\subseteq$ on sort **res{}**. Terms are constructed from variables in $\langle\text{var}\rangle$ and the term constructors, which are introduced below, alongside associating the sorts to specific interpretations.

Sort unit is interpreted by the one-element set $\{\star\}$. Its only constant is $\star$. There are no function symbols.

Sort int is interpreted by the integers with infinity. Constants are the integers plus ∞. Function symbols are the usual $-$: **int** $\rightarrow$ **int** and $+, \cdot, /, \%$: **int** $\times$ **int** $\rightarrow$ **int** (where / and % denote integer division and remainder, respectively).

Sort str is interpreted by the set of strings (over some fixed but unspecified alphabet). Constants are all strings. The only function symbol is $++$: **str** $\times$ **str** $\rightarrow$ **str** (concatenation).

Sort res is interpreted by an arbitrary infinite set (whose elements are termed *resources*). There are no constants, and $\mathit{fromstr}$: **str** $\rightarrow$ **res**, an embedding of strings into resources, is the only one function symbol.

Sort res{} is interpreted by multisets of resources. It features the constant $\emptyset$ (empty multiset) and the function symbols $\cap, \cup, \uplus$: **res{}** $\times$ **res{}** $\rightarrow$ **res{}** (intersection, union and sum of multisets, respectively), $|\_|$: **res{}** $\rightarrow$ **int** (size of a multiset), count : **res{}** $\times$ **res** $\rightarrow$ **int** (counting the multiplicity of a resource in a multiset) and $\{\_:\_\}$: **res** $\times$ **int** $\rightarrow$ **res{}** (constructing a "singleton" multiset containing a given resource with a given multiplicity and nothing else).

Sort $\tau[]$ is interpreted by integer-indexed arrays of elements of sort τ, where an integer-indexed array is a function from an initial segment of the natural numbers to τ. This sort features the constant null (array of length 0) and the function symbols $\mathit{len} : \tau[] \rightarrow$ **int** (length of an array), $\_[\_] : \tau[] \times$ **int** $\rightarrow \tau$ (reading at a given index) and $\_[\_:=\_] : \tau[] \times$ **int** $\times\, \tau \rightarrow \tau[]$ (updating a given index with a given value). Note that the values of $a[i]$ and $a[i{:=}v]$ are generally unspecified if the index i is out of bounds (i. e., $i<0$ or $i \geq \mathit{len}(a)$). As an exception, for $i = \mathit{len}(a)$, the array $a[i{:=}v]$ properly extends a, i. e., $\mathit{len}(a[i{:=}v]) = \mathit{len}(a) + 1$. This models vectors that can grow in size.

Treating the type **mgr** as an alias for the sort **res{}**, type environments can be seen as associating sorts to variables. Given a type environment Γ and constraint $\phi \in \mathcal{L}$, we write $\Gamma \vdash \phi$ if ϕ is well-sorted w. r. t. Γ; note that this entails $\mathit{free}(\phi) \subseteq \mathit{dom}(\Gamma)$, where $\mathit{free}(\phi)$ is the set of free variables in ϕ.

Substitutions. A *substitution* μ maps variables $x \in \langle\text{var}\rangle$ to values $\mu(x) \in \langle\text{val}\rangle$ (which are variables again or constants, not arbitrary terms). We denote the domain of a substitution μ by $\mathit{dom}(\mu)$. Given a type environment Γ, we write $\Gamma\mu$ for the type environment that arises from substituting the variables in Γ according to μ. This is defined recursively: $\emptyset\mu = \emptyset$ and $(\Gamma, x{:}\tau)\mu$ equals $\Gamma\mu, x{:}\tau$ if $x \notin \mathit{dom}(\mu)$, or $\Gamma\mu, \mu(x){:}\tau$ if $\mu(x) \in \langle\text{var}\rangle$, or $\Gamma\mu$ if $\mu(x) \in \langle\text{const}\rangle$. Note that $\Gamma\mu$ need not be linear even if Γ is. Given a formula ϕ such that $\Gamma \vdash \phi$, we write $\phi\mu$ for the formula obtained by substituting the free variables of ϕ according to μ, avoiding capture. Note that $\Gamma \vdash \phi$ implies $\Gamma\mu \vdash \phi\mu$.

Valuations. Let Γ be a type environment. A *Γ-valuation* α maps variables $x \in dom(\Gamma)$ to elements $\alpha(x)$ in the interpretation of the sort $\Gamma(x)$; we call α a *valuation* if we do not care about the particular type environment Γ. We denote the domain of α by $dom(\alpha)$. Note that $dom(\alpha) \subseteq dom(\Gamma)$ but not necessarily $dom(\alpha) = dom(\Gamma)$; we call α a *maximal* Γ-valuation if $dom(\alpha) = dom(\Gamma)$. Given a Γ-valuation α and a set of variables X, we denote the restriction of α to X by $\alpha|_X$; note that $dom(\alpha|_X) = dom(\alpha) \cap X$. Restriction induces a partial order $\succeq$ on Γ-valuations, where $\alpha' \succeq \alpha$ iff $\alpha'|_{dom(\alpha)} = \alpha$. Given n pairwise distinct variables $x_i \in dom(\Gamma)$ and corresponding elements d_i in the interpretation of $\Gamma(x_i)$, we write $\alpha\{x_1 \mapsto d_1, \dots, x_n \mapsto d_n\}$ for the Γ-valuation α' that maps the x_i to d_i and all other $x \in dom(\alpha)$ to $\alpha(x)$. In the special case $dom(\alpha) = \emptyset$, we may drop α and simply write $\{x_1 \mapsto d_1, \dots, x_n \mapsto d_n\}$.

Entailment. Let $\phi, \psi \in \mathcal{L}$ be constraints such that $\Gamma \vdash \phi$ and $\Gamma \vdash \psi$. Given a Γ-valuation α with $\mathit{free}(\phi) \subseteq dom(\alpha)$, we write $\alpha \models \phi$ if α satisfies ϕ. We write $\models \phi$ if $\alpha \models \phi$ for all Γ-valuations α with $\mathit{free}(\phi) \subseteq dom(\alpha)$, and we write $\phi \models \psi$ if $\alpha \models \phi$ implies $\alpha \models \psi$ for all Γ-valuations α with $\mathit{free}(\phi) \cup \mathit{free}(\psi) \subseteq dom(\alpha)$. Entailment induces a theory $\mathcal{T} = \{\phi \mid \mathit{free}(\phi) = \emptyset \wedge \top \models \phi\}$, with respect to which entailment can be reduced to unsatisfiability. Note that unsatisfiability w. r. t. $\mathcal{T}$ is not even semi-decidable as $\mathcal{T}$ contains Peano arithmetic. Thus for reasoning purposes, we will generally approximate $\mathcal{T}$ by weaker theories.

Effects. Let f be a built-in function with $\Pi(f) = \Gamma \rightarrow \Delta$ (viewing argument and return types of f as type environments Γ and Δ, respectively.) An *effect* for f is a pair of constraints ϕ and ψ such that $\Gamma \vdash \phi$ and $\Gamma, \Delta \vdash \psi$. (Note that $\Gamma \rightarrow \Delta$ being a function type implies $dom(\Gamma) \cap dom(\Delta) = \emptyset$, hence Γ, Δ is a type environment.) We write $\phi \rightarrow \psi$ to denote such an effect, and we call ϕ its *precondition* and ψ its *action*.

An *effect environment* maps the built-in functions $f \in dom(\Pi_0)$ to effects for f. Figure 4 displays the effect environment Θ_0, providing an axiomatic, relational semantics for all $f \in dom(\Pi_0)$. This semantics ties most built-in functions to corresponding logical operators in a straightforward way; note the non-trivial preconditions for division, reading and writing arrays, and constructing singleton multisets. The effects of functions operating on resource managers warrant some explanation.

init returns an empty manager m'.

enable non-deterministically adds some sub-multiset of r to manager m, returning the result in manager m'; the complement of the added multiset is returned in r'. In an implementation [3] the multiset to be added to m would be chosen by some *policy*, perhaps involving security profiles or user input; we use non-determinism to abstractly model such policy mechanisms.

split splits the multiset held by manager m and distributes it to the managers m_1' and m_2' such that m_2' gets the largest possible sub-multiset of r.

join adds the multisets held by managers m_1 and m_2, returning their sum in m'.

consume is an explicit destructor for manager m and all its resources; the linear type system means that calls to **consume** are necessary even if m is known to be empty.

assertEmpty acts as identity on managers, but subject to the precondition that m is empty; it will be treated specially by the programming language semantics.

f	$\Pi_0(f)$	$\Theta_0(f)$
$\mathbf{id}_\tau$	$(x{:}\tau) \rightarrow (x'{:}\tau)$	$\top \rightarrow x' \approx x$
$\mathbf{eq}_\tau$	$(x_1{:}\tau, x_2{:}\tau) \rightarrow (i'{:}\mathbf{int})$	$\top \rightarrow i' \approx 1 \wedge x_1 \approx x_2 \vee i' \approx 0 \wedge x_1 \not\approx x_2$
add	$(i_1{:}\mathbf{int}, i_2{:}\mathbf{int}) \rightarrow (i'{:}\mathbf{int})$	$\top \rightarrow i' \approx i_1 + i_2$
sub		$\top \rightarrow i' \approx i_1 + (-i_2)$
mul		$\top \rightarrow i' \approx i_1 \cdot i_2$
div		$i_2 \not\approx 0 \rightarrow i' \approx i_1 \mathbin{/} i_2$
mod		$i_2 \not\approx 0 \rightarrow i' \approx i_1 \mathbin{\%} i_2$
leq		$\top \rightarrow i' \approx 1 \wedge i_1 \leq i_2 \vee i' \approx 0 \wedge i_1 \not\leq i_2$
conc	$(w_1{:}\mathbf{str}, w_2{:}\mathbf{str}) \rightarrow (w'{:}\mathbf{str})$	$\top \rightarrow w' \approx w_1 \mathbin{++} w_2$
fromstr	$(w{:}\mathbf{str}) \rightarrow (c'{:}\mathbf{res})$	$\top \rightarrow c' \approx \mathit{fromstr}(w)$
$\mathbf{null}_\tau$	$() \rightarrow (a'{:}\tau[])$	$\top \rightarrow a' \approx \mathit{null}$
$\mathbf{length}_\tau$	$(a{:}\tau[]) \rightarrow (i'{:}\mathbf{int})$	$\top \rightarrow i' \approx \mathit{len}(a)$
$\mathbf{read}_\tau$	$(a{:}\tau[], i{:}\mathbf{int}) \rightarrow (x'{:}\tau)$	$0 \leq i \wedge i < \mathit{len}(a) \rightarrow x' \approx a[i]$
$\mathbf{write}_\tau$	$(a{:}\tau[], i{:}\mathbf{int}, x{:}\tau) \rightarrow (a'{:}\tau[])$	$0 \leq i \wedge i \leq \mathit{len}(a) \rightarrow a' \approx a[i{:=}x]$
empty	$() \rightarrow (r'{:}\mathbf{res}\{\})$	$\top \rightarrow r' \approx \emptyset$
single	$(c{:}\mathbf{res}, i{:}\mathbf{int}) \rightarrow (r'{:}\mathbf{res}\{\})$	$i \geq 0 \rightarrow r' \approx \{c{:}i\}$
inter	$(r_1{:}\mathbf{res}\{\}, r_2{:}\mathbf{res}\{\}) \rightarrow (r'{:}\mathbf{res}\{\})$	$\top \rightarrow r' \approx r_1 \cap r_2$
union		$\top \rightarrow r' \approx r_1 \cup r_2$
sum		$\top \rightarrow r' \approx r_1 \uplus r_2$
size	$(r{:}\mathbf{res}\{\}) \rightarrow (i'{:}\mathbf{int})$	$\top \rightarrow i' \approx \lvert r \rvert$
count	$(r{:}\mathbf{res}\{\}, c{:}\mathbf{res}) \rightarrow (i'{:}\mathbf{int})$	$\top \rightarrow i' \approx \mathit{count}(r, c)$
include	$(r_1{:}\mathbf{res}\{\}, r_2{:}\mathbf{res}\{\}) \rightarrow (i'{:}\mathbf{int})$	$\top \rightarrow i' \approx 1 \wedge r_1 \subseteq r_2 \vee i' \approx 0 \wedge r_1 \not\subseteq r_2$
init	$() \rightarrow (m'{:}\mathbf{mgr})$	$\top \rightarrow m' \approx \emptyset$
enable	$(m{:}\mathbf{mgr}, r{:}\mathbf{res}\{\}) \rightarrow (m'{:}\mathbf{mgr}, r'{:}\mathbf{res}\{\})$	$\top \rightarrow r' \subseteq r \wedge m \uplus r \approx m' \uplus r'$
split	$(m{:}\mathbf{mgr}, r{:}\mathbf{res}\{\}) \rightarrow (m_1'{:}\mathbf{mgr}, m_2'{:}\mathbf{mgr})$	$\top \rightarrow m_2' \approx m \cap r \wedge m \approx m_1' \uplus m_2'$
join	$(m_1{:}\mathbf{mgr}, m_2{:}\mathbf{mgr}) \rightarrow (m'{:}\mathbf{mgr})$	$\top \rightarrow m' \approx m_1 \uplus m_2$
consume	$(m{:}\mathbf{mgr}) \rightarrow ()$	$\top \rightarrow \top$
assertEmpty	$(m{:}\mathbf{mgr}) \rightarrow (m'{:}\mathbf{mgr})$	$m \approx \emptyset \rightarrow m' \approx m$
assertAtLeast	$(m{:}\mathbf{mgr}, r{:}\mathbf{res}\{\}) \rightarrow (m'{:}\mathbf{mgr})$	$r \subseteq m \rightarrow m' \approx m$

Fig. 4. Types and effects of built-in functions. The subscripts τ indicate families of functions indexed by $\tau \in \langle\text{datatype}\rangle$, except for $\mathbf{id}_\tau$, which is indexed by $\tau \in \langle\text{type}\rangle$.

assertAtLeast acts as identity on managers, but subject to the precondition that the manager m contains the multiset r; will be treated specially by the programming language semantics.

To facilitate the presentation of programming language semantics, we capture the logical semantics of effects directly in terms of valuations. Given a built-in function f with $\Pi_0(f) = \Gamma \rightarrow \Delta$ and $\Theta_0(f) = \phi \rightarrow \psi$, we define $\mathit{Eff}^{\Pi_0}_{\Theta_0}(f)$ to be the set of maximal (Γ, Δ)-valuations such that $\alpha \in \mathit{Eff}^{\Pi_0}_{\Theta_0}(f)$ if and only if $\alpha \models \phi \wedge \psi$.

2.3 Small-Step Reduction Semantics

We present a stack-based reduction semantics (which is essentially a continuation semantics) for our programming language. We will show that reduction preserves the resources stored in resource managers, thanks to linearity. Throughout this section, let Π be a fixed well-typed program.

Stacks. We call a tuple $\langle x_1, \ldots, x_n | \alpha, e \rangle$ a *frame* if $x_1, \ldots, x_n$ is a list of pairwise distinct variables, α is a valuation and e is an expression such that

- $dom(\alpha) \cap \{x_1, \ldots, x_n\} = \emptyset$ and
- $dom(\alpha) \subseteq free(e) \subseteq dom(\alpha) \cup \{x_1, \ldots, x_n\}$.

The roles of e (redex) and α (providing values for the free variables of e) should be clear. The x_i are only present if the frame is suspended waiting for a function to return in which case the x_i act as slots for the return values. A *pre-stack* is either $\lightning$ or ϵ or $F :: S$, where F is a frame and S is a pre-stack. (Pre-stacks essentially correspond to continuations in an abstract machine interpreting λ-terms in ANF [10].) A *stack* (or Π-stack if we want to emphasise the program Π) is a pre-stack of the form $\lightning$ or $\langle | \alpha, e \rangle :: S$. We call $\lightning$ the *error stack*. A stack of the form $\langle | \alpha, \mathbf{ret}\ (x_1, \ldots, x_n) \rangle :: \epsilon$ is called *terminal*. If $F :: S$ is a stack then F is its *top frame*.

Reduction. Figure 5 presents the rules generating the reduction relation $\rightsquigarrow_\Pi$ on stacks. We denote the reflexive-transitive closure of $\rightsquigarrow_\Pi$ by $\rightsquigarrow_\Pi^*$. As usual Π may be omitted if it is understood. Note that reduction performs an eager garbage collection in that it deallocates unused variables immediately by restricting the valuation α in the post stack to the free variables of the expression e.

Reduction is deterministic, except for calls to the built-in function **enable**.

Proposition 2. *For all stacks S_0 there is at most one stack S_1 such that $S_0 \rightsquigarrow S_1$, unless S_0 is of the form $\langle | \alpha, \mathbf{let}\ (m', r') = \mathbf{enable}\ (m, r)\ \mathbf{in}\ e \rangle :: S_0'$.*

Typed stacks. Reduction is untyped since type information is not needed at runtime. However, various properties of reduction are best stated if the type of variables is known. Therefore, we annotate stacks with type environments and conservatively extend reduction to typed stacks.

Given a frame $\langle x_1, \ldots, x_n | \alpha, e \rangle$, we call $\langle x_1, \ldots, x_n | \alpha, e \rangle^\Gamma$ a *typed frame* if Γ is a linear type environment such that

- $dom(\Gamma) = dom(\alpha) \cup \{x_1, \ldots, x_n\}$,
- α is a Γ-valuation, and
- $\Gamma \vdash e : \sigma$ for some product type σ.

A *typed pre-stack* is $\lightning$, or ϵ, or $F{::}\epsilon$ where F is a typed frame, or $F{::}F' :: S'$ where S' is a typed pre-stack and $F = \langle x_1, \ldots, x_m | \alpha, e \rangle^\Gamma$ and $F' = \langle x_1', \ldots, x_n' | \alpha', e' \rangle^{\Gamma'}$ are typed frames such that $\Gamma \vdash e : (z_1'{:}\Gamma'(x_1'), \ldots, z_n'{:}\Gamma'(x_n'))$ for some variables $z_1', \ldots, z_n'$. A *typed stack* is typed pre-stack of the form $\lightning$ or $\langle | \alpha, e \rangle^\Gamma :: S$. Given a typed frame $F = \langle x_1, \ldots, x_n | \alpha, e \rangle^\Gamma$, we denote its underlying frame $\langle x_1, \ldots, x_n | \alpha, e \rangle$ by $F^\natural$. We extend this notation to typed (pre-)stacks, writing $S^\natural$ for the (pre-)stack underlying the typed (pre-)stack S.

The following proposition shows that reduction does not break the invariants maintained by typed stacks.

$$\text{(R-ret)}\ \frac{\alpha'' = \alpha'\{x'_1 \mapsto \alpha(x_1), \ldots, x'_n \mapsto \alpha(x_n)\}}{\langle|\alpha, \mathbf{ret}\ (x_1,\ldots,x_n)\rangle :: \langle x'_1, \ldots, x'_n|\alpha', e'\rangle :: S \ \rightsquigarrow\ \langle|\alpha''|_{\mathit{free}(e')}, e'\rangle :: S}$$

$$\text{(R-let}_1^{\mathrm{tl}}\text{)}\ \frac{\Pi(f) = \boldsymbol{\lambda} e : (z_1{:}\tau_1,\ldots,z_m{:}\tau_m) \to \sigma' \quad \alpha' = \{z_1 \mapsto \alpha(v_1), \ldots, z_m \mapsto \alpha(v_m)\}}{\langle|\alpha, \mathbf{let}\ (x'_1,\ldots,x'_n) = f\ (v_1,\ldots,v_m)\ \mathbf{in\ ret}\ (x'_1,\ldots,x'_n)\rangle :: S \rightsquigarrow \langle|\alpha'|_{\mathit{free}(e)}, e\rangle :: S}$$

$$\text{(R-let}_1\text{)}\ \frac{\Pi(f) = \boldsymbol{\lambda} e : (z_1{:}\tau_1,\ldots,z_m{:}\tau_m) \to \sigma' \qquad e' \neq \mathbf{ret}\ (x'_1,\ldots,x'_n) \quad \alpha' = \{z_1 \mapsto \alpha(v_1), \ldots, z_m \mapsto \alpha(v_m)\}}{\langle|\alpha, \mathbf{let}\ (x'_1,\ldots,x'_n) = f\ (v_1,\ldots,v_m)\ \mathbf{in}\ e'\rangle :: S \rightsquigarrow \langle|\alpha'|_{\mathit{free}(e)}, e\rangle :: \langle x'_1, \ldots, x'_n|\alpha|_{\mathit{free}(e')}, e'\rangle :: S}$$

$$\text{(R-let}_2\text{)}\ \frac{\begin{array}{c}\Pi_0(f) = (z_1{:}\tau_1,\ldots,z_m{:}\tau_m) \to (z'_1{:}\tau'_1,\ldots,z'_n{:}\tau'_n) \\ \alpha_f = \{z_1 \mapsto \alpha(v_1), \ldots, z_m \mapsto \alpha(v_m)\} \qquad \alpha'_f \in \mathit{Eff}^{\,\Pi_0}_{\Theta_0}(f) \qquad \alpha'_f \succeq \alpha_f \\ \alpha' = \alpha\{x'_1 \mapsto \alpha'_f(z'_1), \ldots, x'_n \mapsto \alpha'_f(z'_n)\}\end{array}}{\langle|\alpha, \mathbf{let}\ (x'_1,\ldots,x'_n) = f\ (v_1,\ldots,v_m)\ \mathbf{in}\ e'\rangle :: S \ \rightsquigarrow\ \langle|\alpha'|_{\mathit{free}(e')}, e'\rangle :: S}$$

$$\text{(R-let}_2^{\lightning}\text{)}\ \frac{\begin{array}{c}\Pi_0(f) = (z_1{:}\tau_1,\ldots,z_m{:}\tau_m) \to \sigma' \qquad f \in \{\mathbf{assertEmpty}, \mathbf{assertAtLeast}\} \\ \alpha_f = \{z_1 \mapsto \alpha(v_1), \ldots, z_m \mapsto \alpha(v_m)\} \qquad \forall \alpha'_f \in \mathit{Eff}^{\,\Pi_0}_{\Theta_0}(f) : \alpha'_f \not\succeq \alpha_f\end{array}}{\langle|\alpha, \mathbf{let}\ (x'_1,\ldots,x'_n) = f\ (v_1,\ldots,v_m)\ \mathbf{in}\ e'\rangle :: S \ \rightsquigarrow\ \lightning}$$

$$\text{(R-if}_1\text{)}\ \frac{\alpha(v) \neq 0}{\langle|\alpha, \mathbf{if}\ v\ \mathbf{then}\ e_1\ \mathbf{else}\ e_2\rangle :: S \ \rightsquigarrow\ \langle|\alpha|_{\mathit{free}(e_1)}, e_1\rangle :: S}$$

$$\text{(R-if}_2\text{)}\ \frac{\alpha(v) = 0}{\langle|\alpha, \mathbf{if}\ v\ \mathbf{then}\ e_1\ \mathbf{else}\ e_2\rangle :: S \ \rightsquigarrow\ \langle|\alpha|_{\mathit{free}(e_2)}, e_2\rangle :: S}$$

Fig. 5. Small-step reduction relation $\rightsquigarrow$ (for a fixed program Π). Application of valuations α extends to values $v \in \langle\text{val}\rangle$ in the natural way, i. e., $\alpha(v) = v$ if v is a constant.

Proposition 3. *Let $\hat{S}_0$ be a typed stack and S_1 a stack. If $\hat{S}_0^\natural \rightsquigarrow S_1$ then there is a typed stack $\hat{S}_1$ such that $\hat{S}_1^\natural = S_1$.*

The proposition justifies the view of reduction on typed stacks as a conservative extension of the reduction relation defined in Figure 5, where reduction on typed stacks is defined by $\hat{S}_0 \rightsquigarrow_\Pi \hat{S}_1$ if and only if $\hat{S}_0^\natural \rightsquigarrow_\Pi \hat{S}_1^\natural$; as usual Π may be omitted if it is understood.

We call a stack S_0 *stuck* if there is no stack S_1 such that $S_0 \rightsquigarrow S_1$, and S_0 is neither terminal nor the error stack. Our next result shows that reduction on typed stacks will get stuck only at calls to built-in functions (other than $\mathbf{assertEmpty}$ and $\mathbf{assertAtLeast}$), and only if the preconditions of these calls fail. As the effects listed in Figure 4 reveal, reduction will get stuck only upon attempts to divide by 0, access arrays out of bounds or construct singleton multisets with negative multiplicity.

Proposition 4. *Let $\hat{S}$ be a typed stack. If $\hat{S}^\natural$ is stuck then it is of the form*

$$\langle|\alpha, \mathbf{let}\ (x'_1,\ldots,x'_n) = f\ (v_1,\ldots,v_m)\ \mathbf{in}\ e'\rangle :: S'\ ,$$

$f \in dom(\Pi_0) \setminus \{\mathbf{assertEmpty}, \mathbf{assertAtLeast}\}$, and there is no $\alpha'_f \in Eff^{\Pi_0}_{\Theta_0}(f)$ such that $\alpha'_f \succeq \alpha_f$, where α_f is defined as in rule (R-let$_2$).

Preservation of resources. Given a typed frame $F = \langle x_1, \ldots, x_n | \alpha, e \rangle^{\Gamma}$, we define the multiset $res(F)$ of *resources* in F by $res(F) = \biguplus\{\alpha(x) \mid x \in dom(\alpha), \Gamma(x) = \mathbf{mgr}\}$. We extend *res* to typed non-error stacks by defining $res(\epsilon) = \emptyset$ and $res(F :: S) = res(F) \uplus res(S)$. Proposition 5 states *resource preservation*: The sum of all resources in the system remains unchanged by reduction, unless the built-in functions **enable** and **consume** are called. The former admits increasing (but not decreasing) the resources, whereas the latter behaves the other way round. Obviously, resource preservation depends on the linearity restriction on type **mgr**, otherwise resources could be duplicated by re-using managers.

Proposition 5. *Let S_0 and S_1 be typed stacks such that $S_0 \rightsquigarrow S_1 \neq \lightning$.*

1. *If S_0 is of the form $\langle | \alpha, \mathbf{let}\ (m', r') = \mathbf{enable}\ (m, r)\ \mathbf{in}\ e \rangle^{\Gamma} :: S'_0$ then $res(S_0) \subseteq res(S_1)$.*
2. *If S_0 is of the form $\langle | \alpha, \mathbf{let}\ () = \mathbf{consume}\ (m)\ \mathbf{in}\ e \rangle^{\Gamma} :: S'_0$ then $res(S_0) \supseteq res(S_1)$.*
3. *In all other cases, $res(S_0) = res(S_1)$.*

2.4 Erasing Resource Managers

According to the reduction semantics, a call to **assertEmpty** or **assertAtLeast** either does nothing[1] or goes wrong, and calling one of these two tests is the only way to go wrong. Hence, if we know that a program cannot go wrong (and Section 3 will present a type system for proving just that) then we can erase all calls to these built-ins (or rather, replace them by true no-ops) and obtain an equivalent program.

In fact, we can do more than that. Once the assertion built-ins are gone, it is even possible to remove the resource managers themselves. By the design of the programming language (in particular, the choice of built-in operations on resource managers) the contents of resource managers cannot influence the values of variables of any other type. Informally, this justifies replacing the resource managers themselves by variables of type **unit** whenever we know that a program cannot go wrong. Erasing resource managers also means that the built-in functions acting on managers can be replaced by simpler ones on **unit**: all of which are no-ops, except for **enable** itself.[2] The remainder of the section formalises this intuition.

Figure 6 shows the necessary program transformations to erase resource managers. Most fundamentally, erasure maps the manager type **mgr** to the unit type **unit**. Erasure on types determines erasure on product types, type environments, programs and valuations (where erasure uniformly maps the values of **mgr**-variables to $\star$, the only value of type **unit**), which in turn determines erasure on typed stacks. As outlined

[1] Due to the linearity restriction on resource managers these functions must copy the input manager to an output manager; a true no-op would violate resource preservation.

[2] We do keep the calls in place, so that erasure preserves the structure of programs; this simplifies reasoning, and does not preclude optimising away no-op calls at a later stage.

Erasure τ° of types τ

$\tau^\circ = \mathbf{unit}$ if $\tau = \mathbf{mgr}$
$\tau^\circ = \tau$ otherwise

Erasure Γ° of type environments Γ

$$\emptyset^\circ = \emptyset$$
$$(\Gamma, x{:}\tau)^\circ = \Gamma^\circ, x{:}\tau^\circ$$

Erasure σ° of product types σ

$$(x_1{:}\tau_1,\ldots,x_n{:}\tau_n)^\circ = (x_1{:}\tau_1^\circ,\ldots,x_n{:}\tau_n^\circ)$$

Erasure Π° of programs Π

$dom(\Pi^\circ) = dom(\Pi)$
$\Pi^\circ(f) = \boldsymbol{\lambda} e : \sigma^\circ \longrightarrow \sigma'^\circ$ if $\Pi(f) = \boldsymbol{\lambda} e : \sigma \longrightarrow \sigma'$
$\Pi^\circ(f) = \sigma^\circ \longrightarrow \sigma'^\circ$ if $\Pi(f) = \sigma \longrightarrow \sigma'$

Erasure Θ_0° of effect environment Θ_0

$dom(\Theta_0^\circ) = dom(\Theta_0)$
$\Theta_0^\circ(\mathbf{enable}) = \top \rightarrow r' \subseteq r$
$\Theta_0^\circ(f) = \top \rightarrow \top$ if $\begin{cases} f \in \{\mathbf{init}, \mathbf{split}, \mathbf{join}, \mathbf{consume}\} \cup \\ \quad \{\mathbf{assertEmpty}, \mathbf{assertAtLeast}\} \end{cases}$
$\Theta_0^\circ(f) = \Theta_0(f)$ otherwise

Erasure α° of Γ-valuations α

$dom(\alpha^\circ) = dom(\alpha)$
$\alpha^\circ(x) = \star$ if $\Gamma(x) = \mathbf{mgr}$
$\alpha^\circ(x) = \alpha(x)$ otherwise

Erasure S° of typed stacks S

$\lightning^\circ = \lightning$ $\quad \epsilon^\circ = \epsilon$ $\quad (\langle x_1, \ldots, x_n | \alpha, e\rangle^\Gamma :: S)^\circ = \langle x_1, \ldots, x_n | \alpha^\circ, e\rangle^{\Gamma^\circ} :: S^\circ$

Fig. 6. Erasure of resource managers

above, erasure on effect environments trivialises the effect of resource manager built-ins, except **enable**, and preserves the effects of all built-ins not operating on managers. The effect of **enable** after erasure is to non-deterministically choose a sub-multiset of r and return its complement in r'. This reflects the fact that calls to **enable** provide points of interaction for the policy (e. g., the user) to decide how many resources the system is granted. Erasing resource managers does not mean that policy decisions are fixed, it just removes the managers' book keeping about those decisions.

Lemma 6. *Let Π be a well-typed program and S a typed Π-stack. Then Π° is a well-typed program and S° a typed Π°-stack.*

Erasure makes trivial the effects of **assertEmpty** and **assertAtLeast**, and in particular, replaces their precondition by $\top$. Thus a program cannot go wrong after erasure, as rule (R-let$_2^\lightning$) will never apply.

Proposition 7. *Let Π be a well-typed program and S a Π°-stack S. Then $S \not\rightsquigarrow^*_{\Pi^\circ} \lightning$.*

The next result states that the small-step reduction relation $\rightsquigarrow_\Pi$ of a program Π is almost bisimulation equivalent to the reduction relation $\rightsquigarrow_{\Pi^\circ}$ of its erasure. In fact, it shows that the relation $R = \{\langle S, S^\circ\rangle \mid S \text{ is a } \Pi\text{-stack}\}$ would be a bisimulation if $\rightsquigarrow_\Pi$ could not reduce stacks to the error stack $\lightning$. Put differently, if Π cannot go wrong then $\rightsquigarrow_\Pi$ and $\rightsquigarrow_{\Pi^\circ}$ are bisimulation equivalent. The proof of this theorem is by case analysis on the reduction relation $\rightsquigarrow_\Pi$ of the unerased program. As a corollary, we get that reachability in the erased program is essentially the same as reachability in the unerased one, provided that the unerased program cannot go wrong.

Theorem 8. *Let Π be a well-typed program and $\hat{S}_0$ a typed Π-stack with $\hat{S}_0 \not\rightsquigarrow_\Pi \lightning$.*

1. *For all typed Π-stacks $\hat{S}_1$, if $\hat{S}_0 \rightsquigarrow_\Pi \hat{S}_1$ then $\hat{S}_0^\circ \rightsquigarrow_{\Pi^\circ} \hat{S}_1^\circ$.*
2. *For all typed Π°-stacks S_1, if $\hat{S}_0^\circ \rightsquigarrow_{\Pi^\circ} S_1$ then there is a typed Π-stack $\hat{S}_1$ such that $\hat{S}_0 \rightsquigarrow_\Pi \hat{S}_1$ and $\hat{S}_1^\circ = S_1$.*

Corollary 9. *Let Π be a well-typed program and S_0 a typed Π-stack. If $S_0 \not\rightsquigarrow_\Pi^* \lightning$ then $\{S^\circ \mid S_0 \rightsquigarrow_\Pi^* S\} = \{S \mid S_0^\circ \rightsquigarrow_{\Pi^\circ}^* S\}$.*

What distinguishes erasure of resource managers from other erasure results (e. g., type erasure during compilation, Java generics erasure) is that here, erasure does not completely remove a language construct. Instead, it removes the book keeping but retains the semantically important bit that deals with dynamic policy decisions.

2.5 Big-Step Relational Semantics

The reduction semantics presented in Section 2.3 is good for showing preservation properties, like the preservation of resources. However, it does not easily yield a relational view on functions, relating input and output parameters. This is achieved by a relational semantics, which we will prove equivalent to the reduction semantics. Contrary to the reduction semantics, which was originally untyped and had type environments added conservatively, the relational semantics will be typed from the start. (Types do not hurt here, as the relational semantics is not geared towards execution.)

Throughout this section, we assume that Π is a well-typed program. A *state* β is either the error state $\lightning$ or a normal state $\langle\Gamma;\alpha\rangle$, where Γ is a linear type environment and α a maximal Γ-valuation. Given an expression e, a normal state $\langle\Gamma;\alpha\rangle$ and a state β', we define the judgement $e, \langle\Gamma;\alpha\rangle \Downarrow_\Pi \beta'$ (or $e, \langle\Gamma;\alpha\rangle \Downarrow \beta'$ if Π is understood) by the rules in Figure 7 if $dom(\Gamma) \cap bound(e) = \emptyset$ and there are Γ_e and σ such that $\Gamma \succeq \Gamma_e$ and $\Gamma_e \vdash e : \sigma$. The intended meaning of $e, \langle\Gamma;\alpha\rangle \Downarrow \beta'$ is that evaluating expression e in state $\langle\Gamma;\alpha\rangle$ may terminate and result in state β'.

The reduction semantics deallocates variables once they become unused (an eager garbage collection, so to say), which is essential for the linear variables as otherwise resource preservation would not hold. However, the intermediate values of variables are thus lost. In contrast, the relational semantics names and records all intermediate values, even the linear ones, as $e, \langle\Gamma;\alpha\rangle \Downarrow \langle\Gamma';\alpha'\rangle$ implies $\Gamma' \succeq \Gamma$ and $\alpha' \succeq \alpha$.

By definition, violations of resource safety manifest themselves in reductions ending in the error stack, and hence reductions which diverge or get stuck cannot violate resource safety. Therefore, resource safety is not affected by the fact that the relational semantics ignores such reductions. Under this proviso, Proposition 10 shows the equivalence of reduction and relational semantics.

Evaluation of expressions $e, \langle \Gamma; \alpha \rangle \Downarrow \beta'$

$$\text{(E-ret)}\ \frac{}{\mathbf{ret}\ (x_1,\ldots,x_n), \langle \Gamma; \alpha \rangle \Downarrow \langle \Gamma; \alpha \rangle}$$

$$\text{(E-let}_1\text{)}\ \frac{\begin{array}{c}\Pi(f) = \boldsymbol{\lambda} e : (z_1{:}\tau_1,\ldots,z_m{:}\tau_m) \longrightarrow (z'_1{:}\tau'_1,\ldots,z'_n{:}\tau'_n) \qquad \Gamma_f = z_1{:}\tau_1,\ldots,z_m{:}\tau_m \\ \alpha_f = \{z_1 \mapsto \alpha(v_1),\ldots,z_m \mapsto \alpha(v_m)\} \qquad e, \langle \Gamma_f; \alpha_f \rangle \Downarrow \langle \Gamma'_f; \alpha'_f \rangle \\ \Gamma' = \Gamma, x'_1{:}\tau'_1,\ldots,x'_n{:}\tau'_n \qquad \alpha' = \alpha\{x'_1 \mapsto \alpha'_f(z'_1),\ldots,x'_n \mapsto \alpha'_f(z'_n)\} \\ e', \langle \Gamma'; \alpha' \rangle \Downarrow \beta''\end{array}}{\mathbf{let}\ (x'_1,\ldots,x'_n) = f\ (v_1,\ldots,v_m)\ \mathbf{in}\ e', \langle \Gamma; \alpha \rangle \Downarrow \beta''}$$

$$\text{(E-let}_1^{\lightning}\text{)}\ \frac{\begin{array}{c}\Pi(f) = \boldsymbol{\lambda} e : (z_1{:}\tau_1,\ldots,z_m{:}\tau_m) \longrightarrow \sigma' \qquad \Gamma_f = z_1{:}\tau_1,\ldots,z_m{:}\tau_m \\ \alpha_f = \{z_1 \mapsto \alpha(v_1),\ldots,z_m \mapsto \alpha(v_m)\} \qquad e, \langle \Gamma_f; \alpha_f \rangle \Downarrow \lightning\end{array}}{\mathbf{let}\ (x'_1,\ldots,x'_n) = f\ (v_1,\ldots,v_m)\ \mathbf{in}\ e', \langle \Gamma; \alpha \rangle \Downarrow \lightning}$$

$$\text{(E-let}_2\text{)}\ \frac{\begin{array}{c}\Pi(f) = (z_1{:}\tau_1,\ldots,z_m{:}\tau_m) \longrightarrow (z'_1{:}\tau'_1,\ldots,z'_n{:}\tau'_n) \\ \alpha_f = \{z_1 \mapsto \alpha(v_1),\ldots,z_m \mapsto \alpha(v_m)\} \qquad \alpha'_f \in \mathit{Eff}^{\Pi_0}_{\Theta_0}(f) \qquad \alpha'_f \succeq \alpha_f \\ \Gamma' = \Gamma, x'_1{:}\tau'_1,\ldots,x'_n{:}\tau'_n \qquad \alpha' = \alpha\{x'_1 \mapsto \alpha'_f(z'_1),\ldots,x'_n \mapsto \alpha'_f(z'_n)\} \\ e', \langle \Gamma'; \alpha' \rangle \Downarrow \beta''\end{array}}{\mathbf{let}\ (x'_1,\ldots,x'_n) = f\ (v_1,\ldots,v_m)\ \mathbf{in}\ e', \langle \Gamma; \alpha \rangle \Downarrow \beta''}$$

$$\text{(E-let}_2^{\lightning}\text{)}\ \frac{\begin{array}{c}\Pi(f) = \boldsymbol{\lambda} e : (z_1{:}\tau_1,\ldots,z_m{:}\tau_m) \longrightarrow \sigma' \qquad f \in \{\mathbf{assertEmpty}, \mathbf{assertAtLeast}\} \\ \alpha_f = \{z_1 \mapsto \alpha(v_1),\ldots,z_m \mapsto \alpha(v_m)\} \qquad \forall \alpha'_f \in \mathit{Eff}^{\Pi_0}_{\Theta_0}(f) : \alpha'_f \not\succeq \alpha_f\end{array}}{\mathbf{let}\ (x'_1,\ldots,x'_n) = f\ (v_1,\ldots,v_m)\ \mathbf{in}\ e', \langle \Gamma; \alpha \rangle \Downarrow \lightning}$$

$$\text{(E-if}_1\text{)}\ \frac{e_1, \langle \Gamma; \alpha \rangle \Downarrow \beta'}{\mathbf{if}\ v\ \mathbf{then}\ e_1\ \mathbf{else}\ e_2, \langle \Gamma; \alpha \rangle \Downarrow \beta'}\ \text{if } \alpha(v) \neq 0$$

$$\text{(E-if}_2\text{)}\ \frac{e_2, \langle \Gamma; \alpha \rangle \Downarrow \beta'}{\mathbf{if}\ v\ \mathbf{then}\ e_1\ \mathbf{else}\ e_2, \langle \Gamma; \alpha \rangle \Downarrow \beta'}\ \text{if } \alpha(v) = 0$$

Fig. 7. Big-step evaluation relation (for a fixed program Π)

Proposition 10. *Let* $\langle \Gamma; \alpha \rangle$ *and* $\langle \Gamma'; \alpha' \rangle$ *be states. Let* e *be an expression such that* $\mathit{dom}(\Gamma) = \mathit{free}(e)$ *and* $\Gamma \vdash e : \sigma$ *for some product type* σ*. Then*

1. $e, \langle \Gamma; \alpha \rangle \Downarrow \lightning$ *if and only if* $\langle\!| \alpha, e \rangle^{\Gamma} :: \epsilon \rightsquigarrow^* \lightning$, *and*
2. $e, \langle \Gamma; \alpha \rangle \Downarrow \langle \Gamma'; \alpha' \rangle$ *if and only if there is a typed stack* $\langle\!| \alpha'', \mathbf{ret}\ (x_1,\ldots,x_n) \rangle^{\Gamma''} :: \epsilon$ *such that* $\langle\!| \alpha, e \rangle^{\Gamma} :: \epsilon \rightsquigarrow^* \langle\!| \alpha'', \mathbf{ret}\ (x_1,\ldots,x_n) \rangle^{\Gamma''} :: \epsilon$ *and* $\Gamma' \succeq \Gamma''$ *and* $\alpha' \succeq \alpha''$.

3 Effect Type System

In this section, we will develop a type system to statically guarantee dynamic resource safety, i. e., the absence of reductions to the error stack $\lightning$. We will do so by annotating functions with effects and then extending the notion of effect to a judgement on expressions, which we will define by a simple set of typing rules.

3.1 Effect Type System

We extend the notion of effect $\phi \rightarrow \psi$ from built-in functions to λ-abstractions. To be precise, $\phi \rightarrow \psi$ is an *effect* for f if $\Gamma \vdash \phi$ and $\Gamma, \Delta \vdash \psi$, where $\Pi(f) = [\boldsymbol{\lambda} \ldots]\Gamma \rightarrow \Delta$, regardless of whether f is built-in or a λ-abstraction. In line with this extension, an *effect environment* Θ maps all functions $f \in dom(\Pi)$ to effects $\Theta(f)$ for f.

In order to derive the effects of λ-abstractions, we generalise effects to effect types for expressions and develop a type system for inductively constructing such effect types. Effects relate input and output parameters of functions by logical formulae. Likewise, effect types shall relate input and output parameters of expressions. Here, the input parameters of an expression are its free variables; the output parameters are those variables that are not free yet but will become free during reduction, i. e., the (let-)bound variables. Formally, an *effect type* $\Gamma; \phi \rightarrow \Delta; \psi$ is a pair of constraints ϕ and ψ together with a pair of type environments Γ and Δ such that $dom(\Gamma) \cap dom(\Delta) = \emptyset$ and $\Gamma \vdash \phi$ and $\Gamma, \Delta \vdash \psi$. We call ϕ and ψ *precondition* and *action*, and Γ and Δ *input* and *output (parameters)*, respectively. Given an expression e, we say that an effect type $\Gamma; \phi \rightarrow \Delta; \psi$ is an *effect type for* e if $dom(\Gamma) \cap bound(e) = \emptyset$.

We say that an effect type $\Gamma; \phi \rightarrow \Delta; \psi$ is *stronger than* an effect type $\Gamma'; \phi' \rightarrow \Delta'; \psi'$, denoted by $\Gamma; \phi \rightarrow \Delta; \psi \supseteq \Gamma'; \phi' \rightarrow \Delta'; \psi'$, if $\phi' \models \phi$ and $(\phi' \wedge \psi) \models \psi'$, i. e., the stronger effect type $\Gamma; \phi \rightarrow \Delta; \psi$ has a weaker precondition but stronger action. The stronger-than relation $\supseteq$ is a quasi-order, i. e., reflexive and transitive, and induces an equivalence relation on effect types, the *as-strong-as* relation, which we denote by $\equiv$. Note that for every effect type $\Gamma; \phi \rightarrow \Delta; \psi$ is as strong as an effect type $\Gamma'; \phi \rightarrow \Delta'; \psi$ with linear type environments Γ' and Δ'.

Figure 8 presents the typing rules for deriving effect types. There, the judgement $\Theta \vdash_{\Pi} e : \Gamma; \phi \rightarrow \Delta; \psi$ states that expression e has effect type $\Gamma; \phi \rightarrow \Delta; \psi$ in the context of program Π and effect environment Θ. If Π is understood, we may omit it and write $\Theta \vdash e : \Gamma; \phi \rightarrow \Delta; \psi$ instead. The judgement $\Pi, \Theta \vdash f$ means that the effect type ascribed to a λ-abstraction f by Θ and Π is consistent with the effect type derived for the body of f. We say that Θ is an *admissible* effect environment for a program Π if $\Pi, \Theta \vdash f$ for all λ-abstractions $f \in dom(\Pi) \setminus dom(\Pi_0)$.

Lemma 11. *Let* e *be an expression,* Θ *an effect environment (referring to an implicit program* Π*) and* $\Gamma; \phi \rightarrow \Delta; \psi$ *an effect type. If* $\Theta \vdash e : \Gamma; \phi \rightarrow \Delta; \psi$ *then* $\Gamma; \phi \rightarrow \Delta; \psi$ *is an effect type for* e.

Theorem 12 states soundness of effect typing w. r. t. the big-step relational semantics. The proof is by double induction on the derivation of relational semantics judgements over the derivation of effect type judgements. As a corollary, we get that reduction starting from a state that satisfies the precondition can't go wrong, hence resource managers can be erased. In fact, the untyped reductions in the erased program match exactly the typed reductions in the original program.

Theorem 12. *Let* Θ *be an admissible effect environment for a well-typed program* Π*. Let* e *be an expression and* $\Gamma; \phi \rightarrow \Delta; \psi$ *an effect type such that* $\Theta \vdash e : \Gamma; \phi \rightarrow \Delta; \psi$*. Let* $\langle \Gamma; \alpha \rangle$ *and* β' *be states such that* $e, \langle \Gamma; \alpha \rangle \Downarrow \beta'$ *(which implies* $\Gamma_e \vdash e : \sigma$ *for some* Γ_e*,* σ*). If* $\alpha \models \phi$ *then* $\beta' = \langle \Gamma'; \alpha' \rangle$ *for some* Γ' *and* α' *such that* $\alpha' \models \phi \wedge \psi$*. (In particular, if* $\alpha \models \phi$ *then* $\beta' \neq \lightning$*.)*

Typing of expression effects $\Theta \vdash e : \Gamma; \phi \rightarrow \Delta; \psi$

$$\text{(ET-weak)}\ \frac{\Theta \vdash e : \Gamma; \phi \rightarrow \Delta; \psi}{\Theta \vdash e : \Gamma'; \phi' \rightarrow \Delta'; \psi'}\ \text{if} \begin{cases} dom(\Gamma') \cap bound(e) = \emptyset\ \wedge \\ \Gamma; \phi \rightarrow \Delta; \psi \supseteq \Gamma'; \phi' \rightarrow \Delta'; \psi' \end{cases}$$

$$\text{(ET-ret)}\ \frac{}{\Theta \vdash \mathbf{ret}\ (x_1,\ldots,x_n) : \emptyset; \top \rightarrow \emptyset; \top}$$

$$\text{(ET-if)}\ \frac{\Theta \vdash e_1 : \Gamma; v \not\approx 0 \wedge \phi \rightarrow \Delta; \psi \qquad \Theta \vdash e_2 : \Gamma; v \approx 0 \wedge \phi \rightarrow \Delta; \psi}{\Theta \vdash \mathbf{if}\ v\ \mathbf{then}\ e_1\ \mathbf{else}\ e_2 : \Gamma; \phi \rightarrow \Delta; \psi}$$

$$\text{(ET-let)}\ \frac{\begin{array}{c} \Pi(f) = [\boldsymbol{\lambda}\ldots]\Gamma \rightarrow \Delta \qquad \Gamma = z_1{:}\tau_1, \ldots, z_m{:}\tau_m \qquad \Delta = z'_1{:}\tau'_1, \ldots, z'_n{:}\tau'_n \\ \Theta(f) = \phi \rightarrow \psi \qquad \mu = \{z_1 \mapsto v_1, \ldots, z_m \mapsto v_m, z'_1 \mapsto x'_1, \ldots, z'_n \mapsto x'_n\} \\ \Theta \vdash e' : \Gamma', \Delta'; \phi' \wedge \psi' \rightarrow \Delta''; \psi'' \end{array}}{\Theta \vdash \mathbf{let}\ (x'_1,\ldots,x'_n) = f\ (v_1,\ldots,v_m)\ \mathbf{in}\ e' : \Gamma'; \phi' \rightarrow \Delta', \Delta''; \psi' \wedge \psi''}\ \text{if } (*)$$

$$\text{where } (*) \begin{cases} dom(\Gamma') \cap \{x'_1, \ldots, x'_n\} = \emptyset\ \wedge \\ \Gamma\mu; \phi\mu \rightarrow \Delta\mu; \psi\mu \supseteq \Gamma'; \phi' \rightarrow \Delta'; \psi' \end{cases}$$

Well-typedness of λ-abstraction effects $\Pi, \Theta \vdash f$

$$\text{(ET-lam)}\ \frac{\Pi(f) = \boldsymbol{\lambda} e : \Gamma \rightarrow \Delta \qquad \Theta(f) = \phi \rightarrow \psi \qquad \Theta \vdash e : \Gamma; \phi \rightarrow \Delta; \psi}{\Pi, \Theta \vdash f}$$

Fig. 8. Typing rules for effect types (for a fixed program Π)

Corollary 13. *Let Θ be an admissible effect environment for a well-typed program Π. Let e be an expression and $\Gamma; \phi \rightarrow \Delta; \psi$ an effect type such that $\Theta \vdash_\Pi e : \Gamma; \phi \rightarrow \Delta; \psi$. Let α be a maximal Γ-valuation, and let $\hat{S}_0 = \langle |\alpha|_{free(e)}, e\rangle^{\Gamma|_{free(e)}} :: \epsilon$ be a typed Π-stack (which implies $\Gamma|_{free(e)} \vdash_\Pi e : \sigma$ for some σ). If $\alpha \models \phi$ then*

1. *$\hat{S}_0 \not\rightsquigarrow^*_\Pi \lightning$ and*
2. *for all (untyped) Π°-stacks S, $\hat{S}_0^{\circ\natural} \rightsquigarrow^*_{\Pi^\circ} S$ if and only if there is a typed Π-stack $\hat{S}$ such that $\hat{S}_0 \rightsquigarrow^*_\Pi \hat{S}$ and $\hat{S}^{\circ\natural} = S$. (In particular, $\hat{S}_0^{\circ\natural} \not\rightsquigarrow^*_{\Pi^\circ} \lightning$.)*

3.2 Example: Bulk Messaging Application

To illustrate the use of the effect type system, we revisit the example from Figure 1. The interesting bits of code are in the functions send_bulk and send_msg.

The function send_bulk first builds up a multiset of resources r by converting the strings representing phone numbers in nums into resources. Next it attempts to authorise the use of all resources by having enable add r to an empty resource manager m. If this fails, i. e., the multiset r' returned by enable is of non-zero size, send_bulk terminates (after destroying m' and whatever resources it holds).[3] If authorising all resources succeeds, send_bulk calls send_msgs to actually send the messages while checking

[3] A more sophisticated version of the application could deal more gracefully with enable granting only part of the requested resources. This would require more complex code to inspect the multisets r and r' (but not the resource manager m').

f	$\Theta(f)$
send_bulk	$\top \rightarrow \top$
res_from_nums	$\top \rightarrow \mathsf{r} \approx bagof(map_{fromstr}(\mathsf{nums}))$
res_from_nums'	$0 \leq \mathsf{i} \leq len(\mathsf{nums}) \wedge \mathsf{r'} \approx bagof(map_{fromstr}(subarray(\mathsf{nums}, \mathsf{i}, len(\mathsf{nums}))))$ $\rightarrow \mathsf{r} \approx bagof(map_{fromstr}(\mathsf{nums}))$
send_msgs	$bagof(map_{fromstr}(\mathsf{nums})) \subseteq \mathsf{m} \rightarrow \mathsf{m} \approx \mathsf{m'} \uplus bagof(map_{fromstr}(\mathsf{nums}))$
send_msgs'	$0 \leq \mathsf{i} \leq len(\mathsf{nums}) \wedge bagof(map_{fromstr}(subarray(\mathsf{nums}, 0, \mathsf{i}))) \subseteq \mathsf{m}$ $\rightarrow \mathsf{m} \approx \mathsf{m'} \uplus bagof(map_{fromstr}(subarray(\mathsf{nums}, 0, \mathsf{i})))$
send_msg	$count(\mathsf{m}, fromstr(\mathsf{num})) \geq 1 \rightarrow \mathsf{m} \approx \mathsf{m'} \uplus \{\!\{fromstr(\mathsf{num}){:}1\}\!\}$
prim_send_msg	$\top \rightarrow \top$

$$\forall a : len(map_{fromstr}(a)) \approx len(a)$$
$$\forall a \forall i : 0 \leq i < len(a) \Rightarrow map_{fromstr}(a)[i] \approx fromstr(a[i])$$

$$\forall a \forall j \forall k : 0 \leq j \leq k \leq len(a) \Rightarrow len(subarray(a, j, k)) = k + (-j)$$
$$\forall a \forall j \forall k \forall i : 0 \leq j \leq k \leq len(a) \wedge 0 \leq i < len(subarray(a, j, k)) \Rightarrow subarray(a, j, k)[i] = a[j + i]$$

$$\forall a : |bagof(a)| \approx len(a)$$
$$\forall a : len(a) \approx 1 \Rightarrow bagof(a) \approx \{a[0]{:}1\}$$
$$\forall a \forall k : 0 \leq k \leq len(a) \Rightarrow bagof(a) \approx bagof(subarray(a, 0, k)) \uplus bagof(subarray(a, k, len(a)))$$

Fig. 9. Bulk messaging application: admissible effect environment Θ and axiomatisation of theory extension; for the sake of readability sort information is suppressed in the axioms

that the manager m' contains the required resources. After that, send_bulk checks that send_msgs has used up all resources by asserting that the returned manager m" is empty; failing this assertion will trigger a runtime error. Finally, send_bulk explicitly destroys the empty manager m"' and terminates.

The function send_msg sends one message, checking whether the resource manager m holds the resource required. It does so by converting the string num into a singleton multiset of resources r. Then it splits the manager m into m' and m_r, so that m_r contains at most the resources in r. Next, send_msg asserts that m_r contains at least r; failing this assertion will trigger a runtime error. Succeeding the assertion, send_msg calls the primitive send function, destroys the now used resource by consuming m_r', and returns the remaining resources in the manager m'.

The bulk messaging example is statically resource safe, as witnessed by the admissible effect environment displayed in Figure 9. Of particular interest is the effect $\top \rightarrow \top$ ascribed to the main function send_bulk. This least informative effect expresses nothing about the function itself but implies the absence of runtime errors via Corollary 13.

The effects require an extension of the theory $\mathcal{T}$ (see Section 2.2) by three new functions, axiomatised in Figure 9. The function *map* maps an array of strings to an array of resources, *subarray* takes an array and cuts out the sub-array between two given indices, and *bagof* converts an array of resources to a multiset (containing the same elements with the same multiplicity). Note that the axiomatisation of *bagof* is not complete[4] but sufficient for our purposes.

Effect type checking, e. g., for checking admissibility of the effect environment Θ from Figure 9, requires checking the side condition of the weakening rule (ET-weak),

[4] A complete axiomatisation of *bagof* is possible in the full first-order theory of multisets and arrays but it is much more complicated and unusable in practise.

which involves checking logical entailment w. r. t. to an extension of the theory $\mathcal{T}$. Due to the high undecidability of $\mathcal{T}$, we actually check entailment w. r. t. (an extension of) an approximation of $\mathcal{T}$; in particular, we approximate multiplication and division by uninterpreted functions. For the bulk messaging example, we used an SMT solver [4] that can handle linear integer arithmetic and arrays. We added axioms for multisets and the axioms in Figure 9. Due to an incomplete quantifier instantiation heuristic, we had to instantiate a number of these axioms by hand, yet eventually, the solver was able to prove all the entailments required by the weakening rules.

Even though arising from a single example, we believe that the extension of the theories of multisets and arrays with the functions $subarray$ and $bagof$ is quite generic and could prove useful in many cases.

4 Conclusion

We have presented a programming language with support for complex resource management, close to the standard SSA/ANF forms of compiler intermediate languages [1]. By construction, programs are *dynamically resource safe* in that any attempts to abuse resources are trapped. We have extended the language with an effect type system which guarantees the for well-typed programs no such attempts occur: we have *static resource safety*. In addition, for such programs the bookkeeping required by dynamic resource management can be erased.

Related Work. Many tools and methods have been proposed to assist with resource management at runtime, e.g., in Java, the JRes [9] and J-Seal [8] frameworks. Generally, these aim to enable programs to react to fluctuations of resources caused by an unpredictable environment. Our aim, however is to track the flow of resources through the program, where the environment can influence the availability of resources only at well-understood points of interaction with the program and with clear availability policies. This offers the chance for more precise resource control whose behaviour can be predicted statically.

This paper builds on previous work [3] with a Java library implementing resource managers and focusing on the dynamic aspects of resource management policies. This Java library supports essentially the same operations on resource managers as our functional language, except that state is realised by destructive updates instead of linear types. While [3] does not provide a static analysis to prove static resource safety, it does outline how dynamic accounting could be erased if static resource safety were provable. Our work here shows one way to do just that.

Our approach is in line with a general trend of providing the programmer with language-based mechanisms for security and additional static analyses (often using type systems) which use these mechanisms. This combination provides a desirable graceful degradation: if static analysis succeeds in proving certain properties, then the program may be optimised without affecting security. Yet, even if the analyses fail the language based mechanisms will enforce the security properties at runtime.

The context of our work is the MOBIUS project [5] on proof-carrying code (PCC) for mobile devices. Our effect type system is very simple and in principle well-suited for a PCC setting where checkers themselves are resource bounded. However, the weakening rule relies on checking logical entailment in a first-order theory, which is undecidable in general. Therefore, a certificate for PCC need not only provide a type derivation tree but also proofs (in some proof system) for the entailment checks in the weakening rule. The development of a suitable such proof system is a topic for further research, as is the investigation of decidable fragments of relevant first-order theories.

Acknowledgements. This work was funded in part by the Sixth Framework programme of the European Community under the MOBIUS project FP6-015905. This paper reflects only the authors' views and the European Community is not liable for any use that may be made of the information contained therein. Ian Stark was also supported by an Advanced Research Fellowship from the UK Engineering and Physical Sciences Research Council, EPSRC project GR/R76950/01.

References

[1] Appel, A.W.: SSA is functional programming. SIGPLAN Notices 33(4), 17–20 (1998)
[2] Aspinall, D., Beringer, L., Hofmann, M., Loidl, H.-W., Momigliano, A.: A program logic for resources. Theoret. Comput. Sci. 389(3), 411–445 (2007)
[3] Aspinall, D., Maier, P., Stark, I.: Monitoring external resources in Java MIDP. Electron. Notes Theor. Comput. Sci. 197, 17–30 (2008)
[4] Barrett, C., de Moura, L., Stump, A.: Design and results of the 2nd annual satisfiability modulo theories competition. Form. Meth. Syst. Des. 31(3), 221–239 (2007)
[5] Barthe, G., Beringer, L., Crégut, P., Grégoire, B., Hofmann, M., Müller, P., Poll, E., Puebla, G., Stark, I., Vétillard, E.: MOBIUS: Mobility, ubiquity, security. In: Montanari, U., Sannella, D., Bruni, R. (eds.) TGC 2006. LNCS, vol. 4661, pp. 10–29. Springer, Heidelberg (2007)
[6] Beringer, L., Hofmann, M., Momigliano, A., Shkaravska, O.: Automatic certification of heap consumption. In: Baader, F., Voronkov, A. (eds.) LPAR 2004. LNCS, vol. 3452, pp. 347–362. Springer, Heidelberg (2005)
[7] Besson, F., Dufay, G., Jensen, T.P.: A formal model of access control for mobile interactive devices. In: Gollmann, D., Meier, J., Sabelfeld, A. (eds.) ESORICS 2006. LNCS, vol. 4189, pp. 110–126. Springer, Heidelberg (2006)
[8] Binder, W., Hulaas, J., Villazón, A.: Portable resource control in Java. In: Proc. OOPSLA 2001, pp. 139–155. ACM, New York (2001)
[9] Czajkowski, G., von Eicken, T.: JRes: A resource accounting interface for Java. In: Proc. OOPSLA 1998, pp. 21–35. ACM, New York (1998)
[10] Flanagan, C., Sabry, A., Duba, B.F., Felleisen, M.: The essence of compiling with continuations. In: Proc. PLDI 1993, pp. 237–247. ACM, New York (1993)
[11] Nanevski, A., Ahmed, A., Morrisett, G., Birkedal, L.: Abstract predicates and mutable ADTs in Hoare type theory. In: De Nicola, R. (ed.) ESOP 2007. LNCS, vol. 4421, pp. 189–204. Springer, Heidelberg (2007)
[12] Unknown: Redbrowser. A, J2ME trojan. Identified in February 2006 as Redbrowser. A (F-Secure), J2ME/Redbrowser.a (McAfee), Trojan. Redbrowser. A (Symantec), Trojan-SMS.J2ME.Redbrowser.a (Kaspersky Lab)

Universe Types for Topology and Encapsulation

Dave Cunningham[1], Werner Dietl[2], Sophia Drossopoulou[1], Adrian Francalanza[3], Peter Müller[2], and Alexander J. Summers[1]

[1] Imperial College London
{david.cunningham04,s.drossopoulou,alexander.j.summers}@imperial.ac.uk
[2] ETH Zurich
{Werner.Dietl,Peter.Mueller}@inf.ethz.ch
[3] University of Southampton
af1@ecs.soton.ac.uk

Abstract. The Universe Type System is an ownership type system for object-oriented programming languages that hierarchically structures the object store; it is used to reason modularly about programs.

We formalise Universe Types for a core subset of Java in two steps: We first define a Topological Type System that structures the object store hierarchically into an ownership tree, and demonstrate soundness of the Topological Type System by proving subject reduction. Motivated by concerns of modular verification, we then present an Encapsulation Type System that enforces the owner-as-modifier discipline; that is, that object updates are initiated by the owner of the object.

The contributions of this paper are, firstly, an extensive type-theoretic account of the Universe Type System, with explanations and complete proofs, and secondly, the clean separation of the topological from the encapsulation concerns.

1 Introduction

Imperative object-oriented programming languages, such as C++, Java and C#, use references to build object structures and share state. *Aliasing* allows multiple references to the same object and gives much of the power of object-oriented programming. However, it makes several other programming aspects more difficult, including reasoning about programs, garbage collection and memory management, code migration, parallelism and the analysis of atomicity.

To address these issues, different ownership type systems have been proposed: ownership types [6,9,10], ownership domains [1], Universe Types [15,26] and similar other type systems [2,18]. All have in common that they organise the heap as an *ownership tree* where each object is *owned* by at most one other object. It is common practice to depict ownership through a *box* in an object graph, where all objects that share the same owner are within the box of the owning object. For example, in Figure 1 the dashed box around object 1 of class Bag indicates that it owns objects 2 and 13, while object 2 of class Stack owns

F.S. de Boer et al. (Eds.): FMCO 2007, LNCS 5382, pp. 72–112, 2008.

objects 3, 4 and 5. Objects that are not owned by any other object, such as 1, 6 and 9 are contained within the outermost dashed box labelled root, which gives us a tree.

However, different ownership type systems enforce different *encapsulation policies*, that is, put different restrictions on what references between objects might exist or limit the use of certain references. Ownership types enforce the owner-as-dominator policy, guaranteeing that every reference chain from an object in the root context to an object o goes through o's owner. Ownership domains allow the declaration of flexible encapsulation policies by special *link* declarations. Universe Types enforce the owner-as-modifier discipline that ensures that all modifications of an object are initiated by the object's owner.

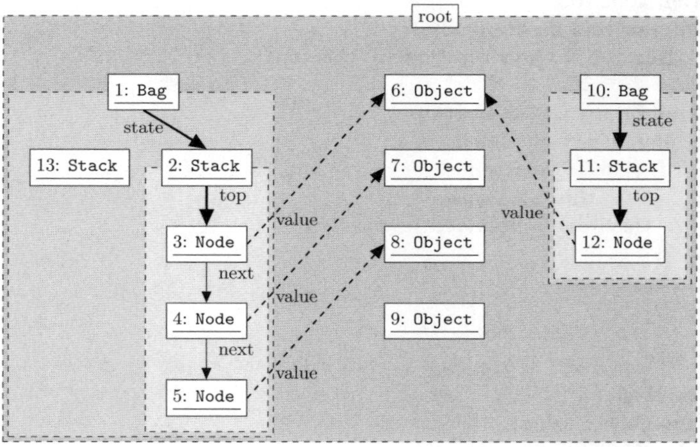

Fig. 1. Depicting object ownership and references in a heap

The hierarchic heap topology and the different encapsulation policies can be exploited in different ways: Andreae et al. [2] speed up garbage collection, because, if the owner-as-dominator policy is enforced, as soon as an owner is unreachable, all owned objects are unreachable, too. Flanagan et al. [18] and Boyapati et al. [5] can guarantee that a program will not have races, because locking an object implicitly locks all owned objects. Cunningham et al. [11] show that Universe Types can be used to guarantee race free programs. Clarke et al. [9] use ownership types to calculate the effects of computations, and thus determine when they do not affect each other. Banerjee et al. [3] use the owner-as-dominator policy to prove representation independence of data structures. Müller et al. [27] use the hierarchic topology for defining modular verification techniques of object invariants.

Universe Types [26,15] were developed to support modular reasoning about programs. The type system is one of the simplest possible in the family of ownership type systems. There are three *Universe Modifiers*: rep, peer and any, which denote the relative placement of objects in the ownership hierarchy. The qualifier rep (short for representation) expresses that the object is owned by the currently active object, while peer expresses that the object has the same owner as the currently active object. The qualifier any abstracts over the object's position in the hierarchy and does not give any static information about the owner.

```
class Bag {
   rep Stack state;
   impure void add(any Object o) { this.state.push(o); }
   pure Bool isEmpty() { return (this.state.top == null); }
}

class Stack {
   rep Node top;
   impure void push(any Object o) {
     this.top := new rep Node(o, this.top);
   }
   impure any Object pop() {
     any Object o := null;
     if (this.top != null) {
       o := this.top.value;
       this.top := this.top.next;
     }
     return o;
   }
}

class Node {
   any Object value;
   peer Node next;
   Node(any Object v, peer Node n) { value := v; next := n; }
}
```

Fig. 2. Code augmented with Universe Modifiers

An example appears in Figure 2. The Stack field state in class Bag is declared as rep and indeed, we see that in Figure 1 the Stack objects 2 and 11 are owned by Bag objects 1 and 10, respectively; similarly, in class Node the field next is declared as peer, and indeed the Node objects 3, 4 and 5 have the same owner. The field value in class Node is declared as any Object and can therefore refer to any object in the hierarchy. In that sense, the Universe Modifier any plays a similar role to that played by the any ownership parameter in [24].

The code in Figure 2 also augments methods with the keywords pure, qualifying methods without side-effects, and impure, for methods that might affect the state of the program; these purity annotations are used to guarantee encapsulation.

In contrast with those ownership type systems that enforce the owner-as-dominator policy [1,2,6,10], Universe Types do not restrict references into the boxes, as long as they are carried out through any references. Thus, a reference from 3 to 12 would be legal through the field value, because this field has the type any Object.

Nevertheless, Universe Types can be used to impose encapsulation, in the sense of guaranteeing that the state of an object can only be modified when the object's owner is one of the currently active objects. This owner-as-modifier discipline [15] is checked by the type system by forbidding all field updates on any references and requiring that only pure methods can be called when the receiver is an any reference. The owner-as-modifier discipline supports modular reasoning by restricting the objects whose invariants can be broken [23,27].

In this paper we give a formal, type theoretical description of Universe Types. We distinguish the Topological Type System from the Encapsulation Type System, and describe the latter on top of the Topological System. The reasons for this distinction are:

- the distinction clarifies the rationale for the type systems;
- some systems, such as those required for race detection, atomicity and deadlock detection, only require the topological properties;
- one might want to add an encapsulation part onto a different Topological Type System or use different encapsulation policies.

Universe Types were already introduced and proven sound [26], but the description was in terms of proof theory, rather than the type theoretic machinery we adopt in this report; they were further described in the context of JML [15,22]. Extensions to Universe Types, such as the addition of generics [14], already use the type theoretic approach, but do not separate topology and encapsulation.

This paper thus aims to fill a gap in the Universe Types literature, by giving a full type theoretical account of the basic type system, proofs, sufficient examples, explanations, and elucidate the distinction between the Topological and the Encapsulation System. We describe Universe Types (UT) for a small Java-like language, which contains classes, inheritance, fields, methods, dynamic method binding and casts.

The rest of the paper is organised as follows: we introduce our base language in Section 2, followed by a discussion of Universe Modifiers and owners in Section 3. In Section 4 we give the operational semantics for our language. Section 5 presents the Topological Type System and states subject reduction. Section 6 covers the Encapsulation Type System. Section 7 discusses related work and Section 8 concludes. Finally, Appendix A gives supporting results and proofs.

2 Source Language

UT models a subset of Java supporting class definitions, inheritance, field lookup and update, method invocations and casting. On top of this core subset, we augment types with Universe Modifiers and method signatures with purity annotations.

Universe Modifiers were originally defined [26] as the set {rep, peer, readonly}. In this paper, we present a generalisation of this approach. Firstly, we replace the modifier readonly with the modifier any, since the name readonly applies only to the intentions of the Encapsulation System, but not to the Topological. Secondly, we extend the set of modifiers with two new values: self and lost, which do not occur in source programs but are key in the operation of the Topological Type System we will present in Section 5.

Universe Modifiers are attached to object references, and provide *relative* information about the location (that is, position in the heap topology) of the referred-to object with respect to the current object. More specifically:

- rep states that the referred object constitutes part of the current object's *direct representation*. Stated otherwise, the current object *owns* the object pointed to by the reference.
- peer states that the referred object constitutes part of the same representation to which the current object belongs. Stated otherwise, the current object and the object pointed to by the reference are *owned* by the same object.
- self is a specialisation of peer, referring to the current object.
- any does not provide information about the location of the referred object. It is a 'don't care' modifier: such a reference may refer to objects with arbitrary owners.
- lost does not provide information about the location of the referred object. It is a 'don't know' modifier: it is used when the type system cannot accurately describe the location of the object[1].

Example 2.1 (Comparing any and lost). *We illustrate the difference between* any *and* lost *using the example from Figure 2 and a reference* node *of type* any Node*. The field access* node.value *has type* any Object *because the declared type of field* value *uses the* any *modifier and therefore permits references to arbitrary objects; the field* doesn't care *about the location of the* value *object. Consequently, an update of* value *is statically safe regardless of the owners of the receiver and the right-hand side. In particular, the update* node.value := y *is legal provided that* y*'s class is a subclass of* Object*. Conversely, the field access* node.next *has type* lost Node *because the declared type of the field requires that the next node and the current node have the same owner. We do not statically know the owner of* node *as its Universe Modifier is* any*. Hence, we cannot express that the* next *field has the same owner. Since we* don't know *the accurate ownership information for* node.next*, the field update* node.next := z *is potentially unsafe and has to be rejected by the type system, as we cannot ensure the topology of the heap would be preserved.*

[1] As we said earlier, Lu and Potter's any ownership parameter [24] is the counterpart to our any Universe Modifier. Their unknown ownership parameter corresponds to our lost Universe Modifier—however, the main motivation for unknown is to preserve effective ownership rather than topology. Furthermore, our Universe Modifiers any and lost introduce a form of existential types [25].

The example above also illustrates that lost variables cannot be assigned meaningful values, therefore our language does not permit any explicit occurrences of lost in the program. Analogously, variables with modifier self can only be aliases of this and so do not add expressibility. For these reasons, when writing source programs we only make use of Universe Modifiers from the set $\{\mathsf{rep}, \mathsf{peer}, \mathsf{any}\}$.

The syntax of our source language is given in Figure 3. We assume three countably infinite, distinct sets of names: one for classes, $c \in Id_c$, one for fields, $f \in Id_f$, and another for methods, $m \in Id_m$. A program P is defined in terms of three partial functions, $\mathcal{F}$, $\mathcal{M}$ and $\mathcal{MBody}$, and a relation over class names $\leq_c$; these functions and relations are global. $\mathcal{F}$ associates field names accessible[2] in a class to types, $\mathcal{M}$ associates method names accessible in a class to method signatures and $\mathcal{MBody}$ associates method names accessible in a class to method bodies. The reflexive, transitive relation $\leq_c$ denotes subclassing.

Types, denoted by t, constitute a departure from standard Java. They consist of a pair, $u\,c$, where class names c are preceded by Universe Modifiers u. Source types, denoted by s are the subset of types t which are allowed to occur in source programs; i.e., they feature only Universe Modifiers from the set $\{\mathsf{rep}, \mathsf{peer}, \mathsf{any}\}$. Method signatures also deviate slightly from standard Java. They consist of a triple, denoted as $p : s_1\ (s_2)$ where s_2 is the type of the (single) method parameter, s_1 is the return type of the method and p is a purity annotation, ranging over the set $\{\mathsf{pure}, \mathsf{impure}\}$. An extension to multiple method parameters is straightforward because each argument can be type-checked independently.

$$
\begin{aligned}
\mathcal{F} &: Id_c \times Id_f \rightharpoonup SrcType \\
\mathcal{M} &: Id_c \times Id_m \rightharpoonup MethSig \\
\mathcal{MBody} &: Id_c \times Id_m \rightharpoonup SrcExpr \\
\leq_c &: Id_c \times Id_c \rightarrow Bool
\end{aligned}
$$

$$
\begin{aligned}
e \in SrcExpr &::= \mathsf{this} \mid \mathsf{x} \mid \mathsf{null} \mid \mathsf{new}\ s \mid (s)\ e \\
&\quad\ \mid e.f \mid e.f := e \mid e.m(e) \\
u \in Universe\ Modifiers &::= \mathsf{rep} \mid \mathsf{peer} \mid \mathsf{self} \mid \mathsf{any} \mid \mathsf{lost} \\
s \in SrcType &::= \mathsf{rep}\ c \mid \mathsf{peer}\ c \mid \mathsf{any}\ c \\
t \in Type &::= s \mid \mathsf{self}\ c \mid \mathsf{lost}\ c \\
MethSig &::= p : s\ (s) \\
p \in Purity\ Tag &::= \mathsf{pure} \mid \mathsf{impure}
\end{aligned}
$$

Fig. 3. Syntax of source programs. The arrow $\rightharpoonup$ indicates partial mappings.

Source expressions, denoted by e, are a standard subset of Java. They consist of the self reference this, parameter identifier x, the basic value null, new object creation new s, casting $(s)\ e$, field access $e.f$, field update $e.f := e$ and method invocation $e.m(e)$.

[2] By "accessible", we mean those which are either defined in the class or inherited from a superclass. We do not formalise visibility; all declarations are implicitly public.

3 Universe Modifiers and Owners

Universe Types structure the heap as an ownership tree. Every object a in a heap is owned by a single owner, o, which is either another object in the heap or the root of the ownership tree, root. The *direct representation* of an object in a heap h is defined to be all the objects it owns (i.e., is the owner of). Ownership is required to be acyclic. When we do not want to refer to a particular heap, we find it convenient to refer to objects as pairs with their owners (a, o). For example, $(1, \mathsf{root})$ and $(2, 1)$, meaning 1 owned by root and 2 owned by 1, respectively.

We recall that the Universe Modifiers self, peer and rep are interpreted with respect to the current object and do not mean anything without this *viewpoint*. One can assign a Universe Modifier to an object (a', o') with respect to another object (a, o) using the judgement

$$(a, o) \vdash (a', o') : u \tag{1}$$

which is defined as the least relation satisfying the rules in Figure 4. It states that, from the point of view of a (owned by o), a' (owned by o') has Universe Modifier u. The lost and any modifiers can always be assigned because they do not express any ownership information.

$$\frac{}{(a, o) \vdash (a, o) : \mathsf{self}}\,(\textsc{Self}) \qquad \frac{}{(\_, o) \vdash (\_, o) : \mathsf{peer}}\,(\textsc{Peer})$$

$$\frac{}{(a, \_) \vdash (\_, a) : \mathsf{rep}}\,(\textsc{Rep})$$

$$\frac{}{(\_, \_) \vdash (\_, \_) : \mathsf{lost}}\,(\textsc{Lost}) \qquad \frac{}{(\_, \_) \vdash (\_, \_) : \mathsf{any}}\,(\textsc{Any})$$

Fig. 4. Assigning Universe Modifiers to objects

Example 3.1 (Universe Modifiers and objects). *In the heap shown in Figure 1, from the point of view of 2 (owned by 1) object 3 (owned by 2) has Universe Modifier* rep *that is*

$$(2, 1) \vdash (3, 2) : \mathsf{rep} \tag{2}$$

Similarly, we can derive

$$(3, 2) \vdash (4, 2) : \mathsf{peer} \tag{3}$$

Each object can view itself as self *or* peer*:*

$$(2, 1) \vdash (2, 1) : \mathsf{self} \qquad (2, 1) \vdash (2, 1) : \mathsf{peer} \tag{4}$$

Also, we can assign any *to any object from any viewpoint using rule* (Any)*:*

$$(3, 2) \vdash (6, \mathsf{root}) : \mathsf{any} \qquad (2, 1) \vdash (3, 2) : \mathsf{any} \qquad (3, 2) \vdash (4, 2) : \mathsf{any} \tag{5}$$

3.1 Universe Ordering

We define the following reflexive ordering for Universe Modifiers $u \leq_u u'$:

$$u \leq_u u \qquad \mathsf{self} \leq_u \mathsf{peer} \leq_u \mathsf{lost} \qquad \mathsf{rep} \leq_u \mathsf{lost} \qquad \mathsf{lost} \leq_u \mathsf{any}$$

It states that peer and rep are smaller (more precise) than lost, self is similarly a specialisation of peer, and any is the least specific modifier. The 'don't care' modifier any is treated as more general than the 'don't know' modifier lost; this is because we want to be able to assign to an any field even those objects whose location cannot be expressed in the type system.

Lemma 3.2 states that the Universe ordering relation ($\leq_u$) is consistent with the judgement of Figure 4. Thus, any object that is assigned rep, peer or self can also be assigned Universe Modifier any or lost, and any object that is assigned self can be assigned Universe Modifier peer, as we have already seen in Example 3.1.

Lemma 3.2 (Universe object judgements respect Universe ordering)

$$\left.\begin{array}{l}(a,o) \vdash (a',o') : u \\ u \leq_u u'\end{array}\right\} \implies (a,o) \vdash (a',o') : u'$$

Proof. By a simple case analysis of $(a,o) \vdash (a',o') : u$. □

Example 3.3 (Subtyping and Universe Modifiers). *We illustrate how the Universe Modifiers of the fields in the classes of Figure 2 characterise the references in Figure 1. For instance, the* Stack *object 2 has the* rep top *field correctly assigned to* Node 3, *since from (2) above we know that 3 has Universe Modifier* rep *with respect to 2. In fact, this reference can only point to (*Node*) objects 3, 4 and 5 since these are the only objects owned by object 2. Similarly,* Node 3 *has the* peer next *field correctly assigned to* Node 4, *which is owned by the same owner as 3; see (3) above. Trivially, the* any value *field of* Node 3 *assigned to* Object 6 *also respects the Universe Modifier because of (5) above. It can however point to any object in the heap since any type t is a subtype of* any Object.

3.2 Viewpoint Adaptation

The ownership information given by Universe Modifiers is *relative* with respect to a particular viewpoint. To adapt Universe Modifiers from one viewpoint to another, we define an operation $u_1 \rhd u_2$ called *viewpoint adaptation* [14]. This operation takes two Universe Modifiers u_1 and u_2, and yields a new Universe Modifier, as defined in Figure 5. The resulting modifier can be intuitively described as follows: "if a_1 sees a_2 as u_1, and a_2 sees a_3 as u_2, then a_1 sees a_3 as $u_1 \rhd u_2$"[3]. If there is no modifier to explicitly describe this relationship, then the operation yields the modifier lost. For example, rep $\rhd$ rep = lost, since there is no modifier to explicitly express that a referred object is in the 'transitive

[3] For readers familiar with work on Ownership Types, this operation is vaguely analogous with the notion there of substitution.

	$u_1 \rhd u_2$	self	peer	rep	any	lost
				u_2		
	self	self	peer	rep	any	lost
	peer	lost	peer	lost	any	lost
u_1	rep	lost	rep	lost	any	lost
	any	lost	lost	lost	any	lost
	lost	lost	lost	lost	any	lost

Fig. 5. Viewpoint adaptation

representation' of the current object. Also note that the modifiers any and lost do not depend on a viewpoint. Therefore, if u_2 is any or lost, the result will again be any or lost, respectively.

In Lemma 3.4, we show that the intuition of $\rhd$ is sound with respect to the interpretation of Universe Modifiers as object ownership in a heap, that is, judgement (1). We also show how we can recover information from a Universe Modifier $u \rhd u'$, so long as it is not lost.

Lemma 3.4 (Sound viewpoint adaptation)

$$\left.\begin{array}{l}(a_1, o_1) \vdash (a_2, o_2) : u_1 \\ (a_2, o_2) \vdash (a_3, o_3) : u_2\end{array}\right\} \Longrightarrow (a_1, o_1) \vdash (a_3, o_3) : u_1 \rhd u_2$$

$$\left.\begin{array}{l}(a_1, o_1) \vdash (a_2, o_2) : u_1 \\ (a_1, o_1) \vdash (a_3, o_3) : u_1 \rhd u_2 \\ u_1 \rhd u_2 \neq \mathit{lost}\end{array}\right\} \Longrightarrow (a_2, o_2) \vdash (a_3, o_3) : u_2$$

Proof. By a case analysis of u_1 and u_2 and inspection of Figures 4 and 5. The argument for the second part depends essentially on the fact that, if there exists a u_2 such that $u_1 \rhd u_2 \neq$ lost then it is unique (in other words, $u_1 \rhd u_2 = u_1 \rhd u_2' \neq$ lost implies that $u_2 = u_2'$). This can be seen by inspection of Figure 5. □

Example 3.5 (Viewpoint adaptation). *From judgements (2) and (3) from Example 3.1, using Lemma 3.4, we derive*

$$(2, 1) \vdash (4, 2) : \mathit{rep} \tag{6}$$

because $\mathit{rep} \rhd \mathit{peer} = \mathit{rep}$*. Conversely, from (2) and (6), using Lemma 3.4 and* $\mathit{rep} = \mathit{rep} \rhd \mathit{peer} \neq \mathit{lost}$*, we recover (3)*

$$(3, 2) \vdash (4, 2) : \mathit{peer}$$

4 Operational Semantics

We give the semantics of our Java subset in terms of a small-step operational semantics. We assume a countably infinite set of addresses, ranged over by a, b.

$$\begin{aligned}
a, b \in \mathit{Addr} \;&:\; \mathbb{N} \\
o \in \mathit{Owner} &::= a \mid \mathsf{root} \\
v \in \mathit{Value} &::= a \mid \mathsf{null} \\[1em]
\mathit{flds} \in \mathit{Flds} \;&:\; \mathit{Id}_f \rightharpoonup \mathit{Value} \\[1em]
h \in \mathit{Heap} \;&:\; \mathit{Addr} \rightharpoonup (\mathit{Owner} \times \mathit{Id}_c \times \mathit{Flds}) \\
\sigma \in \mathit{StackFrame} \;&:\; (\mathit{Addr} \times \mathit{Value}) \\[1em]
e \in \mathit{RunExpr} &::= v \mid \mathsf{this} \mid \mathsf{x} \mid \mathsf{frame}\ \sigma\ e \mid e.f \mid e.f := e \\
&\quad\mid e.m(e) \mid \mathsf{new}\ s \mid (s)\ e \\
E[\cdot] &::= [\cdot] \mid E[\cdot].f \mid E[\cdot].f := e \mid a.f := E[\cdot] \\
&\quad\mid E[\cdot].m(e) \mid a.m(E[\cdot]) \mid (s)\ E[\cdot]
\end{aligned}$$

Fig. 6. Syntax of runtime expressions

At runtime, a value, denoted by v, may be either an address or null. Owners, denoted by o, can be either an address or the special owner root.

Runtime expressions are described in Figure 6. During execution, expressions may contain addresses as values; they may also contain the keyword this and the parameter identifier x. Thus, a runtime expression is interpreted with respect to a heap, h, which gives meaning to addresses, and a stack frame, σ, which gives meaning to the keyword this and parameter identifier x. Evaluation contexts E define expressions with 'holes' [17]; they are used in the semantics to permit reductions to take place below the top level of the expression.

A heap is defined in Figure 6 as a partial function from addresses to objects. An object is denoted by the triple (o, c, flds). Every object has an immutable owner o, belongs to a class c, and has a state, *flds*, which is a mutable field map (a partial function from field names to values). In the remaining text we use the following heap operations:

$$\begin{aligned}
\mathbf{owner}(h, a) &\stackrel{\mathbf{def}}{=} h(a)\!\downarrow_1 & \mathbf{class}(h, a) &\stackrel{\mathbf{def}}{=} h(a)\!\downarrow_2 \\
\mathbf{fields}(h, a) &\stackrel{\mathbf{def}}{=} h(a)\!\downarrow_3 & h(a.f) &\stackrel{\mathbf{def}}{=} \mathbf{fields}(h, a)(f)
\end{aligned}$$
$$h[(a, f) \mapsto v] \stackrel{\mathbf{def}}{=} h\left[a \mapsto \big(\mathbf{owner}(h, a), \mathbf{class}(h, a), \mathbf{fields}(h, a)[f \mapsto v]\big)\right]$$

The first three operations extract the components making up an object, where $\downarrow_i$ is used for the i-th projection. The fourth operation is merely a shorthand notation for *field access* in a heap. The fifth operation is *heap update*, updating the field f of an object mapped to by the address a in the heap h to the value v.

A stack frame σ is a pair (a, v), of an address and a value. The address a denotes the currently active object referred to by this whereas v denotes the value of the parameter x. We find it convenient to define the following operations on stack frames:

$$\sigma(\mathsf{this}) \stackrel{\mathbf{def}}{=} \sigma\!\downarrow_1 \qquad\qquad \sigma(\mathsf{x}) \stackrel{\mathbf{def}}{=} \sigma\!\downarrow_2$$

For evaluating method calls, we require to push and pop new address-value pairs onto the stack. To model this, runtime expressions also include the expression

$\mathsf{frame}\ \sigma\ e$, which denotes that the sub-expression e is evaluated with respect to the inner stack frame σ.

We employ a further operation called *heap extension*, written $\mathbf{alloc}(h, \sigma, s)$, which extends a heap h with a new mapping from a *fresh* address a to a newly-initialised object of type s; it is defined by the following function:

$$\begin{array}{l} \mathbf{alloc}(h, \sigma, u\, c) \stackrel{\mathbf{def}}{=} (h', a) \quad \textit{if}\ u \in \{\mathsf{rep}, \mathsf{peer}\} \\ \quad \text{where} \\ \qquad a \notin \mathbf{dom}(h) \\ \qquad h' = h[a \mapsto (o, c, \mathit{flds})] \\ \qquad o = \begin{cases} \sigma(\mathsf{this}) & \textit{if}\ u = \mathsf{rep} \\ \mathbf{owner}(h, \sigma(\mathsf{this})) & \textit{if}\ u = \mathsf{peer} \end{cases} \\ \qquad \mathit{flds} = \{f \mapsto \mathsf{null} \mid \mathcal{F}(c, f) = \_\} \end{array}$$

The owner is initialised according to the Universe Modifier specified in the type s and the current stack frame σ. The above function is partial: it is only defined for Universe Modifiers rep and peer since the owner of a new object cannot be determined if the Universe Modifier is any. The values of the fields of class c, and all its superclasses, are initialised to null.

Expressions e are evaluated in the context of a heap h and a stack frame σ. We define the small-step semantics

$$\sigma \vdash e, h \leadsto e', h' \tag{7}$$

in terms of the reduction rules in Figure 7. We will use $\leadsto^*$ to indicate a consecutive sequence of (zero or more) small-step reductions.

$$\frac{}{\sigma \vdash \mathsf{x}, h \leadsto \sigma(\mathsf{x}), h}\ (\text{rVar}) \qquad \frac{h' = h[(a, f) \mapsto v]}{\sigma \vdash a.f := v, h \leadsto v, h'}\ (\text{rAssign})$$

$$\frac{}{\sigma \vdash \mathsf{this}, h \leadsto \sigma(\mathsf{this}), h}\ (\text{rThis}) \qquad \frac{e = \mathcal{MBody}(\mathbf{class}(h, a), m)}{\sigma \vdash a.m(v), h \leadsto \mathsf{frame}\ (a, v)\ e,\ h}\ (\text{rCall})$$

$$\frac{(h', a) = \mathbf{alloc}(h, \sigma, s)}{\sigma \vdash \mathsf{new}\ s, h \leadsto a, h'}\ (\text{rNew}) \qquad \frac{\sigma \vdash e, h \leadsto e', h'}{\sigma \vdash E[e], h \leadsto E[e'], h'}\ (\text{rEvalCtx})$$

$$\frac{h, \sigma \vdash a : s}{\sigma \vdash (s)\ a, h \leadsto a, h}\ (\text{rCast}) \qquad \frac{\sigma' \vdash e, h \leadsto e', h'}{\sigma \vdash \mathsf{frame}\ \sigma'\ e, h \leadsto \mathsf{frame}\ \sigma'\ e', h'}\ (\text{rFrame1})$$

$$\frac{}{\sigma \vdash a.f, h \leadsto h(a.f), h}\ (\text{rField}) \qquad \frac{}{\sigma \vdash \mathsf{frame}\ \sigma'\ v, h \leadsto v, h}\ (\text{rFrame2})$$

Fig. 7. Small-step operational semantics

Most of the rules in Figure 7 are straightforward. When creating a new object (rNew) the $\mathbf{alloc}(h, \sigma, s)$ function defined above determines the new heap h' and fresh address a. In (rCall), a method call creates a new stack frame σ'

to evaluate the body of the method, where $\sigma'(\mathsf{this})$ is the receiver object a and $\sigma'(\mathsf{x})$ is the value passed by the call, v. Once a frame evaluates to a value v, we discard the sub-frame and return to the outer frame, as shown in (RFRAME2). We also note that the rule (REVALCTX) dictates the evaluation order of an expression, based on the evaluation contexts $E[\cdot]$ defined in Figure 6. The type judgement in rule (RCAST) expresses that the object at address a has type s; see Subsection 5.3. Note that the source expression null is identical to the value null, which makes a special rule dispensable.

Example 4.1 (Runtime execution). *Let h denote the heap depicted in Figure 1 and the current stack frame be $\sigma = (2, 9)$. Then, if we consider the program in Figure 2, and execute the expression* **this***.push(7) we get the following reductions*[4]*, where the rule names on the side indicate the main reduction rule applied to derive the reduction. We simplify the example slightly, by not mentioning the use of context rules (*REVALCTXT*) and (*RFRAME1*).*

$$
\begin{array}{ll}
\sigma \vdash \textbf{this}.\mathit{push(7)}, h \rightsquigarrow \mathit{2.push(7)},\ h & (\text{RTHIS}) \\
\quad \rightsquigarrow \mathit{frame}\ \sigma'\ \textbf{this}.\mathit{top}{:=}\ \textbf{new rep}\ \mathit{Node(x,}\ \textbf{this}.\mathit{top)},\ h & (\text{RCALL}) \\
\quad \rightsquigarrow \mathit{frame}\ \sigma'\ \mathit{2.top}{:=}\ \textbf{new rep}\ \mathit{Node(x,}\ \textbf{this}.\mathit{top)},\ h & (\text{RTHIS}) \\
\quad \rightsquigarrow \mathit{frame}\ \sigma'\ \mathit{2.top}{:=}\ \textbf{new rep}\ \mathit{Node(7,}\ \textbf{this}.\mathit{top)},\ h & (\text{RVAR}) \\
\quad \rightsquigarrow \mathit{frame}\ \sigma'\ \mathit{2.top}{:=}\ \textbf{new rep}\ \mathit{Node(7,\ 2.top)},\ h & (\text{RTHIS}) \\
\quad \rightsquigarrow \mathit{frame}\ \sigma'\ \mathit{2.top}{:=}\ \textbf{new rep}\ \mathit{Node(7,\ 3)},\ h & (\text{RFIELD}) \\
\quad \rightsquigarrow \mathit{frame}\ \sigma'\ \mathit{2.top}{:=}\ \mathit{14},\ h' & (\text{RNEW}) \\
\quad \rightsquigarrow \mathit{frame}\ \sigma'\ \mathit{14},\ h'[(\mathit{2, top}) \mapsto \mathit{14}] & (\text{RASSIGN}) \\
\quad \rightsquigarrow\ \mathit{14},\ h'[(\mathit{2, top}) \mapsto \mathit{14}] & (\text{RFRAME2})
\end{array}
$$

where $\sigma' = (2, 7)$, $h' = h \uplus \{14 \mapsto (2, Node, \{\mathit{value} \mapsto 7,\ \mathit{next} \mapsto 3\})\}$, and 14 is a fresh address in the heap h.

5 Topological System

In this section, we define the Topological Type System for UT. The formalism is based on earlier work [26,15], but has some differences: as we said in the introduction, we focus here on the hierarchical topology imposed by Universe Types, but do not enforce the *owner-as-modifier discipline* at this stage—this is dealt with in Section 6. The main result of this section is Topological Subject Reduction, stating that a type assigned to an expression and the ownership hierarchical heap structure are preserved during execution.

[4] In order to follow the Java code of Figure 2, the reductions use an object constructor that immediately initialises values to the parameters passed. This is more advanced than the simpler new construct considered in our language, which initialises all the fields of a fresh object to null. These details are however orthogonal to the determination of the owner of the object upon creation, which is the relevant issue for our work. Similarly, we return the value of the method body even if the method is declared to be **void**.

5.1 Subtyping and Viewpoint Adaptation

As was already stated in Section 2, types, t, are made up of two components: a Universe Modifier u and a class name c. Using the Universe ordering $\leq_u$ of Section 3.1 and subclassing $\leq_c$, we define the subtype relation as:

$$u\ c \leq u'\ c' \stackrel{\textbf{def}}{=} u \leq_u u' \text{ and } c \leq_c c' \tag{8}$$

We extend $\triangleright$ defined in Section 3.2 for Universe Modifiers, to an operator on a Universe Modifier and a type, and that produces a type, denoted by $u \triangleright t$:

$$u \triangleright (u'\ c) \stackrel{\textbf{def}}{=} (u \triangleright u')\ c$$

We use this auxiliary operator whenever we need to change the viewpoint of the types.

5.2 Static Types

We type-check UT source expressions with respect to a type environment Γ, which keeps type information for this and the method parameter x. The types in a method signature are meant to be interpreted with respect to this, the currently active object. We assign the self Universe Modifier to $\Gamma(\mathsf{this})$ when type-checking method bodies and note that $\mathsf{self} \triangleright u = u$ for all u.

The use of a specific self Universe Modifier is a variation from previous models of the Universe Type System [14,15,26] and of other ownership type systems. In the work on Universe Types, the expression this was treated separately, viewpoint adaptation was omitted for access through this, and additional checks had to be made to ensure the protection of the representation of an object. This special treatment of the this expression can also be compared to the *static visibility constraint* of Ownership Types [10], which ensures that a type that contains rep is only accessible by this. Even when not enforcing the static visibility constraint, the this parameter in a type needs to be treated specially upon type application [1,4]. The use of a special self ownership modifier makes the special role of the current object more explicit, while at the same time simplifying the overall system[5]. For example, attempting to update the representation of another object using a peer reference results in lost ownership information, i.e., $\mathsf{peer} \triangleright \mathsf{rep} = \mathsf{lost}$ and the update is forbidden. On the other hand, updating the representation of the current object preserves ownership information, i.e., $\mathsf{self} \triangleright \mathsf{rep} = \mathsf{rep}$ and an update is allowed.

Definition 5.1 (Type environment). *A type environment Γ consists of a pair of types, (t, t'), assigning types to the currently active object* this *and the parameter* x*, respectively. We define the following operations on Γ:*

$$\Gamma(\mathit{this}) \stackrel{\mathit{def}}{=} \Gamma{\downarrow_1} \qquad\qquad \Gamma(\mathsf{x}) \stackrel{\mathit{def}}{=} \Gamma{\downarrow_2}$$

[5] Note that in the works mentioned on Ownership Types [10,1,4], types such as A<this> or A<self> do *not* correspond with our Universe Modifier self (which indicates the current receiver): their types would instead be represented in our system by the type rep A.

The source expression type judgement takes the form

$$\Gamma \vdash e : t$$

denoting that expression e has type t with respect to the type environment Γ. Note that we do not restrict t to source types; although only source types may be written explicitly in the program, an inferred Universe Modifier may well be lost, for example. The judgement is defined as the least relation satisfying the rules given in Figure 8. We sometimes find it convenient to use the shorthand judgement notation

$$\Gamma \vdash e : u \qquad\qquad \Gamma \vdash e : c$$

whenever components of the type judgement are not important, that is $\Gamma \vdash e : u\ \_$ and $\Gamma \vdash e : \_\ c$, respectively. Most of the rules are standard, with the exception of the type rules (FIELD), (ASSIGN) and (CALL), which use the auxiliary operation $u \rhd t$ to *adapt* types from one viewpoint to another. For example, consider the rule for field lookup (FIELD). The first premise says that e can be assigned class c, and that from the current point of view, e's position in the heap topology can be described by Universe Modifier u. The second premise states that the field f is declared in class c as having source type s. Since the Universe Modifier of s describes the location of the field with respect to the point of view of e, to assign a type for this field from the *current* point of view, we take into account e's relative position; that is, we adapt the type s with respect to u.

Example 5.2 (Type viewpoint adaptation). *If* $\Gamma \vdash \mathsf{this.top} : \mathsf{rep\ Node}$ *and field* next *in class* Node *has type* $\mathsf{peer\ Node}$*, then using (*FIELD*), the dereference* $\mathsf{this.top.next}$ *has type* $\mathsf{rep} \rhd (\mathsf{peer\ Node}) = \mathsf{rep\ Node}$*, that is*

$$\Gamma \vdash \mathsf{this.top.next} : \mathsf{rep\ Node}$$

*Conversely, we use (*ASSIGN*) to check that when*

$$\Gamma \vdash \mathsf{this.top} : \mathsf{rep\ Node} \qquad \textit{and} \qquad \Gamma \vdash \mathsf{new\ rep\ Node} : \mathsf{rep\ Node}$$

then the assignment $\mathsf{this.top.next} := \mathsf{new\ rep\ Node}$ *respects the field type assigned to* next *in class* Node*. For this calculation we use*

$$\begin{aligned} \mathcal{F}(\mathsf{Node}, \mathsf{next}) &= \mathsf{peer}\ \mathrm{Node} \\ \mathsf{rep} \rhd \mathsf{peer} &= \mathsf{rep}\ \neq \mathsf{lost} \end{aligned}$$

The source expression type judgement allows us to define well-formed classes by requiring consistency between subclasses. In particular, we require that field types in a subclass match those in any superclasses in which the same fields are present (this requirement is trivially met if fields cannot be overridden), and method signatures in subclasses are specialisations of the signatures of overridden methods. In addition to the usual variance on argument and return types, we allow pure methods to override impure methods (but not the opposite).

$$\frac{}{\Gamma \vdash \mathsf{null} : t}(\textsc{Null}) \qquad \frac{}{\Gamma \vdash \mathsf{x} : \Gamma(\mathsf{x})}(\textsc{Var}) \qquad \frac{}{\Gamma \vdash \mathsf{this} : \Gamma(\mathsf{this})}(\textsc{This})$$

$$\frac{\Gamma \vdash e : t}{\Gamma \vdash (s)\ e : s}(\textsc{Cast}) \qquad \frac{u \in \{\mathsf{rep}, \mathsf{peer}\}}{\Gamma \vdash \mathsf{new}\ u\ c : u\ c}(\textsc{New})$$

$$\frac{\Gamma \vdash e : t' \quad t' \leq t}{\Gamma \vdash e : t}(\textsc{Sub}) \qquad \frac{\Gamma \vdash e : u\ c \quad \mathcal{F}(c, f) = s}{\Gamma \vdash e.f : u \rhd s}(\textsc{Field})$$

$$\frac{\Gamma \vdash e : u\ c \quad \mathcal{F}(c, f) = s \quad u \rhd s \neq \mathsf{lost}\ \_ \quad \Gamma \vdash e' : u \rhd s}{\Gamma \vdash e.f := e' : u \rhd s}(\textsc{Assign}) \qquad \frac{\Gamma \vdash e : u\ c \quad \mathcal{M}(c, m) = \_ : s_r\ (s_x) \quad u \rhd s_x \neq \mathsf{lost}\ \_ \quad \Gamma \vdash e' : u \rhd s_x}{\Gamma \vdash e.m(e') : u \rhd s_r}(\textsc{Call})$$

Fig. 8. Source type system

Furthermore, we require that method bodies are consistent with their signatures. A program P is *well-formed* if all the defined classes are well-formed:

Definition 5.3 (Well-formed classes and programs)

$$\frac{\begin{array}{l}\forall c' \ .\ (c \leq_c c' \ \wedge\ \mathcal{F}(c', f) = s) \Longrightarrow \mathcal{F}(c, f) = s \\ \forall c' \ .\ (c \leq_c c' \ \wedge\ \mathcal{M}(c', m) = p' : s'_r\ (s'_x)) \\ \qquad\qquad\qquad\qquad \Longrightarrow \mathcal{M}(c, m) = p : s_r\ (s_x) \\ \qquad\quad \textit{where}\ \ s_r \leq s'_r \ \ \textit{and}\ \ s'_x \leq s_x \\ \qquad\quad\ \ \textit{and}\ \ p' = \mathit{pure} \Rightarrow p = \mathit{pure} \\ \forall m\ .\ \mathcal{M}(c, m) = \_ : s_r\ (s_x) \Longrightarrow (\mathit{self}\ c, s_x) \vdash \mathit{MBody}(c, m) : s_r\end{array}}{\vdash c}(\textsc{WFClass})$$

$$\vdash P \iff (\forall c \in Id_c\ .\ \vdash c)$$

5.3 Runtime Types

We define a type system for runtime expressions. These are type-checked with respect to the stack frame σ, which contains actual values for the current receiver this and the parameter x. Since runtime expressions also contain addresses, we also need to type-check them with respect to the current heap, so as to retrieve the class membership and owner information for addresses.

The runtime Universe Type System allows us to assign Universe Types to runtime expressions with respect to a particular heap h and stack frame σ, through a judgement of the form

$$h, \sigma \vdash e : t$$

It is defined as the least relation satisfying the rules in Figure 9. Once again, we use the shorthand notation $h, \sigma \vdash e : u$ and $h, \sigma \vdash e : c$ whenever the other component of t in the judgement is not important. In the rule (tAddr), the type of an address in a heap is derived from the class of the object and the Universe Modifier obtained using judgement (1) of Section 3. The three rules (tFIELD), (tASSIGN) and (tCALL) use viewpoint adaptation in the same way as their static-expression counterparts in Figure 8. The new rule (tFRAME) also uses viewpoint adaptation to adapt the type of the sub-expression, obtained with respect to the local stack frame, to the current frame's viewpoint.

$$\frac{}{h, \sigma \vdash \mathsf{null} : t}(\text{tNULL}) \qquad \frac{h, \sigma \vdash \sigma(\mathsf{x}) : t}{h, \sigma \vdash \mathsf{x} : t}(\text{tVAR}) \qquad \frac{h, \sigma \vdash \sigma(\mathsf{this}) : t}{h, \sigma \vdash \mathsf{this} : t}(\text{tTHIS})$$

$$\frac{h, \sigma \vdash e : t}{h, \sigma \vdash (s)\ e : s}(\text{tCAST}) \qquad \frac{h, \sigma \vdash e : t' \quad t' \leq t}{h, \sigma \vdash e : t}(\text{tSUB}) \qquad \frac{u \in \{\mathsf{rep}, \mathsf{peer}\}}{h, \sigma \vdash \mathsf{new}\ u\ c : u\ c}(\text{tNEW})$$

$$\frac{\mathbf{class}(h, a) = c \quad (\sigma(\mathsf{this}), \mathbf{owner}(h, \sigma(\mathsf{this}))) \vdash (a, \mathbf{owner}(h, a)) : u}{h, \sigma \vdash a : u\ c}(\text{tADDR})$$

$$\frac{h, \sigma \vdash e : u\ c \quad \mathcal{F}(c, f) = s}{h, \sigma \vdash e.f : u \rhd s}(\text{tFIELD}) \qquad \frac{h, \sigma \vdash e : u\ c \quad \mathcal{F}(c, f) = s \quad u \rhd s \neq \mathsf{lost}\ \_ \quad h, \sigma \vdash e' : u \rhd s}{h, \sigma \vdash e.f := e' : u \rhd s}(\text{tASSIGN})$$

$$\frac{h, \sigma \vdash e : u\ c \quad \mathcal{M}(c, m) = \_ : s_r\ (s_x) \quad u \rhd s_x \neq \mathsf{lost}\ \_ \quad h, \sigma \vdash e' : u \rhd s_x}{h, \sigma \vdash e.m(e') : u \rhd s_r}(\text{tCALL}) \qquad \frac{h, \sigma' \vdash e : t \quad h, \sigma \vdash \sigma'(\mathsf{this}) : u}{h, \sigma \vdash \mathsf{frame}\ \sigma'\ e : u \rhd t}(\text{tFRAME})$$

Fig. 9. Runtime type system

Lemma 5.4 shows that viewpoint adaptation respects the judgements of the runtime type system. The viewpoint adaptations of Lemma 5.4 trivially hold for the case $v = \mathsf{null}$ since rule (tNULL) immediately yields the desired judgements. The proof is relegated to Appendix A.

Lemma 5.4 (Determining the relative Universe Types of values)

(i) *If* $h, \sigma \vdash a : u\ \_$ *and* $h, (a, \_) \vdash v : t$ *then* $h, \sigma \vdash v : u \rhd t$
(ii) *If* $h, \sigma \vdash a : u\ \_$ *and* $h, \sigma \vdash v : u \rhd t$ *and* $u \rhd t \neq \mathsf{lost}\ \_$ *then, for any value* v' *we have* $h, (a, v') \vdash v : t$

Example 5.5 (Relative viewpoints in a heap). *In Figure 1, using* (2) *and* (3) *from Example 3.1 and rule (*tADDR*) we derive*

$$h, (2, \_) \vdash 3 : \mathit{rep\ Node} \qquad \text{and} \qquad h, (3, \_) \vdash 4 : \mathit{peer\ Node}$$

From Lemma 5.4(i) we immediately derive

$$h, (2, \_) \vdash 4 : \mathit{rep\ Node}$$

Conversely, using $h, (2, \_) \vdash 3 : \mathsf{rep\ Node}$, $h, (2, \_) \vdash 4 : \mathsf{rep\ Node}$ *as well as Lemma 5.4(ii), we can recover* $h, (3, \_) \vdash 4 : \mathsf{peer\ Node}$.

We now have enough machinery to define well-formed addresses, heaps and stack frames (Definition 5.7). An address is well-formed in a heap whenever its owner is valid (that is, it is another address in the heap or root) and the types of its fields respect the types of the fields defined in $\mathcal{F}$. A heap is well-formed, denoted as $\vdash h$, if transitive ownership always includes root (this implies that the ownership relation is acyclic, since each address has one owner and root has no owner) and all its addresses are well-formed. Finally, a stack frame is well-formed with respect to a heap if the receiver address it contains is defined in the heap (we make no requirements about the argument on the stack, since these are enforced where necessary by the type system). We use $\mathbf{owner}^+(h, o)$ to denote the transitive closure of $\mathbf{owner}(h, o)$.

Definition 5.6 (Transitive ownership)

$$\boldsymbol{owner}^+(h, o) \stackrel{def}{=} \begin{cases} \{\boldsymbol{owner}(h, o)\} \cup \boldsymbol{owner}^+(h, \boldsymbol{owner}(h, o)) & \text{if } o \neq \mathsf{root} \\ \emptyset & \text{if } o = \mathsf{root} \end{cases}$$

Definition 5.7 (Well-formed addresses, heaps and stack frames)

$$\frac{\begin{array}{l} \boldsymbol{owner}(h, a) \in (\boldsymbol{dom}(h) \cup \{\mathsf{root}\}) \\ \boldsymbol{class}(h, a) = c \\ \forall f \ . \ \mathcal{F}(c, f) = s \implies h, (a, \_) \vdash h(a.f) : s \end{array}}{h \vdash a} (\text{WFADDR})$$

$$\frac{\forall a \ . \ a \in \boldsymbol{dom}(h) \implies \begin{cases} \mathsf{root} \in \boldsymbol{owner}^+(h, a) \\ h \vdash a \end{cases}}{\vdash h} (\text{WFHEAP})$$

$$\frac{\sigma(\mathsf{this}) \in \boldsymbol{dom}(h)}{h \vdash \sigma} (\text{WFSTACK})$$

We conclude the subsection by showing the correspondence between the source type system and runtime type system. Lemma 5.8 below states that, with respect to a suitable stack frame σ, where $\sigma(\mathsf{this})$ and $\sigma(\mathsf{x})$ match the respective type assignments in Γ, a well-typed source expression is also a well-typed runtime expression.

Lemma 5.8 (Source typing to runtime typing)

$$\left.\begin{array}{l} \Gamma \vdash e : t \\ h, \sigma \vdash \mathsf{x} : \Gamma(\mathsf{x}) \\ h, \sigma \vdash \mathsf{this} : \Gamma(\mathsf{this}) \end{array}\right\} \implies h, \sigma \vdash e : t$$

Proof. By induction on the structure of the derivation $\Gamma \vdash e : t$, considering the last rule applied. Comparing the two type systems, all cases follow by straightforward induction except for the rules (VAR) and (THIS). These are guaranteed by the conditions on σ. □

5.4 Subject Reduction

In this subsection, we present the first main result of the paper. It states that if a well-typed runtime expression e reduces with respect to a stack frame σ, and a well-formed heap h, then the resulting expression preserves its type (with respect to the new heap), and the resulting heap preserves its well-formedness as well as the well-formedness of the stack frame. Because our definition of well-formed heaps imposes strong topological constraints in correspondence with the Universe Modifiers in the program, this result means in particular that the implied topology is preserved during execution.

Theorem 5.9 (Topological Subject Reduction)
For well-formed programs, the following property holds:

$$\left.\begin{array}{l} \vdash h \\ h \vdash \sigma \\ h, \sigma \vdash e : t \\ \sigma \vdash e, h \rightsquigarrow e', h' \end{array}\right\} \Longrightarrow \left\{\begin{array}{l} \vdash h' \\ h' \vdash \sigma \\ h', \sigma \vdash e' : t \end{array}\right.$$

Proof. We build up to this result by first proving a number of intermediary lemmas concerning the evolution of the heap under reduction and extracting object information from types (see Appendix A). The owner and class components of an object in a heap are immutable during execution (Lemma A.2). During execution, we never remove existing addresses from the heap (Lemma A.3). Earlier in Section 4, we discussed how reduction rules make use of two operations to update a heap in the form of $\mathbf{alloc}(h, \sigma, s)$ and $h[(a, f) \mapsto v]$. Lemma A.4 shows that the heap extension operation creates a new object with the requested type in the heap. Lemma A.6 states that under appropriate conditions, heap update and heap extension operations preserve heap well-formedness. Lemma A.7 states that the type judgement $h, \sigma \vdash a : u\ c$ implies that the class of a in h is a subclass of c and that a has Universe Modifier u from the current viewpoint $\sigma(\mathsf{this})$. We relegate these five lemmas to Appendix A. The proof uses also Lemma 5.4 and Lemma 5.8 from Section 5.3. The main cases of the Subject Reduction proof are given in Appendix A. □

6 Encapsulation System

In Section 5, we showed how the *Topological* Type System guarantees that the topology of the objects in the heap agrees with the one described by the Universe Types. In this section, we enhance the Topological Type System and obtain the *Encapsulation* Type System. We show that the latter system guarantees the owner-as-modifier discipline [15], which localises the effects of execution in a heap with respect to the currently active object.

We prove two related theorems: the Encapsulation Theorem (6.8) guarantees that an encapsulated expression can only modify objects transitively owned by the owner of the current receiver, while the Owner-as-Modifier Theorem (6.14) guarantees that execution of an encapsulated expression starting from the initial configuration may update an object only when the object's owner is on the call stack. Notice that although related, the two theorems do not follow from each other.

In terms of our running example, the Encapsulation Theorem guarantees that execution of a method by receiver 13 can modify—at most—objects 2, 3, 4, 5 and 13. On the other hand, the Owner-as-Modifier Theorem guarantees that execution of an encapsulated expression starting from the initial configuration may modify 13 only while 1 is on the stack.

6.1 Encapsulation Types

For the subsequent discussion we find it convenient to define contexts $C[\cdot]$ which are generally used to describe the field updates and method calls present within an expression. These are more liberal than the evaluation contexts $E[\cdot]$ previously defined, which are used to specify where evaluation should next take place. For example, x.f.m(·) is a $C[\cdot]$, but not an $E[\cdot]$ context. Like $E[\cdot]$ contexts, $C[\cdot]$ contexts, are restricted to not include frame expressions, which allows us to express relationships between the sequence of stack frames in the expression (e.g., see rule (Enc) in Definition 6.2 below).

Definition 6.1 (Frame-free contexts)

$$\begin{aligned} C[\cdot] ::= & \ [\cdot] \mid C[\cdot].f \mid C[\cdot].f := e \mid e.f := C[\cdot] \\ \mid & \ C[\cdot].m(e) \mid e.m(C[\cdot]) \mid (s)\ C[\cdot] \end{aligned}$$

We will write $\mathbf{pure}(c,\ m)$ to mean that m is declared to be pure in c:

$$\mathbf{pure}(c,\ m) \stackrel{\mathbf{def}}{=} \mathcal{M}(c, m) = \mathsf{pure} : \_\ (\_)$$

The Encapsulation Type System imposes extra restrictions so as to enforce the owner-as-modifier discipline and to guarantee restrictions on the effect of method calls. We define an encapsulation judgement for expressions, $\Gamma \vdash_{\mathbf{enc}} e$, reflecting the expression restrictions needed to enforce the owner-as-modifier discipline. These restrictions state that for an expression e to respect encapsulation, it can only assign to and call impure methods on the current object, on rep receivers or on peer receivers. To determine (conservatively) when a method is actually pure, we require a purity judgement for expressions $\Gamma \vdash_{\mathbf{pure}} e$. An expression e is pure by this judgement if it never assigns to fields and *only* calls methods declared to be pure. We use this very strict notion of purity to simplify the rules. Weaker purity requirements [14,30] suffice to enforce the owner-as-modifier discipline.

Definition 6.2 (Purity and encapsulation for source expressions)

$$\frac{\begin{array}{l}\Gamma \vdash e : t \\ \forall C, e_1, e_2, f \ .\ e \neq C[e_1.f := e_2] \\ \forall C, e_1, e_2, m \ .\ e = C[e_1.m(e_2)] \Longrightarrow \exists c\ .\ \Gamma \vdash e_1 : c \wedge \boldsymbol{pure}(c, m)\end{array}}{\Gamma \vdash_{\boldsymbol{pure}} e} \text{(PURE)}$$

$$\frac{\begin{array}{l}\Gamma \vdash e : t \\ \forall C, e_1, e_2, f \ .\ e = C[e_1.f := e_2] \Longrightarrow \exists u\ .\ \Gamma \vdash e_1 : u \ \wedge \\ \qquad\qquad\qquad\qquad\qquad\qquad u \in \{\mathsf{peer}, \mathsf{rep}\} \\ \forall C, e_1, e_2, m \ .\ e = C[e_1.m(e_2)] \Longrightarrow \exists u, c\ .\ \Gamma \vdash e_1 : u\ c \ \wedge \\ \qquad\qquad\qquad\qquad\qquad (u \in \{\mathsf{peer}, \mathsf{rep}\} \vee \boldsymbol{pure}(c, m))\end{array}}{\Gamma \vdash_{\boldsymbol{enc}} e} \text{(ENC)}$$

Note that if an expression is considered pure, it automatically respects encapsulation; i.e., $\Gamma \vdash_{\mathbf{pure}} e \Rightarrow \Gamma \vdash_{\mathbf{enc}} e$.

In terms of our example code (Figure 2), suppose $\Gamma = (\mathsf{self\ Bag}, \mathsf{any\ Object})$. Then we can derive $\Gamma \vdash_{\mathbf{enc}}$ this.state.push(x), since the expression is typeable, contains no field updates and the only method call has this.state as receiver, where $\Gamma \vdash$ this.state : rep Stack.

A class is well-formed with respect to encapsulation, denoted as $\vdash_{\mathbf{enc}} c$, if and only if all pure methods have bodies that are pure, and all impure methods have bodies that are encapsulated, according to the corresponding definitions above. We recall that according to Definition 5.3, a method declared to be pure can only be overridden by another method declared to be pure. A program P is well-formed with respect to encapsulation if all its classes are encapsulated.

Definition 6.3 (Encapsulated well-formed classes and programs)

$$\frac{\begin{array}{l}\forall m\ .\ \mathcal{M}(c, m) = \mathsf{pure} : s_r\ (s_x) \Longrightarrow \\ \qquad\qquad\qquad (\mathsf{self}\ c, s_x) \vdash_{\boldsymbol{pure}} \mathcal{MBody}(c, m) \\ \forall m\ .\ \mathcal{M}(c, m) = \mathsf{impure} : s_r\ (s_x) \Longrightarrow \\ \qquad\qquad\qquad (\mathsf{self}\ c, s_x) \vdash_{\boldsymbol{enc}} \mathcal{MBody}(c, m)\end{array}}{\vdash_{\boldsymbol{enc}} c} \text{(WFENCCLASS)}$$

$$\vdash_{\boldsymbol{enc}} P \iff (\vdash P \ \wedge\ \forall c \in Id_c\ .\ \vdash_{\boldsymbol{enc}} c)$$

Example 6.4 (Comparing Topological and Encapsulation Systems). *We compare the Topological Type System and the Encapsulation Type System in the context of Example 2.1 (that is, the program from from Figure 2 and a variable* node *of type* any Node*). We explained in Example 2.1 that the update* node.value := y *is valid in the Topological Type System provided that* y*'s class is a subclass of* Object*. Since the viewpoint-adapted type of field* value *is not* lost*, the conditions of rule (*ASSIGN*) in Figure 8 are satisfied. However, the encapsulation rule (*ENC*) in Definition 6.2 forbids the update through the* any *reference* node*.*

We also define encapsulation and purity judgements for *runtime expressions* subject to a heap h and a stack frame σ; these judgements are denoted as $h, \sigma \vdash_{\mathbf{enc}} e$ and $h, \sigma \vdash_{\mathbf{pure}} e$, respectively. Encapsulation and purity for runtime expressions impose similar requirements to those for source expressions but add an extra clause for frame expressions. In particular, encapsulation for frames, $h, \sigma \vdash_{\mathbf{enc}} \mathsf{frame}\ \sigma'\ e'$, requires that the receiver in σ', that is $\sigma'(\mathsf{this})$, is a self, peer or rep of that in σ. This condition is expressed through the predicate $h \vdash \sigma' \preceq_{\mathbf{enc}} \sigma$, defined below.

Definition 6.5 (Frame encapsulation)

$$h \vdash \sigma' \preceq_{enc} \sigma \stackrel{def}{=} \exists u \in \{\mathit{peer}, \mathit{rep}\}\ .\ h, \sigma \vdash \sigma'(\mathit{this}) : u$$

Definition 6.6 (Purity and encapsulation for runtime expressions)

$$\frac{\begin{array}{l} h, \sigma \vdash e : t \\ \forall C, e_1, \sigma_1\ .\ e = C[\mathit{frame}\ \sigma_1\ e_1] \Longrightarrow h, \sigma_1 \vdash_{pure} e_1 \\ \forall C, e_1, e_2, f\ .\ e \neq C[e_1.f := e_2] \\ \forall C, e_1, e_2, m\ .\ e = C[e_1.m(e_2)] \Longrightarrow \exists c\ .\ h, \sigma \vdash e_1 : c \ \wedge\ \boldsymbol{pure}(c, m) \end{array}}{h, \sigma \vdash_{pure} e} \ (\text{RPURE})$$

$$\frac{\begin{array}{l} h, \sigma \vdash e : t \\ \forall C, e_1, \sigma_1\ .\ e = C[\mathit{frame}\ \sigma_1\ e_1] \Longrightarrow \\ \qquad (h \vdash \sigma_1 \preceq_{enc} \sigma \ \wedge\ h, \sigma_1 \vdash_{enc} e_1)\ \vee h, \sigma_1 \vdash_{pure} e_1 \\ \forall C, e_1, e_2, f\ .\ e = C[e_1.f := e_2] \Longrightarrow \\ \qquad \exists u\ .\ h, \sigma \vdash e_1 : u \ \wedge\ u \in \{\mathit{peer}, \mathit{rep}\} \\ \forall C, e_1, e_2, m\ .\ e = C[e_1.m(e_2)] \Longrightarrow \\ \qquad \exists u, c\ .\ h, \sigma \vdash e_1 : u\ c \ \wedge\ (u \in \{\mathit{peer}, \mathit{rep}\} \vee \boldsymbol{pure}(c, m)) \end{array}}{h, \sigma \vdash_{enc} e} \ (\text{RENC})$$

We can show that the source and runtime notions of purity and encapsulation are closely related.

Lemma 6.7 (Source encapsulation to runtime encapsulation)

$$\left.\begin{array}{l} \Gamma \vdash_{pure} e \\ h, \sigma \vdash \mathsf{x} : \Gamma(\mathsf{x}) \\ h, \sigma \vdash \mathit{this} : \Gamma(\mathit{this}) \end{array}\right\} \Longrightarrow h, \sigma \vdash_{pure} e$$

$$\left.\begin{array}{l} \Gamma \vdash_{enc} e \\ h, \sigma \vdash \mathsf{x} : \Gamma(\mathsf{x}) \\ h, \sigma \vdash \mathit{this} : \Gamma(\mathit{this}) \end{array}\right\} \Longrightarrow h, \sigma \vdash_{enc} e$$

Proof. Using Lemma 5.8. □

We now state the Encapsulation Theorem. It says that if an expression respects encapsulation (with respect to some h, σ), then during its execution it will only update objects that form part of the representation of the owner of the currently active object.

Theorem 6.8 (Encapsulation)

$$\left.\begin{array}{l} \vdash_{\textit{\textbf{enc}}} P \\ h, \sigma \vdash_{\textit{\textbf{enc}}} e \\ \sigma \vdash e, h \leadsto^* e', h' \\ a \in \textbf{\textit{dom}}(h) \\ \textbf{\textit{owner}}(h, \sigma(\textsf{\textit{this}})) \notin \textbf{\textit{owner}}^+(h, a) \end{array}\right\} \Longrightarrow h(a) = h'(a)$$

In terms of our running example, the Encapsulation Theorem guarantees, that execution of a method by receiver 2 (i.e., $\sigma(\mathsf{this}) = 2$) will not modify the objects 1, 6, 7, 8, 9, 10, 11 and 12. It may, however, modify the fields in 2, 3, 4, 5 and 13.

On the other hand, consider the further Stack object 13, which is also owned by 1; execution of a method by 13 would be allowed to update the fields of 2, 3, 4 and 5, for instance, by calling an impure method on 2, which in turn would update the fields of 2, 3, 4 and 5. These updates are permissible, according to our theorem, because 1, the owner of 13, is among the transitive owners of 2, 3, 4 and 5.

Before we can prove Theorem 6.8, we need to introduce a number of auxiliary lemmas. In the following lemma we show that execution preserves purity and encapsulation, and that the execution of pure expressions preserves the contents of allocated objects.

Lemma 6.9 (Preservation of purity and encapsulation)
For any program such that $\vdash_{\textit{\textbf{enc}}} P$*, if* $\sigma \vdash e, h \leadsto e', h'$ *then:*

1. *If* $h, \sigma \vdash_{\textit{\textbf{pure}}} e$ *then*
   (a) $h', \sigma \vdash_{\textit{\textbf{pure}}} e'$
   (b) $a \in \textbf{\textit{dom}}(h) \Rightarrow h'(a) = h(a)$
2. *If* $h, \sigma \vdash_{\textit{\textbf{enc}}} e$ *then*
   (a) $h', \sigma \vdash_{\textit{\textbf{enc}}} e'$

Proof. See Appendix A. □

The following definition of extended runtime contexts, $D[\cdot]$, allows for contexts within any number of nested calls: An expression e can be decomposed as $e = D[\mathsf{frame}\ \sigma\ e']$ if and only if it contains a nested method call with receiver and argument as described by σ and method body e'[6].

Definition 6.10 (Extended runtime contexts)

$$D[\cdot] ::= E[\cdot] \ \mid\ E[\mathsf{frame}\ \sigma\ D[\cdot]]$$

6 $D[\cdot]$ contexts are more liberal than $E[\cdot]$ contexts, however no such relation exists between $D[\cdot]$ and $C[\cdot]$ contexts. For example, $\mathsf{x.f.m}(\cdot)$ is a $C[\cdot]$ but not a $D[\cdot]$ context, while $a.\mathsf{m}(\mathsf{frame}\ \sigma\ \cdot)$ is a $D[\cdot]$ but not a $C[\cdot]$ context.

Lemma 6.11 guarantees that the execution of an encapsulated expression e can only modify an object a if it is directly mentioned in one of the nested calls ($e = D[\mathsf{frame}\ \sigma'\ \ E[a.f := v]]$ or $e = E[a.f := v]$, and furthermore, a must be a rep or peer of the receiver of the nested call which causes the modification. In terms of our running example, if execution of an encapsulated expression were to modify object 2, then one of the objects 1, 2 or 13 will be either the outermost receiver, or the receiver in one of the stack frames in the expression itself.

Lemma 6.11 (Encapsulated expressions have limited write effects) *If $\vdash_{enc} P$, and $h, \sigma \vdash_{enc} e$, and $\sigma \vdash e, h \rightsquigarrow e', h'$, and $h(a) \neq h'(a)$ for some $a \in \boldsymbol{dom}(h)$, then there exist $\sigma', f, v, D[\cdot]$, and $E[\cdot]$ such that*

1. $e = D[\mathsf{frame}\ \sigma'\ \ E[a.f := v]]$ *or* ($\sigma' = \sigma$ *and* $e\ = E[a.f := v]$) *and*
2. $h, \sigma' \vdash a : \mathsf{rep}$ *or* $h, \sigma' \vdash a : \mathsf{peer}$

Proof. The proof proceeds by induction on the derivation of $\sigma \vdash e, h \rightsquigarrow e', h'$ considering cases for the last rule applied in the derivation, and using the preservation of encapsulation (Lemma 6.9), and the definition of encapsulated expressions (Definition 6.6). In Appendix A we outline some interesting cases. □

Lemma 6.12 guarantees that for an encapsulated expression e, the outermost receiver ($\sigma(\mathsf{this})$), is either a peer, or a transitive owner of any of the receivers of non-pure method calls in e. In terms of our running example, if an expression e were encapsulated from the point of view of σ and contained a method call with receiver 2, i.e., if $h, \sigma \vdash_{\mathbf{enc}} \ldots \mathsf{frame}\ (2, \ldots)\ \ldots$, then the outermost receiver, i.e., $\sigma(\mathsf{this})$, will be either 13, 2 or 1.

Lemma 6.12 (Owners of receivers precede them on the stack)

$$\left.\begin{array}{l} \vdash_{enc} P \\ h, \sigma \vdash_{enc} e \\ e = D[\mathit{frame}\ \sigma'\ e'] \\ \sigma' = (a, \_) \end{array}\right\} \Longrightarrow \begin{array}{c} h, \sigma' \vdash_{pure} e' \\ or \\ \boldsymbol{owner}(h, \sigma(\mathit{this})) \in \boldsymbol{owner}^{+}(h, a) \end{array}$$

Proof. By induction on the definition of $D[\cdot]$ (c.f., Definition 6.10). We freely use the fact that any evaluation context $E[\cdot]$ is trivially an expression context $C[\cdot]$ (note that neither kind of context contain frames).

(Case: $D[\cdot] = E[\cdot]$) Then $e = E[\mathsf{frame}\ \sigma'\ e']$. By Definition 6.6, we obtain that either $h, \sigma' \vdash_{\mathbf{pure}} e'$ (in which case we are done) or $h \vdash \sigma' \preceq_{\mathbf{enc}} \sigma$. In the latter case, by Definition 6.5, we obtain that either $\sigma(\mathsf{this}) = \mathbf{owner}(h, a)$ or $\mathbf{owner}(h, \sigma(\mathsf{this})) = \mathbf{owner}(h, a)$. In either case, $\mathbf{owner}(h, \sigma(\mathsf{this})) \in \mathbf{owner}^{+}(h, a)$ as required.

(Case: $D[\cdot] = E[\mathsf{frame}\ \sigma''\ D'[\cdot]]$) Then $e = E[\mathsf{frame}\ \sigma''\ D'[\mathsf{frame}\ \sigma'\ e']$. By Definition 6.6, we obtain that either $h, \sigma' \vdash_{\mathbf{pure}} e'$ (in which case we are done) or both $h \vdash \sigma' \preceq_{\mathbf{enc}} \sigma$ and $h, \sigma' \vdash_{\mathbf{enc}} e'$. By induction, we obtain that either $h, \sigma' \vdash_{\mathbf{pure}} e'$ (and we are done) or $\mathbf{owner}(h, \sigma'(\mathsf{this})) \in \mathbf{owner}^{+}(h, a)$. By combining this latter statement with $h \vdash \sigma' \preceq_{\mathbf{enc}} \sigma$, we can show that $\mathbf{owner}(h, \sigma(\mathsf{this})) \in \mathbf{owner}^+(h, a)$ by a similar argument to the previous case. □

Using the lemmas above, we can now prove the encapsulation theorem itself.

Theorem 6.8 (Encapsulation)

$$\left.\begin{array}{l} \vdash_{enc} P \\ h, \sigma \vdash_{enc} e \\ \sigma \vdash e, h \rightsquigarrow^* e', h' \\ a \in \boldsymbol{dom}(h) \\ \boldsymbol{owner}(h, \sigma(this)) \notin \boldsymbol{owner}^+(h, a) \end{array}\right\} \Longrightarrow h(a) = h'(a)$$

Proof. We prove the equivalent assertion that $\vdash_{\mathbf{enc}} P$, and $h, \sigma \vdash_{\mathbf{enc}} e$, and $\sigma \vdash e, h \rightsquigarrow^* e', h'$, and $a \in \mathbf{dom}(h)$, and $h(a) \neq h'(a)$ imply that $\mathbf{owner}(h, \sigma(\mathsf{this})) \in \mathbf{owner}^+(h, a)$. The proof proceeds by induction over the length of the reduction of $\sigma \vdash e, h \rightsquigarrow^* e', h'$.

The base case trivially holds, since we have an execution of length zero, and thus $h = h'$.

For the inductive step, we have $\sigma \vdash e, h \rightsquigarrow^* e'', h'' \rightsquigarrow e', h'$. By application of Lemma 6.9 we obtain $h'', \sigma \vdash_{\mathbf{enc}} e''$.

1st Case $h(a) \neq h''(a)$. The assertion follows from the inductive hypothesis.

2nd Case $h(a) = h''(a)$. Because of the assumption that $h(a) \neq h'(a)$ we obtain $h''(a) \neq h'(a)$. Therefore, by the fact that $h'', \sigma \vdash_{\mathbf{enc}} e''$ and Lemma 6.11, we obtain that there exist $D[\cdot]$, $E[\cdot]$, σ' such that

$$(\ h'', \sigma' \vdash a : \mathsf{rep} \text{ or } h'', \sigma' \vdash a : \mathsf{peer})$$
$$\text{and}$$
$$(e'' = D[\mathsf{frame}\ \sigma' \ \ E[a.f := v]] \text{ or } (\sigma' = \sigma \text{ and } e'' \ = E[a.f := v])).$$

The first part of the conjunction gives $\mathbf{owner}(h'', \sigma'(\mathsf{this})) \in \mathbf{owner}^+(h'', a)$, while the latter, together with the fact that $h'', \sigma \vdash_{\mathbf{enc}} e''$ and application of Lemma 6.12 gives that $\mathbf{owner}(h'', \sigma(\mathsf{this})) \in \mathbf{owner}^+(h'', \sigma'(\mathsf{this}))$. The last two assertions give that $\mathbf{owner}(h'', \sigma(\mathsf{this})) \in \mathbf{owner}^+(h'', a)$, and because a and $\sigma(\mathsf{this})$ were already defined in h, and owners do not change during execution, we also obtain that $\mathbf{owner}(h, \sigma(\mathsf{this})) \in \mathbf{owner}^+(h, a)$. □

6.2 Owner-as-Modifier Discipline

The owner-as-modifier discipline [15] guarantees that any update to the field of an object is initiated by the object's owner. By "initiated", we mean that the owner is still on the stack when the modification takes place. This guarantee can only be made if we consider executions starting at the root of our heap topology, otherwise there is no guarantee that the call-stack will reflect the hierarchy of the heap topology.

We formalise the notion of an initial heap and stack as follows: h_{init} indicates an initial heap which only contains one object (belonging to root) at address 1, while σ_{init} indicates an initial stack, where $\sigma_{\mathsf{init}} = (1, \mathsf{null})$.

Theorem 6.14 states formally the owner-as-modifier guarantee. In terms of our running example, any modification of the fields of, say, the object 4 is, according to the owner-as-modifier discipline, guaranteed to happen only while 2 is on the stack or the outermost receiver (i.e., either a direct or an indirect caller).

We first prove Lemma 6.13 below, which guarantees that, if we consider reductions that begin from an initial heap and stack, then the resulting sequence of stack frames has the property that: either the corresponding expression is pure (in which case the frame may result from a call in an arbitrary position in the heap topology, via an any or a lost reference), or else all of the (transitive) owners (except root which is not an object anyway) of the receiver in the stack frame, are receivers in a preceding stack frame. Note that this is subtly different from the requirements on the sequence of stacks imposed by the judgement $h_{\mathsf{init}}, \sigma_{\mathsf{init}} \vdash_{\mathbf{enc}} e$, which says that *if* a stack frame is in the sequence, *then* it will conform to the restrictions imposed by the $h \vdash \preceq_{\mathbf{enc}}$ relation.

Applying Lemma 6.13 to our running example, execution of an encapsulated expression starting from the initial configuration and leading to an impure expression containing a method call with receiver 12, is guaranteed to have a method call with receiver 10, enclosing the earlier method call.

Lemma 6.13 (All owners are preserved on the stack)

$$\left.\begin{array}{l} \vdash_{enc} P \\ h_{init}, \sigma_{init} \vdash_{enc} e \\ \sigma_{init} \vdash e, h_{init} \rightsquigarrow^* e', h' \\ e' = D[\mathsf{frame}\ \sigma''\ e''] \\ a \in \boldsymbol{owner}^+(h', \sigma''(\mathsf{this})) \setminus \{\mathsf{root}, \mathit{1}\} \end{array}\right\} \Longrightarrow \begin{array}{c} h', \sigma'' \vdash_{\boldsymbol{pure}} e'' \\ or \\ \exists D'[\cdot], D''[\cdot], \sigma \ such\ that \\ D[\cdot] = D'[\mathsf{frame}\ \sigma\ D''[\cdot]], \\ and \\ \sigma(\mathsf{this}) = a \end{array}$$

Proof. By induction on the length of the reduction $\sigma_{\mathsf{init}} \vdash e, h_{\mathsf{init}} \rightsquigarrow^* e', h'$. For the base case, i.e., when $e = e'$, we use induction over the structure of $D[\cdot]$. For the inductive step, i.e., when $\sigma_{\mathsf{init}} \vdash e, h_{\mathsf{init}} \rightsquigarrow^* e'', h'' \rightsquigarrow^* e', h'$ by case analysis over the last step in the derivation. □

We now state the owner-as-modifier guarantee, and prove it using the lemma from above, the preservation of encapsulation (Lemma 6.9), and the fact that encapsulated expressions have limited write effects (Lemma 6.11).

Theorem 6.14 (Owner-as-modifier)

$$\left.\begin{array}{l} \vdash_{enc} P \\ h_{init}, \sigma_{init} \vdash_{enc} e \\ \sigma_{init} \vdash e, h_{init} \rightsquigarrow^* e', h' \rightsquigarrow e'', h'' \\ a \in \boldsymbol{dom}(h') \\ h'(a) \neq h''(a) \\ a' = \boldsymbol{owner}(h', a) \neq \mathsf{root} \end{array}\right\} \Longrightarrow \begin{array}{c} \sigma_{init}(\mathsf{this}) = a' \\ or \\ \exists D[\cdot], D'[\cdot], \sigma, e''' \ such\ that \\ e' = D[\mathsf{frame}\ \sigma\ D'[e''']], \\ and \\ \sigma(\mathsf{this}) = a' \end{array}$$

Proof. If $a' = 1$, then we are done by construction of σ_{init}. Therefore, we can proceed assuming that $a' \notin \{\mathsf{root}, 1\}$.

The first three premises and Lemma 6.9 give that $h', \sigma_{\mathsf{init}} \vdash_{\mathbf{enc}} e'$. This, together with the fourth and fifth premises, and Lemma 6.11 give that there exist f, v, $D_1[\cdot]$, $E_1[\cdot]$, σ' such that

$$(\ h', \sigma' \vdash a : \mathsf{rep} \ \text{or} \ \ h', \sigma' \vdash a : \mathsf{peer} \ )$$

$$\text{and}$$

$$(\ e' = D_1[\mathsf{frame}\ \sigma' \ \ E_1[a.f := v]] \ \text{or} \ \ (\sigma' = \sigma_{\mathsf{init}} \ \text{and} \ e' = E_1[a.f := v]) \ ).$$

The second part of the conjunction above gives the following two cases:

1st Case $\sigma' = \sigma_{\mathsf{init}}$ and $e' = E_1[a.f := v]$. Then, because $h', \sigma_{\mathsf{init}} \vdash_{\mathbf{enc}} e'$, using the definition of encapsulated expressions, we obtain that $h', \sigma_{\mathsf{init}} \vdash a : \mathsf{rep}$ (which gives that $a' = 1$, in which case we are done), or $h', \sigma_{\mathsf{init}} \vdash a : \mathsf{peer}$, (which gives that $a' = \mathsf{root}$, and then we are done again).

2nd Case $e' = D_1[\mathsf{frame}\ \sigma' \ \ E_1[a.f := v]]$. The first part of our conjunction from earlier on gives that either $\sigma'(\mathsf{this}) = a'$, or $\mathbf{owner}(h', \sigma'(\mathsf{this})) = a'$.

2.1st Case $\sigma'(\mathsf{this}) = a'$. We choose $\sigma = \sigma'$, and $D[\cdot] = D_1[\cdot]$, and $D'[\cdot] = E_1[\cdot]$, and $e''' = a.f := v$. This concludes the case.

2.2nd Case $\mathbf{owner}(h', \sigma'(\mathsf{this})) = a'$. Because $a' \notin \{\mathsf{root}, 1\}$ we can apply Lemma 6.13, and obtain that there exist further contexts $D_3[\cdot]$, $D_4[\cdot]$, and frame σ, such that $D_1[\cdot] = D_2[\mathsf{frame}\ \sigma \ \ D_3[\cdot]]$, and $\sigma(\mathsf{this}) = a'$. We now choose $D[\cdot] = D_2[\cdot]$, and $D'[\cdot] = \mathsf{frame}\ \sigma \ \ D_3[\cdot]$, and $e''' = \mathsf{frame}\ \sigma' \ \ E_1[a.f := v]$, and conclude the case. □

7 Related Work

Over the past ten years, there have been a large number of publications on ownership and ownership type systems. In this section, we discuss work that is most closely related to the focus of this paper, namely the separation of ownership topologies from encapsulation policies and the formalisation of ownership type systems.

Most ownership type systems combine the enforcement of an ownership topology and an encapsulation policy. Ownership Types [10] and its descendants [4,6,8,9,29] enforce an ownership topology as well as the owner-as-dominator encapsulation policy, which guarantees that every reference chain from an object in the root context to an object goes through the object's owner. Similarly, Universe Types [14,15,26,28] enforce an ownership topology as well as the owner-as-modifier encapsulation policy, which guarantees that every modification of an object is initiated by the object's owner. In this paper, we showed how to separate the Topological System from the Encapsulation System. This separation is facilitated by distinguishing between the 'don't care' modifier any and the 'don't know' modifier lost because the Topological Type System treats them differently.

Ownership domains [1] was the first ownership system that separated the ownership topology from the encapsulation policy. This is achieved by allowing programmers to distinguish between private and public ownership domains and to declare links between ownership domains. While the Encapsulation Type

System presented in this paper enforces a fixed encapsulation policy, it is possible to combine our Topological System with various encapsulation policies.

Dietl and Müller [16] encoded ownership types on top of Dependent Classes [19]. Dependent Classes are used to enforce the ownership topology, whereas encapsulation has to be enforced separately.

Most ownership type systems have been formalised for a small programming language similar to the one used in this paper. The formalisation of OGJ [29] is based on Java generics. Ownership information is encoded in the type parameters, which makes the formalisation simple.

Dynamic ownership [23] as available in Spec# uses ghost state to encode the ownership topology and the Boogie verification methodology to enforce an encapsulation policy similar to the one of Universe Types. The Topological Type System presented in this paper can be combined with the Boogie methodology.

Type checkers for the Universe Type System are implemented in the JML tools [12,22] and as a pluggable type system for Scala [13].

In this work, in keeping with most works on Universe or Ownership Types, each object is owned directly by at most one other object, and the ownership hierarchy forms a tree. This view can, however, be generalised to allow several direct owners, and the ownership hierarchy to form a DAG [7].

8 Conclusion

We presented UT, a new formalisation of the Universe Type System, which is given in two steps: first presenting a Topological Type System that builds the ownership topology and then augmenting it to the Encapsulation Type System. The two-step formalisation permits a gentler presentation of the mathematical machinery we develop and primarily allows for separation of concerns when extending this work, as some extensions and applications of Universe Types do not require encapsulation properties. Both of these factors facilitate the adoption of the work as a starting point for further work.

We introduced the distinction between the 'don't care' modifier any and the 'don't know' modifier lost. We proved subject reduction (for both the Topological and the Encapsulation Type System) for a small-step operational semantics of a subset of Java. Like UT most ownership type systems have been formalised on paper. We also formalised a version of Universe Types including arrays in Isabelle and proved type safety [21]. The main difference is that there we use a big-step semantics, whereas here we use a small-step semantics.

This formalisation of the Universe Type System is the basis for various future extensions. We plan to extend our work on Generic Universe Types [14] to also separate topology from encapsulation. We are also planning to improve the expressiveness of Universe Types by adding path-dependent types. Adapting the type system to Java bytecode is other future work. This will permit the use of Universe Types for the verification of mobile bytecode in a Proof-Carrying-Code architecture such as the one proposed by the Mobius project [20].

Acknowledgements

We thank our reviewer for extensive feedback and many useful suggestions.

This work was funded in part by the Information Society Technologies program of the European Commission, Future and Emerging Technologies under the IST-2005-015905 MOBIUS project, and the EPSRC grant Practical Ownership Types for Objects and Aspect Programs, EP/D061644/1.

References

1. Aldrich, J., Chambers, C.: Ownership domains: Separating aliasing policy from mechanism. In: Odersky, M. (ed.) ECOOP 2004. LNCS, vol. 3086, pp. 1–25. Springer, Heidelberg (2004)
2. Andreae, C., Coady, Y., Gibbs, C., Noble, J., Vitek, J., Zhao, T.: Scoped types and aspects for real-time java. In: Thomas, D. (ed.) ECOOP 2006. LNCS, vol. 4067, pp. 124–147. Springer, Heidelberg (2006)
3. Banerjee, A., Naumann, D.: Representation independence, confinement, and access control. In: Principles of Programming Languages (POPL), pp. 166–177. ACM Press, New York (2002)
4. Boyapati, C.: SafeJava: A Unified Type System for Safe Programming. PhD thesis, MIT (2004)
5. Boyapati, C., Lee, R., Rinard, M.: Ownership types for safe programming: Preventing data races and deadlocks. In: Object-Oriented Programming, Systems, Languages, and Applications (OOPSLA). ACM, New York (2002)
6. Boyapati, C., Liskov, B., Shrira, L.: Ownership types for object encapsulation. In: Principles of programming languages (POPL), pp. 213–223. ACM Press, New York (2003)
7. Cameron, N., Drossopoulou, S., Noble, J., Smith, M.: Multiple Ownership. In: Object-Oriented Programming, Systems, Languages, and Applications (OOPSLA), pp. 441–460. ACM Press, New York (2007)
8. Clarke, D.: Object Ownership and Containment. PhD thesis, University of New South Wales (2001)
9. Clarke, D., Drossopoulou, S.: Ownership, Encapsulation and the Disjointness of Types and Effects. In: Object-oriented programming, systems, languages, and applications (OOPSLA), pp. 292–310. ACM, New York (2002)
10. Clarke, D., Potter, J., Noble, J.: Ownership types for flexible alias protection. In: Object-Oriented Programming, Systems, Languages, and Applications (OOPSLA), vol. 33(10), pp. 48–64. ACM Press, New York (1998)
11. Cunningham, D., Drossopoulou, S., Eisenbach, S.: Universe Types for Race Safety. In: Verification and Analysis of Multi-threaded Java-like Programs (VAMP), pp. 20–51 (2007)
12. Dietl, W.: JML2 Eclipse plug-in, `http://pm.inf.ethz.ch/research/universes/tools/eclipse/`
13. Dietl, W.: Universe type system tools for Scala, `http://pm.inf.ethz.ch/research/universes/tools/scala/`
14. Dietl, W., Drossopoulou, S., Müller, P.: Generic universe types. In: Ernst, E. (ed.) ECOOP 2007. LNCS, vol. 4609, pp. 28–53. Springer, Heidelberg (2007)

15. Dietl, W., Müller, P.: Universes: Lightweight ownership for JML. Journal of Object Technology (JOT) 4(8), 5–32 (2005)
16. Dietl, W., Müller, P.: Ownership type systems and dependent classes. In: Foundations of Object-Oriented Languages (FOOL) (2008)
17. Felleisen, M., Friedman, D.P., Kohlbecker, E., Duba, B.: A syntactic theory of sequential control. Journal of Theoretical Computer Science 52, 205–237 (1987)
18. Flanagan, C., Qadeer, S.: Types for atomicity. In: Types in Language Design and Implementation (TLDI), pp. 1–12. ACM Press, New York (2003)
19. Gasiunas, V., Mezini, M., Ostermann, K.: Dependent classes. In: Object-Oriented Programming, Systems, Languages, and Applications (OOPSLA), pp. 133–152. ACM Press, New York (2007)
20. Global Computing Proactive Initiative. Mobius: Mobility, Ubiquity and Security. IST-15905, `http://mobius.inria.fr/`
21. Klebermaß, M.: An Isabelle formalization of the Universe Type System. Master's thesis, Technical University Munich and ETH Zurich (2007), `http://pm.inf.ethz.ch/projects/student_docs/Martin_Klebermass/`
22. Leavens, G.T., Poll, E., Clifton, C., Cheon, Y., Ruby, C., Cok, D., Müller, P., Kiniry, J., Chalin, P., Zimmerman, D.M., Dietl, W.: JML reference manual. Department of Computer Science, Iowa State University (2008), `http://www.jmlspecs.org`
23. Leino, K.R.M., Müller, P.: Object invariants in dynamic contexts. In: Odersky, M. (ed.) ECOOP 2004. LNCS, vol. 3086, pp. 491–516. Springer, Heidelberg (2004)
24. Lu, Y., Potter, J.: Protecting Representation with Effect Encapsulation. In: Principles of programming languages (POPL), pp. 359–371. ACM Press, New York (2006)
25. Mitchell, J.C., Plotkin, G.D.: Abstract types have existential type. ACM Trans. Program. Lang. Syst. 10(3), 470–502 (1988)
26. Müller, P.: Modular Specification and Verification of Object-Oriented Programs. LNCS, vol. 2262. Springer, Heidelberg (2002)
27. Müller, P., Poetzsch-Heffter, A., Leavens, G.T.: Modular invariants for layered object structures. Science of Computer Programming 62, 253–286 (2006)
28. Müller, P., Rudich, A.: Ownership transfer in Universe Types. In: Object-Oriented Programming, Systems, Languages and Applications (OOPSLA), pp. 461–478. ACM Press, New York (2007)
29. Potanin, A., Noble, J., Clarke, D., Biddle, R.: Generic ownership for generic Java. In: Object-Oriented Programming Systems, Languages, and Applications (OOPSLA), pp. 311–324. ACM Press, New York (2006)
30. Salcianu, A., Rinard, M.C.: Purity and side effect analysis for java programs. In: Cousot, R. (ed.) VMCAI 2005. LNCS, vol. 3385, pp. 199–215. Springer, Heidelberg (2005)

A Supporting Results and Proofs

Lemma A.1 (Owners are defined in well-formed heap). *If* $\vdash h$ *and* $a \in \boldsymbol{dom}(h)$ *then* $(\boldsymbol{owner}^{+}(h, a) \setminus \{\mathit{root}\}) \subseteq \boldsymbol{dom}(h)$.

Proof. By induction on the definition of $\mathbf{owner}^{+}(h, a)$ using the rule (WFADDR). □

Lemma A.2 (Object owner and class preservation)

$$(i)\quad \left.\begin{array}{l} h(a) = (o, c, \_) \\ (h', a') = \mathbf{alloc}(h, \sigma, t) \end{array}\right\} \Longrightarrow \left\{\begin{array}{l} h'(a) = (o, c, \_) \\ \mathbf{owner}^+(h', a) = \mathbf{owner}^+(h, a) \end{array}\right.$$

$$(ii)\quad \left.\begin{array}{l} h(a) = (o, c, \_) \\ h' = h[(a', f) \mapsto v] \end{array}\right\} \Longrightarrow \left\{\begin{array}{l} h'(a) = (o, c, \_) \\ \mathbf{owner}^+(h', a) = \mathbf{owner}^+(h, a) \end{array}\right.$$

$$(iii)\quad \left.\begin{array}{l} h(a) = (o, c, \_) \\ \sigma \vdash e, h \rightsquigarrow e', h' \end{array}\right\} \Longrightarrow \left\{\begin{array}{l} h'(a) = (o, c, \_) \\ \mathbf{owner}^+(h', a) = \mathbf{owner}^+(h, a) \end{array}\right.$$

Proof.

(i) Immediate from the definition of $\mathbf{alloc}(h, \sigma, t)$, noting it is not possible that $a' = a$ since $a \in \mathbf{dom}(h)$ and $a' \notin \mathbf{dom}(h)$.
(ii) Follows from the definition of $h[(a', f) \mapsto v]$, in which the owner and class information is explicitly preserved.
(iii) By induction on the derivation of $\sigma \vdash e, h \rightsquigarrow e', h'$, using parts (i) and (ii). □

Lemma A.3 (Heap domain inclusion)

(i) If $(h', a) = \mathbf{alloc}(h, \sigma, t)$ *then* $a \notin \mathbf{dom}(h)$ *and* $\mathbf{dom}(h') = \mathbf{dom}(h) \cup \{a\}$
(ii) If $a \in \mathbf{dom}(h)$ *and* $h' = h[(a, f) \mapsto v]$ *then* $\mathbf{dom}(h') = \mathbf{dom}(h)$
(iii) If $\sigma \vdash e, h \rightsquigarrow e', h'$ *then* $\mathbf{dom}(h) \subseteq \mathbf{dom}(h')$

Proof.

(i) Immediate from the definition of $\mathbf{alloc}(h, \sigma, t)$.
(ii) Immediate from the definition of $h[(a, f) \mapsto v]$.
(iii) By induction on the derivation of $\sigma \vdash e, h \rightsquigarrow e', h'$, using parts (i) and (ii). □

Lemma A.4 (Soundness of object creation)

$$\left.\begin{array}{l} u \in \{\mathsf{rep}, \mathsf{peer}\} \\ h \vdash \sigma \\ (h', a) = \mathbf{alloc}(h, \sigma, u\,c) \end{array}\right\} \Longrightarrow h', \sigma \vdash a : u\,c$$

Proof. By case analysis of u, the definition of $\mathbf{alloc}(h, \sigma, u\,c)$ and using rule (TADDR). □

Lemma A.5 (Heap operations preserve value types). *If* $h, \sigma \vdash v : t$ *then*

(i) If $(h', a) = \mathbf{alloc}(h, \sigma, t')$ *then* $h', \sigma \vdash v : t$
(ii) If $h' = h[(a, f) \mapsto v']$ *then* $h', \sigma \vdash v : t$

Proof. There are two sub-cases:

$v =$ **null**: we can still derive the type judgement using (TNULL).

$v = b$: Neither of the operations change the ownership and class information of an existing object in a heap, as we saw in Lemma A.2. Thus we can still derive $h', \sigma \vdash b : t$ in both cases, using (TADDR). □

Lemma A.6 (Heap operations and well-formedness). *If $\vdash h$ and $h \vdash \sigma$ then*

(i) If $u \in \{\mathsf{rep}, \mathsf{peer}\}$ and $(h', a) = \mathbf{alloc}(h, \sigma, u\, c)$ then $\vdash h'$
(ii) If $h, \sigma \vdash a : u\, c$, $\mathcal{F}(c, f) = s$ and $h, (a, \_) \vdash v : s$ then $\vdash h[(a, f) \mapsto v]$

Proof.

(i) First, we notice that by Lemma A.3(i) and Lemma A.2(i) we know:

$$a \notin \mathbf{dom}(h) \;\wedge\; \mathbf{dom}(h') = \mathbf{dom}(h) \cup \{a\} \tag{9}$$

$$\forall b \in \mathbf{dom}(h).\; \mathbf{class}(h', b) = \mathbf{class}(h, b) \tag{10}$$

$$\forall b \in \mathbf{dom}(h).\; \mathbf{owner}(h', b) = \mathbf{owner}(h, b) \tag{11}$$

$$\forall b \in \mathbf{dom}(h).\; \mathbf{owner}^+(h', b) = \mathbf{owner}^+(h, b) \tag{12}$$

We aim to show $\vdash h'$ by rule (WFHEAP, Definition 5.7). By the assumption $\vdash h$, and the form of the rule (which is the only rule which can derive such judgements), we must have:

$$b \in \mathbf{dom}(h) \Rightarrow \mathsf{root} \in \mathbf{owner}^+(h, b) \tag{13}$$

$$\forall b \in \mathbf{dom}(h).\; h \vdash b \tag{14}$$

We show the second premise of (WFHEAP) first; i.e., that $\forall b \in \mathbf{dom}(h').\; h' \vdash b$. To show this, we consider two cases for b:

($b \neq a$): Then by (9), we know $b \in \mathbf{dom}(h)$. By (14) we have $h \vdash b$. From the form of (WFADDR), and using (10) and (11), it suffices to prove (where $\mathbf{class}(h', b) = \mathbf{class}(h, b) = c$) that $\mathcal{F}(c, f){=}s \Rightarrow h', (a, \_) \vdash h'(a.f) : s$. Since $h \vdash b$, we know that $\mathcal{F}(c, f){=}s \Rightarrow h, (b, \_) \vdash h(b.f) : s$. We complete the case by applying Lemma A.5(ii).

($b = a$): We show that the premises of (WFADDR) hold, directly to deduce $h' \vdash b$. Since $h \vdash \sigma$, we have in particular that $\sigma(\mathsf{this}) \in \mathbf{dom}(h)$. By Lemma A.1, we also know that either $\mathbf{owner}(h, \sigma(\mathsf{this})) \in \mathbf{dom}(h)$ or $\mathbf{owner}(h, \sigma(\mathsf{this})) = \mathsf{root}$. From the definition of $\mathbf{alloc}(h, \sigma, u\ c)$ we can then show $\mathbf{owner}(h', a) \in (\mathbf{dom}(h) \cup \{\mathsf{root}\}) \subseteq (\mathbf{dom}(h') \cup \{\mathsf{root}\})$. Furthermore, by Lemma A.4, we know that $h', \sigma \vdash a : u\, c$ as required.

To show the first premise of (WFHEAP), suppose that $b \in \mathbf{dom}(h')$. By (9), we know that either $b \in \mathbf{dom}(h)$ or $b = a$. In the former case, we have (by (13) and (12)), $\mathsf{root} \in \mathbf{owner}^+(h, b) = \mathbf{owner}^+(h', b)$ as required. In the latter case, from the argument above we know that $\mathbf{owner}(h', a) \in (\mathbf{dom}(h) \cup \{\mathsf{root}\})$ Therefore by (13) and the definition of $\mathbf{owner}^{+}(a, h')$, we know that $\mathsf{root} \in \mathbf{owner}^{+}(a, h')$ as required. Thus we have all the premises needed to apply the rule (WFHEAP) and obtain $\vdash h'$.

(ii) Let $h' = h[(a, f) \mapsto v]$ in what follows. We aim to deduce $\vdash h'$ by rule (WFHEAP). By Lemma A.3(ii) we know that $\mathbf{dom}(h') = \mathbf{dom}(h)$. By Lemma A.2(ii), we therefore also know that the ownership and class information defined in h is exactly that defined in h'. Therefore, given the assumption $\vdash h$, and considering the premises of the rules (WFHEAP) and (WFADDR), it suffices to prove that:

$$\left.\begin{array}{l} a' \in \mathbf{dom}(h') \\ \mathbf{class}(h', a') = c' \\ \mathcal{F}(c', f') = s' \end{array}\right\} \implies h', (a', \_) \vdash h'(a'.f') : s'$$

We now consider two cases.

Firstly, if either $a \neq a'$ or $f \neq f'$, then by definition of $h[(a, f) \mapsto v]$, we have $h'(a'.f') = h(a'.f')$. Therefore $h', (a', \_) \vdash h'(a'.f') : s'$ follows from the assumption $\vdash h$ (examining the premises of (WFHEAP) and (WFADDR)).

On the other hand, if both $a = a'$ and $f = f'$ then $c' = \mathbf{class}(h', a') = \mathbf{class}(h, a) = c$ and so $s' = \mathcal{F}(c', f') = \mathcal{F}(c, f) = s$. Therefore, it suffices to prove $h', (a, \_) \vdash h'(a.f) : s$. This follows from applying Lemma A.5(ii) to the assumption $h, (a, \_) \vdash v : s$, noting that by definition of $h[(a, f) \mapsto v]$ we have $h'(a.f) = v$. □

Lemma A.7 (Extracting information from address type judgements) *If $h, \sigma \vdash a : u\ c$ then*

(i) $a \in \mathbf{dom}(h)$
(ii) $\mathbf{class}(h, a) \leq_c c$
(iii) $(\sigma(\mathsf{this}), \mathbf{owner}(h, \sigma(\mathsf{this}))) \vdash (a, \mathbf{owner}(h, a)) : u$

Proof. By induction on the derivation of $h, \sigma \vdash a : u\ c$, specifically using the rules (TADDR), (TSUB) and Lemma 3.2. □

Lemma A.8 (Extracting information from method type judgements) *If $h, \sigma \vdash e_1.m(e_2) : t$ then there exist u_1 and c_1 such that:*

(i) $h, \sigma \vdash e_1 : u_1\ c_1$
(ii) $\mathcal{M}(c_1, m) = p : s_r(s_x)$
(iii) $u_1 \rhd s_x \neq \mathsf{lost}$
(iv) $h, \sigma \vdash e_2 : u_1 \rhd s_x$

Note that we make no requirements on how u_1 and c_1 are related to t; our assumption simply insists that the call is typeable *somehow.*

Proof. By induction on the derivation of $h, \sigma \vdash e_1.m(e_2) : t$, specifically using the rules (TCALL) and (TSUB). □

Lemma A.9 (Viewpoint adaptation preserves subtyping)

$$s \leq s' \implies u \rhd s \leq u \rhd s'$$

Proof. By case analysis of u and the relation $u_1 \leq_u u_2$. □

Lemma 5.4 (Determining the relative Universe Types of values)

(i) If $h, \sigma \vdash a : u\ \_$ and $h, (a, \_) \vdash v : t$ then $h, \sigma \vdash v : u \rhd t$
(ii) If $h, \sigma \vdash a : u\ \_$ and $h, \sigma \vdash v : u \rhd t$ and $u \rhd t \neq \mathsf{lost}$ then, for any value v' we have $h, (a, v') \vdash v : t$

Proof. Uses Lemma A.7(iii) to extract Universe determination judgement for addresses. We have two cases for v:

- If $v = \mathsf{null}$ then we can trivially derive any type judgement using (TNULL).
- If $v = b$ we use Lemma A.7(iii) to extract Universe judgements for the addresses a and b. Then we apply Lemma 3.4 and the rule (TADDR) to obtain the desired judgement. □

Theorem 5.9 (Topological Subject Reduction). *If a program is well-formed, then*

$$\left.\begin{array}{l} \vdash h \\ h \vdash \sigma \\ h, \sigma \vdash e : t \\ \sigma \vdash e, h \rightsquigarrow e', h' \end{array}\right\} \implies \left\{\begin{array}{l} \vdash h' \\ h' \vdash \sigma \\ h', \sigma \vdash e' : t \end{array}\right.$$

Proof. By induction over the structure of

$$h, \sigma \vdash e : t \tag{15}$$

The most interesting cases are when the last rules used to derive (15) are (TFIELD),(TASSIGN) and (TCALL), which we show here. We leave the other cases for the interested reader. In all cases, the conclusion $h' \vdash \sigma$ follows straightforwardly, using Lemmas A.3 and A.7 as necessary.

(tField): From the premise of the rule we know

$$e = e_1.f \tag{16}$$
$$t = u \rhd s' \tag{17}$$
$$h, \sigma \vdash e_1 : u\ c \tag{18}$$
$$\mathcal{F}(c, f) = s' \tag{19}$$

From (16) we know the reduction was derived using either (RFIELD) or (REVALCTXT).
(rField): we know:

$$e_1 = a \tag{20}$$
$$h' = h \tag{21}$$
$$e' = h(a.f) = v \tag{22}$$

From (18) and (20), and applying Lemma A.7(i), we know that

$$a \in \mathbf{dom}(h) \tag{23}$$

From $\vdash h$, the premises of the rule (WFHEAP) and (23), we know in particular that

$$h \vdash a \tag{24}$$

From (24) and the premise of (WFADDR), along with (19) and (22) we deduce

$$h, (a, \_) \vdash v : s' \tag{25}$$

By (21), (20), (18), (25) and Lemma 5.4 we obtain

$$h, \sigma \vdash v : u \rhd s'$$

The resultant heap h' is trivially shown to be well-formed from the assumption $\vdash h$ and (21).

(rEvalCtxt): we know:

$$e' = e_1'.f \tag{26}$$

$$\sigma \vdash e_1, h \leadsto e_1', h' \tag{27}$$

By $\vdash h$, (18), (27) and the inductive hypothesis we know

$$h, \sigma \vdash e_1' : u\ c \tag{28}$$

$$\vdash h' \tag{29}$$

By (28), (19), (17), (26) and (TFIELD) we derive our first required conclusion

$$h, \sigma \vdash e' : t$$

and (29) gives us the second required conclusion.

(tAssign): From the premises of the rule we know

$$e = e_1.f := e_2 \tag{30}$$

$$h, \sigma \vdash e_1 : u\ c \tag{31}$$

$$\mathcal{F}(c, f) = s \tag{32}$$

$$u \rhd s \neq \mathsf{lost} \tag{33}$$

$$h, \sigma \vdash e_2 : u \rhd s \tag{34}$$

From the structure of e, (30), we know the reduction could have been derived using either (RASSIGN) or (REVALCTXT). We here consider the former case, (RASSIGN), and leave the (easier) latter case for the interested reader. From (RASSIGN) we know:

$$e_1 = a \tag{35}$$

$$e_2 = e' = v \tag{36}$$

$$h' = h[(a, f) \mapsto v] \tag{37}$$

Applying Lemma 5.4(ii), using (35), (31), (36), (34), (33), we obtain

$$h, (a, \_) \vdash v : s \tag{38}$$

By the assumption $\vdash h$, (35), (31), (32), (38) and Lemma A.6 we get

$$\vdash h[(a, f) \mapsto v]$$

Also, by (36) and (34) we obtain

$$h, \sigma \vdash e' : u \rhd s \tag{39}$$

and by (39) and Lemma A.5 we get

$$h[(a, f) \mapsto v], \sigma \vdash e' : u \rhd s$$

as required.

(tCall): From the premises of this rule we know

$$e = e_1.m(e_2) \tag{40}$$
$$h, \sigma \vdash e_1 : u_1\ c_1 \tag{41}$$
$$\mathcal{M}(c_1, m) = p : s_1^r\ (s_1^x) \tag{42}$$
$$u_1 \rhd s_1^x \neq \mathsf{lost} \tag{43}$$
$$h, \sigma \vdash e_2 : u_1 \rhd s_1^x \tag{44}$$
$$t = u_1 \rhd s_1^r \tag{45}$$

From the structure of e derived from (40), we know the reduction could have been derived using either (rCall) or (rEvalCtx). We here consider the case for (rCall) and leave the other case for the interested reader. From (rCall) and its assumption we know

$$e_1 = a \text{ and } e_2 = v \tag{46}$$
$$h' = h \tag{47}$$
$$\sigma' = (a, v) \tag{48}$$
$$c_a = \mathbf{class}(h, a) \tag{49}$$
$$e_b = \mathcal{MBody}(c_a, m) \tag{50}$$
$$e' = \mathsf{frame}\ \sigma'\ e_b \tag{51}$$

From (47) and the assumption $\vdash h$ we know that the resulting heap is well-formed. Thus from (51), (45) we only need to show that

$$h, \sigma \vdash \mathsf{frame}\ \sigma\ 'e_b : u_1 \rhd s_1^r \tag{52}$$

The rest of the proof is dedicated to showing this.
From (41), (46), (49) and Lemma A.7 we derive

$$c_a \leq c_1 \tag{53}$$

From (53), (42), the premises of the rule (WFCLASS) and the assumption of well-formed programs, giving $\vdash c_a$, we derive

$$\mathcal{M}(c_a, m) = p : s^r \ (s^x) \tag{54}$$
$$s^r \leq s_1^r \tag{55}$$
$$s_1^x \leq s^x \tag{56}$$

Also, by (50), (54), $\vdash c_a$ and the premises of (WFCLASS) we derive

$$\Gamma \vdash e_b : s^r \tag{57}$$
$$\text{where} \quad \Gamma = (\mathsf{self}\ c_a,\ s^x) \tag{58}$$

Since $\sigma'(\mathsf{this}) = a$ (using (48)), we can use the rule (SELF) (of Figure 4) to derive

$$(\sigma'(\mathsf{this}), \mathbf{owner}(h, \sigma'(\mathsf{this}))) \vdash (a, \mathbf{owner}(h, a)) : \mathsf{self} \tag{59}$$

Using (49), (59) and (TADDR) we derive

$$h, \sigma' \vdash a : \mathsf{self}\ c_a \tag{60}$$

Also, using Lemma 5.4(ii) with (46), (48), (41), (44), we get

$$h, \sigma' \vdash v : s_1^x \tag{61}$$

and by (61), (56) and (TSUB) we derive

$$h, \sigma' \vdash v : s^x \tag{62}$$

By (48), (57), (58), (60), (62) and Lemma 5.8 we derive

$$h, \sigma' \vdash e_b : s^r \tag{63}$$

and by (63), (41), (46),(48) and (TFRAME) we get

$$h, \sigma \vdash \mathsf{frame}\ \sigma'\ e_b : u_1 \rhd s^r \tag{64}$$

From (55) and Lemma A.9 we derive

$$u_1 \rhd s^r \leq u_1 \rhd s_1^r \tag{65}$$

and thus by (64), (65) and (TSUB) we get

$$h, \sigma \vdash \mathsf{frame}\ \sigma'\ e_b : u_1 \rhd s_1^r$$

as required by (52).

□

Lemma 6.9 Preservation of purity and encapsulation. *For any program such that $\vdash_{enc} P$, if $\sigma \vdash e, h \rightsquigarrow e', h'$ then:*

1. *If* $h, \sigma \vdash_{pure} e$ *then*
   (a) $h', \sigma \vdash_{pure} e'$
   (b) $a \in \mathbf{dom}(h) \Rightarrow h'(a) = h(a)$
2. *If* $h, \sigma \vdash_{enc} e$ *then*
   (a) $h', \sigma \vdash_{enc} e'$

Proof. The proof proceeds by induction on the derivation of

$$\sigma \vdash e, h \rightsquigarrow e', h' \tag{66}$$

considering cases for the last rule applied in the derivation. We show here the interesting cases and leave the simpler ones for the interested reader.

(rAssign): Then we know

$$e = (b.f := v) \tag{67}$$

$$e' = v \tag{68}$$

$$h' = h[(b, f) \mapsto v] \tag{69}$$

From (67) we know $h, \sigma \not\vdash_{\mathbf{pure}} e$. So we do not need to consider case (1). To show case (2), we assume

$$h, \sigma \vdash_{\mathbf{enc}} b.f := v \tag{70}$$

By using (70) and unravelling Definition 6.6, we obtain that (for some type t):

$$h, \sigma \vdash e : t \tag{71}$$

By applying the Topological Subject Reduction Theorem 5.9 and using (68), we therefore know

$$h, \sigma \vdash v : t \tag{72}$$

Combining this with (69), we obtain $h', \sigma \vdash v : t$, and then apply Definition 6.6 to obtain $h', \sigma \vdash_{\mathbf{enc}} v$ as required.

(rCall): Let $c' = \mathbf{class}(h, b)$. Then we know

$$e = b.m(v) \tag{73}$$

$$e' = \mathsf{frame}\ (b, v)\ e_b \tag{74}$$

$$e_b = \mathit{MBody}(c', m) \tag{75}$$

$$h' = h \tag{76}$$

We consider the two cases we need to show in turn:
1. $(h, \sigma \vdash_{\mathbf{pure}} e)$**:** From Definition 6.6 we know that:

$$h, \sigma \vdash b.m(v) : t \tag{77}$$

$$h, \sigma \vdash b : c \tag{78}$$

$$\mathbf{pure}(c, m) \tag{79}$$

Using the rule (SELF) of Figure 4, and the rule (TADDR) we can derive

$$h, (b, v) \vdash b : \mathsf{self}\ c' \tag{80}$$

Applying rule (TTHIS), we can then deduce

$$h, (b, v) \vdash \mathsf{this} : \mathsf{self}\ c' \tag{81}$$

From the assumption $\vdash_{\mathbf{enc}} P$ we know $\vdash_{\mathbf{enc}} c$ and thus by (75) and Definition 6.3 we can write:

$$\mathcal{M}(c, m) = \mathsf{pure} : s_r\ (s_x) \tag{82}$$

By (78) and Lemma A.7, we deduce

$$c' \leq_c c \tag{83}$$

By Definition 5.3 and (82) and (83), we obtain:

$$\mathcal{M}(c', m) = \mathsf{pure} : s'_r\ (s'_x) \tag{84}$$

$$s_x \leq s'_x \tag{85}$$

$$s'_r \leq s_r \tag{86}$$

From the assumption $\vdash_{\mathbf{enc}} P$ we know $\vdash_{\mathbf{enc}} c'$ and thus by (75) and Definition 6.3 we know that:

$$(\mathsf{self}\ c',\ s'_x) \vdash_{\mathbf{pure}} e_b \tag{87}$$

Returning to (77), and applying Lemma A.8, we obtain (for some u'', c''):

$$h, \sigma \vdash b : u''\ c'' \tag{88}$$

$$\mathcal{M}(c'', m) = p : s''_r(s''_x) \tag{89}$$

$$u'' \rhd s''_x \neq \mathsf{lost} \tag{90}$$

$$h, \sigma \vdash v : u'' \rhd s''_x \tag{91}$$

We can now take (88), (90) and (91) and apply Lemma 5.4(ii) to obtain:

$$h, (b, v) \vdash v : s''_x \tag{92}$$

By (88) and Lemma A.7, we deduce

$$c' \leq_c c'' \tag{93}$$

Combining this with Definition 5.3 and (89), we obtain in particular:

$$s''_x \leq s'_x \tag{94}$$

By (92), (94), Lemma A.9 and (TSUB), we obtain

$$h, (b, v) \vdash v : s'_x \tag{95}$$

From this, we apply the rule (TVAR) to obtain

$$h, (b, v) \vdash \mathsf{x} : s'_x \tag{96}$$

and as a result of Lemma 6.7, (87), (81) and (96) we get:

$$h, (b, v) \vdash_{\mathbf{pure}} e_b \tag{97}$$

By (77), (66), (74) and the Topological Subject Reduction Theorem 5.9 we get

$$h, \sigma \vdash \mathsf{frame}\ (b, v)\ e_b : t \tag{98}$$

and hence by (97), (98), (74), (76), and Definition 6.6 we obtain

$$h', \sigma \vdash_{\mathbf{pure}} e'$$

which completes the case.

2. **($h, \sigma \vdash_{\mathbf{enc}} e$):** From Definition 6.6 we know we have two sub-cases. The first sub-case states that the method called is pure and the proof then progresses as the previous case for $h, \sigma \vdash_{\mathbf{pure}} e$. Therefore, it suffices to consider the case when, for some $u \in \{\mathsf{peer}, \mathsf{rep}\}$ and source types s_r, s_x, we have:

$$h, \sigma \vdash b : u\ c \tag{99}$$

$$h, \sigma \vdash b.m(v) : t \tag{100}$$

$$\mathcal{M}(c, m) = \mathsf{impure} : s_r\ (s_x) \tag{101}$$

Since the method m is declared impure in c, and we have assumed $\vdash_{\mathbf{enc}} P$ (and thus $\vdash_{\mathbf{enc}} c$), it follows from (75) and Definition 6.3 that we know

$$(\mathsf{self}\ c, s_x) \vdash_{\mathbf{enc}} e_b \tag{102}$$

By similar argument to the previous case, we can deduce from (99) and (100) that

$$h, (b, v) \vdash \mathsf{this} : \mathsf{self}\ c \tag{103}$$

$$h, (b, v) \vdash \mathsf{x} : s_x \tag{104}$$

and thus by (103), (104), (102) and Lemma 6.7 we get

$$h, (b, v) \vdash_{\mathbf{enc}} e_b \tag{105}$$

From (99) we derive (see Definition 6.5):

$$h \vdash (b, v) \preceq_{\mathbf{enc}} \sigma \tag{106}$$

Also, by (100), (66), (74) and the Topological Subject Reduction we know

$$h, \sigma \vdash \mathsf{frame}\ (b, v)\ e_b : t \tag{107}$$

Thus by (107), (106), (105), (74), (76). and Definition 6.6 we conclude

$$h', \sigma \vdash_{\mathbf{enc}} e'$$

as required.

(rFrame2): 1. ($h, \sigma \vdash_{\mathbf{pure}} e$): Similar to the following case.

2. ($h, \sigma \vdash_{\mathbf{enc}} e$): From the rule we know

$$e = \mathsf{frame}\ \sigma'\ v \tag{108}$$

$$e' = v \tag{109}$$

$$h' = h \tag{110}$$

From Definition 6.6 we know that either $h, \sigma' \vdash_{\mathbf{pure}} v$ or

$$h, \sigma \vdash \mathsf{frame}\ \sigma'\ v : t \tag{111}$$

$$h \vdash \sigma' \preceq_{\mathbf{enc}} \sigma \tag{112}$$

$$h, \sigma \vdash_{\mathbf{enc}} v \tag{113}$$

By (111), (66), the Topological Subject Reduction Theorem 5.9 and (109) we get

$$h, \sigma \vdash v : t \tag{114}$$

and by (114), (76), and Definition 6.6 we obtain

$$h', \sigma \vdash_{\mathbf{enc}} v$$

as required. □

Lemma 6.11 (Encapsulated expressions have limited write effects) *If $\vdash_{enc} P$, and $h, \sigma \vdash_{enc} e$, and $\sigma \vdash e, h \rightsquigarrow e', h'$, and $h(a) \neq h'(a)$ for some $a \in \boldsymbol{dom}(h)$, then there exist $\sigma', f, v, D[\cdot]$, and $E[\cdot]$ such that*

1. *$e = D[\mathsf{frame}\ \sigma'\ \ E[a.f := v]]$ or ($\sigma' = \sigma$ and $e\ = E[a.f := v]$).* *and*
2. *$h, \sigma' \vdash a : \mathsf{rep}$ or $h, \sigma' \vdash a : \mathsf{peer}$*

Proof. The proof proceeds by induction on the derivation of $\sigma \vdash e, h \rightsquigarrow e', h'$ considering cases for the last rule applied in the derivation We show here the interesting cases:

(rAssign): Then, because $h(a) \neq h'(a)$, we know that there exists a field f, and value v such that $e = (a.f := v)$, and $h' = h[(a, f) \mapsto v]$. From the latter, the encapsulation property, and the conditions of Definition 6.6 we know there exists $u \in \{\mathsf{self}, \mathsf{rep}, \mathsf{peer}\}$ such that: $h, \sigma \vdash a : u$. We choose $\sigma' = \sigma$ and $E[\cdot] = [\cdot]$, and the rest follows easily.

(rCall): Then $h' = h$, and thus the case is vacuous.
(rFrame2): Then $h' = h$, and thus the case is vacuous.
(rFrame1): Then we know that there exist σ_1, e_1 and e'_1, such that $e = \mathsf{frame}\ \sigma_1\ e_1$, and $\sigma_1 \vdash e_1, h \rightsquigarrow e'_1, h'$, and $e' = \mathsf{frame}\ \sigma_1\ e'_1$. By application of the induction hypothesis, we obtain that there exists a $\sigma', f, v, D_1[\cdot]$, and $E_1[\cdot]$ such that

1. $h, \sigma' \vdash a : \mathsf{rep}$ or $h, \sigma' \vdash a : \mathsf{peer}$
   and
2. $e_1 = D_1[\mathsf{frame}\ \sigma'\ \ E_1[a.f := v]]$, or $(\sigma' = \sigma_1$ and $e_1 = E_1[a.f := v])$.

The second part of the conjunction above gives two cases:

1st Case $e_1 = D_1[\mathsf{frame}\ \sigma'\ \ E_1[a.f := v]]$. We then choose $E[\cdot] = E_1[\cdot]$, and $D[\cdot] = \mathsf{frame}\ \sigma_1\ D_1[\mathsf{frame}\ \sigma'\ \ E_1[\cdot]]$, and the rest follows.

2nd Case $\sigma' = \sigma_1$ and $e_1 = E_1[a.f := v]$. We then choose $E[\cdot] = E_1[\cdot]$, and $D[\cdot] = \mathsf{frame}\ \sigma_1\ E[\cdot]$, and the rest follows. □

COSTA: Design and Implementation of a Cost and Termination Analyzer for Java Bytecode

E. Albert[1], P. Arenas[1], S. Genaim[2], G. Puebla[2], and D. Zanardini[2]

[1] DSIC, Complutense University of Madrid, E-28040 Madrid, Spain
[2] CLIP, Technical University of Madrid, E-28660 Boadilla del Monte, Madrid, Spain

Abstract. This paper describes the architecture of COSTA, an abstract interpretation based COSt and Termination Analyzer for Java bytecode. The system receives as input a bytecode program, (a choice of) a *resource* of interest and tries to obtain an upper bound of the resource consumption of the program. COSTA provides several non-trivial notions of cost, as the consumption of the heap, the number of bytecode instructions executed and the number of calls to a specific method. Additionally, COSTA tries to prove *termination* of the bytecode program which implies the boundedness of any resource consumption. Having cost and termination together is interesting, as both analyses share most of the machinery to, respectively, infer cost *upper bounds* and to prove that the execution length is always *finite* (i.e., the program terminates). We report on experimental results which show that COSTA can deal with programs of realistic size and complexity, including programs which use Java libraries. To the best of our knowledge, this system provides for the first time evidence that resource usage analysis can be applied to a realistic object-oriented, bytecode programming language.

1 Introduction

Research about *automatic cost analysis* goes back to the seminal work by Wegbreit in 1975 [29], which proposes to analyze the performance of a program by deriving *closed-form* expressions for its execution behavior. This approach consists of two phases.

(1) In the first phase, given a program and the description of some *cost measure*, a set of equations is produced, which captures the cost of the program in terms of the *size* of its input data. Such equations are generated by converting the iteration constructs (loops and recursion) of the program into recurrence, and by inferring *size relations* which approximate how the size of arguments varies between calls. This set of equations can be regarded as a set of *Recurrence Relations* (RR for short).
(2) The aim of the second phase is to obtain a *non-recursive* representation (solution) of the equations, known as *closed-form* solution. In most cases, it is not possible to find an exact solution, and the closed-form corresponds to an upper bound.

F.S. de Boer et al. (Eds.): FMCO 2007, LNCS 5382, pp. 113–132, 2008.

There are a good number of cost analysis frameworks for a wide variety of programming languages, including functional, logic and imperative [23,14,3]. Despite such a large amount of work, applying cost analysis to *realistic* languages, and programs with realistic size and complexity, is still an open issue, and, there is a lack of working tools.

Termination analysis [10,19] can be regarded as another kind of resource usage analysis, and it has also been studied in the context of several programming languages. Termination analysis tries to prove that a program cannot infinitely run by considering its iterative and recursive structures and by proving that the number of times they can be executed in a program run is bounded. Putting cost and termination analysis together in the same tool makes sense because of the tight relation between them: proving termination implies that the amount of resources used at runtime is finite. In practical terms, cost and termination analysis share most of the system machinery, as they need to consider and infer roughly the same information about the program. We will use the term *resource usage analysis* (RUA) to refer to either cost or termination analyses.

The present paper describes the design and implementation features of COSTA, a tool which is, to the best of our knowledge, the first RUA tool for an object-oriented, stack-based programming language, namely, *Java bytecode* [21]. The goal of the system is to infer the cost of a program with respect to some cost measure, and to prove its termination. COSTA sets up an accurate RR from the bytecode in an efficient way (phase 1 above) and is connected to a termination prover [1] and to an upper bound solver [2] to carry out phase 2. COSTA can currently work with different *cost models*, formalizing the idea of what a resource is, and how it is consumed at runtime: the *number of instructions*, $\mathcal{M}_{inst}$; the *heap consumption* in bytes, $\mathcal{M}_{heap}$; the *number of calls* to a given method, $\mathcal{M}_{calls}$ (e.g., the library method for sending text messages in mobile phones).

The system allows the user to decide whether the analysis has to consider *libraries* as part of the analyzed program, i.e., if it must go and analyze the library code, or take cost information in the form of *cost interfaces*. Interfaces are needed when some code is not available, or is written in another language. However, they can only be used if it is guaranteed that the *external* code will not generate *call-backs* to the user code. In the absence of interfaces, the system gives symbolic names to the cost of libraries, and they remain as unknown functions in the upper bound. These options make COSTA a flexible RUA tool, as we show in the next example.

Example 1. Figure 1 shows the Java and bytecode of the running example, whose most relevant feature is the use of Java *libraries*. The Java code at the top is only shown for clarity, since COSTA works directly on the bytecode. At the left-middle, we depict the bytecode of the method inter, which computes the intersection of a linked list l and an array a, both non-sorted and containing objects which implement the interface java.lang.Comparable. The class CompList is user-defined, and implements a linked list of Comparable elements in the standard way. The result of the intersection is stored in a java.util.ArrayList object al. The method main (right-middle) allocates memory for a, l and al by means of their constructors.

```
public static void inter(CompList l,Comparable[ ] a,
                         ArrayList al){
 while (l!=null){
  for (int i=0; i<a.length; i++)
     if (a[i].compareTo(l.data)==0) al.add(l.data);
  l=l.next;
 }}
```

```
public static void main (String[ ] args){
  Comparable[ ] a = new Integer[12];
  ArrayList al = new ArrayList();
  CompList l = new CompList();
  loadArray(a);
  loadList(l);
  inter(l,a,al);}
```

```
0  aload_0                       24 ifne 36
1  ifnull 50                     27 aload_2
4  iconst_0                      28 aload_0
5  istore_3                      29 getfield #2
6  iload_3                          //CompList.data
7  aload_1                       32 invokevirtual #4
8  arraylength                      //ArrayList.add
9  if_icmpge 42                  35 pop
12 aload_1                       36 iinc 3, 1
13 iload_3                       39 goto 6
14 aaload                        42 aload_0
15 aload_0                       43 getfield #5
16 getfield #2                      //CompList.next
   //CompList.data               46 astore_0
19 invokeinterface #3            47 goto 0
   //Comparable.compareTo        50 return
```

```
0  bipush 12                     21 astore_3
2  anewarray #6                  22 aload_1
   //Integer                     23 invokestatic #11
5  astore_1                         //loadArray
6  new #7                        26 aload_3
   //ArrayList                   27 invokestatic #12
9  dup                              //loadList
10 invokespecial #8              30 aload_3
   //ArrayList                   31 aload_1
13 astore_2                      32 aload_2
14 new #9                        33 invokestatic #13
   //CompList                       //inter
17 dup                           36 return
18 invokespecial #10
   //CompList
```

With libraries

$\mathcal{M}_{inst}(\mathsf{inter}) = (\mathsf{l}+1)*(\mathsf{a}*(13+c_6+c_2)+6+\max\{12+c_6, 11+c_6+c_2\})+1$

$\mathcal{M}_{inst}(\mathsf{main}) = 24*(123+c_5)+2*c_5+541$

$\mathcal{M}_{heap}(\mathsf{inter}) = (\mathsf{l}+1)*(\mathsf{a}*(c_6+c_2)+c_6+c_2)$

$\mathcal{M}_{heap}(\mathsf{main}) = 26*c_5+612$

Only user-defined code

$\mathcal{M}_{inst}(\mathsf{inter}) = (\mathsf{l}+1)*(\mathsf{a}*(13+c_6+c_2)+6+\max\{12+c_6, 11+c_6+c_2\})+1$

$\mathcal{M}_{inst}(\mathsf{main}) = 24*(13+c_6+c_2)+48+2*\max\{9, 8+c_6\}+2*c_3+12*(10+c_3)+c_4+c_1$

$\mathcal{M}_{heap}(\mathsf{inter}) = (\mathsf{l}+1)*(\mathsf{a}*(c_6+c_2)+c_6+c_2)$

$\mathcal{M}_{heap}(\mathsf{main}) = 24*(c_6+c_2)+2*c_6+14*c_3+c_4+56+c_1$

Fig. 1. The running example, with upper bounds computed for different cost models

Afterwards, calls to static methods loadArray and loadList fill, resp., the array and the list with objects of the library class java.lang.Integer, also implementing java.lang.Comparable. For brevity, the code of both static (user-defined) methods, which terminate and have constant cost, is omitted. Note that parameters a and l of inter are non-null and have constant length, and al is also non-null. At the bottom, we show the upper bounds computed by COSTA for main and inter, with the cost models $\mathcal{M}_{inst}$ and $\mathcal{M}_{heap}$. Variables a and l in the solutions denote, resp., the length of the array a and the maximal *path-length* (Sec. 5) of l. The left column is computed by analyzing all required library methods. In the right column, library methods are not analyzed; instead, their cost appears as $c_1, \ldots, c_6$, where c_1 and c_2 stand for, resp., java.util.ArrayList.ArrayList and java.util.ArrayList.add, and $c_3, \ldots, c_6$ stand for Integer.Integer, Object.Object, System.arraycopy and Comparable.compareTo, all from java.lang. When analyzing libraries, upper bounds for main depend only on the cost of c_5, which corresponds to the *native* Java method arraycopy invoked within ArrayList.add inside inter. When we analyze inter independently of main, c_2 and c_6 are not analyzed, as the objects have not been created and their class is not statically known. When libraries are not considered, c_5 is not reached. While c_1 and c_2 are invoked, resp., in main and inter, c_3 originates from loadList and loadArray, which create Integer objects by invoking their constructor. Due to *inheritance*, c_4 is also required. In $\mathcal{M}_{heap}$, inter does not consume any heap locations by itself, as it does not allocate any object. Yet, analysis considers the heap usage of c_2 and c_6, which could allocate memory. □

2 Architecture of the Cost and Termination Analyzer

Figure 2 shows the overall architecture of the COSTA analyzer. The dashed frames represent the two main phases of the analysis: (i) the transformation of the bytecode into a suitable internal representation; and (ii) the actual resource usage analysis. Input and output of the system are depicted on the left: COSTA takes a Java bytecode program *JBC* and a description of the *cost model*, and yields as output an upper bound *UB* of its cost, and information *TERM* about termination. Ellipses (as *CFG*) represent *what* the system produces at each intermediate stage of the analysis; rounded boxes (as *CFG build*) indicate the *main steps* of the analysis process; square boxes (as *class analysis*), which are connected to the main steps by dashed arrows, denote auxiliary analyses which allow to obtain more precise results or to improve efficiency.

During the first phase, depicted in the upper half of the figure, the incoming *JBC* is transformed into a *rule-based representation* (*RBR*), through the construction of the *control flow graph* (*CFG*). The purpose of this transformation (Sec. 3) is twofold:

(1) to represent the unstructured control flow of the bytecode into a procedural form (e.g., `goto` statements are transformed into recursion); and
(2) to have a uniform treatment of variables (e.g., operand stack cells are represented as local variables).

Several optimizations are performed on the rule-based representation to enable more efficient and accurate subsequent analyses: in particular, *class analysis* is used to approximate the method instances which can be actually called at a given program point in case of virtual invocation; *loop extraction* makes it possible to effectively deal with nested loops by extracting loop-like constructs from the control flow graph; *stack variables elimination*, *constant propagation* and *static single assignment* make the rest of the analyses simpler, more efficient

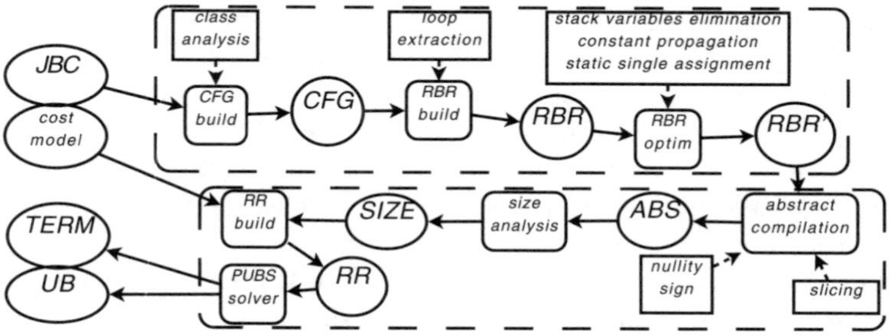

Fig. 2. Architecture of COSTA

and precise. Essentially, the construction of the RBR turns out to be effective for developing a (compositional) RUA (Sec. 3.5).

In the second phase, depicted in the lower half of the figure, the system performs cost and termination analysis on the RBR. *Abstract compilation*, which is helped by auxiliary static analyses, prepares the input to *size analysis*, whose aim is to find interesting relations between execution states (Sec. 5). As usual in object-oriented languages, *nullity* analysis improves the accuracy of size analysis, together with *class analysis*, which was performed previously. Finally, *sign* analysis helps in dealing with operations on integers. Afterwards, COSTA sets up a *Recurrence Relation* (RR) for the selected *cost model*. The latter is given as an input, selected among the available models. It is also trivial to define new cost models in the system by just associating a cost to each bytecode instruction. For the purpose of cost, the system performs *slicing* of the RBR in order to remove those variables which are *useless* to cost analysis. Up to this point, phase (1) in Sec. 1 has basically been achieved. In order to deal with phase (2), COSTA integrates the dedicated *upper bound solver* of [2,1], which finds closed-form solutions for RRs and proves termination (Sec. 6).

3 From the Bytecode to the Rule-Based Representation

Unlike other bytecode analyses performed directly on the CFG, in order to study cost and termination, an essential step is to transform the JBC into an appropriate *recursive* rule-based representation. Basically, this will facilitate the task of identifying loops (necessary for termination), and producing a recurrence relation from (the RBR of) the bytecode which represents its cost.

3.1 The Java Bytecode Language

A (sequential) JBC program consists of a set of *class files*, one for each class. A class file contains information about its name, the class it extends, and the fields and methods it defines. Each *method* has a unique *signature* m containing the class where it is defined, its name and its type. The bytecode associated to m is a sequence $\langle pc_1{:}b_1, \ldots, pc_n{:}b_n \rangle$, where each b_i is a *bytecode instruction* and pc_i is its address. Local variables are denoted by $\langle l_0, \ldots, l_{k-1} \rangle$, where l_0 is the *this* reference (explicit in JBC) and $l_1, \ldots, l_n$, with $n < k$, are the formal parameters of m. Similarly, each *field* f has a unique signature, containing its name and the name of the class it belongs to. It is out of the scope of this paper to provide a thorough description of the JVM (see the specification [21] for details).

Example 2. Let us explain some instructions in Fig. 1 related to object-oriented features. Indexes 0, ..., 3 in the bytecode correspond, resp., to parameters l, a, al and the local variable i. As the method is static, there is no *this* reference. The instruction 15: aload_0 pushes the reference to l on the stack. Next instruction, 16: getfield #2;, fetches the field data from l: the top of the stack l is popped, and #2 is used to build an index of the runtime constant pool (RCP) of the class where the reference to the name is stored. When this reference is fetched, it is pushed on the stack. As another example, 19: invokeinterface #3 pops a[i] and l.data from the stack, and searches the *closest method* with the correct signature, by looking up first in the class of the dispatching object, and then going *up* in the inheritance chain. As before, #3 is used to search the name of the method in the RCP. The method result is then pushed on the stack. □

The execution environment of the JVM consists of a *stack of activation records* and a *heap*. Each activation record contains a program counter, a local operand stack, and a table of local variables. The heap is a global data structure which contains objects (and arrays) allocated by the program. Each method invocation generates a new activation record according to its signature, number and type of local variables, and maximum size of operand stack. Different activation may contain references to the same objects in the heap.

3.2 Generation of Control Flow Graphs Guided by Class Analysis

The control flow of JBC is unstructured. Conditional and unconditional jumps are allowed, as well as other implicit sources of branching such as virtual method invocation and exception throwing. The notion of *Control Flow Graph* (CFG) facilitates reasoning about programs in unstructured languages. COSTA transforms the bytecode of a method into CFGs by using techniques from compiler theory. In particular, the instruction sequence is split into maximal sub-sequences of *non-branching* instructions, which form the *basic blocks* (nodes) of the initial graph. Basic blocks of a method m are given a unique identifier m_i, where i is an index, and are connected by *guarded* edges which describe all possible transitions.

Guarded edges are introduced by considering the last bytecode instruction of each block, and represent the condition for the control going from one block to another one. Edges take the form $\langle m_i \mapsto m_j, \phi_{ij} \rangle$, where m_i and m_j are the source and destination nodes, and ϕ_{ij} is a boolean condition. Branching instructions include conditional jumps, dynamic dispatching and exceptions.

Example 3. Figure 3 depicts the CFGs of method inter (Ex. 1). The edge from inter_1 to inter_2 takes the form $\langle \mathsf{inter}_1 \mapsto \mathsf{inter}_2, \mathsf{ifnonnull} \rangle$, indicating that the top of the stack must be non-null for the control going from *pc* 1 (last instruction of inter_1) to 4 (first one of inter_2). Guards which are always true are left implicit. □

Virtual invocation implies that more than one method can be executed at a given program point. In practice, computing a precise approximation of the *reachable* methods is not trivial, and asking the user to provide such information is not practical. As customary in the analysis of OO languages, COSTA uses *class analysis* [25] in order to precisely approximate this information. First, the CFG of the initial method is built, and class analysis is applied in order to approximate the possible runtime classes at each program point. This information is used to *resolve* virtual invocations. Methods which can be called at runtime are loaded, and their corresponding CFGs are constructed. Class analysis is applied to their body to include possibly more classes, and the process continues iteratively.

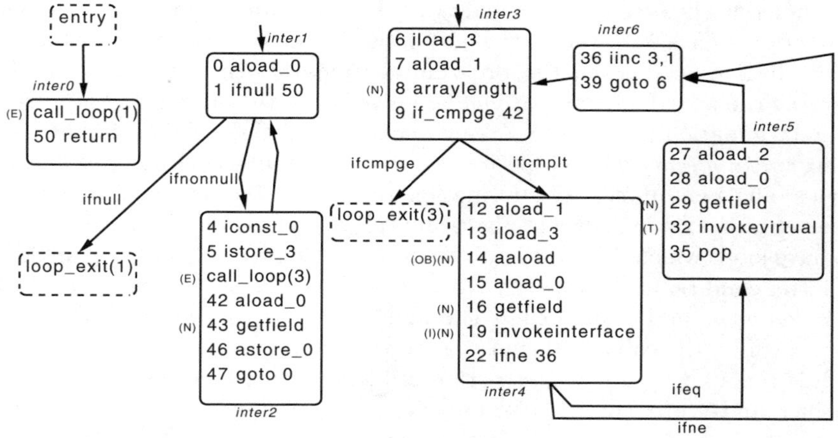

Fig. 3. CFGs for the Java bytecode program in Fig. 1 after loop extraction

Once a fixpoint is reached, it is guaranteed that all reachable methods have been loaded, and the corresponding CFGs have been generated. To handle realistic programs, we implemented a simple class analysis which does not keep class information at the level of reference variables, but just computes the set of reachable classes from any point in the program. This simple class analysis turned out to be crucial for the overall practicality of the analyzer, especially to analyze methods which are defined in the Object class as those found in most libraries. The simple class analysis used drastically reduces the number of methods to be analyzed while remaining quite efficient in practice. In the running example, class analysis detects that only one instance (the one in java.lang.Integer) of compareTo and add can be called resp. at bytecodes 19 and 32, so that virtual invocations invokeinterface and invokevirtual can be actually considered as *non-branching*.

As regards *exceptions*, COSTA handles internal exceptions (i.e., those associated to bytecodes as stated in the JVM specification), exceptions which are thrown (bytecode athrow) and possibly propagated back in methods, as well as finally clauses (even if they are compiled using the bytecode jsr). Exceptions are handled by adding edges to the corresponding handlers. When the type of the exception is not statically known, as it happens when exceptions come from calls to methods, mutually exclusive edges are generated, which capture all possible instantiations. In order to infer resource usage, COSTA provides the options of ignoring only internal exceptions, all possible exceptions or considering them all. In Fig. 3, exceptions are not explicitly shown as edges; instead, they are indicated by marks (*) (see Ex. 4 and 5) in bytecodes producing them. For instance, bytecode 8 might generate a (N) exception if a is null in the call (of a.length).

3.3 Compositional Analysis by Means of Loop Extraction

A subsequent *loop extraction* transformation is applied to the initial CFG in order to separate sub-graphs corresponding to loops. Loop extraction has been well studied in the area of program decompilation [6] and it has been proposed in termination analysis [1]; yet, to the best of our knowledge, its use in cost analysis is new. It is crucial when the program contains *nested loops*, since it allows analyzing the program *compositionally*, in the sense that it is possible to reason on the termination and cost by taking one loop at a time. This is important for finding *ranking functions*, which are required to bound the number of iterations of loops (an essential piece of information for both cost and termination). COSTA implements an existing efficient algorithm [26] to identify the loops, and modifies it to have loops which, in addition to having a single entry, also have a single exit. The latter condition is required to avoid multiple return branches from loops, and is allowed when additional exits correspond to exceptions which can be caught and thrown by the caller. Whenever a loop is extracted, the corresponding sub-graph is replaced by a new instruction $\mathsf{call\_loop}(j, \overline{o})$, where j is a fresh integer identifier, and $\overline{o}$ (often omitted for brevity) is the set of local variables of m which are modified by the execution of the loop. Besides, a new CFG is generated for each sub-graph, whose entry block has m_j as its identifier. Hence, after extracting the loops, there is one CFG which corresponds to the entry of m, and the remaining CFGs correspond to loops.

Example 4. Figure 3 shows the CFGs of inter after applying loop extraction. The middle graph corresponds to the loop called in inter_0 by $\mathsf{call\_loop}(1)$, while the inner loop (right graph) is called from inter_2. The (E) mark indicates that an exception can be generated in the loop and propagated back to the caller block. $\mathsf{loop\_exit}(j)$ denotes the normal exit from loops, which transfers the control to the bytecode following call_loop (bytecode 50, in the case of the outer loop). Exceptional exits from loops are omitted for brevity. □

3.4 Rule-Based Representation

As already mentioned, for a method m and its CFGs, the system obtains a *rule-based representation* (RBR) for m whose purpose is twofold: 1) to transform iteration into recursion; and 2) to *flatten* the operand stack, in the sense that its content is represented as a series of local variables. The latter is possible because, in valid bytecode, the stack height can be statically decided. This is done in one pass on the CFGs, where the stack height is computed at the entry and exit of each block, and saved. The formal translation from a CFG to the rule-based representation can be found in previous work [3,1]. In the present paper, the CFG is different, as class analysis and loop extraction have been introduced in COSTA. This results in a more accurate and compositional representation.

Intuitively, the system computes the rule-based representation of a JBC program by producing, for each basic block m_j of its associated CFGs, a rule which:

(1) contains the set of bytecode instructions within the basic block with the variables (local and stack) it operates on, appearing explicitly in the instructions;
(2) if there is a method invocation within the instructions, includes a call to the corresponding rule; and

(3) at the end, contains a call to a *continuation rule* m_j^c. The definition of a continuation must include mutually exclusive rules to cover all possible continuations from the block, guarded by the respective conditions.

Example 5. When analyzing libraries, and by taking into account exceptions, the RBR for inter contains 59 rules. Let us show the rules associated to block inter_4 in the CFG. For clarity, exception rules are not shown but we just annotate with "%" the instructions susceptible of throwing exceptions. For them, there are rules in the RBR which capture the corresponding behavior.

```
inter4(⟨l, a, al, i⟩, ⟨i⟩)    := aload(a, s1),  iload(i, s2),
                                 aaload(s1, s2, s1),   % NullPointerException, IndexOutOfBoundsException
                                 aload(l, s2),
                                 getfield(CompList.data, s2, s2),   % NullPointerException
                                 nop(invokeinterface(compareTo(⟨s1, s2⟩, ⟨s1⟩))),
                                 Integer_compareTo(⟨s1, s2⟩, ⟨s1⟩),
                                    % NullPointerException and exceptions coming from invocation
                                 nop(ifne(s1)),  inter4c(⟨l, a, al, i, s1⟩, ⟨i⟩).

inter4c(⟨l, a, al, i, s1⟩, ⟨i⟩) := guard(ifeq(s1)),  inter5(⟨l, a, al, i⟩, ⟨i⟩).
inter4c(⟨l, a, al, i, s1⟩, ⟨i⟩) := guard(ifne(s1)),  inter6(⟨l, a, al, i⟩, ⟨i⟩).
```

It can be seen that there are two possible continuations (rule inter_4^c), depending on the result of comparing the method output with zero. The comparison is the bytecode ifne, which is wrapped in a nop mark, meaning that the bytecode must be ignored at this point, but its cost must be taken into account later. The continuation rule may call inter_5 or inter_6, depending on which condition holds at the entry, as made explicit by guards before the calls. □

3.5 Optimizations on the Rule-Based Representation

Several automatic transformations can be done on the RBR, to improve both accuracy and efficiency of the rest of the analysis. Basically, optimizations aim at removing variables to have a simpler program representation.

Static Single Assignment. A *Static Single Assignment* [13] (SSA) transformation is performed on the bytecodes of the RBR. SSA enables simple, yet efficient, denotational program analyses. For example, an instruction $\mathsf{iadd}(s_0, s_1, s_0)$ is transformed into $\mathsf{iadd}(s_0, s_1, s_0')$ where s_0' refers to the value of s_0 *after* the instruction. Our implementation of SSA keeps, for each rule, a mapping from variable names (as they appear in the rule) to new variable names (constraint variables). E.g., the rule for block inter_3 takes the following form after SSA:

```
inter3(⟨l, a, al, i⟩, ⟨i'⟩) := iload(i, s1),  aload(a, s2),  arraylength(s2, s2'),
                              nop(ifcmpge(s1, s2')),  inter3c(⟨l, a, al, i, s1, s2'⟩, ⟨i'⟩).
```

Stack Variable Elimination. While SSA introduces new variables, it also enables the removal of a large number of stack variables which correspond to intermediate states. COSTA *unifies* stack elements, local variables and constants occurring in instructions which move data to and from the stack, as iload, iconst, istore and ireturn. These unifications reduce the number of (distinct) variables which occur in the rule. After stack variable elimination, rule inter_3 becomes:

$$\begin{aligned}\text{inter}_3(\langle l, a, al, i\rangle, \langle i'\rangle) := {} & \text{iload}(i, i),\ \ \text{aload}(a, a),\ \ \text{arraylength}(a, a),\\ & \text{nop}(\text{icmpge}(i, a)),\ \ \text{inter}_3^c(\langle l, a, al, i, i, a\rangle, \langle i'\rangle).\end{aligned}$$

Note that the unification in arraylength does not mean that the length of a is written in a. Actually, this kind of unification is only meant to make size analysis easier. Most stack variables can be removed. In most cases, only those stack variables associated to operations on the heap, such as $\text{aaload}(s_1, s_2, s_1')$, and the return value of methods, as s_1 (s_1' after SSA) in inter_5, are kept in the RBR. Also, arguments which are duplicated in all possible call patterns to a rule can be filtered out. Rules inter_3 and inter_3^c are transformed into:

$$\begin{aligned}\text{inter}_3(\langle l, a, al, i\rangle, \langle i'\rangle) := {} & \text{iload}(i, i),\ \ \text{aload}(a, a),\ \ \text{arraylength}(a, a),\\ & \text{nop}(\text{ifcmpge}(i, a)),\ \ \text{inter}_3^c(\langle l, a, al, i\rangle, \langle i'\rangle).\\ \text{inter}_3^c(\langle l, a, al, i\rangle, \langle i'\rangle) := {} & \text{guard}(\text{ifcmplt}(i, a)),\ \ \text{inter}_4(\langle l, a, al, i\rangle, \langle i'\rangle).\\ \text{inter}_3^c(\langle l, a, al, i\rangle, \langle i'\rangle) := {} & \text{guard}(\text{ifcmpge}(i, a)),\ \ \text{loop\_exit}(3)(\langle l, a, al, i\rangle, \langle i'\rangle).\end{aligned}$$

Note that iload, aload and arraylength in the SSA form of rule inter_3 have no effect here, and can be ignored by size analysis. However, they are not removed since their cost has to be taken into account when generating the recurrence relation.

Inter-Block Constant Propagation. The above optimizations only achieve *intra-block constant propagation*, as variables are unified with values within the scope of a rule (i.e., a block), but are not propagated to other rules. Clearly, *inter-block constant propagation* is interesting in terms of both accuracy (more knowledge about values) and efficiency (less variables to consider). COSTA does a simple, yet effective constant propagation post-process, where constants are propagated forward to continuation rules. In a nutshell, when a block call is found, the current calling pattern is stored and, if it is guaranteed that such block is only invoked from that point, constants in the calling pattern are propagated to its body. For instance, the call pattern to inter_3 from call_loop(3) takes 0 for the counter i. However, this block is also invoked from inter_6, so that the value cannot be propagated. For correctness, constant propagation must be stopped as soon as variables whose value is being propagated are assigned a new value. This is automatically dealt with by using unification in the SSA transformation above.

4 Context-Sensitive (Pre-)Analyses to Improve Accuracy

COSTA implements two context-sensitive analyses based on abstract interpretation [11]: *nullity* and *sign*. The aim of these analyses is to improve the accuracy (and efficiency) of subsequent steps. Both analyses infer information from individual bytecodes, and propagate it via a standard, top-down *fixpoint* computation. They are designed to achieve good performance by implementing abstract operations using *bitmaps*, which allow accessing and updating the analysis information in constant time.

4.1 Nullity Analysis

A simple nullity analysis is performed on the RBR in order to keep track of *non-null* objects. For instance, the bytecode $\text{new}(s_i)$ allows to assign the abstract value *non-null* to s_i. Afterwards, this information can be propagated by means of bytecodes like astore(s_i, l_j), which copies the non-null abstract value of s_i into l_j. The results of nullity analysis often allow to remove rules corresponding to NullPointerException, essentially those guarded by guard(ifnull(s_i)). Nullity analysis is very effective when methods are analyzed *context-sensitively*. For instance, in the main program in Fig. 1, which calls inter with non-null lists l and al, and a non-null array a, nullity analysis of inter guarantees that no NullPointerException can be thrown when accessing fields or invoking methods belonging to the arguments of inter. Thus, bytecode instructions annotated with (N) in Fig. 3 will not generate exception branches. This is clearly beneficial both in terms of precision and efficiency of the remaining analysis steps.

4.2 Sign Analysis

Sign analysis keeps track of the sign of variables. The abstract domain contains the elements $\geq$, $\leq$, $>$, $<$, $= 0$, $\neq 0$, $\top$ and $\bot$, partially ordered in a lattice. Domain operations can be efficiently implemented with bitmaps (three bits for each abstract value). For instance, sign analysis of const(s_i, V) evaluates the integer value V and assigns the corresponding abstract value $= 0$, $>$ or $<$ to s_i, depending, resp., on if V is zero, positive or negative [11]. Information from arithmetic bytecode instructions is inferred as expected.

Knowing the sign of data allows to remove RBR rules associated to arithmetic exceptions which are guaranteed never to be thrown. In addition, sign information plays a crucial role in cost analysis, as it allows obtaining accurate upper bounds for *logarithmic* methods. E.g., consider a method with a simple recursive call of the form void m(int n) { .. m(n/2);..} for which we want to measure number of instructions executed. According to the JVM specification, without knowing the sign of n, it is not possible to know whether $n/2$ will be rounded to the next (if negative) or previous (if positive) integer. Therefore, unless accurate sign information is available, it is not possible to obtain a logarithmic upper bound for m; instead, a less accurate (linear) upper bound is found.

After this step, a post-process on the RBR *unfolds* intermediate rules which correspond to unique continuations. This iterative process finishes when a continuation is not unique, or when direct recursion is reached.

5 Size Analysis of Java Bytecode

From the RBR, size analysis takes care of inferring the relations between the values of variables at different points in the execution. To this end, the notion of *size measure* is crucial. The size of a piece of data at a given program point is an abstraction of the information it contains, which may be fundamental to prove termination and infer cost. The COSTA system uses several size measures:

- *Integer-value* maps an integer value to its value (i.e., the size of an integer is the value itself). It is typically used in loops with an integer counter to approximate the number of iterations by detecting how the size of the counter changes at each pass through the loop body.

- *Path-length* [18] maps an object to the length of the maximum path reachable from it by dereferencing. E.g., null has size 0 and, in a non-null reference x, the size of x is 1 plus the maximum path-length of fields in x which are in turn references. Therefore, for a non-cyclic data structure x, the size of x is greater than the size of any reference field of x, i.e., the size of a data structure decreases as fields are dereferenced. This measure can be used to predict the behavior of loops which go through objects, since the path-length is supposed to strictly decrease through the loop.
- *Array-length* maps an array to its length and is used to predict the behavior of loops which traverse arrays.

Sec. 5.1 shows how it is possible to improve the efficiency of size analysis by simplifying the abstract compilation removing useless information. Finally, a description of the actual size analysis is given in Sec. 5.2 and 5.3.

5.1 Slicing of Useless Variables

When looking at the RBR, it is sometimes possible to note that some variables are not relevant for the specific purpose of getting cost information, and can therefore be removed in order to make the analysis more efficient and the solving process more feasible [4]. In this sense, a variable is *relevant* if it directly or indirectly affects some guards, i.e., the control flow (thus, potentially, the cost), or is needed by the cost model (e.g., in our example, $\mathcal{M}_{heap}$ needs the length of an array created by newarray to infer the allocated memory). Non-relevant variables can be removed from the RBR. As an example, an accumulator variable, which only stores partial results of a computation (e.g., the sum of the elements of a list, where a temporary variable is updated during the loop) is essential to the semantics, but can be removed since, in general, does not affect the cost.

To this end, a variant of *backward program slicing* [27] is used, where variables are removed instead of program statements. The *slicing criterion* consists of the variables occurring in guards or needed by the cost model, which are propagated backwards through the rules by means of a simple dependency calculus, so that variables which directly or indirectly affect the criterion are kept in the slice. As a result, variables which cannot affect the cost are removed.

Unlike in normal slicing, *soundness* is not an issue here: removing variables which are actually relevant may result in a loss of precision, but the correctness of (upper bound) cost and termination results is preserved. In fact, losing precision would make the upper bound bigger (possibly infinite, meaning that it was impossible at all to infer the cost of the program), or make it impossible to prove termination, but such result would not lose correctness (since a bigger upper bound is correct whenever a smaller one is correct, and *not proving* termination is trivially correct). Because of this, the treatment of calls to methods or loop rules can be simplified: when a call to m is found, relevant variables of m are taken (i.e., those which affect its cost), but relevant variables in the caller rule are not propagated through the call (*context-insensitivity*). Such a slicing on the rules is unsound, and different with respect to a previous, analogous algorithm [4], where this information is correctly dealt with (*context-sensitivity*). This results in a less precise and unsound, but more efficient and importantly, scalable slicing.

5.2 Abstract Compilation

The purpose of size analysis is to detect how the size of variables changes during execution [14]. For example, when analyzing a loop where an integer counter i goes from 0 to a threshold, as in the inner loop of Ex. 1, size analysis w.r.t. Integer-value should see that the size of i in the n-th iteration of the loop is greater by 1 than its size in the $n-1$-th iteration. This information is essential for inferring how many times the loop body will be executed, which is a crucial piece of information in cost and termination analyses. Each bytecode, call or guard is *abstracted* by *linear constraints* on the size of its variables: for example, $\mathsf{iadd}(s_0, s_1, s'_0)$ will be abstracted by the constraint $s'_0{=}s_1{+}s_0$, meaning that the size of s_0 after executing the instruction is the sum of the size of s_0 and s_1 before. Similarly, $\mathsf{getfield}(f, s_0, s'_0)$ is abstracted by $s_0{>}s'_0$, meaning that the (Path-length) output size is less than the input size, due to the field access. This only holds if *non-cyclicity* of s_0 can be proven; otherwise, no information can be obtained, and an empty constraint is produced. We refer to [18] for details on path-length and its requirements. This step results in an *abstract constraint program*, or simply *abstract compilation*, which approximates the cost and termination behavior of the original program w.r.t. the chosen size abstractions. E.g., rules inter_3 and inter^c_3, after RBR optimizations, are abstract-compiled into:

$$\begin{array}{l}
\mathsf{inter}_3(\langle l,a,al,i\rangle,\langle i'\rangle) := \{\} \quad \diamond\ \mathsf{inter}^c_3(\langle l,a,al,i\rangle,\langle i'\rangle)\\
\mathsf{inter}^c_3(\langle l,a,al,i\rangle,\langle i'\rangle) := \{i{<}a\}\ \diamond\ \mathsf{inter}_4(\langle l,a,al,i\rangle,\langle i'\rangle)\\
\mathsf{inter}^c_3(\langle l,a,al,i\rangle,\langle i'\rangle) := \{i{\geq}a\}\ \diamond\ \mathsf{loop_exit(3)}(\langle l,a,al,i\rangle,\langle i'\rangle)
\end{array}$$

Expressions in brackets are constraints which describe the behavior of the bytecodes. Abstract rules for the loops in the example are:

$$\begin{array}{lll}
\mathsf{inter}_2(\langle l,a,al,i\rangle,\langle l'',i'''\rangle) & := \{i'{=}0, l{>}l'\} & \diamond\ \mathsf{inter}_3(\langle l,a,al,i'\rangle,\langle i''\rangle),\\
 & & \quad \mathsf{inter}_1(\langle l',a,al,i''\rangle,\langle l'',i'''\rangle)\\
\mathsf{inter}_6(\langle l,a,al,i\rangle,\langle i'\rangle) & := \{i'{=}i{+}1\} & \diamond\ \mathsf{inter}_3(\langle l,a,al,i'\rangle,\langle i'\rangle)
\end{array}$$

The first rule corresponds to the outermost loop, which calls the inner loop with $i = 0$. Note that, provided l is non-cyclic and does not share memory locations in the heap with other variables, size analysis finds a size decreasing in the outer loop. Moreover, by applying the Integer-value measure, it is inferred that i (the counter of the internal loop) increases by one between the input of rule inter_6 and that of inter_3 (the condition of the loop). In both cases, a useful size relation has been found, thus allowing the subsequent cost analysis to understand the behavior of loops.

5.3 Bottom-Up Fixpoint Computation

Linear constraints replacing parts of the program can be propagated via a standard, bottom-up *fixpoint* computation, in order to combine the information about single rules. The goal of this global analysis is to have *size relations* on variables between the input of a rule (i.e., a block in the CFG) and that of another one which can be (directly or indirectly) called by the first one.

In practice, we can often take a trivial over-approximation where for any rules there is no information, i.e., $p(\overline{x}, \overline{y}) \leftarrow true$. This is often enough to prove termination and find upper bounds on the cost of many programs, and results in a more efficient implementation. It is enough in our example, but not in cases where the call modifies the data structure over which a loop of the caller goes. For instance, it would be needed in the example if methods invoked within the loop (either compareTo or add) modify the length of l or the value of i. However, experiments suggest that this is not very likely to occur in imperative programs.

6 Inferring Cost and Termination

Once the bytecode program has been transformed into its RBR (Sec. 3 and 4), and size relations have been inferred (Sec. 5), all the pieces are available to prove termination and infer a *closed-form upper bound* for the cost of the bytecode. To this purpose, COSTA first sets up a recurrence relation system (RR) which captures the cost of the rule-based program and its termination behavior in terms of the input values, and, afterwards, uses a generic RR solver [2] to obtain an upper bound and prove termination.

6.1 Setting Up Recurrence Relations

Setting up a RR from the bytecode culminates the phase 1 of cost analysis (Sec. 1). In particular, for each rule in the RBR, COSTA generates a cost equation of the form $r_p(\overline{x}_p) = exp + [c_j(\overline{x}_j)+]r_q(\overline{x}_q), \varphi$ by using the abstract rule to generate φ, and the original rule together with the selected cost model to generate exp (i.e., the cost expression has to represent the cost of the bytecodes in the rule w.r.t. the model). Here, the optional c_j is the cost of a method invoked from within a rule. Variables $\overline{x}$ are the set of corresponding variables relevant to the cost. Essentially, the equation states that, for given (abstract) values $\overline{v}_p$ such that $\varphi \models \wedge \overline{x}_p = \overline{v}_p$, a *possible* cost for $r_p(\overline{v_p})$ is $exp[x_p \mapsto v_p]$ plus the sum of the costs of $c_j(\overline{v}_j)$ and $r_q(\overline{v}_q)$, where values v_j and v_q are obtained from v_p and the constraints. For example, in $\mathcal{M}_{inst}$, the RR for inter comes to be (as in Ex. 1, c_2 is the cost of add, while c_6 is the cost of compareTo):

$$
\begin{array}{rll}
\mathsf{inter}(l,a) & = 1 + r_1(l,a), & \{\} \\
r_1(l,a) & = 2 + r_2(l,a,l), & \{\} \\
r_2(l,a,l) & = 6 + r_3(a,0) + r_1(l',a), & \{l > l', l' \geq 0, a \geq 0\} \\
r_2(0,a,0) & = 0, & \{\} \\
r_3(a,i) & = 4 + r_4(a,i,i,a), & \{\} \\
r_4(a,i,i,a) & = 6 + c_6 + r_5(a,i,s_1), & \{a > i\} \\
r_4(a,i,i,a) & = 0, & \{a \leq i\} \\
r_5(a,i,s_1) & = r_6(a,i), & \{s_1 \neq 0\} \\
r_5(a,i,s_1) & = 4 + c_2 + r_6(a,i), & \{s_1 = 0\} \\
r_6(a,i) & = 2 + r_3(a,i'), & \{i' = i+1\}
\end{array}
$$

Consider the outer loop: the *execution* of r_1 (corresponding to block inter_1) costs 2 bytecodes plus the cost of r_2. In r_2, 6 bytecodes are executed (those in block inter_2) in the loop body, so that the cost is 6 plus that of the call r_3 to the inner loop, and of r_1. This goes on until a call to $r_2(0, a, 0)$ ends the loop. Note that r_1 is called by r_2 with the first argument decreased, which guarantees termination. The above RR has been simplified by eliminating intermediate equations by means of *unfolding*, as COSTA actually does.

6.2 Finding Closed-Form Upper Bounds and Proving Termination

RRs have a great potential: they are not limited to any complexity class, and can be used for counting different resources. However, unless a *closed-form solution* describing the cost of a program only in terms of its input variables is found (i.e., with no references to other equations), RRs turn out not to be practical (see the applications pointed out in Sec. 9). This is the so-called phase 2 in Sec. 1.

Basically, a RR is a *non-deterministic constraint functional program* which allows to use generic tools both to find closed-form solutions and to prove termination. Non-determinism might occur due to the loss of precision inherent to (static) size analysis. This means that, for given input values $\overline{v}_p$, the query $C_p(\overline{v}_p)$ may result in several solutions. It can be seen in the above example that size relations are inexact: e.g., size analysis has inferred that the size of a data structure l_0 decreases, but does not tell how much. In such cases, size relations cannot be applied; instead, they are kept in the cost equations. Yet, it is guaranteed that (1) one of the solutions corresponds to the actual cost of the rule-based program; and (2) if $C_p(\overline{v}_p)$ has a finite number of solutions and does not lead to any infinite computations, then the original bytecode program terminates for any corresponding concrete input. Due to the *non-decidable* and *non-deterministic* features of RRs, in most cases, it is not possible to obtain an exact solution (see [2]). Rather, the aim is to obtain *non-asymptotic*[1] upper bounds.

Upper bounds. RR are independent of the language in which the original program was written. This traditionally has allowed relying on existing computer algebra systems (e.g., Maple, Mathematica, Maxima) to carry out phase 2 of cost analysis. In our case, COSTA is connected to an existing upper bound solver [2], which is especially designed to handle RR output by automatic cost analysis. The differences between a RR and a standard recurrence equation system are explained in detail in that work. The solver is available on the web (`http://www.cliplab.org/Systems/PUBS`). It is independent of the language the RR is obtained from, and handles a large set of complexity classes, such as *logarithmic*, *linear*, *polynomial*, and *exponential*. In the example, the obtained upper bound is $\mathcal{M}_{inst}(\mathsf{inter})$, shown in Fig. 1. Details of the solving process are rather technical, and are outside the scope of this paper [2].

Termination from RR. As already mentioned, proving termination involves guaranteeing that a *finite upper bound* for the system exists, even if it cannot be

[1] I.e., which hold *for every input value*, not only *for values greater than a threshold.*

found explicitly. As a RR is a non-deterministic constraint functional program, well-studied techniques used for proving termination in such languages can be directly adapted to our setting. The solver actually proves termination on the above representation by using semantic-based techniques, relying on *binary unfolding* combined with *ranking functions*, as those in [10]. In the example, it is able to prove termination of inter alone, and also of main. Termination on the non-deterministic constraint functional representation implies, in turn, termination of the Java bytecode program, as proven in previous work [1].

7 Experimental Results

The COSTA system is implemented in Prolog and, as an external component, it uses the Parma Polyhedra Library [8] for manipulating linear constraints and it is connected to the solver of [2,1] to find upper bounds and prove termination. In contrast to previous experimental work on cost analysis, a main goal of our experiments is to be able to analyze *realistic* programs which are not hand-crafted but rather are taken from different benchmark suites, namely from the own Java libraries and the book [15] and do *not* use predefined assertions but rather analyze all necessary code. The first benchmark, compInter, is our running example which, as we have seen through the paper, uses several classes and interfaces from the Java libraries. The next set of benchmarks stackRev, josephus and arrayMax appear in [15] and all of them use Java libraries. The next three benchmarks are Java libraries: java.util.ArrayList, java.lang.Character and java.lang.Integer.

Table 1 shows the efficiency and accuracy of COSTA on the above examples. For each benchmark, we have two rows: the upper one corresponds to the case where we analyze only user-defined code, and the lower row includes the analysis of all required library methods. The column **#M** shows the number of methods to be analyzed for each benchmark. We can observe that the benchmarks are reasonably large, up to 529 methods analyzed for arrayList (with libraries). The experiments have been performed on an Intel Core 2 Duo 1.86GHz with 2GB

Table 1. COSTA Analysis Times and Results for Benchmarks using Libraries

Bench	#M	CFG	#R	Null	Sign	#R$_r$	AC	SA	#T	#UB
compInter	5	84	146	28	36	113	76	1124	5	5
	19	4600	1997	908	1104	293	216	1828	19	19
stackRev	17	436	496	104	96	332	248	1536	17	17
	27	1848	602	112	112	390	300	1856	27	27
josephus	23	924	986	260	280	780	520	11713	23	23*
	89	6752	2993	1112	1364	2187	1732	16049	77	8
arrayMax	3	120	163	24	28	137	96	536	3	3
	34	3096	1096	344	476	786	588	4504	29	1
ArrayList	34	8917	1649	308	332	1381	1096	3124	33	30
	529	51567	15828	6400	6704	11413	9137	63120	26	23
Character	43	14337	758	116	160	684	364	1684	43	43*
	166	53971	2829	560	464	2464	1544	2296	166	166
Integer	52	24054	2059	784	928	1704	3008	5468	46	43*
	217	49043	8758	5320	6488	4963	11029	29198	103	18

of RAM. Times are in milliseconds and measure the runtime of each of the phases undertaken by the analyzer. In particular, columns **CFG**, **Null**, **Sign**, **AC** and **SA** show, resp., the time of building the CFG, nullity analysis, sign analysis, abstract compilation and size analysis. We argue that analysis times are reasonable given the large size of the benchmarks. Only size analysis is comparatively more expensive. Interestingly, it is often not required in order to prove termination nor to infer upper bounds, in particular, when the loops conditions do not depend on the return value from a method. In the table, we mark the upper bounds with "*" in the three cases when size analysis is required. Columns **#R** and **#R**$_r$ show the number of rules in the RBR of the bytecode program, resp., prior to nullity and sign analysis and after applying them (as explained in Sec. 4). It can be observed that the reduction is significant in all benchmarks. This is crucial for both the efficiency and accuracy of the analysis.

The last two columns **#T** and **#UB** indicate, resp., the number of methods for which we are able to prove termination and infer an upper bound for $\mathcal{M}_{inst}$. We believe our results are quite encouraging. We have proved termination and obtained upper bounds for all methods in compInter, stackRev and Character. As expected, obtaining upper bounds for $\mathcal{M}_{inst}$ is strictly more difficult than proving termination: if we fail to find a well-founded decreasing measure for a loop which ensures its termination, we also fail to bound the number of iterations of such loop. Most of the examples where COSTA fails, e.g., in arrayMax and josephus with libraries, contain loops whose number of iterations depends on the values of fields. This is currently not supported by our size analysis and, moreover, we are not aware of any analysis that can infer such information. In other examples, PUBS [2] fails to find an upper bound because the RR obtained is too large. This happens for some methods in arrayMax, josephus and ArrayList.

Regarding the language, there are some features of Java bytecode that COSTA does not support such as non-sequential, native code, dynamic code generation and reflection. COSTA can still deal with some of them (like native code) by giving symbolic names to their cost, as we have shown along the paper. All in all, we believe that our experiments thus far allow us to conclude that RUA can be applied to a realistic programming language, and to programs with a realistic size and complexity.

8 Related Work

Since the advent of mobile code, Java bytecode analysis has become an active research area, and a number of tools are now available, e.g., the *Soot* framework [28] and the generic analyzer *Julia* [24]. Soot is a framework to develop analyses of Java bytecode, and already includes *points-to*, *purity* and *dynamic data structure* analysis. Similarly to COSTA, such systems transform bytecode into a procedural representation. Indeed, intermediate representations are common practice in JBC analysis (see also *BoogiePL* [20]). The main differences w.r.t. our rule-based representation are: (1) though Soot also performs SSA when generating the *Shimple* representation, neither Shimple nor BoogiePL do the optimizations described in Sec. 3.5: our system can eliminate, in one pass, almost all stack variables in the RBR and, besides, slice out variables which do not affect the cost; this results in a more efficient subsequent size analysis. (2) Neither Soot nor BoogiePL perform loop extraction, which is important for compositionality in cost analysis. Julia provides a generic analysis engine where *sharing*, *class*, *nullity*, *information flow*, *escape* and *static initialization* analyses have been integrated. None of these systems include *resource usage* analysis, though Julia implements some components (in particular class, nullity, sharing and *cyclicity* analyses) which are required by *size* analysis (Sec. 5).

Focusing on *cost* analysis, important effort has been devoted to adapt the general framework by Wegbreit [29] to different languages and programming paradigms. A main goal in this line is defining a setting where RRs can be generated from different languages. In the context of Java bytecode, a cost analysis framework is presented in [3] which shows that standard cost analysis can be performed on Java bytecode. Moreover, the framework has been instantiated to *heap consumption* inference [5]. Essentially, it proposes to (1) transform the bytecode into a high-level recursive representation; and (2) perform size analysis on it to generate the RR. This work has heavily influenced the design of COSTA, which follows the same basic steps. However, though providing convincing arguments for the feasibility of cost analysis in a bytecode language, this work has not yet provided the components needed for the design and implementation of a scalable and realistic resource analyzer. In particular, the recursive representation lacked class analysis (Sec. 3.2), loop extraction (Sec. 3.3) and optimizations in Sec. 3.5, which are fundamental to design a manageable bytecode representation to infer resource usage. The removal of useless variables is the subject of previous work [4], but that algorithm is less efficient, as already discussed in Sec. 5.1. As regards the cost process itself, it lacked the analysis steps described in Sec. 4.1 and 4.2, and did not perform *abstract compilation* to implement the size analysis (Sec. 5.3). All the new components presented in this paper are required to achieve efficient and accurate cost and termination analyses, and apply them to realistic benchmarks.

9 Discussion and Applications

The COSTA system provides a platform for integrating resource usage analysis for Java bytecode by providing the notion of resource as a *black box* component. The analyzer follows the traditional approach to cost analysis, i.e., generating and solving *recurrence relations*. This approach is very powerful, as it is not restricted to any complexity class, and can be used to measure several interesting resources. Also, a unique feature of COSTA is that it works at the bytecode level, which makes it possible to obtain more accurate upper bounds w.r.t. the source level, as compiler optimizations at the level of the JVM are already accounted for. Java bytecode analysis implies problems typically occurring in those arising in the object-oriented paradigm. Our approach handles these issues, and can be applied in the usual fields related to resource usage analysis:

Granularity Control [14,16]. Parallel computers have currently become mainstream with multicore processors. In parallel systems, knowledge about the cost of different procedures in the object code can be used to guide the partitioning, allocation and scheduling of parallel processes.

Performance Debugging and Validation [17]. This is a direct application of cost analysis, where the analyzer checks assertions about the efficiency of the program, written by the programmer. Assertions possibly refer to source code, but can be easily translated to be understandable by the bytecode analyzer. Likewise, analysis results obtained on the bytecode are somehow closer to the actual runtime behavior, and can be easily related to the Java program.

Resource Bound Certification [12,7,9]. It refers to the certification of safety properties involving cost requirements, i.e., that the untrusted code adheres to specific bounds on resource consumption. This is a key point in the design of *Proof-Carrying code* [22] architectures, where the user wants some guarantees that running the code will not take too much an amount of resources. Previous work deals with linear bounds [12,7], semi-automatic techniques [9], or source code [17]. Our approach shows that it is possible to automatically generate *cost-bound* certificates for realistic mobile, Java bytecode languages.

Acknowledgments. This work was funded in part by the Information Society Technologies program of the European Commission, Future and Emerging Technologies under the IST-15905 *MOBIUS* project, by the Spanish Ministry of Education (MEC) under the TIN-2005-09207 *MERIT* project, and the Madrid Regional Government under the S-0505/TIC/0407 *PROMESAS* project. S. Genaim was supported by a *Juan de la Cierva* Fellowship awarded by MEC.

References

1. Albert, E., Arenas, P., Codish, M., Genaim, S., Puebla, G., Zanardini, D.: Termination Analysis of Java Bytecode. In: Barthe, G., de Boer, F.S. (eds.) FMOODS 2008. LNCS, vol. 5051, pp. 2–18. Springer, Heidelberg (2008)
2. Albert, E., Arenas, P., Genaim, S., Puebla, G.: Automatic Inference of Upper Bounds for Recurrence Relations in Cost Analysis. In: Alpuente, M., Vidal, G. (eds.) SAS 2008. LNCS, vol. 5079, pp. 221–237. Springer, Heidelberg (2008)
3. Albert, E., Arenas, P., Genaim, S., Puebla, G., Zanardini, D.: Cost Analysis of Java Bytecode. In: De Nicola, R. (ed.) ESOP 2007. LNCS, vol. 4421. Springer, Heidelberg (2007)
4. Albert, E., Arenas, P., Genaim, S., Puebla, G., Zanardini, D.: Removing Useless Variables in Cost Analysis of Java Bytecode. In: Proc. SAC. ACM Press, New York (2008)
5. Albert, E., Genaim, S., Gomez-Zamalloa, M.: Heap Space Analysis for Java Bytecode. In: ISMM 2007 (October 2007)
6. Allen, F.: Control flow analysis. In: Proceedings of a symposium on Compiler optimization, pp. 1–19 (1970)
7. Aspinall, D., Gilmore, S., Hofmann, M., Sannella, D., Stark, I.: Mobile Resource Guarantees for Smart Devices. In: Barthe, G., Burdy, L., Huisman, M., Lanet, J.-L., Muntean, T. (eds.) CASSIS 2004. LNCS, vol. 3362, pp. 1–26. Springer, Heidelberg (2005)

8. Bagnara, R., Ricci, E., Zaffanella, E., Hill, P.M.: Possibly not closed convex polyhedra and the parma polyhedra library. In: Hermenegildo, M.V., Puebla, G. (eds.) SAS 2002. LNCS, vol. 2477, pp. 213–229. Springer, Heidelberg (2002)
9. Chander, A., Espinosa, D., Islam, N., Lee, P., Necula, G.: Enforcing resource bounds via static verification of dynamic checks. In: Sagiv, M. (ed.) ESOP 2005. LNCS, vol. 3444, pp. 311–325. Springer, Heidelberg (2005)
10. Codish, M., Taboch, C.: A semantic basis for the termination analysis of logic programs. The Journal of Logic Programming 41(1), 103–123 (1999)
11. Cousot, P., Cousot, R.: Abstract Interpretation: a Unified Lattice Model for Static Analysis of Programs by Construction or Approximation of Fixpoints. In: POPL 1977, pp. 238–252. ACM, New York (1977)
12. Crary, K., Weirich, S.: Resource Bound Certification. In: POPL 2000, pp. 184–198. ACM, New York (2000)
13. Cytron, R., Ferrante, J., Rosen, B.K., Wegman, M.N., Zadeck, F.K.: Efficiently computing static single assignment form and the control dependence graph. TOPLAS 13(4) (1991)
14. Debray, S.K., Lin, N.W.: Cost analysis of logic programs. TOPLAS 15(5) (1993)
15. Goodrich, M.T., Tamassia, R.: Data Structures and Algorithms in Java, 3rd edn. John Wiley, Chichester (2004)
16. Hermenegildo, M., Albert, E., López-García, P., Puebla, G.: Abstraction Carrying Code and Resource-Awareness. In: Proc. of PPDP 2005. ACM Press, New York (2005)
17. Hermenegildo, M., Puebla, G., Bueno, F., López García, P.: Integrated Program Debugging, Verification, and Optimization Using Abstract Interpretation (and The Ciao System Preprocessor). Science of Comp. Progr. 58(1–2) (2005)
18. Hill, P.M., Payet, E., Spoto, F.: Path-length analysis of object-oriented programs. In: EAAI 2006, ENTS. Elsevier, Amsterdam (2006)
19. Lee, C.S., Jones, N.D., Ben-Amram, A.M.: The size-change principle for program termination. In: POPL 2001, pp. 81–92. ACM, New York (2001)
20. Lehner, H., Müller, P.: Formal translation of bytecode into BoogiePL. In: Bytecode 2007, ENTCS, pp. 35–50. Elsevier, Amsterdam (2007)
21. Lindholm, T., Yellin, F.: The Java Virtual Machine Specification. Addison-Wesley, Reading (1996)
22. Necula, G.: Proof-Carrying Code. In: POPL 1997, pp. 106–119. ACM Press, New York (1997)
23. Sands, D.: A naïve time analysis and its theory of cost equivalence. Journal of Logic and Computation 5(4) (1995)
24. Spoto, F.: JULIA: A generic static analyser for the java bytecode. In: *FTfJP* 2005. (2005)
25. Spoto, F., Jensen, T.: Class analyses as abstract interpretations of trace semantics. ACM Trans. Program. Lang. Syst. 25(5), 578–630 (2003)
26. Zou, W., Wei, T., Mao, J., Chen, Y.: A new algorithm for identifying loops in decompilation. In: Riis Nielson, H., Filé, G. (eds.) SAS 2007. LNCS, vol. 4634, pp. 170–183. Springer, Heidelberg (2007)
27. Tip, F.: A Survey of Program Slicing Techniques. J. of Prog. Lang. 3 (1995)
28. Vallee-Rai, R., Hendren, L., Sundaresan, V., Lam, P., Gagnon, E., Co, P.: Soot - a Java optimization framework. In: CASCON 1999, pp. 125–135 (1999)
29. Wegbreit, B.: Mechanical Program Analysis. Comm. of the ACM 18(9) (1975)

Active Objects and Distributed Components: Theory and Implementation

Denis Caromel, Ludovic Henrio, and Eric Madelaine

INRIA Sophia-Antipolis, I3S, Université de Nice Sophia-Antipolis, CNRS
{denis.caromel,ludovic.henrio,eric.madelaine}@sophia.inria.fr

Abstract. To achieve effective distributed components, we rely on an active object model, from which we build asynchronous and distributed components that feature the capacity to exhibit various valuable properties, as confluence and determinism, and for which we can specify the behaviour.

We will emphasise how important it is to rely on a precise and formal programming model, and how practical component systems can benefit from theoretical inputs.

1 Introduction

Component models and frameworks have been in use for some years now. This is especially the case for *distributed components* that attempt to handle the inherent complexity of managing distributed systems. However, underlying languages do not seem to feature a strong and adequate programming model with respect to concurrent and distributed behaviour. The communications between distributed entities often take place with a weak semantics. For instance in Java RMI (Remote Method Invocation), the framework does not specify if the servers are executing the incoming calls in parallel or one after another. In C, C# and Java, the concurrency primitives are very low level, with a recognised difficulty to master the correctness of programs, even at the level of a simple, non-distributed program. When you put the two together, distribution and concurrency, the composition does not hold a clear, easy to grasp, semantics. One has to deal with the complexity of such under-specified features, and the behavioural combinatory explosion that occurs when put together.

Moreover, managing parallel and distributed software is now a basic requirement of any programming language. The slowing down of Moore's law, leading to the advent of multi-core processors, is dramatically increasing the pressure on programmers to introduce parallel decomposition in their applications, leading to both distribution and concurrency. Such solution-domain parallelism amplifies the intricacy of code-level behaviour, leading to even vaguer behaviour. The approach taken here is to limit concurrency to concurrent accesses between remote locations: visible concurrency is limited to the one entailed by distribution. However, at the middleware level, several threads have been introduced to introduce parallelism, with the application still behaving as if the *activity* was both the unit of distribution and of concurrency (each active object runs a single service thread).

F.S. de Boer et al. (Eds.): FMCO 2007, LNCS 5382, pp. 133–152, 2008.

These shortcomings prevent us from having a clear semantics at the level of programming the distributed interactions, and in turn preclude from having precise semantics at the component level. When it comes to composite components, composing primitive components made of programming-language code, the semantics issue is even tenser as the imprecision composes into more imprecision. How would it be possible to promote properties at the level of compositions, when we do not have them straight at the inner level? This article advocates the strong need of a simple and sound programming model integrating *distribution, concurrency, and parallelism*, in order to benefit from *soundness and properties* at the level of distributed components.

This paper starts by presenting an active object model featuring asynchronous communications with first-class futures — futures that can be transmitted before having their values. This model is implemented in the ProActive Parallel Suite, available as Open Source within the ObjectWeb Open Source community (http://proactive.ow2.org). An interactive environment, developed as Eclipse plugins, eases the visualisation and control of applications. The next section presents ASP, a generalisation of the ProActive model. Together with a formal semantics, theoretical results on determinacy are detailed. The following section introduces asynchronous distributed components that rely on active objects: primitive components are made of active objects, and the membranes of composite are specified and implemented with active objects as well. An on-going work aiming at defining a joint European component model for Grid computing (GCM) will be summarised. Finally, the paper concludes with challenges at hand with component systems, especially work related to capturing behavioural properties: current work aiming at specifying the architectural and behaviour of components, and guaranteeing their correct behaviour by model-checking methods will be introduced.

Along the course of this article, we would first like to demonstrate how important it is to rely both on practical and theoretical approaches in order to tackle the complexity of today's large-scale distributed systems. The second statement has more to do with a technical orientation: active objects provide a powerful sound foundation for both understanding and programming distributed component systems.

2 Asynchronous Distributed Objects

In order to deal with components, a precise and adequate programming model is needed to adequately build primitive programs to be used as building blocks at composition time. The paper [5] defines ProActive, an object-oriented programming model for concurrent, parallel, and distributed systems.

2.1 Principles

We summarise here the key features of the ProActive programming model:

- *asynchronous calls*, for the sake of hiding latency and decoupling client-server interactions,

- *first-class futures*, for the sake of passing the results of asynchronous calls to other distributed objects without forcing useless synchronisations, also avoiding deadlocks – futures are indeed single assignment variables,
- *wait-by-necessity*, for the sake of using as much as possible data-flow synchronisations of parallel entities,
- *collective synchronisation operations*, for the sake of manipulating synchronisations as first-class entities, e.g., blocking on the availability of all futures in a vector,
- *service primitives*, for the sake of programming in a flexible manner the inner synchronisation of activities,
- *typed asynchronous groups*, for the sake of enabling asynchronous remote method invocations on a group of entities, also a way towards parallel component invocation.

The communication paradigm of ProActive is strongly similar, and somehow inspired by, the actor paradigm [2]. Indeed, active objects communicating by requests and serving them one after the other are similar to actor communicating by messages received in a mailbox and treating them one after the other. More precisely, the active object paradigm can be described as follows. Only active objects can be referenced remotely. A method call on an active object is asynchronous; such a call is stored as a request in a request queue. After a while the active object decides to serve the request[1] and evaluates a result for it. While the result is not computed yet, a *future* [24,31] represents the result of an asynchronous method call. When the result has been computed, it is returned to all the objects holding a reference to the corresponding future.

More recently, programming paradigms relatively similar to ProActive have been developed in different contexts, among them one can distinguish Creol [25,19] and AmbientTalk [20]. Also, X10 [18] can be considered as closed to the ProActive language except that activities in X10 are multi-threaded and X10 does not support futures to our knowledge; whereas ProActive is conceived to have mono-threaded activities which ensures most of its properties and simplifies the programming of active objects.

The features above propose a disciplined way to manage parallelism, and many user operations are achieved in a parallel way without the burden to explicitly build complex synchronisations. Nevertheless, the programming model features a few fundamental properties:

- no interleaving within user code, each primitive component (resp. each active object) is mono-threaded, both concurrency and distribution are the result of the component (resp. active object) composition.
- no sharing of objects between concurrent threads,
- no call-backs, they are replaced by the use of future, which makes programs better structured

[1] Each active object either specifies its service policy using the *Serve* primitive, or uses the default FIFO policy.

Parallelism of operations seems to conflict with the property of not having interleaving within user code. Indeed, parallelism usually leads to interleaving of actions when conducted within a single address space. However, we rely here on the design and implementation of parallel operations within the middleware that have no consequences, whatsoever, for the user. This parallelism is risk-free, intrinsically acting towards confluence, because it does not produce any observable interleaving. Several harmless optimisations are indeed located at various places within ProActive's implementation, e.g., group communications, future updates with automatic continuation. They are increasingly becoming more important with the advent of multi-core processors.

2.2 Environment

The ProActive implementation comes with an environment for deploying, monitoring, and managing distributed applications, based on active objects. For example, Fig. 1 shows a screenshot of IC2D, an application for monitoring the execution of a ProActive application.

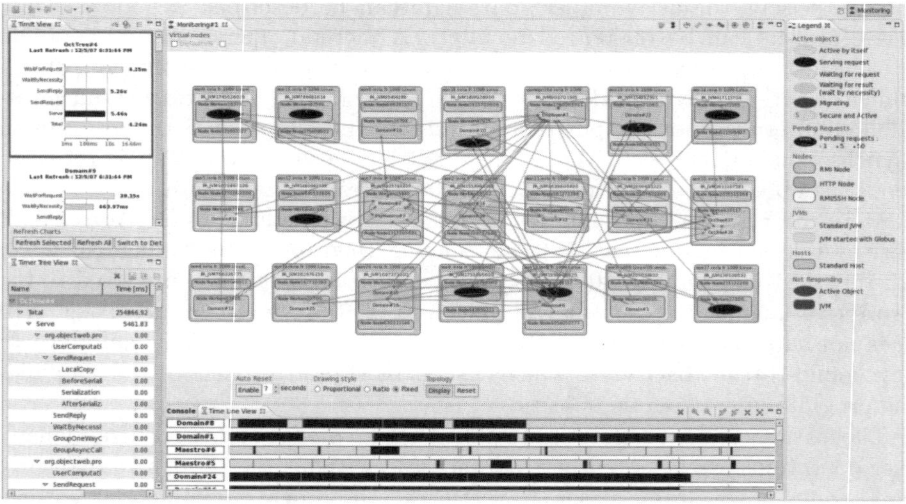

Fig. 1. Screenshot: monitoring a distributed application

Fig. 2 shows a screenshot of the ProActive scheduler. The scheduler is an application written in ProActive that is also part of the ProActive environment, and can be used as a tool administrating the deployment and the maintenance of a list of jobs over various platforms and infrastructures (Grid or P2P infrastructure).

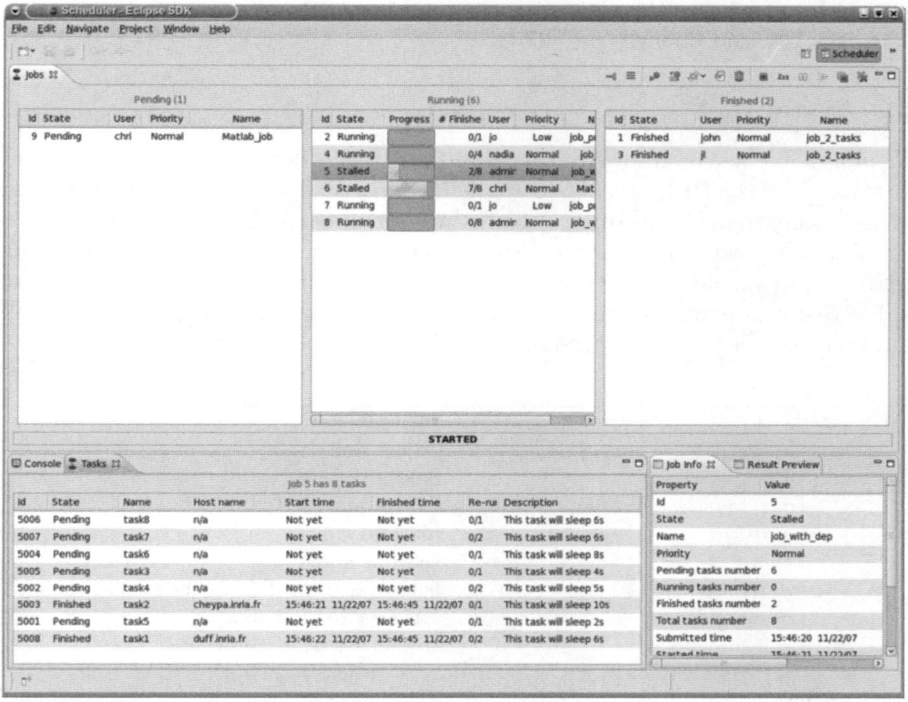

Fig. 2. Screenshot: ProActive scheduler

3 Calculus: Asynchronous Sequential Processes (ASP)

The ASP [17,16] calculus provides a generalisation of the ProActive programming model. It relaxes a few implementation decisions, and provides understanding, and proofs of confluence and determinacy for asynchronous distributed systems. The ASP calculus, is an extension of the **imp**ς-calculus [1,23] with two primitives (*Serve* and *Active*) to deal with distributed objects.

We present here the semantics of ASP in a slightly different version – but equivalent – from our previous publications [17,16]. This new version mainly comes with a more compact syntax. The resulting semantics is more compact than the one presented in our previous publications, but a little further from the implementation concerns. We hope this shorter version will make the semantic rules easier to read. The equivalence between the two versions is trivial, because this new semantics expresses, almost exactly, the same rules on a different syntax.

Concerning related works, futures have been formalised in several settings, generally functional-based [29,19,21]; those developments rely on explicit creation of futures by a thread creation primitive, in a concurrent but not distributed setting. Research on languages ensuring confluence has a long history, the results which are the closest to the ones on ASP are probably the Process Networks [26] and linear types [27].

3.1 Syntax

We first define a syntax for ASP programs: the terms defined as source code that correspond to the ProActive code are defined in Fig. 3, excluding the underlined terms. Compared to the **imp**ς-calculus we added a parameter to methods; we added a primitive *Active* for creating an activity (i.e., a location containing: an active object, some passive ones, plus a queue for incoming requests); we also added *Serve* that filters the unserved receive requests (that are in the queue), and takes the first one corresponding to the filter given as argument.

$a, b \in L ::= x$	variable,
$\mid [l_i = b_i; m_j = \varsigma(x_j, y_j)a_j]_{j \in 1..m}^{i \in 1..n}$	object definition,
$\mid a.l_i$	field access,
$\mid a.l_i := b$	field update,
$\mid a.m(b)$	method call,
$\mid clone(a)$	shallow copy,
$\mid Active(a, m)$	activates a. m defines the service policy
$\mid Serve(M)$	serves a request among the set M of method labels, $M = \{m_1, \ldots, m_k\}$
$\mid \underline{\iota}$	location in store
$\mid \underline{\alpha}$	activity reference
$\mid \underline{f}$	future reference

Fig. 3. Sequential syntax for ASP (underlined terms only occur at run-time)

In the following, l_i range over field labels, m_j over method names, x_i and y_i over variables, and a and b over terms.

Run-time syntax is also shown in Figure 3, but this time both underlined and non-underlined terms are included. Dynamically, one can refer to existing futures, activities or locations in a local store. Thus, we add three new distinct name spaces: activities ($\alpha, \beta, \gamma \in Act$), locations ($\iota$), and futures ($f_i$), and we let run-time syntax refer to them. Note that locations are local to an activity.

Substitution of variables by locations are denoted: $\{\!\{x_i \leftarrow \iota_i'^{\,i \in 1..n}\}\!\}$, and have the usual semantics (i.e., the substitution of the variable x do not enter the binder $\varsigma(x, t)$ or $\varsigma(t, x)$).

3.2 Store and Values

An *object* is said to be entirely *evaluated* if it is of the form: $[l_i = \iota_i; m_j = \varsigma(x_j, y_j)a_j]_{j \in 1..m}^{i \in 1..n}]$, that is all its field have been evaluated and allocated in the store. o range over evaluated objects. A *value* is an evaluated object, a reference to a future, or a reference to an activity: $v ::= o \mid \alpha \mid f_i$

A store is a mapping from locations to values: $(\iota_i \to v_i)^{i\in 1..p}$, it is used to store objects, and modify them. It allows the expression of the imperative nature of ASP. We let σ_α, σ_β, ... range over stores.

Let $\sigma + \sigma'$ update the values defined in σ' by those defined in σ. It is defined on $dom(\sigma) \cup dom(\sigma')$ by

$$(\sigma+\sigma')(\iota) = \begin{array}{ll} \sigma(\iota) & \text{if } \iota \in dom(\sigma) \\ \sigma'(\iota) & \text{otherwise} \end{array}$$

Let $\theta ::= \{\!\{\iota_i \leftarrow \iota_i'^{\,i\in 1..n}\}\!\}$ range over renaming of locations; $\sigma\{\!\{\iota_i \leftarrow \iota_i'^{\,i\in 1..n}\}\!\}$ is the store σ where each occurrence of ι_i is replaced by ι'_i.

We define a function *Merge* which merges two stores (it creates a new store, merging independently σ and σ' except for ι which is taken from σ'):

$$\begin{array}{l} Merge(\iota, \sigma, \sigma') = \sigma'\theta + \sigma \\ \quad \theta = \{\!\{\iota' \leftarrow \iota'' \mid \iota' \in dom(\sigma') \cap dom(\sigma) \backslash \{\iota\}, \iota'' \text{ fresh}\}\!\} \end{array}$$

$copy(\iota, \sigma)$ designates the deep copy of store σ starting at location ι. That is the part of store σ that contains the object $\sigma(\iota)$ and, recursively, all (local) objects that it references.

Moreover, the following operator copies the part of the store σ starting at the location ι at the location ι' of the store σ':

$$Copy\&Merge(\sigma, \iota\,;\, \sigma', \iota') \triangleq Merge(\iota', \sigma', copy(\iota, \sigma)\{\!\{\iota \leftarrow \iota'\}\!\})$$

Those operators are used in the semantics for ASP given in Table 2.

For simplicity of notations, ι_0 is a reserved location in each store where the active object of the activity is stored.

3.3 Structure of Activities

When a request is finished, a result has been calculated for it. The corresponding value is associated to the future identifier for the request: $f_i \to \iota$ means that ι is the location of the value associated with the future f. We denote by F the list of computed futures; it is a list mapping future identifiers to value locations: $F ::= (f_i \to \iota_i)^{i\in I}$ where $I \subseteq \mathbb{N}$.

A current request is a term being evaluated together with the future to which it will be associated: $a \to f_i$ means that a is being evaluated, and when a result will be computed it will be associated with the future f_i. C is a list of current requests: $C ::= (a_i \to f_i)^{i\in J}$ where $J \subseteq \mathbb{N}$.

A pending request is a request that has been received but not served yet. It is denoted by $[m_j; \iota; f_i]$ and consists of:

- the name of the *target method* m_j (invoked method),
- the location of the *argument* passed to the request ι,
- the *future* identifier f_i which will be associated to the result.

R is a list of current requests: $R ::= [m_i; \iota_i; f_i]^{i\in K}$ where $K \subseteq \mathbb{N}$.

:: denotes the concatenation of lists, and appending an element to a list.

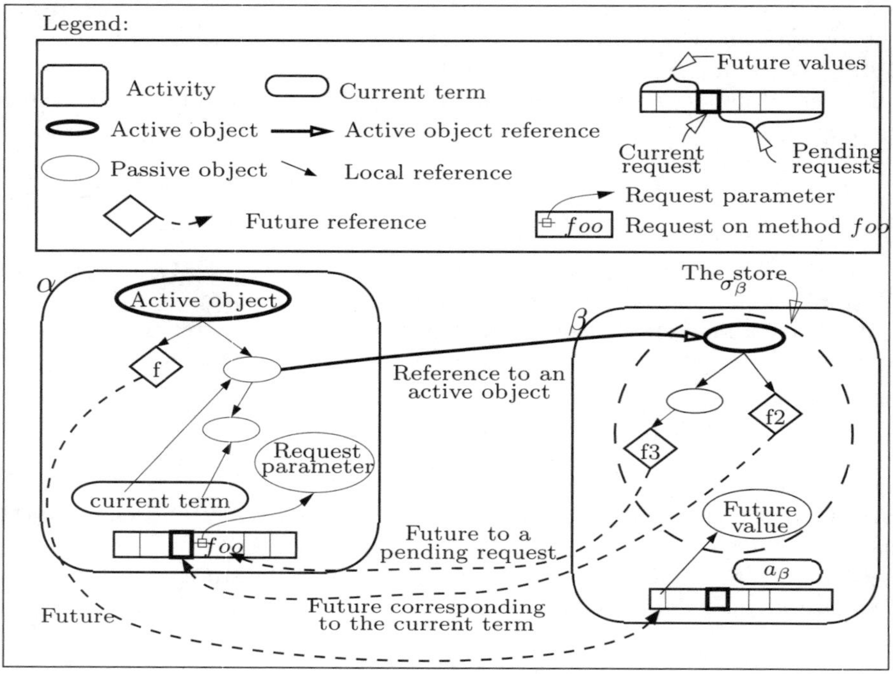

Fig. 4. Example of an ASP parallel configuration

An activity is simply formed of a name (α), a store (σ_α), and a request list containing finished, current, and pending requests ($F \cdot C \cdot R$) denoted by S.

$$S ::= F \cdot C \cdot R$$

A parallel configuration is a set of activities:

$$P, Q ::= \alpha[S_\alpha; \sigma_\alpha] \parallel \beta[S_\beta; \sigma_\beta] \| \ldots$$

Each future identifier is unique: it either belongs to the computed, current, or pending requests of a unique activity. Activities are unique too: there is a single activity with a given name. In practice the unicity of future (resp. activity) identifiers can be ensured by choosing as identifier a composition of the creator of the future[2] (resp. of the activity) with a unique local identifier. Note that activity names and future identifiers only appear at runtime and are used as references to activities or futures, e.g., for sending a request to an activity or receiving a reply from a future.

Configurations are identified modulo the reordering of activities. Figure 4 shows a parallel configuration of the ASP calculus. It shows two activities

[2] To better identify the request one might rather choose the identifier of the activity that treats the request.

α and β, bold ellipses are active objects, squares at the bottom are the requests (S), the bold square being the current requests (C), on the left are computed futures (F), and on the right pending requests (R). Future references are diamonds (and dotted arrows), whereas activity references are bold arrows, simple arrows are local references.

3.4 Contexts

Reduction contexts are expressions with a single hole ($\bullet$) expressing the part in the term where the reduction occurs. We define three reduction contexts:

- one that gives the reduction point in a sequential term,
- one that picks one of the futures an activity has computed, abstracting away the rest of the request list,
- one that gives the (unique) reduction point in the request list.

We first define sequential reduction contexts, allowing to pick the part of a term that is to be evaluated: they simply express a left-to-right call by value evaluation:

$$\mathcal{R} ::= \bullet \mid [l_i = \iota_i, l_k = \mathcal{R}, l_{k'} = b_{k'}; m_j = \varsigma(x_j, y_j)a_j]^{i\in 1..k-1, k'\in k+1..n}_{j\in 1..m}$$
$$\mid \mathcal{R}.m \mid \mathcal{R}.m(b) \mid \iota.m(\mathcal{R}) \mid \mathcal{R}.l := b \mid \iota.l := \mathcal{R} \mid clone(\mathcal{R}) \mid \ Active(\mathcal{R}, m)$$

A future value context extracts one future value, corresponding to a finished request:

$$\mathcal{R}_f ::= F :: \bullet :: F' \cdot C \cdot R$$

A parallel reduction context extracts the current request actually served.

$$\mathcal{R}_c ::= F \cdot (\mathcal{R} \rightarrow f) :: C \cdot R$$

Actually, several requests are being served at the same moment, but only one is active. More precisely, when during the service of a request, a *Serve* primitive is encountered, the service is interrupted, and is stored and a new request, specified by the *Serve* primitive is served. The former current request will be restored when the new current one will be finished. The single point of reduction inside an activity is $\mathcal{R}_c$.

We denote by $\mathcal{R}[a]$ the term obtained by syntactically replacing the hole in the reduction context $\mathcal{R}$, by the term a; note that this substitution allows variables to be captured by a binder. Similarly, we use $\mathcal{R}_f[f \rightarrow \iota]$, and $\mathcal{R}_c[a]$.

3.5 Sequential Semantics

Table 1 recalls the semantics of the **imp**ς-calculus, in the form of a small-step operational semantics.

It has been slightly modified to take into account the second parameter of methods. The semantics do not have to take into account reduction contexts because they will already be used in the parallel semantics.

Table 1. Sequential reduction

STOREALLOC:

$$\frac{o \text{ is of the form } [l_i = \iota_i; m_j = \varsigma(x_j, y_j)a_j]_{j\in 1..m}^{i\in 1..n} \quad \iota \notin dom(\sigma)}{(o, \sigma) \rightarrow_S (\iota, \{\iota \rightarrow o\} :: \sigma)}$$

FIELD:

$$\frac{\sigma(\iota) = [l_i = \iota_i; m_j = \varsigma(x_j, y_j)a_j]_{j\in 1..m}^{i\in 1..n} \quad k \in 1..n}{(\iota.l_k, \sigma) \rightarrow_S (\iota_k, \sigma)}$$

INVOKE:

$$\frac{\sigma(\iota) = [l_i = \iota_i; m_j = \varsigma(x_j, y_j)a_j]_{j\in 1..m}^{i\in 1..n} \quad k \in 1..m}{(\iota.m_k(\iota'), \sigma) \rightarrow_S (a_k\{\!\{x_k \leftarrow \iota, y_k \leftarrow \iota'\}\!\}, \sigma)}$$

UPDATE:

$$\frac{\begin{array}{c}\sigma(\iota) = [l_i = \iota_i; m_j = \varsigma(x_j, y_j)a_j]_{j\in 1..m}^{i\in 1..n} \quad k \in 1..n \\ o' = [l_i = \iota_i; l_k = \iota'; l_{k'} = \iota_{k'}; m_j = \varsigma(x_j, y_j)a_j]_{j\in 1..m}^{i\in 1..k-1, k'\in k+1..n}\end{array}}{(\iota.l_k := \iota', \sigma) \rightarrow_S (\iota, \{\iota \rightarrow o'\} + \sigma)}$$

CLONE:

$$\frac{\iota' \notin dom(\sigma)}{(clone(\iota), \sigma) \rightarrow_S (\iota', \{\iota' \rightarrow \sigma(\iota)\} :: \sigma)}$$

3.6 An Operational Semantics for the ASP Calculus

This section defines the semantics of the ASP calculus. The rules of Table 2 present the formal operational small step semantics of ASP, we explain briefly each of the rules below:

LOCAL performs a local reduction: each activity can perform a step of reduction as specified in Table 1, except that a reference to a future cannot be cloned.

NEWACT creates a new activity. m is the service method (first method executed). For simplicity, and because it is not restrictive in practice, m should have no argument. One could specify for example a FIFO service policy as follows:

$$\begin{aligned} Repeat(a) &\triangleq [repeat = \varsigma(x)a; x.repeat()].repeat() \\ FifoService &\triangleq Repeat(Serve(\mathcal{M})) \end{aligned}$$

where $\mathcal{M}$ is the set of all method labels defined by the concerned active object. Note that the reference to the created activity (γ) is stored in a new location, and thus $\sigma_\alpha(\iota)$ is still a passive object.

REQUEST sends a new request to an active object. It sends a deep copy of the parameter (at location ι'), and associates a new future f to this request.SERVE serves a new request. The current reduction is stopped and stored into the list

Table 2. Parallel reduction(unused variables are grayed)

LOCAL:

$$\frac{(a,\sigma) \rightarrow_S (a',\sigma') \qquad \nexists\iota, (a = clone(\iota) \wedge \sigma(\iota) = f_i)}{\alpha[\mathcal{R}_c[a],\sigma] \parallel P \longrightarrow \alpha[\mathcal{R}_c[a'];\sigma'] \parallel P}$$

NEWACT:

$$\frac{\gamma \text{ fresh activity} \quad \iota' \notin dom(\sigma) \quad \sigma' = \{\iota' \mapsto \gamma\}::\sigma \quad \sigma_\gamma = Copy\&Merge(\sigma,\iota\,;\,\emptyset,\iota_0)}{\alpha[\mathcal{R}_c[Active(\iota,m)];\sigma] \parallel P \longrightarrow \alpha[\mathcal{R}_c[\iota'];\sigma'] \parallel \gamma[\emptyset \cdot (\iota_0.m([]) \rightarrow \emptyset) \cdot \emptyset;\sigma_\gamma] \parallel P}$$

REQUEST:

$$\frac{\begin{array}{c}\sigma_\alpha(\iota) = \beta \qquad \iota'' \notin dom(\sigma_\beta) \qquad f \text{ fresh future} \qquad \iota_f \notin dom(\sigma_\alpha) \\ \sigma'_\beta = Copy\&Merge(\sigma_\alpha,\iota'\,;\,\sigma_\beta,\iota'') \qquad \sigma'_\alpha = \{\iota_f \mapsto f\}::\sigma_\alpha\end{array}}{\alpha[\mathcal{R}_c[\iota.m(\iota')];\sigma_\alpha] \parallel \beta[S;\sigma_\beta] \parallel P \longrightarrow \alpha[\mathcal{R}_c[\iota_f];\sigma'_\alpha] \parallel \beta[S::[m;\iota'';f];\sigma'_\beta] \parallel P}$$

SERVE:

$$\frac{m \in M \qquad \forall[m';\iota';f_l] \in R,\ m' \notin M}{\begin{array}{l}\alpha[F \cdot \mathcal{R}[Serve(M)] \rightarrow f_i::C \cdot R::[m;\iota;f_k]::R';\sigma] \parallel P \longrightarrow \\ \quad \alpha[F \cdot \iota_0.m(\iota) \rightarrow f_k::\mathcal{R}[[]] \rightarrow f_i::C \cdot R::R';\sigma] \parallel P\end{array}}$$

ENDSERVICE:

$$\frac{\iota' \notin dom(\sigma) \qquad \sigma' = Copy\&Merge(\sigma,\iota\,;\,\sigma,\iota')}{\alpha[F \cdot \iota \rightarrow f::C \cdot R;\sigma] \parallel P \longrightarrow \alpha[F::f \rightarrow \iota' \cdot C \cdot R;\sigma'] \parallel P}$$

REPLY:

$$\frac{\sigma_\alpha(\iota) = f \qquad \sigma'_\alpha = Copy\&Merge(\sigma_\beta,\iota_f\,;\,\sigma_\alpha,\iota)}{\alpha[S;\sigma_\alpha] \parallel \beta[\mathcal{R}_f[f \rightarrow \iota_f];\sigma_\beta] \parallel P \longrightarrow \alpha[S;\sigma'_\alpha] \parallel \beta[\mathcal{R}_f[f \rightarrow \iota_f];\sigma_\beta] \parallel P}$$

REQUEST where $\alpha = \beta$:

$$\frac{\begin{array}{c}\sigma(\iota) = \alpha \qquad \iota'',\iota_f \notin dom(\sigma) \qquad f \text{ fresh future} \\ \sigma' = Copy\&Merge(\sigma,\iota'\,;\,\{\iota_f \mapsto f\}::\sigma,\iota'')\end{array}}{\alpha[\mathcal{R}_c[\iota.m(\iota')];\sigma] \parallel P \longrightarrow \alpha[\mathcal{R}_c[\iota_f]::[m;\iota'';f];\sigma'] \parallel P}$$

REPLY where $\alpha = \beta$:

$$\frac{\sigma(\iota) = f \qquad \sigma' = Copy\&Merge(\sigma,\iota_f\,;\,\sigma,\iota)}{\alpha[\mathcal{R}_f[f \rightarrow \iota_f];\sigma] \parallel P \longrightarrow \alpha[\mathcal{R}_f[f \rightarrow \iota_f];\sigma'] \parallel P}$$

of current requests (future f_i, expression $\mathcal{R}[[]]$), and the oldest request satisfying the labels specified in M is treated (future f_k, method m). If no such request is found, the activity is stuck until a matching request is found in the request queue.

ENDSERVICE occurs when the evaluation of a request is finished. It associates in the list of computed results, the current request response to the current future.

The evaluation that had been stopped at the beginning of the request is automatically restored (the second current request becomes first).

REPLY updates the value of a future. It can occur at any time provided an activity refers to a future for which the value has been computed by an(other) activity.

Note that futures remain in the F list, even when all the references to the future have been updated. No notion of garbage collection has been specified for futures in ASP, but it would be easy to adapt existing garbage collection techniques here.

3.7 Properties of the ASP Calculus

Overall, the ASP calculus provides a framework for understanding asynchronous distributed objects, and expressing the various potential implementation strategies that can be implemented in an active object middleware like ProActive. It allows the developer to study which implementation choices can be made without compromising the strong properties of determinacy ensured by the model.

Here we call determinism the fact that a program will always produce the same result (the same configuration), that is no concurrent actions have an impact on the program behaviour. More than determinism properties, our objective is to clearly identify the interferences that can be source of non-determinism. Consequently and more generally, we call partial confluence properties, the properties stating in which conditions two executions of the same programs will lead to the same result, i.e., to the same configuration. Determinism relies on a notion of equality between configurations: configurations are identified modulo alpha conversion[3], and modulo the dereferencing of futures already calculated (roughly, the same configuration before and after the application of a reply rule is considered as identical).

Here are the main properties that were disclosed thanks to the formal ASP model:

- future updates can occur at any time, in any order, as such the delivery of replies can be implemented with an infinity of strategies, in any order,
- the execution of a system is characterised by the order of request senders.

Those properties are further used in order to characterise several sets of deterministic types of programs:

- determinacy of programs based on a dynamic property: a non-deterministic program is a program which can lead to a point where two activities can send at the same time a request to the same third activity;
- determinacy of programs communicating over trees (i.e., programs for which the dependence between activities form a tree).

[3] Alpha-conversion is applied on futures and variables, and activity names are chosen deterministically to simplify the correct formulation of confluence properties.

The determinism properties clearly result from the absence of shared memory between active objects, and the single-threaded nature of ASP. The interested reader could refer to [16] for a detailed descriptions of ASP properties, details on the equivalence relation on ASP terms, and some proofs.

The difficulty when trying to prove properties on specific programs is to statically approximate activities, method calls, and potential services. Shifting to components will provide a statically defined topology: the component structure defines the distribution/concurrency structure.

These properties have massively been used in the development of the ProActive library, for example when implementing future update strategies – as futures can be updated at any time, or fault-tolerance mechanism – as the above properties give a minimal characterisation of a given execution. Globally, the impact of the formal definition and proven properties of the ASP calculus upon the real implementation of the ProActive middleware has proven to be very strong, and influenced both correctness and efficiency.

4 Components

We would like to define a component in a broad sense as:

> *a software module, with a standardised description of what it needs and provides, its accepted parameters for configuration, and to be manipulated by tools for composition and deployment.*

The GCM (Grid Component Model) has been defined in [11,30] by the CoreGrid European Network of Excellence. The GCM is defined as an extension of the Fractal [12] component model, and provides the same basic structure (Figure 5). The main additions that have been made to Fractal in the GCM are 1-to-many

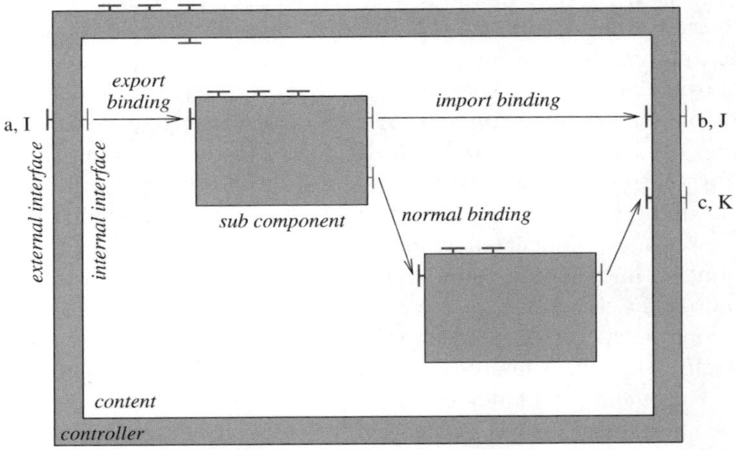

Fig. 5. A Fractal component

and many-to-1 communications, distribution, adaptive component control, and autonomic support.

A reference implementation of the GCM has been implemented in ProActive, overall the components depict the following characteristics:

- Primitive components featuring server and client interfaces,
- Composite components, allowing the hierarchical composition of primitive and composite components to build large and structured configurations,
- Interface specification including external languages such as: Java Interface, C++ .h, Corba IDL, WSDL, etc.
- Specification of Grid aspects such as: parallelism, distribution, virtual nodes, performance needs, QoS, etc.
- Multicast and Gathercast interfaces to manipulate parallel behaviours at the level of interface specification rather than hidden in the code,
- Component controllers, i.e., consider a controller as a sub-component, to provide dynamic adaptation of the component control,
- Autonomic components, the ability for a component to adapt to situations without relying on the outside.

Moreover, the GCM favors *asynchronous method calls.* By default, communications to the server interfaces are supposed to be non-blocking, as proposed in the ProActive implementation. Even in the case of methods returning non-void values, the caller is not supposed to be blocked during the method service. Together with the first-class futures, described above in the framework of ProActive and ASP, it provides the capacity to build both *structured and asynchronous* component configurations.

In the ProActive/GCM implementation, a primitive component is an active object together with passive ones, meaning that the component is the unit of concurrency and distribution. Indeed, as identified before, one of the difficulties towards deterministic distributed programs was to statically approximate activities, topologies, distributed method calls, and services. Shifting to configurations defined through components, and providing a statically defined topology, makes this static approximation a lot easier, very precise (e.g., activities and topologies are known exactly), and very practical. Indeed, the programmer has usually a clear idea about his program topology, therefore trying to discover it makes things unnecessarily complex and non-decidable. Instead of using the topology provided by the programmer, we take a stand to help the programmer achieve what he is willing to do, rather than trying to tell him from scratch the properties of his programs. Concurrency and behaviour are much easier to analyse as the distribution and remote communications are explicit: distribution is given by the component structures, and remote communications are exactly the ones following component bindings. Such explicitly-defined topology and dependencies also help a lot when analysing the behaviour of a component in isolation from its environment, and enhance the reusability of components.

Using the properties proved on the ASP calculus, it becomes possible to identify deterministic components in practice, first based on the detection of deterministic primitive components, further with the characterisation of deterministic composition of primitive components. Overall, components provide a convenient abstraction for statically ensuring determinism.

5 VerCors: Behavioural Specification of Distributed Components

The effort described in [9,10] aims at *behavioural specification and verification* of asynchronous distributed systems; particularly, it deals with asynchronous distributed components based on active objects. That includes dealing with ProActive/GCM components as defined in the section above, specifying the structure and the visible behaviour of components, and generating behavioural models. The objective is then to check properties on this behaviour, using model-checking techniques.

The behavioural model generation is based on compositional modelling of primitive components using Parameterized Networks of Labelled Transition Systems (pNets [7,6]). pNets is a new model, created as a low-level formalism for expressing behavioural semantics of distributed systems, and as a compact and powerful internal format for verification frameworks. It has a hierarchical structure, where basic behaviours are (parameterized) labelled transition systems, and composition of subsystems is expressed by generic constructions in term of (parameterized) synchronisation vectors. Parameters are used to express value passing messages, but also parameterized topologies of systems. As such the pNets model unifies and extends the value-passing CCS of Ingolfsdottir and Lin [28], and the synchronisation networks of Arnold and Nivat [4]. In [6], we have shown how to use pNets for building models of active objects and of distributed components. The models define abstractions for the domains of the application parameters. This way, the models are suitable for use with various model-checking engines, either directly with engines able to deal with parameterized systems, or with finite-state model-checkers. The latter requires another abstraction of parameters, in which we define finite partitions of the domains. through another abstraction, using finite partitions of parameter domains, permitting the generation of finite state-spaces.

In a nutshell, while relying heavily on the results from the ASP formalisation, the approach adopted to achieve successful specification is rather practical. We use several sources of information from which we build the behavioural models: architecture described through ADL (Architecture Description Language) or through graphical diagrams, and behaviour using State Machine diagrams or static analysis of program source code.

The key features and properties coming from ASP that we model, and use, in the behavioural specification framework are:

- the synchronisation by wait-by-Necessity,
- the active objects without shared memory,
- the lack of user- and code-level concurrency and parallelism,

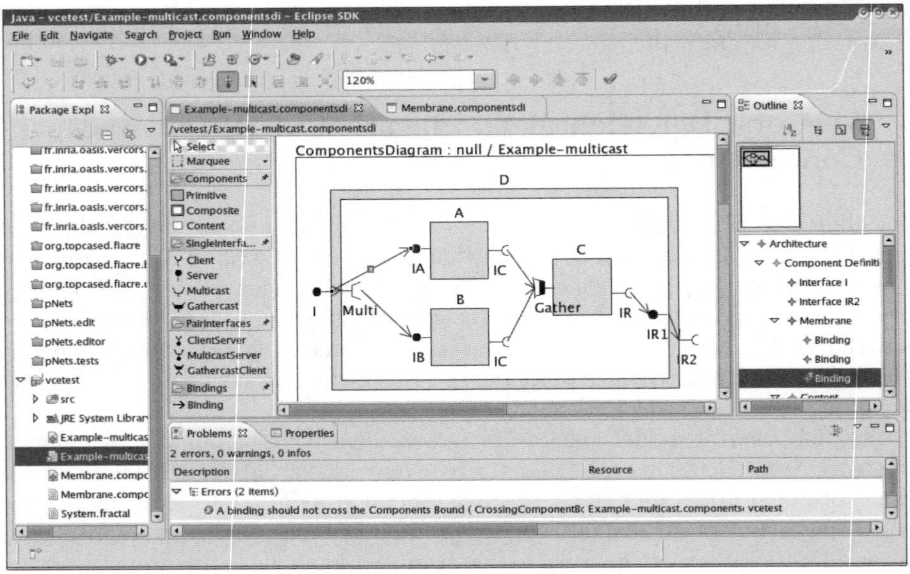

Fig. 6. VerCors Component Editor

- the atomicity of the rendez-vous protocol,
- the insensitiveness of programs w.r.t. distribution/location of activities within address spaces (JVMs).

On the practical side, we are building a specification and verification toolset for Fractal/GCM component systems called VerCors [8], that is freely available for research purposes in our website[4], and that is able to handle mid-size examples. For example in [13] we show how to find behavioural problems, and how to prove properties for a distributed cashdesks system built from over 15 components in 4 or 5 hierarchical layers, with a dozen parameter variables. At specification level, the VerCors platform includes diagram editors (Figure 6) for the architectural and behavioural definition of components [3]. From these diagrams, we build pNet models reflecting the behavioural semantics of the components in terms of communication between components; this includes control- and data-flow within components. This approach this allows us to build and to analyse behaviours of many levels of the ProActive/GCM framework; from active objects and hierarchical components, to non-functional features (deployment and reconfiguration) and group communication.

The model-checking part is done using existing and efficient engines (currently from the CADP toolset [22]). We generate explicit state-spaces both in a distributed and in a by-necessity (on-the-fly) manner. The properties addressed are temporal logic formulas, potentially including all safety properties in the regular μ-calculus. Simpler properties are directly accessible to the non-specialist user,

[4] `http://www.inria.fr/sophia/oasis/index.php?page=vercors`

including deadlock analyses, or reachability of predefined sets of events, typically deployment errors.

We are currently in the process of designing a specification language called Java Distributed Components (JDC)[15]. From JDC, we will allow the generation of both the behavioural models and the skeleton code of the implementation of components. This ensures, by construction, the correctness of the specification relatively to the implementation, and relieves us partially from the imprecision entailed by static analysis techniques.

We are also working on the inclusion of first class futures [14], and on the implementation in the platform of some specific infinite-state model-checking algorithms.

6 Conclusion: Practice in the ProActive Middleware

The ProActive middleware proposes a full-fledged environment with the programming of primitive code, the composition of such codes into composite components, the deployment on various practical infrastructures, and Graphical User Interface (Eclipse Plugin) to help programming, debugging and testing.

One of ProActive's key features is the combination of systematic asynchronous method-call, together with wait-by-necessity and first-class futures. At the level of components, it translates into the strong properties of large assemblage not being blocked by synchronous calls.

Within the GCM, collective operations, so far achieved at the level of programming, are being abstracted into elements of the interface. This shift first represents an achievement in terms of readability, and reuse. Second, functional methods can be used in various contexts, standard non-collective code and at the same time in powerful group interactions. Moreover, it also achieves an important rising with respect to the level of abstraction used by the programmer: interface versus the old API style for controlling parallelism, multicasting and synchronisations. Finally, it permits typing of collective behaviour.

From an historical stand, *modules* then *objects* then *components*, components could be viewed as moving backward in programming evolution. We are moving to a more static topology, while we have shifted from module (static assemblage) to objects where the inter-connection between pieces of code is rather purely dynamic. With components, the interconnection is static, and can only move back to dynamicity using controllers at execution, like binding controllers. In other words, only some specific entities of the architecture authorises to master dynamicity. From this point of view, components can be viewed as *dynamicity under control!*

Why does it scale? Thanks to a few key features like typed, asynchronous (connection-less) communications – somehow RMI+JMS unified, with messages rather than long-living interactions.

Why does it compose? First, because it scales! Indeed one would not be able to scale up to very large component configurations without the benefits of asynchronous method invocations. Second, the model composes because of its typed nature: remote method invocations typed with interfaces. One would not be able to check large systems without some of the guaranties given by a static type system. The absence of unstructured *call-backs* and *ports* makes a tremendous difference with respect to verifying a component system.

As much as possible, we try to use static relations provided by component configurations, avoiding a great deal of static analysis. We believe dynamicity has to be mastered in the future with appropriate controllers, such as binding controllers. As an envisioned perspective, specific properties demonstrated on such controllers can be further used into a dynamically evolving system to prove global properties needed in complex, adaptive reconfigurations.

To conclude, the strategy embraced for verifying real applications is to let the user provide as much information as possible rather than trying to discover non-decidable facts about the programs. We believe that it is impossible to *tell* the user what he is doing, but instead it is possible to *verify* automatically on his behalf what he thinks he is doing. *Rather checking than guessing what the user is doing*, that could summarise our current approach.

This paper presented ASP, a formal model to check general properties at the language level, VerCors, a behavioural specification platform allowing to model-check properties on specific applications, and ProActive/GCM, a middleware for active objects and distributed component implementing the corresponding programming model and benefiting from those formal specifications and verifications. Globally, our objective is to provide safe and efficient distributed hierarchical components that are easy to program, and to be able to guarantee the behaviour both of the middleware, and of the applications.

References

1. Abadi, M., Cardelli, L.: A Theory of Objects. Springer, New York (1996)
2. Agha, G.: An overview of actor languages. ACM SIGPLAN Notices 21(10), 58–67 (1986)
3. Ahumada, S., Apvrille, L., Barros, T., Cansado, A., Madelaine, E., Salageanu, E.: Specifying Fractal and GCM Components With UML. In: Proc. of the XXVI International Conference of the Chilean Computer Science Society (SCCC 2007). IEEE, Los Alamitos (2007)
4. Arnold, A.: Finite transition systems. Semantics of communicating sytems. Prentice-Hall, Englewood Cliffs (1994)
5. Baduel, L., Baude, F., Caromel, D., Contes, A., Huet, F., Morel, M., Quilici, R.: Programming, Composing, Deploying, for the Grid. In: Grid Computing: Software Environments and Tools. Springer, Heidelberg (2005)
6. Barros, T., Boulifa, R., Cansado, A., Henrio, L., Madelaine, E.: Behavioural models for distributed Fractal components. Annals of Telecommunications (to appear, 2008); Research Report INRIA RR-6491, `https://hal.inria.fr/inria-00268965`
7. Barros, T., Boulifa, R., Madelaine, E.: Parameterized models for distributed java objects. In: de Frutos-Escrig, D., Núñez, M. (eds.) FORTE 2004. LNCS, vol. 3235, pp. 43–60. Springer, Heidelberg (2004)

8. Barros, T., Cansado, A., Madelaine, E., Rivera, M.: Model checking distributed components: The Vercors platform. In: 3rd workshop on Formal Aspects of Component Systems, Prague, Czech Republic, ENTCS (September 2006)
9. Barros, T., Henrio, L., Madelaine, E.: Behavioural models for hierarchical components. In: Godefroid, P. (ed.) SPIN 2005. LNCS, vol. 3639, pp. 154–168. Springer, Heidelberg (2005)
10. Barros, T., Henrio, L., Madelaine, E.: Verification of distributed hierarchical components. In: International Workshop on Formal Aspects of Component Software (FACS 2005). Macao, ENTCS (October 2005)
11. Baude, F., Caromel, D., Dalmasso, C., Danelutto, M., Getov, V., Henrio, L., Pérez, C.: Gcm: A grid extension to fractal for autonomous distributed components. Annals of Telecommunications (to appear, 2008)
12. Bruneton, E., Coupaye, T., Leclercq, M., Quéma, V., Stefani, J.-B.: The fractal component model and its support in java. Softw., Pract. Exper. 36(11-12), 1257–1284 (2006)
13. Cansado, A., Caromel, D., Henrio, L., Madelaine, E., Rivera, M., Salageanu, E.: A Specification Language for Distributed Components Implemented in GCM/ProActive. In: Rausch, A., Reussner, R., Mirandola, R., Plášil, F. (eds.) The Common Component Modeling Example. LNCS, vol. 5153. Springer, Heidelberg (2008), `http://agrausch.informatik.uni-kl.de/CoCoME`
14. Cansado, A., Henrio, L., Madelaine, E.: Transparent First-class Futures and Distributed Components. In: 5th workshop on Formal Aspects of Component Systems, Malaga, Spain, ENTCS (September 2008)
15. Cansado, A., Henrio, L., Madelaine, E.: Unifying Architectural and Behavioural Specifications of Distributed Components. In: 5rd workshop on Formal Aspects of Component Systems, Malaga, Spain, ENTCS (September 2008)
16. Caromel, D., Henrio, L.: A Theory of Distributed Object. Springer, Heidelberg (2005)
17. Caromel, D., Henrio, L., Serpette, B.P.: Asynchronous and deterministic objects. In: Proceedings of the 31st ACM SIGPLAN-SIGACT symposium on Principles of programming languages, pp. 123–134. ACM Press, New York (2004)
18. Charles, P., Grothoff, C., Saraswat, V., Donawa, C., Kielstra, A., Ebcioglu, K., von Praun, C., Sarkar, V.: X10: an object-oriented approach to non-uniform cluster computing. In: OOPSLA 2005: Proceedings of the 20th annual ACM SIGPLAN conference on Object oriented programming, systems, languages, and applications, pp. 519–538. ACM, New York (2005)
19. de Boer, F.S., Clarke, D., Johnsen, E.B.: A complete guide to the future. In: De Nicola, R. (ed.) ESOP 2007. LNCS, vol. 4421, pp. 316–330. Springer, Heidelberg (2007)
20. Dedecker, J., Van Cutsem, T., Mostinckx, S., D'Hondt, T., De Meuter, W.: Ambient-oriented programming in AmbientTalk. In: Thomas, D. (ed.) ECOOP 2006. LNCS, vol. 4067, pp. 230–254. Springer, Heidelberg (2006)
21. Flanagan, C., Felleisen, M.: The semantics of future and an application. Journal of Functional Programming 9(1), 1–31 (1999)
22. Garavel, H., Lang, F., Mateescu, R.: An overview of CADP 2001. European Association for Software Science and Technology (EASST) Newsletter 4, 13–24 (2002)
23. Gordon, A.D., Hankin, P.D., Lassen, S.B.: Compilation and equivalence of imperative objects. FSTTCS: Foundations of Software Technology and Theoretical Computer Science 17, 74–87 (1997)

24. Halstead Jr., R.H.: Multilisp: A language for concurrent symbolic computation. ACM Transactions on Programming Languages and Systems (TOPLAS) 7(4), 501–538 (1985)
25. Johnsen, E.B., Owe, O., Yu, I.C.: Creol: A type-safe object-oriented model for distributed concurrent systems. Theoretical Computer Science 365(1–2), 23–66 (2006)
26. Kahn, G.: The semantics of a simple language for parallel programming. In: Rosenfeld, J.L. (ed.) Information Processing 1974: Proceedings of the IFIP Congress, pp. 471–475. North-Holland, New York (1974)
27. Kobayashi, N., Pierce, B.C., Turner, D.N.: Linearity and the pi-calculus. In: Conference Record of the 23rd ACM SIGACT-SIGPLAN (POPL 1996), St. Petersburg, Florida, January 21–24, pp. 358–371. ACM Press, New York (1996)
28. Lin, H.: Symbolic transition graph with assignment. In: Montanari, U., Sassone, V. (eds.) CONCUR 1996. LNCS, vol. 1119, pp. 26–29. Springer, Heidelberg (1996)
29. Niehren, J., Schwinghammer, J., Smolka, G.: A concurrent lambda calculus with futures. Theoretical Computer Science 364(3), 338–356 (2006)
30. OASIS team and other partners in the CoreGRID Programming Model Virtual Institute. Innovative features of gcm (with sample case studies): a technical survey. Technical report, Deliverable D.PM.07 (September 2007)
31. Yonezawa, A., Shibayama, E., Takada, T., Honda, Y.: Modelling and programming in an object-oriented concurrent language ABCL/1. In: Yonezawa, A., Tokoro, M. (eds.) Object-Oriented Concurrent Programming, pp. 55–89. MIT Press, Cambridge (1987)

Self Management for Large-Scale Distributed Systems: An Overview of the SELFMAN Project

Peter Van Roy[1], Seif Haridi[2], Alexander Reinefeld[3], Jean-Bernard Stefani[4], Roland Yap[5], and Thierry Coupaye[6]

[1] Université catholique de Louvain (UCL), Louvain-la-Neuve, Belgium
[2] Royal Institute of Technology (KTH), Stockholm, Sweden
[3] Konrad-Zuse-Zentrum für Informationstechnik (ZIB), Berlin, Germany
[4] Institut National de Recherche en Informatique et Automatique (INRIA), Grenoble, France
[5] National University of Singapore (NUS)
[6] France Télécom Recherche et Développement, Grenoble, France

Abstract. As Internet applications become larger and more complex, the task of managing them becomes overwhelming. "Abnormal" events such as software updates, failures, attacks, and hotspots become frequent. The SELFMAN project is tackling this problem by combining two technologies, namely structured overlay networks and advanced component models, to make the system self managing. Structured overlay networks (SONs) developed out of peer-to-peer systems and provide robustness, scalability, communication guarantees, and efficiency. Component models provide the framework to extend the self-managing properties of SONs over the whole system. SELFMAN is building a self-managing transactional storage and using it for two application demonstrators: a distributed Wiki and an on-demand media streaming service. This paper provides an introduction and motivation for the ideas underlying SELFMAN and a snapshot of its contributions midway through the project. We explain our methodology for building self-managing systems as networks of interacting feedback loops. We then summarize the work we have done to make SONs a practical basis for our architecture: using an advanced component model, handling network partitions, handling failure suspicions, and doing range queries with load balancing. Finally, we show the design of a self-managing transactional storage on a SON.

1 Introduction

It is now possible to build applications of a higher level of complexity than ever before, because the Internet has reached a higher level of reliability and scale than ever before using computing nodes that are more powerful than ever before. Applications that take advantage of this complexity cannot be managed directly by human beings; they are just too complicated. In order to build them, they need to manage themselves. In that way, human beings only need to manage the high-level policies.

F.S. de Boer et al. (Eds.): FMCO 2007, LNCS 5382, pp. 153–178, 2008.

The SELFMAN project is tackling one part of this application space: large-scale distributed systems based on structured overlay networks. Overlay networks are already self managing in the lower layers: they self organize around failures to provide efficient and reliable routing and lookup. We are building a service architecture on top of the overlay network using an advanced component model. To make it self managing, the service architecture is designed as a set of interacting feedback loops. We are building one major service, a distributed transactional storage, that we are using to build two application demonstrators: a distributed Wiki and a media streaming application.

In the rest of this paper, we motivate the need for self-managing systems and we give an overview of our ideas and contributions. The paper is structured as follows:

- Section 2: Motivation for self-managing systems. We give a brief history of system theory and cybernetics. We then explain why programs must be structured as systems of interacting feedback loops.
- Section 3: Presentation of the SELFMAN project. We present SELFMAN's decentralized service architecture and its demonstrator applications.
- Section 4: Understanding and designing feedback structures. We explain some techniques for analyzing feedback structures and we give two realistic examples taken from human biology: the human respiratory system and the human endocrine system. We infer some design rules for feedback structures and present a tentative architecture and methodology for building them.
- Section 5: Introduction to structured overlay networks. We explain the basic ideas of SONs and the low-level self-management operations they provide. We then explain how they need to be extended for self-managing systems. We have extended them in three directions: to handle network partitions, failure suspicions, and range queries.
- Section 6: The transaction service. From our application scenarios, we have concluded that transactional storage is a key service for building self-managing applications. We are building the transaction service on top of a SON by using symmetric replication for the storage and a modified version of the Paxos uniform consensus algorithm for nonblocking atomic commit.
- Section 7: Conclusions and further work. We recapitulate the progress that has been made midway through the project and summarize what remains to be done.

2 Motivation

2.1 Software Complexity

Software is fragile. A single bit error can cause a catastrophe. Hardware and operating systems have been reliable enough in the past so that this has not unduly hampered the quantity of software written. Hardware is verified to a high degree. It is much more reliable than software. Good operating systems provide strong encapsulation at their cores (virtual memory, processes) and this has been polished over many years. New techniques in fault tolerance (e.g., distributed algorithms, Erlang) and in programming (e.g., structured programming, object-oriented programming, more recent methodologies) have arguably kept the pace so far. In fact we are in a situation similar to the Red Queen in Through the Looking-Glass: running as hard as we can to stay in the same place [7].

In our view, the next major increase in software complexity is now upon us. The Internet now has sufficient bandwidth and reliability to support large distributed applications. The number of devices connected to the Internet has increased exponentially since the early 1980s and this is continuing. The computing power of connected devices is continuously increasing. Many new applications are appearing: file sharing (Napster, Gnutella, Morpheus, Freenet, BitTorrent, etc.), information sharing (YouTube, Flickr, etc.), social networks (LinkedIn, FaceBook, etc.), collaborative tools (Wikis, Skype, various Messengers), MMORPGs (Massively Multiplayer On-line Role-Playing Games, such as World of Warcraft, Dungeons & Dragons, etc.), on-line vendors (Amazon, eBay, PriceMinister, etc.), research testbeds (SETI@home, PlanetLab, etc.), networked implementations of value-added chains (e.g., in the banking industry). These applications act like services. In particular, they are supposed to be long-lived. Their architectures are a mix of client/server and peer-to-peer. The architectures are still rather conservative: they do not take full advantage of the new possibilities.

The increase in complexity brings with it a host of problems that must be overcome. For example, one problem is that software errors cannot be eliminated [2,41]. We have to cope with them. There are many other problems: scale (large numbers of independent nodes), partial failure (part of the system fails, the rest does not), security (multiple security domains) [20], resource management (conflicting demands for limited resources), performance (harnessing multiple nodes or spreading load), and global behavior (emergent behavior of the system as a whole). Of all these problems, global behavior is particularly relevant because it is often the primary reason that the system was built. Experiments show that large networks exhibit global behavior that is not easily predicted by the behaviors of the individual nodes (e.g., the power grid [11]). An important question is therefore how to design a system with a desired global behavior.

2.2 Self-managing Systems

What solution do we propose for building a complex software system that overcomes these problems and that has a desired global behavior? For inspiration, we go back fifty years, to the first work on cybernetics and system theory: designing systems that regulate themselves [40,4,5]. A *system* is a set of components (called subsystems) that are connected together to form a coherent whole. Can we predict the system's behavior from its subsystems? Can we design a system with desired behavior? These questions are particularly relevant for the distributed systems we are interested in. No general theory has emerged yet from this work. We do not intend to develop such a theory in SELFMAN. Our aim is narrower: to build self-managing *software* systems. Such systems have a chance of coping with the new complexity. Our work is complementary to [19], which applies

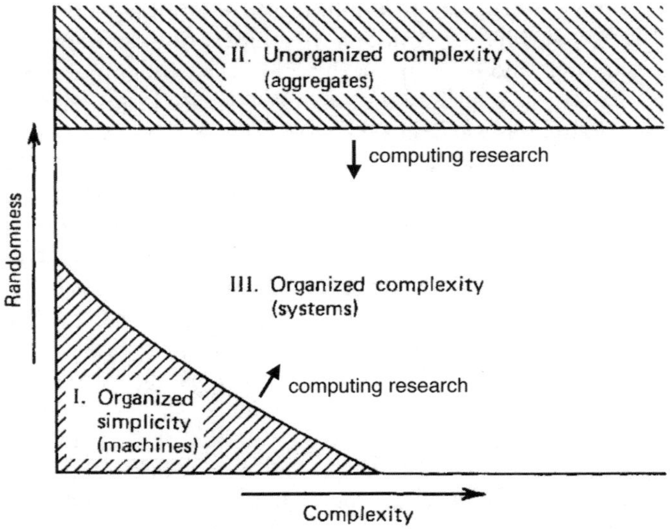

Fig. 1. Randomness versus complexity (taken from Weinberg [38])

control theory to design computing systems with single feedback loops. We are interested in distributed systems with many interacting feedback loops.

Self management means that the system should be able to reconfigure itself to handle changes in its environment or its requirements without human intervention but according to high-level management policies. In a sense, human intervention is *lifted* to the level of the policies. Typical self-management operations include adding/removing nodes, performance tuning, failure detection & recovery, intrusion detection & recovery, software rejuvenation. It is clear that self management exists at all levels of a system: the single node level, the network routing level, the service level, and the application level. For large-scale systems, environmental changes that require recovery by the system become normal and even frequent events. "Abnormal" events (such as failures) are normal occurrences.

Figure 1 (taken from [38]) classifies systems according to two axes: their complexity (the number of components and interactions) and the amount of randomness they contain (how unpredictable the system is). There are two shaded areas that are understood by modern science: machines (organized simplicity) and aggregates (unorganized complexity). The vast white area in the middle is poorly understood. We extend the original figure of [38] to emphasize that computing research is the vanguard of system theory: it is pushing inwards the boundaries of the two shaded areas. Two subdisciplines of computing are particularly relevant: programming research (developing complex programs) and computational science (designing and simulating models). In SELFMAN we do both: we design algorithms and architectures and we simulate the resulting systems in realistic conditions.

2.3 Designing Self-managing Software Systems

Designing self-managing systems means in large part to design systems with feedback loops. Real life is filled with variations on the feedback principle. For example:

- Bending a plastic ruler: a system with a single stable state. The ruler resists with a force that increases with the degree of bending, until equilibrium is reached (or until the ruler breaks: a change of phase). The ruler is a simple self-adaptive system with a single feedback loop.
- A clothes pin: a system with one stable and one unstable state. It can be kept temporarily in the unstable state by pinching. When the force is released, it will go back to (a possibly more complex) stable state.
- A safety pin: a system with two stable states, open and closed. Within each stable state the system is adaptive like the ruler. This is an example of a feedback loop with management (see Section 4): the outer control (usually a human being) chooses the stable state.

In general, anything that has continued existence is managed by a feedback loop. Lack of feedback means that there is a runaway reaction (an explosion or an implosion). This is true at all size scales, from the atomic to the astronomic. For example, binding of atoms to form a molecule is governed by a negative feedback loop: when perturbed it will return to equilibrium (or find another equilibrium). A star at the end of its lifetime collapses until it finds a new stable state. If there is no force to counteract the collapse, then the star collapses indefinitely (at least, until it goes beyond our current understanding of physics). If the star is too heavy to become a neutron star, then it becomes a black hole, which in our current understanding is a singularity.

Most products of human civilization need an implicit management feedback loop, called “maintenance”, done by a human. For example, changing lightbulbs, replacing broken windows, or tanking a car. Each human mind is at the center of an enormous number of these feedback loops. The human brain has a large capacity for creating such loops; they are called “habits” or “chores”. Most require very little conscious awareness. Repetition has caused them to be programmed into the brain below consciousness. However, if there are too many feedback loops to manage then the brain is overloaded: the human complains that “life is too complicated”! We can say that civilization advances by reducing the number of feedback loops that have to be explicitly managed [39]. A dishwashing machine reduces the work of washing dishes, but it needs to be bought, filled and emptied, maintained, replaced, etc. Is it worth it? Is the total effort reduced?

Software is in the same situation as other products of human civilization. In the current state, most software products are very fragile: they require frequent maintenance by a human. This is one of the purposes of SELFMAN: to reduce this need for maintenance by designing feedback loops into the software. This is a vast area of work; we have decided to restrict our efforts to large-scale distributed systems based on structured overlay networks. Because they have low-level self management built in, we consider them an ideal starting point.

SONs have greatly matured since the first work in 2001 [36]; current SONs are (almost) ready to be used in real systems. We are adapting them in two directions for SELFMAN. First, we are extending the SON algorithms to handle important network issues that are not handled in the SON literature, such as network partitioning (see Section 5). Second, we are rebuilding the SON using a component model [1]. This is needed because the SON algorithms themselves have to be managed and updated while the SON is running, for example to add new basic functionality such as load balancing or new routing algorithms. The component model is also used for the other services we need for self management.

3 The SELFMAN Project

The SELFMAN project is building a decentralized service architecture and two demonstrator applications that use the architecture. In this section we introduce the service architecture and the demonstrator applications. We also mention two important inspirations of SELFMAN: IBM's Autonomic Computing Initiative and the Chord system. Section 4.3 explains how the service architecture is used as a basis for self management.

3.1 Decentralized Service Architecture

SELFMAN is based on the premise that there is a synergy between structured overlay networks (SONs) and component models:

- SONs already provide low-level self-management abilities. We are reimplementing our SONs using a component model that adds lifecycle management and hooks for supporting services. This makes the SON into a substrate for building services.
- The component model is based on concurrent components and asynchronous message passing. It uses the communication and storage abilities of the SON to enable it to run in a distributed setting. Because the system may need to update and reorganize itself, the components need introspection and reconfiguration abilities. We have designed a process calculus, Oz/K, that has these abilities in a practical form [25].

This leads to a simple service architecture for decentralized systems: a SON lower layer providing robust communication and routing services, extended with other basic services and a transaction service. Applications are built on top of this service architecture. The transaction service is important because many realistic application scenarios need it (see Section 3.2).

The structured overlay network is the base. It provides guaranteed connectivity and fast routing in the face of random failures (Section 5). It does not protect against malicious failures: our current design is limited in that we must consider the network nodes as trusted. We are exploring how to modify the overlay network to better address security issues; one possibility is to use a small-world network [17]. We assume that untrusted clients may use the overlay as a basic service, but cannot modify its algorithms. See [45] for more on security for SONs and its effect on SELFMAN.

We have designed and implemented robust SONs based on the DKS, Chord#, and Tango protocols [13,32,8]. These implementations use different styles and platforms, for example DKS is implemented in Java and uses locking algorithms for node join and leave. Tango is implemented in Oz and uses asynchronous algorithms for managing connectivity (Section 5.2). We have also designed an algorithm for handling network partitions, which is an important failure mode for structured overlay networks. Network partitioning is handled by a merge algorithm that combines the partitioned subrings back into a single ring (Section 5.1).

The transaction service uses a replicated storage service for reliability (Section 6) and implements optimistic concurrency control. It uses a modified version of the Paxos consensus algorithm to implement nonblocking atomic commit [15]. This algorithm is based on a majority of correct nodes and eventual leader detection (the so-called partially synchronous model). It should therefore be able to cope with failures as they occur on the Internet.

Table 1. Requirements for selected self-managing applications

Application	Self-* Properties	Components	Overlays	Transactions
Distributed Wiki	++	+	++	++
P2P Media Streaming	++	+	++	
M2M Messaging	++	++	+	+
J2EE Application Server	++	++		+

3.2 Demonstrator Applications and Guidelines

The design of the self-management architecture was guided by four application scenarios [12]. Table 1 lists these scenarios and what they need in four areas: self-* properties, components, overlay networks (decentralized execution), and transactions. Two pluses (++) mean strong need and one plus (+) means some need. An empty space means no need for that area. All these applications have a strong need for self-management support. Out of these four scenarios, we are building two application demonstrators:

- A distributed Wiki application (specified by the Zuse Institute Berlin). This is a Wiki (a user-edited set of interlinked Web pages) that is distributed over a SON using transactions with versioning and replication, supporting both editing and search. Our prototype of this application won first prize in the First IEEE International Scalable Computing Challenge (SCALE 2008) [30].
- An on-demand media streaming application (specified by Peerialism). This application provides distributed live media streams with quality of service to large and dynamically varying numbers of customers. Dynamic reconfiguration is needed to handle the fluctuating structure. This application will become a product of the Peerialism company.

The table shows two other applications that were initially considered but subsequently dropped: a machine-to-machine messaging application (specified by France Télécom) and a J2EE application server (specified by Bull). The messaging application was dropped because of resource limitations in the project. The application server was dropped because it does not have any requirements for decentralized execution.

At the end of the project we will provide a set of guidelines and general programming principles for building self-managing applications. One important principle is that these applications are built as a set of interacting feedback loops. A feedback loop, where part of the system is monitored and then used to influence the system, is an important basic element for a system that can adjust to its surroundings. As part of SELFMAN, we are carefully studying how to build applications with feedback loops and how feedback interacts with distribution.

3.3 Related Work

The SELFMAN project is related to two important areas of work:

- IBM's Autonomic Computing Initiative [21]. This initiative started in 2001 and aims to reduce management costs by removing humans from low-level system management loops. The role of humans is then to manage policy and not to manage the mechanisms that implement it.
- Structured overlay network research. The most well-known SON is the Chord system, published in 2001 [36]. Other important early systems are Ocean Store and CAN. Inspired by popular peer-to-peer applications, these systems led to much active research in SONs, which provide low-level self management of routing, storage and smart lookup in large-scale distributed systems.

There is other important related work in ambient and adaptive computing and in biophysics on how biological systems regulate and adapt themselves. For example, [23] shows how systems consisting of two coupled feedback loops behave in a biological setting.

4 Understanding and Designing Feedback Structures

A self-managing system consists of a large set of interacting feedback loops. We want to understand how to build systems that consist of many interacting feedback loops. Systems with one feedback loop are well understood, see, e.g., the book by Hellerstein *et al* [19], which shows how to design computing systems with feedback control, for example to maximize throughput in Apache HTTP servers, TCP communication, or multimedia streaming. The book focuses on regulating with single feedback loops. Systems with many feedback loops are quite different. To understand them, we start by doing explorations both in analysis and synthesis: we study existing systems (e.g., biological systems) and we design decentralized systems based on SONs.

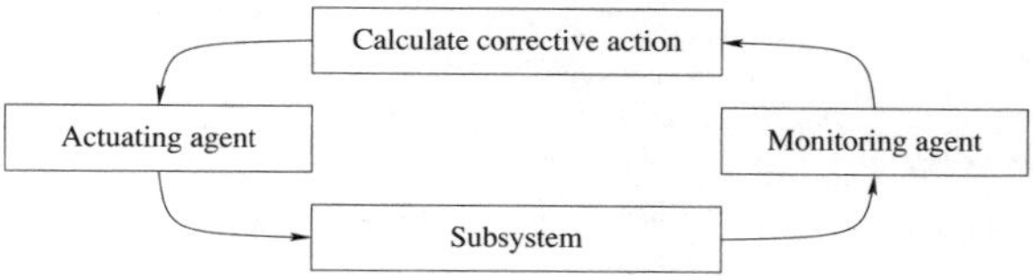

Fig. 2. A feedback loop

A feedback loop consists of three parts that interact with a subsystem (see Figure 2): a monitoring agent, a correcting agent, and an actuating agent. The agents and the subsystem are concurrent components that interact by sending each other messages. We call them "agents" because they can be considered as independent entities in the feedback loop; an agent can of course have subcomponents. As explained in [37], feedback loops can interact in two ways:

- Stigmergy: two loops monitor and affect a common subsystem.
- Management: one loop directly controls another loop.

How can we design systems with many feedback loops that interact both through stigmergy and management? We want to understand the rules of good feedback design, in analogy to structured and object-oriented programming. Following these rules should give us good designs without having to laboriously analyze all possibilities. The rules can tell us what the global behavior is: whether the system converges or diverges, whether it oscillates or behaves chaotically, and what states it settles in.

We start by studying existing feedback loop structures that work well, in both biological and software systems. We then try to understand these systems by analysis and by simulation. Many feedback systems and feedback patterns have been investigated in the literature [24,29,37]. Section 4.1 gives two nontrivial examples from biology. Section 4.2 then presents one approach to analyze these kinds of systems. Section 4.3 outlines a tentative methodology for designing feedback structures. Finally, we address the issue of multiple users that may have conflicting goals. Section 4.4 explains one approach, called collective intelligence, to manage users with conflicting goals.

4.1 Feedback Structures in the Human Body

We investigate two feedback loop structures that exist in the human body: the human respiratory system and the human endocrine system. We then make some observations on the computational architecture of the human endocrine system.

Human respiratory system. Figure 3 (taken from [37]) shows the human respiratory system, which has four feedback loops: three are arranged in a management hierarchy and the fourth interacts with them through stigmergy. This design works quite well. Laryngospasm can temporarily interfere with the breathing reflex, but after a few seconds it lets normal breathing take over. Conscious control can modulate the breathing reflex, but it cannot bypass it completely: in the

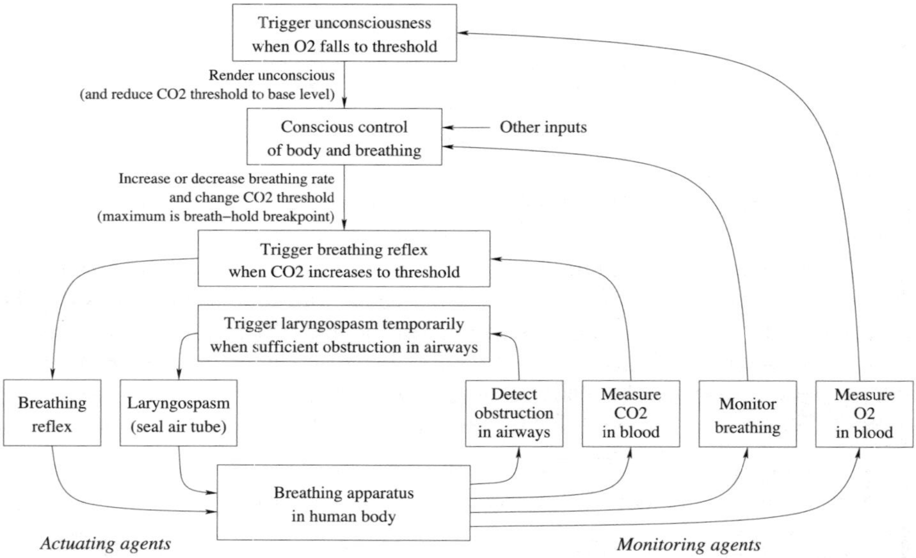

Fig. 3. The human respiratory system

worst case, the person falls unconscious and normal breathing takes over. We can already infer several design rules from this system: one loop managing another is an example of data abstraction, loops can avoid interference by working at different time scales, and since complex loops (such as conscious control) can have an unpredictable effect (they can be either stabilizing or unstabilizing) it is a good idea to have an outer "fail-safe" management loop. Conscious control is a powerful problem solver but it needs to be held in check.

Human endocrine system. The respiratory system is a simple example of a feedback loop structure that works; we now give a more complex biological example, namely the human endocrine system (shown in part in Figure 4) [10]. The endocrine system regulates many quantities in the human body. It uses chemical messengers called *hormones* which are secreted by specialized glands and which exercise their action at a distance, using the blood stream as a diffusion channel. By studying the endocrine system, we can obtain insights in how to build large-scale self-regulating distributed systems. There are many feedback loops and systems of interacting feedback loops in the endocrine system. It provides homeostasis (stability) and the ability to react properly to environmental stresses. Much of the regulation is done by simple negative feedback loops. For example, the glucose level in the blood stream is regulated by the hormones glucagon and insulin. In the pancreas, A cells secrete glucagon and B cells secrete insulin. An increase in blood glucose level causes a decrease in the glucagon concentration and an increase in the insulin concentration. These hormones act on the liver, which releases glucose in the blood. Another example is the calcium

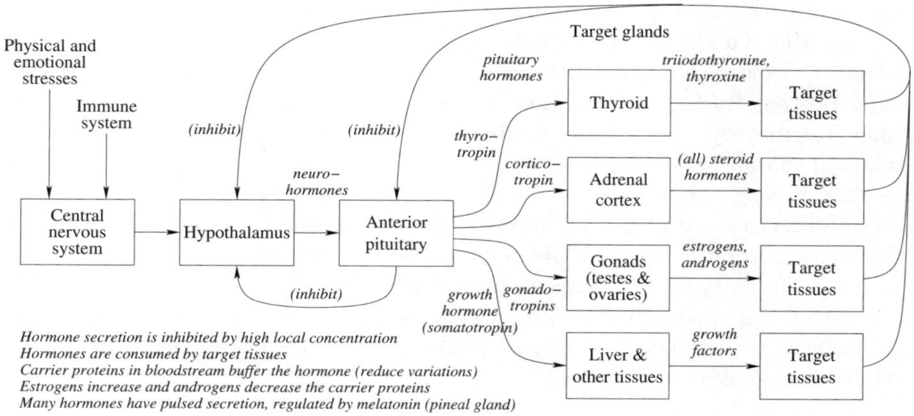

Fig. 4. The hypothalamus-pituitary-target organ axis (in human endocrine system)

level in the blood, which is regulated by parathyroid hormone (parathormone) and calcitonine, also in opposite directions, both of which act on the bone. The pattern here is of two hormones that work in opposite directions (push-pull). This pattern is explained by [23] as a kind of dual negative feedback loop (an NN loop) that improves regulation.

More complex regulatory mechanisms exist in the endocrine system, e.g., the hypothalamus-pituitary-target organ axis. Figure 4 shows its main parts as a feedback structure. This figure is derived from the medical description in [10]. This system consists of two superimposed groups of negative feedback loops (going through the target tissues and back to the hypothalamus and anterior pituitary), a third short negative loop (from the anterior pituitary to the hypothalamus), and a fourth loop from the central nervous system. The hypothalamus and anterior pituitary act as master controls for a large set of other regulatory loops. Furthermore, the nervous system affects these loops through the hypothalamus. This gives a time scale effect since the hormonal loops are slow and the nervous system is fast. The nervous system's input allows to react quickly to external events.

Figure 4 shows only the main components and their interactions; there are many more parts in the full system. There are more interacting loops, "short circuits", special cases, interaction with other systems (nervous, immune). Negative feedback is used for most loops, saturation (like in the Hill equations introduced in Section 4.2) for others. Realistic feedback structures can be complex. Evolution is not always a parsimonious designer! The only criterion is that the system has to work.

Computational architecture. We can say something about the computational architecture of the human endocrine system. There are *components* and *communication channels.* Components can be both local (glands, organs, clumps of cells) or global (diffuse, over large parts of the body). Channels can be point-to-point or broadcast. Point-to-point channels are fast, e.g., nerve fibers from the spinal chord to the muscle tissue. Broadcast is slower, e.g., diffusion of a hormone through the blood circulation. Buffering is used to reduce variations, e.g., the carrier proteins in the bloodstream act as buffers by storing and releasing hormones. Regulatory mechanisms can be modeled by interactions between components and channels. Often there are intermediate links (like the carrier proteins). Abstraction (e.g., encapsulation) is almost always approximate. This is an important difference with digital computers. Biological and social abstractions tend to be leaky; computer abstractions tend not to be. This can have a large effect on the design. In biological systems security is done through a separate mechanism that is itself leaky, namely the human immune system. In computer systems, the security architecture tries to be as nonleaky as possible, although this cannot be perfect because of covert channels.

4.2 Analysis of Feedback Structures

How can we design a system with many interacting feedback loops, like the systems of Figure 3 and 4? Mathematical analysis of interacting feedback loops is quite complex, especially if they have nonlinear behavior. Can we simplify the system to have linear or monotonic behavior? Even then, analysis is complex. For example, Kim *et al* [23] analyze biological systems consisting of just two feedback loops interacting through stigmergy. They admit that their analysis only has limited validity because the coupled feedback loops they analyze are parts of much larger sets of interacting feedback loops. Their analysis is based on Matlab simulations using the Hill equations, first-order nonlinear differential equations that model the time evolution and mutual interaction of molecular concentrations. The Hill equations model nonlinear monotonic interaction with saturation effects. We give a simple example using two molecular concentrations X and Y. The equations have the following form (taken from [23]):

$$\frac{dY}{dt} = \frac{V_X (X/K_{XY})^H}{1 + (X/K_{XY})^H} - K_{dY} Y + K_{bY}$$

$$\frac{dX}{dt} = \frac{V_Y}{1 + (Y/K_{YX})^H} - K_{dX} X + K_{bX}$$

Here we assume that X activates Y and that Y inhibits X. The equations model saturation (the concentration of a molecule has an upper limit) and activation/inhibition with saturation (one molecule can affect another, up to a point). We see that X and Y, when left on their own, will each asymptotically approach a limit value with an exponentially decaying difference. Figure 5 shows a simplified system where X activates Y but Y does not affect X. X has a discrete step decrease at t_0 and a continuous step increase at t_1. Y follows these changes with a delay and eventually saturates. The constants K_{dY} and K_{bY} model saturation of Y (analogous constants exist for X). The constants V_X, K_{XY}, and H model the activation effect of X on Y. We see that activation and inhibition have upper and lower limits.

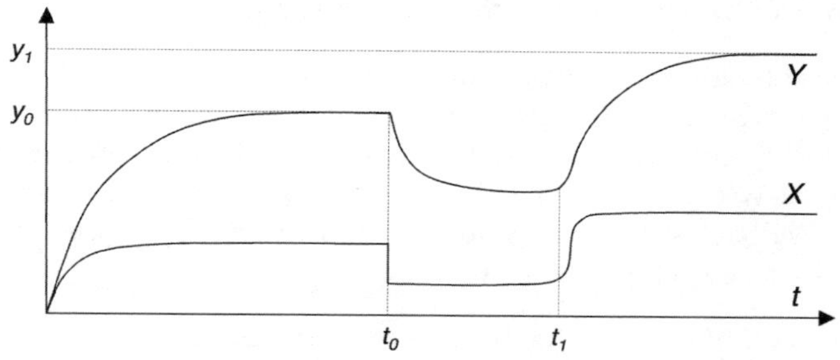

Fig. 5. Example of a biological system where X activates Y

By simulating these equations, Kim *et al* determine the effect of two coupled feedback loops, each of which can be positive or negative.

- A positive loop is bistable or multistable; it is commonly used in biological systems for decision making. Two coupled positive loops cause the decision to be less affected by environmental perturbations: this is useful for biological processes that are irreversible (such as mitosis, i.e., cell division).
- A negative loop reduces the effect of the environment; it is commonly used in biological systems for homeostasis, i.e., to keep the biological system in a stable state despite environmental changes. Negative loops can also show oscillation because of the time delay between the output and input. Two coupled negative loops can show stronger and more sustained oscillations than a single loop. They can implement biological oscillations such as circadian (daily) rhythms.
- A combined positive and negative loop can change its behavior depending on how it is activated, to become more like a positive or more like a negative loop. This is useful for regulation.

These results are interesting because they give insight into nonlinear monotonic interaction with saturation. They can be used to design structures with two coupled feedback loops.

Many patterns of feedback loops have been analyzed in this way. For example, [29] shows how to model oscillations in biological systems by cycles of feedback loops. The cycle consists of molecules where each molecule activates or inhibits the next molecule in the cycle. If the total effect of the cycle is a negative feedback then the cycle can give oscillations. If a cycle shows oscillatory behavior, then its topology (the molecules involved and their interaction types) can be reconstructed from the observed behavior. Many other patterns have been analyzed as well in biological systems, but there is as yet no general theory for analyzing these feedback structures. In SELFMAN we are interested in investigating the kinds of equations that apply to software. In software, the feedback structures may not follow the Hill equations. For example, they may not be monotonic. Nevertheless, the Hill equations are a useful starting point because they model saturation, which is an interesting form of nonlinearity.

4.3 Feedback Structures for Self Management

From the examples given in the previous sections and elsewhere [4,5,37,38,40], we can give a tentative methodology for designing feedback structures. We assume that the overall architecture follows the decentralized structure given in Section 3.1: a set of loosely-coupled services built on top of a structured overlay network. We build the feedback structure within this framework. We envisage the following three layers for a self-managing system:

1. *Components and events.* This basic layer corresponds to the service architecture of Section 3.1: services based on concurrent components that interact through events [1,9]. There can be publish/subscribe events, where any component that subscribes to a published type will receive the events. There is a failure detection service that is eventually perfect with suspect and resume events. There can be more sophisticated services, like the transaction service mentioned in Section 3.1 and presented in more detail in Section 6.
2. *Feedback loop support.* This layer supports building feedback loops. This is sufficient for cooperative systems. The two main services needed for feedback loops are a pseudoreliable broadcast (for actuating) and a monitoring layer. Pseudoreliable broadcast (called best-effort broadcast in [16]) guarantees that nodes will receive the message if the originating node survives [13]. Monitoring detects both local and global properties. Global properties can be calculated from local properties using a gossip algorithm [22] or using belief propagation [42]. The broadcast and monitoring services are used to implement self management abilities.
3. *Multiple user support.* This layer supports competitive systems (users with conflicting goals). This is a general problem that requires a general solution. If the users are independent, one possible approach is to use collective intelligence techniques (see Section 4.4). These techniques guarantee that when each user maximizes its private utility function, the global utility will also be maximized. This approach does not work for Sybil attacks (where one user appears as multiple users to the system). No general solution to Sybil attacks is known. A survey of partial solutions is given in [45]. We cite two of these solutions. One possibility is to validate the identities of users using a trusted third party. Another possibility is to use algorithms designed for a Byzantine failure model, which can handle multiple identical users up to some upper bound. Both solutions give significant performance penalties.

We now discuss two important issues that affect feedback structures: simple versus complex components (how much computation each component does) and time scales (different time scales can be independent). A complex component does nontrivial reasoning, but in most cases this reasoning is only valid in part of the system's state space and should be ignored in other parts. This affects the architecture of the system. At different time scales, a system can behave as separate systems. We can take advantage of this to improve the system's behavior.

Complex components. A self-managing system consists of many different kinds of components. Some of these can be quite simple (e.g., a thermostat). Others can be quite complex (e.g., a human being or a chess program). We define a component as complex if it can do nontrivial reasoning. Some examples are a human user, a computer chess program, a compiler that translates a program text, a search engine over a large data set, and a problem solver based on SAT or constraint algorithms.

Whether or not a component is simple or complex can have a major effect on the design of the feedback structure. For example, a complex component may introduce instability that needs fail-safe protective mechanisms (see, e.g., the human respiratory system) or mechanisms to avoid "freeloaders" (see Section 4.4). Many systems have both simple and complex components. We have seen regulatory systems in the human body which may have some conscious control in addition to simpler components. Other systems, called social systems, have both human and software components. Many distributed applications (e.g., MMORPGs) are of this kind.

A complex component can radically affect the behavior of the system. If the component is cooperative, it can stabilize an otherwise unstable system. If the component is competitive, it can unstabilize an otherwise stable system. All four combinations of {simple,complex} $\times$ {cooperative,competitive} appear in practice. With respect to stability, there is no essential difference between human components and programmed complex components; both can introduce stability and instability. Human components excel in adaptability (dynamic creation of new feedback loops) and approximate pattern matching (recognizing new situations as variations of old ones). They are poor whenever a large amount of precise calculation is needed. Programmed components can easily go beyond human intelligence in such areas. Whether or not a component can pass a Turing test is irrelevant for the purposes of self management.

How do we design a system that contains complex components? If the component is external to the designed system (e.g., human users connecting to a system) then we must design defensively to limit the effect of the component on the system's behavior. We need to protect the system from the users and the users from each other. For example, the techniques of collective intelligence can be used, as explained in Section 4.4. Getting this right is not just an algorithmic problem; it also requires social engineering such as incentive mechanisms [31].

If the component is inside the system, then it can improve system behavior but fail-safe mechanisms must be built in to limit its effect. For example, conscious control can improve the behavior of the human respiratory system, but it has a fail-safe to avoid instability (see Section 4.1). In general, a complex component will only enhance behavior in part of the system's state space. The system must make sure that the component cannot affect the system outside of this part.

Time scales. Feedback loops that work at different time scales can often be considered to be completely independent of each other. That is, each loop is sensitive to a particular frequency range of system behavior and these ranges are often nonoverlapping. Wiener [40] gives an example of a human driver braking an automobile on a surface whose slipperiness is unknown. The human "tests" the surface by small and quick braking attempts, which allows to infer whether the surface is slippery or not. The human then uses this information to modify how to brake the car. This technique uses a loop at a short time scale to gain information about the environment, which is then used to improve the performance at a long time scale.

4.4 Managing Multiple Users through Collective Intelligence

Large systems often have multiple users with conflicting goals. One promising technique to handle this situation is called collective intelligence [43,44]. It can give good results when the users are independent (no Sybil attacks or collusion). The basic question is how to get selfish agents to work together for the common good. Let us define the problem more precisely. We have a system that is used by a set of agents. The system (called a "collective" in this context) has a global utility function that measures its overall performance. The agents are selfish: each has a private utility function that it tries to maximize. The system's designers define the reward (the increment in private utility) given to each of the agent's actions. The agents choose their actions freely within the system. The overall goal is that agents acting to maximize their private utilities should also maximize the global utility. There is no other mechanism to force cooperation. This is in fact how society is organized. For example, employees act to maximize their salaries and work satisfaction and this should benefit the company.

A well-known example of collective intelligence is the El Farol bar problem [3], which we briefly summarize. People go to El Farol once a week to have fun. Each person picks which night to attend the bar. If the bar is too crowded or too empty it is no fun. Otherwise, they have fun (receive a reward). Each person makes one decision per week. All they know is last week's attendance. In the idealized problem, people don't interact to make their decision, i.e., it is a case of pure stigmergy. What strategy should each person use to maximize his/her fun? We want to avoid a "Tragedy of the Commons" situation where maximizing private utilities causes a minimization of the global utility [18].

We give the solution according to the theory of collective intelligence. Assume we define the global utility G as follows:

$$G = \sum_w W(w)$$

$$W(w) = \sum_d \phi_d(a_d)$$

This sums the week utility $W(w)$ over all weeks w. The week utility $W(w)$ is the sum of the day utilities $\phi_d(a_d)$ for each weekday d where the attendance a_d is the total number of people attending the bar that day. The system designer picks the function $\phi_d(y) = \alpha_d y e^{-y/c}$. This function is small when y is too low or too high and has a maximum in between. Now that we know the global utility, we need to determine the agents' reward function. This is what the agent receives from the system for its choice of weekday. We assume that each agent will try to maximize its reward. For example, [43] assumes that each agent uses a learning algorithm where it picks a night randomly according to a Boltzmann distribution following the energies in a 7-vector. When it gets its reward, it updates the 7-vector accordingly. Real agents may use other algorithms; this one was picked to make it possible to simulate the problem.

How do we design the agent's reward function $R(w)$, i.e., the reward that the agent is given each week? There are many bad reward functions. For example, Uniform Division divides $\phi_d(y)$ uniformly among all a_y agents present on day y. This one is particularly bad: it causes the global utility to be minimized. One reward that works surprisingly well is called Wonderful Life:

$$R_{WL}(w) = W(w) - W_{\text{agent absent}}(w)$$

$W_{\text{agent absent}}(w)$ is calculated in the same way as $W(w)$ but where the agent is absent (dropped from the attendance vector). We can say that $R_{WL}(w)$ is the difference that the agent's existence makes, hence the name Wonderful Life taken from the title of the Frank Capra movie [6]. We can show that if each agent maximizes its reward $R_{WL}(w)$, the global utility will also be maximized. Let us see how we can use this idea for building collective services. We assume that agents try to maximize their rewards. For each action performed by an agent, the system calculates the reward. The system is built using security techniques such as encrypted communication so that the agent cannot "hack" its reward.

This approach does not solve all the security problems in a collaborative system. For example, it does not solve the collusion problem when many agents get together to try to break the system. For collusion, one solution is to have a monitor that detects suspicious behavior and ejects colluding users from the system. This monitor is analogous to the SEC (Securities and Exchange Commission) which regulates and polices financial markets in the United States. Collective intelligence can still be useful as a base mechanism. In many cases, the default behavior is that the agents cannot or will not talk to each other, since they do not know each other or are competing. Collective intelligence is one way to get them to cooperate.

5 Structured Overlay Networks

Structured overlay networks are a recent development of peer-to-peer networks. In a peer-to-peer network, all nodes play equal roles. There are no specialized client or server nodes. There have been three generations of peer-to-peer networks, which are illustrated in Figure 6:

- The first generation is a hybrid: all client nodes are equal but there is a centralized node that holds a directory. This is the structure used by the Napster file-sharing system.
- The second generation is an unstructured overlay network. It is completely decentralized: each node knows a few neighbor nodes. This structure is used

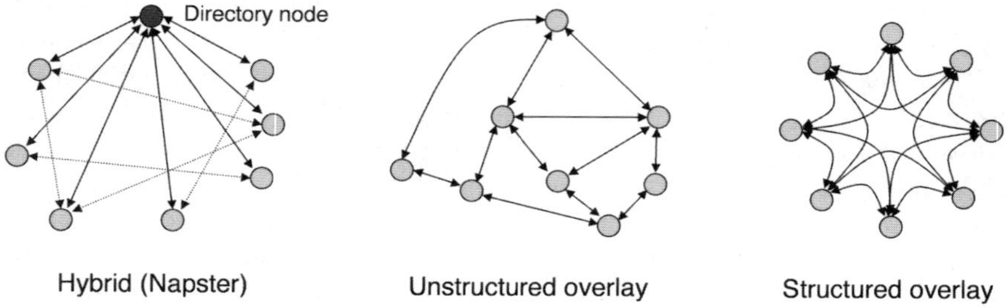

Fig. 6. Three generations of peer-to-peer networks

by systems such as Gnutella, Kazaa, Morpheus, and Freenet. Lookup is done by flooding: a node asks its neighbor, which asks its neighbors, up to a fixed depth. There are no guarantees that the lookup will be successful (the item may be just beyond the horizon) and flooding is highly wasteful of network resources. Improved versions of this structure use a hierarchy with two kinds of peer nodes: normal nodes and super nodes. Super nodes have higher bandwidth and reliability than normal nodes. This alleviates somewhat the disadvantages.

- The third generation is the structured overlay network. A well-known early example of this generation is Chord [36]. The nodes are organized in a structured way called an exponential network. Lookup can be done in logarithmic time and will guarantee to find the item if it exists. If nodes fail or new nodes join, then the network reorganizes itself to maintain the structure. Since 2001, many variations of structured overlay networks with different advantages and disadvantages have been designed: Chord, Pastry, Tapestry, CAN, P-Grid, Viceroy, DKS, Chord#, Tango, etc. In SELFMAN we build on our previous experience in DKS, Chord#, and Tango.

Structured overlay networks provide two basic services: name-based communication (point-to-point and group) and distributed hash table (also known as DHT, which provides efficient storage and retrieval of (key,value) pairs). Routing is done by a simple greedy algorithm that reduces the distance of a message between the current node and the destination node. Correct routing means that the distance converges to zero in finite time.

Almost all current structured overlay networks are organized in two levels, a ring complemented by a set of fingers:

- *Ring structure.* All nodes are connected in a simple ring. The ring must always be connected despite node joins, leaves, and failures.
- *Finger tables.* For efficient routing, extra routing links called fingers are added to the ring. They are usually exponential, e.g., for the fingers of one node, each finger jumps twice (or some other multiple) as far as the previous finger. The fingers can temporarily be in an inconsistent state. This only affects efficiency, not correctness. Within each node, the finger table is continuously converging to a correct content.

Ring maintenance is a crucial part of the SON. Peer nodes can join and leave at any time. Peers that crash are like peers that leave but without notification. Temporarily broken links create false suspicions of failure.

We give three examples of structured overlay network algorithms developed in SELFMAN that are needed for important aspects of ring maintenance: handling network partitioning (Section 5.1), handling failure suspicions (Section 5.2), and handling range queries with load balancing (Section 5.3). These algorithms can be seen as dynamic feedback structures: they converge toward correct or optimal structures. The network partitioning algorithm restores a single ring in the case when the ring is split into several rings due to network partitioning. The failure handling algorithm restores a single ring in the case of failure suspicion of individual nodes. The range query algorithm handles multidimensional range queries. It has one ring per dimension. When nodes join or leave, each of these rings is adjusted (by splitting or joining pieces in the key space) to maintain balanced routing.

5.1 Handling Network Partitioning: The Ring Merge Algorithm

Network partitioning is a real problem for any long-lived application on the Internet. A single router crash can cause part of the network to become isolated from another part. SONs should behave reasonably when a network partition arrives. If no special actions are taken, what actually happens when a partition arrives is that the SON splits into several rings. We need to detect when a split happens and merge the rings back into a single ring when communication is restored [34]. Protocols such as DKS automatically behave as multiple rings when a partition occurs, but they do not automatically merge. We need to extend the protocol with a merge algorithm.

The merge algorithm consists of two parts. The first part detects when the merge is needed. When a node detects that another node has failed, it puts the node in a local data structure called the passive list. It periodically pings nodes in its passive list to see whether they are in fact alive. If so, it triggers the ring unification algorithm. This algorithm can merge rings in $O(n)$ time for network size n. We also define an improved gossip-based algorithm that can merge the network in $O(\log n)$ average time.

Ring unification happens between pairs of nodes that may be on different rings. The unification algorithm assumes that all nodes live in the same identifier space, even if they are on different rings. Suppose that node p detects that node q on its passive list is alive. Figure 7 shows an example where we are merging the black ring (containing node p) and the white ring (containing node q). Then p does a modified lookup operation (`mlookup`(q)) to q. This lookup tries to reduce the distance to q. When it has reduced this distance as much as possible, then the algorithm attempts to insert q at that position in the ring using a second operation, `trymerge`(*pred*,*succ*), where *pred* and *succ* are the predecessor and successor nodes between which q should be inserted. The actual algorithm has several refinements to improve speed and to ensure termination.

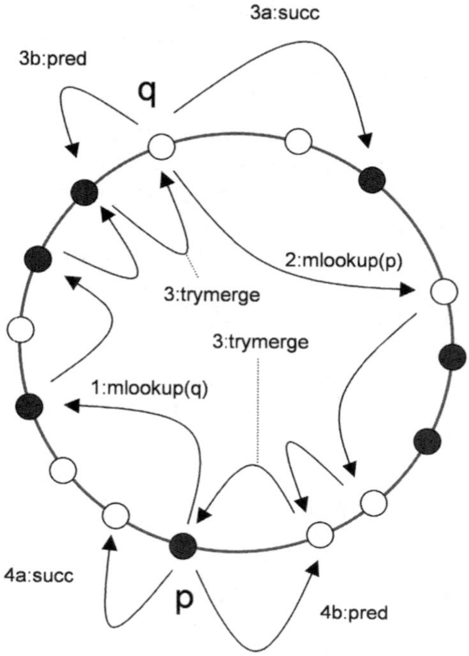

Fig. 7. The ring merge algorithm

5.2 Handling Failure Suspicions: The Relaxed Ring Algorithm

A typical Internet failure mode is that a node suspects another node of failing. This suspicion may be true or false. In both cases, the ring structure must be maintained. This can be handled through the relaxed ring algorithm [26]. This algorithm maintains the invariant that every peer is in the same ring as its successor. Furthermore, a peer can never indicate another peer as the responsible node for data storage: a peer knows only its own responsibility. If a successor node is suspected of having failed, then it is ejected from the ring. However, the node may still be alive and point to a successor. This leads to a structure we call the *relaxed ring*, which looks like a ring with "bushes" sticking out (see Figure 8). The bushes appear only if there are failure suspicions. At all times there is a perfectly connected ring at the core of the relaxed ring. The relaxed ring is always converging toward a perfect ring. The number of nodes in the bushes existing at any time depends on the churn (the rate of change of the ring, the number of failures and joins per time).

5.3 Handling Multidimensional Range Queries with Load Balancing

Efficient data lookup is at the heart of peer-to-peer computing. Many SONs, including DKS and Tango, use consistent hashing to store (key,value) pairs in a distributed hash table (DHT). The hashing distributes the keys uniformly over

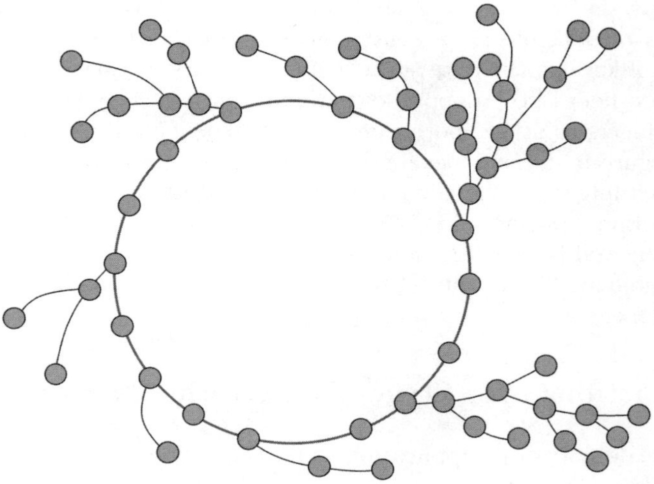

Fig. 8. The relaxed ring structure

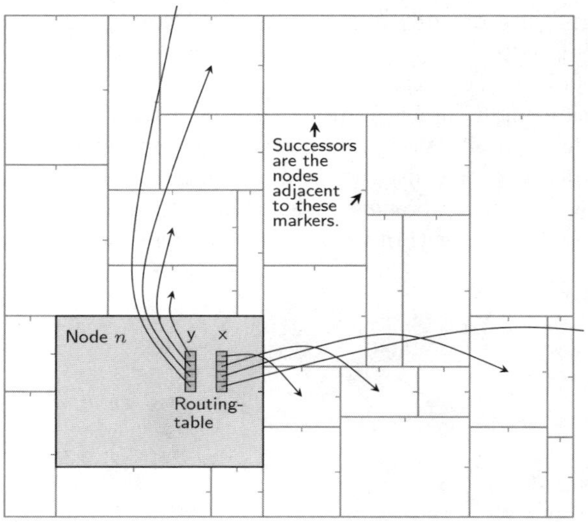

Fig. 9. Two-dimensional routing tables in SONAR

the key space. Unfortunately, this scheme is unable to handle queries with partial information (such as wildcards and ranges) because adjacent keys are spread over all nodes. In this section, we argue that using DHTs is not a good idea in SONs. We support this argument by showing how to build a practical SON that stores the keys in lexicographic order. We have developed a first protocol, Chord#, and a generalization for multidimensional range queries, SONAR [32].

In SONAR the overlay has the shape of a multidimensional torus, where each node is responsible for a contiguous part of the data space. A uniform distribution of keys on the data space is not necessary, because denser areas get assigned more nodes. To support logarithmic routing, SONAR maintains, per dimension, fingers to other nodes that span an exponentially increasing number of nodes. Figure 9 shows an example in two dimensions. Most other overlays maintain such fingers in the key space instead and therefore require a uniform data distribution (e.g., which is obtained using hashing). SONAR, in contrast, avoids hashing and is therefore able to perform range queries of arbitrary shape in a logarithmic number of routing steps, independent of the number of system- and query-dimensions.

6 Transactions over Structured Overlay Networks

For our three decentralized application scenarios, we need a decentralized transactional storage. We need transactions because the applications need concurrent access to shared data. We have therefore designed a transaction algorithm over SONs. We are currently simulating it to validate its assumptions and measure its performance [27,28]. Implementing transactions over a SON is challenging because of churn (rate of node leaves, joins, and crashes and subsequent reorganizations of the SON) and because of the Internet's failure model (crash stop with imperfect failure detection).

The transaction algorithm is built on top of a reliable storage service. We implement this using replication. There are many approaches to replication on a SON. For example, we could use file-level replication (symmetric replication) or block-level replication using erasure codes. These approaches all have their own application areas. Our algorithm uses symmetric replication [14].

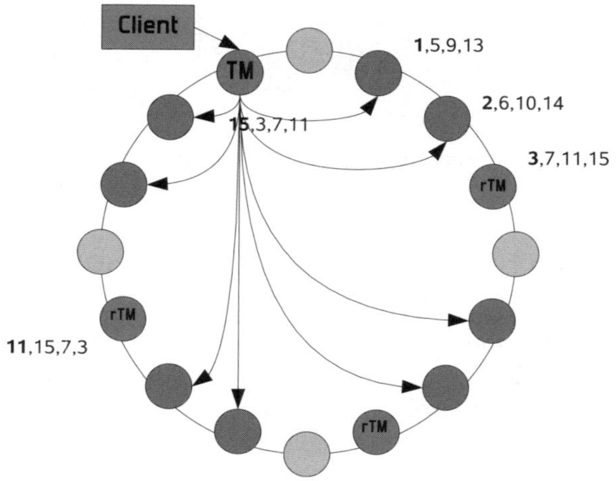

Fig. 10. Transaction with replicated manager and participants

To avoid the problems of failure detection, we implement atomic commit using a majority algorithm based on a modified version of the Paxos algorithm [15]. In a companion paper, we have shown that majority techniques work well for DHTs [35]: the probability of data consistency violation is negligible. If a consistency violation does occur, then this is because of a network partition and we can use the network merge algorithm of Section 5.1.

A client initiates a transaction by asking its nearest node, which becomes a transaction manager. Other nodes that store data are participants in the transaction. Assuming symmetric replication with degree f, we have f transaction managers and each other node participating gives f replicated participants. Figure 10 shows a situation with $f = 4$ and two nodes participating in addition to the transaction manager. Each transaction manager sends a Prepare message to all replicated participants, which each sends back a Prepared or Abort message to all replicated transaction managers. Each replicated transaction manager collects votes from a majority of participants and locally decides on abort or commit. It sends this to the transaction manager. After having collected a majority, the transaction manager sents its decision to all participants. This algorithm has six communication rounds. It succeeds if more than $f/2$ nodes of each replica group are alive.

7 Conclusions and Future Work

The SELFMAN project is using self-management techniques to build large-scale distributed systems. This paper gives a snapshot of the SELFMAN project at its halfway point. We explain why self management is important for software design and we give some first results on how to design self-managing systems as feedback loop structures. We are using structured overlay networks (SONs) as the basis of large-scale distributed self-managing systems. We adapt SONs to a practical setting by extending them to handle network partitioning, failure suspicions, and range queries with load balancing. We are building a transactional storage service running over the SON to support two realistic application scenarios: a distributed Wiki and an on-demand media streaming application. In the rest of the project, we will complete the transactional store and the demonstrator applications and we will evaluate the self-management abilities of our system. The final result will be a set of guidelines on how to build decentralized self-managing applications.

Acknowledgements

This work is funded by the European Union in the SELFMAN project (contract 34084) and in the CoreGRID network of excellence (contract 004265). SELFMAN is a specific targeted research project (STREP) in the Information Society Technologies (IST) Strategic Objective 2.5.5 (Software and Services) of the European Sixth Framework Programme [33]. Peter Van Roy is the coordinator of

SELFMAN. He acknowledges all SELFMAN partners for their insights and research results, some of which are summarized in this paper. He also acknowledges Mahmoud Rafea for encouraging him to look at the human endocrine system and Mohamed El-Beltagy for introducing him to collective intelligence.

References

1. Arad, C., Roverso, R., Haridi, S., Jaradin, Y., Mejias, B., Van Roy, P., Coupaye, T., Dillenseger, B., Diaconescu, A., Harbaoui, A., Jayaprakash, N., Kessis, M., Lefebvre, A., Leger, M.: Report on architectural framework specification. SELFMAN Deliverable D2.2a (June 2007), `www.ist-selfman.org`
2. Armstrong, J.: Making Reliable Distributed Systems in the Presence of Software Errors. Ph.D. dissertation, Royal Institute of Technology (KTH), Stockholm, Sweden (November 2003)
3. Arthur, W.B.: Complexity in economic theory: Inductive reasoning and bounded rationality. The American Economic Review 84(2), 406–411 (1994)
4. Ross, W.A.: An Introduction to Cybernetics. Chapman & Hall Ltd., London, (1956), `pcp.vub.ac.be/books/IntroCyb.pdf`
5. von Bertalanffy, L.: General System Theory: Foundations, Development, Applications, George Braziller (1969)
6. Capra, F.: It's a Wonderful Life. Liberty Films (1946)
7. Carroll, L.: Through the Looking-Glass and What Alice Found There (1872) (Dover Publications reprint 1999)
8. Carton, B., Mesaros, V.: Improving the Scalability of Logarithmic-Degree DHT-Based Peer-to-Peer Networks. In: 10th International Euro-Par Conference, pp. 1060–1067 (August 2004)
9. Collet, R., Lienhardt, M., Schmitt, A., Stefani, J.-B., Van Roy, P.: Report on formal operational semantics (components and reflection). SELFMAN Deliverable D2.3a (November 2007), `www.ist-selfman.org`
10. Encyclopaedia Britannica. Article Human Endocrine System (2005)
11. Fairley, P.: The Unruly Power Grid, IEEE Spectrum (October 2005)
12. France Télécom, Zuse Institut Berlin, and Peerialism AB. User requirements, SELFMAN Deliverable D5.1 (November 2007), `http://www.ist-selfman.org`
13. Ghodsi, A.: Distributed K-ary System: Algorithms for Distributed Hash Tables, Ph.D. dissertation, Royal Institute of Technology (KTH), Stockholm, Sweden (October 2006)
14. Ghodsi, A., Alima, L.O., Haridi, S.: Symmetric replication for structured peer-to-peer systems. In: Moro, G., Bergamaschi, S., Joseph, S., Morin, J.-H., Ouksel, A.M. (eds.) DBISP2P 2005. LNCS, vol. 4125, pp. 74–85. Springer, Heidelberg (2007)
15. Gray, J., Lamport., L.: Consensus on transaction commit. In: ACM Trans. Database Syst., pp. 133–160. ACM Press, New York (2006)
16. Guerraoui, R., Rodrigues, L.: Introduction to Reliable Distributed Programming. Springer, Berlin (2006)
17. Halim, F., Wu, Y., Yap, R.: Security Issues in Small World Network Routing. In: Second IEEE International Conference on Self-Adaptive and Self-Organizing Systems (SASO 2008) (October 2008)
18. Hardin, G.: The Tragedy of the Commons. Science 162(3859), 1243–1248 (1968)
19. Hellerstein, J.L., Diao, Y., Parekh, S., Tilbury, D.M.: Feedback Control of Computing Systems. Wiley-IEEE Press (2004)

20. Hoglund, G., McGraw, G.: Exploiting Online Games: Cheating Massively Distributed Systems. Addison-Wesley Software Security Series (2008)
21. IBM. Autonomic computing: IBM's perspective on the state of information technology (2001) `researchweb.watson.ibm.com/autonomic`
22. Jelasity, M., Guerraoui, R., Kermarrec, A.-M., van Steen, M.: The Peer Sampling Service: Experimental Evaluation of Unstructured Gossip-Based Implementations. In: Jacobsen, H.-A. (ed.) Middleware 2004. LNCS, vol. 3231, pp. 79–98. Springer, Heidelberg (2004)
23. Kim, J-R, Yoon, Y., Cho, K.-H.: Coupled Feedback Loops Form Dynamic Motifs of Cellular Networks. Biophysical Journal 94, 359–365 (2008)
24. Kobayashi, T., Chen, L., Aihara, K.: Modeling Genetic Switches with Positive Feedback Loops. J. theor. Biol. 221, 379–399 (2003)
25. Lienhard, M., Schmitt, A., Stefani, J.-B.: Oz/K: A Kernel Language for Component-Based Open Programming. In: Sixth International Conference on Generative Programming and Component Engineering (GPCE 2007) (October 2007)
26. Mejias, B., Van Roy, P.: A Relaxed Ring for Self-Organising and Fault-Tolerant Peer-to-Peer Networks. In: XXVI International Conference of the Chilean Computer Science Society (SCCC 2007) (November 2007)
27. Moser, M., Haridi, S.: Atomic Commitment in Transactional DHTs. In: Proc. of the CoreGRID Symposium. Rennes, France (August 2007)
28. Moser, M., Haridi, S., Schütt, T., Plantikow, S., Reinefeld, A., Schintke, F.: First report on formal models for transactions over structured overlay networks. SELFMAN Deliverable D3.1a (June 2007), `www.ist-selfman.org`
29. Pigolotti, S., Krishna, S., Jensen, M.H.: Oscillation patterns in negative feedback loops. Proc. National Academy of Sciences 104(16) (April 2007)
30. Plantikow, S., Reinefeld, A., Schintke, F.: Transactions for distributed wikis on structured overlays. In: Clemm, A., Granville, L.Z., Stadler, R. (eds.) DSOM 2007. LNCS, vol. 4785, pp. 256–267. Springer, Heidelberg (2007)
31. Salen, K., Zimmerman, E.: Rules of Play: Game Design Fundamentals. MIT Press, Cambridge (2003)
32. Schütt, T., Schintke, F., Reinefeld, A.: Range Queries on Structured Overlay Networks. Computer Communications 31, 280–291 (2008)
33. SELFMAN: Self Management for Large-Scale Distributed Systems based on Structured Overlay Networks and Components, European Commission 6th Framework Programme (June 2006), `http://www.ist-selfman.org`
34. Shafaat, T.M., Ghodsi, A., Haridi, S.: Dealing with Network Partitions in Structured Overlay Networks. Journal of Peer-to-Peer Networking and Applications (to appear, 2008)
35. Shafaat, T.M., Moser, M., Ghodsi, A., Schütt, T., Haridi, S., Reinefeld, A.: On Consistency of Data in Structured Overlay Networks. In: CoreGRID Integration Workshop. Heraklion, Greece. LNCS. Springer, Heidelberg (2008)
36. Stoica, I., Morris, R., Karger, D.R., Frans Kaashoek, M., Balakrishnan, H.: Chord: A Scalable Peer-to-Peer Lookup Service for Internet Applications. In: SIGCOMM 2001. pp. 149–160 (2001)
37. Van Roy, P.: Self Management and the Future of Software Design. In: Third International Workshop on Formal Aspects of Component Software (FACS 2006), ENTCS. vol. 182, pp. 201–217 (June 2007)
38. Weinberg, G. M.: An Introduction to General Systems Thinking: Silver Anniversary Edition. Dorset House (2001) (original edition 1975)
39. Whitehead, A.N.: Quote: Civilization advances by extending the number of important operations which we can perform without thinking of them

40. Wiener, N.: Cybernetics, or Control and Communication in the Animal and the Machine. MIT Press, Cambridge (1948)
41. Wiger, U.: Four-Fold Increase in Productivity and Quality – Industrial-Strength Functional Programming in Telecom-Class Products. In: Proceedings of the 2001 Workshop on Formal Design of Safety Critical Embedded Systems (2001)
42. Wikipedia, the free encyclopedia. Article Belief Propagation (March 2008), `http://en.wikipedia.org/wiki/Belief_propagation`
43. Wolpert, D.H., Wheeler, K.R., Tumer, K.: General principles of learning-based multi-agent systems. In: Proc. Third Annual Conference on Autonomous Agents (AGENTS 1999). pp. 77–93 (May 1999)
44. Wolpert, D. H., Kevin, R., Wheeler, Tumer, K.: Collective intelligence for control of distributed dynamical systems. Europhys. Lett. (2000)
45. Yap, R., Halim, F., Wu, Y.: First report on security in structured overlay networks. SELFMAN Deliverable D1.3a (November 2007), `www.ist-selfman.org`

Causal Semantics for the Algebra of Connectors
(Extended Abstract)

Simon Bliudze and Joseph Sifakis

VERIMAG, Centre Équation, 2 av de Vignate, 38610, Gières, France
{bliudze,sifakis}@imag.fr

Abstract. The Algebra of Connectors $\mathcal{AC}(P)$ is used to model structured interactions in the BIP component framework. Its terms are *connectors*, i.e. relations describing synchronization constraints between the ports of component-based systems. Connectors are structured combinations of two basic synchronization protocols between ports: *rendezvous* and *broadcast*. They are generated from the ports of P by using a binary *fusion* operator and a unary *typing* operator. Typing associates with terms (ports or connectors) synchronization types: *trigger* or *synchron*.

In a previous paper, we studied interaction semantics for $\mathcal{AC}(P)$ which defines the meaning of connectors as sets of interactions. This semantics reduces broadcasts into the set of their possible interactions and thus blurs the distinction between rendezvous and broadcast. It leads to exponentially complex models that cannot be a basis for efficient implementation. Furthermore, the induced semantic equivalence is not a congruence.

For a subset of $\mathcal{AC}(P)$, we propose a new *causal* semantics that does not reduce broadcast into a set of rendezvous and explicitly models the causal dependency relation between triggers and synchrons. The Algebra of Causal Trees $\mathcal{CT}(P)$ formalizes this subset. It is the set of the terms generated from interactions on the set of ports P, by using two operators: a *causality* operator and a *parallel composition* operator. Terms are sets of trees where the successor relation represents causal dependency between interactions: an interaction can participate in a global interaction only if its parent participates too. We show that causal semantics is consistent with interaction semantics. Furthermore, it defines an isomorphism between $\mathcal{CT}(P)$ and the set of the terms of $\mathcal{AC}(P)$ involving triggers.

Finally, we define for causal trees a boolean representation in terms of *causal rules*.

1 Introduction

Component-based design is based on the separation between coordination and computation. Systems are built from units processing sequential code insulated from concurrent execution issues. The isolation of coordination mechanisms allows a global treatment and analysis.

F.S. de Boer et al. (Eds.): FMCO 2007, LNCS 5382, pp. 179–199, 2008.

One of the main limitations of the current state-of-the-art is the lack of a unified paradigm for describing and analyzing information flow between components. Such a paradigm would allow system designers and implementers to formulate their solutions in terms of tangible, well-founded and organized concepts instead of using disparate coordination mechanisms such as semaphores, monitors, message passing, remote call, protocols etc. A unified paradigm should allow a comparison of otherwise unrelated architectural solutions and could be a basis for evaluating them and deriving implementations in terms of specific coordination mechanisms.

A number of paradigms for unifying interaction in heterogeneous systems have been studied in [1,2,3]. In these works, unification is achieved by reduction to a common low-level semantic model. Interaction mechanisms and their properties are not studied independently of behavior.

We propose a new *causal semantics* for the *Algebra of Connectors* studied in [4]. This algebra considers connectors as the basic concept for modelling coordination between components.

The term "connector" is widely used in the component frameworks literature with a number of different interpretations. In general, connectors have two main aspects: in the *data flow* setting, connectors define the way data is transferred between components; alternatively, in what we call *control flow* setting, connectors rather define synchronization constraints leaving aside or completely abstracting the data flow.

Control flow connectors are often specified in an operational setting, usually a process algebra. In [5], a process algebra is used to define an *architectural type* as a set of component/connector instances related by a set of attachments among their interactions. In [6], a connector is defined as a set of processes, with one process for each role of the connector, plus one process for the "glue" that describes how all the roles are bound together. A similar approach is developed by J. Fiadeiro and his colleagues in a categorical framework for CommUnity [7].

All the above models define connectors that can exhibit complex behavior. That is, computation is not limited to the components, but can be partly performed in the connectors. In [8], an algebra of connectors is developed that allows, in particular, an algebraic translation of the categorical approach used in CommUnity. This algebra allows *stateless* connectors to be constructed from a number of basic ones.

Reo [9,10] is a channel-based exogenous coordination model, which presents both data and control flow aspects. It uses connectors compositionally built out of different types of channels formalized in data-stream semantics and interconnected by using nodes. The connectors in Reo allow computation, but it is limited to the underlying channels. The nodes of connectors realize coordination between these channels.

Our approach is closest to that of [8], as it focuses on stateless connectors in a control flow setting. We consider connectors as relations between ports with synchronization types, which allows one to describe complex coordination patterns with an extremely small set of basic primitives. Thus, our main subject, in this paper, is structuring interactions among components. Although, in the composed system, data exchange can take place upon synchronisation, this is out of the scope of this paper.

In a previous paper [4], we studied an *interaction semantics* for the Algebra of Connectors $\mathcal{AC}(P)$, which is used to model interactions in the BIP component framework [11,12]. Terms of $\mathcal{AC}(P)$ are *connectors.* The interaction semantics defines the meaning of a connector as the set of the interactions it allows.

$\mathcal{AC}(P)$ is defined from a set P of ports. Its terms represent sets of interactions which are non empty sets of ports. Within a connector, an interaction can take place in two situations: either an interaction is fired when all involved ports are ready to participate (strong synchronization), or some subset of ports triggers the interaction without waiting for other ports. Thus, connectors are generated from the ports of P by using a binary *fusion* operator and a unary *typing* operator. Typing associates with terms (ports or connectors) synchronization types: *trigger* or *synchron.* Trigger and synchron terms form connectors as described below.

A *Simple* (or *flat*) connector is an expression of the form $p_1' \ldots p_k' p_{k+1} \cdots p_n$, where primed ports p_i' are triggers, and unprimed ports p_j are synchrons. For a flat connector involving the set of ports $\{p_1, \ldots, p_n\}$, interaction semantics defines the set of its interactions by the following rule: *an interaction is any non empty subset of* $\{p_1, \ldots, p_n\}$ *which contains some port that is a trigger; otherwise (if all the ports are synchrons), the only possible interaction is the maximal one, that is* $p_1 \ldots p_n$. As usual, we abbreviate $\{p_1, \ldots, p_n\}$ to $p_1 \ldots p_n$.

In particular, two basic synchronization protocols can be modelled naturally: 1) *rendezvous*, when all the related ports are synchrons, and the only possible interaction is the maximal one containing all ports of the connector; 2) *broadcast*, when the port that initiates the interaction is a trigger, all other ports are synchrons, and possible interactions are those containing the trigger. Connectors, representing these two protocols for ports s, r_1,r_2, and r_3, are shown in Fig. 1(a, b). Triangles represent triggers, and circles represent synchrons.

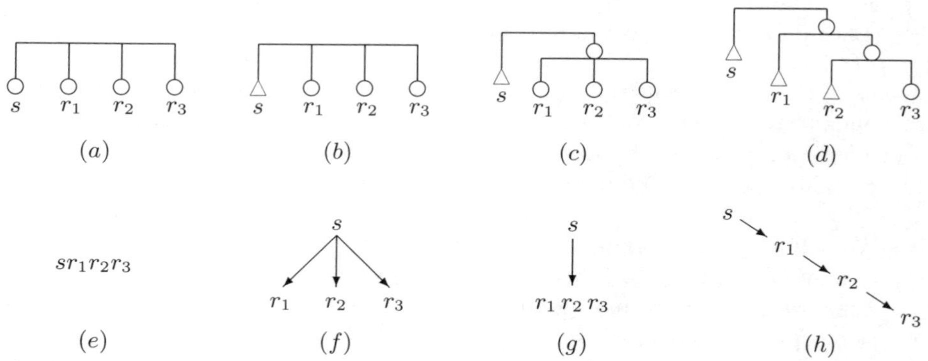

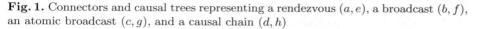

Fig. 1. Connectors and causal trees representing a rendezvous (a, e), a broadcast (b, f), an atomic broadcast (c, g), and a causal chain (d, h)

Hierarchical connectors are expressions composed of typed ports and/or typed sub-connectors. Fig. 1(c) shows a connector realizing an atomic broadcast from a port s to ports r_1, r_2, and r_3. The port s is a trigger, and r_1, r_2, r_3 are strongly synchronized in a sub-connector, itself typed as a synchron. The corresponding $\mathcal{AC}(P)$ term is $s'[r_1r_2r_3]$, and the possible interactions are: s and $sr_1r_2r_3$. Here the term in brackets $[\cdot]$ is a sub-connector typed as a synchron. Primed brackets $[\cdot]'$ denote a sub-connector typed as a trigger. The connector shown in Fig. 1(d) is a causal chain of interactions initiated by the port s. The corresponding $\mathcal{AC}(P)$ term is $s'[r_1'[r_2'r_3]]$, and the possible interactions are s, sr_1, sr_1r_2, $sr_1r_2r_3$: a trigger s alone or combined with some interaction from the sub-connector $r_1'[r_2'r_3]$, itself a shorter causal chain.

As shown in the above examples, interaction semantics reduces a connector into the set of its interactions. This leads to exponentially complex representations. Furthermore, it blurs the distinction between rendezvous and broadcast as each interaction of a broadcast can be realized by a rendezvous. In [4], we have shown that this also has deep consequences on the induced semantic equivalence: broadcasts may be equivalent to sets of rendezvous but they are not congruent.

The deficiencies of interaction semantics have motivated the investigation of a new *causal* semantics for a subset of connectors of $\mathcal{AC}(P)$, formalized as the Algebra of Casual Trees $\mathcal{CT}(P)$. This semantics distinguishes broadcast and rendezvous by explicitly modelling the causal dependency relation between triggers and synchrons in broadcasts. The terms of $\mathcal{CT}(P)$ represent sets of interactions, generated from atomic interactions on the set of ports P, by using two operators:

- A *causality* operator $\rightarrow$ which defines the causal relationship. The term $a_1 \rightarrow a_2 \rightarrow a_3$ is a causal chain meaning that interaction a_1 may trigger interaction a_2 which may trigger interaction a_3. The possible interactions for this chain are a_1, a_1a_2, $a_1a_2a_3$.
- An associative and commutative *parallel composition* operator $\oplus$. A causal tree can be considered as the parallel composition of all its causal chains. For instance, the term $a_1 \rightarrow (a_2 \oplus a_3)$ is equivalent to $(a_1 \rightarrow a_2) \oplus (a_1 \rightarrow a_3)$ (both describing the set of four interactions: a_1, a_1a_2, a_1a_3, and $a_1a_2a_3$).

Terms of $\mathcal{CT}(P)$ are naturally represented as sets of causal trees where $\rightarrow$ corresponds to the parent/son relation. Fig. 1($e - h$) shows the causal trees for the four connectors discussed above.

The main results of the paper are the following:

- We define causal semantics for $\mathcal{AC}(P)$ in terms of causality trees, as a function $\mathcal{AC}(P) \rightarrow \mathcal{CT}(P)$. Causal semantics is sound with respect to interaction semantics. An important result is that the algebra of causal trees $\mathcal{CT}(P)$ is isomorphic to classes of *causal connectors* $\mathcal{AC}_c(P)$ and *causal sets of interactions* $\mathcal{AI}_c(P)$. A causal set of interactions is closed under synchronization. A causal connector has a trigger in each sub-connector (including itself). We have shown that the equivalence and the congruence of $\mathcal{AC}(P)$ coincide for the set of causal connectors $\mathcal{AC}_c(P)$.

- We define for causal trees, $\mathcal{CT}(P)$ a boolean representation by using *causal rules*. Terms are represented by boolean expressions on P. The boolean valuation of port p is interpreted as the presence/absence of a port in an interaction. This representation is used for their symbolic manipulation and simplification as well as for performing boolean operations on connectors. It is applied for the efficient implementation of BIP, in particular, to compute the possible interactions for a given state.

The paper is structured as follows. Sect. 2 provides a succinct presentation of the basic semantic model for BIP and in particular, its composition parameterized by interactions. Sect. 3 presents the Algebra of Connectors, $\mathcal{AC}(P)$, and its global interaction semantics. Sect. 4 presents a semantics for $\mathcal{AC}(P)$ in terms of the Algebra of Causal trees, $\mathcal{CT}(P)$. It also shows how a boolean representation for connectors can be obtained from their representation as causal trees.

2 The BIP Component Framework

BIP is a component framework for constructing systems by superposing three layers of modelling: Behavior, Interaction, and Priority. The lower layer consists of a set of atomic components representing transition systems. The second layer models interactions between components, specified by connectors. These are relations between ports equipped with synchronization types. Priorities are used to enforce scheduling policies applied to interactions of the second layer.

The BIP component framework has been implemented in a language and a tool-set. The BIP language offers primitives and constructs for modelling and composing layered components. Atomic components are communicating automata extended with C functions and data. Their transitions are labelled with sets of communication ports. The BIP language also allows composition of components parameterized by sets of interactions as well as application of priorities.

The BIP tool-set includes an editor and a compiler for generating C++ code from BIP programs. The generated C++ code can be compiled for execution on a dedicated platform (see [11,13]).

We provide a succinct formalization of the BIP component model focusing on the operational semantics of component interaction.

Definition 1. *For a set of ports P, an* interaction *is a non-empty subset $a \subseteq P$ of ports. To simplify notation we represent an interaction $\{p_1, p_2, \ldots, p_n\}$ as $p_1 p_2 \cdots p_n$.*

Definition 2. *A transition system is a triple $B = (Q, P, \to)$, where Q is a set of* states*, P is a set of* ports*, and $\to \subseteq Q \times 2^P \times Q$ is a set of* transitions*, each labelled by an interaction.*

For any pair of states $q, q' \in Q$ and interaction $a \in 2^P$, we write $q \xrightarrow{a} q'$, iff $(q, a, q') \in \to$. When the interaction is irrelevant, we simply write $q \to q'$.

An interaction a is enabled *in state q, denoted $q \xrightarrow{a}$, iff there exists $q' \in Q$ such that $q \xrightarrow{a} q'$.*

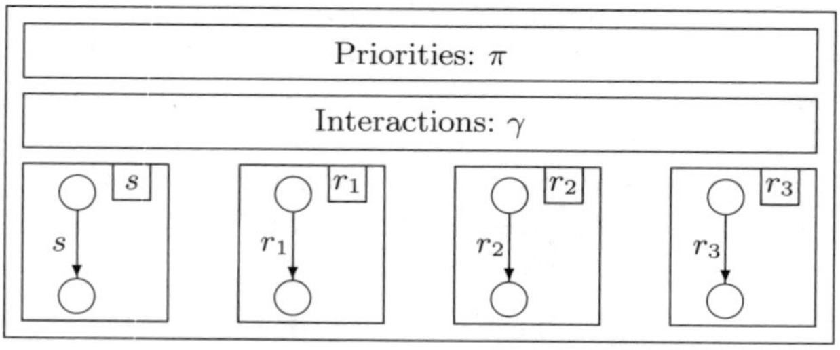

Fig. 2. A system with four atomic components

In BIP, a system can be obtained as the composition of n components, each modelled by a transition system $B_i = (Q_i, P_i, \rightarrow_i)$, for $i \in [1,n]$, such that their sets of ports are pairwise disjoint: for $i, j \in [1,n]$ $(i \neq j)$, we have $P_i \cap P_j = \emptyset$. We take $P = \bigcup_{i=1}^n P_i$, the set of all ports in the system.

The *composition* of components $\{B_i\}_{i=1}^n$, parameterized by a set of interactions $\gamma \subseteq 2^P$ is the transition system $B = (Q, P, \rightarrow_\gamma)$, where $Q = \bigotimes_{i=1}^n Q_i$ and $\rightarrow_\gamma$ is the least set of transitions satisfying the rule

$$\frac{a \in \gamma \quad \wedge \quad \forall i \in [1,n],\ (a \cap P_i \neq \emptyset \Rightarrow q_i \overset{a \cap P_i}{\longrightarrow}_i q_i')}{(q_1, \ldots, q_n) \xrightarrow{a}_\gamma (q_1', \ldots, q_n')}, \tag{1}$$

where $q_i = q_i'$ for all $i \in [1,n]$ such that $a \cap P_i = \emptyset$. We write $B = \gamma(B_1 \ldots, B_n)$.

Notice that an interaction $a \in \gamma$ is enabled in $\gamma(B_1, \ldots, B_n)$, only if, for each $i \in [1,n]$, the interaction $a \cap P_i$ is enabled in B_i; the states of components that do not participate in the interaction remain unchanged.

Several distinct interactions can be enabled at the same time, thus introducing non-determinism in the product behavior. This can be restricted by means of priorities [4,13]. Here, we omit formal definition of priorities, as we only use the *maximal progress* rule, which is implicitly assumed throught the paper: whenever two interactions, a and a', such that $a \subsetneq a'$, are possible, we always choose a'.

Example 1 (Sender/Receivers). Fig. 2 shows a component $\gamma(S, R_1, R_2, R_3)$ obtained by composition of four atomic components: a sender, S, and three receivers, R_1, R_2, R_3 with a set of interactions γ. The sender has a port s for sending messages, and each receiver has a port r_i $(i = 1, 2, 3)$ for receiving them. The following table specifies γ for four different interaction schemes.

Interaction scheme	Interactions
Rendezvous	$sr_1r_2r_3$
Broadcast	s, sr_1, sr_2, sr_3, sr_1r_2, sr_1r_3, sr_2r_3, $sr_1r_2r_3$
Atomic Broadcast	s, $sr_1r_2r_3$
Causal Chain	s, sr_1, sr_1r_2, $sr_1r_2r_3$

Rendezvous means strong synchronization between S and all R_i. This is specified by a single interaction involving all the ports. This interaction can occur only if all the components are in states enabling transitions labelled respectively by s, r_1, r_2, r_3.

Broadcast means weak synchronization, that is a synchronization involving S and any (possibly empty) subset of R_i. This is specified by the set of all interactions containing s. These interactions can occur only if S is in a state enabling s. Each R_i participates in the interaction only if it is in a state enabling r_i.

Atomic broadcast means that either a message is received by all R_i, or by none. Two interactions are possible: s, when at least one of the receiving ports is not enabled, and the interaction $sr_1r_2r_3$, corresponding to strong synchronization.

Causal chain means that for a message to be received by R_i it has to be received by all R_j, for $j < i$. This interaction scheme is common in reactive systems.

Example 2 (Modulo-8 counter). Fig. 3 shows a model for the Modulo-8 counter presented in [14], obtained by composition of three Modulo-2 counter components. Ports p, r, and t correspond to inputs, whereas q, s, and u correspond to outputs. It can be easily verified that the interactions pqr, $pqrst$, and $pqrstu$ happen, respectively, every second, fourth, and eighth occurrence of an input interaction through the port p.

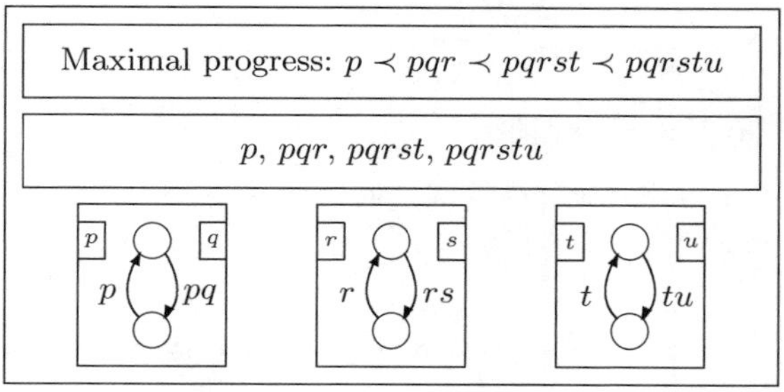

Fig. 3. Modulo-8 counter

Notice that the composition operator can express usual parallel composition operators [4], such as the ones used in CSP [15] and CCS [16]. By enforcing maximal progress, priorities allow to express broadcast.

3 The Algebra of Connectors

In this section, we introduce the *algebra of connectors* $\mathcal{AC}(P)$, which formalizes the concept of connector, supported by the BIP language [11]. For the sake of simplicity, we consider the subset of terms of $\mathcal{AC}(P)$ that do not involve union, that is the subset of *monomial connectors* (cf. [4]).

3.1 The Algebra of Interactions

We introduce the *algebra of interactions* $\mathcal{AI}(P)$, used to define the interaction semantics of $\mathcal{AC}(P)$.

Let P be a set of ports, such that $0, 1 \notin P$. Recall (Def. 1) that an *interaction* is a non-empty subset $a \subseteq P$. We abbreviate $\{p_1, p_2, \ldots, p_n\}$ to $p_1\, p_2 \ldots p_n$.

Syntax. The algebra of interactions $\mathcal{AI}(P)$, is defined by the following syntax

$$x ::= 0 \mid 1 \mid p \in P \mid x \cdot x \mid x + x\,, \tag{2}$$

where $+$ and $\cdot$ are binary operators, respectively called *union* and *synchronization*. Synchronization binds stronger than union.

Axioms

1. Union $+$ is idempotent, associative, commutative, and has an identity element 0;
2. Synchronization $\cdot$ is associative, commutative, has an identity element 1, and an absorbing element 0; synchronization distributes over union. Furthermore, it is idempotent for monomial terms (terms without $+$).

Semantics. The semantics of $\mathcal{AI}(P)$ is given by the function $\|\cdot\| : \mathcal{AI}(P) \to 2^{2^P}$, defined by

$$\begin{aligned}
&\|0\| \;=\; \emptyset, \quad \|1\| \;=\; \{\emptyset\}, \quad \|p\| \;=\; \Big\{\{p\}\Big\},\\
&\|x_1 + x_2\| = \|x_1\| \cup \|x_2\|,\\
&\|x_1 \cdot x_2\| \;=\Big\{a_1 \cup a_2 \,\Big|\, a_1 \in \|x_1\|,\; a_2 \in \|x_2\|\Big\},
\end{aligned} \tag{3}$$

for $p \in P$, $x, x_1, x_2 \in \mathcal{AI}(P)$. Terms of $\mathcal{AI}(P)$ represent sets of interactions between the ports of P.

Remark 1. In Def. 1, interactions are non-empty subsets of P, i.e. $a \in 2^P \setminus \{\emptyset\}$. In the following, we lift this restriction. Thus, $1 \in \mathcal{AI}(P)$ represents a singleton subset $\{\emptyset\} \subseteq 2^P$ (cf. (3)). The term $0 \in \mathcal{AI}(P)$ corresponds to an empty subset of 2^P and does not represent any interaction. Thus interactions correspond to non-zero monomial terms of $\mathcal{AI}(P)$.

Proposition 1 ([4]). *The axiomatization of $\mathcal{AI}(P)$ is sound and complete, that is, for any $x, y \in \mathcal{AI}(P)$, $x = y$ iff $\|x\| = \|y\|$.*

Example 3 (Sender/Receiver continued). The second column of Table 1 shows the representation in $\mathcal{AI}(P)$ for the four interaction schemes of Ex. 1.

Table 1. $\mathcal{AI}(P)$, $\mathcal{AC}(P)$, and $\mathcal{CT}(P)$ representations of four basic interaction schemes

	$\mathcal{AI}(P)$	$\mathcal{AC}(P)$	$\mathcal{CT}(P)$
Rendezvous	$s\,r_1\,r_2\,r_3$	$s\,r_1\,r_2\,r_3$	$s\,r_1\,r_2\,r_3$
Broadcast	$s\,(1+r_1)\,(1+r_2)\,(1+r_3)$	$s'\,r_1\,r_2\,r_3$	$s \rightarrow (r_1 \oplus r_2 \oplus r_3)$
Atomic Broadcast	$s\,(1+r_1\,r_2\,r_3)$	$s'\,[r_1\,r_2\,r_3]$	$s \rightarrow r_1\,r_2\,r_3$
Causal Chain	$s\,(1+r_1\,(1+ +r_2\,(1+r_3)))$	$s'\,[r_1'\,[r_2'\,r_3]]$	$s \rightarrow r_1 \rightarrow r_2 \rightarrow r_3$

3.2 Correspondence with Boolean Functions

$\mathcal{AI}(P)$ can be bijectively mapped to the free boolean algebra $\mathbb{B}[P]$ generated by P. We define a mapping $\beta : \mathcal{AI}(P) \rightarrow \mathbb{B}[P]$ by setting:

$$\beta(0) = \mathit{false}\,, \qquad \beta(x+y) = \beta(x) \vee \beta(y)\,,$$

$$\beta(1) = \bigwedge_{p \in P} \overline{p}\,, \qquad \beta(p_{i_1} \ldots p_{i_k}) = \bigwedge_{j=1}^{k} p_{i_j} \cdot \bigwedge_{i \neq i_j} \overline{p_i}\,,$$

for $p_{i_1}, \ldots, p_{i_k} \in P$, and $x, y \in \mathcal{AI}(P)$, where in the right-hand side the elements of P are considered to be boolean variables. We denote by *false* (resp. *true*) the least (resp. greatest) element in $\mathbb{B}[P]$. For example, consider the correspondence table for $P = \{p, q\}$ shown in Table 2.

Table 2. Correspondence between $\mathcal{AI}(\{p, q\})$ and boolean functions with two variables

$\mathcal{AI}(P)$	$\mathbb{B}[P]$
0	*false*
$1 \quad p \quad q \quad pq$	$\overline{p}\,\overline{q} \quad p\overline{q} \quad \overline{p}q \quad pq$
$p+1 \quad q+1 \quad pq+1 \quad p+q \quad p+pq \quad q+pq$	$\overline{q} \quad \overline{p} \quad \overline{p}\,\overline{q} \vee pq \quad p\overline{q} \vee \overline{p}q \quad p \quad q$
$p+q+1 \quad pq+p+1 \quad pq+q+1 \quad pq+p+q$	$\overline{p} \vee \overline{q} \quad p \vee \overline{q} \quad \overline{p} \vee q \quad p \vee q$
$pq+p+q+1$	*true*

The mapping β is an order isomorphism, and consequently techniques specific to boolean algebras can be applied to the boolean representation of $\mathcal{AI}(P)$ (e.g. BDDs).

Any interaction $a \in 2^P$ defines a valuation on P with, for each $p \in P$, $p = \mathit{true}$ iff $p \in a$. Notice that the constant valuation *false* is associated to the interaction 1, which corresponds to the empty set of ports $\emptyset \in 2^P$ (cf. Rem 1 and Table 2).

Definition 3. *An interaction $a \in 2^P$ satisfies a formula $R \in \mathbb{B}[P]$ (denoted $a \models R$) iff the corresponding boolean valuation satisfies R. A term $x \in \mathcal{AI}(P)$ satisfies R (denoted $x \models R$) iff all interactions belonging to x satisfy R, that is*

$$x \models R \quad \overset{def}{\iff} \quad \forall a \in \|x\|, \quad a \models R\,.$$

Remark 2. Let R_1 and R_2 be two equivalent formulae. They are satisfied by the same interactions:

$$\forall a \in 2^P, \quad a \models R_1 \iff a \models R_2\,.$$

Proposition 2. *An interaction belongs to the set described by an expression $x \in \mathcal{AI}(P)$ if and only if it satisfies $\beta(x)$, that is*

$$\|x\| = \left\{a \in 2^P \,\middle|\, a \models \beta(x)\right\}. \tag{4}$$

Remark 3. As $\|0\| = \emptyset$, according to Def. 3, it satisfies all formulae in $\mathbb{B}[P]$, and in particular $0 \models \mathit{false}$. This is the only term in $\mathcal{AI}(P)$ satisfying the constant predicate *false*. Recall (Rem 1) that $0 \notin 2^P$.

The advantage of $\mathcal{AI}(P)$ over its boolean representation is that it provides a more intuitive description of sets of interactions. For example, the term $p+pq \in \mathcal{AI}(P)$ represents the set of interactions $\{p, pq\}$ for any set of ports P containing p and q. The boolean representation of $p + pq$ depends on P: if $P = \{p, q\}$ then $\beta(p + pq) = p$, whereas if $P = \{p, q, r, s\}$ then $\beta(p + pq) = p\,\overline{r}\,\overline{s}$.

Synchronization of two interactions in $\mathcal{AI}(P)$ is by simple concatenation, whereas for their boolean representation there is no simple context-independent composition rule.

Example 4. Let $P = \{p, q, r, s\}$. The representation of p is $\beta(p) = p\,\overline{q}\,\overline{r}\,\overline{s}$, the representation of q is $\beta(q) = \overline{p}\,q\,\overline{r}\,\overline{s}$, and the representation $\beta(pq) = p\,q\,\overline{r}\,\overline{s}$ of the synchronization pq is obtained by combining the "positive" variables p and q from $\beta(p)$ and $\beta(q)$ respectively with the "negative" variables $\overline{r}$ and $\overline{s}$ belonging to both.

To formalize the above example, let $x, y \in \mathcal{AI}(P)$ be two terms represented respectively by boolean functions

$$\beta(x) = \bigwedge_{p \in P_x} p \cdot \bigwedge_{q \in Q_x} \overline{q}, \quad \text{and} \quad \beta(y) = \bigwedge_{p \in P_y} p \cdot \bigwedge_{q \in Q_y} \overline{q}, \tag{5}$$

where $P_x, P_y \subseteq P$ and $Q_x, Q_y \subseteq P$ are respectively the sets of positive and negative variables in $\beta(x)$ and $\beta(y)$, then the synchronization xy corresponds to

$$\beta(xy) = \bigwedge_{p \in P_x \cup P_y} p \cdot \bigwedge_{q \in Q_x \cap Q_y} \overline{q} \tag{6}$$

In the general case, when the boolean representations of x and y contain multiple summands of the form (5), the representation of their synchronization

xy can be obtained by applying the above operation pairwise to the summands of $\beta(x)$ and $\beta(y)$ and taking the sum of the obtained conjunctions.

On the other hand, the interactions belonging to the intersection of x and y, that is to $\|x\| \cap \|y\|$, are clearly characterized by $\beta(x) \wedge \beta(y)$.

Thus, we have a correspondence between $\mathcal{AI}(P)$ equipped with union, synchronization, and intersection, and $\mathbb{B}[P]$ equipped with disjunction, the operation above described by (5) and (6), and conjunction.

3.3 Syntax and Interaction Semantics for $\mathcal{AC}(P)$

Syntax. Let P be a set of ports, such that $0, 1 \notin P$. The syntax of the algebra of connectors, $\mathcal{AC}(P)$, is defined by

$$\begin{aligned} s &::= [0] \mid [1] \mid [p] \mid [x] \quad (\textit{synchrons}) \\ t &::= [0]' \mid [1]' \mid [p]' \mid [x]' \; (\textit{triggers}) \\ x &::= s \mid t \mid x \cdot x\,, \end{aligned} \tag{7}$$

for $p \in P$, and where $\cdot$ is a binary operator called *fusion*, and brackets $[\cdot]$ and $[\cdot]'$ are unary *typing* operators.

Fusion is a generalization of synchronization in $\mathcal{AI}(P)$. Typing is used to form connectors: $[\cdot]'$ defines *triggers* (which can initiate an interaction), and $[\cdot]$ defines *synchrons* (which need synchronization with other ports).

Definition 4. *In a system with a set of ports P,* connectors *are elements of $\mathcal{AC}(P)$.*

Notation. We write $[x]^\alpha$, for $\alpha \in \{0, 1\}$, to denote a typed connector. When $\alpha = 0$, the connector is a synchron, otherwise it is a trigger.

In order to simplify notation, we will omit brackets on 0, 1, and ports $p \in P$, as well as '$\cdot$' for the fusion operator.

The algebraic structure of $\mathcal{AC}(P)$ inherits most of the axioms of $\mathcal{AI}(P)$.

Axioms

1. Fusion $\cdot$ is associative, commutative, distributive, idempotent, and has an identity element [1].
2. Typing satisfies the following axioms, for $x, y, z \in \mathcal{AC}(P)$ and $\alpha, \beta \in \{0, 1\}$:
   (a) $[0]' = [0]$,
   (b) $\Big[[x]^\alpha\Big]^\beta = [x]^\beta$.

Semantics. The semantics of $\mathcal{AC}(P)$ is given by the function $|\cdot| : \mathcal{AC}(P) \rightarrow \mathcal{AI}(P)$, defined by the rules (we use the product symbol '$\prod$' to denote fusion)

$$|p| = p\,, \tag{8}$$

$$\left|\prod_{i=1}^{n} [x_i]\right| = \prod_{i=1}^{n} |x_i|\,, \tag{9}$$

$$\left| \prod_{i=1}^{n} [x_i]' \cdot \prod_{j=1}^{m} [y_j] \right| = \sum_{i=1}^{n} |x_i| \prod_{k \neq i} \Big(1 + |x_k|\Big) \prod_{j=1}^{m} \Big(1 + |y_j|\Big) , \tag{10}$$

for $p \in P \cup \{0, 1\}$ and $x, x_1, \ldots, x_n, y_1, \ldots, y_m \in \mathcal{AC}(P)$. The sum in (10) is the union operator of $\mathcal{AI}(P)$.

Example 5. Consider a system consisting of two Senders with ports s_1, s_2, and three Receivers with ports r_1, r_2, r_3. The meaning of $s_1' \, s_2' \, r_1 \, [r_2 \, r_3]$ is

$$\begin{aligned} |s_1' \, s_2' \, r_1 \, [r_2 \, r_3]| \; &= \\ &\overset{(10)}{=} |s_1| \, (1 + |s_2|) \, (1 + |r_1|) \, (1 + |r_2 \, r_3|) \; + \; |s_2| \, (1 + |s_1|) \, (1 + |r_1|) \, (1 + |r_2 \, r_3|) \\ &\overset{(9)}{=} \Big(|s_1| \, (1 + |s_2|) \; + \; |s_2| \, (1 + |s_1|) \Big) \, (1 + |r_1|) \, (1 + |r_2| \, |r_3|) \\ &\overset{(8)}{=} \Big(s_1 \, (1 + s_2) \; + \; s_2 \, (1 + s_1) \Big) \, (1 + r_1) \, (1 + r_2 \, r_3) , \end{aligned}$$

which corresponds to the set of the interactions containing at least one of s_1 and s_2, and possibly r_1 and a synchronization of both r_2 and r_3.

Proposition 3 ([4]). *The axiomatization of $\mathcal{AC}(P)$ is sound, that is, for $x, y \in \mathcal{AC}(P)$, the equality $x = y$ implies $|x| = |y|$.*

Example 6 (Sender/Receiver continued). The third column of Table 1 shows the connectors for the four interaction schemes of Ex. 1.

Notice that $\mathcal{AC}(P)$ allows compact representation of interactions and, moreover, explicitly captures the difference between broadcast and rendezvous. The typing operator induces a hierarchical structure.

Example 7 (Modulo-8 counter continued). In the model shown in Fig. 4, the causal chain pattern is applied to connectors p, $q\,r$, $s\,t$, and u. Interactions are modelled by a single structured connector $p' \, \Big[[q\,r]' \, [[s\,t]' \, u] \Big]$:

$$\left| p' \, \Big[[q\,r]' \, \Big[[s\,t]' \, u \Big] \Big] \right| = p + p\,q\,r + p\,q\,r\,s\,t + p\,q\,r\,s\,t\,u \, .$$

These are exactly the interactions of the Modulo-8 counter of Fig. 3.

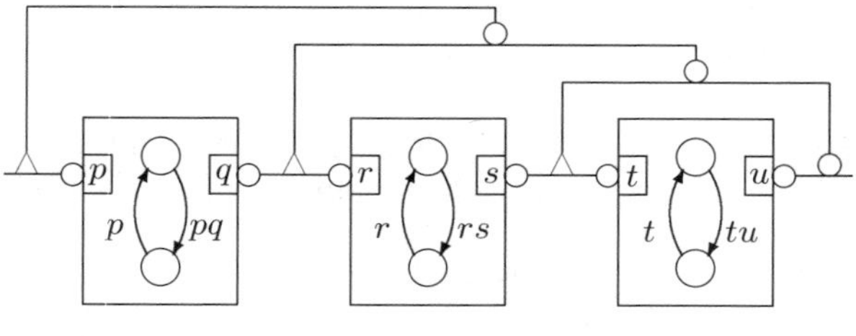

Fig. 4. Modulo-8 counter

Definition 5. *Two connectors $x, y \in \mathcal{AC}(P)$ are* equivalent *(denoted $x \simeq y$), iff they have the same sets of interactions, i.e. $x \simeq y$ if and only if $|x| = |y|$.*

Notice that, in general, two equivalent terms are not congruent. For example, $p' \simeq p$, but $p'q \simeq p + pq \not\simeq pq$, for $p, q \in P$. Furthermore, the following terms are equivalent, but not congruent: pqr, $p[qr]$, and $[pq]r$, as different sets of interactions are obtained, when these terms are fused with a trigger. For instance, $s'[pq]r \simeq s + spq + sr + spqr$, whereas $s'p[qr] \simeq s + sp + sqr + spqr$.

Definition 6. *We denote by '$\cong$' the largest congruence relation contained in $\simeq$, that is the largest relation satisfying*

$$x \cong y \quad \Longrightarrow \quad \forall E \in \mathcal{AC}(P \cup \{z\}),\ E(x/z) \simeq E(y/z)\,, \tag{11}$$

where $x, y \in \mathcal{AC}(P)$, $z \notin P$, $E(x/z)$, and (resp. $E(y/z)$) denotes the expression obtained from E by replacing all occurrences of z by x (resp. y).

Theorem 1 ([4]). *For $x, y \in \mathcal{AC}(P)$, we have $x \cong y$ iff the three following conditions hold simultaneously*

1. $x \simeq y$,
2. $x \cdot 1' \simeq y \cdot 1'$,
3. $\#x > 0 \Leftrightarrow \#y > 0$,

where, for $x = \prod_{i=1}^{n} [x_i]^{\alpha_i}$, we denote by $\#x$ the number of triggers in this fusion, that is $\#x \stackrel{def}{=} \#\{i \in [1, n] \mid \alpha_i = 1\}$.

Corollary 1. *For $x, y \in \mathcal{AC}(P)$, holds $[x]'\,[y]' \;\cong\; \Big[[x]'\,[y]'\Big]'$.*

4 Causal Semantics for Connectors

In this section, we propose a new *causal* semantics for $\mathcal{AC}(P)$ connectors. This allows us to address two important points:

1. (*Congruence*). As we have shown in the previous section, the equivalence relation $\simeq$ on $\mathcal{AC}(P)$ is not a congruence. The causal semantics allows us to define a subset $\mathcal{AC}_c(P) \subsetneq \mathcal{AC}(P)$ of *causal connectors* such that a) every equivalence class on $\mathcal{AC}(P)$ has a representative in $\mathcal{AC}_c(P)$; and b) the equivalence $\simeq$ and congruence $\cong$ relations coincide on $\mathcal{AC}_c(P)$.
2. (*Boolean representation*). In [4], we showed that efficient computation of boolean operations (e.g. intersection, complementation) is crucial for efficient implementation of some classes of systems, e.g. synchronous systems. In this section, we present a method for computing boolean representations for $\mathcal{AC}(P)$ connectors through a translation into the algebra of causal trees $\mathcal{CT}(P)$. The terms of the latter have a natural boolean representation as sets of causal rules (implications). This boolean representation avoids complex enumeration of the interactions of connectors entailed by the method in Sect. 3.2.

The key idea for causal semantics is to render explicit the causal relations between different parts of the connector. In a fusion of typed connectors, triggers are mutually independent, and can be considered *parallel* to each other. Synchrons participate in an interaction only if it is initiated by a trigger. This introduces a causal relation: the trigger is a *cause* that can provoke an *effect*, which is the participation of a synchron in an interaction.

There are essentially three possibilities for connectors involving ports p and q:

1. A strong synchronization pq.
2. One trigger $p'q$, i.e. p is the cause of an interaction and q a potential effect, which we will denote in the following by $p \to q$.
3. Two triggers $p'q'$, i.e. p and q are independent (parallel), which we will denote in the following by $p \oplus q$.

This can be further extended to chains of causal relations between interactions. For example, $(p \oplus q) \to rs \to t$ corresponds to the connector $p'q' \,[\, [rs]' \, t]$. It means that any combination of p and q (i.e. p, q, or pq) can trigger an interaction in which both r and s may participate (thus, the corresponding interactions are p, q, pq, prs, qrs, and $pqrs$). Moreover, if r and s participate then t may do so, which adds the interactions $prst$, $qrst$, and $pqrst$.

Causal trees constructed with these two operators provide a compact and clear representation for connectors that shows explicitly the atomic interactions (p, q, rs, and t in the above example) and the dependencies between them. They also allow to exhibit the boolean *causal rules*, which define the necessary conditions for a given port to participate in an interaction. Intuitively, this corresponds to expressing arrows in the causal trees by implications.

A causal rule is a boolean formula over P, which has the form $p \Rightarrow \bigvee_{i=1}^{n} a_i$, where p is a port and a_i are interactions that can provoke p. Thus, in the above example, the causal rule for the port r is $r \Rightarrow ps \vee qs$, which means that for the port r to participate in an interaction of this connector, it is necessary that this interaction contain either ps or qs.

A set of causal rules uniquely describes the set of interactions that satisfy it (cf. Sect. 3.2), which provides a simple and efficient way for computing boolean representations for connectors by transforming them first into causal trees and then into a conjunction of the associated causal rules.

In the following sub-sections we formalize these ideas.

4.1 Causal Trees

Syntax. Let P be a set of ports such that $0, 1 \notin P$. The syntax of the *algebra of causal trees*, $\mathcal{CT}(P)$, is defined by

$$t ::= a \,|\, t \to t \,|\, t \oplus t \,, \tag{12}$$

where $a \in \mathcal{AI}(P)$ is 0, 1, or an interaction from 2^P, and $\to$ and $\oplus$ are respectively the *causality* and the *parallel composition* operators. Causality binds stronger than parallel composition.

Although the causality operator is not associative, for $t_1, \ldots, t_n \in \mathcal{CT}(P)$, we abbreviate $t_1 \rightarrow (t_2 \rightarrow (\ldots \rightarrow t_n)\ldots))$ to $t_1 \rightarrow t_2 \rightarrow \ldots \rightarrow t_n$. We call this construction a *causal chain.*

Axioms

1. Parallel composition, $\oplus$, is associative, commutative, idempotent, and its identity element is 0.
2. Causality, $\rightarrow$, satisfies the following axioms:
   (a) $t \rightarrow 1 = t$,
   (b) $t_1 \rightarrow (1 \rightarrow t_2) = t_1 \rightarrow t_2$,
   (c) $t \rightarrow 0 = t$,
   (d) $0 \rightarrow t = 0$.
3. The following axioms relate the two operators:
   (a) $(t_1 \rightarrow t_2) \rightarrow t_3 = t_1 \rightarrow (t_2 \oplus t_3)$,
   (b) $t_1 \rightarrow (t_2 \oplus t_3) = t_1 \rightarrow t_2 \;\oplus\; t_1 \rightarrow t_3$,
   (c) $(t_1 \oplus t_2) \rightarrow t_3 = t_1 \rightarrow t_3 \;\oplus\; t_2 \rightarrow t_3$.

Semantics. The *interaction semantics* of $\mathcal{CT}(P)$ is given by the function $|\cdot| : \mathcal{CT}(P) \rightarrow \mathcal{AI}(P)$, defined by the rules

$$|a| = a\,, \tag{13}$$

$$|a \rightarrow t| = a\Big(1 + |t|\Big)\,, \tag{14}$$

$$|t_1 \oplus t_2| = |t_1| + |t_2| + |t_1|\,|t_2|\,, \tag{15}$$

where a is an interaction of 2^P, and $t, t_1, t_2 \in \mathcal{CT}(P)$, and the rules induced by axioms (3a) and (3c). The set semantics of a causal tree $t \in \mathcal{CT}(P)$ is obtained by applying the semantic function $\|\cdot\| : \mathcal{AI}(P) \rightarrow 2^{2^P}$ to $|t|$. We denote $\|t\| \stackrel{def}{=} \|\,|t|\,\|$.

Example 8 (Causal chain). Consider interactions $a_1, \ldots, a_n \in 2^P$ and a causal chain $a_1 \rightarrow a_2 \rightarrow \ldots \rightarrow a_n$. Iterating rule (14), we then have

$$\begin{aligned} |a_1 \rightarrow a_2 \rightarrow \ldots \rightarrow a_n| &= a_1\Big(1 + |a_2 \rightarrow \ldots \rightarrow a_n|\Big) \\ &= a_1 + a_1 a_2\Big(1 + |a_3 \rightarrow \ldots \rightarrow a_n|\Big) \\ &= \ldots \\ &= a_1 \,+\, a_1 a_2 \,+ \ldots +\, a_1 a_2 \ldots a_n\,. \end{aligned}$$

Proposition 4. *The axiomatization of $\mathcal{CT}(P)$ is sound with respect to the semantic equivalence, i.e. for $t_1, t_2 \in \mathcal{CT}(P)$, $t_1 = t_2$ implies $|t_1| = |t_2|$.*

Remark 4. According to the axioms of $\mathcal{CT}(P)$ any causal tree can be represented as a parallel composition of its causal chains (see Fig. 5). Thus an interaction belonging to a causal tree is a synchronization of any number of prefixes (cf. Ex. 8) of the corresponding causal chains, i.e. branches of this tree.

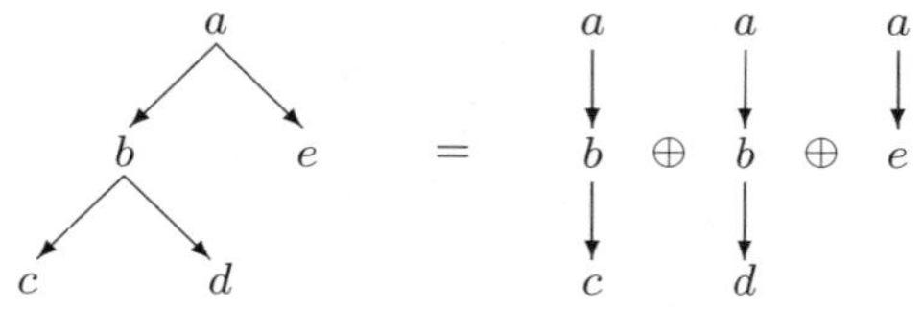

Fig. 5. A causal tree is the parallel composition of its causal chains

Example 9 (Sender/Receiver continued). The fourth column of Table 1 shows the causal trees for the four interaction schemes of Ex. 1.

Example 10 (Modulo-8 counter continued). The connector applied to the three Modulo-2 counter components in Ex. 7 consists of a causal chain pattern applied to rendezvous connectors p, $q\,r$, $s\,t$, and u. Thus, the corresponding causal tree is clearly $p \rightarrow qr \rightarrow st \rightarrow u$. In general, the transformation of $\mathcal{AC}(P)$ connectors into causal trees is presented in the section below.

Definition 7. *Two causal trees $t_1, t_2 \in \mathcal{CT}(P)$ are* equivalent, *denoted $t_1 \sim t_2$, iff $|t_1| = |t_2|$.*

4.2 Correspondence with $\mathcal{AC}(P)$

In order to provide the transformation from $\mathcal{AC}(P)$ to $\mathcal{CT}(P)$, we introduce two helper functions $root : \mathcal{CT}(P) \rightarrow \mathcal{AI}(P)$ and $rest : \mathcal{CT}(P) \rightarrow \mathcal{CT}(P)$ defined by

$$\begin{aligned} root(a) &= a\,, & rest(a) &= 0\\ root(a \rightarrow t) &= a\,, & rest(a \rightarrow t) &= t\,,\\ root(t_1 \oplus t_2) &= root(t_1) + root(t_2)\,, & rest(t_1 \oplus t_2) &= rest(t_1) \oplus rest(t_2)\,, \end{aligned}$$

for $a \in 2^P$ and $t, t_1, t_2 \in \mathcal{CT}(P)$. In general $t \neq root(t) \rightarrow rest(t)$. The equality holds only if t is of the form $a \rightarrow t_1$, for some interaction a and $t_1 \in \mathcal{CT}(P)$.

We define the function $\tau : \mathcal{AC}(P) \rightarrow \mathcal{CT}(P)$ associating a causal tree with a connector. By Cor. 1, any term can be rewritten to have at most one trigger. Therefore, the following three equations are sufficient to define τ:

$$\tau\left([x]' \prod_{i=1}^{n} [y_i]\right) = \tau(x) \rightarrow \bigoplus_{i=1}^{n} \tau(y_i)\,, \tag{16}$$

$$\tau\left(\prod_{i=1}^{n} [x_i]'\right) = \bigoplus_{i=1}^{n} \tau(x_i)\,, \tag{17}$$

$$\tau\left(\prod_{i=1}^{n} [y_i]\right) = \bigoplus_{j=1}^{m} \left(a_j \rightarrow \bigoplus_{i=1}^{n} rest\Big(\tau(y_i)\Big)\right)\,, \tag{18}$$

where $x, x_1, x_2, y_1, \ldots, y_n \in \mathcal{AC}(P)$, and, in (18), a_j are such that

$$\sum_{j=1}^{m} a_j = \prod_{i=1}^{n} root\Big(\tau(y_i)\Big)\,.$$

Example 11. Consider $P = \{p, q, r, s, t, u\}$ and $p'q'\Big[[r's][t'u]\Big] \in \mathcal{AC}(P)$. We have

$$\begin{aligned}\tau\left(p'q'\Big[[r's][t'u]\Big]\right) &= \tau\left(\Big[p'q'\Big]'\Big[[r's][t'u]\Big]\right)\\ &= \tau(p'q') \to \tau\Big([r's][t'u]\Big)\\ &= (p \oplus q) \to \Big(rt \to (s \oplus u)\Big).\end{aligned}$$

We also define the function $\sigma : \mathcal{CT}(P) \to \mathcal{AC}(P)$, associating connectors to causal trees:

$$\sigma(a) = [a], \tag{19}$$

$$\sigma(a \to t) = [a]'[\sigma(t)], \tag{20}$$

$$\sigma(t_1 \oplus t_2) = [\sigma(t_1)]'[\sigma(t_2)]'. \tag{21}$$

Proposition 5. *The functions $\sigma : \mathcal{CT}(P) \to \mathcal{AC}(P)$ and $\tau : \mathcal{AC}(P) \to \mathcal{CT}(P)$, satisfy the following properties*

1. $\forall x \in \mathcal{AC}(P),\ |x| = |\tau(x)|$,
2. $\forall t \in \mathcal{CT}(P),\ |t| = |\sigma(t)|$,
3. $\tau \circ \sigma = id$,
4. $\sigma \circ \tau \simeq id$ *(that is* $\forall x \in \mathcal{AC}(P),\ \sigma(\tau(x)) \simeq x$*).*

The above proposition says that the diagram shown in Fig. 6 is commutative except for the loop $\mathcal{AC}(P) \xrightarrow{\tau} \mathcal{CT}(P) \xrightarrow{\sigma} \mathcal{AC}_c(P) \hookrightarrow \mathcal{AC}(P)$.

In this diagram, $\mathcal{AC}_c(P) \subsetneq \mathcal{AC}(P)$ is the set of *causal connectors*, which is the image of $\mathcal{CT}(P)$ by σ. Note that any connector has an equivalent representation in $\mathcal{AC}_c(P)$. Similarly, $\mathcal{AI}_c(P) \subsetneq \mathcal{AI}(P)$ is the set of *causal interactions*, the image of $\mathcal{CT}(P)$ by the semantic function $|\cdot|$. The following proposition provides a characteristic property of the set of causal interactions.

Proposition 6. *The set of the causal interactions is closed under synchronization, that is $x \in \mathcal{AI}_c(P)$ iff $\forall a, b \in \|x\|,\ ab \in \|x\|$.*

As mentioned above, the semantic equivalence $\simeq$ on $\mathcal{AC}(P)$ is not a congruence. Prop. 7 and Cor. 2 below state that the restriction of $\simeq$ to $\mathcal{AC}_c(P)$ is a congruence. By definition of $\mathcal{AC}_c(P)$, each equivalence class $\simeq$ on $\mathcal{AC}(P)$ has a representative in $\mathcal{AC}_c(P)$.

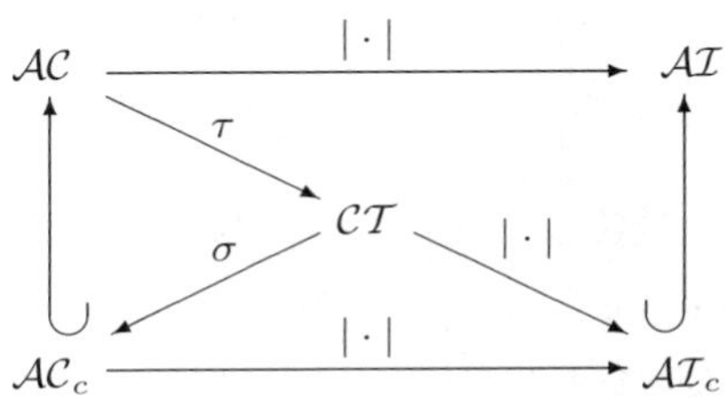

Fig. 6. A diagram relating the algebras

Proposition 7. $\forall t_1, t_2 \in \mathcal{CT}(P),\ t_1 \sim t_2 \Rightarrow \sigma(t_1) \cong \sigma(t_2)$.

Corollary 2. *The $\mathcal{AC}(P)$ equivalence restricted to $\mathcal{AC}_c(P)$ is a congruence, that is, for $x_1, x_2 \in \mathcal{AC}_c(P)$, $x_1 \simeq x_2$ implies $x_1 \cong x_2$.*

4.3 Boolean Representation of Connectors

Definition 8. *A* causal rule *is a $\mathbb{B}[P]$ formula $E \Rightarrow C$, where E (the* effect*) is either a constant, true, or a port variable $p \in P$, and C (the* cause*) is either a constant (true or false) or a disjunction of interactions, i.e. $\bigvee_{i=1}^n a_i$ where, for all $i \in [1, n]$, a_i are conjunctions of port variables.*

Causal rules without constants can be rewritten as formulas of the form $\overline{p} \vee \bigvee_{i=1}^n a_i$ and, by distributivity of $\wedge$ over $\vee$, are conjunctions of dual Horn clauses, i.e. disjunctions of variables whereof at most one is negative.

In line with Def. 3, an interaction $a \in 2^P$ satisfies the rule $p \Rightarrow \bigvee_{i=1}^n a_i$, iff $p \in a$ implies $a_i \subseteq a$, for some $i \in [1, n]$, that is, for a port to belong to an interaction, at least one of the corresponding causes must belong there too.

Example 12. Let $p \in P$, $a \in 2^P$, and $x \in \mathcal{AI}(P)$. Three particular types of causal rules can be set apart:

1. For an interaction to satisfy the rule $true \Rightarrow a$, it is necessary that it contain a.
2. Rules of the form $p \Rightarrow true$ are satisfied by all interactions.
3. An interaction can satisfy the rule $p \Rightarrow false$ only if it does not contain p.

Remark 5. Notice that $a_1 \vee a_1\, a_2 = a_1$, and therefore causal rules can be simplified accordingly:

$$(p \Rightarrow a_1 \vee a_1\, a_2) \ \rightsquigarrow\ (p \Rightarrow a_1)\,. \tag{22}$$

We assume that all the causal rules are simplified by using (22).

Definition 9. *A* system of causal rules *is a set $R = \{p \Rightarrow x_p\}_{p \in P^t}$, where $P^t \stackrel{def}{=} P \cup \{true\}$. An interaction $a \in 2^P$ satisfies the system R (denoted $a \models R$), iff $a \models \bigwedge_{p \in P^t}(p \Rightarrow x_p)$. We denote by $|R|$ the union of the interactions satisfying R:*

$$|R| \stackrel{def}{=} \sum_{a \models R} a\,.$$

A causal tree $t \in \mathcal{CT}(P)$ is equivalent to a system of causal rules R iff $|t| = |R|$.

We associate with $t \in \mathcal{CT}(P)$ the system of causal rules

$$R(t) \stackrel{def}{=} \{p \Rightarrow c_p(t)\}_{p \in P^t}\,, \tag{23}$$

where, for $p \in P^t$, the function $c_p : \mathcal{CT}(P) \to \mathbb{B}[P]$ is defined as follows. For $a \in 2^P$ (with $p \notin a$) and $t, t_1, t_2 \in \mathcal{CT}(P)$, we put

$$c_p(0) = false\,, \tag{24}$$

$$c_p(p \to t) = true\,, \tag{25}$$
$$c_p(pa \to t) = a\,, \tag{26}$$
$$c_p(a \to t) = a\, c_p(t)\,, \tag{27}$$
$$c_p(t_1 \oplus t_2) = c_p(t_1) \vee c_p(t_2)\,, \tag{28}$$

Similarly, we define $c_{true}(t)$ by

$$\begin{aligned} c_{true}(0) &= false\,, \\ c_{true}(1 \to t) &= true\,, \\ c_{true}(a \to t) &= a\,, \\ c_{true}(t_1 \oplus t_2) &= c_{true}(t_1) \vee c_{true}(t_2)\,. \end{aligned}$$

Remark 6. It is important to observe that, for any $t \in \mathcal{CT}(P)$, the system of causal rules $R(t)$, defined by (23), contains exactly one causal rule for each $p \in P^t$ (i.e. each $p \in P$ and *true*). For ports that do not participate in t, the rule is $p \Rightarrow false$. For ports that do not have any causality constraints, the rule is $p \Rightarrow true$.

Proposition 8. *For any causal tree* $t \in \mathcal{CT}(P)$, $|t| = |R(t)|$.

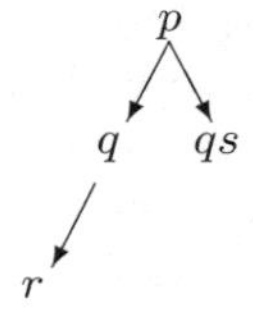

Fig. 7. Graphical representation of the causal tree $t = p \to (q \to r \,\oplus\, qs)$

Example 13. Consider the causal tree $t = p \to (q \to r \,\oplus\, qs)$ shown in Fig. 7. The associated system $R(t)$ of causal rules is

$$\{true \Rightarrow p\,,\quad p \Rightarrow true\,,\quad q \Rightarrow p\,,\quad r \Rightarrow pq\,,\quad s \Rightarrow pq\}\,.$$

Notice that $c_q(t) = p\Big(c_q(q \to r) \vee c_q(qs)\Big) = p \vee ps = p$.

The corresponding boolean formula is then

$$(true \Rightarrow p) \wedge (p \Rightarrow true) \wedge (q \Rightarrow p) \wedge (r \Rightarrow pq) \wedge (s \Rightarrow pq) \;=\; p\,q \vee p\,\overline{r}\,\overline{s}\,.$$

5 Conclusion

The paper provides a causal semantics for the algebra of connectors. This semantics leads to simpler and more intuitive representations which can be used for efficient implementation of operations on connectors in BIP. In contrast to interaction semantics equivalence, the induced equivalence is compatible with

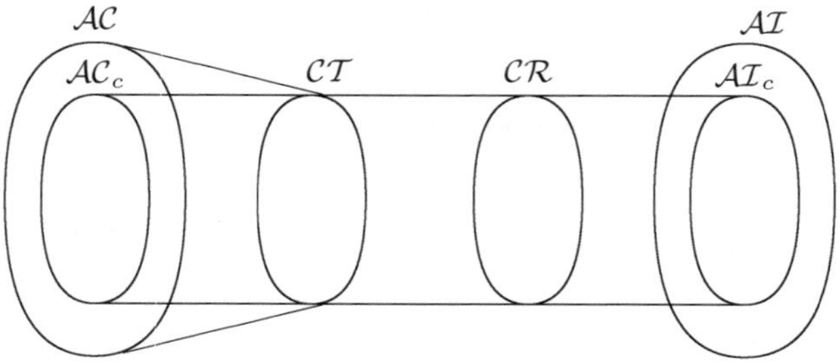

Fig. 8. A graphical representation of the relations between different algebras

the congruence on $\mathcal{AC}(P)$. Causal semantics allows a nice characterization of the set of causal connectors, which is isomorphic to the set of causal trees. The set of causal connectors also corresponds to the set of causal interactions, which are closed under synchronization. The relation between the different algebras is shown in Fig. 8.

The Algebra of Causal Trees, $\mathcal{CT}(P)$, breaks with the reductionist view of interaction semantics as it distinguishes between symmetric and asymmetric interaction. It allows structuring of global interactions as the parallel composition of chains of interactions. This is a very intuitive and alternate approach to interaction modeling especially for broadcast-based languages such as synchronous languages. Causal trees are very close to structures used to represent dependencies between signals in synchronous languages, e.g. [17]. This opens new possibilities for unifying asynchronous and synchronous semantics.

$\mathcal{CT}(P)$ can be extended in a straightforward manner to incorporate guards, necessary for conditional interaction. It is a basis for computing boolean representations for connectors, adequate for their symbolic manipulation and computation of boolean operations. These can be used for efficient implementations of component-based languages such as BIP.

References

1. Balarin, F., Watanabe, Y., Hsieh, H., Lavagno, L., Passerone, C., Sangiovanni-Vincentelli, A.: Metropolis: An integrated electronic system design environment. IEEE Computer 36(4), 45–52 (2003)
2. Balasubramanian, K., Gokhale, A., Karsai, G., Sztipanovits, J., Neema, S.: Developing applications using model-driven design environments. IEEE Computer 39(2), 33–40 (2006)
3. Eker, J., Janneck, J., Lee, E., Liu, J., Liu, X., Ludvig, J., Neuendorffer, S., Sachs, S., Xiong, Y.: Taming heterogeneity: The Ptolemy approach. Proceedings of the IEEE 91(1), 127–144 (2003)
4. Bliudze, S., Sifakis, J.: The algebra of connectors — Structuring interaction in BIP. In: Proceeding of the EMSOFT 2007. Salzburg, Austria, pp. 11–20. ACM SigBED (October 2007)
5. Bernardo, M., Ciancarini, P., Donatiello, L.: On the formalization of architectural types with process algebras. In: SIGSOFT FSE. pp. 140–148 (2000)

6. Spitznagel, B., Garlan, D.: A compositional formalization of connector wrappers. In: ICSE, pp. 374–384. IEEE Computer Society, Los Alamitos (2003)
7. Fiadeiro, J.L.: Categories for Software Engineering. Springer, Heidelberg (2004)
8. Bruni, R., Lanese, I., Montanari, U.: A basic algebra of stateless connectors. Theor. Comput. Sci. 366(1), 98–120 (2006)
9. Arbab, F.: Reo: a channel-based coordination model for component composition. Mathematical Structures in Computer Science 14(3), 329–366 (2004)
10. Arbab, F.: Abstract behavior types: a foundation model for components and their composition. Sci. Comput. Program. 55(1-3), 3–52 (2005)
11. Basu, A., Bozga, M., Sifakis, J.: Modeling heterogeneous real-time components in BIP. In: 4th IEEE International Conference on Software Engineering and Formal Methods (SEFM 2006). pp. 3–12 (invited talk) (September 2006)
12. Sifakis, J.: A framework for component-based construction. In: 3rd IEEE International Conference on Software Engineering and Formal Methods (SEFM05). pp. 293–300 (September 2005) (keynote talk)
13. BIP, `http://www-verimag.imag.fr/~async/BIP/bip.html`
14. Maraninchi, F., Rémond, Y.: Argos: an automaton-based synchronous language. Computer Languages 27, 61–92 (2001)
15. Hoare, C.A.R.: Communicating Sequential Processes, 1985. Prentice Hall International Series in Computer Science. Prentice-Hall, Englewood Cliffs (1985)
16. Milner, R.: Communication and Concurrency. International Series in Computer Science. Prentice-Hall, Englewood Cliffs (1989)
17. Nowak, D.: Synchronous structures. Inf. Comput. 204(8), 1295–1324 (2006)

Multiple Viewpoint Contract-Based Specification and Design*

Albert Benveniste[1], Benoît Caillaud[1], Alberto Ferrari[2], Leonardo Mangeruca[2], Roberto Passerone[2,3], and Christos Sofronis[2]

[1] IRISA / INRIA, Rennes, France
{albert.benveniste,benoit.caillaud}@irisa.fr
[2] PARADES GEIE, Rome, Italy
{alberto.ferrari,leonardo,rpasserone, christos.sofronis}@parades.rm.cnr.it
[3] University of Trento, Trento, Italy
roberto.passerone@unitn.it

Abstract. We present the mathematical foundations and the design methodology of the contract-based model developed in the framework of the SPEEDS project. SPEEDS aims at developing methods and tools to support "speculative design", a design methodology in which distributed designers develop different aspects of the overall system, in a concurrent but controlled way. Our generic mathematical model of contract supports this style of development. This is achieved by focusing on behaviors, by supporting the notion of "rich component" where diverse (functional and non-functional) aspects of the system can be considered and combined, by representing rich components via their set of associated contracts, and by formalizing the whole process of component composition.

1 Introduction

Several industrial sectors involving complex embedded systems design have recently experienced drastic moves in their organization—aerospace and automotive being typical examples. Initially organized around large, vertically integrated companies supporting most of the design in house, these sectors were restructured in the 80's due to the emergence of sizeable competitive suppliers. OEMs performed system design and integration by importing entire subsystems from suppliers. This, however, shifted a significant portion of the value to the suppliers, and eventually contributed to late errors that caused delays and excessive additional cost during the system integration phase.

In the last decade, these industrial sectors went through a profound reorganization in an attempt by OEMs to recover value from the supply chain, by focusing on those parts of the design at the core of their competitive advantage. The rest of the system was instead centered around standard platforms that could be developed and shared by otherwise competitors. Examples of this trend are AUTOSAR in the automotive industry [1], and Integrated Modular Avionics (IMA) in aerospace [2]. This new organization

* This research has been developed in the framework of the European IP-SPEEDS project number 033471.

F.S. de Boer et al. (Eds.): FMCO 2007, LNCS 5382, pp. 200–225, 2008.

requires extensive virtual prototyping and design space exploration, where component or subsystem specification and integration occur at different phases of the design, including at the early ones [3].

Component based development has emerged as the technology of choice to address the challenges that result from this paradigm shift. In the particular context of (safety critical) embedded systems with complex OEM/supplier chains, the following distinguishing features must be addressed. First, the need for high quality, zero defect, software systems calls for techniques in which component specification and integration is supported by clean mathematics that encompass both static and *dynamic* semantics—this means that the behavior of components and their composition, and not just their port and type interface, must be mathematically defined. Second, system design includes various aspects—functional, timeliness, safety and fault tolerance, etc.—involving different teams with different skills using heterogeneous techniques and tools. Third, since the structure of the supply chain is highly distributed, a precise separation of responsibilities between its different actors must be ensured. This is addressed by relying on contracts. Following [4] a contract is a component model that sets forth the assumptions under which the component may be used by its environment, and the corresponding promises that are guaranteed under such correct use.

The semantic foundations that we present in this paper are designed to support this methodology by addressing the above three issues. At its basis, the model is a language-based abstraction where composition is by intersection. This basic model can then be instantiated to cover functional, timeliness, safety, and dependability requirements performed across all system design levels. No particular model of computation and communication is enforced, and continuous time dynamics such as those needed in physical system modeling is supported as well. In particular, executable models such as state transition systems and hybrid automata can be used for the description of the behaviors. On top of the basic model, we build the notion of a contract, which is central to our methodology, by distinguishing between assumptions and promises. This paper focuses on developing a generic compositional theory of contracts, providing relations of contract satisfaction and refinement called dominance, and the derivation of operators for the correct construction of complete systems.

Our key contribution is the handling of multiple viewpoints. We observe that combining contracts for different components and combining contracts for different viewpoints attached to the same component requires different operators. Thus, in addition to traditional parallel composition, and to enable formal multi-viewpoint analysis, our model includes boolean meet and join operators that compute conjunction and disjunction of contracts. To be able to blend both types of operations in a flexible way, we introduce a new operator that combines composition and conjunction to compute the least specific contract that satisfies a set of specifications, while at the same time taking their interaction into account. The operators are complemented by a number of relations between contracts and their implementations. Of particular interest are the notion of satisfaction between an implementation and its contract, and relations of compatibility and consistency between contracts. Specifications are also introduced to model requirements or obligations that must be checked throughout the design process. Our second contribution consists in organizing these relations in a design and analysis methodology that spans a wide range of levels of abstraction, from the functional definition to its final hardware implementation.

The rest of paper is organized as follows. We first review and discuss previous work related to the concept of contract in the context of our contribution in Section 2. We then introduce our model by first motivating our choices, and then by defining formally the notions of component, contract, their implementations and specification in Section 3. In addition, in the same section, we introduce and discuss a number of operators and relations that support the incremental construction and verification of multi-viewpoint systems. After that, we discuss the design methodology in Section 4. Finally, Section 5 presents an illustrative example of the use of the model.

2 Related Work

The notion of contract has been applied for the first time by Meyer in the context of the programming language Eiffel [5]. In his work, Meyer uses *preconditions* and *postconditions* as state predicates for the methods of a class, and *invariants* for the class itself. Preconditions correspond to the assumptions under which the method operates, while postconditions express the promises at method termination, provided that the assumptions are satisfied. Invariants must be true at all states of the class regardless of any assumption. The notion of class inheritance, in this case, is used as a refinement, or subtyping, relation. To guarantee safe substitutability, a subclass is only allowed to weaken assumptions and to strengthen promises and invariants.

Similar ideas were already present in seminal work by Dijkstra [6] and Lamport [7] on *weakest preconditions* and *predicate transformers* for sequential and concurrent programs, and in more recent work by Back and von Wright, who introduce contracts [8] in the *refinement calculus* [9]. In this formalism, processes are described with guarded commands operating on shared variables. Contracts are composed of *assertions* (higher-order state predicates) and *state transformers*. This formalism is best suited to reason about discrete, untimed process behavior.

Dill presents an asynchronous model based on sets of sequences and parallel composition (trace structures) [10]. Behaviors (traces) can be either accepted as *successes*, or rejected as *failures*. The failures, which are still possible behaviors of the system, correspond to unacceptable inputs from the environment, and are therefore the complement of the assumptions. Safe substitutability is expressed as trace containment between the successes and failures of the specification and the implementation. The conditions obtained by Dill are equivalent to requiring that the implementation weaken the assumptions of the specification while strengthening the promises. Wolf later extended the same technique to a discrete synchronous model [11]. More recently, De Alfaro and Henzinger have proposed Interface Automata which are similar to synchronous trace structures, where failures are implicitly all the traces that are not accepted by an automaton representing the component [12]. Composition is defined on automata, rather than on traces, and requires a procedure to restrict the state space that is equivalent to the process called autofailure manifestation of Dill and Wolf. The authors have also extended the approach to other kinds of behaviors, including resources and asynchronous behaviors [13,14]. A more general approach along the lines proposed by Dill and Wolf is the work by Negulescu with Process Spaces [15], and by Passerone with Agent Algebra [16], both of which extend the algebraic approach to generic behaviors introduced by Burch [17]. In both cases, the exact form of the behavior is abstracted, and only the properties of composition are used to derive general results that apply to both asynchronous and synchronous models. An interesting aspect of Process Spaces is the identification of several derived algebraic operators. In contrast, Agent Algebra defines the exact relation between concepts such as parallel composition, refinement and compatibility in the model.

Our notion of contract supports *speculative design* in which distributed teams develop partial designs concurrently and synchronize by relying on the notions of rich component [4] and associated contracts. We define assumptions and promises in terms of behaviors, and use parallel composition as the main operator for decomposing a design. This choice is justified by the reactive nature of embedded software, and by the increasing use of component models that support not only structured concurrency, capable of handling timed and other non-functional properties, but also heterogeneous synchronization and communication mechanisms. Contracts in [8] are of a very different nature, since there is no clear indication of the role (assumption or promise) a state predicate or a state transformer may play. We developed our theory on the basis of assertions, i.e., languages of traces or runs (not to be confused with assertions in [8], which are state predicates).

Our contracts are intended to be abstract models of a component, rather than implementations, which, in our context, may equivalently be done in hardware or software. Similarly to Process Spaces and Agent Algebra, we develop our theory on the basis of languages of generic "runs". However, to attain the generality of a metamodel, and to cover non-functional aspects of the design, we also develop a concrete model enriched with real-time information that achieves the expressive power of hybrid systems. Behaviors are decomposed into assumptions and promises, as in Process Spaces, a representation that is more intuitive than, albeit equivalent to, the one based on the successes and failures of asynchronous trace structures. Unlike Process Spaces, however, we explicitly consider inputs and outputs, which we generalize to the concept of controlled and uncontrolled signals. This distinction is essential in our framework to determine the exact role and responsibilities of users and suppliers of components. This is concretized in our framework by a notion of compatibility which depends critically on the particular partition of the signals into inputs and outputs. We also extend the use of receptiveness of asynchronous trace structures, which is absent in Process Spaces, to define formally the condition of compatibility of components for open systems.

Our refinement relation between contracts, which we call *dominance* to distinguish it from refinement between implementations of the contracts, follows the usual scheme of weakening the assumption and strengthening the guarantees. The order induces boolean operators of conjunction and disjunction, which resembles those of asynchronous trace structures and Process Spaces. To address mutliple viewpoints for multiple components, we define a new *fusion* operator that combines the operation of composition and conjunction for a set of contracts. This operator is introduced to make it easier for the user to express the interaction between contracts related to different viewpoints of a component.

The model that we present in this paper is based on execution traces, and is therefore inherently limited to representing linear time properties. The branching structure of a process whose semantics is expressed in our model is thus abstracted, and the exact state in which non-deterministic choices are taken is lost. Despite this, the equivalence relation that is induced by our notion of dominance between contracts is more distinguishing than the traditional trace containment used when executions are not represented as pairs (assumptions, promises). This was already observed by Dill, with the classic example of the vending machine [10], see also Brookes et al. on refusal sets [18]. There, every accepted sequence of actions is complemented by the set of possible *refusals*, i.e., by the set of actions that may not be accepted after executing that particular sequence. Equivalence is then defined as equality of sequences with their refusal sets. Under these definitions, it is shown that the resulting equivalence is stronger than trace equivalence (equality of trace sets), but weaker than observation equivalence [19,20]. A precise characterization of the relationships with our model, in particular with regard to the notion of composition, is deferred to future work.

3 Model Overview

In the SPEEDS project, a major emphasis has been placed on the development of a model that supports concurrent system development in the framework of complex OEM-supplier chains. This implies the ability to support abstraction mechanisms and to work with multiple viewpoints that are able to express both functional (discrete and continuous evolutions) and non-functional aspects of a design. In particular, the model should not force a specific model of computation and communication (MoCC).

The objective of this paper is to develop a theory and methodology of component based development, for use in complex supply chains or OEM/supplier organizations. Two broad families of approaches can be considered for this purpose:

- Building systems from library components. This is perhaps the most familiar case of component based development. In this case, emphasis is on reuse and adaptation, and the development process is largely in-house dominated. In this case, components are exposed in a simplified form, called their interface, where some details may be omitted. The interface of components is typically obtained by a mechanism of abstraction. This ensures that, if interfaces match, then components can be safely composed and deliver the expected service.
- Distributed systems development with highly distributed OEM/supplier chains. This second situation raises the additional and new issue of splitting and distributing responsibilities between the different actors of the OEM/supplier chain, possibly involving different viewpoints. The OEM wants to define and know precisely what a given supplier is responsible for. Since components or sub-systems interact, this implies that each entity in the area of interaction must be precisely assigned for responsibility to a given supplier, and must remain out of control for others.

Thus each supplier is given a design task in the following form: A goal, also called *guarantee* or *promise*, is assigned to the supplier. This goal involves only entities the supplier is responsible for. Other entities, which are not under the responsibility of this supplier, may still be subject to constraints that are thus offered to this supplier as *assumptions*. Assumptions are under the responsibility of other actors of the OEM/supplier chain, and can be used by this supplier for achieving its own promises. This mechanism of assumptions and promises is structured into *contracts*, which form the essence of distributed systems development involving complex OEM/supplier chains.

3.1 Components and Contracts

Our model is based on the concept of *component*. A component is a hierarchical entity that represents a unit of design. Components are connected together to form a system by sharing and agreeing on the values of certain ports and variables. A component may include both *implementations* and *contracts*. An implementation M is an instantiation of a component and consists of a set P of ports and variables (in the following, for simplicity, we will refer only to ports) and of a set of behaviors, or runs, also denoted by M, which assign a history of "values" to ports. This model essentially follows the Tagged-Signal model introduced by Lee and Sangiovanni [21], which is shown appropriate for expressing behaviors of a wide variety of models of computation. However, unlike the Tagged-Signal model, we do not need a predetermined form of behavior for our basic definitions, which will remain abstract. Instead, the way sets of behaviors are represented in specific instances will define their structure. For example, an automata based model will represent behaviors as sequences of values or events. Conversely, behaviors in a hybrid model will consist of alternations of continuous flows and discrete jumps. Our basic definitions will not vary, and only the way operators are implemented is affected. This way, our definitions are independent of the particular model chosen for the design. Thus, because implementations and contracts may refer to different viewpoints, we refer to the components in our model as *heterogeneous rich components* (HRC).

We build the notion of a contract for a component as a pair of assertions, which express its assumptions and promises. An assertion E is a property that may or may not be satisfied by a behavior. Thus, assertions can again be modeled as a set of behaviors over ports, precisely as the set of behaviors that satisfy it. Note that this is unlike preconditions and postconditions in program analysis, which constrain the state space of a program at a particular point. Instead, assertions in our context are properties of entire behaviors, and therefore talk about the dynamics of a component. An implementation M satisfies an assertion E whenever they are defined over the same set of ports and all the behaviors of M satisfy the assertion, i.e., when $M \subseteq E$.

A contract is an assertion on the behaviors of a component (the promise) subject to certain assumptions. We therefore represent a contract C as a pair (A, G), where A corresponds to the assumption, and G to the promise. An implementation of a component satisfies a contract whenever it satisfies its promise, subject to the assumption. Formally, $M \cap A \subseteq G$, where M and C have the same ports. We write $M \models C$ when M satisfies a contract C. Satisfaction can be checked using the following equivalent formulas, where $\neg A$ denotes the set of all runs that are not runs of A:

$$M \models C \iff M \subseteq G \cup \neg A \iff M \cap (A \cap \neg G) = \emptyset$$

There exists a unique maximal (by behavior containment) implementation satisfying a contract C, namely $M_C = G \cup \neg A$. One can interpret M_C as the implication $A \Rightarrow G$.

Clearly, $M \models (A, G)$ if and only if $M \models (A, M_C)$, if and only if $M \subseteq M_C$. Because of this property, we can restrict our attention to contracts of the form $C = (A, M_C)$, which we say are in *canonical form*, without losing expressiveness. The operation of computing the canonical form, i.e., replacing G with $G \cup \neg A$, is well defined, since the maximal implementation is unique, and it is idempotent. Working with canonical forms simplifies the definition of our operators and relations, and provides a unique representation for equivalent contracts.

In order to more easily construct contracts, it is useful to have an algebra to express more complex contracts from simpler ones. The combination of contracts associated to different components can be obtained through the operation of parallel composition, denoted with the symbol $\|$. If $C_1 = (A_1, G_1)$ and $C_2 = (A_2, G_2)$ are contracts (possibly over different sets of ports), the composite $C = C_1 \parallel C_2$ must satisfy the guarantees of both, implying an operation of intersection. The situation is more subtle for assumptions. Suppose first that the two contracts have disjoint sets of ports. Intuitively, the assumptions of the composite should be simply the conjunction of the assumptions of each contract, since the environment should satisfy all the assumptions. In general, however, part of the assumptions A_1 will be already satisfied by composing C_1 with C_2, acting as a partial environment for C_1. Therefore, G_2 can contribute to relaxing the assumptions A_1. And vice-versa. Formally, this translates to the following definition.

Definition 1 (Parallel Composition). *Let $C_1 = (A_1, G_1)$ and $C_2 = (A_2, G_2)$ be contracts. The parallel composition $C = (A, G) = C_1 \parallel C_2$ is given by*

$$A = (A_1 \cap A_2) \cup \neg(G_1 \cap G_2), \tag{1}$$

$$G = G_1 \cap G_2, \tag{2}$$

This definition is consistent with similar definitions in other contexts [12,10,15]. C_1 and C_2 may have different ports. In that case, we must extend the behaviors to a common set of ports before applying (1) and (2). This can be achieved by an operation of inverse projection. Projection, or elimination, in contracts requires handling assumptions and promises differently, in order to preserve their semantics.

Definition 2 (Elimination). *For a contract $C = (A, G)$ and a port p, the* elimination of p in C *is given by*

$$[C]_p = (\forall p\, A,\ \exists p\, G) \tag{3}$$

where A and G are seen as predicates.

Elimination trivially extends to finite sets of ports, denoted by $[C]_P$, where P is the considered set of ports. For inverse elimination in parallel composition, the set of ports P to be considered is the union of the ports P_1 and P_2 of the individual contracts.

Parallel composition can be used to construct complex contracts out of simpler ones, and to combine contracts of different components. Despite having to be satisfied simultaneously, however, multiple viewpoints *associated to the same component* do not generally compose by parallel composition. Take, for instance, a functional viewpoint C_f and an orthogonal timed viewpoint C_t for a component M. Contract C_f specifies allowed data pattern for the environment, and sets forth the corresponding behavioral property that can be guaranteed. For instance, if the environment alternates the values $\mathtt{T}, \mathtt{F}, \mathtt{T}, \ldots$ on port a, then the value carried by port b never exceeds a given value x. Similarly, C_t sets timing requirements and guarantees on meeting deadlines. For example, if the environment provides at least one data per second on port a ($1ds$), then the component can issue at least one data every two seconds ($.5ds$) on port b. Parallel composition fails to capture their combination, because the combined contract must accept environments that satisfy either the functional assumptions, or the timing assumptions, or both. In particular, parallel composition computes assumptions that are too restrictive. Figure 1 illustrates this. Figure 1(a) shows the two contracts (C_f on the left, and C_t on the right) as truth tables. Figure 1(b) shows the corresponding inverse projection. Figure 1(d) is the parallel composition computed according to our previous definition, while Figure 1(c) shows the desired result. We would like, that is, to compute the conjunction $\sqcap$ of the contracts, so that if $M \models C_f \sqcap C_t$, then $M \models C_f$ and $M \models C_t$. This can best be achieved by first defining a partial order on contracts, which formalizes a notion of substitutability, or refinement.

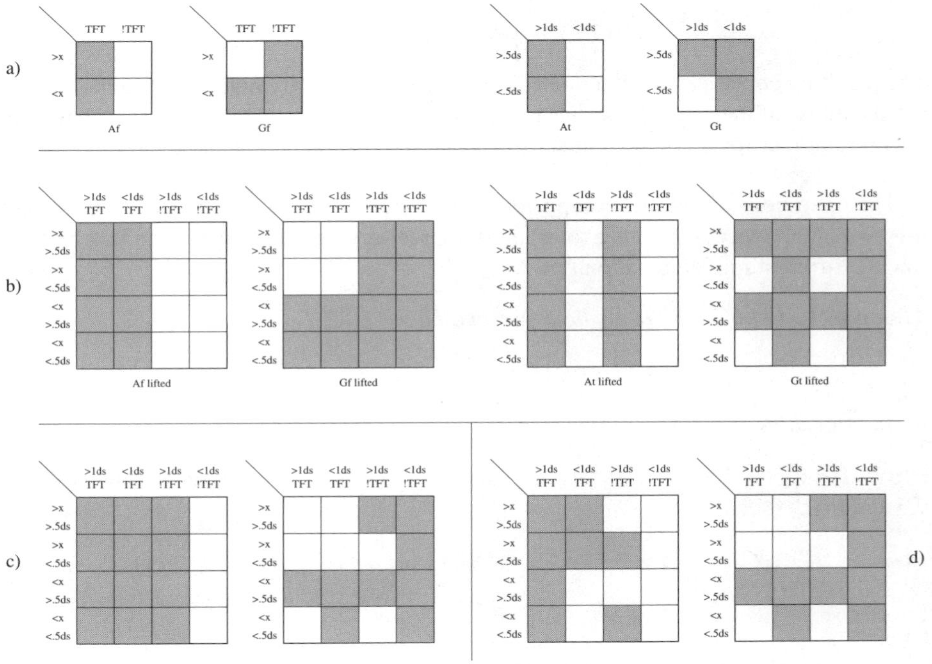

Fig. 1. Truth tables for the synchronization of categories. The four diagrams on the top are the truth tables of the functional category C_f and its assumption A_f and promise G_f, and similarly for the timed category C_t. Note that these two contracts are in canonical form. In the middle, we show the same contracts lifted to the same set of variables b, d_b, x, d_x, combining function and timing. On the bottom, the two tables on the left are the truth tables of the greatest lower bound $C_f \sqcap C_t$. For comparison, we show on the right the truth tables of the parallel composition $C_1 \parallel C_2$, revealing that the assumption is too restrictive and not the one expected.

Definition 3 (Dominance). *We say that* $C = (A, G)$ dominates $C' = (A', G')$, *written* $C \preceq C'$, *if and only if*

$$A \supseteq A', \text{ and}$$
$$G \subseteq G',$$

and the contracts have the same ports.

Dominance amounts to relaxing assumptions and reinforcing promises, therefore strengthening the contract. Clearly, if $M \models C$ and $C \preceq C'$, then $M \models C'$.

Given the ordering of contracts, we can compute greatest lower bounds and least upper bounds, which correspond to taking the conjunction and disjunction of contracts, respectively.

Definition 4 (Bounds). *For contracts* $C_1 = (A_1, G_1)$ *and* $C_2 = (A_2, G_2)$ *(in canonical form), we have*

$$C_1 \sqcap C_2 = (A_1 \cup A_2, G_1 \cap G_2), \quad (4)$$
$$C_1 \sqcup C_2 = (A_1 \cap A_2, G_1 \cup G_2). \quad (5)$$

The resulting contracts are in canonical form. Conjunction of contracts amounts to taking the union of the assumptions, as required, and can therefore be used to compute the overall contract for a component starting from the contracts related to multiple viewpoints.

The operations of parallel composition and conjunction are related by the result below, which allows the designer to relate in a precise way the designs obtained by following different implementation flows:

Theorem 1. *Let* C, C_1 *and* C_2 *be contracts. Then,*

$$(C \sqcap C_1) \parallel (C \sqcap C_2) \preceq C \sqcap (C_1 \parallel C_2)$$

when both sides of the inequality are defined.

Proof. Let $C = (A, G)$, $C_1 = (A_1, G_1)$ and $C_2 = (A_2, G_2)$ be contracts. Then, by (1), (2) and (4),

$$C \sqcap (C_1 \parallel C_2) = (A \cup (A_1 \cap A_2) \cup \neg(G_1 \cap G_2), G \cap G_1 \cap G_2).$$

Similarly,

$$(C \sqcap C_1) \parallel (C \sqcap C_2) = ((A \cup A_1) \cap (A \cup A_2) \cup \neg(G \cap G_1 \cap G_2), G \cap G_1 \cap G_2).$$

Clearly,

$$\neg(G_1 \cap G_2) \subseteq \neg(G \cap G_1 \cap G_2).$$

In addition,

$$A \cup (A_1 \cap A_2) = (A \cup A_1) \cap (A \cup A_2).$$

The result then follows by definition of dominance.

The left hand side of the formula of Theorem 1 yields the contract obtained by first combining viewpoints for each component and then composing the components. On the other hand, the right hand side of the same formula yields the contract obtained by applying the converse flow. Thus, the theorem expresses that component centric design (left hand side) results in less flexibility in the implementations than a viewpoint centric design (right hand side) would do.

3.2 System Obligations

Contracts are not the only way a designer would like to express system's requirements. System obligations are typically high level requirements that the designer would like to hold without considering any environment nor assumption. System obligations are useful for both overall system requirements and for overall properties of the computing platform.

System obligations are formally defined as assertions, i.e., sets of behaviors. An important point is that system obligations should be checked on contracts as early as possible in the design flow, because this significantly reduces the analysis effort, required to prove or disprove the obligation, and the design effort, required to revise the contract if the obligation is not met. To formalize this idea we introduce the *conformance* relation: a contract $C = (A, G)$ *conforms to* a system obligation B if $A \cap G \subseteq B$.

With each contract $C = (A, G)$ we can associate an obligation, that we call the *contract obligation*, defined as $B_C = A \cap G$. Hence, a contract conforms to a system obligation if its contract obligation is contained in (i.e., it is stronger than) the system obligation. There is a simple relationship between the maximal implementation M_C of contract C and the corresponding contract obligation B_C, namely $A \cap M_C = B_C$ and $M_C = B_C \cup \neg A$. Indeed:

$$A \cap M_C = A \cap (G \cup \neg A) = A \cap G = B_C$$
$$B_C \cup \neg A = A \cap G \cup \neg A = A \cap G \cup \neg A \cap G \cup \neg A = G \cup \neg A = M_C$$

The formulation of the conformance relation in terms of the contract obligation suggests an extension of the notion of conformance to contracts: a contract C_2 conforms to a contract C_1 if $B_{C_2} \subseteq B_{C_1}$. This definition ensures that conformance is transitive, thereby implying that contract C_2 conforms to any system obligation which C_1 conforms to. Conformance is compositional with respect to parallel composition. This follows from the fact that $B_{C_1 || C_2} = B_{C_1} \cap B_{C_2}$, i.e., the contract obligation associated with the parallel composition of C_1 and C_2 is the intersection of their contract obligations. This can be shown by using equations (1) and (2) of parallel composition. Contracts and system obligations are specifications that are intended to guide the designer(s) towards a consistent system's implementation. Hence, in the design process we intend to relate implementations to contracts and system obligations. In particular, implementations are used in the contexts defined by contracts and are meant to satisfy all system obligations. In more precise terms, given an implementation that satisfies a contract that conforms to a system obligation, we want that such an implementation also satisfy in some sense to the system obligation. To formalize this we say that an implementation M *satisfies* a system obligation B *through* a contract $C = (A, G)$ if $A \cap M \subseteq B$. It can be readily observed that if an implementation M satisfies a contract $C = (A, G)$, and if C conforms to a system obligation B, then M satisfies B through C.

Conformance and dominance between contracts are complementary, in the sense that one does not imply the other. Nevertheless, there is a strong relationship between the two. Specifically, given two contracts, $C_1 = (A_1, G_1)$ and $C_2 = (A_2, G_2)$, if C_2 dominates C_1, then C_2 conforms to C_1 if and only if $A_2 \subseteq A_1 \cup \neg G_2$, as shown below:

$$G_2 \subseteq G_1 \Rightarrow A_2 \cap G_2 \subseteq G_1 \text{ and } A_2 \subseteq A_1 \cup \neg G_2 \iff A_2 \cap G_2 \subseteq A_1$$

Note that the condition $A_2 \subseteq A_1 \cup \neg G_2$ requires that if a given behavior is not allowed by the contract C_1 (i.e., is not in A_1), but is possible in C_2 (i.e., is in G_2), then it must be disallowed also by contract C_2 (i.e., is not in A_2). This condition together with the dominance relation is called *strong dominance*.

3.3 The Asymmetric Role of Ports

So far we have ignored the role of ports and the corresponding splitting of responsibilities between the implementation and its environment, see the discussion above. Such a splitting of responsibilities avoids the competition between environment and implementation in setting the value of ports and variables.

Intuitively, an implementation can only provide promises on the value of the ports it controls. On ports controlled by the environment, instead, it may only declare assumptions. Therefore, we will distinguish between two kinds of ports for implementations and contracts: those that are *controlled* and those that are *uncontrolled*. Uncontrollability can be formalized as a notion of receptiveness: for E an assertion, and $P' \subseteq P$ a subset of its ports, E is said to be *P'-receptive* if and only if for all runs σ' restricted to ports belonging to P', there exists a run $\sigma \in E$ such that σ' and σ coincide over P'. In words, E accepts any history offered to the subset P' of its ports. This closely resembles the classical notion of inputs and outputs in programs and HDLs; it is more general, however, as it encompasses not only horizontal compositions within a same layer, but also cross-layer integration such as the integration between application and execution platform performed at deployment.

In some cases, different viewpoints associated with the same component need to interact through some common ports. This motivates providing a scope for ports, by partitioning them into ports that are *visible* (outside the underlying component) and ports that are *local* (to the underlying component). The above discussion can be summarized as a *profile* $\pi = (\mathbf{vis}, \mathbf{loc}, \mathbf{u}, \mathbf{c})$, which partitions a set of ports P into subsets such that

$$\begin{aligned} P &= \mathbf{vis} \uplus \mathbf{loc} = \{\text{visible}\} \uplus \{\text{local}\} \\ P &= \quad \mathbf{u} \uplus \mathbf{c} \quad = \{\text{uncontrolled}\} \uplus \{\text{controlled}\} \end{aligned}$$

Thus, in addition to sets of runs, components, implementations and contracts can be characterized by a profile over a set of ports P. As before, for a contract $C = (A, G)$ or an implementation M, the sets A, G and M are constrained to include only runs over P.

The satisfaction and the dominance relations are easily extended to take profiles into account, by simply insisting that the implementations and the contracts that are put in relation have the same profile. Consequently, conjunction (the greatest lower bound) can only be taken between contracts over the same profiles. If two contracts have different profiles, then an operation of inverse projection is required. However, the resulting profiles must be consistent regarding which ports are controlled and which are uncontrolled, and local. This restriction highlights the fact that the logical operations that we have defined are relative to contracts that refer to the same components, and which must therefore treat controlled and uncontrolled ports in the same way.

The situation is different for parallel composition. Here, we enforce the property that each port should be controlled by at most one contract. Hence, parallel composition is defined only if the sets of controlled ports of the contracts are disjoint. However, one contract may regard one port as controlled, and the other as uncontrolled. In this case, we are simply stating that the controlling contract determines the value of the port for the other contract. Thus, in the composite contract, a port is controlled exactly when it is controlled by one of the component contracts. Uncontrolled ports of the contracts remain uncontrolled in the composite provided that they are not already controlled by the other contract. A similar reasoning is applied to visible and local ports. In this case, however, we distinguish between the composition of contracts for the same component, and contracts for different components. In the first case, local ports have no effect on the composition, since the scope of local ports extends to the entire component. In the second case, instead, the set of local ports of one contract must be disjoint from the set of ports of the other contract.

More formally, for contracts $C_1 = (\pi_1, A_1, G_1)$ and $C_2 = (\pi_2, A_2, G_2)$ for the same underlying component, parallel composition is defined if and only if $\mathbf{c}_1 \cap \mathbf{c}_2 = \emptyset$, and in that case is the contract $C = (\pi, A, G)$ defined by:

$$
\begin{aligned}
\mathbf{vis} &= \mathbf{vis}_1 \cup \mathbf{vis}_2, \\
\mathbf{loc} &= (\mathbf{loc}_1 \cup \mathbf{loc}_2) - (\mathbf{vis}_1 \cup \mathbf{vis}_2), \\
\mathbf{c} &= \mathbf{c}_1 \cup \mathbf{c}_2, \\
\mathbf{u} &= (\mathbf{u}_1 \cup \mathbf{u}_2) - (\mathbf{c}_1 \cup \mathbf{c}_2),
\end{aligned}
$$

The formulas are the same for contracts of different components, where composition is defined only if $\mathbf{loc}_1 \cap P_2 = \mathbf{loc}_2 \cap P_1 = \emptyset$.

3.4 Consistency and Compatibility

The notion of receptiveness and the distinction between controlled and uncontrolled ports is at the basis of our relations of consistency and compatibility between contracts. Our first requirement is that an implementations M with profile $\pi = (\mathbf{vis}, \mathbf{loc}, \mathbf{u}, \mathbf{c})$ be $\mathbf{u}$-receptive, formalizing the fact that an implementation has no control over the values of ports set by the environment. For a contract C we say that C is

- *consistent* if G is $\mathbf{u}$-receptive, and
- *compatible* if A if $\mathbf{c}$-receptive.

The sets A and G are not *required* to be receptive. However, if G is not $\mathbf{u}$-receptive, then the promises constrain the uncontrolled ports of the contract. In particular, the contract admits no receptive implementation. This is against our policy of separation of responsibilities, since we stated that uncontrolled ports should remain entirely under the responsibility of the environment. Corresponding contracts are therefore called *inconsistent*.

The situation is dual for assumptions. If A is not **c**-receptive, then there exists a sequence of values on the controlled ports that are refused by all acceptable environments. However, by our definition of satisfaction, implementations are allowed to output such sequence. Unreceptiveness, in this case, implies that a hypothetical environment that wished to prevent a violation of the assumptions should actually prevent the behavior altogether, something it cannot do since the port is controlled by the contract. Therefore, unreceptive assumptions denote the existence of an incompatibility internal to the contract, that cannot be avoided by any environment.

The notion of consistency and compatibility can therefore be extended to pairs of contracts. We say that two contracts C_1 and C_2 are *consistent* or *compatible* whenever their parallel composition is consistent or compatible.

Consistency and compatibility may not be preserved by Boolean operations and by parallel composition. For example, one obtains an inconsistent contract when taking the greatest lower bound of two contracts, one of which promises that certain behaviors will never occur in response to a certain input, while the other promises that the remaining behaviors will not occur in response to the same input. This is because the contracts control the same ports, and composition of promises is by intersection. Similarly, assumptions may become unreceptive as a result of taking the least upper bound. We do not generally use least upper bounds, so we do not elaborate further on this situation. In general, however, the conjunction of compatible contracts is still compatible, since assumptions compose by union.

Another form of inconsistency may arise when taking parallel composition. In this case, certain input sequences may be prevented from happening because they might activate unstable zero-delay feedback loops. The resulting behaviors may have no representations in our model, thus resulting in an empty promise. This problem can be avoided by modeling the oscillating behaviors explicitly (perhaps using a special value that denotes oscillation) [11]. We assume that this kind of inconsistency is taken care of by the user or by the tools.

Assumptions may also become unreceptive as a result of a parallel composition even if they are not so individually. This is because the set of controlled ports after a composition is strictly larger than before the composition. In particular, ports that were uncontrolled may become controlled, because they are controlled by the other contract. In this case, satisfying the assumptions is the responsibility of the other contract, which acts as a partial environment. If the assumptions are not satisfied by the other contract, then the assumptions of the composition become unreceptive. That is, a hypothetical environment that wished to prevent a violation of the assumptions should actually prevent the behavior altogether, something it cannot do since the port is controlled by one of the contract. Therefore, unreceptive assumptions denote the existence of an internal incompatibility within the composition.

Finally, we point out that the operation of transforming a contract to its canonical form preserves consistency (and compatibility), since the promises G are replaced by their most permissive version $G \cup \neg A$.

3.5 Fusion

When several viewpoints and several components are present in a system, combining conjunction and parallel composition may not be trivial. To overcome the problem, we define a unique operator, which combines the operations of conjunction and parallel composition, and results in an overall contract for a system. We call this operation a *fusion* of contracts. The fusion operator takes a finite set of contracts $(C_i)_{i \in I}$ as operand, and a set of ports Q to be eliminated, because internal to the component. The *fusion of* $(C_i)_{i \in I}$ *with respect to* Q is defined by

$$[\![(C_i)_{i \in I}]\!]_Q = \bigsqcap_{J \subseteq I} \left[\,\|_{j \in J} C_j \, \right]_Q, \tag{6}$$

where J ranges over the set of all subsets of I for which composition is defined and, after the composition, no input is contained in Q. In other words, fusion considers only compositions of contracts for which internal connections have been fully established and discharged, and therefore talk only about the global input to output behavior. To guarantee the maximal flexibility in fusion, the subsets J are also chosen to be maximal with respect to containment. By doing so, we avoid considering partial compositions which, when taking the conjunction, restrict the range of accepted environments, and therefore strengthen the assumptions.

Certain particular cases are of interest. For instance, when $Q = \emptyset$, the fusion reduces to the greatest lower bound: $[\![(C_i)_{i \in I}]\!]_\emptyset = \sqcap_{i \in I} C_i$. Likewise, if for $i = 1, 2$,

$$\forall Q \, (A_i \cup \neg G) \supseteq \forall Q \, (A_1 \cup A_2) \tag{7}$$

then fusion reduces to the parallel composition operator: $[\![(C_i)_{i \in \{1,2\}}]\!]_Q = [C_1 \parallel C_2]_Q$. Condition (7) says that the restriction to Q of each contract is a valid environment for the restriction to Q of the other contract. This situation corresponds to two components that interact through ports in Q, which are subsequently hidden from outside. In practice, fusion computes the parallel composition of contracts attached to different sub-components of a composite, whereas contracts attached to the same composite that involve the same inputs and outputs (including their direction) fuse via the operation of conjunction. The general case lies in between and is given by formula (6).

4 Methodology

The aforementioned relations and operations among contracts set the basis for composition and manipulation of components composed of contracts belonging to more than one viewpoint. Moreover, we provide a methodology to orchestrate the usage of the relations and give guidelines to the user on how to design and verify her model against a number of requirements/constraints that follow the laws presented in the previous sections.

We distinguish between the *Design* and the *Analysis* methodology. The former defines the design steps that the user can take for the evolution of her system, while the latter specifies the relations that should be established (or re-established) depending on the corresponding design step.

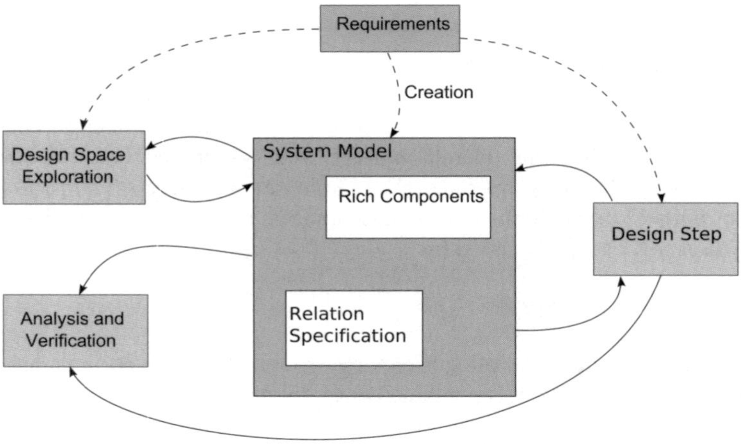

Fig. 2. Abstract view of the design methodology

An abstract representation of the design methodology is shown in Figure 2. Initially, from a set of requirements, we derive a system model composed of rich components and a (initially empty) set of relations between them. From this point, the user may take a number of steps, perform analysis to enhance this set of relations or to perform design space exploration. The latter is subject of future work.

We detail on the design steps later on, after we specify the different elements of the design.

4.1 Elements of the Design

We distinguish between four categories of design elements, as defined in Section 3: contracts, implementations, system obligations, and relations. A rule of thumb to distinguish the relations is that consistency, compatibility and dominance relations are established between two contracts; the satisfaction relation between an implementation and a contract; and the conformance relation between a contract and a system obligation. As part of the design methodology, we consider an organization of those elements in three *design spaces* and furthermore in *layers*. These are: the *implementation space*, the *contract space* and the *system obligation space*. Relations (since they are not syntactic elements of the model) are represented as "connections" between elements of the same or different spaces. For example, dominance "connects" two elements within the contract space, while satisfaction "connects" one element from the contract and one from the implementation space. Note that a relation may "connect" an element with itself, as in the case of the compatibility relation.

Each space may be further subdivided into *layers*. In the context of the SPEEDS project, only the layering of the contract space is relevant, because the main purpose of the HRC model is to represent contracts. However, a layering of the obligation and implementation spaces is also possible.

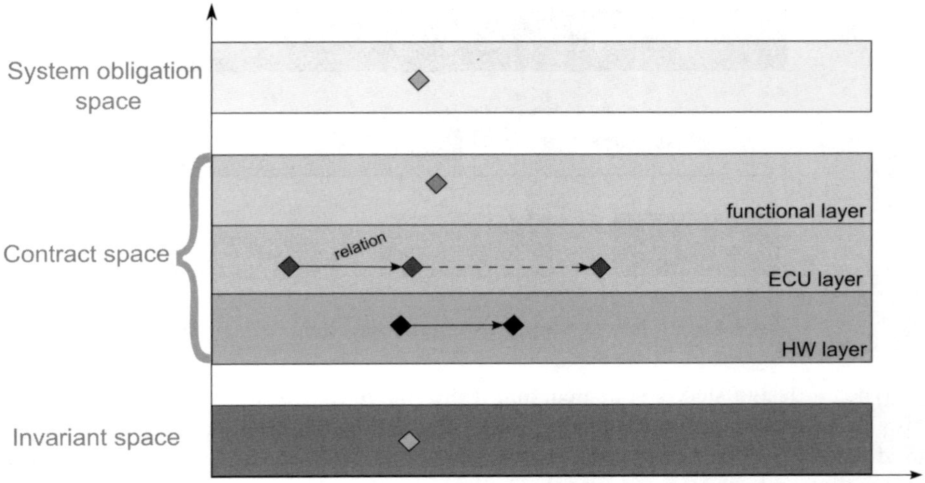

Fig. 3. Organization of spaces and layers

Figure 3 shows a possible layering of the contract space in the case of automotive applications. Here we identify three layers: 1) the functional layer, corresponding to describing the basic functional requirements and guarantees; 2) the Engine Control Unit (ECU) layer, that sets forth the high level timing and architecture assumptions and guarantees; and 3) the Hardware (HW) layer, corresponding to a more detailed description of the individual platform components. In addition, mapping an element from one layer to an element from another will create an element that does not belong to either of the operands' layers. Thus, we have three extra layers for all the possible mappings, as depicted in Figure 4; one layer for the mapping of Function to ECU, one for the mapping of ECU to HW and one for the mapping of all the layers.

4.2 Design Steps

A design step is an evolution of the development of the design, which can be seen also as the evolution of the design in time. We use the elements defined in the previous section to define the basic design steps that a user can follow during design. In principle, a design step is defined as a tuple of *source* and *target* rich components. Moreover, we specify a number of relations that are "required" between the elements of the rich components participating in the step.

A design step is said to be *validated* if the required relations hold. This validation is performed using high-level analysis services which are being developed within the SPEEDS project, and include tools that can check satisfaction, dominance, compatibility and consistency for a variety of models (from pure discrete to hybrid) using both formal and semi-formal (simulation with dynamic property checking) techniques. Moreover, we introduce the notion of *valid rich component*, that is a rich component whose contract is compatible, consistent, it is satisfied by its implementation and conforms to its obligations.

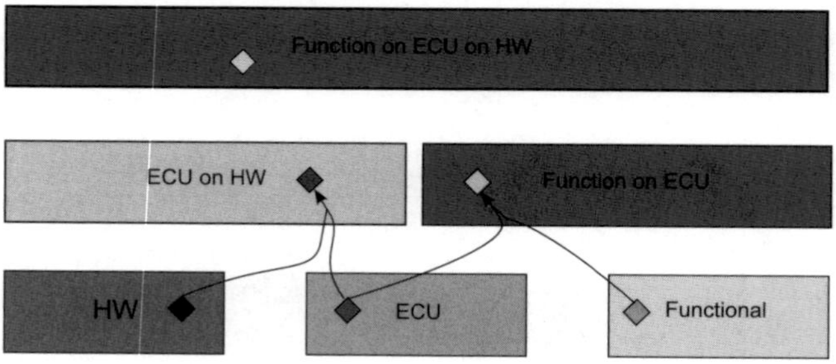

Fig. 4. Layers derived when mapping elements from different layers

When a design step is validated, and if the source rich components are valid, then also the target components are valid, which means that the resulting component can be used "safely" in place of the originating one, i.e., we can substitute without losing any verification and validation results obtained previously.

We subdivide the design steps in two categories:

1. Design steps on single rich components. The first category contains design steps which specify or modify only one element of a rich component, resulting in a new rich component where the remaining elements are unchanged.

Let $RC = \{B, C, M\}$ be the source and $RC' = \{B', C', M'\}$ the target rich components, where B, B' are the system obligations, C, C' the contracts and M, M' the implementation.[1] The design steps and the corresponding relations for their validation are described below.

System obligation modification design step is when $C = C'$ and $M = M'$, whereas $B \neq B'$. For the validation of this step there are two options:
- verify that $B' \subseteq B$

  or
- verify that C' *conforms* to $B \cup \neg B'$

Contract modification design step is when $B = B'$ and $M = M'$, whereas $C \neq C'$. For the validation of this step there are two options:
- verify that C' *strongly dominates* C

  or
- verify that C' is compatible, consistent, *conforms* to C and M' *satisfies* it

Implementation modification design step is when $B = B'$ and $C = C'$, whereas $M \neq M'$. For the validation of this step there are two options:
- verify that M' *refines* M

  or
- verify that M' *satisfies* C

The above steps are called "modifications" even though we may not have prior definition of the "modified" element, in which case, we consider the trivial element.

[1] Even though a rich component may have more than one contract or system obligation, their composition results into a unique one, and thus, without loss of generality, we consider this assumption for the rest of the document.

2. Design steps on multiple rich components. The second category contains those design steps having more than one source or more than one target rich components. Let $RC_n = \{B_n, C_n, M_n\}$ for $n \in [1..\kappa]$ be κ source and $RC'_m = \{B'_m, C'_m, M'_m\}$ for $m \in [1..\lambda]$ be λ target rich components.

Decomposition design step: For the decomposition we have $\kappa = 1$ and $\lambda \geq 2$.
Let $RC'' = \{B'', C'', M''\}$ be the parallel composition of all rich components RC'_m for $m \in [1..\lambda]$. For the validation of this step there are two options:
- verify that C'' *strongly dominates* C_1
  or
- verify that C'' is compatible, consistent, *conforms* to C_1 and M'' *satisfies* C_1

Composition design step: For the composition we have $\kappa \geq 2$ and $\lambda = 1$.
Since parallel composition preserves (strong) dominance, satisfaction and refinement, no verification task is needed for integration.

Mapping design step: Mapping is a composition (fusion) of design elements from different modeling layers and therefore we refer the reader to the discussion for composition.

Using the design steps. The above design steps are all possible actions that can advance the system design and are the "bricks" to build the design methodology. The design methodology that we follow uses these building blocks in a viewpoint centric approach. This means that we should not apply any contract prior to performing decomposition. In that way, and following Theorem 1, we retain a greater level of flexibility for the implementations that should satisfy the decomposed components. We can see this in Figure 5, where component RC, containing two contracts *Cr* and *Cf*, from the real time and functional viewpoints respectively, has two possible decompositions: rich

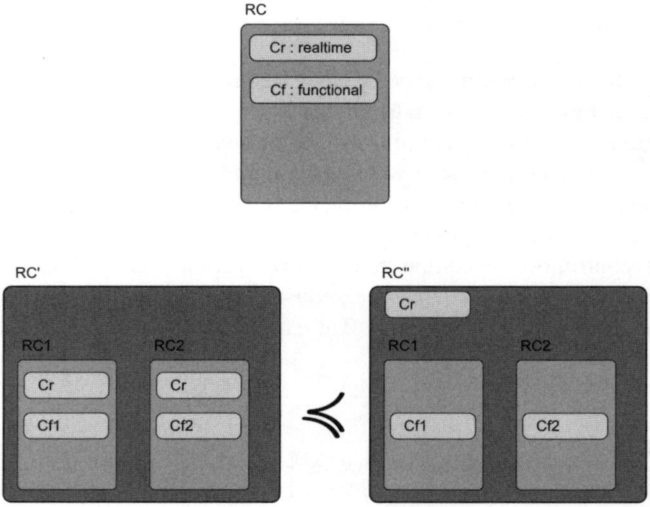

Fig. 5. Two possible decompositions of RC

components RC' and RC''. Therefore, we propose decomposition to RC'', where the real-time viewpoint is not applied (composed) to the decomposed components.

Note that the relations between the different elements of this decomposition should hold according to the definition of the *decomposition design step* above, if we want to have a valid design step. Thus, since we have no implementation or system obligation in our example, the following must hold: $Cf1 \parallel Cf2 \preceq Cf$.

5 Illustrative Example

Our approach aims at supporting component based development of heterogeneous embedded systems with multiple viewpoints, both functional and non-functional. The following simple example illustrates this for the case of functional, timed, and safety viewpoints. The top level view of our system is shown in Figure 6. It consists of a system controller that can let the underlying plant "start", "stop", or "work" (signals r, s, and w). The system controller promises that the mean amount of work performed by the plant does not exceed a maximum and that the work is not paused for too long. A human operator may decide to reinitialize the controller by sending the "reset" message **z**. The system controller, which is the part of the system under design, must conform to the following obligations:

Protocol obligation: "work" requests can be sent only after a "start" and before a "stop". A "stop" must follow a "start" or a "work" request.

Longest idle time obligation: a "work" request must follow a "start" or a previous request at most after τ_{max} seconds.

Maximum mean work obligation: from the last operator "reset", the amount of "work" requests per unit of time must not be greater than $1/\xi$.

Figure 7 shows the automata that specify the obligations. For this example, the notation $[g]s/a$ denotes a transition. It is a triple consisting of a guard g, a triggering event s, and an action a. Action a may, in turn, assign some variables and/or emit some output(s). The idle time and mean work obligations are specified in terms of hybrid automata. These hybrid automata use a timer x bound to physical time, thus satisfying the differential equation $\dot{x} = 1$ (x increases with constant speed 1).

The system controller is decomposed into several components as shown on Figure 8. It consists of a simple controller that is responsible for sending the "start", "stop", and "work" signals to the underlying plant. The controller is deployed over a computing

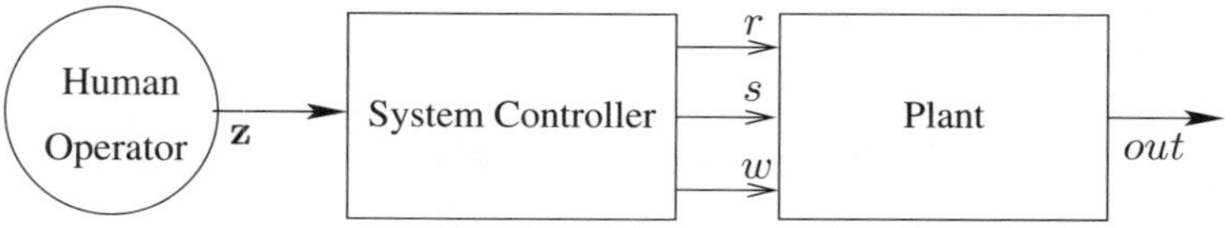

Fig. 6. System view

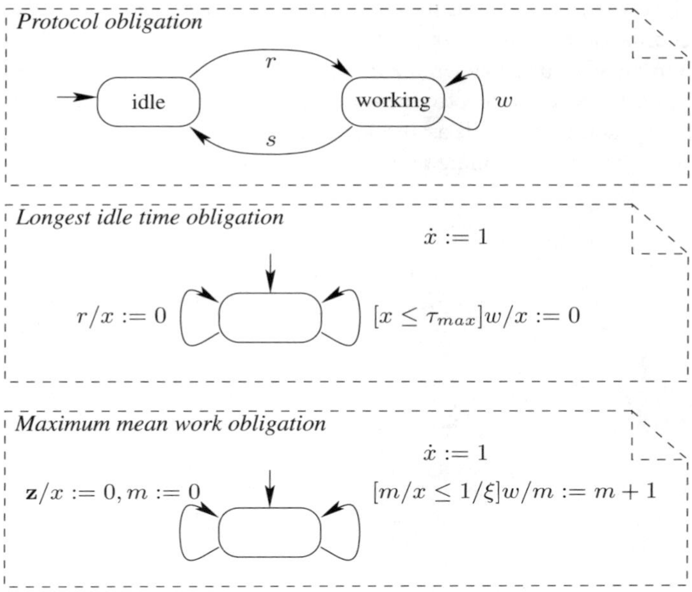

Fig. 7. System obligations

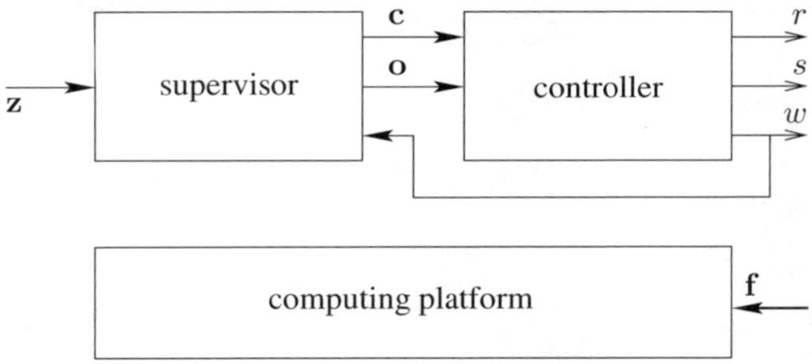

Fig. 8. The decomposition of the system controller

platform subject to "failure" **f**. This component guarantees that the underlying plant receives "work" requests within a maximum amount of time. The supervisor component, instead, limits the "work" requests sent by the controller (the plant has limited capacity) by moving the controller into a "blocked" mode. This is achieved by mimicking the token bucket mechanism used for traffic shaping in communication networks: every unit of time, the supervisor accumulates a token for doing "work"; every request of "work" reduces the token amount by ξ. The supervisor monitors the flow of w's. When they get too frequent, i.e., no token is available, an "overloaded" message **o** is sent to the controller, stopping it from emitting further w requests. Only after an appropriate amount of time, long enough to let a token accumulate, does the supervisor emit a clear "c" message to the controller to enable the emitting of additional w requests. The supervisor resets the accumulated tokens when the human operator sends the "reset" message **z**.

This system involves three viewpoints: functional, Quality of Service (QoS) of timed nature, and safety. The contracts for the different viewpoints are depicted in Figures 9–11. For each contract, we show its assumption (top) and promise (bottom). Assumptions are specified as observers, meaning that the corresponding diagrams define the negation

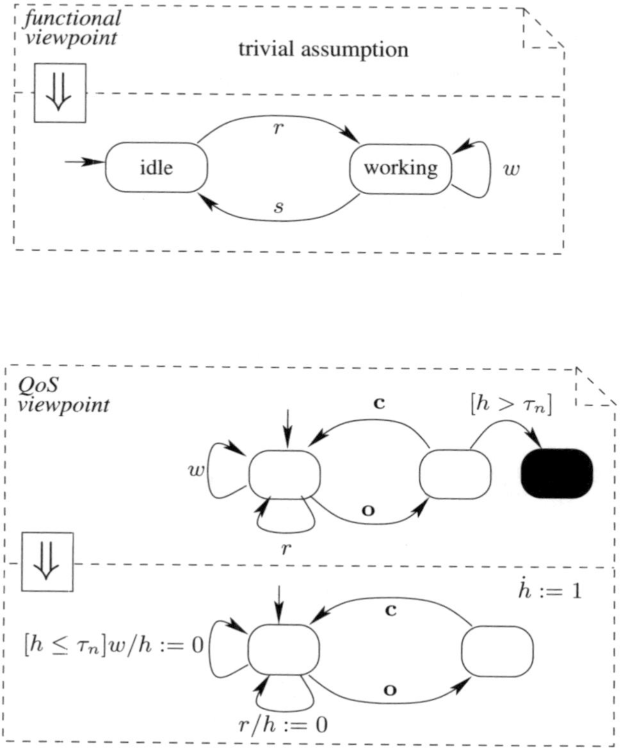

Fig. 9. The two contracts C_{funct} and C_{QoS} specifying the two viewpoints of the controller. The assumption is put on top of the promise and both are separated by the implication symbol $\boxed{\Downarrow}$.

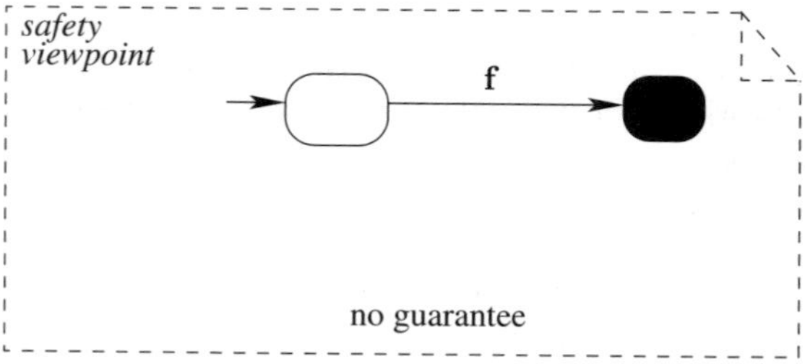

Fig. 10. The contract C_{safety} specifying the contract of the computing platform

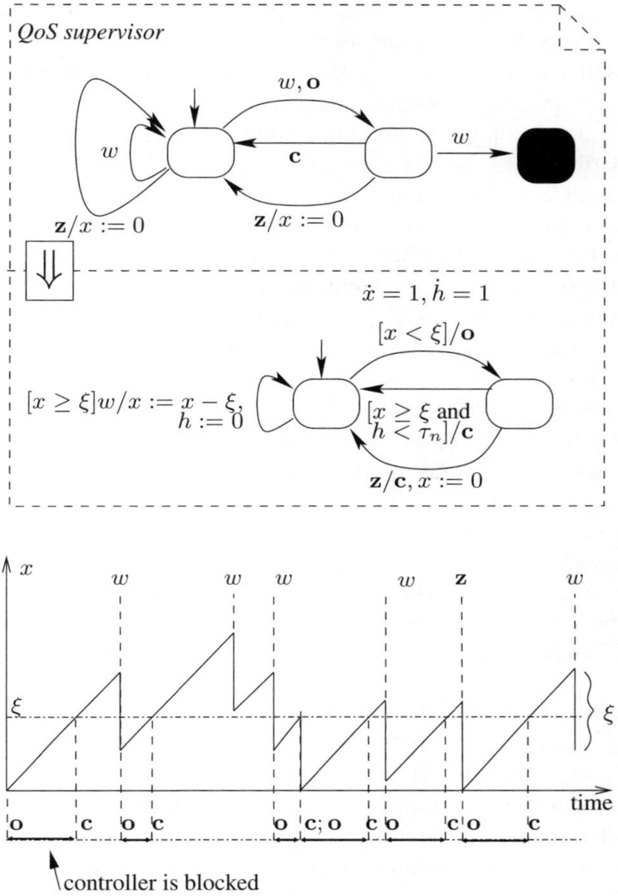

Fig. 11. Contract C_s of the supervisor and its behaviour

of these assumptions. In these diagrams, the circles filled in black denote not accepting states.

Figure 9 depicts the set of contracts associated to the controller. The first contract C_{funct} describes the functional aspect under trivial assumption. The promise of the contract C_{QoS} indicates that there exist two modes: nominal, corresponding to normal operation, and blocked, in which w's are not emitted. Contract C_{QoS} relates to timing. This contract assumes that, if the controller is blocked, it will move to the nominal mode (by receiving an event $\mathbf{c}$) at most τ_n seconds after the last "work" request. If not, the observer will move to a non accepting state. When in nominal mode, the controller guarantees that the time interval between two successive "work" requests is at most τ_n seconds. The timer h is dedicated to computing the elapsed time for both assumption and promise.

Contract C_{safety}, shown in Figure 10, is attached to the computing platform and asserts an assumption of no failure. The failure $\mathbf{f}$ is abstracted and considered as input to the platform itself. The promise is not provided and can be thought as "any" possible behavior (i.e., the "universe"). If a failure event arrives, then the assumption moves to a non accepting state, meaning that nothing could be guaranteed about the provided behavior of the platform. This kind of contracts is useful to introduce assumptions without altering the guarantees of the system.

Figure 11 depicts the QoS contract for the supervisor, which is in charge of avoiding system collapse that may occur when an excessive amount of "work" is supplied to the plant. The assumption says that no w must occur when the system is in the overloaded state. The promise is specified in terms of a hybrid automaton. This hybrid automaton uses two clocks x and h bound to physical time, thus satisfying the differential equation $\dot{x} = 1, \dot{h} = 1$. Timer x is used to implement the token bucket mechanism, while timer h is used to guarantee that a w request will be delayed by at most τ_n seconds. When action w occurs, timer x decreases and, if w occurs too frequently, in the long range x eventually reaches ξ, which causes the emission of message $\mathbf{o}$ and switches the mode to "blocked", where latency is at most the smallest between ξ and τ_n. At some point, when x is again greater than ξ, a cleaning message $\mathbf{c}$ is sent to the controller to switch to mode "nominal". It is guaranteed that the sending of $\mathbf{c}$ is at most τ_n seconds after the last "work" command. It is also guaranteed that, if the operator sends a reset by an event $\mathbf{z}$, then the system resets the timer value x and after ξ seconds the system turns back to its nominal mode.

Contract conformance to the system obligations

As introduced in Section 3.2, system obligations are compositional, i.e., if a contract C_1 conforms to a system obligation B_1 and a contract C_2 conforms to a system obligation B_2, then the parallel composition between C_1 and C_2 conforms to the system obligation $B_1 \cap B_2$. This property allows us to "allocate" system obligations (see Fig. 7) to components in order to check conformance of the corresponding contracts separately, thereby reducing the complexity of the verification task. In order for this check to be successful it is necessary that the system obligation's interface be part of the allocated component's interface. For example, the protocol obligation relates r, s and w, that are outputs of the controller component (see Fig.8). Hence, we can allocate the protocol obligation to the controller for the conformance check. Similarly, the longest idle time obligation relates r and w, so that it can also be allocated to the controller component for the conformance check.

Conversely, the maximum mean work obligation relates $\mathbf{z}$ and w. Hence, this obligation can either be allocated to the supervisor, because $\mathbf{z}$ and w are supervisor's inputs, or to the parallel composition of the supervisor with the controller, because w is also a controller's output. In the former case, the verification task is simpler, because it does not require the parallel composition of the supervisor and the controller. Nonetheless, the conformance check may fail in this case because w is controlled by the controller and not by the supervisor, so that the parallel composition might in the end be necessary to verify conformance to the system obligation.

To illustrate how the conformance check works, we show that the controller's contract conforms to the protocol and the longest idle time obligations. Let us first consider

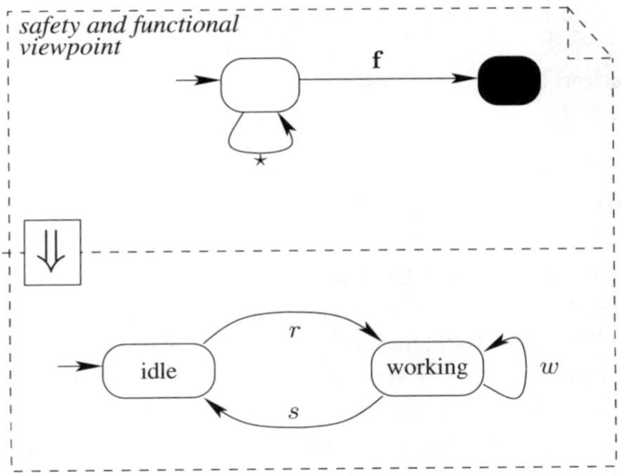

Fig. 12. Composed contract of the functional and safety viewpoints of the system controller

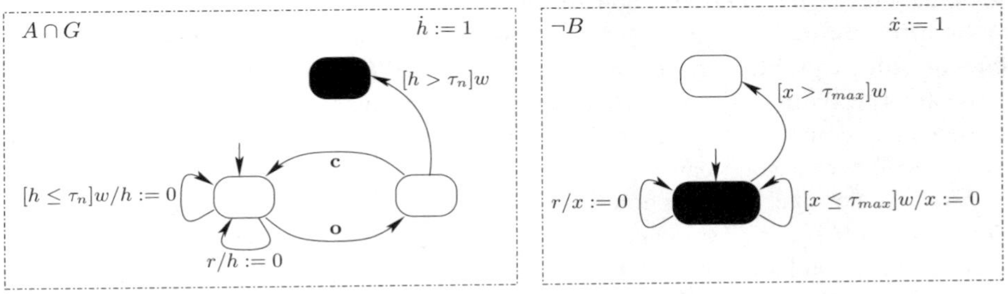

Fig. 13. Controller's contract obligation and negation of the corresponding system obligation

the protocol obligation. Observe that the controller's promise (Fig. 9) is equal to the protocol obligation. Conformance of a contract to a system obligation requires that the contract's promise subject to the contract's assumption (also called the contract obligation) is contained in the system obligation. In formulas: $A \cap G \subseteq B$, where (A, G) denotes the contract and B denotes the system obligation. Since the controller's promise is equal to the protocol obligation, then the controller's contract conforms to the protocol obligation for any assumptions. This shows that the controller's contract conforms to the protocol obligation even after composition with the safety viewpoint (Figs. 10 and 12).

Let us now consider the longest idle time obligation. The conformance check of the controller's contract to this obligation is not as trivial as in the case of the protocol obligation. To verify conformance in this case we need to compute the contract obligation $A \cap G$ and check the containment relation with the longest idle time obligation. To do so we can check that $A \cap G \cap \neg B = \emptyset$. The contract obligation and the negation of the longest idle time obligation are shown in Fig. 13. To compute the negation of the longest idle time obligation, we first complete the obligation's specification with its non-accepting states (not shown for clarity reasons). Since the resulting automaton is deterministic, its negation can be computed by exchanging accepting and non-accepting states. If we now take the intersection of the two automata shown in Fig. 13 we obtain an automaton that has no accepting states if we assume $\tau_n \leq \tau_{max}$, representing therefore the empty assertion. This proves that conformance is met.

6 Conclusion

We have presented mathematical foundations for a contract-based model for embedded systems design. Our generic mathematical model of contract supports "speculative design". This is achieved by focusing on component behavior, via compositions of contracts, with which diverse (functional and non-functional) aspects of the system can be expressed. This enabled a formalization of the whole process of component and multiple viewpoint composition through the general mechanism of contract fusion. A key contribution of our approach is that the incremental consideration of components and viewpoints can be handled with flexibility — whether through a component or a viewpoint centric methodology. The formalism and the design methodology has been illustrated through a multi viewpoint example.

Future work includes the development of effective algorithms to handle contracts, coping with the problems raised by complementation. Taking complements is a delicate issue: hybrid automata are not closed under complementation; in fact, no model class is closed under complementation beyond deterministic automata. To account for this fact, various countermeasures can be considered.

First, the designer has the choice to specify either E or its complement $\neg E$ (e.g., by considering observers). However, the parallel composition of contracts requires manipulating both E and its complement $\neg E$, which is the embarrasing case. To get compact formulas, our theory was developed using canonical forms for contracts, systematically. Not enforcing canonical forms provides room for flexibility in the representation of contracts, which can be used to avoid manipulating both E and $\neg E$ at the same time. A second idea is to redefine an assertion as a *pair* $(E, \bar{E})$, where $\bar{E}$ is an approximate complement of E, e.g., involving some abstraction. In doing so, one of the two characteristic properties of complements, namely $E \cap \bar{E} = \emptyset$ or $E \cup \bar{E} = \top$, do not hold. However, either necessary of sufficient conditions for contract dominance can be given. The above techniques are the subject of ongoing work and will be reported elsewhere.

Acknowledgments

The authors would like to acknowledge the entire SPEEDS team for their contribution to the project and to the ideas presented in this paper.

References

1. Damm, W.: Embedded system development for automotive applications: trends and challenges. In: Proceedings of the 6th ACM & IEEE International conference on Embedded software (EMSOFT 2006), Seoul, Korea, October 22–25 (2006)

2. Butz, H.: The Airbus approach to open Integrated Modular Avionics (IMA): technology, functions, industrial processes and future development road map. In: International Workshop on Aircraft System Technologies, Hamburg (March 2007)
3. Sangiovanni-Vincentelli, A.: Reasoning about the trends and challenges of system level design. Proc. of the IEEE 95(3), 467–506 (2007)
4. Damm, W.: Controlling speculative design processes using rich component models. In: Fifth International Conference on Application of Concurrency to System Design (ACSD 2005), St. Malo, France, June 6–9, pp. 118–119 (2005)
5. Meyer, B.: Applying "design by contract". IEEE Computer 25(10), 40–51 (1992)
6. Dijkstra, E.W.: Guarded commands, nondeterminacy and formal derivation of programs. Communications of the ACM 18(8), 453–457 (1975)
7. Lamport, L.: win and sin: Predicate transformers for concurrency. ACM Transactions on Programming Languages and Systems 12(3), 396–428 (1990)
8. Back, R.J., von Wright, J.: Contracts, games, and refinement. Information and communication 156, 25–45 (2000)
9. Back, R.J., von Wright, J.: Refinement Calculus: A systematic Introduction. Graduate Texts in Computer Science. Springer, Heidelberg (1998)
10. Dill, D.L.: Trace Theory for Automatic Hierarchical Verification of Speed-Independent Circuits. ACM Distinguished Dissertations. MIT Press (1989)
11. Wolf, E.S.: Hierarchical Models of Synchronous Circuits for Formal Verification and Substitution. PhD thesis, Department of Computer Science, Stanford University (October 1995)
12. de Alfaro, L., Henzinger, T.A.: Interface automata. In: Proceedings of the Ninth Annual Symposium on Foundations of Software Engineering, pp. 109–120. ACM Press, New York (2001)
13. Chakrabarti, A., de Alfaro, L., Henzinger, T.A., Stoelinga, M.: Resource interfaces. In: Alur, R., Lee, I. (eds.) EMSOFT 2003. LNCS, vol. 2855, pp. 117–133. Springer, Heidelberg (2003)
14. Henzinger, T.A., Jhala, R., Majumdar, R.: Permissive interfaces. In: Proceedings of the 13th Annual Symposium on Foundations of Software Engineering (FSE 2005), pp. 31–40. ACM Press, New York (2005)
15. Negulescu, R.: Process spaces. In: Palamidessi, C. (ed.) CONCUR 2000. LNCS, vol. 1877. Springer, Heidelberg (2000)
16. Passerone, R.: Semantic Foundations for Heterogeneous Systems. PhD thesis, Department of Electrical Engineering and Computer Sciences, University of California, Berkeley, CA 94720 (May 2004)
17. Burch, J., Passerone, R., Sangiovanni-Vincentelli, A.: Overcoming heterophobia: Modeling concurrency in heterogeneous systems. In: Proceedings of the 2nd International Conference on Application of Concurrency to System Design, Newcastle upon Tyne, UK, June 25–29 (2001)
18. Brookes, S.D., Hoare, C.A.R., Roscoe, A.W.: A theory of communicating sequential processes. Journal of the Association for Computing Machinery 31(3), 560–599 (1984)
19. Engelfriet, J.: Determinacy $\rightarrow$ (observation equivalence = trace equivalence). Theoretical Computer Science 36, 21–25 (1985)
20. Brookes, S.D.: On the relationship of CCS and CSP. In: Díaz, J. (ed.) ICALP 1983. LNCS. vol. 154. Springer, Heidelberg (1983)
21. Lee, E.A., Sangiovanni-Vincentelli, A.L.: A framework for comparing models of computation. IEEE Transactions on Computer Aided Design of Integrated Circuits and Systems 17(12), 1217–1229 (1998)

Coordination: Reo, Nets, and Logic*

Dave Clarke

CWI, Amsterdam, The Netherlands
dave@cwi.nl

Abstract. This article considers the coordination language *Reo*, a Petri net variant called *zero-safe nets*, and *intuitionistic temporal linear logic* (ITLL). The first part examines the semantics of the coordination language Reo in relation to zero-safe nets. Although the external presentations of the two models are quite different, the difference in underlying semantics is rather small. In fact, Reo connectors can be compositionally encoded into zero-safe nets. This means that the tools and techniques developed for Petri nets over the last 30 years, such as various extensions to the zero-safe nets model, such reconfigurable and dynamic nets, can be adapted to the Reo setting. The second part re-examines the idea of using linear logic as a basis for coordination languages. Specifically, we argue that *intuitionistic temporal linear logic* (ITLL) can encode the semantics of Reo and zero-safe nets, by encoding their notion of transaction. Moreover, by adapting the encoding and exploring the additional connectives of ITLL, it can form the basis of an expressive coordination language which goes beyond these models, by introducing means for explicitly reasoning about choices made by the environment and by providing more fine-grained control over the timing of interaction.

1 Introduction

Pundits of coordination languages and models argue that concurrent, component-based software should be broken into two independent parts: the entities performing computation (components), and the entities coordinating the data flow and resource usage between the components. This was crystallised into the equation [23]:

Concurrent Programming = Computation + Coordination.

To date numerous coordination models have been proposed, each realising the philosophy in a different manner [4,37]. The ones we are interested in in this paper endeavour to schedule collections of actions together into multi-party transactions, in the sense that either some desired set of actions occur together or none of them do, possibly at the exclusion of other collections of actions. The following variant of the well-known *holiday booking example* illustrates well what we are after. Consider the following:

* This work is in the context of the EU project IST-33826 CREDO: Modeling and analysis of evolutionary structures for distributed services (http://credo.cwi.nl)

F.S. de Boer et al. (Eds.): FMCO 2007, LNCS 5382, pp. 226–256, 2008.

a flight to Rio a hotel on the beach a dune-buggy	*or*	a flight to Zurich a hotel on the mountain a 4x4	*or*	stay home.

The *goal* is to book, with suitably matching dates, either all the entries in the first box and none of the entries in the second box, *or* all the entries in the second box and none of those in the first box, *or* nothing at all (the third box). Our assumption is that various components (or services) providing the basic functionality for booking flights, hotels, dune buggies, 4x4s, etc. exist, and the task of the coordinator is to plug these together in such a way to achieve the desired goal.

In order to discuss the kind of coordination we are interested in this paper, we first need to establish some terminology. We consider coordination not simply as a one-off event, but rather as an ongoing activity. Conceptually, time is partitioned into a number of contiguous *epochs*, which we consider as the *units of coordination*, meaning that the coordinator attempts to achieve something within each epoch, and that, from the perspective of an external observer, no finer granularity of time is observable. From the perspective of the coordinator, a lot may occur within an epoch.

We say that a set of actions A is *atomic* wrt to another set of actions B if and only if (1) either all of A occur or none of A within an epoch; and (2) the actions A are not interleaved with the actions in B within that epoch. The actions A are said to be *mutually exclusive* with the actions B. It is clear that this notion of atomic can be broken into two part. Indeed, this is how atomicity is conceived in the coordination language Reo [6]. In Reo, and in this article, the notion of *synchrony* is associated with (1), that is, a set of actions are considered *synchronous* if and only if they either all occur or none of them occurs within an epoch. The notion of *asynchrony* or *mutual exclusion* is associated with (2), that is, two sets of actions A and B are *asynchronous* if and only if if some $a \in A$ occurs within an epoch, then no element of B can occur within that epoch, and vice versa. Simply put, two events that *necessarily* occur within the same epoch are considered to be *synchronous*, and two events that *necessarily* occur within different epochs are considered to be *asynchronous*. Synchrony can be also be equated with a primitive notion of transaction.

Using this terminology, we say that the actions underlying the Rio-holiday are synchronous, the actions underlying the Zurich-holiday are synchronous, *and* the Rio-holiday is asynchronous with the Zurich-holiday.

We will work with the following definition of *coordination*:

> *coordination* is the task of (continuously/repeatedly) scheduling groups of dependent actions within temporal epochs.

In this definition, 'scheduling' captures both that actions may be scheduled to occur or to not occur—or perhaps even that they occur and are rolled-back. Furthermore, 'dependent' captures that one action may have temporal or data dependencies on another action, so even though all actions are conceptually considered to happen at the same time (synchronously), there may be a sequential ordering among them, though only the fact that they occur within the same epoch is relevant for our purposes.

The two coordination models considered in this paper are Reo [6] and zero-safe nets [15]. These models, more or less, employ the notions defined above, coordinating by grouping together actions into synchronous epochs at the exclusion of other possibilities. In both cases, the possibilities in different epochs changes due to state changes of the primitive elements of the coordination model.

Reo. Reo is a channel-based coordination designed by Farhad Arbab, and developed extensively by his group at CWI [6]. In Reo component *connectors* are built by plugging together primitive channels.[1] In Reo, channels come in a variety of behavioural variants, but one characteristic persistent across the entire set is that some channels are synchronous, as defined above, whereas others are asynchronous; other channels admit variants of these possibilities or change their behaviour depending upon their state. Channels in Reo can be composed to express a wide range of possible behaviours. Composition occurs at *nodes*—a collection of coincident channel ends—, which consist of a number of channel ends writing data into the node, and a number of ends taking data from the node. The node selects one possible data item written to it *at the exclusion of all others*, and duplicates it to all the ends taking data *synchronously*—thus all ends must be capable of accepting the data. Nodes have the policy that they cannot buffer data, it must be passed onward. The power of Reo comes from the combination of synchronous and mutual exclusion constraints of channels and nodes, resulting in the *propagation of synchrony and exclusion* across a connector. This means, for example, that if two primitives require that their ports a, b, c and d, e, respectively, are synchronised, and they are plugged together, joining c and d, then the synchronisation propagates over the composite of the two primitives, meaning that $a, b, c(= d), e$ will all by synchronised. If action f is mutually exclusive with a, then it will be mutually exclusive with $b, c(= d)$, and e as well after the composition.

Synchronisation and mutual exclusion constraints restrict the possible ways that data can flow through a connector. As we shall see, this means that data cannot simply flow through a connector; rather, only some of the possible ways data can flow are valid. Consider the example in Figure 1(a). Primitives $1(Anpr)$, $3(moB)$, and $7(stC)$ are *replicators*. They move the data synchronously from A, m and s, respectively, to npr, oB, and tc. Primitives $2(nm)$ and $6(rs)$ are *lossy sync* channels. They move data synchronously from n and r to m and s, respectively, *or* simply lose the data at n and r respectively. Primitive $5(otq)$ is a merger. It non-deterministically chooses between moving data from o to q or from t to q. Finally, primitive $4(pq)$ is a *synchronous drain*. It will remove data from p and q synchronously. The semantics of this connector can be understood as the following 'token game': the goal is to move a token from boundary node

[1] We sometimes write *primitive* instead of *channel* to de-emphasise the requirement that they have two ends.

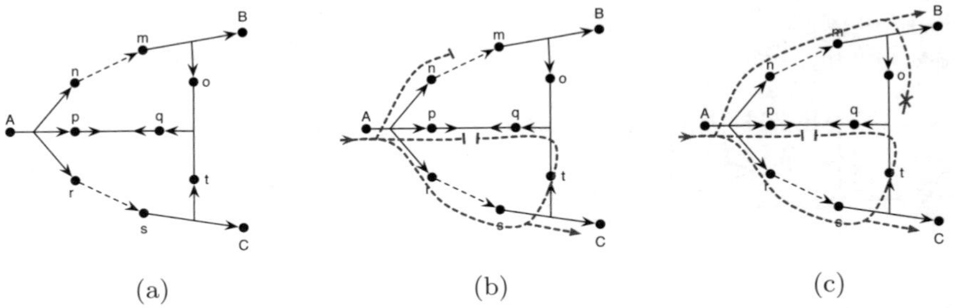

Fig. 1. (a) An exclusive router in Reo. (The numbering of primitives will be used later). (b) Valid data flow. (c) Stuck data flow.

A so that (1) moving it through the connector obeys all the above-mentioned rules imposed by the primitives, (2) no token gets stuck on an internal node $\{n, m, o, p, q, s, r, t\}$, and (3) no primitive is used more than once, so that (4) the token possibly ends up on B and/or C or is lost.

Two of the possible 'plays' are presented in Figures 1(b) and 1(c). The dashed (blue) line marks the path of the token(s) moved through the connector. In the first case, choices were made satisfying the rules of the game, and thus this corresponds to a correct behavioural possibility of the connector. In the second case, we were over-zealous and allowed the data to pass through both lossy syncs nm and rs, because the merger can choose only one item from o and t, hence the token will get stuck on, for example, o, and thus the behavioural possibility indicated (copying data from A to B and C) is invalid. After playing with the various possibilities for this connector, the conclusion should be that it is possible to move the token on A to either B or C, exclusively. This connector is in fact called an *exclusive router.*

Zero-safe Nets. Coordination in zero-safe nets [15] is achieved in a different way. Zero-safe nets are a variant of Petri nets which includes certain places called zero places. These places cannot be observed, meaning that any transition involving a marking of such a place is internal. In contrast, normal places are called *stable.* Only markings of stable places are observable. The basic firing of transitions of a zero-safe net is the same as for an ordinary Petri net. The main difference is that the semantics is expressed as two levels. The *micro*-level is more or less the same as in an ordinary Petri net, except that a micro-step may involve multiple firings. Precisely, it may involve the movement of any number of tokens into and out of zero places, but a token that is moved into a stable place may not be moved out of it again. This way a series of micro-steps makes up a so-called *macro-step*, which models a transaction between observable states. The internal transitions can be seen as synchronising the observable ones. As usual, choice in a Petri net is modelled by the competition between different transitions for the same token.

Figure 2(a) presents and example zero-safe net solving the dining philosophers problem (adapted from Bruni et. al. [15]). A token may be moved from

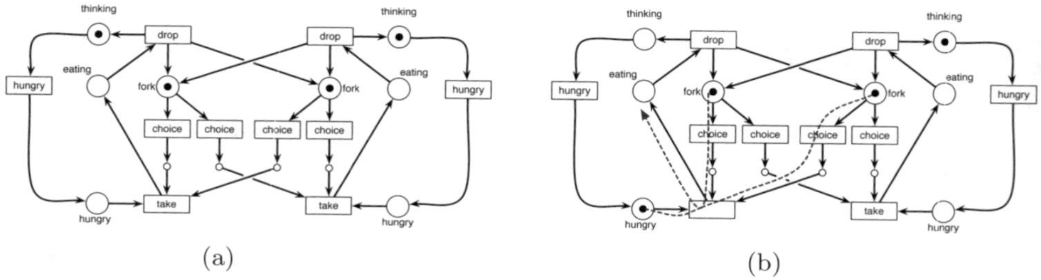

Fig. 2. (a) A Zero-safe Petri net solving the dining philosophers problem. Stable places are represented using large circles. Zero places are represented using small circles. (b) A successful transaction. Notice that it involves multiple internal steps. A stuck configuration would result, for example, if the far right hand *choice* had selected the *fork*.

fork (a stable place) to one of the zero places between the *choice* and the *take* transitions. A *take* transition will fire only if both connected zero places and the *hungry* place have tokens. The transition from having two *fork*s (on the table) to *eating* involves a number of internal transitions. Only combinations of internal transitions that do not get stuck are considered to be valid transactions. Thus, in this example, the two *choice* transitions need to *coordinate* in order to ensure that the transaction succeeds (Figure 2(b)).

This Work. On the surface, the coordination models Reo and zero-safe nets do not look particularly close. We show that they are surprisingly similar by casting their semantic models into a common, simple framework. The semantics of Reo and zero-safe nets are cast in terms of transitions between elements of a pair of monoids. The monoids respectively represent the stable parts of a configuration (states of buffers or stable places) and the internal parts of a configuration (the nodes or the zero places), and transitions represent the synchronous flow of data through Reo primitives or the firing of Petri net transitions. A common set of operational rules gives the semantics for the two models, and the difference is ultimately is in the details of the monoid used. After casting Reo's and zero-safe nets' semantics into a common semantic framework, we show that Reo connectors can be compositionally encoded into zero-safe nets. This result applies to causal Reo models which do not include any notion of context dependence, priority or maximal progress. This creates the opportunity for transferring tools, theoretical results, and implementation techniques for Petri nets to Reo.

The second part of the paper explores the idea of using intuitionistic temporal linear logic [26] as a meta-language for describing coordination models that have a transactional flavour. We then use the logic to encode both Reo and zero-safe nets. Transitions are encoded as linear formula describing the transfer of data between ports and state changes. In addition, the temporal modalities of the logic are used to control in which epochs events may, must and cannot occur. For example, $\Box m \otimes z \multimap \bigcirc\Box m' \otimes z'$, states that connector in state (or stable place) m in the presence of data on node z (or in zero place z) can by synchronously transformed into state (or stable place) m', which cannot be used until the next step or thereafter, and data on node (or in zero place) z, which must be consumed in this epoch. The $\Box-$ modality on the m represents that connector m (or place) may or may not be used in the epoch, and the absence of such a modality on z states that it must be used within the epoch. The semantics of Reo and zero-safe nets are soundly encoded as proofs of judgements of a certain shape, which succeed in either consuming all formulæ that must be consumed within an epoch or by delaying the consumption of formulæ until another epoch. The encoding consists of encoding the common operational framework and showing how the firing of primitive elements can be encoded. A side benefit of using an intuitionistic logic is that our model of Reo does not suffer from *causality* problems which blight most other models of Reo. Finally, we describe how the additional connectors of ITLL can express coordination patterns beyond those expressible in Reo and zero-safe nets, by exploiting the game-like nature of the logic to express choices made by the environment, in contrast to the choices made by the coordinator, and by varying the use of the temporal modalities to change both the specification of the epoch in which an even occurs *and* who decides when it occurs.

Caveat. Many semantic models for Reo have been presented in the literature to address more complex classes of connectors possessing mechanisms such as context dependency [18]. In this article, we take the simplest published semantics of Reo as our basis [8], though the semantics we present does not suffer from any causality problems, so is somewhat closer in spirit to the operational semantics of Mousavi et. al. [35]. In any case, there is no natural semantics for Reo—Reo makes sense only when given a semantic model, and an encoding of channel semantics and composition in that model—so we pursue but a reasonable model of Reo.

Organization. The paper is organized as follows: Section 2 presents a unified semantic framework into which both Reo's and zero-safe nets' semantics are cast, and shows how Reo can be encoded into zero-safe nets. Section 3 describes intuitionistic temporal linear logic. Section 4 describes how both Reo and Zero-safe nets are encoded into ITLL. Section 5 explores ITLL as a coordination model. Section 6 describes related work. Section 7 concludes the paper.

2 Unified Semantic Framework

One of the goals of this paper is to compare the coordination language Reo and zero-safe nets. We do so by casting both formalisms into a common semantic framework. An appropriate, simple framework was developed by Bruni et. al. [13] for studying zero-safe nets, which extends the well-known '*Petri nets are monoids*' approach [34]. Typically, the monoids are so-called *place monoids* modelling the markings of places—essentially, the monoids are multi-sets, with multi-set union as the multiplication operation. The variant adapted for zero-safe nets considers the net as two monoids, one for stable places and one for zero places.

Here we model Reo simply by choosing different (partial) monoids as the basis of the semantics, while keeping the same operational rules as for zero-safe nets. By making the monoid partial, we are able to both place an upper bound on the placement of tokens, modelling the requirement in Reo that nodes (temporarily) have at most one token, and to track the fact that each Reo primitive can *fire* at most once per epoch.

The semantics is based on a two reduction relations, *macro-step reduction* $\Rightarrow_\Delta \subseteq M \times M$ and *mirco-step reduction* $\rightarrow_\Delta \subseteq (M \times Z) \times (M \times Z)$, between configurations capturing the state of a system, where the configurations are elements of M and $M \times Z$, respectively, and M and Z are monoids. Both relations are determined by a set of primitive firings $\Delta \subseteq (M \times Z) \times (M \times Z)$, described below. *External configurations* M represent externally observable states. *Internal configurations* in $M \times Z$ represent, in addition, the internal, unobservable states. M denotes the stable part of a configuration, which persists between epochs, and is externally observable. Z denotes the internal or unobservable part of a configuration. States in Z are used in internal steps to coordinate externally observable transitions, but do not themselves persist from one epoch to another. Thus, *macro-steps* capture what occurs from one epoch to another epoch as far as the outside world is concerned, whereas *micro-steps* capture what occurs within an epoch in order to make a macro-step happen—the coordination. One can think of the macro-step semantics as an extensional description of behaviour, and the micro-step semantics as an intensional description of behaviour.

In Reo, M records the states of the primitive connectors, whereas Z records the data flow on nodes, as the semantics of Reo do not permit data to be (observably) buffered on nodes. The chosen monoids (Section 2.2) will ensure that each primitive can be only in one state and can only fire once per epoch, and that only one data item is permitted on a node.

In zero safe nets, M records the markings of the stable places, whereas Z records the zero-safe places. Only stable places can form part of external configurations. The stable places may change at most once during each epoch. More precisely, each stable token in a zero-safe net may be moved out of a stable place and, eventually, into another stable place at most once per epoch. The zero places are used to coordinate the activities occurring within an epoch. These may be used an arbitrary number of times, and can be fired either sequentially or in parallel.

We now present a generic operational semantics which can be used to give the semantics to Reo and zero-safe nets. The semantic rules are parameterised both by two monoids and a set of transitions, $\Delta \subseteq (M \times Z) \times (M \times Z)$, describing the *firing* of primitives (such as channels and nodes in Reo and transitions in zero-safe nets). Each element of Δ is written as $(m, z)\,[\rangle (m', z')$, where $m, m' \in M$ and $z, z' \in Z$, stating that there is a transition taking internal configuration (m, z) to internal configuration (m', z'). Note that only transitions between internal configurations are provided (though z and z' may be 0, and hence not involve internal states). These form the basis for micro-steps; macro-steps are derived from them using the rules of the operational semantics.

$$\text{(FIRING)}\quad \frac{(m,z)\,[\rangle(m',z') \in \Delta \quad m'' \in M \quad z'' \in Z}{(m \circ m'', z \cdot z'') \to_\Delta (m' \circ m'', z' \cdot z'')}$$

$$\text{(PARALLEL)}\quad \frac{(m_1,z_1) \to_\Delta (m_1',z_1') \quad (m_2,z_2) \to_\Delta (m_2',z_2')}{(m_1 \circ m_2, z_1 \cdot z_2) \to_\Delta (m_1' \circ m_2', z_1' \cdot z_2')}$$

$$\text{(CONCATENATION)}\quad \frac{(m_1,z) \to_\Delta (m_1',z'') \quad (m_2,z'') \to_\Delta (m_2',z')}{(m_1 \circ m_2, z) \to_\Delta (m_1' \circ m_2', z')}$$

$$\text{(COMMIT)}\quad \frac{(m,0_Z) \to_\Delta (m',0_Z)}{m \Rightarrow_\Delta m'}$$

Fig. 3. Operational Semantics Rules. A transition is defined only when each of its constituents parts is defined. $(M, \circ, 0_M)$ and $(Z, \cdot, 0_Z)$ are monoids (Section 2.1).

Figure 3 presents the generic operational semantic rules for the micro- and macro-steps of a system represented by monoids M and Z and primitive transition relation Δ. The rule (FIRING) describes how a primitive firing embeds into the rule format. The rule also can capture parts of a configuration that do not change during a particular micro-step. The rule (PARALLEL) describes two independent micro-steps firing in parallel, in different parts of the connector/net. The rule (CONCATENATION) describes the sequential composition of two series of micro-steps. The two mirco-step sequences typically deal with different parts of the configuration. This rule acts as a coordinator for the various actions which may occur in parallel. The rule (COMMIT) describes macro-steps as a series of micro-steps starting from an external configuration and ending in an external configuration. At the beginning and end of an epoch, the Z component must equal the unit element of the monoid, meaning, in zero-safe nets, that there are no elements on zero-places, and, in Reo, that no data is buffered in nodes.

Some advantages of the monoid-based semantics are that it can define the semantics of a system in a piecemeal fashion and that it can express non-interleaved concurrency. For example, a part of a Reo connector (or zero-safe net) may be described by configuration (m_1, z_1) and another part by (m_2, z_2). The configuration $(m_1 \circ m_2, z_1 \cdot z_2)$ describes the combination of these two connector (net) parts, assuming that it is defined. If we have micro-step transitions $(m_1, z_1) \to_\Delta (m_1', z_1')$ and $(m_2, z_2) \to_\Delta (m_2', z_2')$, the transition $(m_1 \circ m_2, z_1 \cdot z_2) \to_\Delta (m_1' \circ m_2', z_1' \cdot z_2')$ may be possible in the larger connector, depending on certain conditions.

2.1 Partial Commutative Monoids

The generic semantic rules presented above are parameterized by two partial commutative monoids—we will typically just say *monoid* for *partial commutative monoid*. We now define these and present a number of example monoids used in this paper. But first, some notation.

Notation 1. *Recall that* $A^B = \{f : B \to A\}$ *describes the set of functions from* B *to* A*, and that* $B \rightharpoonup A$ *is the partial functions from* B *to* A*. If* $f : B \rightharpoonup A$*, we write* $\mathrm{dom}(f)$ *to be the part of* B *for which* f *is defined, i.e.,* $\mathrm{dom}(f) = \{b \in B \mid f(b) \textit{ is defined}\}$.

Given a set C *and a* C*-indexed collection of sets* $Q_{c \in C}$*, define the* partial dependent function space $C \rightharpoonup\!\!\rightharpoonup Q_{c \in C}$ *to be the subset of the partial functions*

$C \rightharpoonup \biguplus_{c \in C} Q_c$ *such that if* $c \in \mathrm{dom}(f)$*, then* $f(c) \in Q_c$*. Such a function maps each defined* c *to a member of* Q_c*.*

Let $\mathcal{D}ata$ *be a non-empty set representing the data domain.*

Definition 1 (Partial Commutative Monoid). *A partial commutative monoid* $M^\circ = (M, \circ, 1)$ *consists of a set* M*, an unit element* $1 \in M$*, and a partial function* $\circ : M \times M \rightharpoonup M$*, obeying the following axioms:*

- $(a \circ b) \circ c = a \circ (b \circ c)$ *(associativity)*
- $a \circ b = b \circ a$ *(commutativity)*
- $a \circ 1 = 1 \circ a = a$ *(neutral element)*

Definition 2 (Product). *Given two monoids* $M^\circ = (M, \circ, 1_M)$ *and* $N^\cdot = (N, \cdot, 1_N)$*, their product,* $M^\circ \times N^\cdot$ *is defined as* $M^\circ \times N^\cdot = (M \times N, \bullet, 1_{M \times N})$ *where:*

- $(m, n) \bullet (m', n') = (m \circ m', n \cdot n')$*, whenever both components are defined, and undefined otherwise; and*
- $1_{M \times N} = (1_M, 1_N)$*.*

The following two monoids help define semantics for Petri nets. The first models the number of tokens on each place in the net, whereas the second models coloured tokens in coloured variants.

Definition 3 (Place Monoid). *Given a set of places* $\mathcal{P}$*, define the monoid* $PM(\mathcal{P}) = (\mathbb{N}^{\mathcal{P}}, \cdot, 0)$ *as:*

- $(p_1 \cdot p_2)(x) = p_1(x) + p_2(x)$*, and*
- $0(x) = 0$*.*

Definition 4 (Coloured Place Monoid). *Given a set of places* $\mathcal{P}$*, define the monoid* $CPM(\mathcal{P}) = (\mathcal{P} \rightarrow (\mathcal{D}ata \rightarrow \mathbb{N}), \cdot, 0)$ *with*

- $(p_1 \cdot p_2)(x) = \lambda d.(p_1(x)(d) + p_2(x)(d))$*, and*
- $0(x) = \lambda d.0$*.*

Typically, we would require that the function located at each place has finite support—meaning that each place holds a finite multiset of data items.

The following three monoids are used to define the semantic of Reo. The first two model data on nodes: the black-and-white node monoid models the case where data values have no significance (they are *signals*), whereas the coloured node monoid models the case where the data values are of interest. In both cases, elements of the monoid represent a partial mapping of nodes to data values representing the value stored on the node (or just whether it has data in the B/W case). The key point to note is that composition is undefined for two elements of the monoid that give a data value for the same node. The state monoid is similar to the coloured node monoid, in that it describes a partial function; the main difference is that each element of the domain of the function has its own codomain. The domain C is used to represent the primitives and each component Q_c of the codomain $\bigcup_{c \in C} Q_c$ represents the state set of components c. Again, only one state per connector is permitted, so the composition operation is also partial.

Definition 5 (B/W Node Monoid). *Given a set of nodes $\mathcal{N}$, define the monoid $NM(\mathcal{N}) = (2^{\mathcal{N}}, \cdot, \emptyset)$ with*

– $n_1 \cdot n_2 = \begin{cases} n_1 \cup n_2, & \textit{if } n_1 \cap n_2 = \emptyset \\ \textit{undefined}, & \textit{otherwise} \end{cases}$

Definition 6 (Coloured Node Monoid). *Let $\mathcal{N}$ be a set of nodes. A* coloured *node monoid is a triple $CNM(\mathcal{N}) = (\mathcal{N} \rightharpoonup \mathcal{D}ata, \cdot, 0)$, where*

– $f_1 \cdot f_2 = \begin{cases} f_1 \cup f_2, & \textit{if } \mathrm{dom}(f_1) \cap \mathrm{dom}(f_2) = \emptyset \\ \textit{undefined}, & \textit{otherwise} \end{cases}$
– *0 is the nowhere defined function.*

Definition 7 (State Monoid). *Let C be a set, and for each $c \in C$, let Q_c be a non-empty set. Define the monoid $SM(C, Q_{c\in C}) = (C \rightharpoonup Q_{c\in C}, \cdot, 0)$ where:*

– $f_1 \cdot f_2 = \begin{cases} f_1 \cup f_2, & \textit{if } \mathrm{dom}(f_1) \cap \mathrm{dom}(f_2) = \emptyset \\ \textit{undefined}, & \textit{otherwise} \end{cases}$
– *0 is the nowhere defined function.*

2.2 Semantics of Reo

Much of the hard work has now been done to give an operational semantics to Reo connectors. We need simply to instantiate the monoids M and Z, and provide transitions for primitives. We present two variants, a 'black and white' one which ignores data and only sends signals through connectors, and a 'coloured' one which considers data as well.

Let $\mathcal{P}ort$ be a denumerable set of port names. Let $i, o, a, b, \ldots$ range over elements of $\mathcal{P}ort$ and $I, O, A, B, \ldots$ range over subsets of $\mathcal{P}ort$.

A *Reo primitive* P is a 5-tuple $P = (Q, q, I, O, \Delta)$, where Q is a set of states, $q \in Q$ is the initial state, $I, O \subseteq \mathcal{P}ort$ are the sets of input and output ports, respectively, and Δ defines the transition relation. The transitions depend upon whether the model we are interested in is black and white or coloured.

B/W. Initially, transitions will be of the form $\Delta \subseteq (Q \times 2^I) \times (Q \times 2^O)$, satisfying the requirement that if $(q, A)\,[\rangle\,(r, B) \in \Delta$, then $A \cap B = \emptyset$, for causality reasons. The transition $(q, A)\,[\rangle\,(r, B)$ states that in state q the connector can *synchronously* accept input on ports A (excluding ports $I \setminus A$), and output on ports B (excluding ports $O \setminus B$).
Now let $M = SM(\mathbf{1}, Q)$ and $Z = NM(I \cup O)$, where $\mathbf{1}$ is a one element set. It is clear that the following embeddings exists $Q \times 2^I \hookrightarrow Q \times 2^{I\cup O} \hookrightarrow M \times Z$, and similarly for $Q \times 2^O$. Thus we consider the transitions Δ in the desired format as $\Delta \subseteq (M \times Z) \times (M \times Z)$ using these embeddings.

Coloured. This time transitions have the form $\Delta \subseteq (Q \times (I \rightharpoonup \mathcal{D}ata)) \times (Q \times (O \rightharpoonup \mathcal{D}ata))$, where for $(q, f)\,[\rangle\,(r, g) \in \Delta$ we again require that $\mathrm{dom}(f) \cap \mathrm{dom}(g) = \emptyset$, for causality reasons. The transition $(q, f)\,[\rangle\,(r, g)$ states that in state q the connector can *synchronously* accept input on ports $\mathrm{dom}(f)$ (excluding ports $I \setminus \mathrm{dom}(f)$), and output on ports $\mathrm{dom}(g)$ (excluding ports

$O \setminus \mathrm{dom}(g)$). Partial functions f and g describe the actual data that flows. Now let $M = SM(\mathbf{1}, Q)$ and $Z = CNM(I \cup O)$. Given the embeddings $Q \times (I \rightharpoonup \mathcal{D}ata) \hookrightarrow Q \times (I \cup O \rightharpoonup \mathcal{D}ata) \hookrightarrow M \times Z$, and similarly for O, we can consider the transitions Δ in the desired format as $\Delta \subseteq (M \times Z) \times (M \times Z)$ using these embeddings.

Figure 4 presents the firing relations for a number primitives. These consist of Reo's selection of channels, mergers and replicators (to model Reo's n-m nodes), and takers and writers, to model boundary interaction. We assume that the channels are defined over port set $\{a, b\}$, and that mergers and replicators are defined over port set $\{a, b, c\}$.

Primitive	**Arity**	**States**	**Init.**	**B/W Trans.**	**Coloured Trans.**
Sync	$\{a\} \to \{b\}$	$\{\circ\}$	$\circ$	$(\circ, a) [\rangle (\circ, b)$	$(\circ, a \mapsto d) [\rangle (\circ, b \mapsto d)$
SyncDrain	$\{a, b\} \to \emptyset$	$\{\circ\}$	$\circ$	$(\circ, ab) [\rangle (\circ, \mathbf{1})$	$(\circ, a \mapsto d + b \mapsto d') [\rangle (\circ, \mathbf{1})$
SyncSpout	$\emptyset \to \{a, b\}$	$\{\circ\}$	$\circ$	$(\circ, \mathbf{1}) [\rangle (\circ, ab)$	$(\circ, \mathbf{1}) [\rangle (\circ, a \mapsto d + b \mapsto d')$
AsyncDrain	$\{a, b\} \to \emptyset$	$\{\circ\}$	$\circ$	$(\circ, a) [\rangle (\circ, \mathbf{1})$ $(\circ, b) [\rangle (\circ, \mathbf{1})$	$(\circ, a \mapsto d) [\rangle (\circ, \mathbf{1})$ $(\circ, b \mapsto d) [\rangle (\circ, \mathbf{1})$
AsyncSpout	$\emptyset \to \{a, b\}$	$\{\circ\}$	$\circ$	$(\circ, \mathbf{1}) [\rangle (\circ, a)$ $(\circ, \mathbf{1}) [\rangle (\circ, b)$	$(\circ, \mathbf{1}) [\rangle (\circ, a \mapsto d)$ $(\circ, \mathbf{1}) [\rangle (\circ, b \mapsto d)$
LossySync	$\{a\} \to \{b\}$	$\{\circ\}$	$\circ$	$(\circ, a) [\rangle (\circ, b)$ $(\circ, a) [\rangle (\circ, \mathbf{1})$	$(\circ, a \mapsto d) [\rangle (\circ, b \mapsto d)$ $(\circ, a \mapsto d) [\rangle (\circ, \mathbf{1})$
FIFO1	$\{a\} \to \{b\}$	$\{\circ, \bullet\}$	$\circ$	$(\circ, a) [\rangle (\bullet, \mathbf{1})$ $(\bullet, \mathbf{1}) [\rangle (\circ, b)$	$(\circ, a \mapsto d) [\rangle (\bullet(d), \mathbf{1})$ $(\bullet(d), \mathbf{1}) [\rangle (\circ, b \mapsto d)$
Merger	$\{a, b\} \to \{c\}$	$\{\circ\}$	$\circ$	$(\circ, a) [\rangle (\circ, c)$ $(\circ, b) [\rangle (\circ, c)$	$(\circ, a \mapsto d) [\rangle (\circ, c \mapsto d)$ $(\circ, b \mapsto d) [\rangle (\circ, c \mapsto d)$
Replicator	$\{a\} \to \{b, c\}$	$\{\circ\}$	$\circ$	$(\circ, a) [\rangle (\circ, bc)$	$(\circ, a \mapsto d) [\rangle (\circ, b \mapsto d + c \mapsto d)$

Fig. 4. Some Reo Primitives. ab denotes the set $\{a, b\}$. $a \mapsto d + b \mapsto d'$ is a function mapping a to d and b to d'.

A *Reo connector* is simply a set of primitives $P = (Q_n, q_n, I_n, O_n, \Delta_n)_{n \in N}$, where N is used to name the primitives, subject to the conditions (1) for all $a \in \mathcal{P}ort$, if $a \in I_n$ and $a \in I_m$, for $n, m \in N$, then $n = m$, and, similarly, if $a \in O_n$ and $a \in O_m$, for $n, m \in N$, then $n = m$; and (2) for all $a \in \mathcal{P}ort$, if $a \in I_n$ then there is at most one $m \neq n$ such that $a \in O_m$, and if $a \in O_n$, then there is at most one $m \neq n$ such that $a \in I_m$. Condition (1) ensures that the input/output ports are unique for each primitive, and condition (2) ensures that the ports are primitive ports are plugged together 1:1, output to input—that is, if $a \in O_n \cap I_m$, then output port a of n is plugged into input port a of m.

The semantics of a Reo connector is given by taking the two monoids $M = SM(N, Q_{n \in N})$ and $Z = NM(\bigcup_{n \in N}(I_n \cup O_n))$ (or $Z = CNM(\bigcup_{n \in N}(I_n \cup O_n))$ for coloured models) and the transition relation $\Delta = \bigcup_{n \in N} \Delta_n$, where each primitive firing $(q, A) [\rangle (r, B)$ (or $(q, f) [\rangle (r, g)$) is embedded in the obvious fashion.

Figure 5 gives an example derivation for the connector presented in Figure 1.

$$
\dfrac{\dfrac{(1,A)\,[\rangle\,(1,npr)}{(13,A) \to (13,npr)}\,\text{(Firing)} \qquad \dfrac{\dfrac{\dfrac{(2,n)\,[\rangle\,(2,0)}{(2,npr) \to (2,pr)}\,\text{(Firing)} \qquad (*)}{(2567,npr) \to (2567,pqC)}\,\text{(Concat)} \qquad \dfrac{(4,pq)\,[\rangle\,(4,0)}{(4,pqC) \to (4,C)}\,\text{(Firing)}}{(24567,npr) \to (24567,C)}\,\text{(Concat)}}{(1234567,A) \to (1234567,C)}\,\text{(Concat)}
$$

where (*) is

$$
\dfrac{\dfrac{\dfrac{(6,r)\,[\rangle\,(6,s)}{(6,pr) \to (6,ps)}\,\text{(Firing)} \qquad \dfrac{(7,s)\,[\rangle\,(7,tC)}{(7,ps) \to (7,ptC)}\,\text{(Firing)}}{(67,pr) \to (67,ptC)}\,\text{(Concat)} \qquad \dfrac{(5,t)\,[\rangle\,(5,q)}{(5,ptC) \to (5,pqC)}\,\text{(Firing)}}{(567,pr) \to (567,ptC)}\,\text{(Concat)}
$$

Fig. 5. Derivation for Exclusive Router (Figure 1). The primitives are all stateless, so the M (first) component really just records which primitives are used. The Z (second) component records the data flow.

2.3 Zero-Safe Nets

We directly give the semantics of zero-safe nets in terms of monoids, borrowing from (a compressed version of) the development of Bruni et. al. [15].

Definition 8 (Zero-safe net). *A* zero-safe net *is a tuple* $N = (S, T, F, u_{\text{in}}, \mathsf{Z})$ *where*

- *S is the set of* places, $a, a', \ldots$*;*
- *T is the set of* transitions $t, t', \ldots$ *(with $S \cap T = \emptyset$);*
- *$F \subseteq (S \times T) \cup (T \times S)$ is called the* flow relation*; the elements of the flow relation are called* arcs, *and we write $x\ F\ y$ for $(x, y) \in F$;*
- *a finite multiset $u_{\text{in}} : S \to \mathbb{N}$ is the initial marking of N; and*
- *the set $\mathsf{Z} \subseteq S$ is the set of* zero places.

The places $\mathsf{M} = S \setminus \mathsf{Z}$ are called the stable places. *A* stable marking *is a multiset of stable places, and the initial marking u_{in} must be stable.*

A *marking* for a Petri net with places S is a map $S \to \mathbb{N}$ indicating the number of tokens at each place—this can equally be seen as a multiset of places. Each transition, $t \in T$, connects some places ${}^\bullet t = \{s \in S \mid s\ F\ t\}$ with some places $t^\bullet = \{s \in S \mid t\ F\ y\}$. Transitions generate a firing relation $\Delta \subseteq (S \to \mathbb{N}) \times (S \to \mathbb{N})$ such that $f\,[\rangle\,g \in \Delta$ if and only if

$$
f(s) = \begin{cases} 1, & \text{if } s \in {}^\bullet t \\ 0, & \text{otherwise} \end{cases} \qquad \text{and} \qquad g(s) = \begin{cases} 1, \text{if } s \in t^\bullet \\ 0, \text{otherwise} \end{cases}
$$

for some $t \in T$. This could be easily extended to deal with weighted transitions.

We can view markings in $S \to \mathbb{N}$ equivalently as functions from $(\mathsf{M} \times \mathsf{Z}) \to \mathbb{N}$ or as $(\mathsf{M} \to \mathbb{N}) \times (\mathsf{Z} \to \mathbb{N})$, giving the stable and the zero markings. Thus the firing relation $\Delta \subseteq (S \to \mathbb{N}) \times (S \to \mathbb{N})$ can trivially be seen as a relation

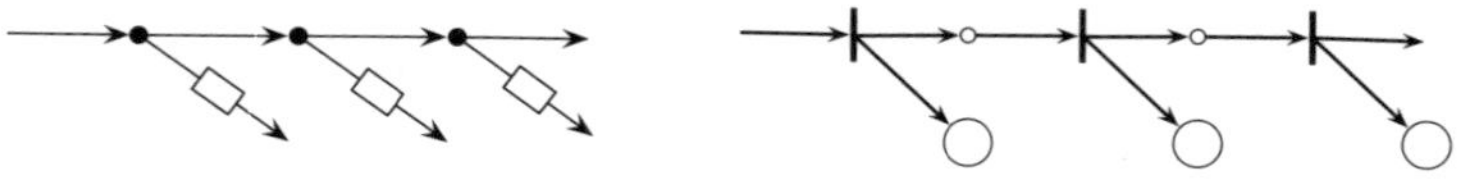

(a) (b)

Fig. 6. (a) Synchronous chain 'coordinating' actions (FIFO-buffers) (b) Again in zero-safe nets

$\Delta \subseteq ((\mathsf{M} \to \mathbb{N}) \times (\mathsf{Z} \to \mathbb{N})) \times ((\mathsf{M} \to \mathbb{N}) \times (\mathsf{Z} \to \mathbb{N}))$, which is a relation between the product of two place monoids, namely, $PM(\mathsf{M}) \times PM(\mathsf{Z})$, so, finally, $\Delta \subseteq (PM(\mathsf{M}) \times PM(\mathsf{Z})) \times (PM(\mathsf{M}) \times PM(\mathsf{Z}))$. Thus, the two monoids underlying the semantic model for zero-safe nets are $M = PM(\mathsf{M})$ and $Z = PM(\mathsf{Z})$, where, as mentioned above, M are the stable places and Z are the zero places. The remainder of the operational semantics is given by the rules in Figure 3.

It is an easy exercise to work out the derivations corresponding to the behaviour demonstrated in Figure 2.

A coloured variant can be easily described, simply by replacing $PM(M) \times PM(Z)$ by $CPM(M) \times CPM(Z)$ and redefining the firing relation Δ.

2.4 Comparision of Reo and Zero-Safe Nets

On the surface, Reo and zero-safe nets look quite different, but delving a little deeper into their semantics reveals that they are in fact very similar in many respects. In fact, we can encode Reo into zero-safe nets.

- Both models enforce a notion of transaction in that valid, externally observable macro-steps consist of a sequence of internal micro-steps, and that not all possible sequences of micro-steps result in a valid macro-step.
- Reo's nodes are akin to zero-safe places and its primitives' states are stable, that is, they are part of the observable configuration. A FIFO buffer behaves similarly to a (bounded/1-safe) place in a Petri net.
- Choice in Reo is handled by merger and primitives such as asynchronous drains (which can in fact be encoded using a merger). Choice in Petri nets is handled by multiple transitions from a place competing for the token.
- Replication in Reo is handled by replicators. Replication in Petri nets is handled by multiple target places of a transition.
- A chain of synchronous channels must fire sequentially at the micro level, within an epoch. This is very similar to how a chain of zero-safe places would fire sequentially. Replication (via replicators or Petri transition) can then be used to coordinate activities, respecting the sequential ordering. Parallel reductions occur in Reo as in zero-safe nets in independent parts of a connector. In both cases, the topology of the connector/net guides the sequential/parallel micro-step reduction. Figure 6 illustrates the idea for both Reo and zero-safe nets.

- The semantics of Reo primitives are expressed externally as a set of transitions, whereas the nature of zero-safe networks is predefined, based on the variant of Petri-net under consideration.
- The major difference between the two is that in any macro-step (epoch), a Reo primitive can participate at most once. Equally, in Reo data may flow through each node at most once in an epoch. On the other hand, a zero-safe net permits each transition to fire an arbitrary number of times in an epoch (though this is easy to control, as we show below).
- In zero-safe nets, places can hold an arbitrary number of tokens. Reo nodes (equivalent to zero-safe places) can hold only one token. Variants of Petri nets exist where places hold at most one token (called 1-safe). Such a variant is closer to Reo.

In order to establish a correspondence between the two models, in one direction at least, we need to demonstrate how to restrict zero places so that they can be used at most once per epoch. This is quite simple, and is illustrated in Figure 7. The stable place is used to ensure that the zero place can fire only once, as the token leaves the stable place when the token enters the zero place, and re-enters the stable place when the token leaves the zero place. After these two steps, the stable place can no longer participate in the epoch.

Figure 8 presents the encoding of each of Reo's primitives into zero safe nets. Each encoded connector uses the above trick to ensure that it fires only once per epoch. The labelled zero places represent the boundary/interface ports of the connectors. Composition of two encoded Reo connectors consists of superimposing the two zero places corresponding to the boundary nodes—that is, the two Reo ends plugged together to form a node are encoded as the same zero place.

Encoding more general Reo primitives based on their semantic description is straightforward, as we simple follow the patterns used in the encodings above. The encoding of FIFO1 demonstrates how to encode a state machine, the encodings of AsyncDrain and LossySync demonstrate how to encode choice, and the encodings of the Sync* demonstrate how to encode synchronisation. Thus, we argue, Reo can be compositionally encoded in terms of zero-safe nets by encoding Reo's primitives, and then composing them.

Now that Reo can be encoded into zero-safe nets, extensions to the zero-safe model such as dynamic and reconfigurable nets [13] can be applied in the context of Reo. Exploring these directions is left for future work. Indeed, reconfiguration of Reo connectors, in particular, when the reconfiguration is caused by dynamic behaviour in the connector, is already an active area of research [17,31].

In the other direction, encoding zero-safe nets into Reo is not possible in general. This is simply because places in zero-safe nets may hold more than one token, and thus zero-safe nets can model multiple interactions on a given port within a single epoch.

Finally, observe that the Reo and zero-safe nets could easily be combined into a single model, simply by taking the product of both their normal and zero components, and by adding non-trivial additional firing rules to link the Reo

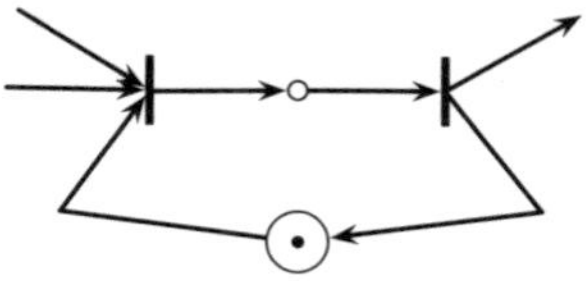

Fig. 7. Ensuring that zero places fire at most once per epoch

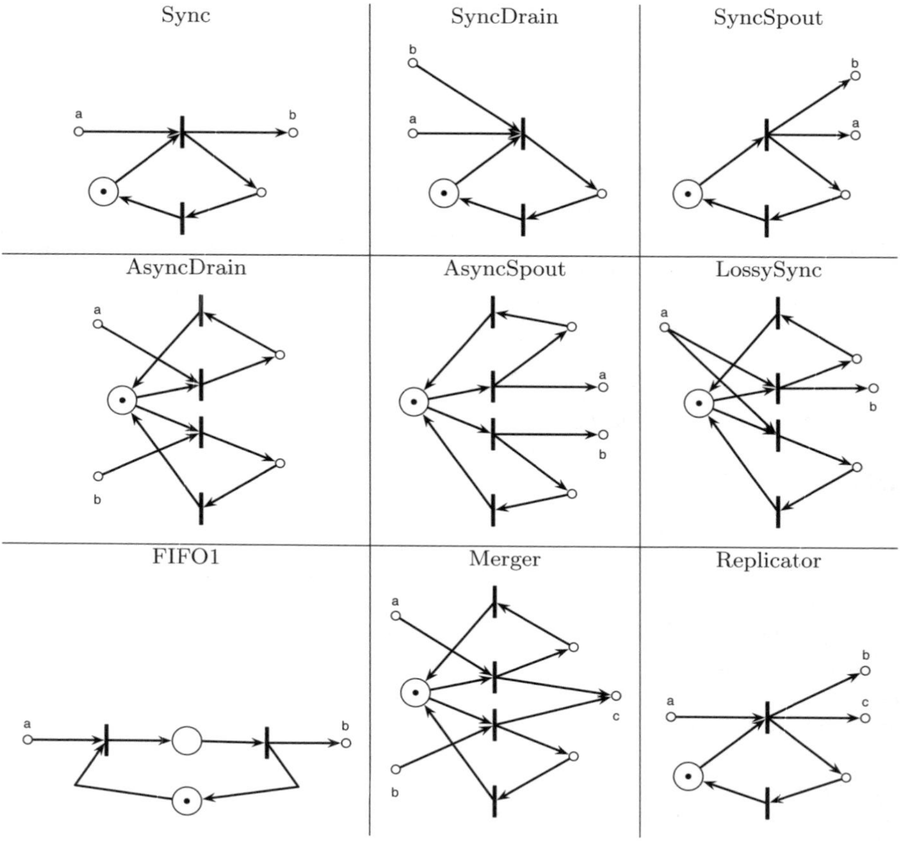

Fig. 8. Zero-safe net Encodings of Standard Reo Primitive. Labelled places represent Reo's ports (ends). Other places are used to ensure that the primitive fires at most once per epoch, plus the buffer for FIFO1 (Compare behaviours with those described in Figure 4).

connector and the zero-safe net, that is, by having transitions from $M_{Reo} \times M_{zsn}$ to $Z_{Reo} \times Z_{zsn}$. This approach is at present being explored to connect Reo and workflow language YAWL [41].

3 Intuitionistic Temporal Linear Logic

We now shift focus away from the Reo and zero-safe nets, and introduce intuitionistic temporal linear logic (ITLL)[2] both as a meta-language for reasoning about the sort of coordination models we are interested in, and as a vehicle for enabling more refined behavioural descriptions beyond those expressible in Reo or zero-safe nets. For example, neither of these models can make the distinction between internal and external choice, whereas in ITLL the formula $A \& B$ expresses an internal choice, and formula $A \oplus B$ expresses external choice.

Intuitionistic temporal linear logic (ITLL) is an extension of linear logic [24], explored by Hirai [26], that includes linear variants of the temporal modalities $\Box-$, $\bigcirc-$, and $\Diamond-$. ITLL is a resource conscious logic with modalities for reasoning about how resource usage changes over time. ITLL has been used to reason about timed Petri nets [25], for modelling agent choices, agent interaction [38,39], and agent negotiation [33], and as a logic programming language [9].

For now, we will consider the following fragment of ITLL (additional connectives will be discussed later):

$$A ::= a \mid \mathbf{1} \mid A \otimes A \mid A \multimap A \mid A \& A \mid A \oplus A \mid \Box A \mid \bigcirc A$$

where a ranges over primitive formulæ. In general, we use lower case letters to range over primitive formulæ and upper case letters to range over formulæ.

Our interpretation of ITLL is that formulæ can describe epochs of time, where within each epoch, formulæ describe resource usage in a linear fashion. Ultimately, we associate coordination (or ability-to-coordinate) with the ability to perform proofs of a certain form. Thus, we base this interpretation on a standard reading of proofs. The standard understanding of the game semantics underlying linear logic formulæ [12], adapted to account for the temporal connectives, has guided our interpretation. The connectives can be read as follows:

a	availability of single resource a, *now*
$\mathbf{1}$	no resources, *now*
$A \otimes B$	availability of (resources) A and B, *now*
$A \multimap B$	availability of a one-time converter of (resources) A to B, *now*
$A \& B$	an internal choice between (resources) A and B, *now*
$A \oplus A$	an external choice between (resources) A and B, *now*
$\Box A$	(resource) A is available *any time*, exactly once
$\bigcirc A$	(resource) A is available in the *next* epoch, exactly once

It is important to note that $\Box A$ does not mean the same as its linear temporal logic (LTL) counterpart. To be compatible with linear logic, Hirai linearised (in the sense of linear logic) the meaning of $\Box A$: *A can be used* ***any time****, but only once.* Note that we have no exponentials ($!A$), though we do suggest how they

[2] A distinguishing feature of intuitionistic linear logic is that judgements allow only a single conclusion. Furthermore, it lacks the *par* connective among others which require multiple conclusions.

can be used as an alternative in our encodings. Further interpretation of ITLL from a coordination perspective will be given in Section 5.

The proof rules for ITLL are presented in Figure 9. Let Γ denote a possibly empty sequence of formulæ. Let $\Box\Gamma = \Box A, \Box B, \ldots$. Similarly for $\bigcirc\Gamma$. Rules are labelled to indicate whether the connective is introduced on the left or right of the turnstile $\vdash$, so, for example, $\multimap_l$ labels the rule introducing $\multimap$ on the left.

$$\frac{}{A \vdash A}\,Ax \qquad \frac{\Gamma \vdash A \quad A, \Delta \vdash B}{\Gamma, \Delta \vdash B}\,Cut \qquad \frac{\Gamma, A, B, \Delta \vdash C}{\Gamma, B, A, \Delta \vdash C}\,Ex$$

$$\frac{\Gamma \vdash A \quad B, \Delta \vdash C}{\Gamma, A \multimap B, \Delta \vdash C}\,\multimap_l \qquad \frac{\Gamma, A \vdash B}{\Gamma \vdash A \multimap B}\,\multimap_r$$

$$\frac{\Gamma, A, B \vdash C}{\Gamma, A \otimes B \vdash C}\,\otimes_l \qquad \frac{\Gamma \vdash A \quad \Delta \vdash B}{\Gamma, \Delta \vdash A \otimes B}\,\otimes_r$$

$$\frac{\Gamma, A \vdash C}{\Gamma, A \,\&\, B \vdash C}\,\&_{1l} \qquad \frac{\Gamma, B \vdash C}{\Gamma, A \,\&\, B \vdash C}\,\&_{2l} \qquad \frac{\Gamma \vdash A \quad \Gamma \vdash B}{\Gamma \vdash A \,\&\, B}\,\&_r$$

$$\frac{\Gamma, A \vdash C \quad \Gamma, B \vdash C}{\Gamma, A \oplus B \vdash C}\,\oplus_l \qquad \frac{\Gamma \vdash A}{\Gamma \vdash A \oplus B}\,\oplus_{1r} \qquad \frac{\Gamma \vdash B}{\Gamma \vdash A \oplus B}\,\oplus_{2r}$$

$$\frac{\Gamma \vdash C}{\Gamma, \mathbf{1} \vdash C}\,\mathbf{1}_l \qquad \frac{}{\vdash \mathbf{1}}\,\mathbf{1}_r$$

$$\frac{A, \Gamma \vdash B}{\Box A, \Gamma \vdash B}\,\Box_l \qquad \frac{\Box\Gamma' \vdash A}{\Box\Gamma' \vdash \Box A}\,\Box_r \qquad \frac{\Box\Gamma, \Gamma'' \vdash A}{\Box\Gamma', \bigcirc\Gamma'' \vdash \bigcirc A}\,\bigcirc$$

Fig. 9. The proof rules for intuitionistic temporal linear logic

The first five rows of rules are standard. From a coordination perspective, the computation interpretation of the rules $\&_l$ and $\oplus_l$ reveals the difference between the two choice connectives. $\&_l$ will enable a proof using $A \,\&\, B$ to go through even if only one of A or B is suitable. The interpretation is the the prover (the coordinator) can choose which. On the other hand, $\oplus_l$ requires that both A and B in $A \oplus B$ can make the proof go through. The coordinator needs to be able to produce an appropriate proof in both cases for coordination to succeed, modelling that the choice can be made externally. This is consistent with existing interpretations of linear logic [1].

Rule $\Box_l$ enables a resource to be used at any time ($\Box A$) to be used *now* (A). Rule $\Box_r$, which we do not use directly, states that a result that depends only on resources that can be used at any time can itself be used anytime. Rule $\bigcirc$ states that reasoning about future epochs (such as the next one) is done by shifting the future (next state) resources to the present state (removing the $\bigcirc$) and then reasoning as per usual. This requires that there are no *now* resources, only $\Box$– and $\bigcirc$– ones.

In the encodings of Reo and zero-safe nets presented later in this section, the proof rules for ITLL are used as the workhorse handling details of the semantic framework, whereas the specific firing rules for the primitives are encoding as externally specified axioms. Let Σ denote a set of axioms of the form $\Gamma \vdash A$. We write $\Gamma \vdash_\Sigma A$ to denote judgements in the proof system extended with axioms Σ and the following rule:

$$\frac{(\Gamma \vdash A) \in \Sigma}{\Gamma \vdash_\Sigma A}\ \Sigma\text{-}axiom$$

Note that proving judgement $\Pi \vdash_\Sigma B$ is equivalent to proving $\Sigma^*, \Pi \vdash B$ in the logic extended with the standard axioms for exponentials along with adaptations of the proof rules above (see [26]), where Σ^* converts each $(\Gamma \vdash A) \in \Sigma$ into the formula $!(\Gamma^\otimes \multimap A)$, and $\Gamma^\otimes$ is the formulæ in Γ connected by an $\otimes$. Thus, if $\Gamma = A_1, \ldots, A_n$, then $\Gamma^\otimes = A_1 \otimes \cdots \otimes A_n$, and if $\Gamma = \epsilon$, then $\Gamma^\otimes = \mathbf{1}$.

3.1 Semantics of ITLL

Hirai [25] presented semantics of ITLL as an adaptation of the original phase space semantics of Girard [24]. No game semantics exists for ITLL. Nonetheless, we can (and have) drawn from game semantics for linear logic when giving our intuitive interpretation of ITLL's connectives. The open question remains: what are the game semantics for full ITLL. Here we provide only some intuition, leaving the complete treatment of game semantics for ITLL for future work.

In games semantics for linear logic [12], one telling feature is the difference between the choice connectives $-\&-$ and $-\oplus-$ is who makes the choice. In the first case, the player needs to only win one of the possible games encoded in the choice in order to win the game. In the second case, the player can only win the game if he can win both games encoded in the choice, as the opponent makes the choice. To extend to deal with the temporal modalities, we anticipate the following changes. Games are played over multiple epochs. $\bigcirc A$ is interpreted as a game that is played in the following epoch. $\Box A$ is a game for which the player (coordinator) can chose which epoch the game corresponding to A is played in — the moves are thus, 'play now' and 'play later', when cast in terms of a game played 'now'. Similarly, $\Diamond A$ is the dual, which means that the opponent (environment) makes the choice when to play the game. Finally, for a player to win a game (= valid/provable judgement), she needs to win every epoch (until the game peters out).

4 Encodings

After investing the effort to cast the semantics of Reo and zero-safe nets into a uniform framework, encoding them into ITLL is quite easy: we need to encode the general framework and then the primitives for each system. The basic assumption we run with is that the elements of the respective monoids can be encoded as primitive formulæ or tensor products ($\otimes$) of such formuæ. We typically do not insert explicit conversions between the elements of the monoid and their representation as formulæ. We demonstrate the soundness of our encoding, but do not give a completeness result. There are two reasons: (1) completeness simply would not hold for the entire class of monoids we consider, though we expect that it will hold for monoids which are not partial and are sufficiently free; and (2) we do not know whether a cut elimination result holds for ITLL, yet this seems to be crucial for proving completeness.

4.1 Encoding Configurations

The encoding of a configuration depends whether it is on the left or right hand side of the arrow.

Given a reduction $(m, z) \rightarrow_{\Delta} (m', z')$, where $m, m' \in M$ and $z, z' \in Z$, the configuration on the left-hand side is encoded as $(\Box m)^{\otimes} \otimes z^{\otimes}$, (or equivalently, as a sequent of form $(\Box m), z$, without the separating $\otimes$), and the configuration on the right-hand side is encoded as $(\bigcirc\Box m')^{\otimes} \otimes (z')^{\otimes}$. Note that the primitive firings themselves are encoded slightly differently, as we shall see in Section 4.2

The reading of $(\Box m)^{\otimes} \otimes z^{\otimes}$ is that (1) any of the elements in m can be used at any time, and (2) all of the elements in z must be used in this step. Similarly $(\bigcirc\Box m')^{\otimes} \otimes (z')^{\otimes}$ states, in addition, that (3) in the next step, but not now, any of the elements of m' can be used at any time. The part involving z' is analogous to (2).

When encoding the left and right hand sides of $m \Rightarrow_{\Delta} m'$, the encodings can be simplified to $(\Box m)^{\otimes}$ and $(\bigcirc\Box m')^{\otimes}$.

4.2 Encoding a Primitive Firing

Each primitive firing $(m, z) \,[\rangle (m', z') \in \Delta$ is encoding as an axiom as follows:

$$[\![(m, z) \,[\rangle (m', z')]\!] = m, z \vdash (\bigcirc\Box m')^{\otimes} \otimes (z')^{\otimes}$$

Proofs for a system with primitive firing relation Δ are carried out in the logic $\Gamma \vdash_{\Sigma} A$, where $\Sigma = [\![\Delta]\!]$.

Example 1. The transition from a Reo replicator $(\circ, a) \,[\rangle (\circ, bc)$ would be encoded as an axiom: $\circ, a \vdash \bigcirc\Box\circ \otimes b \otimes c$.

An alternative approach is to encode the state-machines as a single formula, using an exponential:

$$\begin{aligned}
[\![\Delta]\!] &= !([\![(m_1, z_1) \,[\rangle (m_1', z_1')]\!] \,\&\cdots\&[\![(m_n, z_n) \,[\rangle (m_n', z_n')]\!]) \\
&\qquad \text{where } \Delta = \{(m_1, z_1) \,[\rangle (m_1', z_1'), \ldots, (m_n, z_n) \,[\rangle (m_n', z_n')\} \\
[\![(m, z) \,[\rangle (m', z')]\!] &= m^{\otimes} \otimes z^{\otimes} \multimap (\bigcirc\Box m')^{\otimes} \otimes (z')^{\otimes}
\end{aligned}$$

In this format, the above example would be expressed as $!(\circ \otimes a \multimap \bigcirc\Box\circ \otimes b \otimes c)$.

4.3 Encoding the Semantic Rules into ITLL

We now show how to encode the semantic rules from Figure 3 into ITLL proof fragments. This is the essence of soundness. In our encodings, we will use the exchange rule implicitly on both sides of the turnstile, which implies an implicit use of Cut. We also use $-^*$ to mark multiple applications of a rule or pattern.

Firing. The rule:

$$\frac{(m,z)\,[\rangle(m',z')\in\Delta \quad m''\in M \quad z''\in N}{(m\circ m'',z\cdot z'')\rightarrow_\Delta (m'\circ m'',z'\cdot z'')}\;(\text{FIRING})$$

is encoded as proof:

$$\dfrac{\dfrac{\dfrac{(m,z\vdash_\Sigma(\bigcirc\Box m')^\otimes\otimes(z')^\otimes)\in\Sigma}{m,z\vdash_\Sigma(\bigcirc\Box m')^\otimes\otimes(z')^\otimes}\;\Sigma\text{-AXIOM}}{\Box m,z\vdash_\Sigma(\bigcirc\Box m')^\otimes\otimes(z')^\otimes}\;\Box_l^* \quad \dfrac{(1)}{\Box m''\vdash_\Sigma(\bigcirc\Box m'')^\otimes} \quad \dfrac{(2)}{z''\vdash_\Sigma(z'')^\otimes}}{\Box m,\Box m'',z,z''\vdash_\Sigma(\bigcirc\Box m')^\otimes(\bigcirc\Box m'')^\otimes\otimes(z')^\otimes\otimes(z'')^\otimes}\;\otimes_r^*$$

where (1) is multiple occurrences of the following proof, one for each atom m_a, joined using $\otimes_r$:

$$\dfrac{\dfrac{}{\Box m_a\vdash_\Sigma\Box m_a}\;\text{Ax}}{\Box m_a\vdash_\Sigma\bigcirc\Box m_a}\;\bigcirc$$

and (2) is similar, but simpler.

Parallel. The rule:

$$\frac{(m_1,z_1)\rightarrow_\Delta(m_1',z_1') \quad (m_2,z_2)\rightarrow_\Delta(m_2',z_2')}{(m_1\circ m_2,z_1\cdot z_2)\rightarrow_\Delta(m_1'\circ m_2',z_1'\cdot z_2')}\;(\text{PARALLEL})$$

is encoded as proof fragment:

$$\dfrac{\Box m_1,z_1\vdash_\Sigma(\bigcirc\Box m_1')^\otimes\otimes(z_1')^\otimes \qquad \Box m_2,z_2\vdash_\Sigma(\bigcirc\Box m_2')^\otimes\otimes(z_2')^\otimes}{\Box m_1,\Box m_2,z_1,z_2\vdash_\Sigma(\bigcirc\Box m_1')^\otimes\otimes(\bigcirc\Box m_2')^\otimes\otimes(z_1')^\otimes\otimes(z_2')^\otimes}\;\otimes_r$$

Concatenation. The rule:

$$\frac{(m_1,z)\rightarrow_\Delta(m_1',z'') \quad (m_2,z'')\rightarrow_\Delta(m_2',z')}{(m_1\circ m_2,z)\rightarrow_\Delta(m_1'\circ m_2',z')}\;(\text{CONCATENATION})$$

is encoded as proof fragment:

$$\dfrac{\Box m_1,z\vdash_\Sigma(\bigcirc\Box m_1')^\otimes\otimes(z'')^\otimes \qquad \dfrac{\Box m_2,z''\vdash_\Sigma(\bigcirc\Box m_2')^\otimes\otimes(z')^\otimes}{\Box m_2,(z'')^\otimes\vdash_\Sigma(\bigcirc\Box m_2')^\otimes\otimes(z')^\otimes}\;\otimes_l^*}{\Box m_1,\Box m_2,z\vdash_\Sigma(\bigcirc\Box m_1')^\otimes\otimes(\bigcirc\Box m_2')^\otimes\otimes(z')^\otimes}\;\text{CUT}$$

Commit. The rule:

$$\frac{(m,0) \rightarrow_{\Delta} (m',0)}{m \Rightarrow_{\Delta} m'} \ (\text{COMMIT})$$

is encoded as proof fragment:

$$\dfrac{l_r \dfrac{}{\vdash \mathbf{1}} \qquad \dfrac{\Box m, \mathbf{1} \vdash_{\Sigma} (\bigcirc\Box m')^{\otimes} \otimes \mathbf{1} \qquad \dfrac{\dfrac{\dfrac{}{(\bigcirc\Box m')^{\otimes} \vdash_{\Sigma} (\bigcirc\Box m')^{\otimes}}\ \text{Ax}}{(\bigcirc\Box m')^{\otimes}, \mathbf{1} \vdash_{\Sigma} (\bigcirc\Box m')^{\otimes}}\ \mathbf{1}_l}{(\bigcirc\Box m')^{\otimes} \otimes \mathbf{1} \vdash_{\Sigma} (\bigcirc\Box m')^{\otimes}}\ \otimes_l}{\Box m, \mathbf{1} \vdash_{\Sigma} (\bigcirc\Box m')^{\otimes}}\ \text{Cut}}{\Box m \vdash_{\Sigma} (\bigcirc\Box m')^{\otimes}}\ \text{Cut}$$

An interesting aspect of this encoding is that the main coordination rule (Concatenation) corresponds to *Cut*. Cut elimination in proof theory often is thought of as communication or interaction. Not all proofs go through, however, so coordination is more accurately thought of as *constrained interaction*, as suggested by Wegner [43].

The result we have established is the soundness of our encoding. Specifically, we have the following:

Theorem 1. *Let* $\Sigma = [\![\Delta]\!]$.

1. *If* $(m, z) \rightarrow_{\Delta} (m', z')$, *then* $\Box m, z \vdash_{\Sigma} (\bigcirc\Box m')^{\otimes} \otimes (z')^{\otimes}$.
2. *If* $m \Rightarrow_{\Delta} m'$, *then* $\Box m \vdash_{\Sigma} (\bigcirc\Box m')^{\otimes}$.

More generally, we have show that ITLL is expressive enough to encode both Reo and zero-safe nets. In the next section, we demonstrate through example that ITLL is more expressive.

5 Coordination via ITLL

We have thus far presented, in very general sense, how ITLL can encode the coordination patterns expressible in Reo and in zero-safe nets. Doing so explored only a fraction of ITLL's expressiveness. We now further explore ITLL, mainly focussing on the various pieces of the coordination puzzle, such as the behaviour or protocol of parties involved in coordination, and on variants of how coordination is done in Reo and in zero-safe nets, in particular, with regard to the role of epochs. We assume in addition that two parties are involved in a particular interaction: the *coordinator*, whose choices are controllable, and the *environment* (or *the rest*), whose choices are uncontrollable.[3] After presenting a number of

[3] We ignore the data flowing through connectors/nets—thus we are working in the 'black-and-white' models. Adding colour raises no difficult issues. For example, the filter over a binary domain that accepts only zeros is modelled by: $\Sigma = \{\mathit{Filter} \otimes a(0) \vdash b(0) \otimes \bigcirc\Box \mathit{Filter},\ \mathit{Filter} \otimes a(1) \vdash \bigcirc\Box \mathit{Filter}\}$, where $a(0)$ means that datum 0 is on node a.

variations, we pull all the pieces together into a SoC protocol which would form the essence of a coordinator for the holiday booking problem presented in the introduction.

Choice. ITLL can express choice in two different ways: choices made by the coordinator and choices made by the environment. (This is well-known, and is particularly well exemplified in the game semantics of linear logic [12].) Formulæ of the form $A \,\&\, B$ express a choice between A and B that can made by the coordinator, whereas formulæ of the form $A \oplus B$ express that the choice between A and B is made by the environment.

Progress of Time. ITLL can also express the occurrence of events within epochs. Recapping, a formula of the form A without a preceding modality expresses that A must be dealt with in the current epoch. $\Box A$ expresses an action that the coordinator *may* choose to deal with A in the current epoch. $\bigcirc A$ states that A must be dealt with in next epoch. Combinations of these are possible. For example, $\bigcirc\Box A$ states that the coordinator *may* deal with A in some future epoch (but not now), and $\Box\bigcirc A$ states that the coordinator may deal with A in a future epoch, though the decision must be made one epoch in advance. $\bigcirc^7\Box\bigcirc^7 A$ states that any time after 7 epochs the coordinator may decide, 7 epochs in advance, to deal with A.

Note that a dual to $\Box-$ exists [26]: $\Diamond A$ states that the environment decides *some time* when A must be dealt with.[4] $\Diamond A$ behaves very much like $\Box A$, except that the choice is made by the environment instead of the coordinator.

State Machines (Revisited). An encoding of state machines was hinted at above. It is in fact an adaptation of an existing encoding [29, for example]. The difference here is that we use the modalities to control when transitions may or may not be taken.

An example state machine, in the encoding described above, with 4 states (s, t, u, v) and 4 external actions $(\mathsf{A}, \mathsf{B}, \mathsf{C}, \mathsf{D})$ is encoded as axioms:[5]

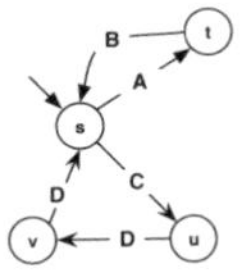

$$\Sigma = \left\{ \begin{array}{cc} s \multimap (\mathsf{A} \otimes \bigcirc\Box t \,\&\, \mathsf{C} \otimes \bigcirc\Box u), & t \multimap \mathsf{B} \otimes \bigcirc\Box s, \\ u \multimap \mathsf{D} \otimes \bigcirc\Box v, & v \multimap \mathsf{D} \otimes \bigcirc\Box s \end{array} \right\}$$

The current state of such an automaton is recorded as a formula of the form $\Box s$,

---

[4] The rules for $\Diamond-$ introduction and elimination are:

$$\frac{\Box\Gamma, A \vdash \Diamond B}{\Box\Gamma, \Diamond A \vdash \Diamond B}\ \Diamond\rightarrow \qquad \frac{\Gamma \vdash A}{\Gamma \vdash \Diamond A}\ \rightarrow\Diamond$$

[5] There are a number of equivalent ways of presenting our axioms. For example, we could write $(s \vdash t \,\&\, u) \in \Sigma$ or $(\mathbf{1} \vdash s \multimap t \,\&\, u) \in \Sigma$ or even $(\mathbf{1} \vdash s \multimap t), (\mathbf{1} \vdash s \multimap u) \in \Sigma$ or $(s \vdash t), (s \vdash u) \in \Sigma$. We typically choose the single formula representation $s \multimap t \,\&\, u$.

meaning that a transition from s can be taken at a time chosen by the coordinator. This particular automaton implements the regular expression $(\mathsf{AB} \mid \mathsf{CDD})^*$ over events, where each event occurs in a different epoch. The fact that the events occur in different epochs is given by the form of the next-state formulæ, namely, $\bigcirc\Box s$. Hence, the automaton is disabled after performing a transition in any given epoch, but it is re-enabled in the next epoch. All Reo primitives would have state machines of this form.

We can change the formulæ describing the state machine behaviour in a number of ways:

- The next state formula can be modified from $\bigcirc\Box s$ to $\Box s$, giving a transition such as $t \multimap \mathsf{B} \otimes \Box s$, to model that the primitive in state t, after making a transition to state s, may optionally perform an additional transition from state s in the given epoch.
- The next state formula can be simply s, giving a transition such as $t \multimap \mathsf{B} \otimes s$, which means that the primitive, after moving from state t to state s, would be forced to perform another transition in this epoch.
  (Applying the two previous the two previous variations to the semantics of a Reo primitive would give primitives that could perform interactions involving more than one step within a given epoch [20]. We will give an example shortly.)
- The choice in transition $s \multimap (\mathsf{A} \otimes \bigcirc\Box t \,\&\, \mathsf{C} \otimes \bigcirc\Box u)$ is determined by the coordinator, as $- \,\&\, -$ is used. An alternative is to use $- \oplus -$, as follows $s \multimap (A \otimes \bigcirc\Box t \oplus C \otimes \bigcirc\Box u)$, meaning that the choice is made externally. This can model, for example, interaction with an external component.

Naturally, other variations are possible.

Boundary Interactions. In Reo, a component interacts with a connector by issuing a write or a take (read) to a port, which is subsequently satisfied by the connector (unless the writer/taker times-out). We can model these in ITLL in a number of ways (showing only a writer, as a taker is quite similar; and ignoring time-out):

1. A Writer has two states $\{\mathit{Writing}, \mathit{NotWriting}\}$ and the following axioms:

$$\mathit{Writing} \multimap \mathsf{a} \otimes \bigcirc(\Box\,\mathit{Writing} \oplus \mathit{NotWriting})$$
$$\mathit{NotWriting} \multimap \bigcirc(\Box\,\mathit{Writing} \oplus \mathit{NotWriting})$$

   Notice that the next state formula $\Box\,\mathit{Writing} \oplus \mathit{NotWriting}$ forces the environment to choose whether the component will be writing or not. When the component is writing, coordinator can determine whether to allow the write to succeed when it chooses. When the component is not writing, the decision whether to write must be made again in the following epoch, determined by the second axiom.
   The initial state is represented by $\Box\,\mathit{Writing} \oplus \mathit{NotWriting}$, forcing the environment to make a choice in the first epoch.

If we were also considering data, the formula stating that data flows on channel a, namely a, would be replaced by $\bigoplus_{d \in \mathcal{D}ata} \mathsf{a}(d)$ to denote that there is a value on the channel and that it is externally selected.

2. An alternative encoding of a Writer exploits $\Diamond-$ to handle the fact that the decision to perform a write is determined by the environment, after which the coordinator decides when the write succeeds (via $\Box-$):

$$\begin{gathered} \mathit{Writing} \multimap \mathsf{a} \otimes \bigcirc \mathit{NotWriting} \\ \mathit{NotWriting} \multimap \Diamond\Box\, \mathit{Writing} \end{gathered}$$

In this case, the initial state is *NotWriting*, which is effectively $\Diamond\Box\, \mathit{Writing}$.

The mode of interaction between the coordinator and the environment need not be restricted to that which is assumed by Reo. For example, interacting by making method calls to standard objects, or by calling web services, are equally useful alteratives, yet distinct from Reo's. In these circumstances the interaction originates with the coordinator, not the environment.

A service/method that takes input described by A and produces output described by B can be modelled by a formula as simple as $A \multimap B$. This, however, makes the assumptions that service is guaranteed to produce a result and that the coordinator must wait for the result. A more asynchronous invariant is modelled by the formula $A \multimap \Diamond B$ or even $A \multimap \Diamond\Box B$. The choice of which model to adopt depends upon the desires of the system builder; the choice of ITLL formula to model the mode of interaction determines the dependency of the coordination on the environment.

Other modes of interaction can be (at least partially) described using ITLL—one way message sends, compulsory interactions, interrupts. A complete study of ITLL's expressiveness and limitations would be very interesting.

User Interaction. ITLL formulæ can capture the essence of synchronous user interaction, which, when combined with the extended Reo we are hinting at, permits coordination of multi-action events that include user interaction, such as obtaining the user's approval of a particular holiday package. A simple formula expressing user interaction is:

$$\mathit{User} \otimes \mathsf{Q} \multimap (\mathsf{Yes} \oplus \mathsf{No}) \otimes \bigcirc\Box\, \mathit{User}$$

User is the (single, uninteresting) state. When asked a question on port Q, a reply can be supplied on either port Yes or port No, where the choice is made by the environment (or user). The question is asked and its answer is given all in the same epoch.

The test to see whether a coordinator can handle both the Yes and No answers is whether certain judgements (of the shape described in Theorem 1) are provable. When the proof does not go through, this means that during coordination-time a choice can be made that the coordinator cannot handle. Roll-back or some sort of recovery would be required when this occurs.

It is worth taking pause to consider whether this kind of user interaction can be handled in Reo. The short answer is that it cannot. External components in

Reo perform either a single write or take in each epoch—this is the only kind of event that the coordinator has to deal with. Any (inter)action that involves multiple steps must be dealt with over multiple epochs in Reo, even though the steps conceptually belong to the same action. Existing implementations of Reo cannot handle a channel whose choices are made externally, within a single epoch (though an attempt was made in the implementation Reolite [16]). Thus the ability to perform multi-step actions, possibly involving external choices, within an epoch goes beyond what Reo can do. Yet, in our opinion, these possibilities makes better use of the abstractions (synchrony and asynchrony) provided by Reo, by enabling more interesting interaction to occur during an atomic step.

A Service-Oriented Computing Protocol. We pull together the ideas presented in this section to give a more realistic example, which ties in with our original holiday booking example. The left hand side of the Figure 10 presents a connector whose job is to monitor a transaction (adopting a simplified version of the WS-Transaction protocol [22]), so that it can be incorporated into a larger Reo connector. An informal description of its behaviour is given by the 'automaton' on the right hand side of Figure 10. This automaton is initiated by a *try* action (try to perform transaction), which results, eventually, in a *success* or *fail* action, the choice of which is made by the environment. Afterwards, the transaction can be *reset* (which also causes a *no* action) or, in the case that it is successful, *committed* (which also causes a *yes* action). The choice of whether to *reset* or *commit* is made by the coordinator.

The key here is that success/failure is externally determined. In order to have this controlled by Reo (or a zero-safe net), we make all steps occur within a single epoch, which would, for example, allow the combination of two or more WC-Transactors to form proper transactions which occur *atomically* within a synchronous slice of time (*i.e.*, epoch).

The ITLL encoding consists of the following formulæ, where the initial state is *Init*: the nodes marked with bold font are on boundary with the user, whereas the others are used to interact with the underlying transaction

$$\Sigma = \left\{ \begin{array}{ll} \mathit{Init} \otimes \mathbf{try} \multimap t, & ps \otimes \mathsf{commit} \multimap \mathbf{yes} \otimes \bigcirc\Box \mathit{Init}, \\ t \multimap s \oplus f, & ps \otimes \mathsf{reset} \multimap \mathbf{no} \otimes \bigcirc\Box \mathit{Init}, \\ s \multimap \mathsf{success} \otimes ps, & pf \otimes \mathsf{reset} \multimap \mathbf{no} \otimes \bigcirc\Box \mathit{Init}, \\ f \multimap \mathsf{fail} \otimes pf & \end{array} \right\}$$

A more compressed variant would replace the $t \multimap s \oplus f$, $s \multimap \mathsf{success} \otimes ps$, and $f \multimap \mathsf{fail} \otimes pf$ by $t \multimap (\mathsf{success} \otimes ps) \oplus (\mathsf{fail} \otimes pf)$.

The Reo-like connector presented in Figure 11(a) combines two WC-Transactors so that either both transactions are committed or neither are. The choice $\bigotimes$ in the middle selects whether to commit or reset both WC-Transactors, giving priority to committing (indicated by !).[6] The simple connector in Figure 11(b) enforces that either exactly one **yes** (using the merger) or two **nos**

[6] Priority was not discussed in this paper. Our work on 3-colouring deals with this fairly effectively [18]. A full treatment of priority in Reo, especially in the present setting, is a whole new kettle of worms that we prefer to leave on the back-burner.

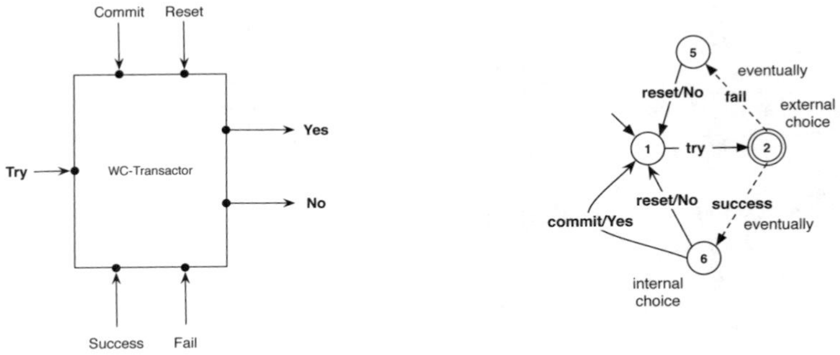

Fig. 10. Coordinator for simplified model of WS-TRANSACTION protocol. There are 7 ports to this coordinator, grouped in the following logical units: **try** initiates part of a transaction; **success & fail** are the results reported by the component being controlled; **commit & reset** commits to the result (only on success), or resets (either on success or failure); and **yes & no** reports whether the transaction succeeded and is committed to.

result, thus ensuring that either one holiday package is booked or none is. This example could be extended with data and user interaction to gain the user's approval of the chosen holiday, but clearly more work would be required to make it completely realistic. In any case, the present example cannot handled by Reo as it exists now, unless the transaction handling is implemented over multiple epochs, and thus failing to fully exploit synchrony.

6 Related Work

Many semantic models for Reo have been presented [7,8,18,35], though all of them, apart from the operational semantics of Mousavi et. al. [35], suffer from causality problems. This problem is avoided in operational models such as the one presented here. The problem is that most models have a non-constructive, classical semantics which would give a semantics to certainly loops stating that data flows in the loop, even though the loop has no source of data. Only the connector colouring model [18] deals with priority. Our semantics is superior to Mousavi et. al.'s on the following counts: the semantics of primitives such as channels are *not* built into our rules, thus we have only 4 rules compared to 16; we more cleanly deal with the treatment of data on nodes and the fact that data flow may occur only in a part of connector; and, perhaps most importantly, our rule format enables an easier comparison with existing systems. On the other hand, Mousavi et. al.'s semantics have a globally defined notion of *maximal progress* for filtering possible behaviours, which we do not consider here.

Many, many variants of Petri nets exists, far too many to review here. Bruni et. al. [13] show how the zero-place approach can be applied to coloured, reconfigurable, and dynamic nets. Given the close correspondence between Reo and zero-safe nets, it would be be fruitful for the development of Reo to transfer these

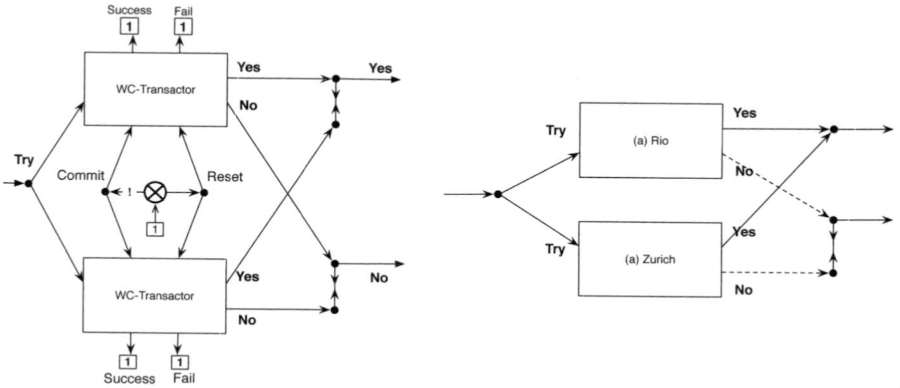

Fig. 11. (a) Combining Two WC-Transactors. The **1** connectors either always offer or accept a signal, depending upon the direction of the arrow. ⊗ denotes an exclusive router, which makes a choice of sending the data to exactly one of its outputs. ! indicates priority. A three-way variant of this can be constructed to implement the coordination for each of the holiday options (ignoring the actual data). (b) The connector combines two instances of the connector in (a), enforcing that either exactly one **yes** or two **no** results, thus ensuring that either one holiday package is booked or none is.

ideas into Reo. More generally, Bruni et. al. [14] present a modular high-level account of the relationship between, in our terms, the mirco- and macro-step levels, demonstrating that the naturalness of the two-level approach to describing transactions.

A large volume of literature considers the relationship between Linear Logic and Petri nets (and other concurrency models) [21,10,42,28, among others]. We adapted a simple encoding of Petri nets to use the temporal modalities of ITLL to model epochs. The closest work to ours, in this respect, is Hirai's thesis and subsequent article [26,25]. Hirai reasons about Timed Petri nets [11] (a model wherein transitions have a waiting time during which they are unusable), whereas we encode zero-safe nets (and Reo), which have a more transactional flavour. A different study of Petri nets uses the logic of bunched implications (BI) [36,40]. From a semantic perspective, it makes a lot of sense to adapt this approach to our domain, as one semantic model of BI involves partial commutative monoids. We would be interested to see what BI could bring to our application domain.

Hirai [26,25] also briefly considers variants of process encodings into ITLL. Specifically, he observes that $\bigcirc\Box-$ can be used to model synchronous message passing, which, he claims, is not expressible in linear logic. Specifically, he compares the pair of linear logic 'processes' $!(p \multimap (m \otimes p))$ and $!(q \multimap (m \multimap q))$ with the ITLL processes $!(p \multimap (m \otimes \bigcirc\Box p))$ and $!(q \multimap (m \multimap \bigcirc\Box q))$. In both cases, the first process sends an m message to the second one, repeatedly. In the LL encoding, the m is sent asynchronously, as both parts of $m \otimes p$ proceed in parallel. In contrast, m is sent and received in the ITLL encoding, as the recursive call to p cannot occur until the next step. Even though we are using the same ingredients, our encoding (or our reading) is quite different, as we equate synchrony with what occurs (necessarily) within some epoch. In fact, we would say that the first case expresses entirely synchronous processes—that is, their entire development occurs within an epoch—whereas the second expresses synchrony for message m, asynchronously with any subsequent behaviour. Because of the different granularity, we typically exploit the parallelism inherent in $-\otimes-$, rather than worry about the asynchrony it introduces.

Küngas [33] and Pham et. al. [38] uses temporal linear logic to model the choices of agents and agent negotiation. Both articles make use of the well-known the distinction between internal $(-\,\&\,-)$ and external $(-\oplus-)$ choice. Formalæ express agent choices and time-sliced resource usage (such as printers). Küngas also models a kind of promise by formula such as $\bigcirc A \multimap B$, meaning that the offer to do A in the next step is traded for B now. Küngas uses partial evaluation (via a technique called *partial deduction*) to give more efficient programs (applicable to the ideas presented here), but also to derive *offers*, so that agents can negotiate the use of resources. Pham et. al. includes reductions corresponding to the choices made by the various choice makers. This feature would be useful in our setting to express the dynamics in the models we considered beyond Reo and zero-safe nets. Both papers only use the $\bigcirc-$ modality, whereas we suggest uses for the whole spectrum.

Kanovich and Ito [30] present an alternative (and earlier) formulation of ITLL. Hirai [26] extends Kanovich and Ito's formulation with the modal storage operator (that is, the exponential !), and removes possible infinite derivations which were at odds with the notion of *passage of time*—specifically, Zeno's paradox could arise.

ITLL has also been used as the basis for a logic programming language [9]. The main goal was to give a more fine-grained control over resources than is possible in linear logic programming languages, and to enable complex data structures which are not entirely available all the time, and thus can be the target for more efficient implementations.

Linear logic has been used as the basis for the coordination language LO (Linear Objects) [5]—though this can equally be seen as a way of combining logic and object-oriented programming—and, its successor, CLF (the Coordination Language Facility) [3]. Both languages have a very strong logic programming flavour and rely on a notion of transaction, so are close in spirit to our logical encoding. Their base language, however, does not have temporal modalities, so they cannot make as fine-grained distinctions as we can.

Several authors [32, for example] have used linear logic to analyse and synthesise planning problems. This corresponds to our intuition that in both Reo and in zero-safe networks one cannot just send the data optimistically through channels or push tokens through the network and hope to arrive at a suitable (external) configuration. Either backtracking, planning or constraint solving [19] is required.

Alexiev [2] presents a now-dated overview of many applications of Linear Logic. One of the key points that he makes is that "everything is connected to everything else." This is certainly made no less true by the present article. Kamide [27] presents linear and affine logics extended with temporal, spatial and epistemic modalities. This looks like very fertile ground for exploring further extensions to coordination language, perhaps even taking on a more agent-like character.

7 Conclusion and Future Work

In this article, we cast both the coordination language Reo and zero-safe nets into a common semantic framework. The key difference between the two models is the choice of monoids used in the framework, demonstrating that, although the two models differ significantly on the surface, they are very similar underneath. In fact, Reo can be compsitionally encoded into zero-safe nets. We then encoded both systems into *intuitionistic temporal linear logic* (ITLL), to explore its applicability as unifying framework for coordination languages. We illustrated this by encoding both Reo and zero-safe nets into ITLL. The meaning of the logical formulæ used in the encodings provided useful intuition into the meaning of configurations and reductions in the respective semantics. In both cases, the reading corresponds to our intuitive understanding of the language being modelled.

In the latter part of the paper, we explored the remainder of ITLL, and demonstrated, mostly through examples, the range of possible behaviour that can be expressed in ITLL, but in neither Reo nor zero-safe nets. In particular, we described more complex *per epoch* behaviour, choices attributable to different players (the coordinator vs. the environment), and optional and compulsory actions. None of these distinctions can be made in Reo or in zero-safe nets.

This work merely scratches the surface of an interesting and useful connection between Reo, zero-safe nets, and ITLL. We hope that this paper will serve as a source of ideas for further developing Reo and the coordination languages that will follow it. A detailed game-semantic study of ITLL is warranted in order to fully elucidate the ideas presented here. In particular, such a model would provide not only a semantics for Reo, but of all the extensions described in Section 5. Additional ideas we would like to investigate include increasing the expressiveness to cover notions such as *co-operation*, wherein the actual possibilities for a choice may be limited by both the coordinator and the environment, but the actual choice is determined by both; the distinction between reversible and irreversible actions; groups and operations on them; and many more.

References

1. Abramsky, S.: Computational interpretations of linear logic. Theor. Comput. Sci. 111(1-2), 3–57 (1993)
2. Alexiev, V.: Applications of linear logic to computation: An overview. Logic Journal of IGPL 2(1), 77–107 (1994)
3. Andreoli, J.-M., Freeman, S., Pareschi, R.: The Coordination Language Facility: coordination of distributed objects. Theory and Practice of Object Systems 2(2), 77–94 (1996)

4. Andreoli, J.-M., Hankin, C., Le Metayer, D. (eds.): Coordination Programming: Mechanisms, Models and Semantics. Imperial College Press (1996)
5. Andreoli, J.-M., Pareschi, R.: Linear objects: logical processes with built-in inheritance. New Generation Computing 9 (1991)
6. Arbab, F.: Reo: a channel-based coordination model for component composition. Math. Struct. in Comp. Science 14(3), 329–366 (2004)
7. Arbab, F., Rutten, J.J.M.M.: A coinductive calculus of component connectors. In: Wirsing, M., Pattinson, D., Hennicker, R. (eds.) WADT 2003. LNCS, vol. 2755, pp. 34–55. Springer, Heidelberg (2003)
8. Baier, C., Sirjani, M., Arbab, F., Rutten, J.: Modeling component connectors in Reo by constraint automata. Science of Computer Programming 61(2), 75–113 (2006)
9. Banbara, M., Kang, K.-S., Hirai, T., Tamura, N.: Logic programming in a fragment of intuitionistic temporal linear logic. In: Codognet, P. (ed.) ICLP 2001. LNCS, vol. 2237, pp. 315–330. Springer, Heidelberg (2001)
10. Bellin, G., Scott, P.J.: On the pi-calculus and linear logic. Theoretical Computer Science 135, 11–65 (1994)
11. Bestuzheva, I.I., Rudnev, V.V.: Timed Petri nets: Classification and comparative analysis. Automation and Remote Control 51(10), 1308–1318 (1990)
12. Blass, A.: A game semantics for linear logic. Annals of Pure and Applied Logic 56, 151–156 (1992)
13. Bruni, R., Melgratti, H.C., Montanari, U.: Extending the zero-safe approach to coloured, reconfigurable and dynamic nets. In: Desel, J., Reisig, W., Rozenberg, G. (eds.) Lectures on Concurrency and Petri Nets. LNCS, vol. 3098, pp. 291–327. Springer, Heidelberg (2004)
14. Bruni, R., Meseguer, J., Montanari, U.: Tiling transactions in rewriting logic. In: WRLA 2002, Rewriting Logic and Its Applications. Electronic Notes in Theoretical Computer Science, vol. 71, pp. 90–109 (April 2004)
15. Bruni, R., Montanari, U.: Zero-safe nets: Comparing the collective and individual token approaches. Information and Computation 156(1-2), 46–89 (2000)
16. Clarke, D.: Reolite implementation (December 2005), `http://www.cwi.nl/~dave/reolite`
17. Clarke, D.: A basic logic for reasoning about connector reconfiguration. Fundam. Inform. 82(4), 361–390 (2008)
18. Clarke, D., Costa, D., Arbab, F.: Connector colouring I: Synchronisation and context dependency. Science of Computer Programming 66(3), 205–225 (2007)
19. Clarke, D., Proença, J., Lazovik, A., Arbab, F.: Deconstructing Reo. In: FOCLASA 2008. ENTCS (July 2008) (to appear)
20. Diakov, N., Arbab, F.: Adaptation of software entities for synchronous exogenous coordination: An initial approach. In: Proceedings of The Second International Workshop on Coordination and Adaptation of Software Entities, W-CAT 2005 (July 2005)
21. Engberg, U.H., Winskel, G.: Linear logic on Petri nets. In: de Bakker, J.W., de Roever, W.-P., Rozenberg, G. (eds.) REX 1993. LNCS, vol. 803, pp. 176–229. Springer, Heidelberg (1994)
22. Cabrera, L.F., et al.: Web Services Atomic Transaction (WS-AtomicTransaction). MSDN Library (November 2004)
23. Gelernter, D., Carriero, N.: Coordination languages and their significance. Commun. ACM 35(2), 97–107 (1992)
24. Girard, J.-Y.: Linear logic. Theoretical Computer Science 50, 1–102 (1987)

25. Hirai, T.: Propositional temporal linear logic and its application to concurrent systems. EICE Transactions on Fundamentals of Electronics, Communications and Computer Sciences (Special Section on Concurrent Systems Technology) E83-A(11), 2219–2227 (2000)
26. Hirai, T.: Temporal Linear Logic and Its Application. PhD thesis, The Graduate School of Science and Technology, Kobe University, Japan (September 2000)
27. Kamide, N.: Linear and affine logics with temporal, spatial and epistemic logics. Theoretical Computer Science 252, 165–207 (2006)
28. Kanovich, M.I.: Linear logic as a logic of computations. Annals of Pure and Applied Logic 67(1–3), 183–212 (1994)
29. Kanovich, M.I.: Linear logic automata. Annals of Pure and Applied Logic 78, 147–188 (1996)
30. Kanovich, M.I., Ito, T.: Temporal linear logic specifications for concurrent processes (extended abstract). In: Twefth Annual IEEE Symposium on Logic in Computer Science, pp. 48–57 (1997)
31. Koehler, C., Costa, D., Proença, J., Arbab, F.: Reconfiguration of Reo connectors triggered by dataflow. In: Electronic Communications of the EASST: Graph Transformation and Visual Modeling Techniques, vol. 10 (2008)
32. Küngas, P.: Analysing AI planning problems in linear logic – a partial deduction approach. In: Bazzan, A.L.C., Labidi, S. (eds.) SBIA 2004. LNCS, vol. 3171, pp. 52–61. Springer, Heidelberg (2004)
33. Küngas, P.: Temporal linear logic for symbolic agent negotiation. In: Zhang, C., W. Guesgen, H., Yeap, W.-K. (eds.) PRICAI 2004. LNCS, vol. 3157, pp. 23–32. Springer, Heidelberg (2004)
34. Meseguer, J., Montanari, U.: Petri nets are monoids. Information and Computation 88, 105–155 (1990)
35. Mousavi, M.R., Sirjani, M., Arbab, F.: Formal semantics and analysis of component connectors in Reo. Electronic Notes in Computer Science 154(1), 83–99 (2006)
36. O'Hearn, P.W., Yang, H.: Petri net semantics of bunched implications(October 1999) (unpublished) (available from Peter's webpage)
37. Papadopoulos, G.A., Arbab, F.: Coordination models and languages. In: Zelkowitz, M. (ed.) The Engineering of Large Systems. Advances in Computers, vol. 46, pp. 329–400. Academic Press, London (1998)
38. Pham, D.Q., Harland, J., Winikoff, M.: Modelling agent's choices in temporal linear logic. In: Baldoni, M., Son, T.C., van Riemsdijk, M.B., Winikoff, M. (eds.) DALT 2007. LNCS, vol. 4897, pp. 140–157. Springer, Heidelberg (2008)
39. Pham, D.Q., Harland, J.: Temporal linear logic as a basis for flexible agent interactions. In: Durfee, E.H., Yokoo, M., Huhns, M.N., Shehory, O. (eds.) 6th International Joint Conference on Autonomous Agents and Multiagent Systems (AAMAS 2007), IFAAMAS (2007)
40. Pym, D.J.: The Semantics and Proof Theory of the Logic of Bunched Implications. Applied Logic Series, vol. 26. Kluwer Academic Publishers, Dordrecht (2002)
41. van der Aalst, W.M.P., ter Hofstede, A.H.M.: YAWL: Yet another workflow language. Information Systems 30(4), 245–275 (2005)
42. Watkins, K., Cervasato, I., Pfenning, F., Walker, D.: A concurrent logical framework: The propositional fragment. In: Berardi, S., Coppo, M., Damiani, F. (eds.) TYPES 2003. LNCS, vol. 3085, pp. 355–377. Springer, Heidelberg (2004)
43. Wegner, P.: Coordination as constrained interaction. In: Ciancarini, P., Hankin, C. (eds.) COORDINATION 1996. LNCS, vol. 1061, pp. 28–33. Springer, Heidelberg (1996)

An Object-Oriented Component Model for Heterogeneous Nets*

Einar Broch Johnsen, Olaf Owe, Joakim Bjørk, and Marcel Kyas

Department of Informatics, University of Oslo, Norway
{einarj,olaf,joakimbj,kyas}@ifi.uio.no

Abstract. Many distributed applications can be understood in terms of components interacting in an open environment. This interaction is not always uniform as the network may consist of subnets with different quality: Some components are tightly connected with order preservation of communicated messages, whereas others are more loosely connected such that overtaking of messages and even message loss may occur. Furthermore, certain components may communicate over wireless networks, where sending and receiving must be synchronized, since the wireless medium cannot buffer messages. This paper proposes a formal framework for such systems, which allows high-level modeling and formal analysis of distributed systems where interaction is managed by a variety of nets, including wireless ones. We introduce a simple modeling language for object-oriented components, extending the Creol language. An operational semantics for the language is defined in rewriting logic, which directly provides an executable implementation in Maude.

1 Introduction

Object-oriented modeling languages [3, 11, 22] aim for a high level of abstraction, and typically capture systems in a *platform independent* manner, as advocated by *model-driven architecture* [24]. Consequently, these languages abstract from low-level communication details such as, e.g., the specific properties of the communication medium components use. However modern distributed applications often require a certain *quality of service*, which cannot be modeled when perfect channels are assumed; e.g., a maximum latency or a minimum throughput. In practice, the properties of a specific connection may even evolve during execution. In particular, connections to other components may appear or disappear, and network components may be shared between several applications with different requirements. Consequently, the quality of a connection between two components may vary over time, and connections to components with the same functional interface may vary significantly in bandwidth or robustness. In many cases, the behavioral properties of the modeled system depend on the specific properties of the net. For such systems, it is desirable to enable *cross-layer designs* [23] by reflecting aspects of the (low-level) connectivity in the high-level modeling language.

In this paper, we develop a light-weight, timed component model with an executable semantics. We present a kernel language, extending our previous work on Creol [11,12].

* This research is in the context of the EU project IST-33826 *CREDO: Modeling and analysis of evolutionary structures for distributed services* (http://credo.cwi.nl).

F.S. de Boer et al. (Eds.): FMCO 2007, LNCS 5382, pp. 257–279, 2008.

Creol is a modeling language for distributed concurrent objects communicating by means of asynchronous method calls. However, this previous work did not address the communication medium in which the concurrent objects live. In this paper, we introduce language primitives to reflect links with different qualities. This allows us to model communication in *heterogeneous nets*; these are nets in which some components may be tightly and reliably connected whereas others may be loosely connected through unreliable or wireless links. This allows certain aspects of the connection quality between components to be taken into account during the analysis of a model. Furthermore, a component may decide on its actions depending on how it is connected to other components. In particular we consider radio communication as well as multicast and broadcast communication, in order to integrate object-oriented modeling with wireless networks. The language abstracts from many implementation details; e.g., it uses a functional sublanguage for side-effect free expressions and execution may be highly nondeterministic. The language has an operational semantics defined in rewriting logic [15] and it is executable on the Maude platform [5], which supports various forms of analysis such as simulation and breadth-first search through the execution space. To illustrate the language and analysis using Maude's simulation support, an example of a simple sensor network is given.

The paper is structured as follows: Section 2 discusses modeling of network aspects, Sect. 3 presents the modeling language, and Sect. 4 provides an example based on wireless medical sensors. Sect. 5 defines the operational semantics of the language, Sect. 6 discusses related and future work, and Sect. 7 concludes the paper.

2 Modeling of Network Information

This paper considers modeling of distributed systems that communicate over different *links*, and introduces a novel framework where such systems may be modeled and simulated, and where system properties may be subjected to formal analysis. When modeling a distributed system, the model should not only describe the components and their behaviors, but also how the different communication media involved are composed, since media properties often affect the overall properties of the system. However, it is not desirable to address all aspects of the network and communication details in a high-level model . We will here focus on safety properties such as "the sender is aware of sent messages that have arrived", but also certain liveness properties such as "a message will arrive at its destination in at most n hops". This means that certain aspects of the communication and network media must be formalized, for instance whether communication preserves the order, whether communication is immediate or delayed, and whether message may get lost. Such factors typically affect overall system properties.

In particular, we consider here *tight*, *loose*, and *wireless* links. A *tight link* between two nodes provides a reliable communication channel that guarantees FIFO ordering of messages sent between the linked objects. A typical example is a serial line link between the two nodes, or a TCP/IP connection. A *loose link* between two nodes is still reliable but it does not guarantee the FIFO ordering; rather some messages take more time than others. A *wireless link* provides synchronous transmission of messages, but

Name		**Description and Examples**	**Simple Model**
Host Layers	7. Application	Web browser, file transfer, mail transfer	3. Application
	6. Presentation	Data representation (MIME, XML) and encryption	2. Transport
	5. Session	Interhost communication (RPC, iSCSI)	
	4. Transport	End-to-end connections & reliability (TCP, UDP)	
Media Layers	3. Network	Path determination & logical addressing (IP)	1. Media
	2. Data link	Physical addressing (802.3 (Ethernet), 802.11a/b/g MAC/LLC (Wireless))	
	1. Physical	Media (100BASE-TX (Ethernet), IEEE 802.11a/b/g PHY (Wireless)), signal, binary coding	

Fig. 1. Network layering model

simultaneous messages may be lost if they are within reach of each other (message collision). A message is received if the sender sends, the message does not collide in transmission, and the receiver receives at the same time; otherwise the message is lost. (Remark that the models considered in this paper are non-deterministic but not probabilistic.) A network built from tight links is called a *tight network*. Analogously, we define *loose networks* and *wireless networks.* A network may have parts that are loose, tight, and wireless. A loose network may have parts that are tight, but not vice versa. We say that a tight link is *better than* any other link.

Our model is based on the *Open System Interconnection Basic Reference Model* (ISO/IEC 7498) [26], OSI model for short. This is considered as one of the standard models for describing networks and applications. It allows application level programming without knowledge of the underlying network protocols. However, the abstractions provided by the OSI model sometimes make it difficult to exploit the capabilities of the underlying network and protocols. For example, applications in wireless networks often have specific requirements on memory and energy use and still need to guarantee their service with a certain quality. Such applications call for *cross-layer designs,* where the abstractions of the OSI model are weakened with APIs that enable the control of aspects of the lower layers (cf. [23] and below). In addition, by using different protocols over the same net, one may obtain different network qualities, such as lossy and fast versus non-lossy and slow, or FIFO and slow versus reordering and fast. In both cases a model design for a given application may benefit from some low-level network (protocol) knowledge, and possibly also from the reprogramming abilities of certain network related aspects. By using the same language for the application level modeling and the network related aspects, such as the programming of network protocols and wireless radio controllers, one may obtain a uniform model with desired properties.

This paper considers a simplified version of the OSI model, which we compare to the original ISO/OSI model (see Fig. 1). Our model allows application level programming as well as the programming of network protocols and wireless radio controllers. Details that are not relevant for high-level modeling and analysis are abstracted away, while other details are included, such as the presence of communication buffers,

Syntactic categories.	*Definitions.*
C, I, m in Names	$IF ::= \texttt{interface}\ I\{\overline{x:I}\}\ \{\texttt{inherits}\ \overline{I}\}$ $\texttt{begin}\ \{\texttt{with}\ I\ \overline{Sg}\}\ \texttt{end}$
n in Network	$CL ::= \texttt{class}\ C\{\overline{x:I}\}\ \{\texttt{inherits}\ \overline{C}\}\ \{\texttt{implements}\ \overline{I}\}$ $\texttt{begin}\ \{\texttt{var}\ \overline{x:I\{=e\}}\}\ \overline{\{\texttt{with}\ I\}\ \overline{M}}\ \texttt{end}$
t in Label	$M ::= Sg == \{\texttt{var}\ \overline{x:I\{=e\}};\}\ \overline{s}$
g in Guard	$Sg ::= \texttt{op}\ m\ (\{\texttt{in}\ \overline{x:I}\}\{\texttt{out}\ \overline{x:I}\})$
p in MtdCall	$n ::= \texttt{loose} \mid \texttt{tight} \mid \texttt{wless}$
s in Stm	$g ::= b \mid t? \mid g \wedge g \mid g \vee g$
x in Var	$p ::= m(\overline{e}) \mid o.m(\overline{e})$
e in Expr	$s ::= (s) \mid s;s \mid x := e \mid x := t.\texttt{get} \mid x := \texttt{new}\ C\{(\overline{e})\}\{\texttt{in}\ o\} \mid \texttt{tick}(n)$
o in ObjExpr	$\mid \texttt{if}\ b\ \texttt{then}\ \overline{s}\ \{\texttt{else}\ \overline{s}\}\ \texttt{fi} \mid \texttt{while}\ b\ \texttt{do}\ \overline{s}\ \texttt{od} \mid \texttt{await}\ g$
b in BoolExpr	$\mid \{t :=\}!p \mid \{x :=\}p \mid \texttt{await}\ x := p \mid !\overline{o}.m(\overline{e}) \mid !\texttt{all} : I.m(\overline{e})$
	$s_{wless} ::= \texttt{send} \mid \texttt{receive}$
	$s_{net} ::= \texttt{link}\ \overline{o}\ n\ \overline{o} \mid \texttt{unlink}\ \overline{o}\ n\ \overline{o}$

Fig. 2. The language syntax. Overlined terms such as $\overline{e}$, $\overline{x}$, and $\overline{s}$, denote lists over the corresponding syntactic categories and curly brackets denote optional elements. Additional constructs for low-level wireless programming are given by s_{wless}, and for network connections by s_{net}.

ordering properties, immediateness of transmission, radio transmission synchronization and messages collision of wireless messages. Our model consists of three levels:

1. the *media layer* is represented by rules in the operational semantics, formalizing the transport of messages in the different nets and which is partly "programmable" in that **link** and **unlink** statements allow to establish and sever links between components, as well as synchronization of radio sending and receiving,
2. the *transport layer* is partly represented by rules of the operational semantics (formalizing the meaning of "tight" and "loose") and partly programmable by language primitives allowing; e.g., the programming of routing in wireless systems,
3. the *application level* represents top level programs. At this level the actual underlying net is invisible, in the sense that one may use the same high-level communication primitives, including broadcast and multicast primitives regardless of the actually used network.

The chosen primitives enable *cross-layer* designs of wireless network applications, which arise from the necessity to adapt properties of lower layers to the applications under design [23]. Such designs allow to adapt the network for better quality of service [19] or to optimize its energy consumption [10]. The framework may be adjusted to cater for other communication properties, such as message loss and packet size.

3 A Modeling Language for Components in Heterogeneous Nets

We introduce an executable modeling language for components in heterogeneous networks, based on the object-oriented language Creol [11, 12]. Creol proposes imperative programming constructs for distributed concurrent objects, based on asynchronous method calls and processor release points. Asynchronous method calls may be seen as triggers of concurrent activity, resulting in new processes in the called object. Objects are dynamically created instances of classes, which are organized in an inheritance hierarchy. Concurrent objects encapsulate an execution thread and an internal process queue. Active behavior, triggered by a *run* method, is interleaved with passive behavior by means of the processor release points. The modeling language includes a standard expression language for values of basic data types, which will not be explained in detail. Objects have unique identities (names); communication takes place between named objects, and object identities may be exchanged between objects. Object variables are typed by interfaces. The language is strongly typed: invoked methods are supported by the called object (when not *null*), such that formal and actual parameters match.

In contrast, the modeling language considered in this paper targets network components in heterogeneous networks. It combines object-oriented components and definitions of actual networks; including tight, loose and wireless networks, and dynamic network changes. Technically, we extend the concurrent object communication model of Creol with representations of components and networks, incorporate a notion of (local and global) time, and introduce multicasts and forms of broadcast. Finally we define primitives for dealing with the special needs of wireless networks inside this model.

Network components. In order to model the units of the heterogeneous network, we introduce a light-weight notion of multi-object *network components*. The objects inside a component are tightly connected and communicate directly with each other. A component supports all interfaces supported by its objects; thus the caller may a call a method on a component if the called method supported by some object in that component. In case several objects in the component support the called method, one of these is chosen non-deterministically. However, if the caller knows the identity of a preferred object inside the component, the caller may call that object directly.

Component creation has the syntax $x := \mathbf{new}\ C(\overline{e})$ where C is the class name and $\overline{e}$ the list of actual class parameters, if any. In fact, this statement creates a network component consisting of a single object. Both components and objects have identity: for an object identity o, the expression component(o) gives the component identity of o (for a component identity c, component(c) $= c$). The statement $x := \mathbf{new}\ C(\overline{e})\ \mathbf{in}\ o$ creates a new (object) instance of C *inside* the component o.

Basic statements. The basic language syntax is given in Fig. 2. A program consists of interface and class declarations. Classes CL contain definitions of attributes x (with initial values) and methods M. A method contains a list of statements s, which may access class attributes, locally defined variables, and the formal parameters of the method (given by the keywords **in** and **out**). An interface IF contains method signatures Sg associated with a *cointerface* I, denoting the (minimal) type of a client of IF (given by a **with** clause). Both classes and interfaces may also contain parameters and inherit other classes and interfaces, respectively. Finally, a class implements a list of interfaces. In order to allow type correct call-backs, a method may use the implicit *caller* parameter, which supports the cointerface of the method. Input parameters, as well as the self-reference *this*, are ready-only. Note that remote attribute access is not permitted, so method interaction is the only means of communication in the language. Assignment and **if**- and **while**-constructs are standard. We assume that purely local operations take no time; local delays may be captured by the statement **tick**(n), for n time units.

In the statement **await** g, the guard g is used to control processor release and may consist of Boolean conditions and return tests (see below). If g evaluates to false in the active process, the process is *suspended* and the execution thread becomes idle. When the execution thread is idle, any enabled process may be chosen from the local process queue. Therefore explicit signaling is not part of the language. The *run* method of an object is called upon creation, and initiates active behavior. Release points in the run method allow processes in the process queue to be handled.

Communication. After making an asynchronous method call $t := !o.m(\overline{e})$, the caller may proceed with its execution without waiting for the method reply. Here o is an object expression and $\overline{e}$ are (data value or object) expressions. The tag t will be assigned a unique tag value identifying the call (relative to the current object), which may later be used to refer to that call in two different ways. First the guard **await** $t?$ suspends the active process unless a return to the call associated with t has arrived. Second the return values are accessed by the blocking *reply statement* $x := t.$**get**, once a return has arrived. We identify certain special cases of these communication primitives: For local calls the dot-notation and o is omitted; e.g., $t := !m(\overline{e})$. If no return value is desired by the caller, the tag may be omitted; e.g., $!o.m(\overline{e})$. The sequence $t := !o.m(\overline{e})$; $x := t.$**get** gives a *blocking call*, abbreviated $x := o.m(\overline{e})$, whereas the call sequence $t := !o.m(\overline{e})$; **await** $t?$; $x := t.$**get** gives a *non-blocking call*, abbreviated **await** $x := o.m(\overline{e})$. A *multicast* $!\overline{o}.m(\overline{e})$ is an asynchronous method call with a set of target objects. The multicast is sent simultaneously to all callees. A *broadcast* **all** : $I.m(\overline{e})$ is an asynchronous method invocation which targets all objects of a certain interface I. For strong typing, I must provide a declaration of the invoked method. The use of these communication primitives is illustrated below and in Sect. 4.

Heterogeneous nets. In a given model, the network connecting the components need not be uniform. Actual nets are defined by means of a number of direct *links* between components, which may have different characteristics. In this paper, we consider three basic forms of links: *wireless*, *loose*, and *tight*. In order to model the heterogeneous net, links are declared by the statements **link** $\overline{o}$ **wless** $\overline{u}$, **link** $\overline{o}$ **loose** $\overline{u}$, and **link** $\overline{o}$ **tight** $\overline{u}$ (for sets of component expressions $\overline{o}$ and $\overline{u}$). These statements respectively add **wless**, **loose**, or **tight** links from each each component in $\overline{o}$ to each component in $\overline{u}$. Correspondingly, links are explicitly broken by, e.g., the statement **unlink** $\overline{o}$ **wless** $\overline{u}$. Remark that (wired) loose or tight links go both ways, but this is not generally the case for wireless links. Furthermore, links to self are redundant.

Example 1. Initial links may be made inside the `run` method of a class `System` from which the initial components are created.

```
op run ==
  var a,b,c,d : Any;
  a:= new Class1; b:= new Class2; c:= new Class3; ...
  link a wless b,c;
  link b,c,d wless a,b,c,d;
```

Here a must use b or c to communicate with d, but d may communicate directly with a.

Wireless communication. A wireless component needs radio functionality to handle the sending and receiving of messages. In order to control the timing of this sending and receiving precisely, we model the radio functionality in a separate radio object in the wireless component. Therefore a component acting in wireless media will consist of at least two active objects; the main processing unit and the radio object. It is the task of the radio object to make wireless messages available for regular processing by the objects inside the component. The objects themselvesact as if they work in a wired network, using the standard primitives for communication. A component acting in a wireless net must be able to wait for and to send a message in a given time interval. We use two explicit non-blocking primitives to capture wireless sending and receiving: **receive** to receive a wireless message and make it available to the component's objects, and **send** to send the first pending wireless message.

Example 2. A cycle of the radio unit of a wireless component could be to receive, then send, receive again, and finally sleep. Instead of defining a controller in the sensor's central processing unit, we use the radio's *run* method to control the cycle.

```
class Radio(sendtime:Nat, sleeptime:Nat, cycle:Nat, sync:Nat)
  implements Controllable
begin var on:Bool := true, timer: Nat := 0
  op run == while on do
    await (clock - sync) rem cycle = 0; *** synchronize
    timer:= clock;
    while clock < timer + sleeptime do
     if clock = timer + sendtime then send else receive fi od od
with Any
  op turnoff == on := false
  op turnon == on := true
  op reset (in time: Nat) == sync := time
  op setSend (in time: Nat) ==
        if time < sleeptime then sendtime := time fi
  op setSleep(in time:Nat) ==
        if sendtime<time<cycle then sleeptime := time fi
end
```

When the radio is turned on, the cycle consists of an active phase where the radio is sending in a specified interval (here of length 1 time unit) and otherwise receiving, followed by a sleeping phase. In addition there are methods to turn the radio on and off, to adjust the sending and sleeping intervals, and for synchronizing the radio cycle. These methods form an interface, *Controllable*, allowing external control of the radio. When sleeping, the processor is released and invocations of the radio methods may be processed. For simplicity, we here assume a fixed cycle length (set at creation time).

4 Example: A Model of a Wireless Sensor Network

A typical biomedical sensor network consists of a number of sensors, a sink, and users. The example in Fig. 3 has five sensors and one sink connected by wireless links. The sink sends signals which are sufficiently strong for all sensors to receive them. The sensors, which could be inside patients, run on battery, and save power by reducing their signal strength, which again limits their range. Hence some sensors are not directly connected with the sink and depend on other sensors to forward their messages. The sink is connected to the end users by a tight network. The interfaces of the system components are given in Fig. 4. The `Forwarder` interface declares a forward operation, and

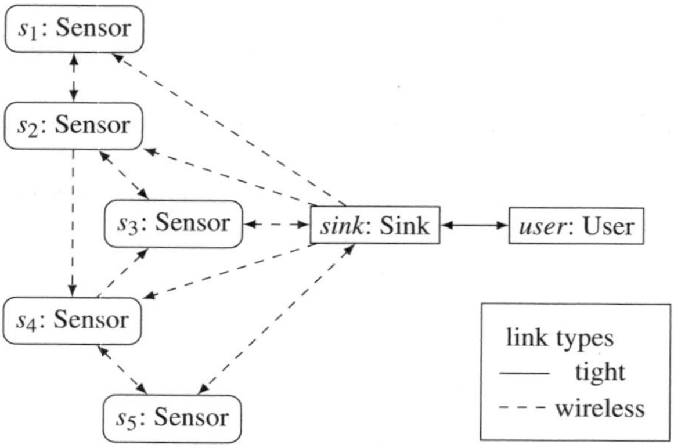

Fig. 3. Typical sensor network

is inherited by both the `Sink` and the `Sensor` interfaces. Methods of `Forwarder` have `Forwarder` as cointerface (given by the **`with`** clause) because a `Forwarder` object should communicate with another `Forwarder` object. The `Sensor` interface adds a method for updating the distance to the sink, which is accessible only to sink objects, as `Sink` is the cointerface. The `User` interface declares a `newData` method for receiving data from the sink.

The `run` method of the `System` class constructs the system model by creating all objects and setting up the initial network (not given here). A sensor component is created as in

```
s1:= new TempSensor(10); r1:= new Radio(t1,6,10,1) in component(s1);
```

and similarly for the sink component, ensuring that the sending intervals of the different radios are disjoint, by appropriate radio parameter values. It also reconfigures the network at runtime to simulate the patients' movements. For example, we express that sensor `s5` moves too far to reach the sink after 200 time units by severing the link:

```
await clock > 200; unlink s5 wless sink;
```

The sensors, sink, and users are described by the classes `TempSensor`, `Sink`, and `User` in Fig. 4. The sensors operate in cycles with a period given by the class parameter `interval`. In each cycle a sensor reads the current temperature by calling an instance of the `TempMeter` interface, using a non-blocking call. The `TempMeter` interface models access to the hardware.

After reading the temperature, the sensor sends a message with the temperature to all reachable components that implement the `Forwarder` interface by the statement

```
!all:Forwarder.forward(this, distToSink + 2, 1, clock, temp)
```

Here, *reachable* means that there is a direct link from the caller to the callee. If there is more than one link from the two components, the best link is selected. If the link is tight, the message will move directly from the caller's out-queue to the callee's in-queue. If the link is wireless then the radio unit transports the message.

```
interface Forwarder begin with Forwarder op forward(...) end
interface Sensor inherits Forwarder
   begin with Sink op setDistToSink(...) end
interface Sink inherits Forwarder begin ... end
interface User begin with Sink op newData(...) end

class TempSensor(interval:Nat) implements Sensor
begin var forwarded:List[Oid*Nat] := emp, distToSink:Nat := 10,
      distUpdTime:Nat := 0, timer:Nat, temp:Int, tempm:TempMeter
  op run == tempm := new TempMeter in component(this);
   while true do timer := clock; await temp := tempm.getTemp();
     !all:Forwarder.forward(this, distToSink + 2, 1, clock, temp);
     await clock > timer+interval od
 with Sink
  op setDistToSink(in time:Nat, dist:Nat) ==
   if distUpdTime < time ∨(distUpdTime = time ∧ dist < distToSink)
   then distToSink := dist; distUpdTime := time fi
 with Forwarder
  op forward(in origin:Oid,htl:Nat,steps:Nat,timestamp:Nat,data:Int)==
   if not((origin, timestamp) in forwarded) ∧ origin ≠ this ∧
      htl > distToSink then if length(forwarded) > 9
        then forwarded := after(forwarded, length(forwarded)-9) fi;
     forwarded := forwarded⊢(origin, timestamp);
     !all:Forwarder.forward(origin, htl-1, steps+1, timestamp, data) fi
end

class Sink() implements Sink
begin var forwarded:List[Oid*Nat*Int] = emp
 with Forwarder
  op forward(in origin:Oid, htl:Nat, steps:Nat,
                 timestamp:Nat, data:Int) ==
   !origin.setDistToSink(timestamp, steps);
   if not((origin, timestamp) in forwarded) then
      if length(forwarded) > 9
       then forwarded := after(forwarded, length(forwarded)-9) fi;
      forwarded := forwarded⊢(origin, timestamp);
      !all:User.newData(origin, timestamp, data) fi
end

class User(criticalLow:Nat, criticalHigh:Nat) implements User
begin var allData: List[Oid*Nat*Nat*Int] := emp;
  op alarm()...
 with Sink
  op newData(in origin:Oid, timestamp:Nat, data:Int) ==
    var i:Nat := 1;
    if data < criticalLow ∨data > criticalHigh then alarm() fi;
    while i <= length(allData)
          ∧ index(index(allData, i),1) ≠ origin do i := i+1 od;
    while i <= length(allData)
          ∧ index(index(allData, i),1) = origin
          ∧ index(index(allData, i),2) < timestamp do i := i+1 od;
    allData :=
      insertAtIndex(allData, i, (origin, timestamp, clock, data))
end
```

Fig. 4. Model of the temperature sensor, the sink, and a user. We here use ⊢ for list append.

In class `Sink`, the `forward` method has the following parameters: `origin` gives the identity of the sensor that has provided the data; `htl` (hops to live) gives the number of remaining hops the message should live; `steps` gives the number of hops this message has taken so far; `timestamp` stores the time when the origin sent this message; and `data` is the temperature measured in degrees centigrade. When a sensor receives a `forward` call, it adds the message to `forwarded` and forwards the call to all reachable forwarders, unless the message has already forwarded. The length of `forwarded` is limited to ten entries, a common limit of, e.g., biomedical sensors.

The distance to the sink from a sensor may be measured by the minimum number of hops needed. Because sensors may move, this distance may change. When the sink gets a message, it sends the number of hops taken by this message to the original sender, using `setDistToSink`. If the data are new to the sink, they are broadcasted to all users. The user stores data in a list `allData`, which is sorted by sensor name and sending time to simplify queries. Observe that none of the remote calls made in any class are blocking; consequently, the system is deadlock free (assuming that local calls always terminate).

5 Operational Semantics

The operational semantics of the language is defined using rewriting logic (RL) [15]. A *rewrite theory* is a 4-tuple $\mathscr{R} = (\Sigma, E, L, R)$, where the signature Σ defines the function symbols of the language, E defines equations between terms, L is a set of labels, and R is a set of labeled rewrite rules. A state configuration in RL will be modeled as a multiset of terms representing local system states, of given types. These types are specified in (membership) equational logic (Σ, E), the functional sublanguage of RL which supports algebraic specification in the OBJ [9] style. RL extends algebraic specification techniques with transition rules: The dynamic behavior of a system is captured by rewrite rules, supplementing the equations which define the term language. Assuming that all terms can be reduced to normal form, rewrite rules transform terms modulo the equations of E. A rewrite rule $t \longrightarrow t'$ **if** c may be seen as a *local transition rule* allowing an instance of the pattern t to evolve into the corresponding instance of the pattern t', where the optional condition c is a conjunction of rewrites and equations which must hold for the main rule to apply. If several rules can be applied to distinct subconfigurations, they can be executed in a *concurrent rewrite step*. As a result, concurrency is implicit in rewriting logic semantics. Rules in RL may be formulated at a high-level of abstraction, similar to a compositional operational semantics. In fact, RL provides a semantic framework unifying equational and operational semantics [16]. Many concurrency models have been successfully represented in RL [15,5]; including Petri nets, CCS, Actors, and Unity. RL also offers its own model of object orientation [5].

In RL, objects are commonly represented by terms $\langle o : C \mid a_1 : v_1, \ldots, a_n : v_n \rangle$ where o is the object's identity, C is its class, the a_i's are the names of the object's fields, and the v_i's are the corresponding values [5]. We adopt this form of presentation and define the elements of our semantics as RL objects. When auxiliary functions are needed, these are defined in equational logic and evaluated in between transitions [15]. Whitespace is used as the associative and commutative constructor of multisets with identity element empty, whereas semicolon is used as the associative constructor of lists, also with identity element empty. Variables of the operational semantics are written in upper case letters, whereas variables of the modeling language (as well as auxiliary functions) are written in lower case letters. As before, variables for lists or multisets are written $\overline{M}$ for semantic construct M.

5.1 Configurations, Local and System Transitions

The modeling language considered in this paper depends on a notion of time. For timed distributed systems, time is either modeled by a global clock (or equivalently, local clocks which evolve with the same rate), or by local clocks. For simplicity we use a so-called *fictitious clock model* [1] based on a global clock, which allows us to ignore clock synchronization between objects. In this clock model, the clock value is just a number that serves to group simultaneous events. The values need not correspond to values of real clocks, and are therefore usually chosen to be natural numbers that count steps. Effects such as radio broadcast are confined to a particular instance of time, and disappear as soon as time advances. Local clocks coordinate the objects' behavior with the global progress of time, enforcing the invariant that an object may only make a step when the local time is less than or equal to the global time. The global clock advances as soon as its value is less than the values of all local clocks.

A state *configuration*, of sort *Configuration*, is a multiset which consists of objects, classes, interfaces, queues, messages, and links. The empty configuration is denoted *empty*. A basic link is written $[O\ N\ O']$, where O and O' range over object identities and N over networks (i.e., wless, tight, and *lossy*). In order to capture the global clock in RL, we let a term $@C$ clock(N)@ of sort *System* include a configuration C with at least one object and a (global) clock, denoted *clock*(N), where the variable N ranges over natural numbers. There are three different kinds of rewrite rules:

- *Code execution rules* correspond to the different program statements;
- *Transport rules* move messages between objects, components, and the network;
- *System level rules* manage low-level activities such as global clock update and table lookup for classes and interfaces

Remark that code execution and transport rules apply to local configurations and allow concurrent execution, whereas system level rules apply to the whole system.

Components consist of tightly connected objects, and are represented by a naming discipline: a component name may be extracted from every object identity by a function *component* : *Oid* → *Cid*, where the component name is of sort *Cid* (a subsort of *Oid*). The objects with the same component name form a component. From outside a component, one may then refer to an object by its identity or by its component name. A component O has one *in-queue* object $\langle O$: InQu | EvQ: $\overline{M}\rangle$, where the queue $\overline{M}$ is FIFO ordered, and one *out-queue* object $\langle O$: OutQu | EvQ: $\overline{M'}$, Tag: $K\rangle$, where $\overline{M'}$ has a simple form of priority ordering and the tag K (together with the object identity) is used to uniquely identify outgoing messages. (Other forms of priority queues could be considered in more specialized settings; e.g., LIFO out-queues would give priority to fresh messages.) The queues have the same name as the component, and provide (a controlled form of) shared data structures for the component's objects. The queues may interact with the net at the same time as internal actions inside the component's objects. The specific message processing depends on the different networks linked to an object. Remark that by using the same component name for all objects in a component, we need no further encapsulation syntax for components. In many cases, including the examples in this paper, full object names are not needed and component names suffice.

A *concurrent object* is represented by $\langle O : C \mid \text{Pr: } Q, \text{PrQ: } \overline{Q}, \text{Att: } \overline{V}\rangle$, where O is the object identity, of sort *Oid*, C the class name, *Pr* the active process (which includes code and local variables), *PrQ* a multiset of suspended processes with unspecified queue ordering, and *Att* the object state variables, including some predefined system variables such as *clock* which represents the *local clock* of the object. A *process* is modeled as a pair consisting of code and local state, $(\overline{S}, \overline{W})$, where $\overline{S}$ is a statement list and $\overline{W}$ is a state mapping from (local) variable names to values, using + for concatenation (and overwriting) and $\_ \mapsto \_$ for constructing variable-to-value associations. The suspended processes in the process queue represent remaining parts of method activations. Programs have read-only access to the clock, so the programmer may not assign to the clock variable. Let $[\![E]\!]_{\overline{V}}$ denote the evaluation of an expression E in the state $\overline{V}$.

Example. A wireless sensor may have one radio object $O2$ responsible of sending and receiving wireless messages in interaction with the network, together with a main object $O1$ doing the main computations. Such a component may have the form:

$$\langle O : \text{InQu} \mid \text{EvQ: } \overline{M}\rangle\ \langle O : \text{OutQu} \mid \text{EvQ: } \overline{M}', \text{Tag: } K\rangle$$
$$\langle O1 : C \mid \text{Pr: } Q_1, \text{PrQ: } \overline{Q}_1, \text{Att: } \overline{V}_1\rangle\ \langle O2\text{: Radio} \mid \text{Pr: } Q_2, \text{PrQ: } \overline{Q}_2, \text{Att: } \overline{V}_2\rangle$$

where component(O1) = component(O2) = O, and a class *Radio* defines active behavior controlling the wireless sending and receiving of messages (see Section 4).

In a *class* $\langle C : \text{Cl} \mid \text{Ifc: } \overline{I}, \text{Inh: } \overline{C}, \text{Par: } \overline{Y}, \text{Att: } \overline{V}, \text{Mtds: } \overline{P}\rangle$, C is the class name, *Ifc* is the list of interfaces supported by the class, *Inh* is the list of superclasses, *Par* the list of class parameters, *Att* a list of attributes with initial values, and *Mtds* a multiset of methods (including the initialization method *init* and a method *run* defining active object behavior). The attributes include a system variable *token* used for unique naming of generated objects. When an object needs a method, it is loaded from the *Mtds* multiset of the object's class. Similarly, in an *interface* $\langle I : \text{Ifc} \mid \text{Inh: } \overline{I}\rangle$ I is the name, $\overline{I}$ the inherited interfaces. The inheritance list is used for broadcasts at run-time to determine all (connected) objects of a given super-interface. Method and cointerface declarations in an interface are used for type checking purposes and may be ignored at run-time.

Heterogeneous networks are represented by sets of links. We let *Link* be a subsort of *Config*, thereby allowing (multi)sets of links directly in the configuration, with terms $[O\ N\ O']$ (where N denotes a net; i.e., either wless, tight, or loose). We assume that the transmission strength in a wireless link may vary, in contrast to a wired link. Consequently, wireless links are directed and not symmetric, whereas wired connections are both symmetric and transitive. In the multiset of links, duplicates as well as links to self are ignored (i.e., we have the equations $CN\ CN = CN$ and $[O\ N\ O]\ \overline{U} = \overline{U}$, where CN denotes some link and O a component). The link statements described in Sect. 3 result in changes of link configurations.

We define a function bestcon : Oid Oid Configuration $\rightarrow$ Net$^+$ to identify the best connection between two objects, exploiting the transitivity and symmetry of wired

$$@ \langle O : C \mid \text{PrQ: } \overline{Q} \rangle \; \langle O : \text{InQu} \mid \text{Ev: invoc m}(\overline{E}); \overline{M} \rangle \; \overline{U} \; @$$

(BIND) $$= @ \langle O : C \mid \text{PrQ: } \overline{Q}; \text{bind}(\text{m}, \overline{E}, \text{C}, \overline{U}) \rangle \; \langle O : \text{InQu} \mid \text{Ev: } \overline{M} \rangle \; \overline{U} \; @$$

$$\textbf{if} \;\; \text{supports}(\text{C, m}, \overline{U})$$

$$\langle O : \text{C} \mid \text{Pr: (await G ; } \overline{S}, \overline{W}), \text{PrQ: } \overline{Q}, \text{Att: } \overline{V} \rangle \; \langle O : \text{InQu} \mid \text{Ev: } \overline{M} \rangle$$

(GUARD) $$\longrightarrow \langle O : \text{C} \mid \text{Pr: } (\overline{S}, \overline{W}), \text{PrQ: } \overline{Q}, \text{Att: } \overline{V} \rangle \; \langle O : \text{InQu} \mid \text{Ev: } \overline{M} \rangle$$

$$\textbf{if} \;\; \text{enabled}(\text{G}, (\overline{V} + \overline{W}), \overline{M})$$

$$\langle O : \text{C} \mid \text{Pr: } (\overline{S}, \overline{W}), \text{PrQ: } \overline{Q}, \text{Att: } \overline{V} \rangle \; \langle O : \text{InQu} \mid \text{Ev: } \overline{M} \rangle$$

(SUSPEND) $$\longrightarrow \langle O : \text{C} \mid \text{Pr: idle, PrQ: } \overline{Q}; (\overline{S}, \overline{W}), \text{Att: } \overline{V} \rangle \; \langle O : \text{InQu} \mid \text{Ev: } \overline{M} \rangle$$

$$\textbf{if not} \;\; \text{enabled}(\overline{S}, (\overline{V} + \overline{W}), \overline{M})$$

$$\langle O : \text{C} \mid \text{Pr: idle, PrQ: } (\overline{S}, \overline{W}); \overline{Q}, \text{Att: } \overline{V} \rangle \; \langle O : \text{InQu} \mid \text{Ev: } \overline{M} \rangle$$

(PRQ-READY) $$\longrightarrow \langle O : \text{C} \mid \text{Pr: } (\overline{S}, \overline{W}), \text{PrQ: } \overline{Q}, \text{Att: } \overline{V} \rangle \; \langle O : \text{InQu} \mid \text{Ev: } \overline{M} \rangle$$

$$\textbf{if} \;\; \text{enabled}(\overline{S}, (\overline{V} + \overline{W}), \overline{M})$$

$$\langle O : \text{C} \mid \text{Pr: idle, PrQ: } \overline{Q}, \text{Att: } \overline{V} \rangle \; \langle O : \text{InQu} \mid \text{Ev: } \overline{M} \rangle \; \text{clock(T)}$$

(IDLESTEP) $$\longrightarrow \langle O : \text{C} \mid \text{Pr: idle, PrQ: } \overline{Q}, \text{Att: advance}(\overline{V}) \rangle \; \langle O : \text{InQu} \mid \text{Ev: } \overline{M} \rangle \; \text{clock(T)}$$

$$\textbf{if not} \;\; \text{enabled}(\overline{Q}, \overline{V}, \overline{M}) \; \textbf{and} \; [\![\text{clock}]\!]_{\overline{V}} = \text{T}$$

Fig. 5. Rules for process queue handling. In the rules we omit object fields not relevant for the rule. Note that matching is modulo associativity, commutativity, and identity for the multiset constructor, and modulo associativity and identity for the list constructor.

networks. The sort Net^+ extends the sort *Net* with the constant noNet and we define $\text{bestcon}(O, O', \overline{U}) = \text{noNet}$ if there is no connection path from (the component of) O to (the component of) O'. Otherwise, the connection between the two objects is tight if there is a connection path from O to O' consisting of tight direct connections only; loose if there is one or more loose direct connections in the path; and wless if there is a wireless connection between O and O'. Objects in the same component are always tightly connected:

$\text{bestcon}(O, O', \overline{U}) = \text{tight}$ **if** $\text{component}(O) = \text{component}(O')$

For example, bestcon(o1, o3, [o1 wless o3][o1 tight o2][o3 loose o2]) = loose, whereas bestcon(o1, o3, [o1 wless o3][o1 tight o2]) = wless.

Messages. There are three different kinds of message bodies *MB*: these have the form *invoc m*(*par*) for *invocation messages*, where *m* is the name of the called method and *par* are actual parameters; *comp* (*par*) for *completion messages*; and *error* (*name*) for *error messages*, capturing network errors or other kinds of errors. The actual parameters include system generated parameters such as the *caller* identity and tag value. With full header information, a message has the form *MB* **from** O **to** $\overline{O}$ **by** *NET*, where O is the sender object, $\overline{O}$ the destination (either a single object or a list of objects), and *NET* is the network to be used: loose, tight, wless, or noNet. For simplicity, we omit sender information from messages inside out-queues and keep only message bodies inside in-queues. The network information of a message is determined when the message is placed in the out-queue (by means of an equation taking the total network into consideration). Remark that messages by noNet cannot be sent.

5.2 The Rewrite Rules

The operational semantics ensures that clock values increase, and that the global clock is less than or equal to each local clock. The global clock is updated by the rule (CLOCK) in Fig. 6, in which the variable $\overline{U}$ ranges over configurations, clockmin gives the smallest local clock value in $\overline{U}$, and *refresh* removes any remaining receive statements and wireless messages from the configuration (since such messages are not persistent). The function clockmin is defined by the following equations (where *OB* denotes an object):

$$\begin{aligned}
\text{clockmin}(OB\ OB'\ \overline{U}) &= \text{min}(\text{clockval}(OB), \text{clockmin}(OB'\ \overline{U}))\\
\text{clockmin}(OB\ \overline{U}) &= \text{clockval}\,(OB)\ \textbf{otherwise}\\
\text{clockval}\,(\langle O : C \mid \ldots \text{ Att: } \overline{V}\rangle) &= [\![\text{clock}]\!]_{\overline{V}}
\end{aligned}$$

Note that in RL, equations marked by **otherwise** only apply when no other equations are applicable [5]. In general, an object may only compute when its local clock value equals the global clock. Thus a rule modeling object behavior typically has the form

$$\text{object}\ \ \text{clock}(T) \longrightarrow \text{object}'\ \text{clock}(T)\ \textbf{if}\ \text{clockval}(\text{ object }) \ = T$$

where *object* is a pattern representing an object (possibly with its associated in-queue) and *object′* is the resulting object state, typically with local time increased. In particular the rule (IDLESTEP) in Fig. 5 increases the local time of objects that are *idle*; i.e., objects with no active process in which no processes in the process queue are enabled. Similarly, the rule (NO REPLY) in Fig. 6 increases local time when the active process is blocked (i.e., `x:=t.get`) with no matching label value in the in-queue. In addition, all communication statements increase the local clock (see Fig. 6); e.g., send, receive, method calls, return, link, and unlink.

The principle that local computation requires the local and global clock values to be the same, may be relaxed for *internal* object actions; i.e., by allowing local actions of object which do not involve any interaction (affected by or affecting other objects). For example, assignments to local and state variables do not need to depend on the global clock. Thus, the assignment rule, which may be given by

$$\begin{array}{lll}
 & & \langle O : C \mid \text{Pr: } (X{:=}E;\overline{S},\overline{W}), \text{ Att: } \overline{V}\rangle\\
(\text{ASSIGN}) & \longrightarrow & \textbf{if}\ \ X\ \textbf{in}\ \overline{V}\ \textbf{then}\ \langle O : C \mid \text{Pr: } (\overline{S},\overline{W}), \text{ Att: } \overline{V} + (X \mapsto [\![E]\!]_{(\overline{W}+\overline{V})})\rangle\\
 & & \qquad\qquad \textbf{else}\ \langle O : C \mid \text{Pr: } (\overline{S},\overline{W}+(X \mapsto [\![E]\!]_{(\overline{W}+\overline{V})})), \text{ Att: } \overline{V}\rangle\ \textbf{fi}
\end{array}$$

does not increase the local time. The **`tick`**(n) statement evaluates as an assignment on the local clock; i.e., $clock := clock + n$. The rules for **`if`** and **`while`** (omitted here), as well as guards and process queue handling do not involve clocks, except (IDLESTEP) (given in Fig. 5). The (BIND) rule additionally uses the class hierarchy to bind methods, and the supports function checks if a class supports a method in a given class hierarchy.

To simplify, object names in the rules are abstracted to component names. This allows a direct matching by names ($O = O'$) rather than matching by component name (as in component(O) = component(O')). Note that method binding based on component names is non-deterministic when the component has several objects supporting the method. With this simplification, all remote calls are made to components. For many practical purposes, including the sensor example, this simplification works well.

(CLOCK)
$$@\ \text{clock}(T)\ \overline{U}\ @ \longrightarrow @\ \text{clock}(\text{clockmin}(\overline{U}))\ \text{refresh}(\text{T},\ \overline{U})\ @$$
$$\textbf{if}\ \ T < \text{clockmin}(\overline{U})$$

(NET)
$$@\ \langle O : \text{OutQu}\ |\text{Ev: } \overline{M};\ (MB\ \textbf{to}\ O');\ \overline{M'}\ \rangle\ \overline{U}\ @$$
$$= @\ \langle O : \text{OutQu}\ |\text{Ev: } \overline{M};\ (MB\ \textbf{to}\ O'\ \textbf{by}\ \text{bestcon}(O, O', \overline{U}));\ \overline{M'} \rangle\ \overline{U}\ @$$

(NONET)
$$\langle O : \text{OutQu}\ |\text{Ev: } \overline{M};\ (MB\ \textbf{to}\ O'\ \textbf{by}\ \text{noNet}) \rangle$$
$$= \langle O : \text{OutQu}\ |\text{Ev: } \overline{M};\ (\text{error(``noNet'')}\ \textbf{to}\ O\ \textbf{by}\ \text{tight}) \rangle$$

(MULTIMSG1)
$$\langle O : \text{OutQu}\ |\text{Ev: } \overline{M};\ (MB\ \textbf{to}\ (O'\ ;\ \overline{O})) \rangle$$
$$= \langle O : \text{OutQu}\ |\text{Ev: } \overline{M};\ (MB\ \textbf{to}\ O');\ (MB\ \textbf{to}\ \overline{O}) \rangle$$

(MULTIMSG2)
$$\langle O : \text{OutQu}\ |\text{Ev: } \overline{M};\ (MB\ \textbf{to}\ \text{empty}) \rangle\ = \langle O : \text{OutQu}\ |\text{Ev: } \overline{M}\ \rangle$$

(MULTIMSG3)
$$@\ \langle O : \text{OutQu}\ |\text{Ev: } \overline{M};\ (MB\ \textbf{to}\ \text{all: } I) \rangle\ \overline{U}\ @$$
$$= @\ \langle O : \text{OutQu}\ |\text{Ev: } \overline{M};\ (MB\ \textbf{to}\ \text{all}(O, I, \overline{U})) \rangle\ \overline{U}\ @$$

(MULTICAST)
$$\langle O : C\ |\text{Pr: } (!\overline{O}.m(\overline{E})\ ;\ \overline{S}, \overline{W}),\ \text{Att: } \overline{V}\ \rangle\ \langle O : \text{OutQu}\ |\text{Ev: } \overline{M},\ \text{Tag: } K\ \rangle\ \text{clock}(T)$$
$$\longrightarrow \langle O\text{: C}\ |\text{Pr: }\ (\overline{S}, \overline{W}),\ \text{Att: advance}(\overline{V})\ \rangle$$
$$\langle O : \text{OutQu}\ |\text{Ev: } \overline{M};\ \text{invoc m}(O, K, [\![\overline{E}]\!]_{(\overline{V}+\overline{W})})\ \textbf{to}\ [\![\overline{O}]\!]_{(\overline{V}+\overline{W})}),\ \text{Tag: } K{+}1\ \rangle$$
$$\text{clock}(T)\ \textbf{if}\ [\![\text{clock}]\!]_{\overline{V}}\ = T$$

(UNICAST)
$$\langle O : C\ |\text{Pr: } (L{:=}!O.\text{m}(\overline{E})\ ;\ \overline{S}, \overline{W}),\ \text{Att: } \overline{V}\ \rangle\ \langle O : \text{OutQu}\ |\text{Ev: } \overline{M},\ \text{Tag: } K\ \rangle\ \text{clock}(T)$$
$$\longrightarrow \langle O : C\ |\text{Pr: } (L := K;\ \overline{S}, \overline{W}),\ \text{Att: advance}(\overline{V})\ \rangle$$
$$\langle O : \text{OutQu}\ |\text{Ev: } \overline{M};\ \text{invoc m}(O, K, [\![\overline{E}]\!]_{\overline{V}+\overline{W}})\ \textbf{to}\ [\![O]\!]_{\overline{V}+\overline{W}})),\text{Tag: } K{+}1\ \rangle\ \text{clock}(T)$$
$$\textbf{if}\ \ [\![\text{clock}]\!]_{\overline{V}}\ = T$$

(BROADCAST)
$$\langle O : C\ |\text{Pr: } (!\ \text{all: }\ I.\text{m}(\overline{E})\ ;\ \overline{S}, \overline{W}),\ \text{Att: } \overline{V}\ \rangle\ \langle O : \text{OutQu}\ |\text{Ev: } \overline{M},\ \text{Tag: } K\ \rangle$$
$$\text{clock}(T)$$
$$\longrightarrow \langle O : C\ |\text{Pr: } (\overline{S}, \overline{W}),\ \text{Att: advance}(\overline{V})\ \rangle$$
$$\langle O : \text{OutQu}\ |\text{Ev: } \overline{M};\ \text{invoc m}(O, K, [\![\overline{E}]\!]_{(\overline{V}+\overline{W})})\ \textbf{to}\ \text{all: } I,\ \text{Tag: } K{+}1\ \rangle\ \text{clock}(T)$$
$$\textbf{if}\ \ [\![\text{clock}]\!]_{\overline{V}}\ = T$$

(RETURN)
$$\langle O : C\ |\text{Pr: } (\text{return}(\overline{E})\ ;\ \overline{S}, \overline{W}),\ \text{Att: } \overline{V} \rangle\ \text{clock}(T)\ \langle O : \text{OutQu}\ |\text{Ev: } \overline{M},\ \text{Tag: } K\ \rangle$$
$$\longrightarrow \langle O : C\ |\text{Pr: } (\overline{S}, \overline{W}),\ \text{Att: advance}(\overline{V})\ \rangle\ \text{clock}(T)$$
$$\langle O : \text{OutQu}\ |\text{Ev: } \overline{M}\ ;\ \text{comp}\ ([\![(\text{label}, \overline{E})]\!]_{\overline{V}+\overline{W}})\ \textbf{to}\ [\![\text{caller}]\!]_{\overline{W}}),\ \text{Tag: } K\ \rangle$$
$$\textbf{if}\ \ [\![\text{clock}]\!]_{\overline{V}}\ = T$$

(REPLY)
$$\langle O : C\ |\text{Pr: } (\overline{X} := L?\ ;\ \overline{S}, \overline{W}),\ \text{Att: } \overline{V}\ \rangle\ \text{clock}(T)$$
$$\langle O : \text{InQu}\ |\text{Ev: } \overline{M};\ \text{comp}(K, \overline{E});\ \overline{M'}\ \rangle$$
$$\longrightarrow \langle O : C\ |\text{Pr: } (\overline{X} := \overline{E};\ \overline{S}, \overline{W}),\ \text{Att: advance}(\overline{V})\ \rangle\ \text{clock}(T)$$
$$\langle O : \text{InQu}\ |\text{Ev: } \overline{M};\ \overline{M'}\ \rangle$$
$$\textbf{if}\ \ [\![\text{clock}]\!]_{\overline{V}}\ = T\ \textbf{and}\ K = [\![L]\!]_{(\overline{V}+\overline{W})})$$

(NO REPLY)
$$\langle O : C\ |\text{Pr: } (\overline{X} := L?\ ;\ \overline{S}, \overline{W}),\ \text{Att: } \overline{V}\ \rangle\ \text{clock}(T)\ \langle O : \text{InQu}\ |\text{Ev: } \overline{M}\ \rangle$$
$$\longrightarrow \langle O : C\ |\text{Pr: } (\overline{X} := L?\ ;\ \overline{S}, \overline{W}),\ \text{Att: advance}(\overline{V})\ \rangle\ \text{clock}(T)\ \langle O : \text{InQu}\ |\text{Ev: } \overline{M}\ \rangle$$
$$\textbf{if}\ \ [\![\text{clock}]\!]_{\overline{V}}\ = T\ \textbf{and not}\ \text{inqueue}([\![L]\!]_{(\overline{V}+\overline{W})}, \overline{M})$$

Fig. 6. Rewrite equations and rules for message processing

(TIGHT1) $\langle O : \text{OutQu} \mid \text{Ev: } (MB \textbf{ to } O' \textbf{ by } \text{tight}); \overline{M}\rangle\ \langle O' : \text{InQu} \mid \text{Ev: } \overline{M'}\rangle$
$= \langle O : \text{OutQu} \mid \text{Ev: } \overline{M}\rangle\ \langle O' : \text{InQu} \mid \text{Ev: } \overline{M'}; MB\rangle$

(TIGHT2) $(M1 \textbf{ to } \overline{O1} \textbf{ by } \text{wless}); (M2 \textbf{ to } \overline{O2} \textbf{ by } N)$
$= (M2 \textbf{ to } \overline{O2} \textbf{ by } N); (M1 \textbf{ to } \overline{O1} \textbf{ by } \text{wless}) \textbf{ if not } N = \text{wless}$

(LOOSE1) $\langle O : \text{OutQu} \mid \text{Ev: } (MB \textbf{ to } O' \textbf{ by } \text{loose}); \overline{M}\rangle$
$= \langle O : \text{OutQu} \mid \text{Ev: } \overline{M}\rangle\ (MB \textbf{ from } O \textbf{ to } O' \textbf{ by } \text{loose})$

(LOOSE2) $(MB \textbf{ from } O \textbf{ to } O' \textbf{ by } \text{loose})\ \langle O' : \text{InQu} \mid \text{Ev: } \overline{M}\rangle \longrightarrow \langle O' : \text{InQu} \mid \text{Ev: } \overline{M}; MB\rangle$

Fig. 7. Tight and loose networks

Basic Statements and Creation. The rules for basic statements, such as **`skip`**, **`if`**, **`while`**, **`link`**, and **`unlink`**, are straightforward (see Fig. 9). The rule for object creation creates a new object and associated queues. In case of a new object in a given component, the component identity is reused for the new object and no further queues are created. Local calls are defined by remote calls to self (by the obvious equation). For simplicity, the rules for reentrance are ignored in this paper.

Network processing. The rewrite rules for network processing are given in Fig. 6. In the equation (NET), the network determines how to send messages. Notice that the equation is on the total system, such that all possible connections are considered. The equation represents network actions, realized by hardware or the operating system. Equation (NONET) reflects that messages to noNet cannot be sent. Such messages may represent serious communication failures and should be communicated to the caller. In our framework this is indicated by an *error* message. Message sending to multiple destinations is defined by means of messages to single destinations in equation (MULTIMSG1), and by ignoring messages sent to empty destination lists in (MULTIMSG2). The rules for *tight* and *loose networks* are given in Fig. 7. A tight network from o to o' is defined by a transport equation (TIGHT1) which takes the first message from the out-queue of o marked by "tight", directly into the in-queue of o'. We let wired messages in out-queues have priority over wireless ones, as stated in equation (TIGHT2). Loose networks are modeled by using an equation to move messages from an out-queue into the configuration, and by a (nondeterministic) rule taking a message from the configuration into the appropriate in-queue ((LOOSE2)). Messages over loose nets are automatically sent to the network (i.e., placed in the configuration multiset) by the equation (LOOSE1).

Communication. Messages in the out-queue are created by call and return statements in the associated objects. We consider uni-cast, multicast, and broadcast; the rules are given in Fig. 6. Of these, only *labeled uni-casts* allow the caller to request a result of the call. We have seen that blocking (synchronous) methods calls are understood in terms of labeled asynchronous method calls: $t := !o.m(\overline{e})$ where o is an object expression. The label value provides a way of identifying the call and the reply. In rule (UNICAST), a labeled call has only one callee, which ensures that there is a unique reply. A call's result value is communicated in rule (RETURN) as a completion message, caused by a

(WSEND1)
$\langle O : C \mid \text{Pr: (send ; } \overline{S}, \overline{W}), \text{ Att: } \overline{V}\rangle \text{ clock}(T)$
$\langle O : \text{OutQu} \mid \text{Ev: } (MB \textbf{ to } O' \textbf{ by } \text{wless}) \text{ ; } \overline{M}\rangle$
$= \langle O : C \mid \text{Pr: } (\overline{S}, \overline{W}), \text{ Att: advance}(\overline{V})\rangle \text{ clock}(T) \langle O : \text{OutQu} \mid \text{Ev: } \overline{M}\rangle$
$(MB \textbf{ from } O \textbf{ to } O' \textbf{ by } \text{wless}) \textbf{ if } [\![\text{clock}]\!]_{\overline{V}} = T$

(WSEND2)
$\langle O : C \mid \text{Pr: (send ; } \overline{S}, \overline{W}), \text{ Att: } \overline{V}\rangle \text{ clock}(T) \langle O : \text{OutQu} \mid \text{Ev: empty}\rangle$
$\longrightarrow \langle O : C \mid \text{Pr: } (\overline{S}, \overline{W}), \text{ Att: advance}(\overline{V})\rangle \text{ clock}(T) \langle O : \text{OutQu} \mid \text{Ev: empty}\rangle$
$\textbf{if } [\![\text{clock}]\!]_{\overline{V}} = T$

(COLLIDE)
$(M1 \textbf{ from } O1 \textbf{ to } O \textbf{ by } \text{wless}) (M2 \textbf{ from } O2 \textbf{ to } O \textbf{ by } \text{wless})$
$= (\text{error}(\text{"collision"}) \textbf{ from } \text{null} \textbf{ to } O \textbf{ by } \text{wless})$

(RECEIVE)
$@ \langle O : C \mid \text{Pr: (receive ; } \overline{S}, \overline{W}), \text{ Att: } \overline{V}\rangle \langle O : \text{InQu} \mid \text{Ev: } \overline{M}\rangle$
$(M \textbf{ from } O' \textbf{ to } O \textbf{ by } \text{wless}) \text{ [O' wless O] clock}(T) \overline{U} \ @$
$= @ \langle O : C \mid \text{Pr: } (\overline{S}, \overline{W}), \text{ Att: advance}(\overline{V})\rangle \langle O : \text{InQu} \mid \text{Ev: } \overline{M} \text{ ; } M\rangle \text{ [O' wless O]}$
$\text{clock}(T) \overline{U} \ @ \textbf{ if } [\![\text{clock}]\!]_{\overline{V}} = T \textbf{ otherwise}$

(REFRESH1) $\text{refresh (T, } (MB \textbf{ from } O \textbf{ to } O' \textbf{ by } \text{wless}) \overline{U}) = \text{refresh (T, } \overline{U})$

(REFRESH2)
$\text{refresh (T,} \langle O : C \mid \text{Pr: (receive; } \overline{S}, \overline{W}), \text{ Att: } \overline{V}\rangle \overline{U})$
$= \langle O : C \mid \text{Pr: } (\overline{S}, \overline{W}), \text{ Att: advance}(\overline{V})\rangle \text{ refresh}(T, \overline{U}) \textbf{ if } [\![\text{clock}]\!]_{\overline{V}} = T$

(REFRESH3) $\text{refresh (T, } \overline{U}) = \overline{U} \textbf{ otherwise}$

Fig. 8. Wireless communication

return statement in the callee, where *caller* and *label* are the implicit local parameters identifying the caller and the tag. A blocking reply statement is captured by the rule (REPLY), when the corresponding completion has arrived. Otherwise, the rule (NO REPLY) ensures that the local clock progresses. A similar rule ensures the progress of the local clock when an object is idle without any enabled process in the queue.

Unlabeled calls may have multiple destinations, given by a list $\overline{O}$ of object expressions. These are captured by rule (MULTICAST), where $advance(\overline{V})$ is defined by $\overline{V} + (\text{clock} \mapsto [\![\text{clock}]\!]_{\overline{V}} + 1)$. We let semicolon denote both concatenation and append, for sequences of statements as well as of messages. Notice that the caller O and tag-value K are added as implicit parameters. *Broadcast*, captured by the rule (BROADCAST), is restricted to all objects of a given interface, using the notation *all* : I. This restriction is needed to maintain strong typing. A broadcast message MB **to** *all* : I should arrive (in a single copy) to all I-objects in the system which are connected to O. The *all* : I expression is expanded by means of the equation (MULTIMSG3) on the total system, using a function *all* to collect all objects of interface I (or better) in a configuration:

$\text{all}\,(O, I, \overline{U} \ \langle O' : C \mid ...\rangle) = O'; \text{all}(O, I, \overline{U})$
$\quad \textbf{if} \ \text{supports}\,(C, I, \overline{U}) \textbf{ and } \text{bestcon}(O, O', \overline{U}) \neq \text{noNet}$
$\text{all}\,(O, I, \overline{U}) = \text{empty } \textbf{otherwise}$

Here, supports $(C, I, \overline{U})$ checks whether class C implements interface I, or a subinterface of I, in the configuration $\overline{U}$.

(LINK)
$$\langle O:C \mid \text{Pr: } (\overline{W}, (\text{link E NW E'}); \overline{S}), \text{Att: } \overline{V}\rangle \longrightarrow \langle O:C \mid \text{Pr: } (\overline{W}, \overline{S}), \text{Att: } \overline{V}\rangle \;\; \text{component}([\![E]\!]_{\overline{V}+\overline{W}}) \text{ NW component}([\![E']\!]_{\overline{V}+\overline{W}})$$

(UNLINK)
$$\langle O:C \mid \text{Pr: } (\overline{W}, (\text{unlink E NW E'}); \overline{S}), \text{Att: } \overline{V}\rangle \; [\text{O' NW O''}] \longrightarrow \langle O:C \mid \text{Pr: } (\overline{W}, \overline{S}), \text{Att: } \overline{V}\rangle \;\; \textbf{if } \text{component}([\![E]\!]_{\overline{V}+\overline{W}}) = \text{O'} \textbf{ and } \text{component}([\![E']\!]_{\overline{V}+\overline{W}}) = \text{O''}$$

(IF-EL)
$$\langle O:C \mid \text{Pr: } (\overline{W}, \text{if E then } \overline{S1} \text{ else } \overline{S2} \text{ fi ; } \overline{S}), \text{Att: } \overline{V}\rangle \longrightarrow \textbf{if } [\![E]\!]_{\overline{V}+\overline{W}})) \textbf{ then } \langle O:C \mid \text{Pr: } (\overline{W}, \overline{S1} \text{ ; } \overline{S}), \text{Att: } \overline{V}\rangle \;\; \textbf{else } \langle O:C \mid \text{Pr: } (\overline{W}, \overline{S2} \text{ ; } \overline{S}), \text{Att: } \overline{V}\rangle \textbf{ fi}$$

(WHILE)
$$\langle O:C \mid \text{Pr: } (\overline{W}, \text{while E do } \overline{S1} \text{ od ; } \overline{S2})\rangle \longrightarrow \langle O:C \mid \text{Pr: } (\overline{W}, (\text{if E then } (\overline{S1} \text{ ; while E do } \overline{S1} \text{ od) else skip fi}); \overline{S2})\rangle$$

(NEW1)
$$@ \; \langle O:C \mid \text{Pr: } (\overline{W}, (X := \text{new C' } (\overline{E}); \overline{S})), \text{Att: } \overline{V}\rangle \; \overline{U} \; @ \longrightarrow @ \; \langle O:C \mid \text{Pr: } (\overline{W}, (X := \text{O'}); \overline{S}), \text{Att: } \overline{V} + (\text{token} \mapsto [\![\text{token}]\!]_{\overline{V}} + 1)\rangle \; \overline{U} \;\; \langle \text{O'} : \text{C'} \mid \text{Pr: init (C' } [\![\overline{E}]\!]_{\overline{V}+\overline{W}}, \overline{U}), \text{PrQ: empty, Att: (clock} \mapsto [\![\text{clock}]\!]_{\overline{V}}) + (\text{this} \mapsto \text{O'}) + \text{inherit(C' } ([\![\overline{E}]\!]_{\overline{V}+\overline{W}}, \overline{U}))\rangle \;\; \langle \text{O'} : \text{InQu} \mid \text{Ev: noMsg}\rangle \; \langle \text{O'} : \text{OutQu} \mid \text{Tag: } 1, \text{ Ev: noMsg}\rangle \; @ \;\; \textbf{if } \text{O'} := \text{newId}(O, [\![\text{token}]\!]_{\overline{V}})$$

(NEW2)
$$@ \; \langle O:C \mid \text{Pr: } (\overline{W}, (X := \text{new C' } (\overline{E}) \textbf{ in } \text{E}); \overline{S}), \text{Att: } \overline{V}\rangle \; \overline{U} \; @ \longrightarrow @ \; \langle O:C \mid \text{Pr: } (\overline{W}, (X := \text{O'}); \overline{S}), \text{Att: } \overline{V} + (\text{token} \mapsto [\![\text{token}]\!]_{\overline{V}} + 1)\rangle \; \overline{U} \;\; \langle \text{O'} : \text{C'} \mid \text{Pr: init (C' } [\![\overline{E}]\!]_{\overline{V}+\overline{W}}, \overline{U}), \text{PrQ: empty, Att: (clock} \mapsto [\![\text{clock}]\!]_{\overline{V}}) + (\text{this} \mapsto \text{O'}) + \text{inherit(C' } ([\![\overline{E}]\!]_{\overline{V}+\overline{W}}, \overline{U}))\rangle \; @ \;\; \textbf{if } \text{O'} := \text{component}([\![E]\!]_{\overline{V}+\overline{W}})$$

Fig. 9. Rules concerning basic statements and object creation. The function newId is used to create new object identities (composed by the parent object and a counter). The auxiliary functions inherit and init are used to define multiple inheritance and initial code. An if-clause of the form $O' := E$ represents a let expression.

5.3 Wireless Sending and Receiving

The two language primitives **`send`** and **`receive`** model synchronized wireless communication. Their operational semantics, given in Fig. 8, depends on the refresh function, used in the (CLOCK) rule, which erases wireless messages and receive statements as time passes. The equation (WSEND1) defines the semantics of sending; the first wireless message in the out-queue is sent, making the **from**-part of the message header explicit. When there is no message to send, a send message is skipped in rule (WSEND2). Recall that wireless messages in a network (i.e., configuration) disappear when global time advances. This is captured by an equation (REFRESH1) on the *refresh* function used in the global clock rule. Two wireless messages with the same destination which occur in the configuration at the same time, cause a collision and destroy each other. We model this by an equation (COLLIDE), which results in an *error* message. The equation detects collisions of two or more messages. The receiving itself is modeled by an equation (RECEIVE). Here, the **otherwise**-clause implies that the equation should have lower priority than

(COLLIDE). Therefore, the left hand side considers the system state and includes all possible matches of the (COLLIDE) rule. The rule also checks that there is a wless connection, since it may have been disconnected after the message was sent. By advancing the local clock, we ensure that two wireless messages cannot be received at the same time.

Notice that the condition on the clocks implies that the receiving of a message happens at the same time as its sending, thereby modeling *synchronous transmission*. Recall that *refresh* applies whenever the global local is advanced, which should also happen when the local time of receiving objects is equal to the global time. We therefore add an equation for this case

$$\text{clockval}(\langle O : C \mid \text{Pr: (receive ; } \overline{S}, \overline{W}\text{), Att: } \overline{V}\rangle) = [\![\text{clock}]\!]_{\overline{V}} + 1$$

and otherwise use the previous equation for clockval.

5.4 Simulation and Search

The operational semantics outlined above is executable on the RL platform Maude [5], and thus form the basis for an analysis tool for the modeling language of Sect. 3. We illustrate this by showing how to perform some simple simulations of the wireless sensor network example of Sect. 4 in Maude.

The model of Sect. 4 focuses on the behavior of the components. A special class `System` is used to set up the system model by creating components and establishing the links between components. The initial `System` object can later be used to modify these links, thus changing the topology of the network.

Interesting behaviour of the communication medium may be investigated by simulating the system given in Fig. 4; e.g., can message overtaking occur in this net? By message overtaking, we mean that a message arrives at the user before an older one from the same sender. This may happen, if an additional link from the sensor s_1 to the `sink` in the network of Fig. 3 is introduced at runtime and the interval between two measurements is sufficiently short. To exhibit this behaviour, the following code is added to the `run` method of the `System` class:

```
await (clock > int(25)); connect s1 wless sink;
```

Now the link between s_1 and the `sink` is added when the local clock has reached 25 time units. Simulating the system will then show that a later message may overtake an earlier message, because the earlier message is waiting to be forwarded at sensor s_2, while the later message is sent directly to the sink via the newly established link.

Maude also allows to search in a breadth-first manner through all possible executions from a given initial state. The state space of concurrent and distributed systems is huge, usually growing exponentially in the number of components. In order to make searching feasible, abstractions that reduce the state space are needed, preferably by eliminating components. For example, objects of class `TempSensor` may be replaced by equations for forwarding messages, moving these from in-queues to out-queues while updating the "step" and the "hops to live" attributes. This way, simple searches about communication patterns may be perfortmed while abstracting from the internal functionality of the sensors.

6 Related and Future Work

Our approach is based on modelling with active objects. Active objects have been used to model mobile ad-hoc networks, which are similar to our biomedical sensor networks, in [7]. However, in contrast to our work, cross-layer design is not considered, because no means for reasoning about the network are provided.

Formal automata models have been used analyse protocols and channels. The properties of communication media are usually modelled as automata, too. For example, Nancy Lynch models communication media by processes in [14]. A lossy channel is modeled by a process that randomly drops messages. In contrast to these approaches, which apply ad-hoc techniques to model various kinds of links and networks, our modelling language fully integrates into the modelling language a set of primitives to describe dynamically evolving network topologies.

TinyOS [6] is a popular operating system for wireless sensor nodes. The associated programming language nesC [8] takes an approach similar to ours: Programs in nesC are structured in components. However, the number of components in nes C is statically fixed and each component ressembles a single Creol objects. In contrast, our components may be created dynamically and contain a number of concurrent objects. In nesC tasks correspond to our processes and are cooperatively scheduled, because sensor nodes usually do not permit dynamic scheduling. In contrast, our approach abstracts from particular scheduling schemes; in fact, our models could be refined with application-specific schedulers (see [21]). This may be starting point for a development technique for applications which target TinyOS. We are currently investigating the relationship between our models and nesC programs in more detail.

For the analysis of networks, the current state of the art focuses on discrete event simulation software, such as OMNet++ [25], that defines accurate models of wireless communication networks and channels. These simulators target the *quantitative* aspects of the model, such as throughput figures, whereas we are mainly concerned with *functional* aspects, e.g., the correctness of the deployed protocol and sensor functionality.

Verisim [2] is a simulator similar to OMNet++, which is used to validate functional properties of wireless networks. Verisim allows models from discrete event simulations to be used directly, and integrates well with established design methods. Monte-Carlo simulation is used to record traces of events, which may be queried using a special language. In contrast, our approach is based on a simple, high-level modeling language with a formal semantics. Furthermore, the integration with Maude makes it possible to customize the simulation strategy, as well as to apply search techniques to the models.

Ölveczky and Thorvaldsen [18] have shown how Real-Time Maude [17] can be applied to model and analyse advanced wireless sensor network algorithms, using, e.g., Monte Carlo simulations for performance evaluation for networks with up to 800 nodes. Rodriguez [20] has similarly used Real-Time Maude to analyse flooding in WSN protocols. These papers focus on the modeling and analysis of protocol algorithms. Our work complements this approach by emphasising sensor functionality and behavior, as well as heterogeneous media. However, we intend to investigate how their techniques for simulation may apply in our setting.

Compared to earlier work on Creol [11, 12], the main contribution of this paper is the extension to heterogeneous networks and the introduction of language abstractions suitable for a unified modeling of network components and different kinds of networks. In particular, the extension consists of the notion of *network components* with tightly connected objects sharing in- and out-queues, specification of different and dynamic networks architectures, including *wireless networks* and *radio programming*, multi- and broadcasts, as well as the extension to a *timed semantics*. The proposed primitives are useful to establish connections at the network level but may also be exploited at the application level, for instance in service-oriented architectures [4].

Since our approach allows the radio level to be programmed inside the modeling language, we may experiment with different radio solutions. For instance, the active radio object used in the example of Sect. 4 may be replaced by a passive radio model. This can be done by letting the sensor class inherit a passive radio class, and letting the sensor object control the radio sender and receiver. Furthermore our approach may be adjusted to allow more realistic models of wireless communication by considering factors like battery capacity, power consumption of sending and receiving, signal strength, and location. Stochastic modeling, however, is less trivial, but might be addressed using the probabilistic Maude tool [13] as a basis for the operational semantics.

7 Concluding Remarks

The main contribution of this paper is a modeling framework for heterogeneous networks. The framework allows the unified modeling of network components in different kinds of networks, as well as network changes. In particular, we consider wireless networks and radio communication, as well as loosely and tightly connected wired networks. Our approach extends the object-oriented paradigm by suggesting novel language abstractions related to heterogeneous networks, using Creol as an underlying language for concurrent and distributed objects. The extended language may be used for high-level application programming (without knowledge of the particular network available) as well as for network-aware programming such as radio controllers. Our framework is based on formal methods and may serve as a basis for reasoning about system properties and semantical analysis. The formal semantics of the language is presented through a high-level operational semantics, defined in rewriting logic. The operational semantics is executable, allowing simulation and formal analysis by means of the Maude tool. The language is demonstrated through an example of a wireless sensor network, and some initial simulations and analysis have been performed.

The value of a formal framework as a basis for intuitive understanding of a language and towards practical modeling and reasoning, depends crucially on the simplicity of the semantics. The presented operational semantics consists of 32 rules or equations, apart from auxiliary function definitions. This covers the semantics of basic statements and object-oriented issues such as object creation, inheritance, late binding, and (asynchronous) method calls and replies, as well as extensions for heterogeneous networks, including broad- and multicast, timing (with global and local clocks), programming and re-programming of network links, and primitives for wireless receiving and sending. The semantical simplicity may also be taken as an argument for the appropriateness of the proposed abstractions and their integration within the object-oriented paradigm.

The long term goal of this work is to adapt the object-oriented paradigm to the setting of modern distributed systems by exploring suitable language abstractions and constructs that at the same time support simplicity both in reasoning and in semantics. The present paper may be seen as a first step in the direction of high-level, object-oriented, and formal modeling of heterogeneous systems where properties of the different networks are directly modeled.

Acknowledgments. We are grateful for comments by Wolfgang Leister and Xuedong Liang on sensor network modeling and analysis.

References

1. Alur, R., Henzinger, T.A.: Logics and models of real time: A survey. In: Huizing, C., de Bakker, J.W., Rozenberg, G., de Roever, W.-P. (eds.) REX 1991. LNCS, vol. 600, pp. 74–106. Springer, Heidelberg (1992)
2. Bhargavan, K., Gunter, C.A., Kim, M., Lee, I., Sokolsky, O., Viswanathan, M.: Verisim: Formal analysis of network simulations. IEEE Transaction on Software Engineering 28(2), 129–145 (2002)
3. Booch, G., Rumbaugh, J., Jacobson, I.: The Unified Modeling Language User Guide. Addison-Wesley, Reading (1999)
4. Clarke, D., Johnsen, E.B., Owe, O.: Concurrent Objects à la Carte. In: Correctness, Concurrency, and Components: Festschrift for Willem-Paul de Roever. LNCS. Springer, Heidelberg (to appear, 2008)
5. Clavel, M., Durán, F., Eker, S., Lincoln, P., Martí-Oliet, N., Meseguer, J., Quesada, J.F.: Maude: Specification and programming in rewriting logic. Theoretical Computer Science 285, 187–243 (2002)
6. Culler, D.E., Hill, J.L., Buonadonna, P., Szewczyk, R., Woo, A.: A network-centric approach to embedded software for tiny devices. In: Henzinger, T.A., Kirsch, C.M. (eds.) EMSOFT 2001. LNCS, vol. 2211, pp. 114–130. Springer, Heidelberg (2001)
7. Dedecker, J., Belle, W.V.: Actors for mobile ad-hoc networks. In: Yang, L.T., Guo, M., Gao, G.R., Jha, N.K. (eds.) EUC 2004. LNCS, vol. 3207, pp. 482–494. Springer, Heidelberg (2004)
8. Gay, D., Levis, P., von Behren, J.R., Welsh, M., Brewer, E.A., Culler, D.E.: The nesC language: A holistic approach to networked embedded systems. In: Proc. Conf. on Programming Language Design and Implementation PLDI 2003, pp. 1–11. ACM, New York (2003)
9. Goguen, J.A., Winkler, T., Meseguer, J., Futatsugi, K., Jouannaud, J.-P.: Introducing OBJ. In: Goguen, J.A., Malcolm, G. (eds.) Software Engineering with OBJ: Algebraic Specification in Action, Advances in Formal Methods, ch. 1, pp. 3–167. Kluwer Academic Publishers, Dordrecht (2000)
10. Goldsmith, A.J., Wicker, S.B.: Design challenges for energy-constrained ad hoc wireless networks. IEEE Wireless Communications 9(4), 8–27 (2002)
11. Johnsen, E.B., Owe, O.: An asynchronous communication model for distributed concurrent objects. Software and Systems Modeling 6(1), 35–58 (2007)
12. Johnsen, E.B., Owe, O., Yu, I.C.: Creol: A type-safe object-oriented model for distributed concurrent systems. Theoretical Computer Science 365(1–2), 23–66 (2006)
13. Kumar, N., Sen, K., Meseguer, J., Agha, G.: A rewriting based model for probabilistic distributed object systems. In: Najm, E., Nestmann, U., Stevens, P. (eds.) FMOODS 2003. LNCS, vol. 2884, pp. 32–46. Springer, Heidelberg (2003)

14. Lynch, N.A.: Distributed Algorithms. The Morgan Kaufmann Series in Data Management Systems. Morgan Kaufmann Publishers, Inc, San Francisco (1996)
15. Meseguer, J.: Conditional rewriting logic as a unified model of concurrency. Theoretical Computer Science 96, 73–155 (1992)
16. Meseguer, J., Rosu, G.: Rewriting logic semantics: From language specifications to formal analysis tools. In: Basin, D., Rusinowitch, M. (eds.) IJCAR 2004. LNCS, vol. 3097, pp. 1–44. Springer, Heidelberg (2004)
17. Ölveczky, P.C., Meseguer, J.: Specification of real-time and hybrid systems in rewriting logic. Theoretical Computer Science 285(2), 359–405 (2002)
18. Ölveczky, P.C., Thorvaldsen, S.: Formal modeling and analysis of the OGDC wireless sensor network algorithm in Real-Time Maude. Theoretical Computer Science (to appear, 2008)
19. Raisinghani, V.T., Iyer, S.: Cross-layer design optimizations in wireless protocol stacks. Computer Communications 27(8), 720–724 (2004)
20. Rodríguez, D.E.: On modelling sensor networks in Maude. In: Denker, G., Talcott, C. (eds.) Proc. 6th Intl. Workshop on Rewriting Logic and its Applications (WRLA 2006). Electronic Notes in Theoretical Computer Science, vol. 176, pp. 199–213. Elsevier, Amsterdam (2007)
21. Schlatte, R., Aichernig, B., de Boer, F., Griesmayer, A., Johnsen, E.B.: Testing concurrent objects with application-specific schedulers. In: Fitzgerald, J.S., Haxthausen, A.E., Yenigun, H. (eds.) ICTAC 2008. LNCS, vol. 5160, pp. 319–333. Springer, Heidelberg (2008)
22. Smith, G.: The Object-Z Specification Language. In: Advances in Formal Methods, Kluwer Academic Publishers, Dordrecht (2000)
23. Srivastava, V., Motani, M.: Cross-layer design: A survey and the road ahead. IEEE Communications Magazine 43(12), 112–119 (2005)
24. Mellor, A.U.S.J., Scott, K., Weise, D.: Model-driven architecture. In: Bruel, J.-M., Bellahsène, Z. (eds.) OOIS 2002. LNCS, vol. 2426, pp. 233–239. Springer, Heidelberg (2002)
25. Varga, A.: Omnet++. IEEE Network Interactive 16(4) (July 2002)
26. Zimmermann, H.: OSI reference model—the ISO model of architecture for open system interconnection. IEEE Transactions on Communication 28(4), 425–432 (1980)

Coordinating Object Oriented Components Using Data-Flow Networks

Mohammad Mahdi Jaghoori*

CWI, Amsterdam, The Netherlands
jaghouri@cwi.nl

Abstract. We propose a framework for component-based modeling of distributed systems. It provides separation of concerns between computation (in object oriented components), coordination (via connectors) and dynamic reconfiguration (by the network manager). This framework builds upon the object oriented modeling language Creol for modeling the components, and uses the ideas of Reo for exogenous coordination using data-flow networks.

1 Introduction

Internet and systems distributed over internet, such as service oriented software, are nowadays becoming more popular. This brings about the need for modeling and analysis of these systems before implementation. The growing size of such systems favors use of high level languages supporting component-based design techniques. Internet based software usually consists of loosely coupled components, possibly provided by different parties, interacting with each other.

Components-based software development has been proposed by several authors as a solution to the increasing complexity of software development. Components are assumed to be individual and independent units of functionality and deployment and thus to turn them into an application, a mechanism for component composition is needed.

In this paper, we propose a framework for component-based modeling based on Creol [10]. The basic concept of standard Creol is to provide a formal object-oriented solution for modeling distributed systems. Creol objects have their own processors and communicate by asynchronous method calls. Although Creol is suitable for distributing objects over different processors, it does not in itself separate the coordination issues from computation. Nonetheless, we can translate our component models to standard Creol allowing us to use all the techniques developed for Creol. Furthermore, we get the formal semantics of the model for free.

Our work is on integrating the data-flow network modeling to an object oriented modeling language, namely Creol, by providing a syntax for modeling components consisting of objects. For modeling a distributed system in this framework, three different perspectives should be considered. First of all, one

* This work has been funded by the European IST-33826 STREP project CREDO on Modeling and Analysis of Evolutionary Structures for Distributed Services.

F.S. de Boer et al. (Eds.): FMCO 2007, LNCS 5382, pp. 280–311, 2008.

should define the components in the system. The inside of a component is modeled as a number of (standard Creol) objects communicating by message passing. Every component implements some facades, which in turn declare (disjoint) sets of ports. The objects inside the component may read, write or wait for a signal on the ports. The computation inside a component does not depend on how ports will be connected; hence, allowing the modeling of reusable off-the-shelf components.

The second perspective focuses on the exogenous coordination of components and their communication. At this level, as proposed in [15], a software component is considered a static abstraction (black box) with plugs (called ports here). We use connectors to connect components. A connector has a fixed number of connector-ends, which can be plugged into component ports. In other words, component ports are to be bound to connector-ends. Connectors are independent of any specific components. We have developed a library of mobile connectors for some basic coordination patterns. A connector is mobile in the sense that its ends can move during execution, i.e., connect different components at different times. Mobility together with dynamic creation of connectors (and components) provide the means for a dynamically reconfigurable network, in a similar way as modeled in π-calculus [14].

The third perspective of modeling addresses reconfiguration. Reconfiguration policies are defined in network managers. In addition to ports, a component facade specifies the events it may raise, e.g., a request/announcement for a specific service. Events are handled by the network manager. As a result of a sequence of events (possibly from different components), the network manager may reconfigure the network (by creating new connectors and/or changing port bindings). For a given system, one or more network managers can be developed modeling different reconfiguration policies. This shows the level of decoupling in the component based framework.

1.1 Related Work

The object based modeling languages based on method calls [1,10,19] are more suitable for modeling and analysis of the internals of the components rather than the communication between independently developed components. On the other hand, languages like [2,5,8] consider components as black boxes and focus only on the interactions between them. In our model, these aspects can be modeled and analyzed separately as well as integrated into a Creol model and analyzed together as a whole.

The data flow networks in our model are inspired from Reo [2]. We can compare our work with the implementations of Reo mobile channels (MoCha) in Java [16] and π-calculus [17]. Mocha, like our framework, allows for modeling component behavior as a separate issue from coordination. The main difference is that we also propose a syntax for modeling components. In addition, we allow for modeling dynamic reconfigurations in the network.

We can also compare our work with JCSP [20] as both bring channel based communication to the world of object oriented languages. The difference is in the fact that JCSP processes are connected by and synchronize upon a small set of primitives - such as message-passing channels and multiway events. However, we allow construction of complex connectors (independently from the components) which provide exogenous coordination.

Another difference with the two works above is the underlying concurrency model is different, i.e., multi-threaded Java vs. concurrent objects in Creol. One may also use Creol features like dynamic upgrades [22] or its executable semantics [10].

Among other component-based modeling frameworks are BIP [4] and Ptolemy II [6]. BIP provides an algebraic formalization of connectors, wherein atomic components are modeled as a set of transitions. Ptolemy II, implemented in Java, is aimed at modeling heterogeneous components. In Ptolemy, the components communicate by contacting the *receiver* object of one another, whereas in our model components are exogenously coordinated. Furthermore, we use an operational formalization of components and connectors using the object oriented language Creol.

1.2 Paper Structure

In the next section, the basics of Creol and Reo are described. Then we explain how Creol can be lifted up to the level of component-based modeling in Section 3. Section 3.1 covers the syntax proposed for modeling the components. Section 3.2 describes how coordination can be modeled using connectors. A case study demonstrates the typical use of the framework in Section 4. Section 5 concludes the paper.

2 Preliminaries

2.1 Creol

The basic concept of the Creol modeling language is to provide a formal object-oriented solution for modeling distributed systems. The (simplified) syntax of Creol is given in Fig. 1. A complete presentation of the formal semantics of Creol (given in rewrite logic) in [10] is beyond the scope of this paper. Here we overview some Creol characteristics.

Creol objects have dedicated processors and communicate by asynchronous method calls. The caller can choose to wait for an answer, thus simulating synchronous method calls. Creol objects are typed by interfaces, whereas classes can implement as many interfaces as necessary. The notion of co-interfaces can be used to restrict who can call the operations provided in interfaces. As a result, the callee can communicate with the caller in a type-safe way.

Fig. 2 shows a very simple Creol model. The Simple interface defines a callMe operation that can be called only by instances of type Simple, while the response operation does not require any co-interface. The run method in a class defines its active behavior; thus the class Easy starts with calling its own callMe operation.

$$
\begin{array}{lll}
\mathit{IF} & ::= & \textbf{interface}\ N\{(\mathit{Par})\}^?\{\textbf{inherits}\ \mathit{Inh}\}^? \\
 & & \textbf{begin}\ \{\textbf{with}\ N\ \mathit{Msig}^+\}^?\ \textbf{end} \\
\mathit{Inh} & ::= & \{N\{(E)\}^?\}^+_, \\
\mathit{Par} & ::= & \{\{v\}^+_, : N\}^+_, \\
\mathit{Msig} & ::= & \textbf{op}\ N\{(\{\textbf{in}\ \mathit{Par}\}^?\ \{\textbf{out}\ \mathit{Par}\}^?)\}^? \\
\mathit{CL} & ::= & \textbf{class}\ N\{(\mathit{Par})\}^? \\
 & & \{\textbf{implements}\ \mathit{Inh}\}^?\ \{\textbf{inherits}\ \mathit{Inh}\}^? \\
 & & \textbf{begin}\ \mathit{Vdcl}^?\{\{\textbf{with}\ N\}^?\ \mathit{Mtd}\}^*\ \textbf{end} \\
\mathit{Vdcl} & ::= & \textbf{var}\ \{\{v\}^+_, : N\{= e\}^?\}^+_,
\end{array}
$$

$$
\begin{array}{lll}
\mathit{Mtd} & ::= & \{\mathit{Msig} == \{\mathit{Vdcl};\}^?\ S\}^+ \\
g & ::= & b \mid t? \mid \neg g \mid g \wedge g \\
p & ::= & x.m \mid m \\
S & ::= & \epsilon \mid s; S \\
s & ::= & (S) \mid V := E \mid \textbf{skip} \\
 & & \mid v := \textbf{new}\ N(E) \mid !p(E) \\
 & & \mid t!p(E) \mid t?(V) \mid p(E;V) \\
 & & \mid \textbf{if}\ b\ \textbf{then}\ S\ \textbf{else}\ S\ \textbf{end} \\
 & & \mid \textbf{await}\ g \mid \textbf{await}\ t?(V) \\
 & & \mid \textbf{await}\ p(E;V) \mid \textbf{release}
\end{array}
$$

Fig. 1. BNF grammar for Creol. Curly brackets are used as meta parenthesis, superscript ? for optional parts, superscript * for repetition zero or more times, whereas $\{...\}^+_,$ denotes repetition one or more times with , as delimiter. Identifiers N denote interface, class, type, or method names. Capitalized terms such as E, V, and S, denote lists of the syntactic categories of the corresponding lower-case terms [10,11].

```
interface Simple begin
    with Simple op callMe
    with Any op response
end

class Easy implements Simple begin
    op run == await this.callMe()
    with Simple op callMe == ! caller.response()
    with Any op response == skip
end
```

Fig. 2. A simple Creol model

It 'awaits' until the requested operation is accomplished (synchronous method call with releasing the processor). The **this** keyword can be used to refer to the same object. The **caller** keyword refers to the object calling the current method, and it is typed by the co-interface used. The callMe method calls the caller back asynchronously (denoted by the ! sign).

Each object in Creol, shows reactive behavior upon receiving messages. As an object receives a message, a new process is created inside the object for responding to the message. The processes inside an object are interleaved. Any of the enabled processes can be scheduled to run (nondeterministically) when the current process finishes. Alternatively, the currently executing process may, at its own discretion, release the processor (at some predefined processor release point using the **await** keyword) allowing other enabled processes to start execution.

Releasing processor can be unconditional (via the **release** command) or guarded by boolean expressions. These guards can also test whether an asynchronous call has been accomplished. This is handled implicitly by the semantics with a completion notification. An example of a release point is '**await this**.callMe()' in Fig. 2. In general, the caller may expect a return value, thus simulating synchronous method calls. Notice that waiting for a return value without releasing the processor blocks the objects, disallowing other processes in the object to use the processor.

To make a system run, one should provide the initialization script. In the Creol convention, one can have a class for the initialization. This is similar to the class containing the main method in Java.

Creol is backed by its formal operational semantics and its strong typing allows for dynamic class upgrades [22]. Since Creol semantics is given in rewrite logic [13], Creol specifications can be readily executed and analyzed on the Maude [7] platform. Maude is a rewrite engine that can perform analysis like simulation, model checking, etc., on transition systems specified using rewrite logic.

2.2 Reo: A Coordination Language

Reo is a model for building component connectors in a compositional manner. It allows for modeling the behavior of such connectors, formally reasoning about them, and once proven correct, automatically generating the so-called glue code from the specification. Reo's notion of components and connectors is depicted in Figure 3, where component instances are represented as boxes, channels as straight lines, and connectors are delineated by dashed lines. Each connector in Reo is, in turn, constructed compositionally out of simpler connectors, which are ultimately composed out of primitive channels.

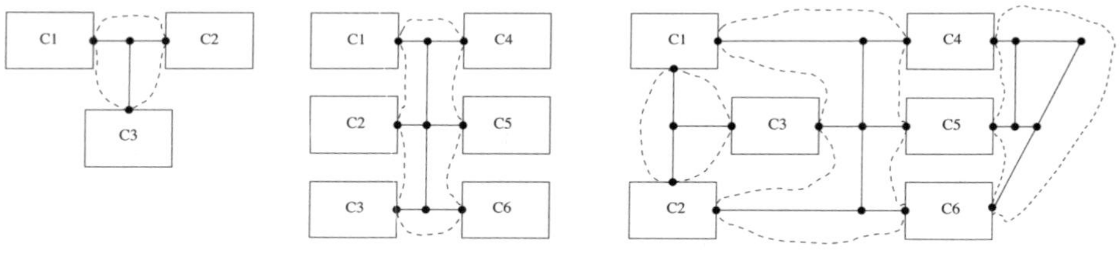

(a) a 3–way connector (b) a 6–way connector (c) two 3–way connectors and a 6–way connector

Fig. 3. Components and Connectors

Reo is a compositional approach to defining component connectors. Reo *connectors* (also called *circuits*) are constructed in the same spirit as logic and electronics circuits: take basic elements (e.g., wires, diodes and transistors) and connect them. Basic connectors in Reo are *channels*. Each channel has exactly two ends, which can be a *sink* end or a *source* end. A *sink* end is where data flows out of a channel, and a *source* end is where data flows in a channel. It is possible that the channel ends of a channel are both sink or both source. A channel must support a certain set of primitive operations, such as I/O, on its ends; beyond that, Reo places no restriction on the behavior of a channel. This allows an open-ended set of different channel types to be used simultaneously together in Reo, each with its own policy for synchronization, buffering, ordering, computation, data retention/loss, etc.

Channels are connected to make a circuit. Connecting channels is putting channel ends together in a *node*. So, a *node* is a set of channel ends. A node in Reo has a certain semantics: for all the source channel ends on a node, a fork operation takes place which is copying the outgoing data to all the channel ends (*replicator*); for all the sink channel ends on a node, a merge operation takes place which is a nondeterministic choice between incoming data (*merger*).

3 Mobile Connectors Framework

In this section, we explain how components and mobile connectors can be modeled in Creol. Fig. 4(a) shows the class diagram of the general framework. We have extended the standard notation of class diagrams with a dotted arrow with black head (┈►) between two interfaces (shown as ovals) which represents the required co-interfaces. This arrow should not be confused with dashed arrows (with white heads) showing that a class implements an interface (cf. Fig. 8).

As shown in Fig. 4(a), every component must implement the Component interface to have access to connector ends. In the next subsection, we provide an abstract syntax for modeling a component hiding these details. A component modeled using these abstractions can be automatically translated into the model in Fig. 4(a).

Then we explain modeling mobile connectors, which are the basic elements for constructing a reconfigurable network. Connectors can transfer data between components and/or synchronize their actions.

Each connector provides a fixed number of connector-ends, to which component ports can be bound. Fig. 4.(b) shows the object diagram of a connector

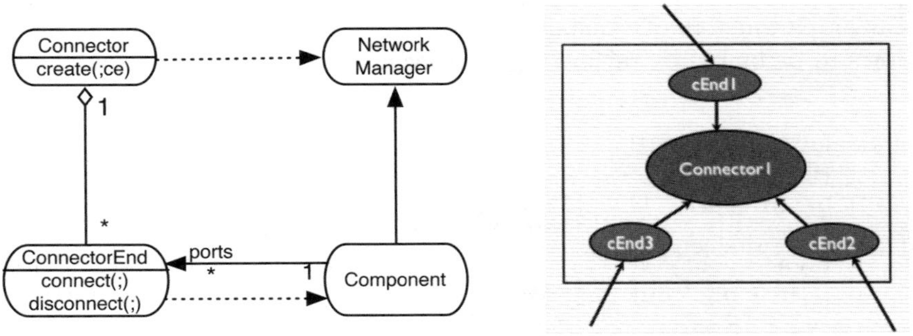

(a) General class diagram (b) Object diagram for a connector

Fig. 4. The general model of the framework

with three ends. We model each connector-end with an object, while the behavior of the connector is provided by another object. Connector-end objects are similar to the buttons of a coffee machine, where the coffee machine resembles the connector object. The output of the machine depends on the button pressed, i.e., the machine needs to distinguish between its input buttons to be able to produce the correct behavior. Similarly, since a connector needs to distinguish between the connector-ends, we have used one object per connector-end.

This object scheme is especially necessary because of the mobility of the connector, i.e., the components attached to each connector may change dynamically. For a connector, however, the connector-end objects do not change during its whole life time. Therefore, the connector object only needs to establish the proper synchronization and data flow paths among its fixed connector-end objects.

3.1 Component View

A component provides one or more facades. Facades encapsulate the internal behavior of a component, in the same way as interfaces encapsulate the internals of a class. A facade declares a set of ports and events. Fig. 5 shows the extensions to Creol syntax for defining facades and components. Furthermore, a class can be defined to be *inside* (the facade of) a component to be able to raise events and access the ports of that component.

A port is essentially just a reference to a connector-end and is used for communication with other (anonymous) components. The actual binding of ports (to connector-end objects) is beyond component's control. In addition to communicating with other components, components may raise events. Event examples include a request/announcement for a specific service, reporting a time-out for a given request, or simply acknowledging that a request accomplished successfully. These events guide possible reconfigurations of the *context-aware* network. Since components have no explicit reference to the network manager, an event can be raised by the abstract command **raise_event**.

There are three types of ports. Objects inside a component may read from inports, write to outports and wait for synchronization on syncports. These actions are performed synchronously. Apart from these basic operations, ports can only appear as parameters of events. Whenever necessary, the component requests its ports to be bound by raising a proper event (at the so called reconfiguration

$$
\begin{array}{lll}
Fcd & ::= & \textbf{facade}\ N\{(Par)\}^? \\
 & & \{\textbf{inherits}\ Inh\}^? \\
 & & \textbf{begin}\ \{Pdcl\}^*\ \{Edcl\}^*\ \textbf{end} \\
Pdcl & ::= & \textbf{port}\ \{\{v\}^+_{,}\ :\ N\}^+_{,} \\
Edcl & ::= & \{\textbf{sync\_event}\}^?\ N \\
 & & \{(\{\textbf{in}\ Par\}^?\ \{\textbf{out}\ Par\}^?)\}^?
\end{array}
\qquad
\begin{array}{lll}
CL & ::= & \textbf{class}\ N\{(Par)\}^? \\
 & & \{\textbf{inside}\ N\}^? \ldots \\
Cmp & ::= & \textbf{component}\ N \\
 & & \{\textbf{implements}\ Inh\}^? \\
 & & \textbf{begin}\ \{N := \textbf{new}\ N(E)\}^+\ \textbf{end} \\
S & ::= & \ldots \mid \textbf{raise\_event}\ N(E\{;V\}^?)
\end{array}
$$

Fig. 5. Extended syntax for modeling the component view. The type of a port variable in *Pdcl* can only be inport, outport or syncport. Triple dots are used to avoid repeating the parts similar to Fig. 1.

points). Ports cannot be used elsewhere, e.g., cannot be assigned explicitly as normal variables in the code, or may not be sent around as message parameters.

Events are by default asynchronous. However, some events especially those expecting some return values (e.g., reconfiguration points) can be declared synchronous (using the keyword **sync_event**).

Fig. 6 shows the facade of a component in a peer2peer system. This example is explained in detail in Section 4. The facade Peer inherits the ports and (synchronous) events defined in ServerSide and ClientSide facades. In addition, Peer adds two asynchronous events. A peer component (providing a client and a server side) can use the ports and raise the events declared in these facades.

Having defined the facade and the internal interfaces of a component, one can implement the internal classes to provide the functionality of the component. A concrete component is obtained by instantiating these classes. Fig. 7 shows a Node component based on the classes in Appendix B implementing the Peer facade. Notice that the classes used in this component are defined to be *inside* a Peer. Section 4 elaborates more on this example.

A class can have access to the ports defined in a facade only if it defined to be inside that facade. Notice that a class can be inside only one facade. A class can raise an event only if it is inside a facade declaring that event. Section 3.4 will explain how facade and component definitions can be translated to normal Creol syntax adhering to the diagram in Fig. 4.

3.2 Coordination View

Coordination is modeled in a network consisting of connectors. In general, every connector should provide a create() method that can be called by the network manager (as the co-interface). This method should create the necessary connector-end objects and return the list of their references.

The behavior of a connector is completely independent of the components and the rest of the system. This makes them suitable for reuse. A library of connectors has been developed and Appendix A includes the Creol code for some of these connectors.

From the connectors point of view, a connector-end object represents the component port(s) attached to that end. However, more than one component ports may be attached to a connector-end (i.e., have a reference to the object). This sharing is handled by the connector-end object by forwarding only one request to the connector object at a time.

Connectors may offer three types of connector-ends. *Source* and *Sink* connector-ends are used for writing to and reading from a connector, respectively. A *Signal* connector-end is used when only a signal is to be provided. For example, a Synchronizer connector (see Fig. 8) provides (rendezvous) synchronization between (the components attached to) its Signal connector-ends.

The ConnectorEnd interface contains connect and disconnect operations to be implemented by all types of connector-ends. A component may use the connect operation to have exclusive access to a connector-end. If more than one component try to connect to one connector-end, nondeterministically one of them will

```
facade ClientSide
begin
  port myReq : outport
  port myAns : inport
  sync_event openClient(in k:Data, reqi:outport, ansi:inport
                    out reqo:outport, anso:inport, f:Boolean)
  sync_event closeClient(in reqi:outport, ansi:inport
                         out reqo:outport, anso:inport)
end
```

```
facade ServerSide
begin
  port exReq : outport
  port exAns : inport
  sync_event openServer (in reqi:inport, ansi:outport
                         out reqo:inport, anso:outport)
  sync_event closeServer(in reqi:inport, ansi:outport
                         out reqo:inport, anso:outport)
end
```

```
facade Peer inherits ClientSide, ServerSide
begin
  register (in keyList : List[Data]) // async_event
  update (in keyList : List[Data])   // async_event
end
```

Fig. 6. The facade of a component in peer2peer system

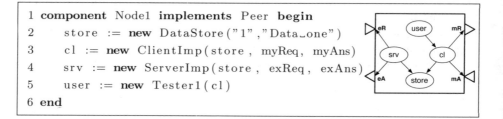

```
component Node1 implements Peer begin
    store := new DataStore("1","Data_one")
    cl := new ClientImp(store, myReq, myAns)
    srv := new ServerImp(store, exReq, exAns)
    user := new Tester1(cl)
end
```

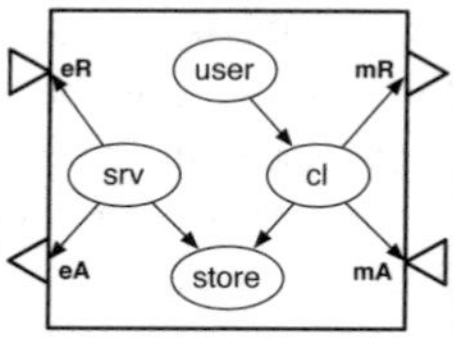

Fig. 7. A concrete component definition and its component-object diagram

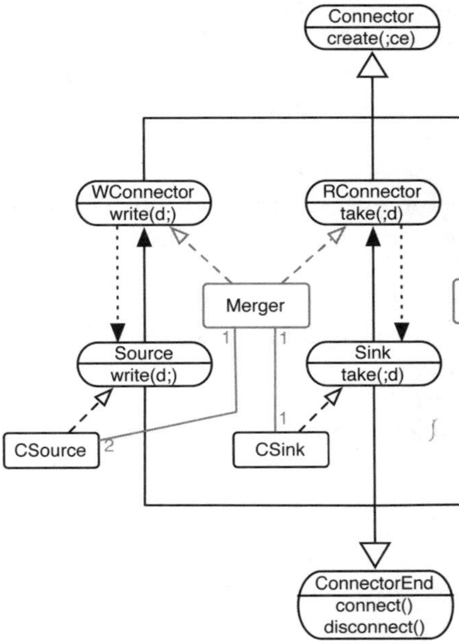

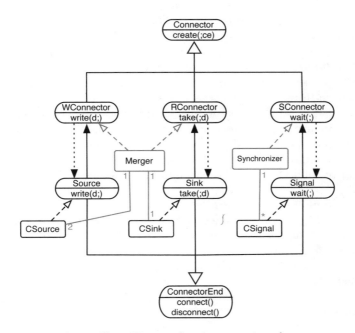

Fig. 8. Class diagram for connector interfaces

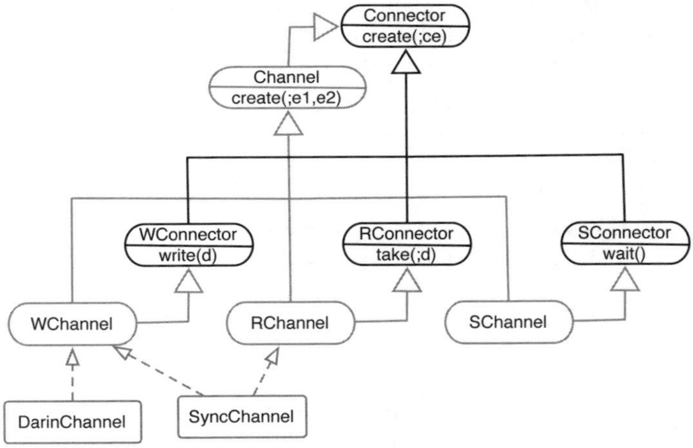

Fig. 9. Class diagram for channels with two ends

be selected (by the Creol scheduler). Other connect messages will be granted after the first one disconnects.

Each connector-end sub-type introduces its specific operation. The write on a Source takes an input, a take on a Sink produces an output, while the wait operation on a Signal has no parameter. Accordingly, connectors should provide (a subset of) the same operations. For instance, the WConnector interface provides a write operation to a Source connector-end. In Fig. 8, this is reflected with a co-interface (dotted arrow) relation. Therefore, a connector with source ends needs to implement the WConnector interface. Similarly, a connector with sink (resp. signal) ends needs to implement the RConnector (resp. SConnector) interface, which in turn provides a take (resp. wait) operation.

A channel is a special connector with exactly two ends. This fact is reflected in the model by overloading the create method (cf. Fig. 9). Since channels have exactly two ends, this method returns exactly two connector-ends instead of a list. Channel interfaces can be used for modeling the equivalents for Reo channels. Similar to connectors, the Channel interface has three sub-types for different operations.

To define connectors and channels, one needs to implement the proper interfaces shown in Fig. 8 and 9. A merger has two sources and one sink. It propagates the data on one of its two input sources onto its output sink. Therefore, it should provide write and read capabilities (by implementing WConnector and RConnector). A drain channel only has two sources and only needs to implement the WChannel interface.

3.3 Network Manager

The network manager is the entity responsible for reconfigurations in the network. It is context-aware in the sense that it performs reconfigurations based on the events raised by the components. A network manager must provide event handlers for all of the events defined in the facades of the components in the model. This can be implemented in different ways providing different strategies.

```
with NetworkManager
    op create(out ce:List[ConnectorEnd]) ==
        sig := new CSignal(this);
        snk := new CSink(this);
        src := new CSource(this);
        ce := nil |- src |- snk |- sig
```

Fig. 10. A typical create method

The list of event declarations in a facade is a contract between components and the network manager. This list, in fact, shows the event handlers that must be implemented in the network manager. A special event initPorts is implicitly sent by all components upon creation. This event informs the network manager of a new component in the system whose ports may need to be initialized. Note that a facade does not include the initPorts event, which must be handled by the network manager.

Unlike connectors and components, a network manager is designed specifically for a particular system. It creates the necessary connectors by calling their create methods (Fig. 11.a). Each connector returns the list of its connector-ends to the network manager. A typical create method is shown in Fig. 10.

The network manager, knowing the components and having the references to the connector-ends, binds component ports to connector-ends properly. Fig. 11.b depicts a specific configuration of the system. Later on, as the system evolves, and after certain (complementary) events are raised (possibly by different components), the network configuration may change. This takes place by reassigning connector-end references to the ports of components. The network manager can change port bindings in response to events raised at reconfiguration points, i.e., events that have ports as parameters.

3.4 Translation to Creol

The model provided in the higher-level syntax (in Section 3.1) can be translated to normal Creol syntax such that the Creol interpreter can be used to run (simulate, analyze, etc.) the model. This also shows the formal semantics of our model in terms of Creol's operational semantics. The algorithm for translation is given below.

- '**facade** N(P)' results in:
  - **interface** N(mgr:NetworkManager, P)
    - each event is changed into an operation with cointerface 'Any'
  - **class** N_Boundary(mgr:NetworkManager, P) **implements** N(mgr, P)
    - change **port**s to **var** declaration.
    - add **op** run == **await** mgr.initN(;allPorts)
    - implement each event as forwarding the message to the network manager.
- '**component** M(P) **implements** N' results in:
  - **class** M_Boundary(mgr:NetworkManager, P) **inherits** N_Boundary(mgr, P)
    - 'V := **new** T (Args)' generates '**var** V : T'
  - add a run method
    - every 'V := **new** T (Args)' is added.
- '**class** C(P) **inside** N' results in:
  - **class** C(b:N_Boundary, P)
  - change **raise_event** to '**await** b.' (for sync events) or '! b.' (for async events)

In a nutshell, events are translated to operations and ports to connector-end references (inport to Sink, outport to Source, and syncport to Signal). Notice that this step is transparent to the modeler. A *boundary* class will be automatically generated for each facade and each component concrete definition (cf. Fig. 7). For instance, Fig. 12 shows the boundary for the client side facade. A similar boundary class is created for any facade in the model. This boundary class initializes the ports defined in that facade. It also provides the definitions for operations corresponding to events.

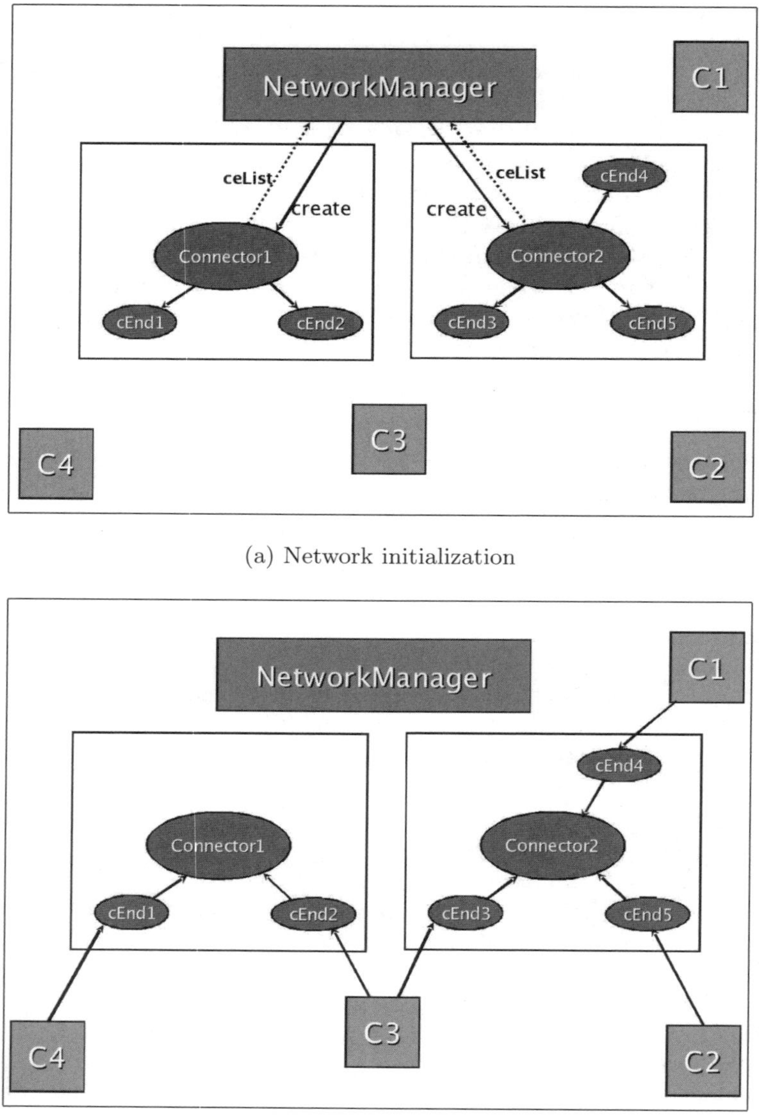

(a) Network initialization

(b) Running network configuration

Fig. 11. Network Manager. Components are viewed as black boxes here.

Fig. 12 shows the boundary class for Node1 (cf. Fig. 7). One instance of the boundary class will be created per instance of the component. A boundary object creates the objects as specified in the component definition (see the run method in Fig. 12, compared to Fig. 7). It also receives all the events raised (by the internal objects), and forwards them to the network manager. This ensures that

```
interface ClientSide(mgr:NetworkManager)
inherits Component(mgr)
begin
  with Any op openClient(in k:Data, reqi:Source, ansi:Sink
                          out reqo:Source, anso:Sink, f:Boolean);
  with Any op closeClient(in reqi:Source, ansi:Sink
                                  out reqo:Source, anso:Sink);
end

class ClientSide_Boundary(mgr:NetworkManager)
implements ClientSide(mgr)
begin
  var myReq : Source
  var myAns : Sink
  op run ==
     await mgr.initClientSide(;myReq,myAns);
  with Any op openClient(in k:Data, reqi:Source, ansi:Sink
                          out reqo:Source, anso:Sink, f:Boolean) ==
     await mgr.openClient (k, reqi, ansi; reqo, anso, f)
  with Any op closeClient(in reqi:Source, ansi:Sink
                                  out reqo:Source, anso:Sink) ==
     await mgr.closeClient (reqi, ansi; reqo, anso)
end
```

```
class Node1_Boundary (mgr:NetworkManager)
inherits PeerBoundary(mgr)
begin
   var store : Store
   var cl : Client
   var srv : Server
   var user : User
   op run ==
      store := new DataStore("1","Data_one", this);
      cl := new ClientImp(store, myReq, myAns, this);
      srv := new ServerImp(store, exReq, exAns, this) ;
      user := new Tester1(cl , this)
end
```

Fig. 12. Boundary classes for ClientSide facade and a Node component

the '**caller**' of all events from the same component remains unique. In other words, if each object (inside the component) was set up to send an event directly to the manager, the **caller** of the events would be different objects, whereas the manager should see them coming from one component.

The implementation of the classes inside a component must be changed such that a reference to the boundary object, say 'b', is provided as a parameter to the class definitions. The boundary object is, in turn, provided (as parameter) with a reference to the network manager, to which it sends the raised events. Finally, raising an event should be replaced with a call to the boundary object; i.e., **raise_event** will become '**await** b.' for sync events, and '! b.' for async events.

4 Case Study

Peer-to-peer networks are now a commonly used way of sharing data. In such networks, each node shares some data and in return can (search for and) get the data on other nodes. We model a hybrid p2p architecture (like that of Napster [18]) in which there is a central server (called the *broker*) that keeps track of (the keywords for) the data in every node. Each node, upon creation, registers its data with the broker. Later it may query the broker for some new data (using their keywords), and the broker connects it to the node who has the data.

```
interface Store
begin
    with Client op add (in key:Data, info:Data)
    with Server op find (in key:Data out info:Data)
end
/*************************************************/
interface Client (store:Store, req:outport, ans:inport)
begin
    with User op search(in key:Data out result:Data)
end
/*************************************************/
interface User (cl:Client)
begin
end
/*************************************************/
interface Server (store:Store, req:inport, ans:outport)
begin
end
```

Fig. 13. Interfaces of objects inside a Peer component

```
interface Broker inherits NetworkManager
begin
    with Peer async_event register
              (in keyList : List[Data])
    with Peer async_event update
              (in keyList : List[Data])
    with Peer sync_event openServer
              (in reqi:inport ,ansi:outport
               out reqo:inport ,anso:outport)
    with Peer sync_event closeServer
              (in reqi:inport ,ansi:outport
               out reqo:inport ,anso:outport)
    with Peer sync_event openClient
              (in k:Data, reqi:outport , ansi:inport
               out reqo:outport , anso:inport , f:Boolean)
    with Peer sync_event closeClient
              (in reqi:outport , ansi:inport
               out reqo:outport , anso:inport)
end
```

Fig. 14. The Broker interface

4.1 A Peer Component

The facade of a peer component, including a server and a client side, was defined in Fig. 6, Section 3.2. A component implementing Peer may raise events inherited from ClientSide or ServerSide, as well as 'register' and 'update' declared in Peer itself. In this model, openClient/closeClient and openServer/closeServer are reconfiguration points; because, every time a node asks for some data (as a client) or services a request (as a server), it is *possibly* connected to different nodes, i.e., its port bindings may (or may not) be updated. Note that in reconfiguration points, ports are used as **in/out** parameters of the event.

We consider four interfaces for the internal objects of peer components (Fig. 13). The 'User' object represents the interface of the component to a user who can ask for new pieces of data; and, in turn, it drives the 'Client' object. The client object uses the two ports myReq and myAns from the ClientSide facade. As a client, a node writes its request on myReq and expects the result on myAns. The local store is updated upon acquiring the requested data using the 'add' operation in the 'Store' interface.

Each node also shares its data; i.e., it can service the requests from other nodes. A component implementing the ServerSide facade, reads a request ('key' to some data) from exReq and writes the data corresponding to the given key

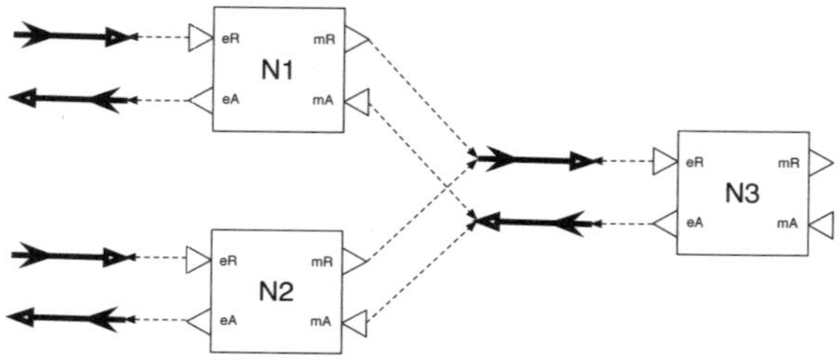

(a) Two nodes requesting data from the same node with the SimpleBroker

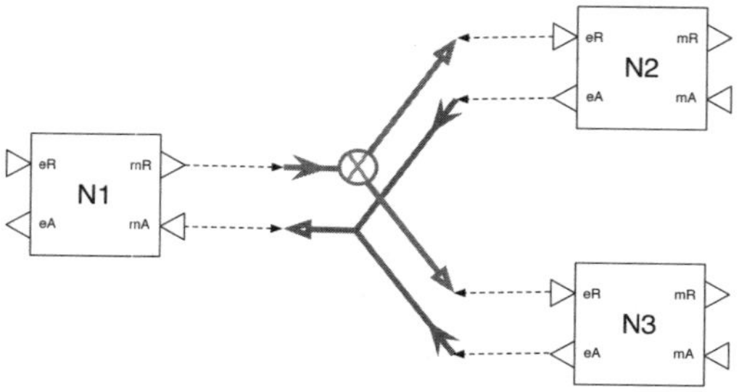

(b) Two nodes providing the requested data with the AlternateBroker

Fig. 15. Peer-to-peer network configurations

on exAns. A server, therefore, needs to query the local data store for existing information. The implementation of these classes is given in Appendix B.

The final step in defining the components is to instantiate the objects inside a component. The Clinet and Server objects are the same. The Store objects are initialized with different data. Different implementations of the User interface can be used for testing the model. Fig. 7 shows the definition of a component Node1 which is based on a specific implementation of User in the class Tester1. Components Node2 and Node3 are defined similarly using Tester2 and Tester3 classes as User. The implementation of these classes is given in Appendix B.

4.2 Network Manager and System Setup

A network manager must provide event handlers for the events defined in the facade of the components (Peer in this example). Fig. 14 shows the Broker interface that handles all the events that a Peer may raise. This interface can be implemented in different ways providing different strategies. A simple broker connects the requesters with at most one provider (possibly using a shared connection shown in Fig. 15.a), while an alternate broker may connect a requester to all the nodes that can provide the requested data (Fig. 15.b). Appendix B includes the implementation of SimpleBroker.

To make the whole system run, one should provide the initialization script. As in the Creol convention, one can have a class for the initialization. The only things needed are to instantiate a network manager, and some components.

```
class NetOne begin
    op init ==
        var mgr : Broker;
        var n1  : Peer;
        var n2  : Peer;
        var n3  : Peer;
        mgr := new SimpleBroker;
        n1  := new Node1(mgr);
        n2  := new Node2(mgr);
        n3  := new Node3(mgr)
end
```

Fig. 16. The system setup

Fig. 16 shows a possible system setup using the simple broker. For simplicity, one instance of each component type is created.

After translating to normal Creol syntax (cf. Section 3.4) and generating the Maude code for the model (using Creol compiler), one can perform different kinds of analyses in Maude. The simplest analysis is to run (simulate) the model. As defined in the tester classes in Appendix B.1, the data store in node one should get data '2' and similarly the data store in node three gets data '1' and '2', in addition to their initial data.

As explained before, one can run NetOne (see Fig. 16) to see how the simple broker implementation works. To do so one can execute the command 'rew[100000] init main("NetOne", emp) .' in Maude. By examining the Maude output, we can see that using the simple broker, the nodes will finally receive the requested data.

5 Conclusions and Future Work

In this paper, we presented a framework for component-based modeling of distributed systems with dynamic reconfigurable networks using mobile connectors in Creol. Components communicate anonymously, i.e., they allow the connectors to exogenously decide how they should communicate with other components in the system. The task of network reconfiguration is left to the network manager. This separates the issues of modeling (and analysis of) computation, coordination, and reconfiguration.

Components and connectors are modeled independently and can be reused in other system models. We have implemented a library of connectors. These connectors provide a variety of basic coordination schemes and can be used in modeling different systems. Nevertheless, the framework is not restricted to the currently implemented set of connectors and can be expanded by introducing new connectors.

However, a network manager should be modeled specifically for each system. The network is context aware, in the sense that reconfigurations depend on the events raised by components. Different network managers can be designed modeling different reconfiguration policies. In addition to automatic discovery of services (from a component's point of view), the framework allows for modeling different ways to connect the components.

One can use all characteristics of Creol in modeling the inside of a component, for example dynamic class upgrades. In the end, the component-based model can be translated to standard Creol. Thus we obtain an executable high-level modeling language, and can use all the techniques developed for analyzing Creol.

5.1 Future Work

The first thing to consider is adding a type-system. We are working on protocol types as an extension of session types [9]. A protocol type should be attached to each facade specifying abstractly how ports in that facade will be used. The object manipulating the ports in that facade should be type correct with respect to this protocol. This allows analyzing the network based on the protocol types of the participating components without looking into the component implementations.

We are working on allowing components to create ports dynamically when needed. For example, a service provider should preferably create new ports upon request, so that more requests can be serviced in parallel. Protocol types for each facade can be used to ensure type-safety.

In this paper, we focused on implementing the components as pliant entities. It remains to do more research on systematic implementation of network managers. One approach is to study a high-level way of specifying the network manager, for example by broadcast and late binding of anonymous messages, implemented for instance using Maude reflective programming techniques, so as to avoid keeping redundant information about all objects and components.

Another trend for future work is real time modeling. Timing constraints such as time-out on performing a network operation can be added to the model. On the other hand, schedulability of real time tasks on each component is being studied.

Acknowledgement

I would like to thank Frank de Boer, Tom Chothia, the anonymous reviewers and others who provided ideas and comments on developing this framework.

References

1. Agha, G.: The structure and semantics of actor languages. In: Proc. the REX Workshop, pp. 1–59 (1990)
2. Arbab, F.: Reo: A channel-based coordination model for component composition. Mathematical Structures in Computer Science 14, 329–366 (2004)

3. Basu, A., Bozga, M., Sifakis, J.: Modeling heterogeneous real-time components in bip. In: Proc. Software Engineering and Formal Methods (SEFM 2006), pp. 3–12. IEEE Computer Society, Los Alamitos (2006)
4. Bliudze, S., Sifakis, J.: The algebra of connectors: structuring interaction in bip. In: Proc. Embedded software (EMSOFT 2007), pp. 11–20. ACM Press, New York (2007)
5. Bowles, J.K.F., Moschoyiannis, S.: Concurrent logic and automata combined: A semantics for components. ENTCS 175(2), 135–151 (2007)
6. Cervin, A., Eker, J.: The control server: A computational model for real-time control tasks. In: Proc. Real-Time Systems ECRTS 2003, pp. 113–120. IEEE Computer Society Press, Los Alamitos (2003)
7. Clavel, M., Durán, F., Eker, S., Lincoln, P., Martí-Oliet, N., Meseguer, J., Quesada, J.F.: Maude: specification and programming in rewriting logic. Theoretical Computer Science 285(2), 187–243 (2002)
8. Cook, W.R., Misra, J.: Computation orchestration, a basis for wide-area computing. Software and Systems Modeling 6(1), 83–110 (2007)
9. Honda, K., Vasconcelos, V.T., Kubo, M.: Language primitives and type discipline for structured communication-based programming. In: Hankin, C. (ed.) ESOP 1998. LNCS, vol. 1381, pp. 122–138. Springer, Heidelberg (1998)
10. Johnsen, E.B., Owe, O.: An asynchronous communication model for distributed concurrent objects. Software and Systems Modeling 6(1), 35–58 (2007)
11. Johnsen, E.B., Owe, O., Yu, I.C.: Creol: A type-safe object-oriented model for distributed concurrent systems. Theoretical Computer Science 365(1-2), 23–66 (2006)
12. Lau, K.-K., Wang, Z.: A survey of software component models (second edition).Technical Report CSPP-38, School of Computer Science, The University of Manchester (2006)
13. Meseguer, J.: Conditioned rewriting logic as a united model of concurrency. Theoretical Computer Science 96(1), 73–155 (1992)
14. Milner, R.: Communicating and Mobile Systems: The π-Calculus. Cambridge University Press, Cambridge (1999)
15. Nierstrasz, O., Dami, L.: Component-oriented software technology. In: Object-oriented software composition, pp. 3–28. Prentice Hall, Englewood Cliffs (1995)
16. Scholten, J.G., Arbab, F., de Boer, F.S., Bonsangue, M.M.: Mobile channels, implementation within and outside components. ENTCS 66(4) (2002)
17. Scholten, J.G., Arbab, F., de Boer, F.S., Bonsangue, M.M.: Mocha-pi, an exogenous coordination calculus based on mobile channels. In: Proc. the 2005 ACM Symposium on Applied Computing, pp. 436–442. ACM Press, New York (2005)
18. Shirky, C.: Listening to Napster. In: Peer-to-Peer: Harnessing the power of disruptive technologies. O'Reilly, Sebastopol (2001)
19. Sirjani, M., Movaghar, A., Shali, A., de Boer, F.S.: Modeling and verification of reactive systems using Rebeca. Fundamamenta Informaticae 63(4), 385–410 (2004)
20. Welch, P.H., Brown, N., Moores, J., Chalmers, K., Sputh, B.: Integrating and extending JCSP. In: Proc. Communicating Process Architectures (CPA 2007), pp. 349–370. IOS Press, Amsterdam (2007)
21. Welch, P.H., Martin, J.M.R.: A CSP model for Java multithreading. In: Proc. Software Engineering for Parallel and Distributed Systems (PDSE), pp. 114–122 (2000)

22. Yu, I.C., Johnsen, E.B., Owe, O.: Type-safe runtime class upgrades in creol. In: Gorrieri, R., Wehrheim, H. (eds.) FMOODS 2006. LNCS, vol. 4037, pp. 202–217. Springer, Heidelberg (2006)

A Connectors Implementation

In this appendix, the Creol implementation of the three connector-end types are given. In addition, the implementation details of some connectors are explained. These implementations are based on the class diagram in the main paper in Fig. 8.

Each instance of a ConnectorEnd, upon creation, should be supplied with a reference to the connector object to which it belongs. This parameter is specialized in sub-types of ConnectorEnd to sub-types of Connector. On the other hand, instances of Source (similarly Sink or Signal), at creation, must be provided as parameter, a reference to a WConnector (RConnector or SConnector, respectively). In other words, the sub-types of the ConnectorEnd interface, specialize their parameters. This allows them to have access to proper operations of the connectors.

In order to prevent requests of different components from being mixed, a connector-end should propagate to the connector only one request at a time. This is achieved by using a blocking synchronous call such as `cnct.write(d;)`. After the current request finishes, nondeterministically, one of the suspended requests is chosen and propagated to the connector[1].

If one component needs to perform a sequence of actions on a connector-end atomically, it can first request an uninterruptible connection to the connector-end (via the connect method). In this case, the variable cc holds the identity of (i.e., a reference to) the currently connected component. After this connection is made, the connector-end, suspends any requests from other components, until the connected component explicitly disconnects (via the disconnect method). When no component is connected, cc is null, which allows any request from any component to be accepted. Note that the implementation of the disconnect operation allows only the currently connected component to perform this operation.

The implementation of Sink and Signal is essentially the same as Source. Fig. 17 depicts how to implement these connector-ends. The main difference is replacing the call to write with take and wait for sink and signal, respectively. Other issues, for example, the connect and disconnect operations, which are not shown in Fig. 17, are completely the same in all three types of connector-ends.

Sync Channel. The synchronous channel is the simplest connector. This connector has a source and a sink connector-ends. It allows any data written to its source to be taken from its sink. The actions on its ends need be synchronized.

Fig. 18 shows the implementation of the synchronous channel. As shown in the figure, the channel implements the two forms of the create method, i.e., the one for general connectors and the one specific to channels. For returning the

[1] A nondeterministic choice made by Creol scheduler from the enabled processes.

```
class CSource(cnct:WConnector) implements Source(cnct)
begin
   var cc:Component := null

   with Component op write(in d:Data) ==
      await (caller=cc || cc=null);
      cnct.write(d;);

   with Component op connect ==
      await cc=null;
      cc := caller

   with Component op disconnect ==
      if (caller = cc) then
         cc := null
      end
end

class CSink(cnct:RConnector) implements Sink(cnct)
begin
   var cc:Component := null
   with Component
      op take(out d:Data) ==
         await (caller=cc || cc=null);
         cnct.take(;d)
   // connect and disconnect are the same as Source
end

class CSignal(cnct:SConnector) implements Signal(cnct)
begin
   var cc:Component := null
  with Component
      op wait ==
         await (caller=cc || cc=null);
         cnct.wait(;)
   // connect and disconnect are the same as Source
end
```

Fig. 17. The implementation of connector-ends

```
class SyncChannel implements RChannel, WChannel
begin
    var end1 : ConnectorEnd
    var end2 : ConnectorEnd
    var dd : Data
    var ready : Boolean

    op init == ready := false

    with Sink op take(out d:Data)==
        await ready;
        d := dd;
        ready := false // synchronize with 'write'

    with Source op write(in d:Data)==
        dd := d;
        ready := true;
        await ~ ready // wait for next take

    with NetworkManager
        op create (out e1:ConnectorEnd, e2:ConnectorEnd)==
            end1 := new Source(this);
            end2 := new Sink(this);
            e1 := end1;
            e2 := end2

    with NetworkManager
        op create(out ce:List[ConnectorEnd])==
            end1 := new Source(this);
            end2 := new Sink(this);
            ce := nil |- end1 |- end2

end
```

Fig. 18. Synchronous channel

connector-ends as a list, it first creates the connector-ends by calling the channel-standard create operation. This implementation of the create operations is the same in all channels with a source and a sink connector-ends.

A variable of type Data (namely dd) is used to store the value written to the source end. Using the type Data enables passing values of any type. The boolean variable ready is used for synchronizing the actions on the two ends. The write action sets this variable indicating that there is some data available. This makes is possible for the take action to proceed (if there is a take action pending). After the take succeeds, it resets the ready flag, enabling the write to continue. On the other hand, if a take action happens first, it cannot proceed until the next write action appears.

Note that each connector-end propagates only one action at a time. Therefore, the connector is not concerned about situations where two write (or take) actions arrive consecutively on the same connector-end before the previous one has succeeded. Furthermore, for synchronization, we have used an extra flag (ready) rather than using a constraint on the value of dd. This allows passing any value (including 'null') as data along the channel.

Replicator. A replicator connector has one source and can have any number of sinks. It replicates the data written to its source on all its sink ends. The actions on all connector-ends need to be synchronized. It is interesting to note that by using a simple sync channel, and letting many components have a reference to the sink end, no replication takes place. In that case, each component attached to the sink end, has a chance to synchronize with the source end, and take the data. Nevertheless, only one component (from those sharing the reference) can participate in this procedure at a time. In other words, the take operations are serialized instead of being synchronized.

Fig. 19 shows the implementation of a replicator. The parameter n to the class shows the number of the sink ends; so, the connector has n+1 ends in total. A naive solution to the problem of synchronizing all the sinks is to let each sink set its corresponding flag and wait until all flags are set. With this approach, only the last sink can continue, and as soon as it resets its flag, other sink will remain suspended. Instead, every sink, except the last one, should set its flag to true and wait until it is reset, which is in fact reset by the last sink.

All the calls to the take operation, except the last one, need to wait for the last call (at line 27). The last call knows that it's the last, by checking if all the elements of the arrive flag are set. It then waits for the source end. After that, releases all the sinks (by resetting all the elements of arrive) as well as the source (by resetting the ready flag). On the other hand, the source can proceed with the write operation, only after the last sink arrives (i.e., all sinks arrive).

The last sink also makes a copy of the data (line 25), because after synchronization, the source may overwrite the data (dw), as a result of the next write action, before other sinks had a chance to read the previous value (which is now kept in dr and read in line 29). It is worth noting again that each connector-end propagates only one request at a time, thus the consecutive requests from the same end are not confused.

This connector has a parametric number of sink ends. Therefore, one needs to write a recursive function for creating 'n' sinks. Note that in Creol while and for loops are not allowed. A similar function is defined in all connectors with parametric number of connector-ends. This function is called synchronously so that all the connector-ends are created in one step.

```
class SyncReplicator(n:Nat) implements WConnector,RConnector
begin
   var sinkEnd : List[ConnectorEnd] := nil
   var arrive : List[Boolean] := nil
   var src : ConnectorEnd := null
   var dw, dr : Data := null
   var ready : Boolean := false
   op createNSink (in m:Nat)==
      var s : Sink;
      if (m > 0) then
         s := new CSink(this);
         sinkEnd := sinkEnd |- s;
         arrive := (arrive |- (false));
         createNSink(m-1;)
      end

   with Sink op take(out d:Data) ==
      var i:Nat;
      i := index (sinkEnd, caller);
      arrive[i] := true;
      if (arrive = true) then
         await ready; ready := false;
         arrive := false; dr := dw
      else
         await arrive[i] = false // wait for the last sink
      end;
      d := dr

   with Source op write(in d:Data) ==
      dw := d; ready := true;
      await ~ ready // wait for next take

   with NetworkManager
      op create(out ce:List[ConnectorEnd])==
         src := new CSource(this);
         createNSink(n;);
         ce := src -| sinkEnd
end
```

Fig. 19. Synchronous Replicator

```
class NMerger(n:Nat) implements WConnector,RConnector
begin
    var srcList  : List[Source] := nil
    var snk      : Sink := null
    var ready    : Boolean := false
    var written  : Boolean := false
    var dd       : Data := null

    op createNSource (in m:Nat)==
        var s : Source;
        if (m > 0) then
            s := new CSource(this);
            srcList := srcList |- s;
            createNSource(m-1;)
        end

    with Sink op take(out d:Data)==
        ready := true;
        await written;
        written := false;
        d := dd

    with Source op write(in d:Data)==
        await ready;
        ready := false;
        dd := d;
        written := true

    with NetworkManager
        op create(out ce:List[ConnectorEnd])==
            createNSource (n;);
            snk := new CSink(this);
            ce := srcList |- snk

end
```

Fig. 20. General nondeterministic merger

Nondeterministic Merger. A nondeterministic merger can have any number of inputs (source ends), but has one output (sink end). Whenever a take appears on the sink, it should synchronize with exactly one of the sources, if there is some data available on the source (a write action pending). If more than one source is ready, one of them should be chosen nondeterministically. The data from the chosen source will flow to the sink. Besides, the write action on that source and the take on the sink will succeed.

Creol supports a binary choice operator, which nondeterministically chooses one of its enabled operands. It would suspend (and possibly release the processor) if none is enabled. The main problem is that in the general case, the number of entities participating in the choice is not statically known. Therefore, the choice operator cannot be used.

To solve the problem of general nondeterministic choice between dynamic number of entities, we make use of the nondeterministic choice of Creol scheduler from among enabled processes. To this end, we make all available writers into a process, one of which succeeding to synchronize with the reader.

Fig. 20 shows the implementation of this connector. In this implementation, n is the number of source ends. When a source tries to write, it is suspended until the ready flag becomes true. When there is a take action, the ready flag is set to true. This enables exactly one writer process, because immediately afterwards, the writer resets the ready flag back to false.

The sink can continue when some data is written. This is indicated by the written flag. If there are more than one writer pending, the Creol scheduler selects one nondeterministically. If there is no writer available, the sink waits until the first source provides some data.

The current implementation of Creol uses a completely nondeterministic choice between the processes in an object. It is interesting to note that when Creol allows defining schedulers for objects, one can use a particular scheduler for the merger object to implement different policies in making its choice, e.g., to have priorities in its choice.

B Peer to Peer Implementation

B.1 Sample Components Implementing Peer

The implementation of a component, among other things, includes the implementation of its internal objects (i.e., classes implementing the interfaces of the internal objects). The interfaces of these objects are given in Fig. 13.

The client provides the search operation for the user interface. It can be invoked with a given key. The openClient and closeClient events are reconfiguration points in the Client. After the openClient, the client expects to be connected to (at least) one node that has the requested data. It then writes the 'key' for the required data on the 'req' port and expects the result on the 'ans' port. Finally, it updates the local store by adding the new (key,ans) pair of data. If no node has the data, the manager returns a 'false' and the client does not continue with the session.

From openClient until closeClient, the current process must enter a *critical region*. That is to disallow concurrent 'search' operations. Suppose the first search is waiting for a server to read the 'key'. If another search can be interleaved, it

```
class ClientImp (store:Store, req:outport, ans:inport)
      inside Peer implements Client(store, req, ans)
begin
   var busy : Boolean
   op init == busy := false

   with User op search(in key:Data out result:Data) ==
      var found : Boolean;
      await ~ busy;
      busy := true;
      raise_event openClient(key,req,ans; req,ans,found);
      if (found) then
         await req.write(key;);
         await ans.take(;result);
         ! store.add (key, result)
      end;
      raise_event closeClient(req, ans; req, ans);
      busy := false

end
```

```
class ServerImp (store:Store, req:inPort, ans:outPort)
      inside Peer implements Server(store, req, ans)
begin
   var busy : Boolean
   op init == busy := false

   op run ==
      var key, result:Data;
      await ~ busy;
      busy := true;
      raise_event openServer (req, ans;req, ans);
      await req.take(;key);
      await store.find (key; result);
      await ans.write(result;);
      raise_event closeServer (req, ans;req, ans);
      busy := false;
      ! run ()

end
```

```
class DataStore (key:Data, info:Data)
      inside Peer implements Store
begin
   var infoLst : List[Data]
   var infoKey : List[Data]

   op init ==
      infoLst := empty |- info;
      infoKey := empty |- key

   op run ==
      raise_event register(infoKey)

   with Client op add (in key:Data, info:Data) ==
      infoLst := infoLst |- info;
      infoKey := infoKey |- key;
      raise_event update(infoKey)

   with Server op find (in key:Data; out info:Data) ==
      info := nth (infoLst, index(infoKey, key))
end
```

```
class Tester1 (cl:Client) inside Peer implements User (cl)
begin
   op run ==
      var reply : Data;
      await ! cl.search("2";reply)
end

class Tester2 (cl:Client) inside Peer implements User (cl)
begin
end

class Tester3 (cl:Client) inside Peer implements User (cl)
begin
   op run ==
      var reply : Data;
      ! cl.search("0");
      ! cl.search("1");
      ! cl.search("2")
end
```

may reconfigure the network and change the port assignments. This results in the first search taking the answer from a wrong connection.

After the openServer event is performed, a server is connected to a client. The server receives a key to some data on 'req' port. It then finds the data associated to the key, and writes the answer onto 'ans' port. To find the data, the server queries the store object. After servicing a request, the server invokes its 'run' method again to be able to service other requests. Since a server has a fixed number of ports, it can service one request at a time.

The store keeps the data residing in the current node. The implementation is provided with a (key, info) pair as the initial data in the node. It first tries to register (the keys to) its local data at the broker. Later the client can add the new acquired data to the store ('add' operation). Then the store should update the broker's information. A server can try and find some data in the store ('find' operation).

The user represents the entity who invokes the search on the client. Three different implementations of the User interface are provided in this example. By putting these implementations in different Peer components, one can make different components behave differently. The three implementations are to be used as test cases. One can provide different implementations to test the model.

B.2 Broker Implementation

In a simple broker, (the client side of) the requesting node and (the server side of) the providing node are connected by synchronous channels. One channel is used to connect the 'req' ports and another channel connects the 'ans' ports. Therefore, a client is connected to at most one server. Fig. **??** shows the implementation of a simple broker with this policy.

When a node is added to the system, it requests initialization. For a server, in initServer, the simple broker creates two synchronous channels for the new node, and assigns the server side ports (exReq and exAns) accordingly (see Fig. 15.a). When a node raises an openClient event, along with the desired keyword, the network manager finds the node who has the data (matching the given key) and assigns the client side ports (myReq and myAns) of the requester to point to the channels of the node with the data.

Fig. 15.a shows a particular configuration of 3 nodes, where both nodes N1 and N2 try to read some (possibly different) data from N3. The network manager is not shown in this figure. But as can be seen, each node has two pairs of in-/outports, and a pair of synchronous channels are associated to the server side ports. The dashed arrows are used to show references to the connector-ends.

The requesting node sends its keywords to the channel, which is taken by the node on the other end (the server object) via its extReq port. And then the response goes from the extAns port of the latter to the myAns port of the former. Note that, even if more than one node is trying to request some data from the same node (as in Fig. 15.a), each node gets the correct data, due to the synchronous nature of the channels.

```
class SimpleBroker implements Broker
begin
    var nodeList  : List[Peer]
    var dataList  : List[List[Data]]
    var srcList   : List[Source]
    var snkList   : List[Sink]

    op init ==
        nodeList := nil;
        dataList := nil;
        srcList := nil;
        snkList := nil

    // find in datalist
    op findFirst (in key:Data; out ind:Nat) ==
        subFindFirst(1, key, dataList; ind)

    op subFindFirst (in k:Nat, key:Data, lst:List[List[Data]]
                          out ind:Nat) ==
        if lst = nil then
            ind := 0
        else
            if has(head(lst), key) then
              ind := k
            else
              subFindFirst(k+1, key, tail(lst); ind)
            end
        end

    with Peer op initClient(out myReq:Source, myAns:Sink) ==
        skip

    with Peer op initServer(out exAns:Source, exReq:Sink) ==
        var c1 : Source;
        var k1 : Sink;
        var temp: SyncChannel;
        temp := new SyncChannel; temp.create(;c1,exReq);
        temp := new SyncChannel; temp.create(;exAns,k1);
```

Fig. 21. A simple Broker implementation

```
        nodeList := nodeList |- caller;
        dataList := dataList |- nil;
        srcList := srcList |- c1;
        snkList := snkList |- k1

    with Peer op register (in lst:List[Data]) ==
        dataList:=replace(dataList,index(nodeList,caller),lst)

    with Peer op update(in lst:List[Data]) ==
        dataList:=replace(dataList,index(nodeList,caller),lst)

    with Peer op openServer (in reqi:Sink,ansi:Source
                             out reqo:Sink,anso:Source) ==
        reqo := reqi; anso := ansi

    with Peer op closeServer (in reqi:Sink,ansi:Source
                              out reqo:Sink,anso:Source) ==
        reqo := reqi; anso := ansi

    with Peer op openClient(in k:Data,reqi:Source,ansi:Sink
                        out reqo:Source,anso:Sink,f:Boolean) ==
        var i : Nat;
        findFirst (k ; i);
        if i = 0 then
            f := false
        else
            f := true;
            reqo := nth(srcList, i);
            anso := nth(snkList, i)
        end

    with Peer op closeClient (in reqi:Source,ansi:Sink
                              out reqo:Source,anso:Sink) ==
        reqo := reqi; anso := ansi

end
```

Fig. 21. *(continued)*

Author Index

Albert, Elvira 113
Arenas, Puri 113
Aspinall, David 52

Barthe, Gilles 1
Benveniste, Albert 200
Beringer, Lennart 25
Bjørk, Joakim 257
Bliudze, Simon 179

Caillaud, Benoît 200
Caromel, Denis 133
Clarke, Dave 226
Coupaye, Thierry 153
Crégut, Pierre 1
Cunningham, Dave 72

Dietl, Werner 72
Drossopoulou, Sophia 72

Ferrari, Alberto 200
Francalanza, Adrian 72

Genaim, Samir 113
Grégoire, Benjamin 1

Haridi, Seif 153
Henrio, Ludovic 133
Hofmann, Martin 25

Jaghoori, Mohammad Mahdi 280
Jensen, Thomas 1
Johnsen, Einar Broch 257

Kyas, Marcel 257

Madelaine, Eric 133
Maier, Patrick 52
Mangeruca, Leonardo 200
Müller, Peter 72

Owe, Olaf 257

Passerone, Roberto 200
Pavlova, Mariela 25
Pichardie, David 1
Puebla, German 113

Reinefeld, Alexander 153

Sifakis, Joseph 179
Sofronis, Christos 200
Stark, Ian 52
Stefani, Jean-Bernard 153
Summers, Alexander J. 72

Van Roy, Peter 153

Yap, Roland 153

Zanardini, Damiano 113

Printing: Mercedes-Druck, Berlin
Binding: Stein + Lehmann, Berlin